IN
# CONFIDENCE

# ANATOLY DOBRYNIN

## IN
# CONFIDENCE

### MOSCOW'S AMBASSADOR
### TO AMERICA'S SIX
### COLD WAR PRESIDENTS
### (1962–1986)

TIMES 𝕿 BOOKS

RANDOM HOUSE

*With love to my wife Irina,*
*who shared it all and made this book possible*

LIBRARY OF CONGRESS CATALOGING-IN-PUBLICATION DATA
Dobrynin, Anatoliy Federovich
   In confidence : Moscow's ambassador to America's six Cold War
presidents / by Anatoly Dobrynin.—1st ed.
      p.   cm.
   Includes index.
   ISBN 0-8129-2894-6
   1. Dobrynin, Anatoliy Federovich, 1919–   .  2. Ambassadors—
Soviet Union—Biography.   3. United States—Foreign relations—
Soviet Union.   4. Soviet Union—Foreign relations—United States.
5. United States—Foreign relations—20th century.   6. Soviet Union—
Foreign relations—1953–1975.   7. Soviet Union—Foreign relations—
1975–1985.  I. Title.
DK275.D63A3   1995
327.2'092—dc20
[B]                                                          95-11611

*Designed by Beth Tondreau Design / Robin Bentz*
Random House website address: http://www.randomhouse.com/
Printed in the United States of America on acid-free paper
9  8  7  6  5  4  3  2
First Edition

# CONTENTS

# ACKNOWLEDGMENTS

I am deeply indebted to all those who gave me the wonderful opportunity to work in the diplomatic service for half a century and thus opened to me the exciting world of diplomacy and international relations which are the focus of this book. I am grateful for the cooperation and friendship of my colleagues in the Foreign Ministry of the Soviet Union and of the Russian Federation.

I also acknowledge with gratitude the support for this book from the Harriman Institute of Columbia University in New York and the Kennan Institute of the Woodrow Wilson Center for Scholars in Washington. The support and warm interest of my friends Dwayne Andreas and Donald Kendall also helped make this book possible.

In the process of organizing the material and reflecting on it through successive drafts to produce a book, I want especially to acknowledge the help of the writer and journalist Lawrence Malkin. His immediate and persistent enthusiasm was seasoned with demanding critiques, and he gave me a lift that was deeply appreciated. Peter Osnos, my publisher, was invaluable in shepherding this book through its birth and bringing it to life. Both mixed support with wise comment about the book's structure, helping to enliven it and make it more accessible to the reader. They were joined by Don Oberdorfer, from whose expert and thoughtful reading of the manuscript we all benefited. I am also grateful to Irina Balakina, for her diligent help to me in putting the book into English. Peter Smith of Times Books ably participated in editing the book and Venka Macintyre was the copyreader. All made the publication of this book a pleasure, and I am deeply grateful to everyone at Times Books.

My sincere thanks are also due to William Hyland and Robert Levgold for deep and useful comments and suggestions, and to my literary agent Morton Janklow, always a wise counselor.

# IN
# CONFIDENCE

# INTRODUCTION

My life and work as a diplomat spanned a unique and decisive period in the history of my country and the world. We know it as the Cold War. My career in the Soviet Diplomatic Service began at the end of World War II, when I had just graduated from Diplomatic School in Moscow and entered the Foreign Ministry. It continued from the time of Joseph Stalin through to the downfall of Mikhail Gorbachev in the Soviet Union, and in the United States from the presidency of Harry S. Truman to that of George Bush. Altogether my association with Soviet diplomacy lasted almost half a century, and about half of that time I served as the ambassador of the Union of Soviet Socialist Republics to the United States. I participated in preparations for all the summit meetings between the leaders of the United States and the Soviet Union from the first one in Geneva in 1955 until the summit between Bush and Gorbachev in 1990, the only diplomat to witness all these landmarks in international relations. My term as ambassador in Washington began in 1962 and lasted until 1986, the longest term in such a position in Soviet and indeed the whole of Russian diplomatic history before the Revolution. The best years of my life were devoted to this work.

During this quarter-century relations between our two countries remained highly unstable. They usually improved after summit meetings and deteriorated during periods of crisis in various parts of the world. The arms race far outpaced the disarmament negotiations that were designed to control it. Local conflicts erupted. It so happened that the task of maintaining confidential contact at the highest levels between both governments fell primarily on me as the Soviet ambassador in Washington. I saw my fundamental task as one of helping to develop a correct and constructive dialogue between the leaders of both countries and maintaining the positive aspects of our relations whenever possible. I did my best to resist the impulsive emotions caused by diplomatic reverses, misunderstandings, and failures of policy, of which I witnessed plenty.

In writing this book I have not just relied on my memory. I have consulted the Soviet diplomatic archives in Moscow as well as my own diaries, none of which has ever been published before. My most important formal meetings and private conversations with presidents, secretaries of state, national security advisers, senators, and political and public figures in the United States have found their way into these pages, as well as many of my dealings with my superiors and our leaders in Moscow, including the meetings of the Politburo that I attended. I have concentrated on matters in which I personally participated.

I have tried to reflect the spirit of those times and the evolution of Soviet-American relations in a way that I believe is unique because doors were open to me in both the White House and the Kremlin. In addition to the recollections of my early career in the Soviet Foreign Ministry, the United Nations, and the embassy in Washington, the eyewitness accounts here span six American presidencies, from John F. Kennedy to Ronald Reagan. I met with all of them many times. I also knew Presidents Truman, Eisenhower, and Bush. All these leaders were quite different in their temperament and in their knowledge and ability to deal with affairs of state. Some were outstanding public figures who remain vivid in my memory, and each was, without doubt, a notable personality.

In my own country, I closely observed Nikita Khrushchev and Leonid Brezhnev during their years in power, as well as their successors through Mikhail Gorbachev, who brought me back to Moscow in 1986 to serve first as party secretary in charge of international affairs and then as an adviser on American affairs. I then retired. On August 1, 1991, I returned to the Soviet Foreign Ministry, which later became the Foreign Ministry of the Russian Federation, where as of this writing in 1995, I serve as a consultant.

I hope this memoir will be of use to all those who are interested in the complex history of Soviet-American relations and at the same time serve as a warning against any recurrence of the sad mistakes of this century. I also mean it to be a personal history of how affairs of state were conducted by the White House and the Kremlin.

My American interlocutors still wonder whether I was a true believer in the Soviet system, and indeed Ronald Reagan was not quite sure whether I really was a communist (I was). The fact is that I served my country to the best of my ability as citizen, patriot, and diplomat. I tried to serve what I saw as its practical and historic interests and not any abstract philosophical notion of communism. I accepted the Soviet system with its flaws and successes as a historic step in the long history of my country, in whose great destiny I still believe. If I had any grand purpose in life, it was the integration of my country into the family of nations as a respected and equal partner. But for this it is always necessary to consider the realities of the world and one's own country.

In my everyday activity as ambassador I reported to the Politburo in general and of course directly to Andrei Gromyko, often exploring openings in a way that he as foreign minister could not. I was closely connected with a whole gallery of secretaries of state and national security advisers, among them Dean Rusk, William Rogers, Henry Kissinger, Cyrus Vance, Edmund Muskie, Zbignew Brzezinski, Alexander Haig, George Shultz, and Brent Scowcroft. We saw many conflicts emerge and saw them resolved, but not without strained negotiations, claims and counterclaims, and emotional debates. But through all this we managed as a rule to maintain good, businesslike relations and in some cases were even on close and friendly terms. I think of most of my American partners with warm feelings, and I still keep in touch with some of them.

I also recall with affection and deep gratitude my embassy colleagues—many of whom later served as ambassadors or in senior diplomatic posts of the Russian Federation—Yuli Vorontsov, Aleksandr Bessmertnykh, Georgi Kornienko, George Mamedov, Vladlen Vasev, Oleg Sokolov, Vitaly Churkin, Victor Komplektov, Victor Isakov, and many others with whom I shared our difficult tasks during my long term in Washington.

We all strived always to keep open the lines of communication to the other side, although our success varied, depending on the state of relations. They alternated from dangerous, during the Cuban missile crisis; to more constructive, during the period of detente under Richard Nixon and Henry Kissinger; to uncertain and confused, during the Ford and Carter administrations; to positively frigid after the invasion of Afghanistan and during the Reagan arms buildup. Despite all this I luckily found myself useful in the command posts of both sides in the Cold War. In Washington I was granted access that others found astonishing for the ambassador of the Soviet Union. By our own government in Moscow I was given rather unprecedented latitude, although I must say one reason was that I myself often decided to take it, and it evidently suited my superiors for me to do so.

Another principal purpose of this memoir has been to discover the pattern of my career by retracing it for myself as well as my readers. One of its lessons is how profoundly human nature and indeed human relations affect the outcome of events; diplomacy, after all, is not just a public and professional skill but also a very private and individual one.

I believe that one reason for my success in communicating with most people was that we were prepared to deal with each other on an equal basis to search for better understanding. I liked communicating with them as well, and I showed it; this is essential. I dealt with them as human beings, whatever our political and philosophical differences—and believe me, they were profound. Nevertheless I was curious about their motives, and I never failed to show that I could be sympathetic to their ideas when we found areas of mutual interest.

On a professional level, it never crossed my mind that I should be excessively cautious in action or expression, although I always tried to be prudent. As a result of all this, the Kremlin came to rely on my judgment, while not always accepting it by any means. To both sides, I tried to be a reassuring presence in a very strained world.

Yet in going through this book readers may wonder how so many people in and out of government were persuaded to talk frankly to the representative of the government that was, after all, the principal adversary of the United States in the world. There was no great secret to it; building a close personal relationship was a matter of character, mutual respect, professionalism, and good human relations in general. A bit of humor helps, too. But above all, many of those who spoke to me sincerely wanted better relations with the Soviet Union, and that formed the basis of our mutual communications.

From the start I had decided to develop less formal relations with high officials of the American administration than was the custom under Gromyko. From the president on down, I usually visited American officials without anyone accompanying me from the embassy as a witness to a meeting with a foreigner, a tradition dating from Stalin's times. I knew that if I appeared alone it would encourage confidentiality and the exploration of new ideas beyond our often frozen official positions. At the same time I wanted to avoid unnecessary confrontations with my American interlocutors, especially over ideology, in order to promote better personal relations and by extension create a better climate to work in during both calm and troubled times.

As a professional, I always tried to find the right person around each president, although it was not possible to develop proper personal chemistry with everyone. Robert Kennedy was certainly close to his brother, but he was a difficult person to deal with. He would come with a message of complaint in the name of the president, and that was that. Instead, I tried to find someone who was as interested as I was in improving Soviet-American relations and in compromising to reach solutions to the difficult problems that separated us. Then, if necessary, we would each report separately to the president and to the Politburo on how far we had gone. This worked well with the Kennedy administration's Soviet affairs specialist, Llewellyn Thompson, and especially later on with Kissinger and Vance. While Robert McNamara was Lyndon Johnson's defense secretary he once invited me to his house for lunch; we played chess, then met again, and gradually began to talk frankly and without any official authorization about disarmament, a field in which he had many fresh and interesting ideas.

I had good personal connections in other administrations and a wide circle of acquaintances among businessmen, members of Congress, and the press, all of which helped to overcome the sense of isolation we felt inside the embassy during the Cold War. The heavy heritage of Stalin made this openness relatively rare among my diplomatic colleagues in other countries. I also participated in Washington's social life and in the activity of the diplomatic corps, of which by reason of longevity of service I eventually became dean.

But sociability was not the most important part of my life as an ambassador. It was also important that I maintained good connections with the political establishment in Moscow, first of all with the Politburo and the general secretary of the Communist Party (I was a member of the Central Committee of the party). I knew the people in charge of political and military intelligence, and I of course knew what was being discussed within our Foreign Ministry about our relations with the United States. I could speak with all of them frankly.

The officials in Washington with whom I developed confidential relations understood that what they told me would in due course find its way back to the Kremlin. What they gave me were not state secrets but principally political information, personal views, and their ideas about how to solve difficult problems. In return I had to supply them in the same coin about a subject that would interest them. People do not invite you back if you just ask questions and do not tell them anything in return.

So I was prepared to tell them information about my country that would interest the secretary of state, or defense, or the vice president, so they would want to meet with me again. I thus felt at liberty, although within certain limits, to probe for new ideas that might find their way into formal negotiations and would be useful to both sides. With Kissinger, for instance, this process was developed successfully.

No one in Moscow ever warned me to pull back and keep my distance from the Americans—not the successive chiefs of the KGB, whom I knew, nor even the Politburo's arch ideologue Mikhail Suslov. Through my confidential and unorthodox talks they often received views directly from the highest levels in Washington. Such relations rarely existed in other capitals, and hence there was little information of this kind. Few Soviet ambassadors were prepared to take the risk and go beyond just trading official information. I was a bit cautious, too, but I knew I had a rather strong position at home. Besides, I was not a politician and was not out for anybody else's job in Moscow. I was more than content to remain an ambassador, and my superiors knew it.

I think my behavior as ambassador also suited the Americans. Officials who spoke with me often wanted their ideas and proposals to reach the appropriate level in the Soviet Union in an unofficial way through my channels. They knew that when I returned to the Soviet Union on vacation I was not just going to the Crimea but would be stopping in Moscow to speak to members of the Politburo and other high officials in the Kremlin. Henry Kissinger, who in his memoirs chides me in jest for being in Moscow when he wanted to convey something of urgency through me, knew very well that my frequent trips home for consultations, party conferences, or my annual vacation were part of my usefulness to him as a pipeline to the Kremlin. We both knew that we could frankly and in complete confidence explore the possibility of resolving our troubles and always tried to play them down, not play them up.

I managed to make Washington understand that whenever an administration initiated something through me even unofficially, I had the persistence to carry it through and the ability to be heard in the Foreign Ministry and the Politburo where the decision would be made. I could not of course guarantee that any proposal would be adopted, but they knew that if something was proposed, and we had explored it in Washington, I would have at least an opportunity to put it to high officials in Moscow and I would return with an answer, either officially or unofficially. Even if it was not quite an acceptable one, it usually would leave room for us to continue the dialogue.

All of this was part of the essential mechanism of what we came to call the confidential channel. Through it passed the principal efforts by Washington and Moscow to resolve the disputes of the Cold War; until now the full extent of its operations has never been publicly detailed. If I had been accompanied by anyone in my meetings with presidents, secretaries of state, or national security council advisers, with some of their people present, it would have been much more difficult to exchange unofficial opinions, to lay the groundwork for negotiation, or actually to bargain between both governments. In front of his own people I could not have said—as we did with Kissinger—things like, "Come on, Henry, this is a bluff, a nonsense. What are you trying to do?" Nor would he have said the same sort of thing—and even stronger—to me or about my leaders in front of my own people without either of us causing offense. Much later I found myself meeting with George Shultz when he was Ronald Reagan's secretary of state, always flanked by a phalanx of his own assistants. I wondered why the two of us could not just talk privately. It was only later I realized that at the beginning of his tenure, he was not at liberty to explore with me new ideas about improving our relations because the president was not at that time interested in doing so, and one sign was that Shultz would not meet me alone for a confidential talk. During Reagan's second term, we cooperated quite well with Shultz.

I also knew my high access in Washington annoyed American ambassadors in Moscow because many of the most important exchanges took place right over their heads. As a diplomat I sympathized with their position, but there probably was no other solution at that time. Gromyko simply would not enter into the kind of free discussions that could form the basis for a confidential exchange. As for the U.S. ambassador, what could he possibly say unofficially to the uncommunicative Gromyko? So ambassadors would deliver a note from Washington, explain it in front of a number of officials from both sides who sat there translating, taking notes, or observing the conversation. A confidential chat in Moscow to exchange inside political information was just not possible with our strict sense of secrecy in the Kremlin and the formal way in which we conducted our foreign affairs. In this sense, Washington was the better place to work.

The nature of the relations between the Soviet Union and the United States was unique because the two countries were both adversaries in their rival claims to represent the future of mankind and partners in their common responsibility for the fate of life on our planet, which either could extinguish at the touch of a button. Looking back, I regret that the quarter of a century of my service as ambassador in Washington fell mainly during the complex period of Soviet-American rivalry, even hostility. If only it had been possible then to build a sensible foundation of trust between our two nations, how much could have been done and could still be done by both sides to bring our nations closer together.

Although the past cannot be judged by the events of today, the lessons of the past should be remembered. The world has entered a new age. For the first time in decades and perhaps centuries we have no great power rivalries to threaten peace or, as in much of our own century, the very existence of civilization on earth. We must do everything in our power to preserve this situation. Yet we still have an unsettled and indeed unstable world, and the confusion and danger we now suffer should be seen as part of the price both sides are paying for the Cold War.

# BEFORE
# WASHINGTON

# I. My Diplomatic Career Begins

*From Engineering to Diplomacy*

I became a diplomat at the age of twenty-five quite unexpectedly and in a very unusual way. On a summer day in 1944, my whole life was changed by a sudden phone call to the aircraft plant where I worked as an engineer. The Communist Party Central Committee summoned me to its headquarters the next day. I had never before been to places of such high authority and spent the day guessing why I, an ordinary engineer, was needed there. When I arrived, I was directed to the Personnel Department.

I was received by an unsmiling, imposing, and stern man who had little difficulty impressing such a young and inexperienced person as I was then. I even remember his name. He presented himself as "Sdobnov, CPSU Central Committee instructor for personnel." It was obvious that he had no intention of entering into a long conversation or even a discussion about the matter at issue. He declared, "There is an opinion to send you to study at the Higher Diplomatic School."

I should note that the Russian expression *yest mnieniye,* or there is an opinion—without ever clarifying whose opinion it was—used to be quite popular in the vocabulary of the Communist Party and Soviet government. It had a touch of secrecy and power: you did not know to whom you could appeal, and the only way out was to consent.

The proposal left me completely bewildered. After graduating from the Moscow Aviation Institute I was working as a designer at Experimental Aircraft Plant No. 115, which was headed by the famous aircraft designer Aleksandr Yakovlev. His fighter planes made up a considerable part of the Soviet Air Force. I liked my job and had never even thought of becoming a diplomat, or anything else for that matter.

Observing that I was not at all excited by the news and was even trying to object, Sdobnov snapped, "It is wartime and the party knows better where and how to use its people. Actually, this question has already been settled.

However, you may think it over till tomorrow. I'll be expecting you in the morning."

What worried me most in this situation was the fact that I came from a plain working-class family and had no connections either in the Communist Party or in the government. I was a person no one knew. Why had I been chosen to be a diplomat? Entirely confused, I went home to discuss things at a family council. At that moment my wife Irina, also as an aircraft engineer, was graduating from her institute, which had been evacuated for the duration of the war to the city of Alma-Ata far off in Kazakhstan.

That left my father as my only adviser. He was a plumber. My mother was essentially unlettered. She was a housewife and also worked as an usher at the Moskovsky Malyi Theatre, which staged the best dramas in the capital. Through her I not only saw all the Russian plays at this theater, but by carrying a note identifying myself as her son and a poor student, I gained admission to all of Moscow's theaters. One of my aunts was married to a mathematician, and I was also fond of mathematics, winning second prize in the Moscow mathematic Olympiad, which led to my recommendation for admission to Moscow University after I graduated from high school in 1937. But my father urged me to attend the Moscow Aviation Institute. "Oh, come on," he said. "At university you just sit and read books, but at the Aviation Institute you work in real life."

Thus my father had always dreamed that his son would become an engineer. He viewed my becoming a diplomat as nonsense and of course was against it. People like him believed that diplomats mingled in high society and were either crooks or liars, and he could not bear the thought of his son spending his life doing that. Naturally I was more well-read than my father, but I still had only a vague idea about what diplomats really do. Not that I needed any clarification: I had an interesting job and did not intend to change it. In short, by evening I was all set to turn down the strange proposal.

My answer the next day enraged Sdobnov. He told me that I was too young to realize what a great honor it was to be sent to study at the Higher Diplomatic School, and if I was unable to understand well-meant advice, I should regard the proposal as a wartime order that had to be fulfilled unconditionally.

I then turned for advice to my boss, Chief Designer Aleksandr Yakovlev (he had the rank of a lieutenant-general). What else was I to do? I knew that he liked me and was closely following my work at the plant. He expressed his regret at the turn of events and remarked that he had hoped to see me rise to become his deputy in eight or ten years. But he said there was no way of refusing a Central Committee decision, which had to be obeyed whether I liked it or not.

That is how I parted with the plant and with designing aircraft, an occupation I never stopped loving and whose progress I tried to follow even after I had become a diplomat. I must say that the years I had spent in aviation were finally not wasted. My engineering skills helped me a great deal in my diplomatic work during Soviet-American disarmament talks on many types of aircraft and missiles. It was much easier for me to master this quite complicated technical field than for my diplomatic colleagues who had no technical education. Besides, I think my technical training also helped bring me to the pragmatic, nonideological bent that characterized my approach to diplomacy and my diplomatic work.

For many years I wondered whose "opinion" it had been that changed my life so drastically. Only by mere chance was I able to find out when I was already ambassador to the United States. On vacation in Usovo, a place in the environs of Moscow where many government dachas are located, I was out walking when I quite unexpectedly ran into Vyacheslav Molotov, the once powerful former minister of foreign affairs. He had been living in Usovo since 1957, when Nikita Khrushchev removed him from his post. At the time of our meeting Molotov was over eighty, but he still had a clear mind and excellent memory. He also retained all the convictions of the Old Bolshevik that he was and thoroughly disapproved of any sort of *perestroika* or other reform; to the end of his days he denounced Khrushchev and Brezhnev and praised Stalin.

During our conversation I recalled the events of my "enlistment" to the Higher Diplomatic School in 1944 (it was later renamed the Diplomatic Academy). Once again I expressed my bewilderment at having been chosen despite the fact that I had not been known to anyone in the party leadership. Molotov still remembered what had happened. At one of the Politburo sessions in the summer of 1944, after discussing the successful offensive of the Soviet Army at the front, Stalin had suddenly changed the subject and started talking about the necessity to prepare new diplomatic cadres because Hitler would soon be defeated and Soviet diplomacy had to be ready for the rapid revival of foreign affairs. New ties would be established with many states, and it would also be necessary to solve a lot of postwar problems. In short, the Soviet Union would very soon need a large and fully qualified diplomatic corps. Even though it was the peak of the war and almost all of the young men had been called up by the armed forces, Stalin told Molotov that a diplomatic school had to be established at once.

"But where shall we get students?" Molotov asked Stalin. "Especially those who have studied liberal arts and languages." Stalin replied that it was not necessary to find candidates educated in the humanities; they could learn that later. Right now, he said, the Foreign Ministry could take young engineers from defense plants. He said to be sure to choose those who got along well with workers: "Both engineers and workers are leading a very hard life; they receive only 700 grams of black bread, and many of them practically live at the plants and don't see their families for days." Stalin reasoned that if a young engineer managed to handle the difficult day-to-day problems and conflicts that were inevitable in those hard times, and the workers still respected him, he was a real diplomat, or at least had the necessary abilities to become one.

And indeed our first class of close to fifty students consisted of young engineers, mostly from the aircraft industry. Before the war the aviation institutes had been considered the nation's most prestigious, and the majority of ambitious young people tried for admission. This was what we called the "Stalin enrollment" to diplomacy, although hardly anyone knew about it at the time. Moreover, Stalin had deeper motives. Having got rid of the old generation of diplomats in the purges just before the war, he wanted to be sure that the old ways of thinking would not return. Even those of the old guard who managed to survive the purges, like Maxim Litvinov, the former Menshevik who was useful during the wartime alliance with the United States and Britain because of his contacts and reputation in the West, were watched closely. The young Andrei Gromyko was sent abroad to be trained as minister-counselor in the Washington embassy and to back up Litvinov. But Litvinov never liked Gromyko, and old-timers at our foreign ministry recalled that in his annual personnel rating the ambassador wrote, Gromyko "is not fit for high diplomatic service." True or not, the report is missing from the archives.

Like me, most of the new people were technicians who were in no way affected by the old ways of thinking. We did not feel particularly vulnerable to Stalin's excesses, about which we knew only vaguely at the time. All of my family were ordinary people, and we did not have a single intellectual except my uncle, who was a professor of mathematics anyway. We felt as secure in Stalin's time as anyone could feel. When the call came, you had no choice; you had to accept. Fear or no fear, you went.

## Diplomacy from Litvinov: Table Manners from Princess Volkonsky

The Higher Diplomatic School was located in a small two-story building not far from the Krasnye Vorota (Red Gate) subway station. It had two departments: Western (two years of study) and Oriental (three years). The main subject was a foreign language, since most of us could speak only Russian. We had to learn it in the shortest possible time in order to start speaking and to be able to read newspapers and political literature. I was included in the

English section with seven other students. This was my own preference. The English-speaking world had become our ally during the war, and I also had studied under one professor at the Aviation Institute who had worked in the United States for several years and liked it there very much.

The school had good professors. Some language teachers were British and their Russian was not too good, so we had to learn to understand each other. Well-known professors—Skazkin, Khvostov, Krylov, Lebedev—and others lectured on world history and the history of diplomacy. Our seminars with such distinguished diplomats of the time as Litvinov, Troyanovsky, Stein, Gusev, and others who had practiced the craft as ambassadors, also helped us a great deal. Ambassadors who visited Moscow on business also occasionally spoke at our school. They did not teach us specifically in terms of the ideological conflict between communism and capitalism, but in terms of the classical and practical diplomacy of dealing with different countries—how to defend or adjust policy in the interests of the state.

At the same time we were provided mostly with communist foreign periodicals for reading, which was a great flaw in our English studies. Major bourgeois newspapers such as the *New York Times* and London *Times,* or magazines such as *Time* and *Newsweek,* could only be obtained with special permission from the dean, or by graduate students if their thesis topic demanded it. Such was the ideological atmosphere and approach toward everything foreign, although the school was supposed to train people for work abroad. No wonder that the school's graduates who were sent to work at our embassies in the West found it quite difficult to adapt themselves to the language and terminology of the mainstream Western press and their readers.

The same applied to spoken language. Our graduates could easily participate in a conversation on a *Marxist* topic with our "friends," which is how foreign communists were referred to in party jargon. However, they found themselves at a loss during discussions on serious political or economic issues with foreign diplomats or merely with common people of the country they were working in. They had to catch up on their studies on their own, and quickly, so as to be able to fulfill their duties at the embassy efficiently.

During our first year at the school we also had a class in etiquette, that is, manners and rules of behavior in the society into which we would soon be plunged as diplomats, and about which we only knew from books. Our lessons resembled a theatrical performance: we had to imagine ourselves at diplomatic receptions, luncheons, and dinners, of which none of us had the slightest experience. The lessons were conducted by an elderly aristocratic lady from the famous family of the princes Volkonsky.

We were usually seated at a large and well-set table with all the necessary spoons, knives, forks, and wine glasses. Everything was real except for one thing: no food or wine was served (it was wartime and there was a tremendous food shortage). Imaginary waiters brought in imaginary dishes for which we had real porcelain plates, which, unfortunately, remained empty.

Our lady-in-waiting would announce, "Let's start with the soup. Imagine that you've been served vichyssoise." Then followed a description of this and other possible soups. Next came the fish course and various meat dishes with the most intricate names. We were also instructed how to use this or that particular fork and knife and how to speak to our neighbors at table. Much emphasis was placed on wines—Burgundy, Bordeaux, Rhine wine, and Soviet wines—which were supposedly poured into our glasses according to ritual with the appropriate fish, meat, dessert, or other delicacy, all of which only increased those young appetites starved by meager food rations.

In 1946, after two years of studies at the Higher Diplomatic School, we were to take our final examinations. Maxim Litvinov, at the time deputy minister of foreign affairs and formerly ambassador to Washington, was the chairman of the examining board, which he conducted in English. He understood and spoke the language very well, but his pronunciation was terrible. After only two years of study, the poor students were not too fluent and they were often flustered in the presence of such a famous diplomat. Our teachers usually came to our rescue, reinterpreting his questions into a more simple and understandable English. Litvinov overlooked the teachers' attempts to help us and gave us good marks saying that practical work abroad would "teach us everything." That was his way of wishing us good luck.

On Molotov's order, the school's graduates were assigned to various departments of the Soviet Ministry of Foreign Affairs. I was the only one to remain at the diplomatic school for another year. And there was a reason for that. At our graduation party I had gotten into a friendly discussion with our director Professor Vladimir Khvostov, who specialized in the history of international relations. He was a decent person, though a dry-as-dust pedant. But after some wine he was talking with us, his students, in the relaxed atmosphere of the party. The conversation was informal and quite free. Someone wondered which occupation was more difficult—a historian's or an engineer's? Our opinions differed. I was somewhat excited after a good graduation dinner and found myself holding an opinion opposite to the director's. I tried to prove how difficult my first occupation had been and found, as I thought, a weighty argument. I announced that although I was an engineer, I could write and defend a thesis in history and become a doctor in history within a year, whereas no historian could do that in a year in the field of engineering. Everyone began to shout, trying to prove his own point. Soon we forgot all about our argument.

About a week later, the minister's order was posted at the school, assigning the graduates to jobs at the Ministry of Foreign Affairs. It said that student Dobrynin was to spend another year there. I was struck dumb. Having forgotten completely about our argument, I rushed to see the director. He smiled slyly and said that he had conveyed to Molotov my "wish" to remain at the school for another year and prepare to defend a thesis. He assured me that he himself had supported my "wish." As an exception Molotov had agreed.

There was no way I could back out. I had to spend another ten months at the school and write my thesis. It was based on my diploma paper, which was about U.S. Far East policy during the Russo-Japanese War, and I successfully defended it. It was devoted mainly to Russian-American diplomatic relations during the war and to President Theodore Roosevelt's role as mediator, and my work led me to study the diplomatic history of the United States.

A year later it was published as a separate book, but under the pen name Dobrov since employees of the Foreign Ministry were not permitted to publish under their own names. This allowed me to become an assistant professor and to lecture on the history of U.S. foreign policy at the Institute of International Relations while I continued with my principal job at the Ministry of Foreign Affairs. There I served as the assistant chief of the Education Department, an appointment I obtained because of my doctoral degree.

My department in the Foreign Ministry had hardly anything to do with practical diplomacy, and after several months I found myself up to my neck in various instruction manuals and began to hate the work. I had hoped that one day I would plunge into real diplomatic activity. But as a result of a foolish argument with the school's director I had ended up with this loathsome job.

## My Apprenticeship at the Ministry

A year had passed, and the new minister of foreign affairs, Andrei Vyshinsky, summoned me to his office and offered me the position of the head of the Education Department. The prospect of spending the rest of my life or at least a greater part of it in that department terrified me so much that I refused on the spot. My reply irritated the minister very much because the position he had offered me, that of a counselor, was equal in rank to a general's. There was a real uproar. Vyshinsky, who had been the vitriolic prosecutor at the Moscow purge trials of the 1930s, was equally notorious for the lash of his tongue on his subordinates.

"You're just a beginner! And refusing a general's position!" he shouted at me. "Do you know how many people in the ministry would jump at the opportunity to receive such a post?"

After giving me a piece of his mind, he roared, "You may go!" and savagely crossed out the memorandum on my appointment and threw it to the head of the Personnel Department, Peter Strunnikov, who was accused of "utter incompetence and presentation of unreasoned proposals."

One can only imagine my state of mind after this personal introduction to my formidable minister. I returned to being a rank-and-file drudge at the Education Department.

However, I soon had a stroke of luck. Several months later Valerian Zorin, one of our most experienced diplomats, became a deputy foreign minister. He had previously been our ambassador in Czechoslovakia, where he had played a role in the fall of its postwar pro-Western government. He needed his own secretariat of professional diplomats. The head of my department, Aleksandr Popovkin, was on good terms with Zorin. Knowing how anxious I was to become a diplomat, my chief recommended me to his friend. Although Zorin was a vigorous debater against his adversaries, and became well known as such while later serving as Soviet representative at the United Nations during the 1960s, he was an intelligent and kind person.

I worked for Zorin for five years until 1952, having started as a second secretary and finally becoming his first assistant. I learned a lot from him. Whenever I presented him different documents from various departments of the ministry for his consideration, he asked for my opinion and increasingly relied more and more on my judgments. That made me examine the materials much more carefully. I followed and learned the procedures for the solution of important issues, especially those that were sent to the top—to Vyshinsky, Molotov, and even Stalin—and then returned to us with their comments and instructions. I thus obtained broad experience in how our policies were developed and formulated. Things I did not understand, I asked Zorin about at opportune moments. He always took the time to explain why this or that question had been solved in a particular way.

I must note that at the time the work of the entire state machine was organized in a very strange and bizarre way, "in keeping with Stalin." Stalin used to start his working day at 4 or 5 P.M. (nobody knew why for sure). Vyshinsky and Molotov, accordingly, showed up in the ministry at about 1 or 2 P.M., and their deputies were at their desks an hour or so earlier than that. Those of us in the Secretariat took turns working around the clock. The first assistants came to work at 9 or 10 A.M. to sort out and prepare the incoming documents. Ministers' deputies and their assistants worked until 3 or 4 A.M., that is, up to the moment when Stalin went to bed. God forbid if someone was not on the job when Stalin phoned him after midnight. We were all exhausted, including our chiefs. We would catch some sleep on the office couch, taking turns with the other assistants, and then go on working again.

As assistants of the deputy minister, we never personally contacted Stalin. Nevertheless, his name made us shudder. Only once in my life had I met with Stalin face to face. That day a Politburo meeting was to be held to which Zorin had been summoned. He found that he needed some additional document before the meeting convened. So he phoned me from the Kremlin and asked me to bring it immediately from the ministry. I was walking briskly along a Kremlin corridor to the Politburo hall when I suddenly saw Stalin and his guards slowly approaching from the other end of the long corridor. The corridors in the Kremlin have high ceilings, but they are long and narrow, with a lot of space between the doors. I quickly glanced first to the left, then to the right: there was neither a door nearby nor a side corridor down which I could disappear. So I pressed my back against the wall and stood there waiting for Stalin to pass by.

He did not fail to notice my confusion. When he came over to me he asked who I was and where I worked. Then, stressing his words by slowly moving a finger of his right hand in front of my face, he said, "Youth mustn't fear comrade Stalin. He is its friend." With this he nodded and proceeded to where he was going.

Late that night I told Zorin about what had happened to me. At first he became worried, but on learning that Stalin had behaved in quite an amicable manner, he stopped worrying. Nevertheless he remarked, "Stalin is unpredictable and it is better to stay away from him."

He had good reason to know. At times Stalin arrived at rather drastic decisions concerning the Ministry of Foreign Affairs. I remember Zorin once returning from a Politburo session in a state of shock. He said he was sure that it was the end of Gromyko and him, because Stalin had gotten dangerously angry with them. This is what had happened: a document on the exchange rate of the Chinese yuan for Soviet rubles had been prepared by the Ministry of Foreign Affairs in coordination with the Ministry of Finance. At the time Zorin was dealing with Chinese affairs. He submitted the document to Gromyko (who was a first deputy minister and at the moment performing the duties of the minister) for final approval. Gromyko took his time. On the one hand, he did not want to disturb Stalin because in his opinion the ruble-yuan rate was not a very significant matter. But on the other, Gromyko's innate circumspection made him hesitate.

The Chinese government and our embassy in Beijing once again began pressing for a decision. Once again Zorin supported them. Gromyko finally approved, though quite unwillingly, because he was dubious about the matter, which was meant as a friendly gesture toward the new communist government of Mao Zedong, but without Stalin's knowledge. Some time later Stalin learned about the decision and put it on the agenda of a Politburo meeting. At the meeting Stalin labeled Gromyko's and Zorin's actions as "flagrant overstepping of authority by conceited Ministry of Foreign Affairs officials" and asked the Politburo members what punishment the two deserved. Since no one knew what Stalin was driving at, everyone remained silent. For Gromyko and Zorin, it was a terrifying moment.

Having uttered some very strong words, Stalin declared to the Politburo that Gromyko should be removed from the position of first deputy and be sent (here he paused) as ambassador to England, and that Zorin should be subjected to a severe reprimand and warning. It was so decided. Gromyko went to Great Britain where he spent nine months until Stalin died. Nikita Khrushchev restored him to his former position of first deputy minister. Zorin escaped with an oral reprimand.

It was still worse when Stalin, without consulting anyone, made "resolute" decisions on his own. They did a lot of damage to our foreign relations, such as in the turn toward the Cold War, our actions against Tito in Yugoslavia, and our decision to boycott the United Nations Security Council during the Korean War in 1951.

Yet on the whole Stalin was quite favorably disposed toward Gromyko and took his opinion into consideration. After Stalin's death, Gromyko, who was otherwise a very reserved person, spoke of him with admiration during our personal conversations. He recalled that Stalin had always prepared all his own speeches, including summary reports at party congresses, for which he drew upon a vast range of materials. He also used to write his own articles for the press. Not without praise did Gromyko remember that when diplomatic notes drafted at the Foreign Ministry were considered by the Politburo, Stalin not only criticized them but, if necessary, dictated his own wording, which Gromyko took down right there.

Gromyko recalled that in sending him as ambassador to Washington, Stalin had given him a piece of advice. Upon learning that Gromyko did not know English too well, Stalin advised him to go to American churches on Sunday and listen to the sermons. He said that the preachers spoke a language understandable to plain people and since the sermons reflected their congregations' everyday needs and aspirations, in this way he would be able to get an idea of the domestic situation. (Stalin seemed to have based this advice on his experience as a young seminarian years before.)

Of course, once in Washington Gromyko did not dare visit churches, but as he later confessed, he had regularly listened to the sermons of popular preachers on the radio.

Gromyko recalled an episode at the 1945 Potsdam summit meeting of Stalin, Truman, and Winston Churchill. After receiving the cable that the atomic bomb had been successfully exploded, Truman casually mentioned that the United States had tested a weapon with huge destructive power (without naming the atomic bomb). Stalin nodded and said nothing. Churchill wrote in his memoirs that Stalin evidently had not understood the importance of the news. But Churchill was wrong.

When Stalin returned to his headquarters, he immediately called Igor Kurchatov, chief of our own supersecret atomic bomb project, and, citing Truman, ordered him to speed up his work. Kurchatov complained about his difficulties: first, the project was consuming huge amounts of electric power, then in very short supply in our war-devastated country, and second, he did not have enough tractors to clear the Siberian forest to build nuclear plants.

Stalin made his decision on the spot. First, power was simply switched off in several large, populated areas—except for their factories—and diverted to the atomic project, and second, two tank divisions were placed at Kurchatov's disposal to work as tractors clearing the place.

Early in 1952 I decided to speak to Zorin about my future work. I had been in his secretariat for close to five years and wanted a job somewhere at an embassy. Zorin approved, saying that a real diplomat must have experience in work abroad. After a while he told me that there would soon be a vacant position as the minister at our embassy in Switzerland and that he would recommend me for it.

According to the tradition that existed in those times, all recommendations for the highest positions in each country were considered by the foreign minister in the presence of all his deputies and the nominees themselves. The urgent questions of the day were also decided at such sessions, which were called "the minister's conferences with his deputies" and were held almost daily. They usually started at midnight. Foreign Minister Vyshinsky was practically the sole speaker at these meetings (he liked to speak on these occasions and often initiated the discussion, where he could demonstrate his striking rhetorical talents).

My appointment to Switzerland was to be discussed at one of these night sittings, which was my second face-to-face meeting with Vyshinsky. When my turn came, he at once remembered that I was the one who had refused the prestigious position at the Education Department.

"Oh yes, at that time you told me about your wish to be an active diplomat and work abroad," he said with sarcasm. "I see you've chosen a very active spot, Switzerland, to which only pensioners are appointed or those who are soon going to retire."

I explained that I did not choose that country but rather had been offered a post there. I also said that I was ready to go to any other country.

"That's different," Vyshinsky said. "Where should we send this young and strong fellow, so he can put in some work instead of relaxing?"

No one said anything. Then, as if a brilliant idea had just come into his head, he said, "Let's send him as a counselor to our embassy in Washington. Our relations with the Americans are very bad, so let him try to improve them."

And that was what they decided.

This was how, quite unexpectedly, I found myself in the sphere of Soviet-American relations, which I have never regretted and where I remained from 1952 to 1992, for almost the entire period of my diplomatic career.

At the time the staff of the Ministry of Foreign Affairs did not travel to the United States by plane, which was expensive, but by boat to New York. We had embarked on the splendid ocean liner *Ile de France,* and for the first time we were to take a course in etiquette not at school, but in real life. Everything came off quite smoothly except for a small embarrassing episode when my wife and I came into the dining room and were handed an elegantly printed menu with a long list of dishes. Most were absolutely unfamiliar, and, besides, all the names were in French. We studied the menu and bravely ordered different dishes so as to learn more quickly. While giving my order I sensed that something was wrong, but the waiter took it with an unruffled air, and I ended up with two different soups. We took the menu with us to our room and studied it thoroughly with the help of a dictionary.

In this connection I should probably say a few words about our knowledge of foreign languages. Although I had graduated from the diplomatic school with good grades in English, when I arrived in the United States, things did not turn out to be that simple. It was especially difficult to attune our ears to regional accents and the patter of American street talk. When we were traveling from New York to Washington, the train stopped at a big city. We asked the conductor what it was. "Bolmor," he answered. We asked again because we had never heard of such a city. The answer was the same. We looked it up on the railroad map but could not find it. Only later we realized that he had been talking about Baltimore.

# II. My First Look at the United States

*Learning the Diplomatic Ropes*

I arrived in the United States for the first time in September of 1952. As a career diplomat, I had of course read a great deal about the country, its history, its political and economic system, science, and culture. I was well acquainted with the state of our current relations with Washington through almost daily reading of the cables from our embassy there and regular exchanges with our officials responsible for American affairs. I knew that the United States was a great country, very versatile and unique in its own way, but not too easy for a foreigner to understand.

The reality surpassed my expectations. A vast and beautiful country, great cities, many cars on the highways, modern factories, the energetic rhythm of life, the high standard of living, an active political and public life, the diversity of press and opinion—all these were my first impressions of life in America. It differed so much from my own country that it took me quite a time to get accustomed to this new country and eventually to like it. After almost thirty years, life in America has become, so to speak, second nature to me.

But I must confess that my entry to this new world was neither easy nor cloudless. I arrived at the very height of the Cold War, too close indeed to a hot war. Stalin was still alive and many in the United States blamed him for the war that was under way in Korea and the Cold War in general. The division of Europe was a reality of the continental landscape, perhaps to last for centuries. And so the party leadership and diplomatic corps of the Soviet Union were inspired to believe that no cardinal changes in the world were possible in any future they could foresee. As for the United States, it was at the moment of my arrival in the midst of a presidential campaign in which the eventual winner, General Dwight D. Eisenhower, was said to be thinking about using nuclear weapons in Korea and the entire country was going through a period of anti-communist and anti-Soviet hysteria.

So coming to Washington was for me something in the nature of entering enemy territory. I was a true believer in Marxism-Leninism. I believed in the ultimate victory of socialism over capitalism. My mind was clogged by the long years of Stalinism, by our own ideological blunders, by our deep-seated beliefs and perceptions, which led to our misconstruing all American intentions as inherently aggressive.

Stalin saw U.S. plans and actions as preparation for an all-out war of aggression against the Soviet Union. As his successor Nikita Khrushchev later recalled, the Soviet leadership then believed that the United States, with its superiority in nuclear weapons, would ultimately go to war with the Soviet Union. Soviet diplomacy was heavily influenced by this Stalinist dogma about the inevitability of a world war, and this of course affected our relations with the United States at that time. But the dogma itself was also strengthened by the permanent postwar hostility of the United States and its own intransigence toward the Soviet Union.

After Stalin's death on March 5, 1953, the Soviet Union entered a period of uncertainty which also offered new opportunities. Unfortunately a distorted image of our adversary and its intentions was the most lasting legacy Stalin left for his successors. The Kremlin could not break with Stalin's foreign policy during that transitional period. An additional cause of uncertainty and worry was the new Republican administration, with Eisenhower's secretary of state, John Foster Dulles, as its principal cold warrior. The administration's policies helped strengthen the already deeply held convictions of the new Soviet leaders that they could neither hope nor attempt to change the anti-Soviet attitudes in Washington. As a result—and with the help of our own cold warriors such as Molotov—Stalin's successors seemed to have decided early on that it would be impossible to achieve a breakthrough in relations with the new administration. They did not venture beyond the minimal steps necessary to avoid direct conflicts with the United States and to project an image of themselves as strong, but more peaceful than Stalin. So the Cold War continued in full swing.

I began working at our embassy in Washington on September 27, 1952. Our ambassador was Georgi Zarubin, a veteran diplomat who had previously served as an ambassador to Canada and Great Britain. He had the stern and strict appearance of a typical representative of "Stalin's school," although in general he was a pleasant and fair person. He had one secret which he tried to conceal by all possible means. Despite the fact that for more than ten years he had been an ambassador to a number of English-speaking countries, his knowledge of the language was rather poor. However, he had a good reputation at the ministry where it was understood that he spoke English fluently.

As I realized later, the ambassador's secret accounted for a fairly strange work schedule in the embassy. Every morning he gathered us for a meeting where we were to report the gist of the American newspapers to which each of us had been assigned. That took up almost all of the morning. I tried to convince the ambassador that it was a mere waste of time, and it would be much more efficient if each of us studied the press on his own, choosing the most significant articles. But all was in vain, and our "collective" studies of the press continued for his whole term of office, under the pretext that the diplomatic staff had to be well informed about the contents of the entire American press and not just of certain newspapers. Only later did I understand that it was he who needed these surveys. At these meetings he usually chose the most interesting topics and asked us to prepare reports on them for Moscow.

Apart from the ambassador there were four other senior officials at the embassy—a minister-counselor, Boris Karavaev, and three counselors. Two were from the Ministry of Foreign Affairs—I was one and Konstantin Fedoseev the other—and the third, Vladimir Vladykin, came from the intelligence service. At first I had to deal with internal political affairs and the economy of the United States. I was not particularly happy with this assignment because, like all young diplomats, I wished to deal with high matters of foreign policy. But there was nothing I could do but obey. So I was appointed chief of the embassy's department that handled these matters. I must admit that later I appreciated my first assignment by Ambassador Zarubin to those supposedly dull domestic questions of which most of the Foreign Ministry staff, including myself, had only a very vague idea. In Washington I was able to study them quite thoroughly, which served me in my future diplomatic work.

Nevertheless, my reputation as a foreign policy expert was also growing within the embassy. When important requests for information or other messages were prepared for Moscow, the ambassador always discussed them with the counselors. At these conferences it soon became evident that although I was not as well informed about some spheres of U.S. internal affairs as my colleagues, I was very much at home in questions of grand policy. This was a result of my experience in the Ministry Secretariat in Moscow, where we were used to handling all kinds of important issues. Moreover, in Moscow we tended to discuss them in depth, and outside of the orthodox thinking of official policy, which was a must for people who had to defend it in the embassies. I therefore was used to thinking more broadly (within strict limits, of course), although it demanded some courage to state an opinion. As a whole, it helped my diplomatic career.

At one point the ambassador had received from Moscow in close succession two important requests for the embassy's recommendations on current issues of our relations with the United States. As we were preparing answers, our opinions differed: I suggested one option and the other counselors another. In both cases the ambassador took the side of my colleagues. When Moscow cabled us our instructions on the two issues, they were almost identical to the options I had proposed at our meetings.

Soon the ambassador received a telegram with a direct request from Stalin seeking the embassy's recommendation about the American presidential campaign. Such things happened very rarely, because requests of this kind were usually routed to the Ministry of Foreign Affairs and not to the embassies. An answer was being prepared urgently. The discussion in the ambassador's office assumed the same pattern as the previous ones, and once again I was left in the minority. After much hesitation the answer of the majority was sent by the ambassador to Moscow. The reply was quite unpleasant: "Your recommendations are insufficiently considered."

After that the ambassador invited me for a private conversation. He wanted to know how I guessed Moscow's ideas. I said I was not really guessing and there was no special secret: intuition and experience had accumulated during quite a long period of witnessing how important decisions had been made. Soon after, the ambassador entrusted me with approving all the draft cables to Moscow before they were submitted to him. On July 24, 1954, I was promoted to minister-counselor of our Washington embassy at the age of thirty-four.

## Across the Country with Molotov

The next year Molotov came to the United States to head our delegation for the celebration of the tenth anniversary of the founding of the United Nations in San Francisco, where the United Nations charter had been signed in 1945. Having arrived in New York by ship, he decided to take a train to San Francisco and see the country on his way. He took Ambassador Zarubin with him, and Zarubin took me, since I had become familiar with the United States and could be useful during the trip.

Our train journey lasted three days and two nights. Molotov, though with a certain degree of his characteristic reserve, commented quite favorably on the enterprise of the Americans and on the scope of their industrial and agricultural development. At that time Soviet-American relations were far from friendly, and the Cold War was in full swing, which of course strongly influenced public opinion. A lot of curious people used to gather at the railroad stations, hoping to catch a glimpse of the "real Molotov."

Our stops at the stations were rare and short and, luckily, there were no unpleasant incidents. People were merely curious and did not express any favorable or unfavorable emotions except at one place, Chicago, where a large and agitated crowd had gathered. Chicago had many immigrants from Slavic and Eastern European countries who resented the domination of Moscow. The city was also the headquarters of many trade unions that were hostile to the Soviet Union. When Molotov looked out of the window, the people started booing (without any other manifestations of protest). When the train started off, Molotov asked Zarubin what the crowd had meant.

"That is an American way of greeting," the ambassador explained without batting an eye. Molotov looked rather puzzled and noted that this surely was a strange way of greeting foreigners. It was not surprising to me, but I said nothing so as not to let Zarubin down.

We had some difficulties sending coded cables to Moscow. At the time we did not have our own consulate in San Francisco and had to rent a house for Molotov near the city. Our security service was sure that the Americans had stuffed it with all kinds of undetected bugs. So our cipher clerks worked lying on the beds while we held blankets over them, so the Americans would not be able to "take pictures from the ceiling."

Fears of being spied on were mutual. At a conference of foreign ministers in Moscow's Sovietskaya Hotel (before the revolution it used to be the famous Yar hotel) the American delegation was provided with offices on the second floor, just above two restaurants. In the evening of the opening day the diners noticed with alarm that the huge chandelier in the center of the ceiling was shaking. A team of mechanics was immediately sent upstairs. At first the Americans refused to open up, and when they did we learned that the American security officers had been checking the premises for bugs. In the center of the floor their devices detected a large amount of metal, whereupon they opened the parquet and saw some kind of a metal structure with wires. They began to take it apart, unscrewing one part after another. That turned out to be the chandelier, which began swaying until our men arrived and stopped it.

In San Francisco I had to accompany Molotov everywhere and interpret for him. His own staff interpreter and my friend, Oleg Troyanovsky, had to leave urgently for Moscow to attend his father's funeral. Oleg Troyanovsky had been raised partly in the United States and attended American schools, and his English was flawless. I must say that only when I had to fill in for him did I realize how hard an interpreter's work actually was, although on the surface it always seemed to be so easy. All the smallest details of a conversation had to be translated with scrupulous exactness, because they usually carried an important diplomatic and political meaning. Although I could speak English rather fluently, I was hardly ready for the job of a professional interpreter. The most difficult part was writing the minutes of Molotov's talks from memory in order to send his reports to Moscow: unlike professional interpreters, I was unable to make shorthand notes. But on the whole I managed satisfactorily.

While interpreting the tough discussions between Molotov and John Foster Dulles, President Eisenhower's secretary of state and a moralist every bit as committed to capitalism and the Christian religion as Molotov was to the ideas of Marxism-Leninism, I had a feeling that they resembled a dialogue of the deaf *and* the blind, although all the rules of a diplomatic conversation were strictly obeyed. This was a highly symbolic confrontation of the two most outstanding representatives of the world's two ideological systems. It was obvious that as long as they and people like them were endowed with power, the Cold War would never end, and Soviet-American relations would not improve. They disagreed about everything, and they spoke in an uninspired language that you could read in any newspaper—the American press for Dulles and *Pravda* for Molotov.

They had no sense of trying to feel each other out, or trying to discuss details in the traditional and private diplomatic way. Molotov and Dulles completely avoided the traditional diplomatic give-and-take through which one side can hint at something new to the other. This was not Molotov's way of doing things, and he used to act the same with us. As we used to say, he was dry, dry as toast—and so was Gromyko later, unless you knew him quite well.

Here is another minor episode that reveals Molotov's state of mind. On the train from New York to San Francisco we were accompanied by an official representative of the State Department, who traveled in his own compartment. He was an obliging person who never annoyed us and was invariably helpful. At one point Molotov became interested in the land we were passing and asked for a map. Unfortunately, none of us had such a map. He called us "brainless" and stopped talking to us. What were we to do?

I went to the State Department escort and told him about our problem. He told me not to worry, we would get a map at the next station. And indeed he soon brought us a colorful map with the railroad line and the stations on our way. It also showed the location of large army camps and bases and the stations that served them.

We gave this map to Molotov. He was terrified by the sight of the camps and bases. He declared that we had purposely been given a secret map as a provocation so that the American newspapers could write that Molotov had been collecting secret information during his journey. He ordered us to return the map immediately, so I sought out the State Department man, who laughed and said it wasn't a secret map at all. On the contrary, it was given out free at all railroad stations for tourists "like you" but especially to help servicemen reach their bases. No one made any secret of their location.

At the next station he got us another map at a post office. This one did not show any camps or bases. We handed it to Molotov who was quite proud of his "vigilance." Without telling him I kept the old map as a memento.

Since Troyanovsky had not returned from Moscow, Molotov informed me that I was to accompany him on the *Queen Mary* during his return trip to Europe. This time there was little work for me to do because Molotov stayed in his stateroom practically all the time, and even his meals were brought to him there. He was not choosy and ordered the simplest dishes. For breakfast he only ate his cereal which his cook brought from Moscow and prepared for him. The ship's chef, whose professional pride was somewhat hurt, offered to make "any kind of porridge Mr. Molotov wished," since the ship was provided with all imaginable foodstuffs. However, our boss stubbornly refused all these offers.

Every morning an odd procession could be seen in the ship's corridors. It consisted of three people: I was the first, in case there should be any need to communicate with the outside world. Next came our cook with his kettle. Colonel Alexandrov, the head of Molotov's guard, brought up the rear. Our cook would enter the big kitchen and the chefs would stare at him fussing over his pot of Molotov's special porridge. Then he would wrap it in a warm towel, and we solemnly returned to the minister's stateroom.

## Back to Moscow as Molotov's Assistant

After seeing Molotov off to Moscow I flew back to Washington where I returned to my duties at the embassy. However, several weeks later an order came appointing me one of Molotov's assistants and instructing me to come back to Moscow. At that time it was only natural that no one had even thought of asking my opinion. Frankly speaking, I had come to like my work at the embassy. I became acquainted with many Americans and established contacts with many diplomats from other countries. I had discovered a new and fascinating world and was not at all willing to return to the rigid work schedule at the Ministry Secretariat with the same colleagues. But an order is an order, and I had to obey.

After working for Molotov for about a year, I had to admit that from the psychological point of view it was the most difficult period in my whole career. Relations between Molotov and Khrushchev were worsening with each passing day. This was making Molotov irritable and suspicious, and his behavior was unrestrained toward people who worked for him.

He was a very orderly and punctilious person—that I remember as one of his few good traits. The large desk in his Kremlin office was divided into eight sections, although these sections were marked out only in his mind (and of course, ours). We, his assistants, were to place all the incoming materials in these sections in strict order to prepare them for the Politburo, the Council of Ministers, Ministry of Foreign Affairs, and so on. When he arrived in his office he first looked through the papers for the most important destinations. God forbid if any of us had put some document or a coded cable in the wrong section. When he had the time, he used to lie down in the back room for forty-five minutes' rest. Not a minute more nor a minute less. During these breaks the head of his guard stood at the door and prevented anyone from disturbing him. He was also very punctual with visitors or people he had summoned. He disliked long speeches or disputes at meetings. His own reports were always unemotional, short and to the point.

Molotov's positions in foreign policy were utterly dogmatic. Not only had he zealously supported Stalin's policy when the latter was alive, but he actually followed it after Stalin's death in 1953. At the time the Politburo was heatedly discussing the question of a peace treaty with Austria. This was eventually to mean the withdrawal of the U.S., British, and French troops from that country and a formal end to World War II as far as Austria was concerned in exchange for its neutrality in the ideological and diplomatic battles between East and West. Molotov was against this on the ground that the withdrawal of Soviet troops from Austria would considerably weaken the USSR's position in the center of Europe and would deprive the nation of a large part of its gains in World War II. But by that time the political atmosphere in Europe was quite different, and the dominant tendency was the promotion of stable relations between the wartime allies, something Moscow had to take into account. As a result, Molotov was left in the minority, and the treaty with Austria was signed on May 15, 1955. That was a serious blow to his prestige in the field of foreign policy, where until then he had made virtually all the decisions.

As relations with the West continued to improve, that left Molotov increasingly isolated and at odds with Khrushchev. We at the Secretariat could not help feeling that Molotov's star was falling, and finally he was dismissed as minister of foreign affairs, although he still remained a member of the Politburo. Khrushchev appointed Dmitri Shepilov as minister of foreign affairs. He was Molotov's antipode: sociable, accessible, and by no means dogmatic. But he was removed after only one year along with members of the Politburo who had coalesced in opposition to Khrushchev: Molotov, Nikolai Bulganin, Lazar Kaganovich, and others of the old guard. Shepilov, who at first was Khrushchev's protégé, had made the mistake of joining them and had to pay for it. The opposition formed after Khrushchev's famous secret speech about Stalin, followed by "the thaw" in politics and his attempt at domestic reforms. A growing internal struggle was finally resolved with complete victory for Khrushchev and dismissal from the Politburo of all his opponents by virtue of his overwhelming support within the Central Committee of the Communist Party.

Khrushchev did not bring any new conception of foreign policy, although he was open to new ideas and from time to time improvised impulsively in the field. He chose Gromyko as his foreign minister because he respected his professionalism and recognized him as a very disciplined official. He could be trusted utterly to carry out the orders of Khrushchev and the Politburo, indeed to "sit on a block of ice if I tell him to," as Khrushchev once said of him. But this was only half of the story. The rest was that inside the Politburo Gromyko was the generator and daily administrator of Soviet foreign policy. During discussions in the Politburo or one-on-one with Khrushchev he did not hesitate to express and defend his views. But once the final decision was taken, Gromyko would conscientiously and stubbornly fulfill all the instructions of the Politburo and the CPSU general secretary, not allowing himself to deviate from them even an inch, although at times during negotiations the situation would call for some flexibility.

It appears that it was his sense of discipline and lack of any aspirations to other posts in the party and government leadership that made it possible for him to remain in the post of a minister for almost thirty years. His high competence was beyond doubt. But above all, he possessed an excellent intuition which helped him to figure out who was going to win the next of the regular battles for power. Gromyko unerringly chose the winning side at the right time even to the very end of his career when he supported the appointment of Mikhail Gorbachev as general secretary in 1985 with his famous phrase—"a man with a nice smile and iron teeth"—although Gorbachev certainly did not stand for the same things as Gromyko and soon got rid of him.

## A Tour at the United Nations

Gromyko inherited me as an assistant, and I was on good terms with him from the very beginning. He acceded to my request for a transfer to a diplomatic job in the field. On his recommendation, Secretary General Dag Hammarskjold appointed me an undersecretary general for special political affairs at the United Nations. At the same time the Presidium of the Supreme Soviet gave me the rank of ambassador extraordinary and plenipotentiary. I temporarily left my job at the Soviet Foreign Ministry and became an international civil servant, as did some of my Western diplomatic colleagues. Although at first the prospect of dealing with a heap of dull UN resolutions did not seem too attractive, Gromyko solved my problem by granting me the right to send independent correspondence from New York, bypassing our diplomats in New York and Washington.

At that time about 150 Soviet employees worked at the UN Secretariat, although by size and budget contribution the Soviet Union was entitled to about twice that number. However, there was an obvious shortage of candidates, and not all of our professional diplomats were willing to take this highly specific job. During the Cold War Russians also were prevented by Western officials in the UN Secretariat from signing on, especially for high posts. My principal task was to ensure that the Soviet view was not ignored by the secretary general of the UN.

It was also a more or less open secret that our quota of UN officials was partly filled by people from the intelligence services. We, diplomatic professionals, knew each other fairly well, and it was not very difficult to know who was who among the Soviet personnel, although no one outside intelligence knew exactly what it was doing. This cast an unpleasant shadow on all Soviet employees in the Secretariat.

There was another negative factor. We Soviet citizens in the Secretariat were paid much more than diplomats at the Soviet Mission to the United Nations, and to "eliminate this injustice" someone in the Soviet government had arrived at a brilliant decision: All Soviet UN employees were secretly ordered to hand over to the Mission's bookkeepers a sum equalizing the difference, even though we got none of their perks such as subsidized housing and automobiles. Each month I parted with over half my salary. Finally in 1990 Soviet UN personnel revolted against this racket and it was stopped.

Moscow's conservatism also manifested itself in a seemingly quite simple matter. All employees of the UN Secretariat were paid by checks drawn on the UN's payroll account at the Chemical Bank of New York, one of the largest American banks, and of course we got checkbooks. When this became known at the Personnel Department of the Central Committee, it exploded: Soviet employees of the United Nations had checkbooks just like capitalists! I argued for several months on behalf of my colleagues against these absurd accusations, and we were finally allowed to keep our checkbooks.

Hammarskjold and I established a peculiar personal relationship. I was his only deputy who did not depend on him as an employer, since I had been "loaned" from active diplomatic service and could return at any moment. I therefore could sometimes afford to disagree tactfully with Hammarskjold during the regular Friday conferences of his deputies. One day he confided to me that I was the only one at the meetings who posed complex and delicate questions to which he could not always provide clear and frank answers.

He suggested that each time I had any serious questions, or when he himself was not sure about Moscow's position, we should meet together privately in the evenings. Of course, I agreed, and these conversations became routine. At times he even read from the private diary of his official visits, which, as might be expected from such an aristocratic intellectual, had their sarcastic side. These talks also made it possible to establish a channel between him and the Soviet leadership during my term.

Because of Hammarskjold's background and demeanor, Khrushchev was not overfond of him, which gave rise to awkward episodes. Hammarskjold wanted to visit the Soviet Union, and I arranged for an invitation. I advised him to address Khrushchev in simple words, and especially not to bring up his ideas for a radical restructuring of the United Nations on the lines of a world government. Hammarskjold seemed to understand. I accompanied him on the trip, and you can imagine my surprise when during their meeting I heard Hammarskjold plunge into a long and boring description of the future world order and the UN's role in it, all this in reply to Khrushchev's simple question, "What's new at the United Nations?"

After about twenty minutes of Hammarskjold's monologue, Khrushchev became visibly irritated. With his characteristic rudeness he told the interpreter, "Ask Mr. Hammarskjold if he wants to go to the bathroom."

The interpreter hesitated. Khrushchev told him to translate exactly what he had said, and without "any diplomatic tricks." Hammarskjold, taken aback, said finally that if Mr. Prime Minister suggested it, he had no objection.

After that Khrushchev suggested they take a break and go for a ride in a boat (all this was taking place on the Black Sea coast). Hammarskjold expected a big launch and gladly agreed. When they reached the pier they saw a small four-oar dinghy. Khrushchev took two oars and handed the other two to the secretary general, who had no idea how to use them. In the end Khrushchev was the one who rowed. He took Hammarskjold for quite a long ride in the open sea. The guards were ordered not to approach closely. After an hour the boat returned. Khrushchev got out and said, "We had such a nice talk." (Khrushchev did not know English, Hammarskjold did not speak Russian, and the interpreter had been left ashore.) Khrushchev must have realized that he had gone too far, and over a good breakfast, they discussed issues facing the United Nations in a businesslike manner, but Hammarskjold was nevertheless left quite shaken by his adventures.

These were not the only misunderstandings at the UN, and I especially recall one exchange at the Trusteeship Council. A Nigerian, engaged in a heated discussion with a titled English delegate, suddenly addressed him: "Sir, why should argue? We are almost blood brothers."

The Englishman, a lord, was taken aback. "You? My blood brother?"

The Nigerian confirmed he certainly was by asking the Englishman, "Who was your grandfather?"

"My grandfather was the commander of the expeditionary corps sent to Africa by Queen Victoria. He perished there but was posthumously awarded the highest British order."

"And my grandfather was the chief of the tribe that defeated your grandfather's troops. Since at the time he was not too civilized, he ate your grandfather. So, as you see, we are blood brothers."

On the whole, I look back at my work at the United Nations with satisfaction. I increased my fluency to the point where I could edit UN documents in English, and while I was living in New York I enjoyed freedom from normal diplomatic constraints and acquired a large number of friends and acquaintances from the most diverse circles of American society. This greatly helped me during my work later as ambassador in Washington; I still meet with many of them. No less important was that my wife and I lived for two years in a residential hotel on the Upper West Side of Manhattan, far from the Soviet mission, and we got accustomed to everyday American life.

From time to time I sent Moscow my own observations about political life in the United States from New York, where I had established numerous contacts. As I later learned, parts of my dispatches were circulated by Gromyko to members of the Soviet government. Perhaps that was why, three years later, at the beginning of 1960, I was suddenly recalled from the United Nations and appointed a member of the Board of the Ministry of Foreign Affairs and chief of the American Department.

Before we returned to Moscow, my wife and I spent two weeks (and our remaining dollars) on a tourist trip to California. We flew to San Francisco, rented a car, and drove down the picturesque Highway 1 along the Pacific Coast to Los Angeles and San Diego, and from there to Phoenix in Arizona, hoping to visit the Grand Canyon. We were blocked by a snowstorm that also grounded air traffic, so we boarded a bus that took three days to cross the United States from Phoenix to New York. We still remember the incomparable geography and customs of the various states of this wonderful country. Later on as ambassador, I traveled extensively throughout the country, and eventually we visited all fifty states.

# III. Summits: The View from the Other Side of the Peak

*The Geneva Summit: Eisenhower and Khrushchev*

Summit meetings always played a very important role in Soviet-American relations, and I participated at all summit meetings involving the Soviet Union from 1955 to 1990. The summit was the ultimate court, where heads of state entrusted with the highest authority could try to solve the most difficult questions in international relations. Great hopes were always attached to these meetings. At the same time, summits, if they failed, carried serious consequences for relations between Washington and Moscow and for the international situation as a whole. When that happened, both sides would try to cover it with propaganda attacks, which did not help diplomatic relations in the least.

Some in the West believed that Moscow was interested in summit meetings only or mostly for the propaganda they might generate. This was only partly true. I can testify that Brezhnev and Gromyko would never consent to a summit with an American president until they were sure they could achieve something concrete and positive from it that would improve relations. That was one reason they were prepared to wait a year or two before agreeing to a summit.

Khrushchev was a bit different. He also sought positive results but often did not think out carefully how to achieve them. He was committed to the peace process but could not often translate that commitment into concrete agreements. His improvisation, his inclination to bluff, and his bad temper were all overlaid by a strong ideology, and this helped turn his discussions with American presidents into heated disputes without helpful results, although I must add that his partners in these disputes also did not make the process any easier. Perhaps the time was not yet ripe for agreements, and the summits attended by Khrushchev, however colorful they may have been, were hardly productive milestones in the history of Soviet-American relations.

After the armistice ending the fighting in Korea in 1953, the French withdrawal from Indochina in 1954, and finally the Austrian State Treaty in 1955, there was a steady relaxation of international tension that made the first peacetime summit meeting possible. Prime Minister Winston Churchill had coined the phrase "a meeting at the summit," but his term of office did not last long enough for him to participate in the first summit meeting since those in Yalta and Potsdam in the closing days of World War II. That meeting was held on July 18–23, 1955, in Geneva, which then held a reputation as a center for peaceful mediation because it was the prewar home of the League of Nations. I was then serving as Molotov's assistant, and it was the first time in my career that I took part in a meeting at such a high level.

The Soviet delegation was led by Premier Nikolai Bulganin, although he only delivered the speeches that had been prepared beforehand. Khrushchev, as general secretary of the Communist Party, played the most active role. President Eisenhower of course led the U.S. delegation, but it was obvious to us that foreign policy was handled by Dulles. Britain and France made up the rest of the Big Four, and the principal topics were the division of Germany and the reduction of arms.

Eisenhower favored unifying Germany on the basis of elections and then including it in the Western security system. Khrushchev, as far as I know, did not really believe in the possibility of reunifying Germany in his lifetime and wanted the German Democratic Republic to remain separate from West Germany as "a state of workers." This issue remained essentially unresolved until the Cold War ended.

The Soviet Union proposed agreements to reduce arms and armed forces, prohibit the testing of nuclear weapons, and commit the Big Four not to use nuclear weapons first—items that remained on the agenda of East-West diplomacy throughout the Cold War, although a limited treaty banning nuclear tests was signed in 1963.

Eisenhower's abiding concern in arms control was with mutual inspection to guard against surprise attack, an almost obsessive theme in American diplomacy because of the 1941 Japanese attack on Pearl Harbor. He proposed that the Soviet Union and the United States exchange information on the location of their armaments and send inspectors to verify them on the ground. Each country would also photograph the territory of the other from the air, which came to be known as the "Open Skies" plan. The Americans were well aware that such close monitoring had long been out of the question for the Soviet leadership because it was convinced that the United States would exploit the process to gather military information. This created a vicious circle lasting three decades, and our rejection seemed to suit Washington perfectly, making it the winner at least on propaganda points.

When the idea was discussed at one Politburo session, Khrushchev insisted that the Eisenhower administration was bluffing, and that no one in the U.S. Congress would agree to allow Soviet planes to fly over, say, the Capitol in Washington. He therefore suggested we accept the proposal and watch the White House squirm in the propaganda spotlight. But the Politburo would not even hear of letting American planes fly over Soviet territory and rejected Khrushchev's tactic.

Even with such deadlocks, our Foreign Ministry rated the Geneva summit favorably, partly because the meeting ended in smiles all around and a so-called Spirit of Geneva was often invoked later to help calm disputes.

It was obvious to me that on the American side it was Dulles who ran the show. The president seemed to be quite helpless in foreign policy matters, since from the very start he had entrusted them to Dulles and had not shown any real interest. Eisenhower often found himself in a difficult situation during debates on specific issues, and Dulles repeatedly had to come to his aid with the details. At one point we claimed that NATO was an aggressive bloc plotting a war against the Soviet Union. Eisenhower denied that. Suddenly Khrushchev asked him: "Then why have you refused to admit us to NATO?"

"Have you applied?" Eisenhower asked, surprised.

"Several months ago," Khrushchev replied.

Eisenhower was obviously at a loss.

The point was that a while back, on Khrushchev's initiative and purely for propaganda purposes, the Foreign Ministry had raised the possibility of Soviet membership in NATO in one of its notes to Western states. As expected, Dulles immediately refused but had not bothered to inform the president. At Geneva he had to explain the situation to the president in a whisper, while others exchanged glances, trying to hide their smiles. To Eisenhower's relief, Khrushchev dropped the subject.

During recesses Khrushchev and Eisenhower engaged in lively conversation on personal topics, and by the end of the conference they seemed to take a liking to each other. Eisenhower was invited to visit the Soviet Union, and Khrushchev had returned from Geneva thinking highly of him. At one of the Politburo sessions he had said, "I cannot judge how good Eisenhower is as a president. It is for the American people to decide that. But as a father and grandfather I would gladly entrust my kids to him at school or a day care center." This was a typical example of Khrushchev's humor but he became genuinely convinced that Eisenhower would never allow a major military confrontation between the Soviet Union and the United States. In this he trusted him like "one war veteran would trust another."

But such camaraderie was not sufficient to crack the central issue of arms control, which during the whole of postwar history represented the core of Soviet-American relations. The process was also cynically used by both sides for propaganda. So, for many years our mania for secrecy allowed the West to use control and inspection as a battering ram to convince the world that the cause of disarmament was hopeless. When we ourselves began to advance the issue, the Americans moved backwards, for example, by trying to exempt their warships from inspections.

## The Collapse of the Paris Summit

The next Big Four summit was scheduled for Paris on May 16, 1960. I had just returned from New York and resumed my work at the Foreign Ministry as head of the American Department. We were busy preparing for the meeting, which was to consider disarmament, nuclear tests, a peace treaty with Germany, and relations between East and West.

But even before it began, the prospects for the meeting were uncertain at best because American U-2 reconnaissance planes had been sent high over Soviet territory on April 9 and May 1. The second one had been brought down near the city of Sverdlovsk by one of our missiles, and its pilot, a Central Intelligence Agency contract flier named Francis Gary Powers, had bailed out and fallen into our hands. We knew that the U-2s had been flying over the Soviet Union for some time but remained silent about this intrusion because our artillery had until then been unable to shoot down one of these extraordinary planes, which flew at an altitude of more than 80,000 feet.

Although the U-2 episode was eventually to wreck the Paris summit, even before that it caused an unexpected scandal in the central apparatus of the Soviet Ministry of Foreign Affairs. It involved a well-known Soviet diplomat, Yakov Malik, who at that time was a deputy minister of foreign affairs. After the U-2 had been hit and Powers had been captured, Khrushchev forbade everyone to say anything about it at all, hoping that the Americans would consider him dead and would start putting forth various face-saving stories to explain his flight over Soviet territory. Afterward Khrushchev intended to unmask the whole illegal operation and ridicule the administration through Powers's own words.

For several days everything proceeded according to plan. But at a diplomatic reception Malik blabbed out the story. It immediately became known to the U.S. Embassy in Moscow, and from there to official Washington, although Ambassador Llewellyn Thompson's cable arrived in Washington minutes too late for Washington to amend its official version of the incident. Once he learned the story, an enraged Khrushchev removed Malik from his post at the ministry and excluded him from the party. For three weeks poor Malik went to everyone he knew in Moscow expressing his utter repentance.

Even that might not have been enough if Gromyko had not personally intervened and persuaded Khrushchev to pardon his talkative deputy.

On May 14, the Soviet delegation consisting of Khrushchev, Gromyko, and our defense minister, Marshal Rodion Malinovsky, arrived in Paris. I was the delegation's counselor. The American delegation was led by Eisenhower, accompanied by Christian Herter, who had succeeded Dulles as secretary of state upon the latter's death from cancer.

The preliminary meeting of the four heads of government took place on May 16 as scheduled. Khrushchev was the first to speak. He was in an angry mood and loudly demanded that the American government should first denounce "the inadmissible provocative actions" of its own air force toward the Soviet Union and second, publicly renounce any similar actions against the Soviet Union in the future.

"Until this is done by the U.S. government," Khrushchev stressed, "the Soviet government sees no possibility of productive talks with the U.S. government at the summit conference." He continued that the provocative flights of American planes over Soviet territory as declared national policy created "new conditions in international relations under which the Soviet delegation cannot participate in any kind of negotiations and even in the consideration of urgent issues." Khrushchev therefore proposed postponing the summit conference for about six or eight months and put off Eisenhower's previously agreed trip to the Soviet Union as well. He said it could be rescheduled "when the required conditions appear."

Khrushchev's emotional speech and especially its second part was a real surprise to Eisenhower and, besides, made him feel uncomfortable, since it had been delivered in the presence of his main allies, Prime Minister Harold Macmillan of Great Britain and President Charles de Gaulle of France, who as host was chairman of the meeting.

After an awkward pause, Eisenhower made a short statement in which he tried to justify himself, saying that the flights of American planes over the Soviet territory "did not pursue any aggressive object and were aimed at preventing the United States from being attacked by surprise." This only increased Khrushchev's indignation, as did Eisenhower's remark that "these flights had been suspended after the recent incident and would not be renewed."

Khrushchev announced that the Soviet delegation would take part in the conference only after "the American government declares that it denounces such actions and commits itself not to carry out any spying flights over the Soviet territory."

That evening the American delegation issued a statement by Eisenhower announcing that he had given instructions to discontinue the flights of

American military planes over the territory of the Soviet Union. In private talks with Khrushchev, Macmillan and de Gaulle tried to convince him that Eisenhower had fulfilled his demands. Macmillan reminded Khrushchev that he had three requests: that the flights be denounced, that they no longer take place, and that the denunciation be made in public. The first two requests, he argued, had been fulfilled by President Eisenhower—"But try to understand: Can a head of state censure himself and his nation?"

Khrushchev replied, "We want him to condemn the guilty."

Later in the evening Khrushchev held a conference with the Soviet delegation. He was very excited. He was sure that if not Eisenhower himself, then the president's close associates had intended to humiliate Khrushchev, personally and as the head of the Soviet government, by sending planes across Soviet territory and thus demonstrating to the whole world his helplessness and inability to protect his country's borders. He even recalled Stalin's words to the Politburo in his last years that "soon after my death, the arrogant Americans would wring your necks, like chickens."

Marshal Malinovsky supported Khrushchev's unyielding position; he had not forgotten that after the first successful U-2 flight over Soviet territory, he and the Soviet Armed Forces had been roundly criticized by the Politburo for not being able to destroy the planes and stop the flights.

Gromyko held a more reserved position. He agreed that "Eisenhower has to be taught a good lesson," but he feared that the summit conference would collapse and was trying to find a way out. But Khrushchev remained firm, probably remembering his promise at the Politburo on the eve of the conference "to teach the Americans, who had gone beyond all limits, a good lesson."

To better understand Khrushchev's behavior it should be said that from the very beginning he was convinced that Eisenhower would not allow the conference to collapse and would find a way out by sacrificing one of his generals "who had gone too far." But Eisenhower had spoiled this scenario by declaring that he, as commander in chief, was responsible for the operations of his armed forces, although he personally had not ordered the flight of the U-2 plane over Sverdlovsk. (In fact, Eisenhower's biographer, Professor Stephen E. Ambrose, records that the president alone authorized the schedule of every U-2 flight and wanted to ground them well before the summit but finally yielded to the pleas of the CIA for just one more in the month before the summit. Eisenhower agreed but clouds delayed the flight and it took place on the last day he would permit, which happened to be May 1.)

On May 17 the heads of governments of the three Western states gathered for a meeting at the Elysée Palace, home of French presidents. Since the Soviet delegation had not been explicitly informed whether the meeting was preliminary or the formal opening of the summit conference, it did not arrive. Khrushchev stayed away, still hoping that Eisenhower would give in.

That evening the public recriminations began.

Eisenhower's press secretary, James Hagerty, announced that the summit conference was to have begun its work that day but had not done so since the Soviet representative had been absent. The president of the United States therefore considered the conference closed. Khrushchev's press office immediately released a statement saying that "the government of the United States, which had taken a number of aggressive actions against the USSR on the eve of the summit conference and which had stubbornly refused to take responsibility for these actions, was the one which had blocked the conference, which the peoples of the whole world had awaited with hope."

After the collapse of the summit conference of 1960, Soviet-American relations deteriorated considerably. They were confined to partial fulfillment of a program of scientific, technical, and cultural exchange. Eisenhower's presidential trip to the Soviet Union never took place. A hunting lodge, specially built for his visit on the beautiful shore of Lake Baikal, was locally known as "Eisenhower's Cottage," but he never saw it.

Some American historians have argued that Khrushchev came to Paris with the intention of wrecking the summit so he could make propaganda. That was not so, and I can testify to it. Our delegation brought with it extensive directives for each item on the agenda, all of them approved after active deliberation within the Politburo. So we left Moscow with the expectation of lengthy if uneasy discussions in Paris.

While it is true that Khrushchev asked for and received authorization from the Politburo to criticize American behavior strongly for arrogantly sending the U-2 into our airspace just before the summit, he had no instructions to demand a personal apology from Eisenhower. That happened because of Khrushchev's emotional attempt to bluff an apology out of Eisenhower by threatening to ruin the summit. He failed. So the Big Four summit, the last in history of the four wartime allies—should be remembered as a summit of lost opportunities.

## Khrushchev and Kennedy at Vienna

In his first speeches after winning the 1960 presidential election, John F. Kennedy announced that his administration intended to improve relations with the USSR and solve problems by negotiation. In its turn the Soviet government sent a message of greetings to the new president on the day of his inauguration expressing the hope that the two nations would be able to make a "radical improvement of relations" and "to normalize the international situation in general." On January 24, only four days into the new government, Washington sent an official note confirming that President Kennedy had given an order forbidding American planes to intrude in Soviet airspace. It was clear that the two leaders wanted to seek an early meeting to discuss improving relations.

On March 9, 1961, the American ambassador in Moscow, Llewellyn Thompson, handed Khrushchev a confidential message from Kennedy proposing a summit conference between the leaders of the two superpowers. After brief negotiations—I was still head of the Foreign Ministry's American Department—we agreed to hold the meeting on July 3–4, 1961, in Vienna.

On specific questions, Kennedy was seeking accommodation in Laos, a distant nation in Southeast Asia that entangled both governments into backing rival factions. He also wanted to explore the possibilities of a treaty banning nuclear tests in the atmosphere. But most of all he was searching out the Soviet Union's true motives for its persistent pressure on Berlin and wanted to discover whether it was prepared to go to war over the city with the NATO nations. Khrushchev had warned that he might sign a peace treaty with the German Democratic Republic, thus handing over the Soviet Union's occupation rights to the GDR and leaving the U.S., British, and French allies surrounded in West Berlin; if they then chose to preserve their own rights, they would have to use force. Kennedy recognized that maintaining those rights would be a supreme test of the resolve of the United States and the value of its commitments—he even told Khrushchev so at Vienna. But Khrushchev wished to measure the resolve of this young, new president who even in his own country still retained something of a reputation, whether deserved or not, as a political dilettante.

Shortly after the delivery in March of the initial note about the meeting, something else also made the sky seem less cloudless. On April 17, 1961, landing parties of Cuban counterrevolutionaries invaded Cuba under the protection of American warships. Most of the fighting took place at the Bay of Pigs. The Soviet Union protested vigorously, many nations denounced the United States, and Kennedy had to admit his mistake publicly and take responsibility for it. Later at Vienna he blamed it on bad information from the CIA, but in any case the Cuban problem had become a constant irritant in Soviet-American relations; it finally culminated in the Cuban missile crisis the following year.

Approximately ten days before the meeting in Vienna the Politburo met in special session to discuss the Soviet position at the summit conference. I was present at this session as the counselor of the Soviet delegation, which was headed by Khrushchev and consisted of Gromyko as foreign minister and Mikhail Menshikov, then ambassador to Washington.

Khrushchev delivered a report describing the course he was going to follow during his meeting with Kennedy. I must say that from the very beginning it was based on an erroneous postulate: that under the pressure of Soviet troops in Europe the young and inexperienced American president could be made to concede, in particular on Berlin. From the very first, American journalists and later American historians suspected that Khrushchev came to Vienna intending to exert as much pressure on President Kennedy as possible in regard to the principal issues, German affairs especially. This is essentially correct. He hoped that after the failure of the American-backed invasion of Cuba by exile forces the American president would yield to his pressure.

Most of the Politburo members, not knowing Kennedy well enough and being unaware of the situation, supported Khrushchev's tactics. Anastas I. Mikoyan, the deputy prime minister, was the only one to express certain doubts. He argued that our attitude toward the new, young, and open-minded president should not be based on attacks and pressure, but rather on entering into a reasonable and constructive dialogue which would lead to a positive development of Soviet-American relations. Furthermore, he warned, a policy of pressure could turn out to be harmful if the president was revealed as a man of strong character.

Khrushchev became excited, insisting that this was a favorable situation that must be exploited. Realizing that he was in the minority, Mikoyan stopped arguing and said that he was "for a cautious approach." After the Politburo meeting I spoke privately with Gromyko and told him I thought Mikoyan was right. But he did not want to discuss it, although I got the feeling that he had doubts of his own about Khrushchev's course.

The two-day summit began in Vienna on July 3.

Kennedy noted that he was disturbed by the fact that the Soviet Union was striving to do away with the capitalist system in other countries and to eliminate American influence where it had traditionally existed. Khrushchev replied that the Soviet Union did not intend to interfere in the internal affairs of other countries or to force its ideas upon them. He declared that he was against the export of revolutions, but also against the export of counter-revolutions.

Kennedy stated that "at present the Sino-Soviet bloc on the one hand, and the United States and its West European allies on the other, formed a certain balance from the point of view of correlation of forces." And that was why any "sharp change in the balance" would become a "matter of concern" to the United States.

As we had foreseen, the German question was both the central question of the meeting and the most tense. In his typically determined tone Khrushchev presented his idea for a solution. In fact, he confronted Kennedy with a dilemma: either they would sign an agreement acknowledging the existence of two Germanys or he would be compelled to sign a separate peace treaty with East Germany not later than in December. After that the occupation rights of the Western states in Berlin and their free access to the city would "cease to exist." West Berlin would still be able to exist, but its communications with the world would be controlled by East Germany, and Moscow would no longer recognize America's rights in Berlin. There could be no delay, and any attempt by the West to interfere with this plan, he clearly implied, could lead to an armed clash.

Kennedy admitted that the situation in West Berlin and Germany was on the whole an unnatural one, but the time had not yet come for Khrushchev's suggested changes to take place. He appealed to Khrushchev "not to change the existing balance of forces." The president insisted on postponing the consideration of the German question, while Khrushchev insisted on the necessity to take actions before it was too late.

According to the American participants at the meeting, the extended exchange on Berlin and Khrushchev's aggressive, almost threatening, tone disturbed Kennedy, and the president himself left no doubt of his worries. Right after the meeting he met James Reston of the *New York Times,* who wrote a widely noted article reporting that the president believed that a prolonged crisis was inevitable in his relationships with Khrushchev over the German question.

I must note that Khrushchev's threatening posture was a result both of his impulsive character and of his attempt to convince Kennedy that he regarded Berlin as a serious situation that had to be decided along Moscow's lines. In reality, when all these questions were being discussed at the meetings of the Politburo, no one even thought of the possibility of a military confrontation with the United States. That was absolutely excluded from our plans. The objective was to exert as much pressure as possible on Kennedy in Vienna. That tactic was Khrushchev's own idea and not that of the rest of the Soviet leadership, although most except Mikoyan went along with him. Khrushchev was obviously bluffing, whether consciously or because of his emotional makeup is still hard to say. But I must repeat that Khrushchev actually feared a new war and never considered a possibility of one waged over Germany or other international disputes.

This check on Khrushchev's temper was never fully understood in the West. An unnecessary fear of war over Berlin affected U.S. diplomacy for many years, starting with Kennedy himself. The question continued to resemble a smoldering fuse, and Kennedy, who believed that Khrushchev's threats were serious, began to prepare for military countermeasures. Khrushchev continued to maintain a rather tough stand without stepping across a dangerous line. The discussion of the German question and West Berlin was extremely strained, and the tension around these issues was not to cease for many months, at times relaxing and at times reaching a state of conflict.

My personal impression, as an eyewitness to the summit meeting, was that Kennedy was prepared to find a compromise, and one of the American participants later confided the same view to me. But Khrushchev was not patient enough to explore all the possibilities and continued to press his own proposals.

At Vienna Kennedy and Khrushchev also discussed banning nuclear tests, an issue that turned on verification. They wrangled over the number and type of inspections. For the first time, Khrushchev indicated that three annual inspections on Soviet territory and three each in the United States and Britain would be sufficient to monitor an agreement. Kennedy insisted on stricter controls and a larger number of inspections. Both also discussed the idea of banning *all* nuclear tests but failed to agree. As a result, only a partial test ban was concluded in 1962: a ban on atmospheric tests, which were the cause of a public uproar because of their radioactive fallout.

On the whole, the meeting in Vienna between Khrushchev and Kennedy (it was their first and last) had a significant effect. Khrushchev continued, to a certain degree, to underestimate Kennedy's ability to defend his position, although his opinion of the young president had improved considerably. And it seemed that Kennedy overestimated the readiness of Khrushchev and his allies to take decisive actions on Berlin, the most aggressive of which really was the erection of the Berlin Wall two months after the Vienna summit. The status of the city complicated and aggravated our relations until a four-power agreement regulated it in 1971, immobilizing it as one of the great monuments of the Cold War until the wall came down in 1989 and the isolation of the city finally ended with the reunification of Germany.

## Surprise: I Am Appointed Ambassador to the United States

At the end of the 1950s Khrushchev had introduced a new and more open procedure for considering foreign policy issues at the meetings of the Politburo. Before that only the minister of foreign affairs was present, but Khrushchev started inviting the heads of principal Foreign Ministry departments to attend when issues in their areas were on the agenda. They were generally young or middle-aged people, like myself.

Khrushchev often asked their opinions, and he invariably did so before asking the minister's opinion in the hope of discovering what they really thought. Once a minister spoke, few subordinates would dare to contradict him. In this way they had to think by themselves and express their own ideas, and these often were quite interesting.

Sometimes I would be subjected to such questioning in my area of American affairs. Khrushchev used to offer the most diverse ideas, especially after a weekend during which he, in his own words, "had been walking and thinking." These ideas ranged from the genuinely interesting to the impractical and bizarre.

It was not always easy to persuade him how unreal some of his ideas were, especially in the presence of other Politburo members. I had to make him understand diplomatically. For example, "Your proposal is interesting, but I am afraid the Americans won't understand and accept it." Such replies usually displeased him, but after receiving responses from officials in Washington that often came rather close to mine because of my experience there, he continued asking for my point of view.

I was invited to a Politburo session in January 1962 that was to consider a number of foreign policy issues. At the end of the discussion Khrushchev said that one question remained that was not on the agenda: the appointment of a new ambassador to the United States to succeed Menshikov, who was going to retire.

I expected Khrushchev to ask me to suggest a successor and feverishly began turning over the likely candidates in my mind. However, Khrushchev did not ask anyone; the members of the Politburo had already discussed that question among themselves.

Khrushchev said that he knew of one candidate and half-jokingly added that it would be best to appoint someone who could guess the Americans' reaction to Khrushchev's own proposals. He pronounced my name and asked those present for their opinion.

The Politburo members started smiling and saying that they supported "this candidate." Khrushchev congratulated me with my new appointment.

I thanked him, but I was at a loss about what else to say. I was only forty-two years old, and I had never before been an ambassador to any country. And here I was being given the number one appointment in the Soviet diplomatic corps.

When I came home and told my wife, she at first thought I was kidding her. Nor could I get accustomed to the idea easily. Only when Gromyko phoned us at home and congratulated me, did we begin to realize what a change was about to take place in our life and work.

That is how I became the ninth Soviet ambassador to the United States (after Troyanovsky, Umansky, Litvinov, Gromyko, Novikov, Paniushkin, Zarubin, and Menshikov). Of course I could not imagine that I was going to occupy this post for almost a quarter of a century, from 1962 to 1986, and that this would be, in a way, a record not only in Soviet, but in all of Russian diplomatic history.

That was the beginning of a completely new period of my life.

# WASHINGTON

## I. Finding My Way Around Washington

*Instructions from Moscow*

Shortly before leaving Moscow early in March of 1962 I called on Gromyko who, I thought, might give me instructions for Washington. He wished me a warm farewell but said that he was not going to give me any specific new directions, since "for the last two years we have been seeing each other about American matters almost every day" while I was serving as chief of the Foreign Ministry's American Department. But he had some personal advice: not to be hasty in judging actions of the American administration, even if they might at times seem rather dramatic.

He explained that, as I certainly knew, members of the Politburo sometimes viewed the events in Soviet-American relations in different and even emotional ways—the latter was a hint at Khrushchev. So my task was to provide Moscow with serious, solid, and sensible information without going into unnecessary details and sensational stories.

Although Gromyko was known as "the iron minister," always fulfilling the decisions of the Central Committee from A to Z and never deviating an inch from them in negotiations with Washington, his advice did not surprise me. Gromyko was never an eager supporter of confrontation with the United States and tried to avoid it whenever possible. He appreciated the elements of stability in this relationship. To give Gromyko his due, in his private conversations with Khrushchev he expressed his position candidly. But he never pushed it to the point of grave dispute, especially when other members of the Soviet government were present.

Of course I also had to visit Khrushchev before leaving for Washington. His guidelines were energetic: to protect and promote the interests of the Soviet Union with all firmness and to "resist temptation when provoked." This led to a piece of advice that was rather unusual coming from him: "Don't ask for trouble." He plainly told me that I should always bear in mind that war with the United States was inadmissible; this was above all.

Then he reviewed our relations with the United States. As always, he spoke emotionally and at length. From what he said it was clear that he regarded the problems of Germany and West Berlin as the principal issue in

Soviet-American relations, and he wanted them solved along the lines he had laid out to Kennedy at their meeting in Vienna. In his solution, there would be peace treaties with the then two separate German states, the Federal Republic and the German Democratic Republic, known in the West as "West" and "East" Germany, and West Berlin would be made a "free city." This was supposed to ensure stability in postwar Europe and somewhat restrict American influence in Germany as the country recovered from the devastation of the war. German revival preoccupied Soviet leaders, particularly because they feared Germans gaining access to nuclear arms.

Khrushchev also sharply criticized the American endeavor to attain strategic nuclear superiority because it made the United States, as he put it, "particularly arrogant." He cited in particular the stationing of American nuclear missiles in Turkey, "under the very nose of the Soviet Union." These missiles were to play a major role in unraveling the Cuban missile crisis, but if he was already hatching his plans to deploy our missiles there, he never mentioned them to me during our conversation. Without elaboration, he said of the United States and its nuclear reach, "It's high time their long arms were cut shorter."

Khrushchev also spoke of John F. Kennedy with more esteem than, say, the year before when they met for the first time in Vienna and admitted that although young, the American president was "a man of character." Nevertheless he did not conceal his belief that putting pressure on Kennedy might bring us some success. He believed that a second meeting with Kennedy could prove useful though it needed to be thoroughly prepared.

Judging by this conversation, Khrushchev did not seem to believe a major conflict with the United States was possible in the near future, though he assumed there would be occasional tensions in the relations between the two countries, mainly because of differences over Germany—which really represented the front line in the confrontation between the superpowers in Europe. On the whole, however, Khrushchev did not seem too preoccupied with our relations with the United States at the time, and he gave me his blessing in my new job.

## The Confidential Channel

During the period between Ambassador Menshikov's departure on January 4 and my arrival in Washington on March 15, a private exchange was going on between Khrushchev and Kennedy. This confidential channel between them had been set up and was being handled in Washington by Georgi Bolshakov and the president's brother Robert Kennedy, as well as by the president's press secretary Pierre Salinger. Although nominally the chief of the

Washington Bureau of our Tass news agency, Bolshakov was also an officer of our military intelligence, holding the rank of colonel. He was strictly forbidden to do anything except operate this communication back channel. He had established friendly relations with these close associates of the president, played tennis with them, and visited them at their homes.

Bolshakov was a diligent officer who knew how to keep his communication channel secret. Even Ambassador Menshikov was unaware of it because Bolshakov sent his reports through our military attaché and received instructions in the same way. But Bolshakov had a grave flaw: he knew little of the diplomatic side of our relations with the Kennedy administration and nothing of the details of some negotiations and our positions in them. While serving as a good mailbox for the leaders of the two nations, he was nevertheless unable to provide us with substantial additional information because he could not converse with Robert Kennedy and Salinger on an adequate level. Sometimes he even misinterpreted their words. As a result of all this, before my departure Gromyko had instructed me, with Khrushchev's approval, to take over Bolshakov's connections gradually but to keep on using him on special occasions. Gromyko of course disliked the very existence of a special channel run by the Defense Ministry and not by him.

Let me say a few words about the confidential channel, which will figure significantly in this story and has never been fully documented or explained until now. It referred to the methods used by the White House and the Kremlin for the direct exchange of information and views, in strict confidence and outside the normal diplomatic channels that existed in the State Department and our Foreign Ministry. Americans know of it mainly through the memoirs of Henry Kissinger, when it served its most active role in superpower diplomacy. Richard Nixon used it to circumvent the diplomatic bureaucracy he so distrusted and even bypass his own secretary of state, William Rogers. He was able to rely on our confidentiality because I had built up a good record. "One good thing I know about you," he told me at the start of his presidency, "there has not been a single leak."

This mode of communication existed for many years while I served as ambassador, continuing with varying intensity, although it was more restricted during the Reagan era when all contacts went through the secretary of state. Those who used it generally referred to it privately as "the channel" or "the confidential channel." It provided the freedom of personal chemistry, which is an essential of diplomacy, and made it possible to explore uncharted diplomatic territory, which was often precisely what was needed to break the stalemates that characterized the Cold War.

So, during the first few months of my work in Washington there were still two of these confidential channels: the old one running through Bolshakov and the new one that was starting to function through me. My channel soon became the principal one in the search for a solution to the Cuban crisis through the president's brother, Robert Kennedy, and then in negotiations between Washington and Moscow throughout the years I served as ambassador.

Bolshakov's channel was less systematic. His coded messages (sent through our military attaché in Washington) were received in Moscow only by the head of Soviet Army Military Intelligence, who reported them directly to the defense minister. Because of the unflagging competition between the ministries, the defense minister would report Bolshakov's messages to Khrushchev personally, while giving the foreign minister a brief oral summary or not bothering to inform him at all. As a result, Khrushchev commented on the messages and gave his instructions on them to the defense minister, who then passed the remarks on to Bolshakov. On some occasions Khrushchev talked things over with Gromyko; on other occasions, when he believed the matter to be clear, he did not. Gromyko naturally disapproved of this channel and tried to redirect it through me.

Besides, when Bolshakov came to Moscow on vacation or business, he would meet members of Khrushchev's inner circle; he knew Anastas I. Mikoyan and Khrushchev's son-in-law, Alexei Adzhubei, quite well. They would readily give him advice on how he ought to act when dealing with Robert Kennedy or the president's other close associates. At times, Mikoyan coordinated his suggestions with Khrushchev and occasionally even passed on the premier's oral messages to the president's associates via Bolshakov. As a rule, the Foreign Ministry, including the minister himself, knew very little about all this. Bolshakov would inform me of his most important conversations with Robert Kennedy, but I had no idea just how accurate his information was. No wonder our actions suffered from a certain lack of coordination.

As a result of all this, the White House initially obtained information through two separate channels, which to some extent might have been at variance with each other. I suspect that on the eve of the Cuban crisis the Bolshakov channel was increasingly used by our intelligence (I should think it was done with Khrushchev's blessing) for misinforming Kennedy's administration about our military preparations in Cuba. I must admit, however, that the Soviet leadership used the official diplomatic channels in practically the same way, which left them badly damaged. Much effort was needed after the Cuban crisis to restore trust.

## An Ambassador's Life

I arrived in Washington on March 15, 1962, as the ambassador of the Soviet Union. Riding by train from New York, I found I was, in a manner of speaking, a fellow traveler with, of all people, the director of Central Intelligence, Allen Dulles, although we did not converse. As we got off the train in Washington, we saw a large group of journalists waiting on the platform. Frankly speaking, I thought they were expecting Dulles. And to all appearances he must have been thinking the same thing. They seemed, however, to be waiting for the new Soviet ambassador. Dulles was visibly disappointed. For me what followed was my first trial by press. All ended well: I knew some of the journalists from my previous tour in Washington and was on good terms with them. The tone of their inquiries turned out to be friendly.

The embassy where I was to live and work was located in an old four-story mansion on 16th Street, just three blocks north of the White House. Geographically it happened to be closer to the president's residence than any other embassy. Alas, politically it was so far removed that it might as well have been on the other side of the globe.

The house itself had been purchased by the czar's government back in 1913 from the family of George Pullman, the famous American manufacturer of the railroad sleeping cars. For the small czarist embassy staff the mansion had been quite spacious. Besides an ambassador (who then held the rank of minister), it had consisted only of one counselor and two secretaries, as well as a coach-driver and some servants. By the time I came, the embassy housed about a hundred diplomats and technical staff. What a squeeze it was! Apart from the ambassador himself, only his deputy, the minister-counselor, had an office for himself. The other rooms accommodated five to seven persons. This had been going on for many years.

My own office was hardly luxurious. In Franklin Roosevelt's time almost thirty years before, when our two countries had just reestablished relations, the office had had two large windows looking out across the lawn to the street. But during the Cold War a mutual spying mania had escalated into a war of the secret services, and the spacious windows had been tightly bricked up from the inside. From the outside they still looked like ordinary windows with glass panes, but sure enough they could not be opened anymore. A new room was built inside the old one. Between the outer and inner walls there was a magnetic field as a defense from outside monitoring. The whole thing was supposed to be a protected zone. I never received any foreign visitors in this office, only in an outer reception room.

I have no idea how effective all this was, but for almost a quarter of a century I had to work in this windowless cell surrounded by constant magnetic radiation. Not to mention the psychological effect of this continuous solitary confinement (I literally could not tell day from night), there may well have been some physical consequences. Yet nothing was scientifically proven, and thus such conditions were permitted.

The office was on the second floor. On the third, there was a modest ambassadorial apartment, consisting of three rooms and a kitchen, which was close to the roof of the house next door. It did not belong to the embassy, and an intruder could easily gain access to our apartment. This was exactly what happened six months before I arrived in Washington. Someone had penetrated the apartment from the adjacent roof, stolen some things and, before leaving, set the ambassador's bedroom on fire. Fortunately, one of the embassy's guards saw the blaze just in time, and the fire was put out by the embassy staff.

Surveillance cameras were subsequently placed around the building and inside it. The guard posts were reinforced as well. Before the incident, the ministry had been saving hard currency at the expense of the special protection for the embassy that the staff had requested. The arsonist helped to solve that problem, and nothing of the kind has happened since. As the old Russian saying goes, "Until it thunders, the muzhik won't bother to cross himself."

It is worth mentioning that for more than ten years I had no bodyguards in Washington. Usually I moved around alone with just a driver. On weekends I used to dismiss him and drive the car myself, taking my wife and, some years later, my granddaughter out of town or shopping. However, anti-Soviet campaigns heated up in the United States, and there were a number of terrorist acts against Soviet organizations in Washington and New York. (Rabbi Meir Kahane's group was especially violent.) So our government assigned a bodyguard who was to accompany me every time I left the embassy. I refused his services, for I was sure that one guard would make no difference. Moreover, his constant presence was somehow embarrassing and only made me feel uneasy. Having learned that I was not making use of the bodyguard, the Politburo sent me an unusual cable: "You belong not to yourself but to the country and, as an ambassador, are valuable to the nation. So please carry out the resolution of the government." I had to obey the order.

A painful issue for all Soviet embassies abroad was our low wages. The state was very frugal with its foreign currency, and this affected salaries in our embassy. They were considerably lower than both American rates and salaries in embassies of other countries. Most ambassadors in Washington earned two to three times as much as I did. (Incidentally, the salary of the American ambassador to Moscow had always been four to five times higher than mine.) Among the embassies of the socialist countries of Eastern Europe, we shared the bottom step on the pay scale with Bulgaria. And there was no in-dexation of wages for inflation.

In the quarter-century I spent as ambassador, we got a pay increase only once. Even this happened in rather an unconventional manner. In the late 1970s I made my regular performance report to a Politburo meeting. Having endorsed our work, Leonid Brezhnev, then the general secretary, asked whether the embassy needed any help. I told him that the only thing we needed was a pay raise. I added that our requests to the Ministries of Foreign Affairs and Finance were repeatedly declined with the standard wording—"no currency"—even though Stalin, in discussing the postwar financing of embassies, had said that "as for the United States, it should be double." I pointedly noted that after the last salary increase at the Romanian Embassy, their ambassador's driver was getting as much as our counselor. This compar-ison to the Romanians finally made an impression, and our wages were raised by 25 percent. The next raise did not come until the 1990s.

As soon as I arrived at the embassy I joined in its work, started getting acquainted with the staff at conferences, and prepared to report my first im-pressions and observations to Moscow. My work was made easier at the be-ginning by my previous stay in the United States. I already knew this country, was familiar with its principal institutions, customs, and media, and had many American friends and acquaintances. As an ambassador, I saw my principal aim as establishing the largest possible number of contacts within the Kennedy administration (which was new to me), the diplomatic corps, business circles, and the Washington establishment in general.

Officially, however, I was unable to act as an ambassador until I pre-sented my credentials to President Kennedy. Before that I had to meet with the secretary of state, Dean Rusk, whom I had already met several times when he was director of the Rockefeller Foundation in New York and I was at the United Nations. Our first meeting at the State Department, on March 29, was therefore informal; Rusk said that he was glad to renew our acquain-tance. Unfortunately, he admitted, he had failed to establish personal contact with my predecessor, Mikhail Menshikov, which made it impossible to dis-cuss issues occasionally in an unofficial way. But he hoped to be able to do this with me. We could meet outside the State Department, for instance, at his place in the evenings and sometimes even aboard the president's yacht on weekends. This could be a useful addition to our official dialogue.

I completely agreed to his proposals. We refrained from discussing any serious political questions at our first meeting until I could present my cre-dentials to the president. Thus started my active and close cooperation with Dean Rusk on an official as well as an unofficial level that was to last for al-most seven years, through the end of the administration of Lyndon Johnson.

A lot would happen in the world during that period—the crises over Berlin and Cuba, the Vietnam War, the invasion of Czechoslovakia, and our attempts at disarmament—but we always managed to keep intact our good personal relations, and that enabled us to talk frankly and informally whenever necessary.

Rusk was conservative in his views and persistent in advocating them—no less persistent than even Gromyko—and he was not very imaginative. He was dogmatic and stubborn. Rusk was not an engineer of new ideas; he left that to the president. He certainly never rushed to change his views in foreign affairs. In that sense the confidential channel never really operated with Rusk. Yet he never resorted to cheap propaganda or deceptive tricks. His word could be trusted. Whether you agreed or disagreed with him, he was always clear about his position. He was also very prudent and avoided unnecessary conflicts but not rational polemics. In short, he was a real gentleman from Georgia.

## Meeting President Kennedy and the Washington Establishment

On March 31 I presented my credentials to President Kennedy. I have to admit that I was somewhat nervous before the ceremony, the first one in my diplomatic career. In Moscow it was a grand ritual. Our president or vice president received a new foreign ambassador in one of the Kremlin's most beautiful halls. Our ministry's officials, who were present at the ceremony, wore the full dress uniform of black and gold that had been instituted by Stalin. After the presentation there had to be a conversation with the ambassador, usually a formal one, though in some cases serious business was discussed.

At the State Department I was told that the White House ceremony was much simpler. Indeed, when I arrived at the White House, I was met by the chief of protocol, who accompanied me past two saluting marines directly into the president's office. The president was already there. His manner was informal and friendly. There were no usual formalities of presenting credentials. He just took my credentials and said he had already read them (duplicates had been delivered to the Department of State according to established practice). Because of his bad back he was sitting in a rocking chair near the couch where he invited me to sit. He was alone, and I had also come alone.

By arriving without an interpreter or diplomatic counselors I broke a long-standing tradition of Soviet ambassadors in Washington, which had grown out of two conditions. First, most of my predecessors could not speak English fluently, and second, it had been deemed inappropriate in Stalin's time to talk with foreigners unless witnesses were present. I was not bound by those constraints. And above all, a conversation without a bureaucratic note-taker tends to be less formal and more frank. I later followed this practice in talking to most higher officials of the American administration, and I was greatly helped by a good memory, which allowed me to write a record of conversations practically word for word as soon as I returned to the embassy. Anyway, not a single time in my long years in Washington did anyone dispute the precision of my account of the other side's viewpoint.

Over a cup of coffee, Kennedy got right to the point. As soon as I had communicated Khrushchev's regards and best wishes and he responded with the same courtesy, he started to talk animatedly about their "interesting meeting" a year before in Vienna, where I had also been present. The president said that he hoped to meet with Khrushchev again. It was difficult, he added, to set the date for such a meeting at the time. Now he would like to see at least something either agreed upon beforehand or ready to be signed by heads of state at the next summit meeting.

I asked what he thought could be prepared in advance of another summit, and Kennedy said that remained to be seen, but in any case he was sure that the discussion would unavoidably turn to Germany and Berlin. He said that he hoped this meeting would take place as early as that same year. To all appearances, he remarked, there was a need for it. I seconded the idea.

The president did not discuss specific questions, saying that we would be able to do it later and that I could count on his cooperation in my work as an ambassador. He also asked me to let Moscow know that he very much appreciated its concern for his ailing father, who had received the medical opinion and detailed advice of our leading physicians.

At the end of the meeting the president conducted me to the offices of his principal aides: McGeorge Bundy, his national security adviser; Theodore Sorensen, his principal domestic adviser; and Pierre Salinger, his press secretary. He introduced each one of them to me with a wisecrack at their expense. He also showed me some gifts he had received on various occasions and pointed out a model ship made of a walrus tusk given to him by Khrushchev. Among the pictures, I spotted two small canvasses by Aivasovski, a distinguished Russian painter of seascapes; which were interesting because he had taken urban landscapes as his subject and painted winter scenes in St. Petersburg. Both pictures had been loaned to the White House by a private collector.*

---

* Through Bolshakov, Robert Kennedy had made one unconventional request. Rudolph Ivanovich Abel, the Soviet intelligence officer convicted of espionage, had drawn a very good portrait of John F. Kennedy while in federal prison in Atlanta. Would Mr. Abel mind if this portrait was taken to the White House? Robert Kennedy added that Mr. Abel was a very talented artist. My reply was that they should address their request directly to Mr. Abel. After all, the painting was his property, not ours.

Compared to the Kennedy of last year in Vienna, the president now looked like a man in full command. Judging by our exchanges, he had mastered the issues of Soviet-American relations quite well, which distinguished him from some of his predecessors in the White House. So, I reported to Moscow, "On the American side we are dealing with a worthy opponent."

As soon as I met with any important American official, I used to write up a dispatch and send it in code to Moscow. I tried to keep to the salient highlights and sometimes would condense a conversation of three hours in two pages. I did not dictate my cables to a stenographer or to one of my diplomatic staff but wrote my dispatches myself, which was always my habit. This also helped keep my exchanges private. Only a minister-counselor, who would have to fill in as chargé d'affaires in my absence, was kept fully informed. (Subsequently those ministers—Georgi Kornienko, Yuli Vorontsov, Aleksandr Bessmertnykh, Vladlen Vasev, Oleg Sokolov among them—became outstanding diplomats themselves.) There were, however, certain personal cables that only an ambassador was authorized to handle. If a cable or a conversation called for any actions on the part of the embassy, I would instruct an officer orally.

Having presented my credentials, I started functioning as a full-fledged ambassador. I had a number of introductory meetings with leading representatives of Kennedy's administration where specific questions were often discussed in detail. Those conversations left me with a general impression that there was neither visible progress in Soviet-American relations nor any prospect of it, although the sides kept discussing a number of issues over and over again.

In their efforts to find a way out of the impasse, both sides tried to extend their connections with the help of members of their respective inner circles. Late in the previous year Khrushchev had received through Bolshakov President Kennedy's confidential offer to send his brother Robert to Moscow for informal talks. Khrushchev had agreed. Simultaneously, Adzhubei's trip to Washington was arranged and quickly took place, but Robert Kennedy's voyage was repeatedly postponed by the Americans. At last, in the middle of January, the president regretfully informed Khrushchev that plans for Robert Kennedy's heretofore confidential visit to Moscow had leaked through the American press and he was being falsely attacked by American hard-liners. Therefore he was going to postpone the trip temporarily but not going to withdraw his consent. (At our very first meeting when I presented my credentials, the president had complained to me about the American press. "Here I envy the Soviet leaders," he said. "Whatever I do, 80 percent of the American media comes out against me.")

It so happened that I had not yet met Robert Kennedy, although I was informed about correspondence that was being sent from the president through him. In fact, by that time we both wanted to establish direct contact outside Bolshakov's channel.

On May 3 the president gave a reception at the White House in honor of the diplomatic corps. These receptions had always played an important part in Washington politics, and the Kennedys were good at organizing them and enjoyed them. During the reception the president came up to me with his brother and introduced him jokingly as "an expert in confidential contacts with the Soviet Union" whom I "ought to know better." In the same tone I answered that I would without fail take his advice.

A week later Robert Kennedy invited my wife and me to a relaxed lunch at his beautiful house in McLean, a wealthy suburb just across the Potomac River in Virginia. Political issues were virtually ignored. We were surrounded by his large and rather tumultuous family of nearly a dozen children. When we mentioned that our embassy staffers were at that moment having a picnic to fry a big fish caught in the Potomac, Kennedy's wife was horrified. She explained that the river was so badly polluted that it was dangerous to eat anything caught in it. I rushed to the phone to pass on the warning. Alas, the fish had already been consumed and been duly praised by all. No one got sick.

Thus started my personal acquaintance with Robert Kennedy. He was a complex and contradictory person who often lost his temper; at such moments he behaved rudely and was unpleasant to deal with. Having met with a rebuff, however, he usually took hold of himself but could easily wind himself up again. That is why a conversation with him tended to be uneven and broken. He did not know the foreign policy questions in detail, but apparently thought himself to be an expert in them. This at times complicated the dialogue, particularly when he spoke on behalf of the president. But his clear intimacy with his brother made him a very valuable channel of communication.

Robert Kennedy never made a trip to the Soviet Union, although the possibility was discussed with us several times. I believe that the main reason was his own indecision. On one hand, he strove to prove himself to us, to the president's entourage, and to the American public as a substantial political figure. In his heart, however, he evidently remained unsure whether he was able to master this complicated assignment, especially talking with Khrushchev, who already had a notorious reputation in the United States for bombast.

I knew the columnist Walter Lippmann, who was a patriarch of Washington's intellectual elite and whose views on U.S. relations with the

Soviet Union were moderate and pragmatic. The president often talked with him. The elite itself was not at all homogeneous in its views and convictions, especially on Soviet-American relations, a sober view of which in many cases was obstructed by hard-core anti-communism. Prominent representatives of this trend were the Alsop brothers, Joseph and Stewart.

Rather curious was the transformation undergone by Drew Pearson, another well-known columnist. For a long time he had been one of America's most ardent anti-communists. But after two visits to the Soviet Union (one of them aboard a yacht accompanied by the widow of the *Washington Post*'s owner, Agnes Meyer, who was friendly toward our country), and after two meetings with Khrushchev, Pearson's own attitude toward the Soviet Union grew more sympathetic. This was increasingly reflected in his widely syndicated articles.

In the summer, when I visited his farm, he showed me a bed of peas grown from seeds that had been given to him by Khrushchev. In the next bed American peas were growing. "I am the first American," Pearson smiled, "who is practicing peaceful coexistence and peaceful competition. By the way, the Soviet peas, at least from outside, look better."

From this I must digress with a companion story about Llewellyn Thompson's attempt to engage in peaceful competition in agriculture while serving as U.S. ambassador in Moscow while I was head of the American section of the Foreign Ministry. One July 4 he was holding the annual Independence Day reception at his ambassadorial residence. Guests were strolling in his small garden, where a small plot of magnificent corn had caught everyone's attention. Khrushchev, a guest at the reception, could not help but notice it. Corn was his hobby and he tried to have it cultivated in Russia wherever possible, even where the conditions were unsuitable. Moscow's climate was certainly unfit for this crop, and he had been told so by Soviet specialists, but he did not trust them.

As soon as Khrushchev saw Thompson's plot of corn, he summoned his minister of agriculture. The premier immediately took him in hand. In front of the assembled guests he plainly told the poor man that this fellow Thompson—a diplomat, incidentally, and not a farmer—had managed to grow this superb corn right there in the capital while the minister kept assuring him that it was impossible in the Moscow region.

After the reception, Thompson, laughing softly, admitted to me that his beautiful plot of corn—every separate stem of it!—had been cultivated by the embassy's agriculture counselor for the sole purpose of surprising Khrushchev if an opportunity presented itself, which on that July 4 it finally did.

Thompson was called back to Washington by Kennedy, who valued his advice and installed him at the State Department as counselor and principal adviser on Soviet affairs. We had known each other for a long time, so we often spoke freely. In Moscow, Thompson had gained the respect of Soviet leaders, who readily talked with him at state receptions. He was a considerate, pleasant person who knew how to win people over and a competent professional who spoke Russian well. He was a true supporter of the idea of improving our relations and showed far less ideological bias than many other American ambassadors. I think he was the best American ambassador in Moscow during the entire period of the Cold War.

## The Diplomatic Stalemate over Germany and Berlin

Our relations with the United States seemed to move in a perpetual circle around the questions of Germany and arranging a ban on nuclear tests. Germany and Berlin overshadowed everything; Germany was, of course, the historic balance at the center of Europe, as well as our historic enemy, the cause of two world wars, and now the main battleground of the Cold War, with Berlin, literally, as the front line. They became a constant subject of my frequent meetings with Secretary of State Rusk (as well as Thompson's meetings with Gromyko in Moscow before his recall). But there appeared to be no progress or change in positions on both sides. In the course of meetings those positions were only being reiterated.

Rusk made it a rule to meet with me once every two or three weeks on Saturdays in strictly unofficial surroundings—"without ties and over a glass of whiskey"—for a free discussion of all issues. (This is how I learned to drink bourbon, his favorite drink.) We met at the State Department or at his house, aboard a yacht, or at my place. These meetings proved to be very useful for better understanding on a number of subjects, but on Germany and West Berlin we came to a complete deadlock. We repeated our arguments and counterarguments as if they had been learned by heart—and finally, they were—and repeating them became monotonous. Once Rusk jokingly suggested we could save time in our discussions by assigning a number to each question and each answer for both sides. He explained, "After I say, for instance, 'I have asked question number five,' you would reply, 'Answer number six,' and so on. Then you can send home a detailed report, and I can inform the president about the meeting."

Rusk's witticism was well-meant, but it reflected the dead-end situation surrounding West Berlin. On April 10 a good demonstration of how the American administration itself assessed the situation was provided by Rusk himself in a confidential briefing for a private group of leading columnists, the details of which circulated quickly around town. Rusk said frankly that the U.S. government did not see any real practical reason for a recent Soviet proposal to conclude a nonaggression treaty between NATO and the Warsaw Pact. Such a treaty would be feasible only after some understanding had been reached with the Soviet Union on the status quo in Europe, including an agreement on West Berlin. But he saw no prospect of such an agreement yet. Rusk said the United States would apparently have to make further substantial appropriations to modernize and improve its armaments, and he hoped that this would sooner or later help bring both sides to a solution, for such an enormous military burden could not be borne indefinitely.

I was not surprised by this statement. My own assessment of the American position was rather close to Rusk's. It was clear that without a solution in Berlin that was acceptable to both sides, the tension would continue. President Kennedy was prepared to accept the division of Germany into two states—he had already hinted he might be ready to recognize the German Democratic Republic in three to five years if Berlin receded as an issue—but he opposed any changes in the status of West Berlin that would entail the withdrawal of American troops from the city, as sought by Khrushchev. Such a withdrawal, he believed, would be considered in the West and in the United States as a sign of weakness by him. And that is what I reported to Moscow.

But Moscow at the time overlooked a very important point: President Kennedy's readiness to reach an understanding on the status quo in Europe. Had that happened, it would have been one of the highest achievements of Soviet diplomacy and might have been an introduction to detente in the postwar period. But Khrushchev believed he had a chance to shift the status quo in his favor through Berlin. Soviet leaders therefore exerted pressure on the Kennedy administration, a mistaken strategy that only promoted international tension and the arms race.

In May Khrushchev intensified his pressure with a warning to the American ambassador in Moscow that raised the possibility of a new Berlin crisis. On June 3 Robert Kennedy sought to convince us through Bolshakov that the president was unable to change his position on West Berlin—he just "cannot do it"—but if Moscow would recognize this, there was a possibility of agreements on other important questions. The president's brother cautiously inquired whether anyone in the Soviet government favored a showdown with the United States even though it might lead to war.

The reply was that there was no such faction, and he was asked in turn whether the American administration contained any advocates of a Soviet-American showdown. "No, not in the administration," Robert Kennedy replied, but there were some people like this among the military in the Pentagon—although "not McNamara himself," referring to Robert McNamara, the secretary of defense. Kennedy added that some time before this conversation the military had submitted to the president a confidential report arguing that since the United States had a greater military potential than the Soviet Union, a direct test of strength might be possible in extreme circumstances. But the president, he said, had a more realistic view on the balance of forces and firmly turned back all attempts by "overzealous advocates" of a showdown to persuade his administration to adopt their views. One of these was the senior Democratic statesman, Dean Acheson, secretary of state under President Truman. His report to the president on Berlin of June 28, 1961, was submitted a few weeks after the Vienna meeting and declassified in 1994, and it said, "There is a substantial chance . . . that the preparations for war and negotiation outlined here would convince Khrushchev that what he wants is not possible without war, and cause him to change his purpose. There is, also, a substantial possibility that war might result."

Before long Bolshakov reported back to Robert Kennedy that Moscow urged the president to rein in "the overzealous heads in the Pentagon." Robert Kennedy vigorously insisted that they had no influence whatsoever over the administration and, along with the rest of the Pentagon, were strictly under control of the White House. He proposed to freeze the Berlin question, at least for some time, or to reach a temporary understanding— written or oral—that would provide for leaving American troops in West Berlin for a certain period (apparently until the president was reelected to a second term). Moscow, however, kept insisting on its terms, and tension mounted inexorably in Berlin, where American and Soviet troops were practically confronting each other.

On July 13 Rusk drew my attention to frequent Soviet statements hinting that the United States might start a preventive war against the Soviet Union and said that if Soviet leaders actually believed this propaganda they were living under a very dangerous delusion. I told the secretary of state that such fears of a militant America were circulating in Moscow, but the Soviet leadership was not worried about a surprise attack, although it was really concerned about the arms race pursued by the United States and the explosive situation in Berlin. Rusk replied by citing American fears about the Soviet Union's newly intensified pressure on Berlin.

Such were the anxieties raised on both sides by the confrontation over Berlin, which may seem like a mere footnote to history so many years later. But it was seen with deep seriousness and even dread at the time, affecting much of our diplomatic relations and behavior. Two months later the Berlin Wall was erected, the most notorious symbol of the Cold War division of Europe.

Rusk also raised what he called "a very delicate point"—which he could do because the two of us were talking alone. Many in the United States, Kennedy's circle included, believed that he as secretary of state was using "excessively mild language" in dealing with the Soviet Union. And indeed, Rusk admitted, he was not a partisan of strong words. But lately, due to the toughening of the Soviet position toward the United States, Rusk said he was being subjected to additional pressure to toughen his own tone. He himself was beginning to worry that the Soviet-American dialogue could revert to the Cold War vocabulary of "Dulles's times," of which he, Rusk, had always disapproved. That was exactly what could happen as rhetoric heated up in the midterm election campaign in the autumn, and it had to be prevented.

I must admit that Rusk was partly right. Our official language was increasingly influenced by Khrushchev, who was not fastidious in his choice of words, especially when he became excited in public. McNamara told me that Khrushchev's graphic remark about a new Soviet missile that could "hit a fly in space" turned American intelligence inside out in search of some Soviet technological breakthrough, of which they could find no evidence.

Gromyko disliked such language but barely resisted it, not daring to contradict his master. Khrushchev's messages and letters to the American president were usually prepared by the Ministry of Foreign Affairs. They were legally accurate, correctly and professionally worded, but their style was tedious, all of which reflected Gromyko's own personality.

Khrushchev, vivacious as he was, preferred spoken language and used to scold his minister, whom he would put down as "a dry old stick" of a man. Once in a while he set out to rephrase the prepared text, and in an unconventional manner. Khrushchev disliked dictating to a stenographer or an aide and was not good at it anyway. Nor could he write well. Undaunted, he started talking, loudly and with a lot of gesticulation, as though he were addressing the president in person: "My dear Mr. President, I cannot agree with your position. . . ." His words turned into a lengthy monologue, as if he were engaged in a real conversation. He reached out into Russian folklore as well as other, rather colorful and more popular expressions that at times went beyond the limits of diplomatic correspondence. Redrafting the letter was no easy task, especially when Khrushchev remembered what he had said and became infuriated at "the bureaucrats" who smoothed out his language. Gradually he began to understand the necessity of diplomatic drafting. So, as time went by he came to rely more on Gromyko's texts—but there still was enough of the original Khrushchev in them to raise the temperature higher than a professional such as Rusk would like. Or, for that matter, myself.

President Kennedy himself decided to cut into the heated diplomatic discussion in person to explain his position confidentially. On June 17 he invited me to meet with him in the White House alone to give me his reaction to Khrushchev's proposals on Germany and Berlin.

"If we, the United States, agree to leave West Berlin," he said, "then no one is going to trust Washington's word anymore, and all our obligations toward other countries will turn into a worthless piece of paper. If we are forced out of Berlin in any way, all our guarantees to Western Europe will lose any sense. And this affects our basic interests, for the alliance with Western nations is the keystone of American foreign policy.

"I hope that Prime Minister Khrushchev will understand me correctly. We don't want the Berlin crisis of last year to be repeated, and we trust that this is not going to happen. That crisis cost us over three billion dollars, and the Soviet Union must have spent a lot as well."

Then the president made a comparison between Cuba and Berlin that would become increasingly vivid in the next few months. "I wish," Kennedy added, "I were able to get rid of Castro's Cuba under our nose, but I have to put up with its existence, as both sides have to put up with the existence of other things they don't like. Each serious aggravation of the Berlin problem brings with it fresh demands in Western Europe to provide themselves with their own nuclear weapons. But the United States is as opposed to this idea of 'independent nuclear forces' in Europe as is the Soviet Union."

This discussion of Berlin with the president did not, and could not, produce any specific results. The Kremlin was insisting on granting West Berlin the status of a "free city," which would even have given its population the right to choose its way of life, but on one condition—all Western troops had to be withdrawn. Kennedy made it clear that he would not consent and was willing to face a direct conflict on it with us, although he was not explicit about what that meant. Moscow gave credit to the president's determination, but Khrushchev personally and mistakenly hoped that constant pressure would eventually force him to yield. The principal result of the whole course of this Berlin policy was long-standing and, in the end, unnecessary tension.

The president then also asked if Khrushchev was going to agree to sign a treaty banning nuclear tests in the atmosphere after the current Soviet test series. I replied that Khrushchev's position was to ban all forms of nuclear testing and have the ban monitored by each nation on its own territory. (This was clearly a maximalist and even a propaganda-oriented position, since it was perfectly obvious that Washington would not assent.)

The president observed that Khrushchev's recent remark about the new missile that supposedly could hit a fly in space had produced a fresh wave of disputes within the American military and scientific elites about Soviet military achievements as a whole and the results of the latest tests, especially high-capacity and high-altitude explosions. The president ended the conversation in a conciliatory tone, expressing his hope that both countries still would soon be able to agree on a comprehensive nuclear test ban.

The conversation left me with a clear impression of the president's concern over our new round of pressure on Germany, but nevertheless he evidently assumed the dispute would not come to a major conflict provided he maintained sufficient military force in the region. That was his policy after the difficult Vienna summit with Khrushchev in 1962, and he was determined to follow it.

In late August I had a private conversation with Theodore Sorensen, the president's personal assistant. His main duty at the White House, he told me, was monitoring political feeling to promote the president's personal appeal, win support for his policies, and develop the president's strategy for supporting the Democratic Party in the congressional election campaign that was just getting into high gear.

The Soviet Union, Sorensen said, could potentially influence the outcome of the campaign by increasing pressure on Berlin. In this case, regardless of the president's actions, the result would be some additional points for the Republicans. He implied that Kennedy would prefer the Soviet Union to stay neutral during the election. This could pave the way toward another meeting with Khrushchev after the election, unless the prospects for an agreement on some specific issue arose in the meantime.

This appeal was clearly unusual and could not but attract Moscow's attention. Some days later I informed Sorensen that the contents of our conversation had been reported to Khrushchev. The Soviet side, I told him, regarded "the president's wishes" with understanding and was not going to undertake any actions that could complicate the international situation and intensify tension between our countries, especially over Germany and Berlin, on the eve of the election.

Sorensen noted the importance of the message. Only on Cuba, he said, was the message somewhat belated, since it had already become a campaign issue. The president would be compelled to assume a more active position on Cuba during the elections than he had intended.

At that time I did not know that the secret Soviet preparations that were to result in the missile crisis were already under way. So Khrushchev's promises not to complicate the international situation on the eve of the election were deliberately misleading. Khrushchev thus continued gambling.

## Cuba Looms

Cuba came up again more forcefully on September 4 when I met one-on-one with Robert Kennedy to discuss Khrushchev's latest position on a nuclear test ban. In a highly agitated manner, Robert Kennedy diverted the conversation to the question of Soviet military aid to Cuba. The American administration, he said, was following with growing concern the increase of Soviet military deliveries to Cuba and the arrival there of Soviet military personnel.

The U.S. government was especially concerned by the appearance in Cuba of ground-to-air missiles even though they remained under the control of Soviet military personnel. But what would happen, Robert Kennedy said, after they were passed into the hands of "impulsive Cubans?" A much more serious question would arise for the security of the United States itself, he added, if events continued along a logical path: Wouldn't still more powerful missiles arrive, capable of reaching U.S. territory from Cuban soil? And wouldn't they carry nuclear warheads? If this were to happen, the American administration was definitely not going to leave the security of the United States dependent on decisions by the present government of Cuba. All this, Robert Kennedy concluded, emphasized the great importance the administration attached to Soviet military deliveries to Cuba.

In response, I pointed out that Cuba had a right to defend itself. As far as nuclear warheads were concerned, the Soviet Union fully favored the expeditious conclusion of a nuclear nonproliferation treaty. At the same time I avoided the subject of missiles in general and military personnel. I neither confirmed nor denied the reports, since I had no information about them whatsoever until the very beginning of the Cuban crisis only about six weeks later.

At that point I never even imagined the idea of stationing our *nuclear* missiles in Cuba. I also proceeded from the assumption that the missiles did not have the range to reach U.S. territory. Yet I was well aware of the importance of the issues Robert Kennedy had raised, and I urgently asked Moscow for instructions. Moscow answered curtly: "In talking to the Americans you should confirm that there are only *defensive* Soviet weapons in Cuba." * That was all. No further explanations were given to the Americans or to me personally. Moreover, Bolshakov, who had just returned from his vacation at home, had been instructed to tell Robert Kennedy the same thing and invoke Khrushchev's name. So I continued to repeat to American officials what

---

* This was a misleading answer. In our military jargon the word "defensive" meant that all the weapons were to be used "for the defense of Cuba." The Americans understood this term to mean weapons that could be used for Cuba's defense against an invasion and therefore only within Cuba or its territorial waters.

I had been instructed to say until the crisis erupted in October, at which point I realized that the term "defensive weapons" meant something entirely different to Moscow from the way Washington took it.

On September 18, I gave Robert Kennedy an account of Khrushchev's new oral message to President Kennedy. This message ran some fifteen pages when it was transmitted and was the most detailed and significant statement of the Soviet leadership's views about relations with the Kennedy administration shortly before the Cuban crisis.

The nature of an "oral message," which is customary in diplomatic practice, needs some explanation. It is used in order to make a communication sound less official and informal, and closer to colloquial language. The text is sometimes passed to the other side typed on a sheet of paper, but not in the form of an official document. On other occasions it is not made available, and the party to which it is recounted is supposed to make its own notes.

In Khrushchev's time this way of communicating with President Kennedy was used rather often, for it allowed Khrushchev to narrate his messages freely. This made his messages long, so without asking Moscow, I resorted to translating these messages into English beforehand. Then I would give the addressee a brief oral account and hand over a strictly unofficial but complete text of this "oral" message. This suited Rusk, Robert Kennedy, and the president fine. In their replies they would not refer to a written document (which officially did not exist), but only to the more manageable "oral message" that I had delivered.

Khrushchev's message commented on President Kennedy's concern over Soviet-American relations and insisted that "the aggravation is not our fault." He blamed it first of all on the "unnatural situation" in Berlin but promised to freeze matters until after the election, whereupon the dialogue could resume. In his characteristic manner of blowing hot and cold, he turned to the "nice conversation" he had had with Stewart Udall, the secretary of the interior, who had visited Moscow in the company of his friend the poet Robert Frost, "And what I least expected," said Khrushchev, "was that at this very moment you would decide to ask Congress to call out 150,000 reservists." He insisted that the Soviet Union was doing nothing to provoke tensions while the United States was making "piratical demands" to inspect Soviet ships heading for Cuba.

I was preparing myself for an unpleasant and probably stormy conversation as I went to meet Robert Kennedy with this message in my hands. So I was rather surprised when he contented himself with saying, somewhat gloomily, that he was going to pass the message to his brother on the same day. He refrained from discussing any specific questions apart from saying that it would be a good idea for both countries to refrain from any action, including action in Berlin, that could aggravate the situation before the congressional elections. This conversation and another I had with Llewellyn Thompson, who had just returned from a successful tour as ambassador in Moscow, made me realize that only ten days before the Cuban crisis the Kennedy administration seemed to regard Berlin and not Cuba as the principal threat to Soviet-American relations.

In retrospect I ask myself whether the tension surrounding Berlin was a deliberate diversion by Khrushchev from Cuba. I have no concrete proof from our archives, but I suspect that he kept both in his mind to exercise pressure on President Kennedy in the hope of extracting concessions from him. This illusion ended very shortly.

## II. The Cuban Crisis

*Khrushchev Offers Nuclear Missiles to Cuba: Castro Accepts*

The Cuban missile crisis was the most dramatic moment of my quarter-century in Washington, but more important, it was the most dramatic event of the Cold War. By drawing both great powers as close to nuclear war as they dared, it became the watershed in understanding how far they could go and taught us a major lesson in what had to be done to prevent nuclear war. For the next thirty years, these became the rules and the limits of the nuclear game, and of the important, volatile, and dangerous relationship between Moscow and Washington.

It may be useful to review how we came to be poised on the brink of war because of this small island ninety miles from the American mainland. American pressure on Cuba had risen steadily after the collapse of the invasion in April 1961 by exiles supported by the Central Intelligence Agency. In January 1962 the United States arranged Cuba's expulsion from the Organization of American States and set up a trade blockade of Cuba. In the summer and fall of 1962 the situation in the Caribbean became even more aggravated. Numerous American warships headed toward the Cuban coast, and the island's air space was patrolled around the clock by U.S. military planes. As later became known, the Central Intelligence Agency and the Pentagon had prepared, and President Kennedy had approved, a secret plan known as "Mangusta" to undermine and ultimately overthrow Fidel Castro's regime. This intensifying psychological pressure on Cuba went hand in hand with an American propaganda campaign warning the Soviet Union of the risks of its military and economic aid to Cuba. On September 11, the Soviet Union replied with a strong statement issued through our Tass news agency denouncing the American campaign and warning that "this time one cannot attack Cuba and count on going unpunished."

What was not known at that time was that five months before, in May of 1962, the Soviet leadership had reached important secret agreements with Fidel Castro in the strictest confidence. Aleksandr Alexeyev, counselor of the Soviet Embassy in Cuba and a KGB man, was unexpectedly called from

Havana to Moscow and summoned to Khrushchev. Alexeyev spoke Spanish and had set up friendly and confidential relations with Castro, who preferred dealing with him to doing business with our ambassador, Sergei Kudryavtsev. The ambassador had failed to establish proper contact with the Cuban leader, and this did not go unnoticed in Moscow.

When Alexeyev arrived, Khrushchev suddenly informed him that he was being named ambassador. Years later Alexeyev gave me some of his notes from the time and said that Khrushchev had told him: "Your appointment is linked with our decision to site nuclear-tipped missiles there. This is the only way to safeguard Cuba against an outright American invasion. Do you think Fidel Castro will agree to such a move on our part?"

Greatly astonished, Alexeyev answered after some hesitation that Castro had built his entire strategy of defending the Cuban revolution on his and Cuba's solidarity with other Latin American nations and was therefore hardly likely to agree to our proposed action. And even if he did, the Americans would use the Soviet military presence in Cuba as an excuse for completely isolating him and his government from the rest of Latin America.

The following day was a Sunday. Khrushchev nevertheless called in the Politburo and several military leaders. Andrei Gromyko was also summoned although he did not become a member of the Politburo until 1973. They were invited for a "cup of tea" at his dacha. "Alexeyev has told me," Khrushchev said, "that Fidel Castro will be scared by our decision and is unlikely to agree to the stationing of missiles. I have been thinking about this and come to the conclusion that rather than tell Castro that we have already adopted a decision, we ought perhaps to declare to him that to save the Cuban revolution it is imperative to take a bold step, and that since the alignment of forces in the region is unfavorable to us, the Soviet government might even consider stationing Soviet missiles in Cuba provided that Fidel finds this acceptable."

Khrushchev continued: "We must deliver and deploy the missiles quietly, taking all precautions so as to present the Americans with an accomplished fact. It is imperative to see that no information is leaked to the press before the end of the campaign for the American [congressional] elections on November 4 if we are to avoid aggravating the situation there. Once the elections are over and electoral tensions have eased, the Americans will have no choice but to swallow this bitter pill. Aren't we compelled to put up with the American missiles in Turkey?"

Khrushchev said further that he had long been pondering ways and means of defending the Cuban revolution against outright American aggression and that the idea of deploying our missiles in Cuba had occurred to him while he was vacationing in Varna, a seacoast resort in Bulgaria.

Was Khrushchev's decision prompted only by his desire—and it was a sincere one—to defend Cuba? I doubt it. The move was part of a broader geopolitical strategy to achieve greater parity with the United States that would be useful not only in the dispute over Berlin but in negotiations on other issues.* But at that meeting they only discussed Cuba.

When Alexeyev returned to Cuba, he was accompanied by Marshal Sergei Biryuzov, who traveled incognito with several other missile specialists. The new ambassador was surprised that Castro reacted calmly to the suggestion to station our missiles in Cuba. After a brief pause he said, "That's a very bold move. Before we make it, I must consult my closest associates. But if making such a decision is indispensable for the Socialist camp, I think we will agree to the deployment of Soviet missiles on our island. May we be the first victims of a showdown with U.S. imperialism!"

Alexeyev reemphasized that the only reason for the proposal was to defend Cuba against possible American aggression.

In June, Raul Castro, Fidel's brother and his defense minister, paid a working visit to Moscow, where he and Defense Minister Rodion Malinovsky initialed a secret treaty to deploy Soviet missiles in Cuba. He was followed later by Ernesto (Che) Guevara, another close associate of Castro from his days as a guerrilla and his principal spokesman in Latin America. Guevara presented some amendments proposed by Castro to the treaty, which had been initialed but not yet signed. Khrushchev accepted them without qualification, but the two sides never formally signed the treaty because shortly afterward the Caribbean crisis arose.

According to Ambassador Alexeyev and General Anatoly Gribkov, who participated in the planning and handling of the operation in Cuba, altogether forty-two nuclear missiles of intermediate range were stationed in Cuba, accompanied by a Soviet force of about forty thousand men to guard them. The missiles could hit major American cities up to the Canadian border. The nuclear warheads had the explosive power of the bomb that devastated Hiroshima and two had megaton explosives. All these missiles remained under strict Soviet control, and all kinds of precautions were taken to prevent Cubans from getting hold of them. General Gribkov reported that more than eighty-five ships were secretly used to transport men and materiel to Cuba, and they made more than 183 runs from different ports under false cover.

* At that time the balance of strategic forces favored the United States. The Soviet Union had 300 nuclear warheads against the Americans' 5,000. Khrushchev hoped to redress the nuclear balance by moving our intermediate-range missiles to a point from which they could strike the United States.

## Soviet Embassies Are Left Out of the Loop

As I have already mentioned, all these dangerous developments were kept secret not only from the public but also from the Soviet diplomatic service. Even Valerian Zorin as permanent representative to the United Nations, and I as ambassador to the United States, knew absolutely nothing at all about them. What is more, we had received repeated instructions of a general nature to the effect that we should answer any questions about missiles in Cuba by saying that the Soviet Union supplied Cuba with "defensive weapons" only, without going into any details whatever. We proceeded from the assumption that the Soviet missiles in Cuba did not have the range to reach American territory. But we had no official confirmation from Moscow, and although I accurately reported to Moscow all my answers to American officials on the subject of missiles, I was never corrected by either Khrushchev or Gromyko.

In seeking to keep the secret, Moscow not only failed to inform me of so dramatic a development as its plans to station nuclear weapons in Cuba but virtually made its ambassador an involuntary tool of deceit, for I kept stubbornly telling the Americans that we had nothing but defensive weapons in Cuba. Zorin found himself in an even more embarrassing situation, for he kept saying as much publicly at meetings of the UN Security Council.

Years later Dean Rusk told me that as soon as American reconnaissance photographs of Cuba revealed the existence of our missiles and ignited the crisis, a discussion took place at the White House about whether the government should insist on Moscow recalling me for "deliberately misleading" the U.S. administration. They finally came to the conclusion that I lacked detailed information and that it would therefore be unfair to accuse me of duplicity.

There was another curious episode in the many postmortems we held of this historic crisis. During the summer of 1989 Moscow hosted a Soviet-American seminar on the Cuban crisis. The participants included Gromyko and me. One of the Americans asked me directly whether I had advance knowledge of the missiles in Cuba. I said no and asked Gromyko for comment. He answered, "Of course, it is strange that you had not been informed, Anatoly Fyodorovich. Nothing should have been kept secret from you."

Gromyko was not telling the truth. One reason for keeping us uninformed was that the entire Cuban operation was so secret that Moscow may have decided not to communicate any information about it to Zorin and me via telegram, which might have been monitored and deciphered. The second, and more cynical one, was that without knowing the facts, we could better defend the government's false version of its strategy in Cuba. This deliberate use of an ambassador by his own government to mislead an American administration remained a moral shock to me for years to come and left me more cautious and critical of the information I received from Moscow.

The American administration, I now believe, was every bit as surprised as I was when it learned about the missiles placed in Cuba through aerial reconnaissance several days before I did. Quite indicative of the general mood in the White House on the eve of the crisis was a briefing held by President Kennedy in mid-October for a group of leading editors reviewing the international situation. He put far greater emphasis on Berlin than Cuba as a likely source of crisis and said no military operations would be launched against Cuba unless it actually acted against its neighbors in the Western Hemisphere. The purpose of U.S. policy was to make the maintenance of Cuba economically as costly as possible for the Soviet Union—and there could be no deal with the Soviets to renounce their bases in Cuba in return for America abandoning its bases elsewhere.

Kennedy of course had to reappraise this assessment of Cuba with wrenching urgency only a few days later. On October 14 U-2 airplanes flown by air force pilots spotted and photographed launch sites in Cuba for medium-range missiles. On October 16 the photographs were submitted to the president by photo reconnaissance and missile experts who positively identified our missiles on Cuban soil. The White House became the venue of feverish meetings of a crisis team of the National Security Council under the president himself that later became known as the Ex Comm, or Executive Committee. The most hawkish members declared themselves in favor of an immediate bombing of the launch sites, to be followed by a landing of U.S. troops in Cuba. Some generals were believed even to have mentioned the possibility of using nuclear weapons, but I believe this idea was never discussed in earnest. After some deliberation the president evidently concluded that, while military pressure was necessary, diplomacy, talks, and compromise should be given preference. The situation could have been much more explosive if Washington had known that the Soviet missiles had nuclear warheads.

Although my government had earlier left me out of the loop, as the Washington expression goes, I became the principal private channel to Moscow for the president's closest confidant during the crisis, his brother Robert Kennedy. Bolshakov was virtually abandoned as a channel because he was deemed not competent to handle the serious and delicate communications between the two governments. During the crisis, Robert Kennedy and

I had almost daily conversations. He kept dropping hints about the highly charged atmosphere among members of the presidential crisis team. Occasionally he seemed to overdramatize somewhat the pressure from the military, and the president's resistance to it, in order to get the Soviet Union to withdraw its missiles. But in general he rather correctly reflected the tense mood inside the White House. I reported this to Moscow, and it helped Khrushchev understand the seriousness of the situation he had set in motion. The dispatches obviously reached him and had their intended effect, because some are cited vividly in his memoirs.

Simultaneously President Kennedy started a series of consultations with a number of European leaders, including President Charles de Gaulle of France and Konrad Adenauer, the chancellor of the Federal Republic of Germany. It was amidst these secret consultations with his allies that the president met with Foreign Minister Gromyko on October 18. Gromyko had come down to Washington from New York, where he was attending the regular autumn session of the United Nations General Assembly.

I was present at this far from routine meeting. Many years later, Gromyko admitted in his memoirs that it could well have been the most difficult conversation of all that he had with nine American presidents in his forty-eight years of diplomatic service. The conversation abounded in abrupt turns and omissions. Both Kennedy and Gromyko were nervous, although both tried to conceal it. The discussion turned around Soviet and U.S. policies toward Cuba and Cuba itself. The president kept implying that the situation was being increasingly aggravated by deliveries of Soviet military equipment to Cuba, yet his manner was not particularly aggressive. He even repeated his confession, originally made in Vienna, that last year's invasion of Cuba had been a mistake.

The dialogue fitted into the rather classic diplomatic framework of an argument over "defensive" versus "offensive" weapons in Cuba—and without any mention whatsoever by either side of missiles by name. Gromyko repeated that the Soviet Union would not introduce offensive weapons in Cuba. The president did not once refer to the Soviet missiles deployed in Cuba, although we later learned that the air force photographs of missiles' launching sites were in his desk drawer at that very moment. "And so I was spared the need of answering the question whether these weapons were present in Cuba," as Gromyko later tried to excuse himself to the readers of his memoirs. Gromyko always insisted afterward that he was not *asked* specifically about missiles, and that is why he said nothing about them. Was this duplicitous, as the president and his staff later said? Judge for yourself. And why did the president himself say nothing about the missiles? There is no answer to this question, but I think he had not yet worked out a clear plan of action and therefore preferred to refrain from a pointless discussion with Gromyko.

In the course of the conversation, Gromyko, on behalf of the Soviet leadership, suggested a Soviet-American summit meeting. Kennedy reacted favorably, but later that same day Gromyko was informed by a telephone call from Rusk that if the meeting were held the following month there would not be enough time to prepare for positive results. In this way Washington, while not rejecting the idea of a summit meeting as such, postponed it indefinitely. The German problem, for example, was only touched on in general terms by Kennedy and Gromyko.

On the whole Gromyko was pleased with the meeting. He was completely misled by Kennedy's conduct, as evidenced by the optimistic report he cabled immediately afterward to the Politburo. Gromyko wrote: "All that we know about the U.S. position on the Cuban question warrants the conclusion that, by and large, the situation is quite satisfactory. This is confirmed both by formal statements on the part of U.S. officials, including President Kennedy through his statement in conversation with us on October 18, and by the whole body of information reaching our diplomats through unofficial channels. There is reason to believe that the United States has no current plans for an invasion of Cuba. Instead it banks on raising obstacles to economic relations between Cuba and the Soviet Union in order to disrupt the Cuban economy, cause hunger in this country and thus provoke a revolt against the regime."

With some pride, he boasted that this American stance arose from Washington's amazement "at the boldness of the Soviet action intended to help Cuba." The administration's line of reasoning, he wrote, was that Moscow was aware not only of the vast importance the Americans attached to Cuba and its location, but of the extent to which the issue was painful to America. But if, even knowing this, the Soviet Union had decided to render aid to Cuba, then the Soviet Union was the more resolved to offer resistance should the Americans invade Cuba. According to Gromyko, opinions varied on where and how this resistance would be mounted, but nobody doubted that it would be.

Gromyko went on that the anti-Cuban campaign in the United States had been scaled down somewhat and emphasis was shifting to Berlin in order to divert public attention from Cuba—and not without the White House doing its share. It was even rumored, Gromyko reported, that the Soviet Union was given to understand that it might moderate its position on Cuba if the United States did the same on West Berlin. He warned, however, that while there was still no guarantee against reckless American moves on Cuba, all the objective factors and official assurances that the United States had no plans to invade Cuba—which he felt unquestionably tied Washington's hands—made it safe to presume that the Americans would hardly venture on a military gamble against Cuba. I tried to persuade him to hedge his assessment with some caution, but he would not listen. Evidently he wanted to please Khrushchev.

## The Crisis Erupts: In the Center of the Settlement

On Monday, October 22—the start of that fateful week—I flew to New York to see Gromyko off on his special flight home to Moscow. He still said nothing about our missile deployment in Cuba. (I must admit that I did not ask him in detail either; for me it was enough to know that our weapons were only "defensive.") Literally as his plane took off at noon, a staff member of the U.S. mission to the United Nations handed me, right at the airport, a request from Rusk to call on him at the State Department at 6 P.M. that day. I had a business appointment in New York the same evening, so I asked Rusk's messenger if the meeting could be put off until the following day. He appeared to have the secretary of state's explicit instructions to ensure that by whatever means I kept the appointment in Washington that evening. Although Rusk's emissary said he knew nothing about the subject, it was clear enough that something serious was afoot. Never before had Rusk insisted so resolutely on a definite hour; on the contrary, he used to meet me halfway on timing our meetings. So I sensed that something important had happened, but was uncertain whether it had to do with Cuba or West Berlin.

I returned to Washington at once by plane and stepped into Rusk's office at the appointed hour—6 P.M. on October 22. Rusk looked unusually serious. He said that he had been instructed by the president to forward through me a personal message to Khrushchev on the Cuban question, as well as to hand me, for our information, the text of the address the president would be making to the American people on television and radio at 7 P.M. Rusk warned that this time he had instructions neither to answer any questions about the two texts nor to comment on them.

"The documents speak for themselves," he said.

In his address to the nation that evening Kennedy warned that the emplacement of Soviet missiles in Cuba threatened the security of the nation and announced a "strict quarantine on all offensive weapons being shipped to Cuba." In his personal letter to Khrushchev, the president pointed out that, as in the case of Berlin, he had publicly stated that if certain developments took place in Cuba, the United States would take all measures necessary to protect its own and its allies' security. Despite that, the Soviet Union had proceeded with long-range missile bases and other offensive weapons in Cuba. "I have to tell you that the United States is determined to remove this threat to the security of our hemisphere," the president wrote. He added that his action was only a "necessary minimum" and hoped that the Soviet government would refrain from any moves bound to deepen this already grave crisis, which would help resolve it in a peaceful way, by means of negotiations.

I expressed my surprise to Rusk that neither the president nor Rusk had found it necessary to discuss all this with Gromyko when they had met just four days before; and now the administration was creating a serious crisis by raising a storm of propaganda. Rusk, clearly in a state of nervous tension, observed that for the time being they were not planning to publish Kennedy's personal message to Khrushchev although that could not be ruled out. In effect that ended the meeting.

We were clearly facing a major, highly dangerous crisis in our relations with the United States. I returned immediately to the embassy, but first I spent about a quarter of an hour just sitting in my office alone and trying to cool down and assess the situation as accurately as I could. I was severely confused, since I had no instructions or advance warning of any sort from my government. Without delay I reported to Moscow on my conversation with Rusk, fully aware that this was going to be a great and uncomfortable surprise after Gromyko's reassuring cable. Never before had the experienced and cautious Gromyko made so grave a miscalculation!

Of course the fatal miscalculation was made by Khrushchev himself. He did not anticipate that his adventurous thrust would be discovered in time for Kennedy to organize a sharp reaction, including the threat of a direct confrontation. He had no fallback plan to deal with such a reverse and was forced to improvise, awkwardly as it turned out, which cost him dearly by eventually cutting short his political career. He was so confused that he did not play the one good card in his hand—Kennedy's agreement to withdraw U.S. missiles from Turkey. This could have been presented to the public as a deal trading their bases for ours, which Kennedy and Rusk would have swallowed as their last resort for a settlement. If Khrushchev had managed to arrange this, the resolution of the crisis need not have been seen as such an inglorious retreat for him.

But he grossly misunderstood the psychology of his opponents. Had he asked the embassy beforehand, we could have predicted the violent American reaction to his adventure once it became known. It is worth noting that Castro understood this. He had proposed to Khrushchev that Havana and Moscow formally and publicly agree to base missiles in Cuba through a legal agreement—just as the United States was doing on the soil of its allies

KENNEDY AND THE CUBAN CRISIS ■ 83

in Europe. But Khrushchev wanted to spring a surprise on Washington; it was he who got the surprise in the end when his secret plan was uncovered.

As soon as I had sent my cable about the meeting with Rusk, I summoned the senior staff of the embassy. Having instructed them to monitor developments closely, I stressed the gravity of the situation, which might have complications for the embassy itself. Diplomats staffed the embassy around the clock. Diplomatic families who lived off the embassy's premises were warned to be especially cautious. I held a separate conference with the senior intelligence staff to discuss the impending crisis and how to coordinate the information we would provide to Moscow. The mood in the embassy was of course uneasy but without any panic or disorder. The embassy kept functioning as efficiently as it normally did. Some Western commentators have reported that we burned our files—the classic sign of an imminent break in relations or war—but that was not true.

Tuesday, October 23, Khrushchev replied to Kennedy describing the president's measures as aggressive toward Cuba and the Soviet Union, and as inadmissible interference in Cuba's internal affairs and an encroachment on its right "to defend itself against aggression." It rejected the right of the United States to control navigation in international waters. He expressed the hope that the measures announced by Kennedy would be called off to prevent "catastrophic consequences for the whole world."

Meanwhile our embassy cabled Moscow on the same day that a nationwide campaign had been launched in the United States to dramatize the situation following the president's address. McNamara had categorically declared at a briefing Monday that the United States would not hesitate to sink Soviet ships delivering offensive weapons to Cuba should they refuse to follow orders given by American warships. According to our information from personal contacts and technical intelligence, the president's actions on Cuba followed intensive backstage debates in the top echelon of the administration. There was a growing belief around the president that the international balance of power was tipping in favor of the Soviet Union, and this must be reversed in order to prevent Moscow from getting the impression that Washington lacked the will to resist Soviet pressure in various parts of the world. Central to the debates, we reported, was the strategic question of whether it wouldn't be better for the United States to force the Soviet Union to backtrack by doing battle over Cuba, which offered the United States an advantage over Berlin in the field of American public opinion as well as the more obvious geographical and military-strategic factors. It was on the Cuban issue that President Kennedy was urged to stand firm and show his character.

The embassy also reported that tension throughout the capital was mounting. We observed that the Americans were getting nervous as they waited for the first Soviet ship to draw near Cuba and—many Americans put this question directly to the embassy—what was going to be the outcome of this first trial of strength? The atmosphere grew more tense as the presidential decree went into effect at 2 P.M., Washington time, imposing a quarantine on deliveries of "offensive" weapons to Cuba. I must confess that I was also getting nervous because I had not received any instructions about our reaction to the quarantine or any information at all from Moscow.*

In the late hours of October 23 Robert Kennedy called on me. He was in a state of agitation, and what he said was markedly repetitious. It may be summarized as follows.

He had come on his own initiative in order to explain just what had led to the current grave state of events. What preoccupied him most was the serious damage that had been done to the personal relationship between the president and the Soviet premier, a relationship that meant so much. The president had virtually "staked his political career" on the Soviet assurances about Cuba by publicly declaring that the arms were purely defensive— although some Republicans had warned otherwise. And now Soviet medium-range missiles had appeared in Cuba, where their range covered almost the entire territory of the United States. Surely those were not the "defensive" weapons which the ambassador, Gromyko, the Soviet government, and Khrushchev had been talking about. The president saw that as a deliberate deceit which had also compromised the confidential channel, for "even the Soviet ambassador, who is fully trusted by his government, as far as we can say, was unaware that medium-range missiles capable of

---

* I did not know it at the time, but on October 22, Oleg Penkovsky, a colonel of Soviet Central Military Intelligence and a secret agent of British and American intelligence, was arrested in Moscow. A vainglorious man, he had insisted on being awarded the American rank of colonel, and on his business trips to London and Washington he asked to be presented to Queen Elizabeth II and President Kennedy. As was later recounted by Raymond L. Garthoff of the Brookings Institution, who began his government career as a Soviet analyst with the CIA and ended it as U.S. ambassador to Bulgaria, Penkovsky's American handlers had allotted him two coded telephone signals, one to signal immediate danger of arrest, the other to signal an imminent Soviet attack on the United States. Before his arrest Penkovsky had several minutes to send a signal, and he sent the one warning of an attack. It seems he decided he would rather go down in the company of the whole world!

Penkovsky's CIA handlers had already learned of his arrest through other channels and reported it immediately—but they never mentioned his signal that war was imminent. In so doing they assumed a great responsibility. But they also fully recognized their agent's exaggerated notion of his influence over international events. It is both difficult and frightening to imagine the catastrophic turn that events could have taken at the height of the Cuban crisis had Penkovsky's intelligence handlers not known their man and had they passed on his alarm to their superiors.

hitting the United States have already been delivered to Cuba and that they were not intended to defend Cuba against attack on the approaches to that country. It follows that even the ambassador himself had no reliable information at the time of our earlier meeting." He was right, and I had not much to say to him in reply except to confirm that I had no real information from my government. The conversation was tense and rather embarrassing to me.

Before leaving, he seemed to have calmed down and asked, almost in passing, what instructions the masters of Soviet ships bound for Cuba had received following the president's address and quarantine order, which extended to the use of force to prevent more offensive missiles from reaching Cuba. I replied that I knew about strict instructions issued earlier: shipmasters were not to bow to any unlawful demands for a search on the high seas, for this would be contrary to international laws of freedom of navigation. I added that those instructions still stood, as far as I knew. Robert Kennedy wondered how it all would end, for the Americans were set on stopping our ships by force.

"But that would be an act of war," I prompted. He shook his head and left.

After some hesitation I conveyed all of Robert Kennedy's harsh statements to Moscow word by word, including those that were not at all flattering to Khrushchev and Gromyko. I wanted to give Moscow an idea of the genuine state of agitation in the president's inner circle. I considered this important, so that the Kremlin could visualize overall the nervous atmosphere in Washington. (Afterward, Gromyko's aides told me that he had instructed them not to circulate my report among members of the Soviet leadership, since he was going to set it out to Khrushchev personally. What had happened to it next remains unknown, but he never returned it to his assistants, nor could I find it in the archives.)

In order to keep our meetings during the Cuban crisis strictly confidential, Robert Kennedy and I usually arranged them after midnight, from about 1 A.M. to 3 A.M. We met either at my embassy or in his office at the Department of Justice. When he visited me, I used to meet him at the entrance, and we ascended to the third floor to my sitting room where we proceeded to talk in the perfect silence of the night. Never was anyone else present at those meetings apart from the two of us. My wife used to leave coffee for us and go to bed. All this made the ambiance somewhat mysterious and at the same time reflected the tense atmosphere of Washington in those days. This tension was accentuated by the fact that Robert Kennedy was far from being a sociable person and lacked a proper sense of humor—always a great help whenever discussions become complicated, as these certainly were. Moreover, he was impulsive and excitable. Nevertheless we managed to keep our conversations, which as a rule were lengthy, strictly businesslike.

Even then Moscow continued to tell our embassy nothing. No instructions to answer Robert Kennedy. Complete silence. Vassily Kuznetsov, our deputy foreign minister, later told me that my lack of concrete information could be explained by the sense of total bewilderment that enveloped Khrushchev and his colleagues after their plot had taken such an unexpected turn.

After my first meeting with Robert Kennedy, the president sent Khrushchev another message on October 23. It expressed his hope that Khrushchev would immediately instruct Soviet vessels to observe the terms of the quarantine. That same day Khrushchev replied that the Soviet government regarded violation of freedom of the seas and international airspace as "an act of aggression which pushes mankind toward the abyss of nuclear missile war." The Soviet government could consequently not instruct its shipmasters to obey orders from U.S. naval forces blockading Cuba. It went without saying, the message read, that "we will not remain simple bystanders with regard to piratical acts by American ships on the high seas. We will then be forced to take our own measures that we consider essential and adequate in order to protect our rights. We have all necessary means to do so."

Wednesday, October 24, was probably the most memorable day in the whole long period of my service as ambassador to the United States. As if it were yesterday, I can recall the enormous tension that gripped us at the embassy as we all watched the sequences on American television showing a Soviet tanker as it drew closer and closer to the imaginary line which, if crossed, would imply a violation of the quarantine against Cuba. This would thus permit American warships to stop and detain it—even by shelling if the master refused to halt.

In a voice choked with emotion, the television announcer counted down the miles as the ship approached the line, escorted by U.S. destroyers and warplanes. Four, three, two, finally one mile was left—would the ship stop? Finally, the ship crossed the line without the destroyers opening fire. There was a general sigh of relief, primarily among the staff of our embassy. But we did not know at that moment that all other cargo ships received secret orders to remain outside the quarantine line. We, in the embassy, were again not informed of this by Moscow. So our emotions remained high.

The threat of an immediate direct clash at sea was thus delayed. But the confrontation still looked very real.

Our embassy told the government that most people in Washington feared a further escalation of the crisis. Press reports said the administration was considering the possibility of destroying the launch sites under construction in Cuba by carrying out a massive bombing raid. Some sources described Robert Kennedy, Bundy, and the military as the warmongers of the administration who insisted on showing firmness in order to eliminate the Cuban missile bases and on going as far as invading the island if necessary. Our cable suggested that this information could have been officially inspired to put additional pressure on us. But we also warned that the president himself, like a gambler, actually was staking his reputation as a statesman, and his chances for reelection in 1964, on the outcome of this crisis. That was why we could not rule out—especially given the more aggressive members of his entourage—the possibility of a reckless reaction such as a bombing raid on the Cuban missile bases or even an invasion, although the latter was clearly less likely.

The embassy also pointed to a general stoking of tension in the United States through the media, which was reporting that various states were placing the civil defense system and nuclear bomb shelters on full alert and were storing food and other necessities for the population. We also reported that Rusk had called leading American journalists to the State Department the same day to tell them that the tendency of some newspapers to register a certain lessening of tension (after the first Soviet ship had run the blockade) was at variance with the real state of affairs. The administration was as determined as ever to use "any" means to bring about the dismantling of the Cuban missile bases, Rusk stressed. He also denied a report published by the influential columnist Walter Lippmann that the Kennedy administration was weighing the pros and cons of dismantling American missiles based in other countries, such as Turkey, in exchange for the withdrawal of Soviet missiles from Cuba. This exchange turned out to be one of the key elements of the settlement of the crisis, but at that stage Rusk did not want to plant this compromise with us or with American public opinion.

Late Thursday, we received a letter from Kennedy to Khrushchev arguing that the United States had not been the first to challenge the situation in Cuba because the Soviet government had delivered military supplies, invariably described as defensive. But missiles capable of striking the United States justified his latest actions toward Cuba, he said, and called for a "restoration of the earlier situation."

Throughout Friday, October 26, the embassy reported, the American media, obviously taking their cue from high places, claimed with increasing persistence that Cuba was continuing to build missile sites and put missiles on operational status. By the end of that day, the State Department and White

House made formal statements transparently hinting that this might lead to more drastic U.S. measures against Cuba. The press was insisting that an invasion of Cuba was still possible, but there was greater emphasis on the possibility of bombing the missile bases.

Some American authors report that Bolshakov passed on an oral message from Mikoyan to Robert Kennedy insisting that none of the missiles in Cuba had the range to hit the United States. I could find no sign of any such message in our archives. But things like this could happen under Khrushchev, especially when he was under stress. If any such message existed, it certainly was as ill-advised as it was incorrect—but Robert Kennedy never mentioned it to me.

According to a report from our ambassador to Havana, Fidel Castro arrived at the Soviet Embassy on Friday night and stayed there until 5 A.M. on Saturday, October 27. He was deeply disturbed by the lack of any prospects for an end to the crisis. Both sides stood pat. Castro admitted to the possibility of an American bombing strike on Cuba. He even suggested that our ambassador withdraw with him to the bunker built at the command post in a cave near Havana. Castro sent Khrushchev a message proposing that the Soviet Union, in its negotiations with the United States, should try to trump any American threat to Cuba by threatening to use its nuclear arms against the United States.

But far from stiffening Khrushchev's resolve, this merely confirmed him in his determination to seek a compromise and avoid nuclear war. In any case this decision had already been taken before Castro's message was received in Moscow on Saturday. The day before, the U.S. Embassy in Moscow had been handed a detailed letter from Khrushchev to Kennedy. It reaffirmed that Soviet missiles sent to Cuba were purely defensive and had been sent at the request of the Cuban government. Khrushchev again criticized the American quarantine and assured the president that Soviet ships en route to Cuba at the moment were carrying no military supplies whatsoever. The Soviet Union had no intention of attacking the United States because a war between the two countries would be suicidal. Ideological differences should be settled by peaceful means, so "let us normalize our relations."

Khrushchev called for a mutual demonstration of common sense. He proposed that the Soviet Union declare its ships bound for Cuba would carry no military supplies whatever while the United States declare that it would refrain from armed intervention in Cuba and equally refrain from supporting any invasion forces. Khrushchev hinted that such a solution would entirely remove the cause for siting Soviet missiles in Cuba. This important hint showed that Khrushchev was seeking a political compromise in what was his first conciliatory letter.

■ ■ ■

Saturday was a day of dynamic diplomatic activity. Without waiting for an answer to Friday's letter, Khrushchev sent Kennedy a further urgent message proposing a more concrete compromise: the Soviet side would be willing to remove from Cuba the weapons Kennedy had branded as offensive in return for the withdrawal of similar American weapons from Turkey. The mutual commitments would be formalized through the UN Security Council and special representatives of both governments.

What was the riddle of the two messages? Khrushchev was anticipating an American air strike on the missile bases in Cuba at any moment. At first he had been afraid to complicate the urgent search for settlement by insisting on the removal of American missiles from Turkey. But on second thought, under pressure from some of his colleagues, he made a desperate, last-minute attempt to obtain a deal to swap his missiles in Cuba for the American missiles in Turkey.

When Kennedy replied that same Saturday, he deliberately ignored Khrushchev's second message offering a mutual missile exchange between the two nations' client states. Sensing Khrushchev's confusion and hesitancy, the president plainly intended not to engage in a discussion of the missiles in Turkey for the time being. Kennedy's message welcomed Khrushchev's desire to seek a prompt solution, but he insisted that first all work on missile sites in Cuba should be stopped and all offensive weapons in Cuba should be rendered inoperable under international control. At the same time, he expressed his readiness to reach an accord on a permanent settlement of the Cuban crisis on the following basis: the Soviet Union would remove all missiles and other offensive weapons from Cuba; the United States would lift its blockade and give assurances that there would be no invasion of Cuba either by the United States or other countries of the Western Hemisphere.

## A Timely Question and Answer Break the Deadlock

Late Saturday night, Robert Kennedy invited me to meet him for an urgent tête-à-tête at the Justice Department. It turned out to be a decisive conversation that sent the signal to Khrushchev that he could save face by eventually arranging for a missile trade in Cuba and Turkey.*

The president's brother began by stating that the Cuban crisis was rapidly worsening. A report just received said that an unarmed U.S. aircraft

---

* This account of the meeting is based on my contemporary report in our archives, which was written immediately afterward and is to be regarded as authoritative.

had been shot down on a reconnaissance flight over Cuba, and now the American military was demanding permission from the president to retaliate. The United States, Robert Kennedy explained, could not discontinue these flights because they were sent out to obtain timely information on the missile bases in Cuba that threatened America's national security. But answering fire with fire would provoke a chain reaction that would be very difficult to stop.

This also applied to the essential issue of Cuban missile bases. The U.S. administration was resolved to get rid of the bases and was prepared to bomb them as a serious threat to American security if it came to the worst. But Robert Kennedy also recognized that bombing the bases might also lead to Soviet casualties, which would undoubtedly induce the Soviet government to retaliate in Europe. Then a real war would break out, and millions of Americans and Russians would perish. The American side wanted to avoid this by all means, and he was sure the Soviet government did, too. Yet delay in finding a way out entailed great risks that the situation could spin out of control. To underline this, he remarked almost in passing that a lot of unreasonable people among American generals—and not only generals—were "spoiling for a fight."

That was why the president believed, Robert Kennedy continued, that Khrushchev's first message of October 26 and the president's reply dispatched that day, October 27, could provide a suitable basis to settle the crisis. For the Americans, the important thing was to secure the Soviet government's early agreement to stop all further construction at the missile sites in Cuba and the adoption of international controls making it impossible to fire them. In return, he said, the U.S. government would not only be willing to call off the Cuban quarantine but to offer assurances against another invasion of Cuba. The United States also was certain that other countries in the Western Hemisphere would be willing to give similar assurances.

I thought for a moment. The principal shortcoming of this compromise—as well as of the president's reply that day—was that it did not include a "base-for-base" exchange of missiles. I still had no relevant instructions from Moscow and had not yet received from Moscow the full text of Khrushchev's second message because it had been handed to the U.S. Embassy in Moscow only that day. Nevertheless I decided to inquire: What about the missile bases in Turkey?

It turned out that Robert Kennedy was ready with an answer. It had been authorized by the president but had not yet been given to Khrushchev. He replied that if the missiles in Turkey represented the only obstacle to a settlement on the terms that had just been outlined, the president saw no insurmountable difficulties. His main problem was a public announcement:

the siting of missile bases in Turkey had been a result of a formal decision adopted by the NATO Council. For the president now to announce a unilateral decision to withdraw the missiles from Turkey would damage the structure of NATO and the position of the United States as its leader. Nevertheless, President Kennedy was ready to come to terms with Khrushchev on this subject as well.

"I believe," Robert Kennedy said, "that it will probably take four to five months for the U.S. to withdraw its missiles from Turkey. This is the minimum time the administration will require in view of rules of procedure within NATO. The discussion of the whole Turkish aspect of the problem can be continued through you and myself. Right now, however, there is nothing the president could say publicly about Turkey in this context."

He warned that what he was telling me about Turkey was strictly confidential and that only a couple of people in Washington, besides his brother and himself, were aware of it. That was all that the president had asked him to convey to Khrushchev, he concluded, and the president was also asking Khrushchev to give an explicit, substantive reply by the next day—Sunday— through our private channel rather than become involved in a complex debate that could merely cause delay. Regrettably, the situation was shaping up in a way that left very little time for the solution of the whole problem, and Robert Kennedy said his brother hoped that the head of the Soviet government would not misunderstand him and think the United States was issuing an ultimatum. It was simply that time was of the essence.

Before we parted, Robert Kennedy gave me a telephone number so I could ring him directly at the White House. Throughout the whole meeting he was very nervous; indeed, it was the first time I saw him in such a state. He did not even try to argue with me over various points as he normally did; he just kept repeating that time was pressing and we should not waste it. After the meeting, he at once drove to the president with whom, he had said, he now spent nearly all the time.

In his memoirs, Khrushchev leaves no doubt that my report of this conversation turned the tide in Moscow. He called it the "culminating point of the crisis." By that time, alarming reports about American plans to bomb Cuban missile bases were snowballing. Soviet intelligence sources got information that bombing raids were believed to be set for October 29 or 30, the following Monday and Tuesday. In both Moscow and Washington, tension was mounting. Nervousness increased still more among Khrushchev and his colleagues when, in the wake of my telegram reporting my conversation with Robert Kennedy, word came that the president was expecting an answer from Moscow the following day—Sunday, October 28—at the latest.

The climax of the conflict was in sight. In the Kremlin, this was a moment of "great anxiety" over possible American military strikes on Cuba, as I was later told by Mikoyan, and there was a frantic search for a solution. The Politburo had gone into session at Khrushchev's dacha Saturday evening, there to remain until Sunday. After receiving my report, Khrushchev immediately told the Politburo: "Comrades, now we have to look for a dignified way out of this conflict." It was then decided without further delay to accept President Kennedy's proposals, all the more since his consent to remove American missiles gradually from Turkey made it possible to justify our retreat.

At 4 P.M. on Sunday, October 28, I received an urgent cable from Gromyko. It read, "Get in touch with Robert Kennedy at once and tell him that you have conveyed the contents of your conversation with him to N. S. Khrushchev. Khrushchev herewith gives the following urgent reply: 'The suggestions made by Robert Kennedy on the president's instructions are appreciated in Moscow. The president's message of October 27 will be answered on the radio today, and the answer will be highly positive.' The principal point that worries the president, namely, the issue of dismantling missile bases in Cuba under international control, raises no objections and will receive ample coverage in Khrushchev's address."

I have to admit that upon reading this cable I breathed a sigh of great relief. The prospect of a military showdown receded, and the strain of the last days somehow just vanished. It became clear that the critical point of the conflict had been safely passed, and we could relax a little.

I immediately called Robert Kennedy, and we at once arranged to meet. Within an hour I had relayed Khrushchev's reply to him. After he had listened to it with close attention and thanked me, he said that he was going directly to the White House to advise the president of the "important reply" sent by the head of the Soviet government. In spite of himself he added that the news was "a great relief." "At last, I'm going to see the kids. Why, I've almost forgotten my way home." And, for the first time since the crisis began, I saw him smile.

It was quite obvious that Robert Kennedy had learned the news of Khrushchev's reply with satisfaction and deep emotion. Before leaving he once again asked me to maintain strict secrecy about the accord on Turkey. I answered that apart from me not a soul in the embassy knew about my conversation with him the day before.

Somewhat later that same Sunday, Radio Moscow on Khrushchev's direct orders quickly broadcast an English version of Khrushchev's promised message to Kennedy; its text was handed simultaneously to the U.S. Embassy. This unusual step was taken to forestall the bombing of the missile sites Khrushchev feared was imminent. It was an answer to Kennedy's message of October 27. Khrushchev's detailed address, intended in part to justify publicly the Soviet government's actions in the Cuban crisis, contained the most important point: the Soviet side accepted the terms of settling the crisis proposed by the U.S. president. Turkey, however, was not mentioned. Kennedy replied almost at once, hailing Khrushchev's message as an important contribution to peace. Soviet citizens were stunned by the broadcast of Khrushchev's message, for they had heard nothing official during the entire week about our missiles in Cuba.

On Monday, October 29, I handed Robert Kennedy a confidential message to the president from Khrushchev. The Soviet premier said he realized that a public discussion about eliminating American missile bases in Turkey would be a rather sensitive matter for the president, and he agreed not to discuss it openly but would continue discussing the subject confidentially through Robert Kennedy and the Soviet ambassador. The message highlighted the idea that the Soviet leadership was accepting the terms of the accord on Cuba after the president's agreement to decide the question of American missile bases on Turkey. It expressed the hope that an accord would become a further step of no small importance toward easing international tension.

The next day, October 30, Robert Kennedy informed me that the president confirmed the accord on closing American missile bases in Turkey, and that while we could be sure that the appropriate steps would be taken, no connection was to be drawn in public between his decision and the events surrounding Cuba. He said that the White House was not prepared to formalize the accord, even by means of strictly confidential letters, and that the American side preferred not to engage in any correspondence on so sensitive an issue. Very privately, Robert Kennedy added that some day—who knows?—he might run for president, and his prospects could be damaged if this secret deal about the missiles in Turkey were to come out.

I relayed the Kennedy reply to Moscow. Two days later, I told Robert Kennedy that Khrushchev agreed to those considerations and had no doubt that the president would keep his word.

The important part about this dialogue with Kennedy on the confidentiality of the accord on Turkey was the fact that at the most critical moment of the crisis, the president himself had been prepared to declare his commitment to it in public if necessary, using the United Nations secretary general, U Thant, as an intermediary. Many years later Rusk disclosed that as soon as Robert Kennedy had left for his Saturday meeting with me, Rusk himself talked alone with the president. Rusk suggested, and the president agreed, that if needed they could undertake one more move. Rusk would call Andrew Cordier, a close friend and an undersecretary general of the United

Nations, and pass on to him the text of a statement to be published by the secretary general himself. U Thant's statement would contain a proposal to withdraw both the Soviet missiles from Cuba and the American ones from Turkey. Cordier was to give this statement to U Thant only upon receiving a special additional signal from Rusk himself. Yet the rapidly changing situation made it unnecessary, as Khrushchev agreed to a confidential accord. The whole idea of floating the "base-for-base" exchange through U Thant had remained a deep secret known only to the president, Rusk, and Cordier. The full details did not leak out for years.

Khrushchev's failure to insist on a public pledge by Kennedy cost him dearly. Kennedy was proclaimed the big winner in the crisis because no one knew about the secret deal. Khrushchev had been humiliated into withdrawing our missiles from Cuba with no obvious gain. In fact, the terms of the final settlement were neither a great defeat nor a great victory for Kennedy or Khrushchev. Kennedy accomplished his main purpose: the restoration of the status quo ante in Cuba, although he had to accept the presence of Soviet military personnel there. Khrushchev fell short of shifting the strategic balance more in our favor, but he obtained a pledge from Washington not to invade Cuba, which had been sought by him and Castro, and withdrawal of American missiles from Turkey, which was also in our interest.

## After the Crisis: Lessons and Footnotes

It was not until January 7, 1963, after nearly two months of intensive diplomatic bargaining and top-level correspondence, that Vassily Kuznetsov, Soviet deputy foreign minister, and Adlai Stevenson, U.S. permanent representative to the United Nations, sent a joint letter to the UN Secretary General U Thant proposing that the Cuban question be struck off the Security Council agenda in view of the settlement of the Cuban crisis.

All subsequent U.S. administrations confirmed in one way or another their readiness to abide by the 1962 accords. On the other hand, the Americans repeatedly presented us with various claims attempting to interpret the accords more broadly, that is, in their own interest. They tried to take advantage of the fact that the understanding had never been formalized in writing. Kennedy had abstained from formalizing his commitment not to attack Cuba because Castro had refused to allow the Americans to monitor the removal of Soviet offensive weapons on site. Khrushchev had to content himself with the understanding that the United States would not attack Cuba unless Soviet offensive weapons were deployed there.

On November 29, Mikoyan, who was on his way to visit Cuba, stopped off in Washington and met with the president in the White House. Their conversation lasted for about three and one-half hours, and virtually all of it was devoted to Cuba. At times the discussion tended to be intense, yet its participants parted in a conciliatory mood.

Mikoyan reported to the Politburo that the president claimed that Cuba was turning "into a springboard of Soviet policy for undermining the situation in Latin America." Kennedy stressed that he was not referring as much to Cuba itself—"how could it hurt us in earnest?"—as to the expansion of the Soviet influence in this part of the world through an attempt to change the existing balance of power. His goal was quite transparent: the United States would prefer the Soviets to limit their activities to their own country and their domestic social structure, and the United States would do the same.

"What we have now," the president went on, "is quite the contrary: although our two countries don't challenge each other directly we keep running into each other almost everywhere, which in our nuclear age is fraught with serious dangers for world peace. As soon as the first spark of revolution appears any place, so you appear saying, 'Here we are!' We both ought to avoid aggravating the situation in all parts of the globe. And the most important thing is for Khrushchev and me to comprehend each other."

Mikoyan replied: "We favor solving questions, not suspending them. What 'spark of revolution' are you talking about? Originally we had no connections in Cuba whatsoever. [Kennedy agreed.] Revolutions have always been and they will always be. Eventually they are going to prevail in the American countries, and here, in the U.S.A. revolution will prevail. Even you may one day find yourself in Castro's shoes, who, not being a Marxist, is nevertheless leading Cuba toward socialism."

The president laughed, "Not I, but my younger brother may indeed."

Then Mikoyan and Kennedy engaged in a heated debate about the American wording of a nonaggression guarantee for Cuba. The Americans were clearly trying to avoid anything explicit. Kennedy insisted they should confine themselves to separate declarations by the two heads of government outlining all settled and unsettled issues, and not a joint UN declaration. But when asked by Mikoyan directly, the president confirmed that the United States would not invade Cuba and that it was not deviating from the positions it took during the crisis. "I have already said," the president remarked, "the United States is not going to attack Cuba and won't allow others. Khrushchev and I understand each other, and I will fulfill the commitments I assumed."

Besides Cuba, the most important part of the conversation for Mikoyan was the president's observations, and not for the first time, on the desirability of maintaining what might be called a global status quo. As a cautious person, Mikoyan kept his own comments on this idea out of his report on the meeting, but it was not lost on him that within a year President Kennedy had twice proposed agreement on maintaining the status quo. Khrushchev, however, having burnt his fingers on Cuba, still was not prepared to consider the question seriously. He was captive to ideological illusions: He believed that socialism was advancing on a world scale with the Soviet Union in the lead, and that capitalism, with the United States in charge, was retreating. But he never really thought of war.

I cannot overemphasize the vast significance of the Cuban crisis for the subsequent development of Soviet-American relations. Those days revealed the mortal danger of a direct armed confrontation of the two great powers, a confrontation headed off on the brink of war thanks to both sides' timely and agonizing realization of the disastrous consequences. It was this insight that made the political settlement possible, and a substantial role was played by a direct confidential channel between the leaders of the two countries. Even now that so many years have passed, the political and diplomatic solution at which the two states jointly arrived may be regarded as a model of successfully controlling a crisis. It showed that a third world war can be avoided.

The Cuban crisis also had serious negative long-range consequences. The Soviet leadership could not forget a blow to its prestige bordering on humiliation when it was forced to admit its weakness before the whole world and withdraw its missiles from Cuba. Our military establishment used this experience to secure for itself a new large-scale program of nuclear arms development. This was bound to lead to a new stage in the arms race between the United States and the Soviet Union, the repercussions of which were to be felt for nearly thirty years, despite the attempts made to contain it.

In addition, the crisis affected Khrushchev's political career and helped bring him down. In 1964, as Khrushchev's dismissal was being agreed upon in the plenary meeting of the Central Committee, many delegates strongly criticized his personal role in creating the Cuban crisis.

But both sides also were left keenly conscious of the need to ease tension. In 1963 Moscow and Washington signed a series of agreements, including a limited test ban treaty and an agreement on establishing a "hot line" to communicate high-level messages directly and instantaneously between the two capitals. Besides, no further serious situations arose out of the dispute over another dangerous seat of tension, Berlin, either in 1963 or later. The construction of the Berlin wall two years earlier had in its own perverse way given Kennedy confirmation of the status quo that he sought in that area, although it could never be publicly acknowledged. Nor was Cuba exposed to any further threat of an American invasion.

The importance of the confidential channel was proven as well. I cannot tell how the Cuban crisis would have ended if these contacts had not been there, and if it had ended badly, the consequences could have been truly disastrous. The whole experience also provided guidelines for my future diplomatic activity, which I followed for the remainder of my quarter-century as an ambassador. I tried to be an active participant in the constantly functioning confidential channel at the highest level, in order to ensure possibilities for a candid if not always pleasant dialogue between the leaders of both countries. I venture to think that at times this appeared to be the only way of preventing the Cold War from turning into a hot one. The later history of our relations in this book testifies to this.

There are certain requirements for the confidential channel to be effective. It has to be permanently available, and its immediate participants must possess a certain level of diplomatic and political experience and knowledge. Above all, the channel should never be used by any government for the purpose of misinformation. Of course, a diplomatic game is always being played, but deliberate misinformation is inadmissible, for sooner or later it is going to be disclosed and the channel will lose all its value.

That was what happened to Bolshakov who, together with Robert Kennedy, used to participate in the confidential channel between the White House and the Kremlin. After the Cuban crisis, our embassy learned that an article about it was being prepared by Charles Bartlett, a journalist with contacts close to the Kennedys, and Stewart Alsop, a leading columnist. The article would mention for the first time Bolshakov's meetings with Robert Kennedy. Bolshakov rushed to Robert Kennedy and asked him to prevent publication of the article, which would devalue their channel. But Kennedy's response was unexpectedly angry and rude: "We believe that in the Cuban crisis we have been deceived by everybody, including you. If you want to keep on using this channel, it's up to you from now on." The article was published, and Bolshakov was duly recalled. He paid a farewell call on Robert Kennedy, who gave a hypocritical performance of parting with "his friend," regretting his departure and asking Bolshakov to let him know "how he was getting on" in Moscow. Bolshakov returned home, where he continued working for twenty years and then retired.

Another scenario gained credence in the American press, according to which an important role in resolving the crisis was played by John Scali, a television journalist who, allegedly with the knowledge of the White House, maintained contact with the resident of our intelligence service in Washington, Alexander Fomin (his real name was Feklisov). Fomin contacted Scali because he regarded him, rightly or wrongly, as an important CIA agent. In the Washington restaurant where the two met during the crisis, an enterprising owner has even hung a sign saying that this was "The

Place." I was briefed on these contacts by Fomin, who also held the rank of counselor in our embassy, but I found their importance was relatively insignificant in view of my direct and ongoing dialogue with Robert Kennedy. As far as I could determine, our intelligence did not have any significant regular connections within President Kennedy's immediate entourage or other important sources, and the KGB in Washington failed to obtain any significant information during the crisis. Fomin himself was soon recalled.

After the crisis subsided, Robert Kennedy complained to me that the Soviet side should not have searched for other channels apart from his own. He observed that Scali had been acting on his own initiative, without any approval on the part of the White House. Scali and Fomin each claimed the other had sought him out first as a contact. In a December 14 letter to Khrushchev, President Kennedy seconded his brother's point, noting that it was risky to establish confidential links through a journalist, since neither side could be sure of what might suddenly appear in public. Personally, I think that the real reason behind all this was that both intelligence services were looking for contacts with each other during the crisis in a desperate search for information. In any case, that was the end of the Fomin-Scali affair, and nothing like it ever occurred again. When they met by chance many years later at a seminar for participants in the Cuban crisis, they were not even on speaking terms, and both gave contradictory versions of their meetings during the crisis itself.

At the annual reception for the diplomatic corps at the end of 1962, I was chatting with the president about the crisis, and he expressed his satisfaction at the way the whole crisis was being wound down. He called over Llewellyn Thompson, pointed at him, and said, "Now I have a very good, cautious, and experienced adviser on Soviet affairs."

I commented that, having such able advisers, it was also a good idea to listen to them. Reflecting on the depth of Khrushchev's ideological commitment recalls an episode during a session of the UN General Assembly. That day the item on the agenda was not especially important, so only junior diplomats were there—and so few of them that the chairman checked for a quorum by calling the roll in alphabetical order. He started with Australia, which answered yes, meaning that its representative was present. "Byelorussia?" the president went on. "No!" the republic's representative promptly replied. Greatly astonished, the chairman asked again and got the same answer. Still surprised and now amused, the chairman turned to the clerk keeping the minutes. "Please put down that the Byelorussian representative, though he is sitting here, insists that he is absent." After the meeting we asked the young diplomat why he had acted in this odd way. He explained that this was his first General Assembly session and he was not sure what was going on. Yet he knew his job. As long as Australia, a member of all kinds of hostile pacts, was saying yes, he had to say no.

I find this incident has a moral for more exalted politicians: you will never agree on anything if you are already tuned in to a specific notion and cannot or will not hear the other side. This was one important lesson of the Cuban crisis.

# III. Learning to Live Together

*Setting Up the "Hot Line"*

After the Cuban crisis, our relations with the Kennedy administration began settling into a more realistic mode in which the emphasis had to be on communication, discussion, negotiation, and continuous adjustment if not solution of the differences between what were now beginning to be seen as the world's two superpowers. Cuba continued to be an irritant, especially the Castro government's ventures in Latin America and later in Africa, but despite the almost unanimous desire of the American public to get rid of Castro, there was no taste in the U.S. government for doing so at the risk of provoking a war with the Soviet Union. There also appeared among the public a dread of nuclear war, which I had not observed before the Cuban crisis.

It became obvious that among other things we needed a complete overhaul and modernization of communications on both sides in order to help defuse another confrontation in time. This became known as the "hot line," a direct communication channel between the Soviet and American governments reserved for emergencies.

Nowadays one can hardly imagine just how primitive were our embassy's communications with Moscow in the dreadful days of the Cuban crisis, when every hour, not just every day, counted for so much. When I wanted to send an urgent cable to Moscow about my important conversation with Robert Kennedy, it was coded at once into columns of numbers (initially this was done by hand and only later by machine). Then we called Western Union. The telegraph agency would send a messenger to collect the cable. Usually it was the same young black man, who came to the embassy on a bicycle. But after he pedaled away with my urgent cable, we at the embassy could only pray that he would take it to the Western Union office without delay and not stop to chat on the way with some girl!

This primitive means of communication accounted for the rather unconventional methods used by Khrushchev to send his urgent answer to President Kennedy on that decisive day, Sunday, October 28. Since the

Kremlin thought there was a deadline and the outcome of the crisis hung on his answer, Khrushchev not only sent me his urgent reply as a coded cable and dispatched a duplicate to the American Embassy in Moscow, but instructed that the English text be broadcast immediately by Radio Moscow. At great speed, with sirens shrieking, a motorcade headed by Khrushchev's assistant raced off from Khrushchev's dacha to the radio station, where the message to President Kennedy was broadcast at once. It was from this broadcast that I myself heard Khrushchev's full reply, not by the cable with the text that arrived at the embassy via Western Union two hours later.

The American Embassy in Moscow also communicated with Washington by commercial cable in the same way we did with Moscow. Both embassies had long been forbidden to install the huge roof aerials that are necessary for radio communication because the intelligence services of each side feared the other would use the aerials to eavesdrop on radio conversations within government and other offices in their respective capitals. As we learned many years later, one of the motives for the stubborn refusal of the American Embassy in Moscow to move to another, more spacious and scenic site (the Soviet authorities had proposed a mutual exchange of sites to erect larger modern embassy buildings) was the fact that the old embassy building was situated near the Kalininsky Prospect, the main highway in Moscow, along which our bosses were driven to work from their dachas. After their cars were equipped with radio telephones—but not scramblers—Khrushchev, and especially President Nikolai Podgorny, on their way to work used to talk with their colleagues, discussing business and gossiping. Because of their location near their route, the American Embassy in Moscow could intercept and record this radio traffic without a huge rooftop aerial, which would have given away what they were doing. In Washington, where our embassy was only half a dozen blocks from the White House, our intelligence services likewise tried to comb the surrounding airspace for whatever transmissions it could pick up, but it appeared that the Americans had left us behind in the field of technology, as the U.S. government's radio conversations were for the most part coded.

With a healthy regard for the communications problems that had suddenly surfaced at the climactic moments of the Cuban crisis, Khrushchev and Kennedy recognized the urgency of establishing a direct connection between Moscow and Washington. On June 20 a memorandum was signed in Geneva establishing this communications hot line "to be used in case of emergency."

It provided for the installation of an around-the-clock telegraph channel between both capitals via Helsinki-Stockholm-Copenhagen-London to transmit urgent messages. Simultaneously a wireless around-the-clock channel from Moscow to Washington via Tangier was set to be used for backup

communication and for the coordinating channel operating between the ter-
minals. Later, a second telegraph line was installed after a Finnish farmer inadvertently cut the first and only telegraph line while tilling his land, which
understandably caused a lot of commotion in Moscow and Washington. In
the end, Moscow and Washington installed a radio-telephone line that operated via satellite.

## The Old Problems Reappear

The old problems nevertheless began to reappear on the political scene—the
German and Berlin questions, the quest for a nuclear test ban, and the other
points that had long remained at issue between us. On March 12, about six
months after the Cuban crisis, Robert Kennedy and I had a long private dinner to review relations. One rather interesting footnote to history emerged
during the conversation: when John Kennedy first became president he had
suggested to Robert that his brother start learning Russian, because he was
thinking about appointing him ambassador to Moscow. The venture was
later abandoned, although Robert Kennedy never said why.

The president, Robert Kennedy said, first and foremost had a heartfelt
desire to conclude a treaty banning all nuclear tests "not for himself, but
rather for the sake of his children and grandchildren," and he considered it
would help normalize the international situation. He also raised the possibility of another summit meeting to discuss the test ban treaty and the remaining Soviet military personnel in Cuba. The two leaders could discuss other,
more complex international issues such as Germany and Berlin, which he
believed could only be resolved at the summit and not through ordinary
diplomacy.

After I reported on our meeting, Moscow asked me how serious I
thought the Kennedys were about a summit. I replied that they were indeed
weighing the idea but that in my opinion the president was looking at it primarily for domestic considerations. If the meeting turned out to be a success,
or even could be presented as one, it would definitely bring Kennedy victory
in 1964. At the same time I told Moscow that Robert Kennedy's statements
about Germany and Berlin gave no hint of compromise at a summit or elsewhere, so I recommended to Moscow that we wait for further clarification
from "more experienced people" such as Rusk or Thompson.

But Khrushchev was still stubbornly trying to have his own way on
Germany and Berlin despite the fact that he came out of the Cuban crisis
with his position weakened. Even though I believed the discussion was most
unlikely to succeed because Khrushchev was asking for too much, I had been
instructed to take part in lengthy and complex exchanges. The diplomatic

dialogue was nevertheless useful enough in itself by providing the opportunity to remove emotional antagonism.

The discussion was initiated in a detailed conversation with Rusk on March 26. As instructed, I informed him of our position, which was based on Khrushchev's well-known proposals. Upon hearing them, Rusk observed that there were many who did not see much sense in discussing this deadlocked question, but President Kennedy was prepared to continue searching for a solution, or at least for ways to diminish its attendant risks.

Then Rusk started simultaneously probing our position and reassuring me that the relaxation of tension on Germany was real. In the end he asked me directly: Didn't we believe that "time would take care of settling a number of questions" and that the risks would gradually diminish by themselves? Indeed, this was the essence of the American approach to the Germany and Berlin issues, which was to maintain the status quo and wait and see what was to be done next. Without explicit instructions from Moscow, how could I reply to him?

This was how Rusk and I set out on a new marathon on these questions, which in time became so monotonous and repetitive that the ritual gave rise to Rusk's joke numbering our questions and answers.

But on another level, our relations became more friendly. Despite our government's reluctance to have foreigners witness the launching of Soviet spaceships, I was invited to a launching at Cape Canaveral, which I found breathtaking. With the express permission of President Kennedy I was also taken through the restricted facilities at the Massachusetts Institute of Technology where engineers were developing the technology for landing on the moon. I was permitted to sit in the cockpit model for the lunar landing craft. As an engineer by training, I was genuinely impressed by American technology, and I so reported to Moscow.

## Negotiations on the Nuclear Test Ban

An important element in Soviet-American relations during 1963 was the negotiations on banning nuclear tests. Kennedy sought to conclude an agreement to prohibit them completely, in part because he realized the danger of nuclear proliferation more profoundly than his predecessors. An agreement to prohibit tests by the nuclear powers could be part of an effective deterrent to the spread of nuclear weapons to those countries that did not have nuclear weapons. Another issue was the danger of radioactive fallout from atmospheric tests; it was also gaining momentum in public opinion in both countries, although in the Soviet Union it had less force because the tests were conducted in much greater secrecy.

Khrushchev meanwhile started contemplating the feasibility and utility of stopping nuclear tests. The crisis in the Caribbean, with all its excesses, had already shown the world that there were two nuclear powers. The conclusion of a treaty between them to stop nuclear testing would in a sense be another confirmation of the Soviet Union's place as a superpower alongside the United States. Moreover, a number of Soviet scientists and military leaders believed that further tests would only benefit the United States in upgrading the quality of its nuclear weapons, rather than helping the Soviet Union catch up.

But the key obstacle to the treaty was still the problem of monitoring to ensure all sides would fulfill its prohibitions. Here Khrushchev had his own grave doubts, and he was influenced by his advisers. They could not decide among the options: monitoring by national means, which meant self-enforcement; limited use of automated stations (so-called black boxes) on the territories of both countries; or monitoring by foreign experts who would be permitted as observers to visit the territory of the signatories. There was a technical problem. While tests on land or sea and in outer space could be detected scientifically in other countries by their radioactive fallout, the tell-tale signs of an underground test could be confused with seismic data reporting earthquakes. To be certain of a violation, it was occasionally necessary to send an expert to inspect the site where seismographs had recorded a disturbance and determine whether what had taken place was an earthquake or a nuclear explosion. It was these visits that were at the heart of the problem. For Khrushchev, this was first of all a political and not a scientific problem: whether or not to allow inspectors to enter our country.

Khrushchev's opening gambit to resolve the issue came soon after the Cuban crisis. In a conciliatory mood, he informed President Kennedy through the confidential channel—now exclusively operated by Robert Kennedy and me—that for the first time the Soviet government would agree to two to three inspections a year on the territory of each nuclear power.

Unfortunately, the Kennedy administration failed to seize the opportunity and instead started a prolonged dispute about increasing the number of inspections. The American side did not appreciate how psychologically difficult and innovative for Moscow was this very first decision to permit even a few foreign observers onto the Soviet territory (many Politburo members were far from agreement).

So the president answered Khrushchev that he welcomed the Soviet consent to on-site inspection, but he indicated rather than two or three inspections a year, the United States wanted a quota of eight to ten, which Khrushchev rejected as too many.

In March I had a number of revealing talks with Robert McNamara and with prominent American scientists such as J. Robert Oppenheimer, Leo

Szilard, and Jerome Wiesner, who was the president's science adviser. McNamara told me that American nuclear physicists had told the president that from the military and technological point of view, there did not appear to be much sense in continuing the nuclear testing race. But from the political viewpoint, McNamara went on, both Congress and the general public were still convinced—largely by the loud polemics on the issue—that a continuation of tests would give the United States an irrevocable lead in nuclear weapons. Paradoxically, he said, the government's own poll shown that the dread of nuclear war augmented by the Cuban crisis had increased support for advancing nuclear arms and continuing tests despite the fear of radioactive fallout. All this was being expertly used by the Republicans and scientists like Edward Teller supporting them.

Oppenheimer and Szilard in their turn told me that they were troubled by these sentiments. They urged us to seek a reasonable compromise on a treaty stressing that "time was against all of us" if we wanted to help prevent a race toward more complex and deadly nuclear weapons. Wiesner implied that five or six inspections was a likely number to be agreed on by the United States.

Early in April, Thompson privately told me he was worried over the drift in relations between the Kremlin and the White House and said he was thinking of suggesting that the president send one of his close associates to Moscow to meet with Khrushchev, perhaps Rusk, Robert Kennedy, or ambassador-at-large W. Averell Harriman. I liked the idea and told him I was prepared to support it; in my view the best candidate was Rusk.

Thompson said that it was essential for the president to build his election campaign upon specific issues, and those close to him believed that a test ban treaty was among the most promising possibilities, to be followed by a meeting between Kennedy and Khrushchev in August or September, when they would exchange instruments of ratification, discuss the international situation, and perhaps sign bilateral documents, such as a civil aviation treaty. There would also be discussions on Germany and disarmament to provide direction to both sides' negotiators. Kennedy adopted most of this in a message to Khrushchev on April 11.

A few days later Rusk gave me a draft of a joint declaration that would be signed by the four nuclear powers (the United States, the Soviet Union, Britain, and France) pledging not to transfer nuclear weapons, either directly or indirectly through military alliances, to any nation that did not possess them, and also pledging they would not assist them in producing nuclear arms. On April 29 I passed on a message to Kennedy that Khrushchev was ready to receive the president's special representative for an informal exchange of views.

But the road toward a test ban was not to be smooth. At about the same time in Moscow, Khrushchev met with the U.S. and British ambassadors, both of whom brought identical messages from President Kennedy and Prime Minister Harold Macmillan urging him to agree to a larger number of inspections—between three and seven.

"So you want us unilaterally to open entire regions of our country to foreign intelligence?" Khrushchev replied. "Even after the Soviet government had agreed to two or three inspections, the Western powers made an effort to include all but half of the country into the area covered by this inspection. We will not agree to this. I am already displeased with myself for agreeing to these two or three inspections on the Soviet territory. Now I see that we should take this proposal back. To provide all necessary monitoring it's enough to establish two or three automated seismic stations. And thanks to you I made a fool of myself, because as soon as we made our proposal we were answered with a demand to agree to eight to ten, and now seven inspections a year, which the Soviet Union can't accept. All further concessions would not be to Kennedy, but to [Republican Sen. Barry] Goldwater and other 'hawks.' "

(Glenn Seaborg, the distinguished American scientist who had headed the U.S. Atomic Energy Commission, later told me with regret that it had been he who had convinced Kennedy to bargain for more inspections; eight to ten inspections a year was his opening offer. He had been sure that the two sides would reach a compromise somewhere in the middle at about five or seven. If he had known then, Seaborg told me, that Khrushchev could even take back his proposal of two to three visits a year, he would have definitely advised the president to accept.)

Nevertheless plans for an exchange of personal representatives went ahead, and the president decided to send Rusk to Moscow as his personal representative—a choice also favored by Thompson—although he would not arrive until July 28. Simultaneously, negotiations would resume in Moscow on a nuclear test ban treaty, and as his representative the president picked Harriman, an experienced diplomat who enjoyed considerable respect in Moscow and with Khrushchev personally.

Harriman was a reliable negotiator with direct access to the top, which is always an advantage in such complex discussions. On the final day of negotiations, with Gromyko standing his ground on a particular point, Harriman said, as though speaking to himself, that the dispute did not really raise a matter of principle and that the United States could meet the wishes of the Soviet side. He then asked to be put through by phone to President Kennedy right away. The negotiations were taking place in a Ministry of Foreign Affairs residence on Alexei Tolstoy street. Harriman's request caused some commotion there, since calling the White House directly from Moscow was without precedent. Yet a half-hour later they reached the president. Harriman, still sitting at the negotiating table, explained the situation and asked the president to approve his proposal for resolving it. After asking a couple of questions, Kennedy agreed. All members of the Soviet delegation were duly impressed by this pace of decision-making at the top of American government.

President Kennedy held Harriman in high respect, and Harriman paternally watched over Kennedy and invariably supported him strongly. His long experience with us dated back to his wartime term as Roosevelt's ambassador in Moscow, and in this capacity he acquired great respect and liking in our country, which was shared by successive leaders and lasted until the end of his long life. This respect was well-deserved: a true citizen and patriot, he nevertheless sought to find common points that could unite our two nations, not separate them. Yet this never prevented him from frankly expressing his opinion about things he disagreed with. This only made him more popular with both the Soviet leaders and President Kennedy. Among friends and close associates the president jokingly called Harriman the "crocodile" because of his persistence in defending his convictions. As a birthday present the president once gave him a little bronze crocodile with a corresponding inscription, and Harriman was very proud of it.

My wife and I were frequent visitors to Harriman's house in Georgetown, famed as a sort of a permanent meetingplace in the capital for Washington's Establishment of cabinet members, Congressmen, diplomats, journalists, and public and political figures. After his wife died he married the widow of Winston Churchill's son, an intelligent, energetic and fascinating woman, Pamela, who soon became not only an American citizen but a most active benefactor of the Democratic Party.* We cherish the memory of our friendship with the Harrimans.

The negotiations in Moscow were conducted by Gromyko, Harriman, and the British Conservative politician Lord Hailsham. They lasted about two weeks and resulted in an agreement on a limited test ban in three spheres—the atmosphere, on land, and in the sea—but excluded underground tests because these alone could not be monitored without on-site inspections. The agreement was signed in Moscow on August 5.

The extent of the problem of inspection was well demonstrated on July 15 when Khrushchev held a decisive meeting with Harriman and

---

* President Clinton appointed her U.S. ambassador to France.

Hailsham and presented the Soviet arguments with his characteristic earthiness.

"The Soviet Union will not agree to inspection, even if only two or three inspections are proposed," he said. "We are ready to agree to cease all nuclear tests, but without inspections, with monitoring only by means of 'black boxes.' We shall not accede to even one inspection in any form. As to the nuclear tests in those spheres where there is no need for inspections, we are able to sign such an agreement. As regards espionage, it seems that we have different conceptions of what it means. We have difficulty in believing the assertions of Western states in this respect. When the cat promises that he is only going to catch mice and won't touch the lard, it is likely that he really believes in what he says, but there is little doubt that he will grab the lard as well when no one is looking."

By failing to agree on a underground test ban because of the issue of on-site inspections, the nuclear powers lost a significant chance which still has not been regained, one of so many missed opportunities in the long history of Soviet-American relations. An agreement to prohibit nuclear tests completely could have decisively limited the arms race. There probably would have been no multiple warhead, or MIRV, missiles and no nuclear-tipped cruise missiles because their new warheads could not have been tested. Looking back, this failure looks like serious thoughtlessness on the part of our leaders of that period, who were not ready for such openness. Nowadays hundreds of inspections on foreign territories are carried out each year in accordance with various treaties.

On August 5 the treaty banning nuclear tests in the atmosphere, outer space, and underwater was signed in Moscow—the first concrete step toward slowing the arms race and protecting the world from nuclear fallout. Rusk participated in the ceremony and then traveled to the Caucasus where Khrushchev was vacationing at Pizunda on the Black Sea. They had a lively conversation but achieved no obvious breakthroughs—none were expected so soon after signing the test-ban treaty—but when Rusk raised the question of a summit Khrushchev supported the idea but said the meeting would have to be duly prepared.

The meeting at Pizunda was remarkably informal. To the delight of photographers they even played badminton together. My wife Irina, a great home-movie enthusiast, kicked off her shoes and filmed the match from the top of the negotiating table. Khrushchev remarked with a smile that she had definitely absorbed the American spirit of enterprise.

## My Last Meeting with John F. Kennedy

In mid-August Khrushchev entrusted me with conducting a detailed discussion with President Kennedy on a broad range of issues. He accompanied this assignment with a special message that I was to pass to the president. On August 26 I met alone with President Kennedy at the White House; it was to be my last conversation with him. He started the conversation by asking about Khrushchev's health, but before I could answer he added with a smile that the question seemed to be unnecessary in view of Rusk's vivid account of his badminton match with Khrushchev.

Kennedy expressed his satisfaction with the nuclear test ban treaty signed in Moscow, but he turned gloomy when we came to talk about the Senate ratification hearings. "What can I do with people like [Edward] Teller or Senator Goldwater?" Kennedy said, "Along with de Gaulle, they yield to no reasoning and talk themselves into absurdity. Yet I want to note that both the administration and I want to build on the success of signing the treaty, and I will make every effort to do so. You can assure Moscow of this."

I delivered Khrushchev's message expressing the need to consolidate our relations, and the president agreed that as soon as the treaty was ratified, there should be an exchange of views on, first and foremost, measures to prevent surprise attack and a declaration prohibiting weapons of mass destruction in outer space, to be followed by other issues.

In accordance with my instructions I again raised the questions of a peaceful settlement in Germany. I said that, although the situation was less intense from our point of view in the two years since the building of the Berlin Wall and the establishment of the border between East and West Germany, the Soviet government believed that the question of a peace treaty with Germany was still an issue. Essentially, I said, everybody agreed that existing borders could not be altered by war, at which the president nodded. In this case it was best to be consistent and recognize the borders de jure because the world was changing rapidly, and people might lose patience and hope. I reminded Kennedy that he himself had confidentially told Gromyko that he recognized existing German borders de facto—so let us take the next step and sign a peace treaty.

Kennedy confirmed what he had told Gromyko but said the U.S. government was not yet ready to agree to a formal declaration. The most it could concede was a commitment not to use force to alter borders. The main problem for Kennedy remained the position of America's allies, especially with the Federal Republic of Germany and France. In discussing with me a nonaggression pact, the president also tried to shift the blame to his allies, in the first place on Bonn and de Gaulle, and especially de Gaulle. The French president, he said, opposed any such pact and was difficult to talk to altogether, and French-American relations remained strained.

On his own initiative, Kennedy raised several other issues that seemed to show he was seeking better relations with us. He said he hoped to expand trade between our two countries and had instructed the State Department and the Department of Commerce to deal with this immediately. He also asked me to let Khrushchev know that it would be mutually advantageous for both countries to cooperate more actively in outer space, thus sharing our huge investment; in due course there might be a Soviet-American flight to the moon, although he made this suggestion lightly.

Then President Kennedy turned to Cuba and asked me about Soviet military personnel there. I said our troops had been withdrawn and only instructors and other military specialists would remain until the Cubans had mastered the use of our military equipment. He inquired if it was true that Khrushchev was going to visit Cuba, and I told him that he was. The president voiced a cautious hope that when Khrushchev talked with the Cubans and when he spoke there in public, he would bear in mind how extremely sensitive the whole issue was in the United States, especially with him facing reelection the following year. My meeting concluded with the president asking me to convey his appreciation to Khrushchev and his wife for their condolences on the death of his newborn son, Patrick. Then he proposed that we coordinate the information for the press about our meeting by disclosing Khrushchev's message expressing his hope that the nuclear test ban would lead to more agreements—a hope that Kennedy stressed he shared. I agreed and briefed the press in essentially the same way as I left the White House.

It became clear during the autumn that the administration was pursuing a more active and conciliatory diplomacy toward the Soviet Union. Thompson sounded me out on the idea of a gradual reduction of troops to be monitored by international control posts not only on Soviet and West European territory but even in the East Coast ports of the United States as a guarantee against another invasion of Cuba—an intriguing idea in which Kennedy lost interest because Moscow ignored it out of a traditional distaste for inspections. Meanwhile, the United States advanced the idea of an agreement to prohibit nuclear weapons in outer space, which was supported by a Soviet-American resolution approved unanimously by the UN General Assembly. And on November 15 Robert Kennedy, speaking in confidence with the president's knowledge, told me that relations between our two countries depended to a large extent on the development of good personal relations and mutual understanding between his brother and Khrushchev, and another meeting between them would be useful if they could "calmly sit and talk everything over" for two or three days.

This was the first time the possibility of a summit had been raised by the Americans in the year since the Cuban missile crisis. Robert Kennedy also suggested an exchange of visits, with the president to go first to the Soviet Union, perhaps as early in the following year. But it was not to be. Our meeting took place one week before John Kennedy's fateful visit to Dallas.

## President Kennedy's Assassination

On November 22 I dispatched to Moscow an urgent and tragic cable: "It has just been announced on the radio that President Kennedy has died of wounds inflicted as a result of an attempt on his life in the state of Texas. Johnson automatically becomes president of the USA."

The events that day unfolded dramatically. In the morning I had an appointment with my dentist. While sitting in the dentist's chair, I heard the radio in an adjoining room playing music. Then the music stopped, and excited voices were heard repeatedly mentioning Kennedy's name. I could not hear very well what was being said, so I asked the dentist to turn up the sound. He left but presently returned and said, rather calmly though, that the president had been assassinated. After that he asked me to open my mouth again so he could continue with his work.

It goes without saying that at the moment I could not have cared less about my teeth. I had to leave immediately for the embassy. To my great surprise, the dentist, having remarked that "it was too bad the president was killed," added that he was not one of Kennedy's supporters because the president had paid too much attention to the rights of blacks and "spoilt them badly." This, he said, accounted for racial disorders in the country. He hoped that the new president was not going to "play the democrat" too much. Later an American newspaper found out about my visit to the dentist and said, "Now the American secret service will get everything from the horse's mouth." Little did they know what the dentist had said.

Things happened at great speed and affected us in a way that no one could have imagined. The day of the assassination, November 22, police in Dallas arrested a twenty-four-year-old American, Lee Harvey Oswald, on suspicion of the president's murder. Oswald was reported to be a chairman of a local branch of the Fair Play for Cuba Committee. The radio also reported that some time previously Oswald had been to the Soviet Union and had married a Russian woman. Oswald was officially charged on November 23 with Kennedy's murder.

With the anti-communist and anti-Cuban campaign gaining momentum in the United States, it was obvious that we would be suspected as part of a plot, even if there was none. Rusk, anxious and worried, discussed the possible international repercussions with Lyndon Johnson right away. The embassy received some threatening letters. Rumors of a new crisis in Soviet-American relations began to spread. As the situation grew more alarming, I remained convinced that the Soviet Union had nothing to do with this American drama. Even the most tenuous connection would shake Soviet-American relations to their foundation.

I quickly summoned the embassy's chief of intelligence. He assured me that they had no links with Oswald and that I could proceed from this in my talks with the American authorities. (Years later I was told in Moscow that when Oswald first arrived in the Soviet Union and settled in Minsk, the state security services showed some interest in him. Soon, however, he was left alone because of his mediocrity and shrewishness. At the radio plant where he worked he was considered a good-for-nothing, despite his claims to be a technical expert. Oswald enthusiastically attended the factory's shooting club but regularly took the last place in every competition. Deemed quarrelsome and shiftless, he encountered no official opposition from Soviet officials when he decided to return to the United States, and no one in our embassy maintained any contact with him later.)

I urgently informed Moscow of all this, stressing this unexpected Soviet element through Oswald, which was appearing in the dramatic American accounts of Kennedy's assassination. I also reported that according to our embassy's consular department Oswald had been for some years living in Minsk where he had married one Marina Prusakova, and in July of 1962 they had returned to the United States. In March of 1963, just nine months before the assassination, Oswald's wife and daughter had applied for permission to come back to the Soviet Union, and he wanted to accompany them. Their application was refused because nobody in the Soviet Union wanted any more trouble from them. The consular department had kept all of its correspondence with the Oswalds, and it contained nothing blameworthy. I suggested to our government that this correspondence be made available to the Americans, and Moscow quickly approved.

We immediately handed over copies to Rusk, who expressed his thanks for our initiative and asked if the documents could be sent to the commission headed by Chief Justice Earl Warren which was investigating Kennedy's assassination. I told Rusk that I was leaving this entirely to his judgment.

The secretary of state was clearly unprepared for our unusual act and did not conceal his satisfaction. Rusk looked very tired, his eyes were red for lack of sleep—"no more than three or four hours a night," he said—but he was animated, optimistic, and looked altogether like a man who was sure of his present situation notwithstanding the change of presidents. He took whatever steps he could to preserve the ties we had patiently constructed during the Kennedy administration. The State Department issued a statement that its information showed that neither Russia, Cuba, nor any other foreign country had anything to do with the assassination. I was told by Salinger that the statement had been approved by Rusk to minimize any international complications.

On the day after the assassination, I spoke with Thompson and found him highly depressed. Kennedy's death, he said, was a grave blow to the relations between our two nations and especially to the unique confidential connection between our two heads of state, which had proven its value. Thompson said that he had no idea how things would turn out. He also suggested that for security reasons Mikoyan, who was to join the many senior foreign representatives as our representative at the funeral, should not remain in Washington afterward. For my part, I had already sent personal letters of condolence to Jacqueline Kennedy, Robert Kennedy, and Rusk.

The next day, November 24, I had another long conversation with Thompson. He informed me that President Johnson knew of most of the personal correspondence between Kennedy and Khrushchev, but not of all of it. For instance, he knew nothing about their unwritten agreement concerning missiles deployed in Turkey that had been reached during the Cuban crisis. Johnson had been present at many of the president's foreign policy meetings and had spoken on several occasions but mostly just kept silent.

Thompson expected that in the field of foreign policy the relationship between Johnson and Rusk was going to be similar to that of Eisenhower and Dulles. Yet Rusk was not Dulles, and Johnson was not Eisenhower. Johnson was more tough, ambitious, and quick-tempered than Eisenhower. Johnson, he supposed, was going to pay principal attention to domestic policy and the administration's relations with Congress, where he had been the Senate majority leader. I was also told that Johnson had definitely decided to run for president in 1964 and was preparing himself for the campaign, and that Thompson had heard Johnson remark that he probably should think about putting Robert Kennedy on the ticket to run with him as vice president, but this was too soon to talk about it. Rusk had just told Thompson that Johnson instructed him to carry on with the main lines of Kennedy's foreign policy, and Thompson was to remain Rusk's chief adviser on Soviet-American relations. His one personal concern was that as ambassador in Moscow he had given Oswald permission to return to the United States and he hoped this minor incident would not surface and cause him trouble, which in fact it never did.

▪ ▪ ▪

On November 25 Kennedy's impressive funeral took place. Huge crowds of Americans in deep grief watched the cortege. Many were crying. The coffin was followed by the president's relatives and close friends, numerous delegations from all the world headed by presidents, prime ministers, members of the diplomatic corps, members of the cabinet and Congress, public and political figures, and military units. Mikoyan was among those in the front ranks following the cortege on foot.

That night there was a commemorative reception at the White House. The hall, so familiar as a place of festivities and official ceremonies, was quiet and doleful. Foreign delegations in their turn presented their condolences to the president's widow, who rarely said anything, only nodded; she made a strong impression on everybody with her self-control and composure. But when Mikoyan and I approached Jacqueline Kennedy and conveyed the deep condolences of Khrushchev and his wife, she said with deep feeling and with tears in her eyes, "The day my husband was murdered, early in the morning before breakfast he suddenly told me in our hotel room that everything should be done to get things under way with Russia. I don't know why he said those words just then, but they sounded like they were a result of some deep reflection. I am sure that Prime Minister Khrushchev and my husband would have been successful in their search for peace, and they both sought it. Now our governments must go on with this and bring it to an end."

We, Mikoyan and myself, were deeply moved. To me, her account of her husband's words about Russia sounded like a continuation of what Robert Kennedy had told me on his behalf only a week before.

Mrs. Kennedy then sent a handwritten letter to Khrushchev citing their mutual respect and fear of nuclear war, and giving her very moving and personal assurance that Johnson would continue a policy of "control and restraint" to which her husband had been deeply committed. Khrushchev was genuinely touched and circulated the letter among all the members of his cabinet. For us, it was the last page of the tragic chronicle of John F. Kennedy's presidency.

### The Kennedy Era Reconsidered

Kennedy's assassination had a great impact in the Soviet Union. State television broadcast the funeral ceremony. The newspapers were full of mournful articles. Crowds of tearful people waited in long lines outside the American Embassy to sign the book of condolences. Those sorrowful days helped create something of a Kennedy mystique among the Soviet people, although politically the Kennedy era had not done too much to improve Soviet-American relations. Little was known then of the confidential correspondence between Kennedy and Khrushchev; the confidential channel between them was a matter of strictest secrecy.

The president as I remember him was in the prime of his life, seemed full of optimism, and was facing the future with confidence. During two years of contact with him I had seen how quick was his progress as the chief executive of his country. After just a few months in office, he demonstrated in his talks with me about Soviet-American affairs a detailed knowledge of the principal topics, which favorably distinguished him from some other American presidents. He was well informed on European affairs and readily discussed the complex questions of arms control. Yet his conception of the Soviet Union was rather conservative. He knew how to contain his emotions during his conversations and, unlike his brother Robert, used to construct them so as to avoid excessive tension. At the same time he skillfully stood his ground while conducting a dynamic dialogue on various international issues.

During his presidency there were many important and tumultuous events—the Cuban crisis, the nuclear test-ban treaty, tensions over West Berlin, and an agreement on Laos—which meant that our relations underwent huge fluctuations from the brink of nuclear war to the first of our agreements limiting the curse of nuclear weapons.

Despite all this, the Soviet public generally held a favorable view of the president. In my view, the main reason for this paradox lay in the Cuban crisis and in the personal tragedy of the assassination. For a week the world was on the verge of war, and both our nations were in an excruciating state of strain. Everybody was shocked. So the successful outcome of the crisis was a great relief. This gradually created an atmosphere of expectation and optimism, upon which more might have been built and of which Kennedy was the symbol. The assassination abruptly terminated all this and, apart from natural human feelings of compassion and sympathy, left a deep psychological trauma in the conscience of both nations. Subconsciously people believed (especially in the Soviet Union) that the likable young president had fallen while trying to improve the international situation and especially relations with the Soviet Union.

And what was the Soviet leadership's view of his death? The KGB on Khrushchev's orders prepared a top secret report. Its principal conclusion was that the assassination arose from a plot hatched by ultraconservative groups and the Mafia in the United States with the goal of strengthening the reactionary and aggressive elements of American policy.

If Kennedy had lived—how often we who lived in those times think about that!—I believe those relations would actually have been improved, particularly if the summit meeting had taken place the following year. Khrushchev as well as Kennedy looked forward to this meeting. Moreover, like

Kennedy he did not want a repetition of the painful and damaging 1961 meeting in Vienna. It would have been unacceptable for his own political reputation to have two unsuccessful meetings with the president of the United States. He had to demonstrate some success for public opinion in his country.

This was the reason for Khrushchev's last confidential instructions to Gromyko to lay the groundwork for a successful new meeting with Kennedy. Likewise those were Gromyko's instructions to me. For both Gromyko and Khrushchev, Kennedy's assassination was a serious shock and setback to their policy, for they had already established personal relations, and the actions of each side were gradually becoming mutually predictable to the other. With a new president everything had to start over.

Then were there any distinctive features at all to Soviet-American relations in Kennedy's time? One must admit that Kennedy's foreign policy preserved the main directions of his predecessors, that is, global confrontation with the Soviet Union. This course was still actively advocated by the conservative circles that had laid the foundation of the Cold War and were still adamant opponents of improving our relations.

Yet times were gradually changing in the world. In the late 1950s the United States lost its monopoly on nuclear arms. A major military confrontation with the Soviet Union under these conditions would thus threaten not only the security of the Soviet Union, but of the United States as well. President Kennedy's understanding of this danger led to his gradual acceptance of the existing reality—an approximate "balance of terror" (as it came to be called)—that arose from the growing equilibrium of the two countries' nuclear forces.

Proceeding from this, President Kennedy concluded that it was essential to create some safeguards in relations with the Soviet Union in order to prevent our confrontation from turning into a nuclear conflict. In order to achieve this goal, Kennedy knew that the United States had to cooperate with the Soviet Union in specific areas where their interests coincided. Before becoming president, he wrote that these areas could be a ban on nuclear tests, a check on the proliferation of nuclear weapons, and purely bilateral disputes. This was not exactly a customary American view at the height of the Cold War.

Khrushchev in fact shared these opinions. Kennedy's principal rival naturally welcomed the fact that for the first time in the postwar period Washington accepted Moscow as a nuclear power on a global scale. Moreover, Washington appeared to look for areas of coinciding interest, which approached Khrushchev's idea of "peaceful coexistence."

Kennedy went even farther. He started to suggest cautiously that the strategic and political status quo had to be maintained and that each side had to avoid taking steps which might lead to any significant upset in the balance of power between East and West by infringing on the vital interests of the other side. Kennedy said this explicitly during his meetings with Khrushchev in Vienna and with Mikoyan in Washington.

In itself this principle seemed eminently sound, but in the world of real policy of the time it was hardly practicable. The United States continued to do all it could to follow a policy based on the global containment of communism. The Soviet Union's exertions were directed toward what it saw as fighting imperialism and promoting wherever possible its ideas of socialism, since it believed that the future belonged to these ideas. Unflagging ideological confrontation between the two nations thus remained the main obstacle to any dramatic improvement of their relations.

Likewise, it was far from easy to apply this status quo principle in regions where both sides saw their most vital interests were engaged, most surpassingly in Europe. Kennedy waged his fiercest struggles over the status of Germany, which lies at the heart of Europe, and especially over yielding anything in West Berlin, which would have upset the intricate balance throughout Europe—as indeed proved finally to be the case thirty years later when the Berlin Wall came down, the balance shifted, and Germany was reunified. It was first of all Berlin and Germany that Kennedy always had in mind when speaking with Khrushchev and Mikoyan about the importance of maintaining the status quo. But the status quo at that time no longer suited the leaders in Moscow, who aimed at the creation of two German states, thus consolidating and legitimizing the partition of Germany.

In short, the status quo could only be selective. Under the circumstances of the Cold War both Kennedy and Khrushchev found it difficult to isolate Soviet-American relations from other events or to reconcile the two principal and yet conflicting aspects of the foreign policies of both countries—the necessity to diminish the threat of nuclear war and to seek compromise on one hand, and the desire on the other hand by each nation to expand its own influence in the world by all means available short of nuclear war. This contradiction was to underlie Soviet-American relations as one leader succeeded another in both the Kremlin and in the White House for another quarter of a century.

A significant, at times decisive, role was played in this respect by the specific political situation in each country. In the Soviet Union there was no particular controversy regarding the course of Soviet-American relations, the principal goal of which was seen in Moscow as the relaxation of tension with Washington. But this was not so in the United States. After the Cuban crisis the polarization of political forces in American society became even more pronounced. Open disagreements on issues of political strategy and tactics toward the Soviet Union intensified. Hostile campaigns were pursued in the areas of human rights and Jewish emigration. In both countries the emphasis on specific nuclear and general military strategies was developed as a part of political strategy. The defeat in Cuba intensified the buildup of Soviet nuclear arms, which was already under way to catch up to the United States. Meanwhile the United States was gradually militarizing its policy against the North Vietnamese, who were our allies.

All this to a greater or a lesser extent kept undermining our relations until the middle of the 1980s, when they were stabilized in part by significant breakthroughs in agreements to control nuclear and conventional arms, but mostly through the change in the internal politics of the Soviet Union.

Looking back at the Kennedy years from the perspective of the 1990s, one can only come to the conclusion that mankind, and the great powers of the Soviet Union and the United States in particular, behaved rather irrationally and irresponsibly, to put it mildly. Trillions were to be spent by the two countries on military forces. Numerous international crises with rapidly growing nuclear potential had to be overcome in order to arrive at the far-reaching agreement between the United States and Russia early in 1993 on a drastic reduction of their strategic forces by two-thirds—that is to say, back to levels comparable to the Kennedy-Khrushchev period. So why did we insist on all these sacrifices if, after having made this long and costly journey, we were essentially to return to our starting point?

Many opportunities were wasted that could have made this journey far shorter even from the time of Kennedy and Khrushchev. But the same applies to the subsequent years when, as we shall see, this process was effectively hindered by the ideological, psychological, and imperial considerations of both states and their governments in the Kremlin and the White House. Although the decisive factor finally was the fundamental change within my own county, nearly one-third of a century would pass before the two principal participants understood the depravity and destructiveness of the Cold War, recognized the imperative of ending it, and began efforts for a transition to mutual understanding, cooperation, and partnership.

# THE JOHNSON PRESIDENCY, 1963–1969

## I. Getting to Know the New President

*Johnson's Foreign Policy*

As vice president Lyndon Johnson had been excluded from the Kennedy inner circle and compelled to remain a passive spectator to great events, a galling situation for this dynamic man. Through the tragic event of assassination, Johnson's torments and patience were rewarded by destiny, but a strange destiny it turned out to be. A master of domestic policy and backstage deals in Congress, he tried to unite the nation with his Great Society programs and legislation on civil rights. He seemed to believe that the raw goodwill that activated his desire to serve as "president of all the people" could somehow work the same magic in foreign affairs. But in Vietnam this became his quagmire, his personal obsession, and the tragedy of his presidency as well as of the country.

From the start, both Moscow and Washington hoped to broaden the dialogue that had been opened by Kennedy—and indeed, our dialogue on disarmament continued, and number of limited bilateral agreements were concluded between us. But Johnson mistakenly believed he could isolate Vietnam from the other world problems that concerned us such as arms control and European security. As American military intervention expanded, his dialogue with us turned into an almost desperate appeal for the Soviet Union to serve as an intermediary in Vietnam, without realizing that our hands were almost as closely tied by our own ideological loyalties to Hanoi as his were by his diehard opposition to it.

When Johnson assumed the presidency, about fifteen thousand American troops were already deployed in South Vietnam. In the Vietnam relay race he had accepted the baton from Kennedy. But in contrast to Kennedy, who seemed to have been considering a withdrawal of his troops, Johnson—urged on by the election campaign, militant conservatives in his party, and by the Pentagon—became more deeply involved in the conflict and hoped to settle it from a position of strength. Moscow, on the other hand, sympathized with North Vietnam, for the latter was "waging a liberation war." Besides, Moscow had no intention of applying strong diplomatic pressure on Ho Chi Minh lest it drive him into the arms of the Chinese. Although

Johnson and Khrushchev both tried to separate the Vietnam War from the sphere of Soviet-American relations, this grew more and more difficult.

But why did both sides allow themselves to become entangled by their client states instead of trying to form some sort of diplomatic front to settle the problem—or at least back away from it—and get on to more vital questions of disarmament, European security, and the rest? First, each side approached the conflict over the unification of Vietnam from a completely different ideological perspective: Was it liberation, as the Soviet side saw it, or aggression, as the United States saw it? Would a unified state be socialist or capitalist? The second reason was geopolitical: Washington was trying to draw a line in Southeast Asia against communism.

During Johnson's presidency I repeatedly wondered what it was that drove him in his stubborn desire to wage the Vietnam War to a victorious end. Indeed, at the time he unexpectedly became president he was bound by no commitments in Vietnam, unlike his predecessor. Moreover, America's military involvement was relatively limited and the issue had not yet attracted any significant popular attention in the United States outside the public policy elites in Washington and New York. As a new president, Johnson had a clear opportunity not to draw the nation any further into military operations in Vietnam. I doubt he would have been blamed for holding back.

Yet to the surprise of many, Johnson quickly and voluntarily assumed the dubious role of Vietnam's protector. As soon as he arrived at the White House, he committed himself to the cause, although American interests in this former French colony were insignificant. Senator J. William Fulbright, the chairman of the Senate Foreign Relations Committee, confided to me that on the very day of Kennedy's funeral, the new president had firmly told the American ambassador to South Vietnam, Henry Cabot Lodge, that he had "no intention of losing Vietnam to the communists, like China."

Unlike his predecessors Truman and Eisenhower, who used to hold the military on a tight leash, Johnson came to believe strongly in their competence and increasingly relied on their advice, as well as on the counsel of those of his confidants who advocated a military solution in Vietnam. And it was the military path that Johnson began to follow insistently and even stubbornly.

What can possibly explain this conduct? His anti-communism? His conviction that the tremendous military might of the United States would make victory easy in Vietnam? His intention to demonstrate that he, like Kennedy of whom he was not very fond, possessed a strong will and was capable of accepting and mastering a challenge in Vietnam as Kennedy had in Cuba? Or his emotional nature and his inability to anticipate all consequences of the war in Vietnam?

There seems to be no single answer. Each factor must have played its role. As the war dragged on, it increasingly became a personal matter for him, a kind of self-test. Who would win? Johnson or Ho Chi Minh? Johnson or Mao Zedong? A couple of times I actually heard him say something like this. This war was turning into his personal war. Having taken the wrong path he was unable to turn away from it. Johnson's emotional nature and his obsession contributed to the senseless adventure in Vietnam going on and on. In the end it cost him his second term, inflicted deep wounds on the nation, harmed Soviet-American relations, and diminished the chances for disarmament.

Aside from Vietnam, Johnson did not at first involve himself in foreign affairs but directed Rusk, whom he kept on as secretary of state (as Rusk had predicted to me he would), to follow Kennedy's guidelines in foreign policy. Practical implementation was largely entrusted to Rusk, and in part to McGeorge Bundy, the director of the National Security Council and also a Kennedy holdover. The secretary of state's influence grew substantially, and behind the scenes he tended to be more conservative in relations with the Soviet Union than some other presidential advisers and even Johnson himself. Rusk, with his stubbornness and his basically conservative political views, carried an important share of the responsibility for the tragedy in Vietnam. Later he was courageous enough to admit that he had not always been right about the war.

I met Bundy in December and he expressed an interest in a summit meeting provided it would lead to some kind of agreement lest a failure endanger Johnson's election campaign the next year. He also warned us not to expect them to pull out of Vietnam, because "this would be equivalent to Johnson's political suicide." But Rusk never mentioned a summit when we met, so it seemed Bundy's probe had been his own, although checked in advance with Johnson. In Moscow, Khrushchev and Mikoyan were interested, but Gromyko was not, fearing Khrushchev might be carried away and ruin relations from the start without careful advance preparation.

In the new year, Bundy reversed his position by telling me that the president was too busy for a summit in an election year and could not leave the country without a sitting vice president. Later we learned that it was Rusk who had more or less discouraged Johnson from taking part in the meeting: the secretary of state considered he was not ready for it yet. This episode was by no means the last of its kind and clearly demonstrated Johnson's impulsive nature, and his inability to calculate his moves to the end. It appeared that initially he was eager to meet Khrushchev, but after a few days he began hesitating, then lost his interest and postponed the matter indefinitely.

Moscow was, to put it mildly, puzzled by this conduct. A meeting between the two never took place, which was one more missed opportunity.

I made it my business to find out more about Johnson's personality, and in the first few months of his presidency I heard incisive descriptions from his close associates.

Abe Fortas, his friend for more than twenty years and personal legal adviser, gave a psychological picture. After two heart attacks in the 1950s, Fortas said that Johnson was now living in constant but well-concealed fear of another attack. This was typical of people who suffered from heart disease, and it had left its traces. Johnson instinctively avoided matters that demanded long and complicated decision making, as well as those with grave and unforeseen consequences; he often tried to put them off. On the other hand, he readily dealt with "more pleasant" business like promoting his popularity, or with other matters that did not demand physical and mental exertion. In order to come to a decision on a complicated or controversial subject, he needed time and opportunity to think it over comfortably. In a difficult situation such as an international crisis, when he would be pressured from all sides to take urgent decisions in the heat of the moment, Fortas said that Johnson could lose control and do things he would later regret.

Jack Valenti, Johnson's closest aide (who later became famous for his saying that he could sleep peacefully at night because he knew Johnson was president), told me that Johnson was staking his election on domestic issues while the Republicans were focusing on foreign policy. That was why the president tried at least for the present to maintain the international status quo, improving the relations where possible, but avoiding anything that might aggravate the international situation to the benefit of the Republicans.

Pierre Salinger singled out Vietnam and Cuba as the most potentially dangerous foreign policy issues for Johnson's election. He said the main threat in South Vietnam would be some unforeseen reversal that could force Johnson to make a painful political decision at the height of the campaign. Salinger saw the United States as "stuck fast" in South Vietnam, but because of the campaign Johnson also felt he had no choice but to follow the present line; he was certain that pulling out would cost him the election. Johnson disliked holding large and especially televised press conferences, Salinger said, because he feared being trapped by some foreign policy issue of which he had little knowledge. That was why the Republicans kept challenging him to televised debates and he was in no hurry to agree.

George Reedy, who soon replaced Salinger as press secretary, told me Johnson read many newspapers, focusing on domestic topics. He disliked reading books. Valenti would report urgent news during the day. As national security adviser, Bundy's task was to keep the president up to date on the latest foreign policy developments, but lately the president had begun discussing these questions directly with Rusk, who would often come to the White House for a working lunch with Johnson. Yet on the whole Johnson, unlike Kennedy, considered that the White House did not need to interfere with the work of federal departments on a daily basis.

## My First Meeting Alone with Johnson

On April 17 I met for the first time alone with the president at the White House at his invitation. We talked tête-à-tête in the same Oval Office where I had met with Kennedy, but the atmosphere of the room had changed. The late president's favorite mementos of the sea and some elegant touches of his own were not there anymore and had been replaced by less sophisticated but more colorful things, from the American West.

Johnson was very friendly. He asked me to convey his best wishes to Khrushchev for his seventieth birthday. The president showed me the White House's garden and his favorite dogs. He told me that hunting was his hobby, and he knew the Soviet premier was a sportsman: "It would be a good thing to compete with him in hunting. Golf is not for me. I like to ride and to hunt." His powerful build made me believe him.

Then we returned to the Oval Office. Here Johnson told me that for a long time he had wanted to talk with the Soviet ambassador about the relations between our countries. In general he was satisfied with them, he said, and then he asked, "What about you?"

I agreed that "some preconditions" had indeed been created for the improvement of the international situation and of Soviet-American relations, but we needed to proceed and especially limit the arms race. I said I assumed the reason was that the administration was busy with elections.

Johnson immediately agreed, "Oh, yes, for now American foreign policy is determined by just these considerations." Just a few days before, he said, when he had publicly welcomed Khrushchev's peace statement, a major Chicago newspaper had accused him of "publicly hugging a communist" for his pains. And this was not the only example, Johnson added. He was also subjected to frenzied attacks by Goldwater and his allies. White House polls indicated that public opinion was inclined toward better relations between the two nations, but many people still listened to Goldwater, Richard Nixon, and the right wing of the Republican Party, which opposed any agreements with the Soviet Union and in essence argued for even worsening our relations. Their influence, he said, was not to be underestimated.

The president said he would like to announce some move, even a small

one, to demonstrate clearly to the American public that he intended to follow a different path. Therefore he wanted to pass to Khrushchev a new message proposing a cutback in the production of fissionable materials for
military purposes. It so happened that I already had with me a similar proposal from Khrushchev which suggested bringing in France and Britain, the
other Western nuclear powers, but Johnson conceded that he had little influence with "that guy in Paris" (meaning President de Gaulle of France), so he
was asking Khrushchev to consent to a bilateral commitment without waiting for the others to join in. A joint statement to that effect was soon made.

Johnson also proposed an exchange of televised addresses with
Khrushchev in the two countries and replied to our previous complaint that
American planes were violating Soviet borders to provoke and thereby locate
Soviet air defenses. He said the U.S. Air Force had already received strict or-
ders not to violate Soviet air space and asked us "not to resort to extreme mea-
sures," if American planes strayed over the border in "unintended mistakes."
(Khrushchev expressed his satisfaction with this in a reply on May 15.)

It is worth noting that very little was said about Vietnam, although
President Johnson was rather loquacious, which distinguished him from
practically all other presidents I have known. He gesticulated often, and at
the most important moments of his statements he used to bring his face
close to the face of the person he was talking to, practically touching the
other's nose. Johnson looked directly into the eyes of his interlocutor, often
pulling him closer by the lapel of his suit in a heroic effort at persuasion. He
was genuinely interesting to talk with, not so much about diplomatic topics
(here he was visibly bored) as on general subjects such as domestic politics
and Congress, matters on which Johnson was very eloquent. He was invariably friendly and avoided sharp edges, trying to do his best for both sides to
remain satisfied with each other.

But he left little doubt that all his energies and aspirations were focused
on his election and he viewed international events through the same political
prism, which meant that the principal issues in Soviet-American relations
would have to wait. Thompson told me straightforwardly that was exactly
the case.

Khrushchev, however, did not intend to waste the whole year waiting for the
elections. On June 5 he sent Johnson a detailed confidential message which I
passed orally to Thompson. He covered a number of issues—mutual troop
reductions in Europe, American attacks on Cuba, the German problem, and
Southeast Asia.

"I am aware that it is an unpleasant subject for both of us," Khrushchev
said in his message, "but everyone needs peace equally." He deemed it essen-

tial to extinguish tension, specifically in South Vietnam and Cambodia, where the systems created by Geneva agreements of 1954 and 1962 threatened to collapse. The German problem was fundamental, the message also said, because our armed forces were concentrated there, facing each other. If the German problem were settled, there would be no more "great confrontation between John and Ivan." Khrushchev went on to express his unshakable conviction that West Germany would never succeed in absorbing the German Democratic Republic: "Even if in a hundred years the capitalist system is still there, they, the revanchists, will not be able to achieve what they would like to achieve, that is to seize the GDR. This is the reality, and everyone has to face it." It is evident that Khrushchev was not a great prophet.

But Khrushchev pressed ahead, and on June 10 he entrusted me with confidentially informing President Johnson of the decision made by the governments of the USSR and the GDR to sign an agreement known as the Treaty of Friendship, Cooperation, and Mutual Assistance. I passed the message to Rusk, who did not attempt to conceal his displeasure. He confined himself to a sarcastic remark that Soviet foreign policy, as he had long suspected, evidently came down to quite a simple formula: "What's mine is mine, and what's yours is to be divided between us."

But in fact a few months later, over dinner with Bundy in October devoted to "shop talk" about the Johnson administration, I heard quite a different view. In a curious confession, he said the administration's foreign policy planners assumed that Germany could only be reunified if it became a neutral state outside the North Atlantic Alliance, because they recognized that Moscow would never agree to a reunited Germany inside NATO. They wondered why the Soviet Union did not propose a neutral, reunified Germany, which would at least give Moscow some good propaganda points. (Indeed, the Polish foreign minister, Adam Rapacki, made quite a name for himself and his country by proposing something very similar.)

The answer to this can now be disclosed, and it is quite simple: Khrushchev opposed the reunification of Germany on any terms, for he had staked his policy on a separate "German state of workers." Subsequent Soviet leaders, too, never discussed the question of Germany's neutralization in earnest, because they simply could not conceive of a unified German state.

But Germany and European security were not in the forefront of the administration's concerns at that time; it increasingly devoted its attention to Southeast Asia. After I had passed on Khrushchev's urgent message, Rusk in turn, passed me Johnson's message on Laos, which pointed out that the agreements on Laos represented a personal understanding between Khrushchev and President Kennedy, and it now was necessary to achieve quick and full compliance with the Geneva agreements on Laos to share power among various factions. Rusk justified U.S. military action in Laos by saying that Washington wanted to signal the Communist Pathet Lao and the neighboring government in Hanoi that they could not take over the country.

All this—Johnson's message, Rusk's reasoning, and the expansion of military operations in Southeast Asia—were typical examples of how peripheral issues kept interfering with the development of Soviet-American relations, creating tensions and putting off the settlement of really important problems.

On July 12, two hours before I was to take a plane to Moscow for vacation, Bundy invited me to the White House to give me "some information for your meetings in Moscow with the Soviet leaders." Goldwater clearly was going to be Johnson's opponent in the elections, and Bundy wanted to assure us that the president did not intend to abandon his attempts to reach an understanding with the Soviet Union. But he wanted me to warn the Kremlin that in the polemics with Goldwater, Johnson might have to say some things that might displease Moscow. Moscow must therefore realize that rhetoric in the heat of the campaign would in no way signify any change in Johnson's position toward the Soviet Union. Moreover, Bundy hinted that the Johnson camp would not mind if the Soviet side, too, sometimes criticized Johnson, although he requested it to be kept "within reasonable limits" lest excessively sharp attacks adversely affect the state of our relations.

I was well aware of the role of such anti-communist rhetoric in American politics, and I learned how to read it, so as to determine when it was serious and when it was mere posturing. But explaining all this to Moscow was sometimes more difficult. I told Moscow about Bundy's warning—that it was evidently part of a campaign (not unusual in the United States) to protect Johnson's flanks from Goldwater's charges that he was "soft on communism." They may have had their doubts but they recognized me as someone who knew something more about American politics and accepted my explanation.

## Life as a Soviet Diplomat

It is often hard to remember how we lived in those days, under such tight controls and in isolation that was partly self-imposed and partly imposed upon us by the suspicion of our hosts. I tried my utmost to break out of these constraints, and the story of my life as an ambassador would not be complete without some idea of how I dealt with them on other levels as well as those of the grand policies and international diplomacy that are the focus of this book.

As I have already mentioned, our small embassy building in Washington was overcrowded. At last, after long consideration, the Soviet government appropriated money to buy a lot for a new building in the American capital.

The search for an appropriate location took several years. Several times we encountered anti-Soviet prejudice by property owners and their neighbors, who would kick up a row. They protested that they would be forced to live in the vicinity of the Soviets, who were supposed to surround their embassy with barbed wire and armed guards, and whose trained dogs would savage their children—a typical Hollywood conception of a Soviet institution.

Wild and terrifying stories circulated widely about us. The most notorious held that we had our own atomic bomb in the embassy, and one version of this tale even reached the president. On the thirtieth anniversary of Kennedy's assassination, *Time* magazine published a reminiscence by Hugh Sidey, its White House correspondent during the 1960s, recalling that Kennedy once intrigued his dinner guests with a report that we had assembled a bomb from parts sent to us by diplomatic pouch. "If war breaks out, they push the button and destroy Washington," the president told his guests at a dinner in Palm Beach while vacationing in Florida after the Vienna summit with Khrushchev in 1961. Sidey was never quite sure how true the story was—and neither, apparently, was Kennedy—so he decided not to publish it at the time. But its mere existence and the exalted levels of its circulation were indicative of the charged atmosphere in which we Soviet diplomats lived at the height of the Cold War.

Twice our lawyers and a real estate agency had to sue the opponents of a prospective purchase after we had found a suitable property. We won a judgment in the lower court but the neighborhood association succeeded in overturning it on appeal. Some disputes were really amusing. The owner of a lot adjoining the territory of Mount Vernon National Park (the site of George Washington's historic estate) agreed to sell us his plot near the Potomac. The owner had no quarrelsome neighbors, and his own attitude toward the Soviet Union was not hostile; during World War II he had captained a destroyer escorting convoys with vital war supplies to Murmansk. For years he also been trying to sell the lot to the National Park Service, which dragged out the negotiations, pleading financial problems. As soon as the owner informed the park management that he was going to sell the land to the Soviet Embassy, the money to buy it was found as if by magic, and we were once again left empty-handed.

Then we managed to find a suitable plot in the suburbs, farther up the Virginia side of the Potomac near McLean. Now it was the Central Intelligence Agency that interfered, claiming that the location was too close to its headquarters.

To do justice to the American government, both the Kennedy and Johnson administrations tried to help us. When our case was under consideration in the appeals court, the secretary of state sent a letter to the court supporting our case. Alas, that did not help either.

We were going to appeal to an even higher court but Rusk advised us against it because, he said, the case was already receiving too much publicity and the media had turned the matter into a scandal. The administration then promised to find a site on federal property. At long last, but not until the Nixon administration, the government offered us a building site on Wisconsin Avenue where the old federal Mount Alto hospital had been located. The Soviet government then allocated a site in Moscow for a new American Embassy. New embassy buildings were duly erected in both Washington and Moscow, but neither could be occupied long after the problem first was raised because of scandals arising from the secret installation of microphones and transmitters in both buildings during construction.

Once our listening devices were discovered in the framework of the American building in Moscow, the U.S. Congress categorically forbade the use of the new embassy facilities there and blocked further construction of the new Soviet embassy in Washington. Both new buildings were closed down (and an angry dispute commenced about Soviet compensation for the structure in Moscow, which the Americans said could never be securely used).

By that time I had left Washington, and in December of 1991 I was having lunch in Moscow with Robert Strauss, a Washington acquaintance of many years who was then serving as American ambassador in Moscow. Smiling enigmatically, he asked me to guess which Soviet leader he had visited earlier in the day, I gave up after a short time and he declared solemnly, "I called on Bakatin, the head of the KGB." I was somewhat surprised and asked what they had discussed.

"You'll never guess," he replied. He said the KGB boss provided him with information on the design and location of the Soviet bugging equipment in the new American Embassy building, apparently part of the new Soviet policy of *glasnost* or openness. He said this was no small surprise to Washington, "but it is welcomed in every way."

"Well, what about returning the favor?" I asked the ambassador, alluding to our new embassy in Washington with its American bugging equipment. He laughed it off and said the Americans were not yet ripe for openness. In fact, the matter was settled a few years later. When I visited Washington in 1994 for the preparation of this book, I was finally able to stay at the new building at Mount Alto on Wisconsin Avenue just above Georgetown—more than thirty years after I had first started looking for a new site.

■ ■ ■

The visits to America by our world-famous musicians and ballet and opera companies were a pleasant exception to the rather tense atmosphere surrounding our relations with the United States. Among them were Sviatoslav Richter, the pianist; the prima ballerina Maya Plisetskaya; the cellist Mstislav Rostropovich and his wife, the soprano Galina Vishnevskaya; the Bolshoi Ballet from Moscow; the Leningrad Opera and Ballet, the Moiseyev Dance Ensemble, and other groups. They invariably enjoyed great and well-deserved success. To no small degree this was also a merit of an American impresario from prerevolutionary Russia, Sol Hurok.

I still remember the coming of Richter, not from the artistic point of view (although his performance was beyond praise), but in connection with humiliating customs that accompanied our artists' tours and visits abroad at the time. In all these tours they were always escorted by intelligence officers under various pretexts and in various disguises. Their task was to spy on the artists, watch their contacts, and prevent any attempts to stay abroad, which, by the way, never stopped those who really wanted to defect.

The overwhelming majority of performers were patriots, and the surveillance insulted them. Richter, an extremely sensitive and highly cultured man, was among those who took it especially hard. He was accompanied by an "administrator" who poked his nose into all Richter's affairs, even in his private life. (Richter's mother lived in West Germany and he often telephoned her.)

My wife and I felt that the artist, whom we knew well, was close to a nervous breakdown. So I sent an urgent cable to Moscow insisting that his "companion" be returned home and Richter left alone. In Moscow they seemed to understand the situation, and Richter's intelligence officer was recalled. It was moving to see his relief when I told him that he could continue his concerts in America wherever he wanted and without any "company." Some time later, with Richter in mid-Atlantic en route home aboard a British liner, my wife received a large bouquet of roses he had ordered in gratitude for our hospitality and for saving him from his official guardian.

But all Soviet citizens going abroad, either on a short trip or on a long-term assignment to embassies or trade delegations, were thoroughly checked by various authorities. The final decision was to be made by a special department of the Communist Party Central Committee. Every individual leaving the country was called to this department for an interview on his or her public positions and private life, as well as on "Rules of Conduct for Soviet Citizens Abroad." These rules had been approved by the Central Committee; they consisted of written instructions, and anyone going abroad had to sit through an explanation and sign a statement saying he had read and understood them.

Most of the rules listed things that were prohibited or not recommended for Soviet citizens in foreign countries. They were supposed to prevent us from "being provoked and recruited by foreign intelligence" on the street and in stores, at the movies and theaters, at the receptions and other events to which we might be invited. Actually, it would have been easier to list things that were permitted than enumerate all the rules. Breaking them meant either being sent home immediately or refused permission to travel abroad again.

Sometimes the situation created by the rules ran to absurdity. The wife of a newly appointed ambassador was called for the standard interview about the rules. She had been abroad many times with her husband. As the instructor read to her all the rules and then asked her to sign the declaration that she understood how to behave, the lady grew indignant and asked him if he had ever been abroad. Informed that he had not, she refused to continue the interview, insisting that she did not want to listen to bureaucrats who knew life only through written instructions. The scandal reached higher levels. The lady was advised to "exercise more self-control in the Central Committee headquarters," and the instructor was told that he had been "overzealous" to call an ambassador's spouse for an interview.

Far more amusing was an episode involving the head of this very department on a trip to Paris. This senior bureaucrat, Barannikov by name, traveled to Paris with some delegation. When he arrived he confided to the ambassador that his greatest wish was to visit the Folies Bergère. But the notorious rules prohibited visits to such places. The ambassador quietly advised Barannikov to see the Folies' famous showgirls incognito and offered as a guide his assistant, who knew Paris well. The assistant did his best and bought tickets for the front row. During the performance a *danseuse* descended from the stage and approached the department chief, inviting him to dance with her. She took him by the hand, but Barannikov, totally shaken, tore himself away. The dancer shrugged and left him. The excursion seemed to pass unnoticed, to the great satisfaction of both the ambassador and his high-ranking guest.

A couple of weeks later the French Department of the Ministry of Foreign Affairs in Moscow received its regular shipment of newspapers from Paris. In one of them the diplomats of the French Department saw a photo of the Central Committee department chief with a cabaret dancer. His name was not mentioned, and the text identified him only as some "foreigner who behaved oddly."

At first the ministry officials thought that it was a provocation—a photomontage published with the aim of discrediting an important Communist Party official. They even planned a protest to the French government. Before that could happen, our ambassador in Paris had to interfere and explain to the minister what had happened. The matter was hushed up and never reached the very top. But the diplomats had a lot of fun thanks to the expert in "Rules of Conduct."

## II. Moscow and Vietnam

*A Palace Coup in Moscow*

In October 1964 intrigues within the Soviet leadership succeeded in forcing the dismissal of Nikita Khrushchev. It was a real palace revolution. The Plenum of the Communist Party Central Committee was convened only after Khrushchev had been called back from vacation and made to resign at a meeting of the Presidium, which later was called the Politburo. The full Central Committee was summoned only to confirm the decision and make it look legitimate.

By that time Khrushchev had lost his popularity; many of his decisions turned out to be half-baked and his policies had produced inconsequential results. Granted, he unmasked, criticized, and tried to overcome Stalinism, but he was not ready for substantive reform. Khrushchev was unable to imagine that anything else could exist in his country apart from the system based on the Communist Party's domination. He, too, was a product of his time.

The principal architects of the coup were Nikolai Podgorny, Mikhail Suslov, and Leonid Brezhnev, aided by a few others. They were neither united by common political objectives, nor did they share any new political platform. Rather, they were motivated by personal interests, first and foremost their desire to gain or retain power, or by a fear of losing their high posts. In foreign policy they did not suggest any changes whatsoever. Without delay the new leaders took steps to consolidate their position internationally. I received an urgent instruction to meet with President Johnson and explain the situation.

On October 16, in the morning, I visited the president at the White House and informed him of Khrushchev's resignation and the election of Brezhnev as first secretary of the Central Committee and Alexei Kosygin as chairman of the Council of Ministers. In accordance with my instructions I said that the general direction of the Soviet foreign policy would not change.

For Johnson, as for everybody else, all this was a clear surprise. He immediately asked about Khrushchev's fate, not so much out of personal sympathy for Khrushchev, whom he had never met, but out of natural curiosity.

He was far more interested in the new Soviet leaders and the direction of their policies and was impressed by the fact that they had urgently instructed me to meet with him and assure him of their desire to develop good relations with him. He said he appreciated that and wished them success.

Then, expressing his own intention to expand contacts with the new leadership, he asked me to relay his own thoughts, which he expressed in his characteristically earthy language. He reiterated his commitment to Kennedy's policies of peace. If returned to the White House he said he expected to achieve progress in disarmament. He wanted to be clearly understood: "We do not want to bury the Soviet Union, but at the same time we do not want to be buried." (This was an allusion to Khrushchev's celebrated threat to overtake and bury the capitalist world.) Neither side had any reason to fear the other, he said, and he was "ready to spend a night at the Soviet ambassador's house without a pistol under my pillow"—and was sure the ambassador would do the same. The problem was to convince both our nations of this, so that public funds could be spent on the vital needs of people instead of the military, and for this it was essential "to abandon old antagonisms." He confirmed he was ready to go anywhere and talk with anyone, if only this would bring positive results.

Turning to Vietnam, Johnson expressed his conviction that the Soviet Union was going to have even more problems than the United States with those who aimed at domination in that region (that is, with the Chinese), but that was no concern of his. One of the things that must have been on his mind was the news that China had detonated its first nuclear device that very day.

This was not the first time he had invoked China in connection with Vietnam and attempted to involve us. In August Khrushchev had sent a note questioning the American version of a supposed North Vietnamese attack on American destroyers in the Tonkin Gulf, which was used as the legal basis for the president to widen the war. In response, the president said that any step the Soviet Union could take to restrain North Vietnam or Beijing from further irresponsible actions would be helpful. That was the first clear effect of the Vietnam War on our relations.

Initially, the new Soviet leadership differed mainly in the names of those who constituted it. Khrushchev's place as first secretary of the Communist Party was now occupied by Leonid Brezhnev, who was no novice in politics. He had occupied one of the leading positions in the party as a member of the Presidium, although his had not been the number two post. That belonged to "the gray cardinal," Mikhail Suslov, the second secretary of the CPSU Central Committee. Yet, Suslov never aspired to become number one, preferring to stay in the shadows as kingmaker rather than king. Suslov was a very dull, highly dogmatic, and ideologically narrow-minded person. But for many years he dominated the whole apparatus of the Central Committee of the Communist Party, and this was his real strength. He disliked reform and in general tried to avoid any surprises that might destabilize the domestic situation. He was largely responsible for the fall of Khrushchev, who in the opinion of his colleagues had become uncontrollable in his emotions and willful in making decisions.

Leonid Brezhnev was the exact opposite of his predecessor. This was a politician who knew the Kremlin's corridors of power very well and was a team-player, not an individualist. Brezhnev was cautious and unhurried and was used to listening to his colleagues. He was neither as gifted by nature nor such an impulsive innovator as Khrushchev. He avoided sudden turns and radical innovations, preferring predictable stability. One cannot call him a great man, or a strong character, or even a strong personality. At the beginning he seemed to be just an amicable man. He wanted to be liked, loved to tell stories, and enjoyed having a drink with his cronies.

In Khrushchev's Politburo before Brezhnev became general secretary, he supervised the military-industrial complex and its production of armaments and knew the field thoroughly. Brezhnev was fond of the military, and they of him. If they wanted to show him some new development, they would invite him to the factory, and he would eagerly visit. Outer space projects were also his domain. He had done much to achieve strategic arms parity with the United States, although this race exhausted the national economy. He was proud of himself in his field marshal's uniform; I once visited him at home and he told me to sit with my cup of tea while he vanished. He reappeared in his grand uniform with all his medals and asked: "How do I look?" I replied, "Magnificent"—what else could I say?

Brezhnev did not care much for the problems of ideology, yet he firmly adhered to the dogmas of Marxism-Leninism. He was 100 percent orthodox and thus never interfered with Suslov in his ideological domain. He also knew little about foreign policy; initially this area attracted him mainly by its superficial, ceremonial side—the guards of honor, the grand receptions for foreign leaders in the Kremlin, the fulsome publicity, and all the rest. He wanted his photo taken for his albums, which he loved to show. He much preferred a fine ceremony signing final documents rather than working on them. But basically, he stood for better relations with America, and that was what mattered.

When I visited Moscow, I would personally tell Brezhnev about American events in detail (he was always interested in America). Then I would ask him for his "instructions for the future." Brezhnev would invariably answer, "What instructions do you need?—you know better than I how to deal with the Americans. Let there be peace; that's the main thing."

From the beginning until the end of his career Brezhnev relied on Gromyko in all substantial matters of foreign policy, apart from the issues of strategic arms reduction, in which his background in our armaments industry gave him much expertise. Gromyko played for him practically the same role as Dulles had for Eisenhower, yet our cautious minister tried not to show his superiority among his colleagues in the Politburo. Andrei Gromyko remained a diplomat even when dealing in the upper echelons of power in his own country, which only emphasized his special role in foreign policy. Contrary to Khrushchev, who at times imposed his will on Gromyko (as well as on his other colleagues), Brezhnev gave his foreign minister full rein because he was sure that Gromyko was a better specialist in international affairs than he was. Besides, Brezhnev and Gromyko were friends. This friendship was based on their joint hunting trips (practically every week) to Brezhnev's dacha at the village Zavidovo, about 120 kilometers from Moscow. Gromyko had never before cared for hunting, and some spiteful tongues claimed he became an "inveterate sportsman" at the age of fifty in order to be closer to Brezhnev's ear.

In general, though, Gromyko's influence on Brezhnev was positive. Being an intelligent man, he expertly fulfilled the general secretary's desire for stable foreign policy without the emotional outbursts characteristic of Khrushchev. One might disagree with some of Gromyko's views, but to give him his due, he was always consistent and predictable in his policy. Henry Kissinger once half-jokingly called it "the policy of a heavy road-roller stubbornly moving towards its destination." As long as the destination was right, this could even be considered a compliment. But Gromyko's principal distinction as a statesman was that he was forever striving to prevent his country's involvement in military conflict with the United States. No one could ever accuse him of being demonstrative about this policy, but in his heart he always favored improving relations with Washington, while never allowing himself to overstep major ideological barriers.

Johnson and Brezhnev never met. But in some sense they were alike. Both were of approximately the same age, both came from plain families, both were masters of the domestic political game, and both lacked a deep knowledge of the issues of foreign policy—a failing that they unfortunately did not take to heart. Both adored hunting and fast cars, both had no interest in books but watched a lot of television, both were fond of westerns and football, both had nothing against tossing back a glass or two, both liked to tell jokes and show off in public (or in front of an interlocutor), and both tried to conduct a conversation so that each side was satisfied. They were quick-tempered (though not in public) and rancorous, yet at the same time they liked to demonstrate their kindness and compassion.

Both adored publicity and being photographed for the press. Johnson even issued special instructions for television cameramen to shoot him from the left side because he believed that was his more photogenic profile. Soviet newspaper photographers knew that Brezhnev wanted the numerous orders and medals he wore on his chest to be seen clearly in his pictures. Johnson, eager to look more attractive on television, replaced his glasses with contact lenses and used special stage make-up and an electronic prompter. Brezhnev did not employ such props, but not because he was humble. There were no such things in the Soviet Union at the time. As soon as he learned why Johnson did not have to read his speeches from a text on paper and was able to look directly at the audience, Brezhnev instructed his aides to buy a teleprompter. (It was later given to him as a present by Armand Hammer, the American industrialist who claimed his connections with the Kremlin leadership stretched back to Lenin.) But Brezhnev never could get used to reading in this new, televisual way and soon returned to his notes.

One difference between Johnson and Brezhnev was the American president's active pursuit of personal publicity. During the first year of his presidency Johnson made more TV appearances than Kennedy had during almost three years in the White House. Over five years Johnson held 126 press conferences, most of which took place during the first two years of his term of office, before the Vietnam War turned against him. Brezhnev firmly refused to hold any press conferences. He was aware of his clumsy style and dreaded speaking without a prepared text. At the same time he was fond of delivering extensive, well-written speeches, and he enjoyed good publicity.

Both liked favorable media reviews of their speeches. This of course presented no problem for Brezhnev at home in the Soviet Union, but abroad things were different. Brezhnev's aides sorted out the most advantageous articles and photos of their master, and even ambassadors, knowing this weakness of Brezhnev's, used to send complimentary cuttings from foreign periodicals. He always read them and sometimes cited them at Politburo meetings. Johnson's situation was not quite so simple because of the independence of the American press, and he was always trying to tame journalists in the hope that they would present him in a favorable light. He would invite small, select groups to the White House and deploy his formidable personal charms. That technique worked surpassingly well during the early years of the Great Society and the civil rights battle but, like so much else, backfired as the war in Vietnam went from bad to worse and he was blamed for it.

It is hard to tell how a personal meeting of these two men would have proceeded, yet I should think it would have been more successful than the one between Khrushchev and Kennedy. To make a long story short, both of them were rather colorful figures, but Brezhnev stayed at the top too long. His last, senile years were not a pleasant sight. But that was to happen almost two decades later.

## Johnson's Triumphant Election

Brezhnev was so pleased by Johnson's favorable reaction to his accession to power that the Politburo then decided to send Johnson a detailed reply even before his election. (The Kremlin always watched American and other major elections so as not be left out on a limb by backing losers.) On November 3—election day—I handed Thompson the text of the Soviet government's note to the president, who was at his ranch in Texas. The note seized on Johnson's idea of reducing military expenditures. Why not have both sides simultaneously reduce them further—even more than the year before—without formal agreements? The Soviet government suggested further mutual troop reduction in Europe, both sides just having reduced their numbers by about a division. The note also said the government was convinced that there was great potential for improvement in such fields as disarmament and European security. It was essential, the message said, that all states—both large and small, both your and our friends—be able to benefit from detente. (In Russian, we do not use the French word "detente," which is favored in the West, but prefer the Russian equivalent of the words that mean "lessening of tension.")

"We would like to reaffirm that the Soviet government appreciates its relations of trust with President Johnson and considers it mutually advantageous to maintain and develop them, including through established confidential channels," the letter concluded. Thompson told me that he would pass this to Johnson without delay because the president would especially appreciate the fact that Soviet leaders had expressed their ideas even before the election results became known. Some in Moscow had their doubts about the wisdom of the timing without knowing the outcome of the election, but Brezhnev wanted to give Johnson moral support. He prevailed and was vindicated when Johnson triumphed over Goldwater the next day by a huge margin of sixteen million votes.

Thus ended 1964, the year when both Johnson's presidency and Soviet-American relations were influenced by the fact that Johnson became president in tragic circumstances, which made him look and feel like some kind of temporary president. Now all this was over and, with his presidency legitimized by an overwhelming majority of the electorate, Lyndon B. Johnson became a full-fledged president—"president of all the people," as he liked to say.

## Brezhnev versus Kosygin. Vietnam Escalates

On January 14, 1965, Thompson handed me a personal message from the president replying to the preelection message that had so pleased him. He in effect upped the ante for slowing down the arms race and notified the Kremlin that for the new fiscal year the U.S. government would request $2 billion less in military appropriations. He also suggested that a member of the Soviet leadership visit the United States for a full discussion face-to-face. Thompson diplomatically expressed the hope that this would not be interpreted as a rash sign of hasty interest in a visit, and he explained that Johnson had used the broad term "Soviet leadership" on purpose to enable the Soviet side to decide on who would actually come. An exchange of messages followed, and the Soviet leaders came to prefer a visit by Johnson to Moscow in part because they could not agree which among them should go to Washington, although the question soon became moot as hostilities in Vietnam aggravated abruptly.

But there was a more fundamental reason for addressing the message ambiguously to "the Soviet leaders"—and not to Brezhnev or Kosygin personally. After Khrushchev's resignation Johnson began receiving messages from Moscow without any signature at all, and his advisers therefore had no idea how to address the president's letters to his opposite number in Moscow.

The reason for their perplexity was a behind-the-scenes power struggle between Brezhnev and Kosygin as to who was to sign messages to foreign leaders. Kosygin claimed that honor to be his, since as the head of government he would be entitled by normal international protocol to send messages to foreign heads of government. Brezhnev was itching to play a role on the world stage, but Kosygin argued that Brezhnev as party leader was in no position to usurp his function as the public representative and spokesman for the Soviet state. Initially, Kosygin gained the upper hand within the Soviet leadership and was authorized to sign the messages, yet the battle was not over. Gromyko quietly supported Brezhnev, having secretly instructed ambassadors to explain discreetly to the leaders of their host countries "who was who" in the Soviet leadership. As a result, Brezhnev eventually got the upper hand, but during the Johnson administration the correspondence was still addressed to Kosygin.

A few words about Alexei Kosygin. He remains an enigma in the West and is often considered to have been a dour man without much humor. This was far from the reality. But having survived Stalin's times, Kosygin had learned how to keep to himself and preferred not to be too close to anyone. He did not work in the party apparatus, only in the government, and this to some extent weakened his political standing.

Kosygin was an honest, intelligent, and extremely knowledgeable man, highly competent in handling government business, very much at home with the economy, industry, and finance. Just one example of his administrative acumen and prudence. Soviet scientists had been researching the possibility of peaceful nuclear explosions on such tempting projects as reversing the great Siberian rivers to flow into the arid regions of Central Asia instead of the Arctic Ocean. Convincing estimates of cost and effectiveness were presented by atomic scientists and irrigators to the Council of Ministers, with Kosygin presiding. But quite unexpectedly, prompted by one of the scientists, Kosygin asked for reliable prognoses of the effects on the atmospheric temperature and the overall ecology if comparatively warmer rivers ceased to fall into the cold ocean. No one was able to give an accurate answer of what would happen in this area rich in fish and minerals. Kosygin had the project sent back "for revision." Happily, it never returned, because the real objection was the deadly radioactive fallout that would have contaminated the soil for years to come.

Kosygin was not a demagogue by nature, and for all this he was respected in the party and the nation. He was not an expert in foreign affairs, but thanks to his common sense, he could handle discussions and negotiations with foreign partners better than any other member of the Politburo except Gromyko, and certainly better than Brezhnev. Leonid Brezhnev was well aware of this. In his heart he envied Kosygin and disliked him. But it was common knowledge that Kosygin had no desire to be the top man in the party as general secretary. He stayed out of power struggles, and Brezhnev therefore tolerated him as prime minister.

I was invited to two very private dinners at a Black Sea resort by Kosygin, who also happened to be vacationing there. After drinks we had long, relaxed conversations, lasting into the night. He asked many straight questions about the United States, its society and its people, its lifestyles and traditions. He was a devoted communist, but a rather open-minded one. Sitting in his dacha, he told me how our highest leadership lived and operated.

By coincidence Kosygin was visiting Hanoi when, on February 10, a large Vietcong force launched a surprise attack on the U.S. army barracks near the city of Pleiku in South Vietnam. Johnson retaliated by ordering a heavy bombing of North Vietnam while Kosygin was still there. Senator Fulbright told me later in confidence that Johnson hesitated over whether to bomb

North Vietnam at once or to wait until Kosygin's departure. Many of his advisers recommended an immediate start to the bombing. They argued that while this would without doubt temporarily aggravate relations with the Soviet Union, the raid would at the same time demonstrate American determination to North Vietnam, China, and the Soviet Union. Moreover, they argued that a sharp exacerbation of the situation would make it easier to negotiate a settlement and produce a more favorable one for the United States. To his associates Johnson reaffirmed that he was against worsening relations with Moscow. But he also told them, Fulbright reported, that "in the eyes of the whole world he had to oppose the challenge of China and Mao Zedong himself with America's will."

When I met with Rusk he was fully aware of the sensitivity of the situation. So he kept telling me that the president did not want to impair our relations, that he wished for their improvement, that the United States was ready to withdraw from Vietnam if Hanoi stopped its interference, and so on. I declined to accept these excuses. The fact remained that they had bombed the country while our premier was there.

Shortly afterward the Soviet government sent a rather strongly worded confidential message to President Johnson condemning American actions in Vietnam. Kosygin bitterly resented the bombing that had taken place while he was in Vietnam and turned against Johnson, although previously he had been more favorably disposed toward him in Kremlin meetings.

The North Vietnamese had also done their unseemly bit by launching their offensive just when Kosygin was in Hanoi, without giving us advance notice. Indeed, they were doing their utmost to foster enmity between Washington and Moscow. The situation was absurd. On the one hand, the Soviet leaders were well aware of the game the Vietnamese were playing and cursed them behind their backs, especially Brezhnev, who, like Gromyko, did not want to aggravate Soviet-American relations without reason. Of course, there remained the hope that we could divert Washington's attention from Europe through its involvement in Southeast Asia, but in the last analysis, it was ideological dogmatism in Moscow that inexorably drove our country along a faulty and wanton course.

Our Cuban friends did not leave us in peace either. They tried to bring pressure to bear on the White House through our embassy. At Fidel Castro's confidential request, Moscow instructed me to make still another official statement to Thompson regarding the growing number of "provocative actions launched by the United States against Cuba," including some military actions from the Guantanamo naval base located in an American enclave on the island of Cuba.

In short, the behavior of our allies in two major trouble spots in our relations with the United States—Vietnam and Cuba—systematically blocked any rational discussion of other problems that were really of key importance to both of us.

## The War Party in Washington

On March 2 I had another meeting with Rusk. In a rather agitated manner he claimed that both direct and indirect contacts with Beijing and Hanoi had made it clear that Hanoi was not going to stop its activities in Southeast Asia. It now was actively using the territory of Laos to infiltrate into South Vietnam in violation of the Geneva agreements. The Soviet Union was responsible in part for ensuring they were carried out. We kept criticizing the United States for intervening in Southeast Asia, but Rusk kept stubbornly reducing the matter to North Vietnam meddling in South Vietnam.

Meanwhile, a controversy was growing inside Washington, with many senior officials seeing the war in a broader and more threatening geopolitical context.

Senator Mike Mansfield, the Senate majority leader and a respected authority on Asia, said to me that the architects and principal promoters of the interventionist American policy in Vietnam were McNamara, the Bundy brothers (William Bundy was the assistant secretary of state for Asia), and General Maxwell Taylor, chairman of the Joint Chiefs of Staff. The Pentagon members of this group believed that China's direct involvement would provide a good pretext for bombing Chinese nuclear facilities and thus indefinitely exclude China from the ranks of the nuclear powers. Senator Fulbright also told me of an active "war party" in Washington uniting officials in the Pentagon and State Department. Since the election, Fulbright said, the president had become hard to talk to, notwithstanding the fact that they were old friends. Johnson hardly listened to his interlocutors, but cut them short and did the talking himself, trying to impress his listeners with his mountains of facts, eloquent rhetoric, and sound statesmanship. He would only listen to Pentagon military experts and certain high-ranking officials from the State Department, mainly people like Rusk and, at the beginning, his deputy George Ball, until he resigned his office.

Fulbright characterized the president's position as follows: Johnson wanted to stop China before it was too late. Giving up South Vietnam would not help stabilize Asia but precisely the reverse, because the Chinese leadership would not stop at Vietnam. The West therefore had to "give battle" without delay, while Beijing still was not a major military power and its capacity for expansion in Asia was still fairly limited. Hanoi was fully subordinate to Beijing and practically shared its conception of the future development in

Southeast Asia and beyond. Hence, Johnson believed, the United States had to keep up the military pressure with aerial bombardment and continue this until Vietnam accepted a peaceful settlement within the framework of the 1954 Geneva accords. This was, of course, the notorious "domino theory" that the fall of Vietnam would spread to all of Southeast Asia.

Hervé Alphand, the French ambassador, who had served as de Gaulle's representative in New York during World War II, was quite close to the French president and had tried to impress on Johnson and Rusk the sad lessons of his country's involvement in Vietnam. But he told me that Johnson saw himself joined in a global struggle against communism, and that meant literally drawing a line on a world scale like the one that divided Europe between the two camps. He told me the White House was confident that Moscow would not dare to risk a substantial aggravation of its relations with Washington over Vietnam because of the growing hostility between the Soviet Union and China.

I followed up this theme at a private lunch on March 12 with Vice President Hubert Humphrey, who said the administration had come to believe that Beijing discounted the United States as a "paper tiger," and that both the Chinese and North Vietnamese had therefore invested the conflict in Vietnam with a geopolitical dimension which the U.S. government could no longer ignore. The United States therefore could not permit itself a forced withdrawal without a suitable political settlement, and this was why Washington flatly rejected Hanoi's precondition that U.S. troops quit South Vietnam before negotiations.

The president's position boiled down to a barter deal: if Hanoi would halt its military operations against the South, the United States would stop its operations against North Vietnam; then negotiations could begin. The Johnson administration was ready to accept any government in South Vietnam even if eventually it turned socialist, he said, but the main point for the administration was that the United States would never give in to Beijing's pressure. He added that one of the reasons the president was ready for a peaceful settlement was to avoid any further deterioration of Soviet-American relations. Johnson realized that the Soviet Union had to give military assistance to North Vietnam, but he knew that would only lead to a greater involvement of both the Soviet Union and the United States in Vietnam. And Beijing wanted to pursue the war in order to avoid a rapprochement between Moscow and Washington.

While listening to Humphrey I was thinking that his analysis was good, and in a broad sense it would actually respond to the real interests of the Soviet Union to end the war and improve relations with the United States. Yet Hanoi stubbornly refused to accept this kind of gradual settlement and to halt its military operations to unify the whole of Vietnam under the banner of socialism. It took Hanoi more than a decade of intense combat to achieve this goal. Could they have accomplished it earlier and more easily by accepting the compromise in 1964? Nobody can ever know.

Rusk, of all people, put out a peace feeler to me in the most tentative, unofficial, and personal manner. On May 8 he spoke with me about Vietnam during the State Department's annual reception for the diplomatic corps. Emphasizing that neither the United States nor the Soviet Union should be enslaved by its own partners, he gave me to understand that our countries might join forces (without publicizing it) to reach a stage-by-stage settlement. Suppose, he said, a confidential agreement on Vietnam could be reached privately between Washington and Moscow. The United States would not regard it as a challenge if the Soviet Union simultaneously gave North Vietnam a solemn military guarantee against American bombardment. On the whole, the developments might look like a compromise reached in the face of imminent confrontation between the two superpowers. This, among other things, would be a major setback for China.

Rusk's words about the undue ideological dependence of both governments upon their allies appeared all too true. My conversation left me with the impression that, for all its big talk about the high geopolitical stakes, the administration was starting to feel alarmed at the way the Vietnam crisis was turning into an impasse. In my report to Moscow I emphasized the importance of what Rusk had told me.

Two days later Rusk asked me to inform the Soviet government urgently that, in response to our appeals, air raids against North Vietnam were to be halted for what he called a limited probation period. Washington hoped that Hanoi would reciprocate by reducing its military operations in South Vietnam. If it did not, the United States would resume its attacks.

Not surprisingly, Brezhnev became interested in Rusk's ideas and told Gromyko to think about them. Gromyko's conclusion was essentially that Rusk's suggestions would be hard to put into practice. North Vietnam was dead against any mediation by third parties in negotiating with the Americans; Hanoi wanted to deal with them directly. If Washington had any concrete proposals, they could be passed to Hanoi. Rusk pushed his proposals again, first when he met Gromyko at the tenth anniversary celebration of the Austrian State Treaty in Vienna in mid-May and again through Ambassador Foy Kohler in Moscow. Gromyko said bluntly that the Soviet Union did not and would not negotiate on Vietnam with anyone, including the United States.

## Our Own Vietnam Syndrome

On July 3, before going on vacation, I had a lengthy conversation with Rusk. He said that Southeast Asia was of key importance, but the Soviet approach to the problem kept the U.S. government guessing, and Moscow took no initiative in searching for ways to solve the problem. The United States, he said, wondered whether Moscow had voluntarily accepted Hanoi's veto. He remarked that Gromyko had told the American ambassador in Moscow that unless the United States stopped bombing North Vietnam, there would be no chance for a peaceful settlement. But when Kohler asked what was likely to happen if the raids stopped, all Gromyko would say was something like, "You stop first, then we'll see."

Rusk wanted Moscow to know that all American attempts to establish confidential channels with Hanoi to discuss a peaceful settlement had failed. The American side realized that Moscow had its own headaches just like Washington, but in spite of everything the American government was deeply convinced that the destinies of war and peace were, in the last analysis, in the hands of the Soviet Union and the United States. Both appeared interested in settling Vietnam gradually to improve their own relations.

But following my instructions, I informed Rusk of the analysis I had just received from Moscow, which was that in recent months American policy had undergone grave changes for the worse and was basically at variance with the principles of the Kennedy administration. I must admit that this criticism was not at all well founded, and Rusk clearly was hurt by the comparison, which he found unwarranted and wrong. There had been enough sharp aggravations during Kennedy's time over Berlin or Cuba, and Rusk was anxious to prove (not without reason) that many of our disputes, including Vietnam itself, had started in Kennedy's time. On the whole, the conversation was anything but pleasant for both of us.

During my stay in Moscow I attended several Politburo meetings and talked with Brezhnev, Gromyko, and other leaders. They all agreed that Vietnam and its effect on our relations with the United States were among the principal issues of our foreign policy. Yet our leadership unanimously recognized that our relations with the United States were a priority, while Vietnam was not that vital to our national interests. Nor had the Soviet public ever known much about this faraway country. Our political course therefore should have been evident, but the powerful factor of ideology— "international solidarity with the socialist republic of Vietnam"—was deeply ingrained in the minds of the Kremlin leaders. It kept affecting our relations with the United States, at times to the detriment of our own basic interests. Many Soviet leaders, including Brezhnev, admitted this in private conversations with me. But when it came to practical action, the Soviet Union had its own Vietnam syndrome, which remained a heavy burden on our relations with America and for years hampered detente between us.

# III. Trying to Juggle Peace and War

*Johnson Stakes His Presidency on Ending the War*

By 1966, the strength of the U.S. armed forces in South Vietnam had increased sharply to about 400,000, and the American army finally became the principal force confronting the national resistance in the country. The bombing of North Vietnam was expanding, with air strikes against Hanoi and Haiphong soon to follow.

As the United States escalated the war, meanwhile also increasing its nuclear arms and missile forces to ensure its global superiority, it became difficult to prevent Vietnam from impairing Soviet-American relations. Still, some specific questions in Soviet-American relations were solved or at least explored. Both governments resumed their confidential exchanges of messages and examined such ideas as the use of nuclear energy for mining and earthmoving projects, and the peaceful exploration of the moon and outer space. After a long delay we signed an agreement at the end of 1966 opening direct air traffic between the two countries. In January 1967, we signed another agreement on the principles of exploration and the peaceful use of outer space. But most important, the administration expressed serious interest in an agreement to restrain the deployment of antiballistic missile systems in both countries in order to counter rising pressures by some members of Congress and the military-industrial complex for this new step in the arms race.

Johnson in fact was beginning to realize that unless the war ended in 1967 he could hardly count on being reelected for another term; as the war widened, so did opposition to it across the country. Fulbright explained to me that was why the president felt that greater military pressure had to be applied to North Vietnam to force it to settle. The columnist Walter Lippmann, who increasingly and bitterly challenged the president's war policies, told me at lunch in his home early in June that Johnson and Rusk were no longer interested in a peaceful settlement now and were pinning their hopes on a military solution to end the war before the 1968 elections.

I also learned of another person in the president's inner circle who was an active champion of escalation. Late in May Harriman warned over dinner at his home that the new national security adviser, Walt Rostow (who succeeded Bundy), was the administration's most dangerous hawk. He enjoyed unqualified support of the Joint Chiefs of Staff and called for expanding the air raids, to "bring home to Hanoi that American means it," as Harriman put it. Johnson, supported by McNamara, did not accept this aerial escalation, yet he agreed with Rusk that the policy of limited bombing should continue. He bet on success in the ground war; more troops were scheduled to be sent to Vietnam in 1966 to enable the United States to defeat the main Vietcong forces by the following year.

Early in June I had a get-acquainted lunch with Rostow. Sounding rather optimistic, he argued that things were going better in Vietnam. He admitted that all their attempts had failed to obtain help directly from the Chinese to reach a peaceful solution in Vietnam; the question had been raised at the regular meetings of the U.S. and Chinese ambassadors in Warsaw, which was the only direct contact between the two governments. But he stressed that a tacit understanding had been established between Washington and Beijing: the United States would not attack or bomb mainland China, and China would at least not use its armed forces to interfere in the Vietnam War. The Chinese leadership was rather "vociferous," but "extremely careful about the matters likely to lead to a direct confrontation with the United States." Underlying the power struggle that was going on in China—that was the time of the Cultural Revolution—Rostow said, was the process of defining China's future foreign and domestic political course.

President Johnson was also closely following developments in Europe and relations with the Soviet Union, Rostow said, but he recognized that as long as the Vietnam War continued, "one could hardly expect" greater progress in European affairs. The national security adviser evinced no interest in disarmament, and he never showed any in our subsequent conversations. In general, I got the impression that he was on guard, anxious not to give away too much to a Soviet ambassador, and in that connection I remember an amusing story.

On one occasion Rostow wanted to give me a confidential letter from President Johnson to Prime Minister Kosygin and asked me to pick it up at his home at about 11 P.M. He lived somewhere on the outskirts of Washington. When I got there, I read through the letter and spotted one rather ambiguous passage. I pointed it out to Rostow and asked him, "What is the right way to interpret this so as not to cause misunderstanding in Moscow?" Rostow replied that he was not authorized to interpret the president's letter. I told him that I was not asking for an interpretation but a clarification. But he was adamant. Since the question was important, I asked him to call the president and clarify it on the phone. Rostow refused, saying it was too late to disturb the president.

I asked if I could use his phone, dialed the number of the duty officer at the White House, whom I knew, and asked if the president had gone to bed. Impressed by my determination, Rostow snatched the receiver from my hand and asked what the president was doing. The officer replied that Johnson was watching television.

Reluctant and diffident, Rostow called the president. Johnson told Rostow to pass the receiver to me. I asked the president to clarify the meaning of the passage in the letter, which he did most willingly. "Rostow is too fond of playing diplomatic games. He can't speak with foreigners in plain language," Johnson said. "He knows perfectly well what my letter means."

The president then gave me his personal phone number in the White House so I could call him directly on urgent matters, rather than go through Rostow. Later I had to use it a couple of times, most notably to arrange an urgent appointment on a Sunday to inform him of the Soviet invasion of Czechoslovakia.

## Moscow's Concern about Vietnam

In Moscow there was no less consternation than in Washington over the effect of the Vietnam War on relations with the United States and indeed other important nations. Privately, in conversation with me and among themselves, many Politburo members cursed the Americans, the Chinese, and the Vietnamese for their unwillingness to seek a compromise in Vietnam. Brezhnev once told me angrily that he had no wish "to sink in the swamps of Vietnam." The Soviet leadership welcomed Johnson's attempts to separate relations with Moscow from the grave effects of his stubborn policies in Vietnam, but it nevertheless stuck to the ideological principle of "proletarian internationalism" in support of Hanoi and could not fully accept the administration's approach of trying to normalize our relations in general while disregarding the war in Vietnam.

I got a taste of our public perplexity when I attended the Twenty-Third Congress of the Communist Party as a delegate in May 1966. In preparing its report to the congress, the Politburo devoted great attention to formulating its position on Soviet-American relations. In its summary report, the congress blamed the war on the United States but said, "We have repeatedly stated our readiness to develop our relations with the United States of America, and we still hold to the same position. But this requires that the United States stop its policy of aggression." Thus our basic public sympathies still lay with a small socialist country that had challenged a mighty superpower for the sake of national reunification. But realpolitik demanded a more flexible position in our relations with the United States. The Politburo understood this but saw no clear way out of the impasse.

Needless to say, the party congress was followed in Washington with great attention, and Thompson shared with me the American analysis of the results, which was that the Soviet government was not changing its foreign policy and planned to concentrate on building the country's economic and military power.

Rusk showed a personal interest in the congress and said the administration had noted that Brezhnev and Kosygin had sharpened their words about Vietnam. He advised me: "Moscow ought to take into account that Hanoi leaves the United States no alternative but to follow the present course." At our most recent meetings, Rusk could barely keep his temper when it came to Vietnam. I could not help feeling that there was a growing tension on Vietnam within the administration, and Rusk had to deal with it on a day-to-day basis without any obvious way out of the deadlock. This had started to tell on the mood and emotions of this otherwise even-tempered man.

On October 10 Gromyko and Johnson had the traditional White House meetings during the annual sessions of the United Nations General Assembly. They began by wrangling over whose fault it was that relations had deteriorated, with Johnson saying how upset he was by the personal attacks on him in the Soviet Union, especially in the press.

When the conversation settled into a more even temper, Johnson said he would be glad to receive Soviet leaders in the United States or to visit the Soviet Union himself. "The more we meet, the better it will be for us all," he said.

Johnson once again said he remained ready to negotiate with North Vietnam and asked the Soviet Union to help bring its friends to the table. Gromyko replied that all the U.S. statements on negotiating an end to the war contained preliminary conditions utterly unacceptable to the other side, since they amounted to nothing less than capitulation.

"The question is," Gromyko went on solemnly, "what will happen if the United States continues with the same course? Other countries, the Soviet Union included, will understandably render assistance to Vietnam on an ever greater scale. In that case the United States and in some way the Soviet Union will find themselves involved in these developments. Can it be that history has sealed our fate like that? The key to the earliest possible termination of the war is in the hands of the United States. It depends upon your policy."

The first thing to do, he insisted, was for the United States to stop bombing North Vietnam. But the most curious thing was that, apart from that simple demand, the Soviet government did not have any clear plan for settling the conflict. It merely relied on Hanoi, and Hanoi did not confide in Moscow with its specific plans. Terms for ending the conflict in Vietnam remained just as unresolved after the conversation as before. Yet, on the whole, the meeting was useful in helping Washington and Moscow review the outlook and consider potential dangers.

At the end of the conversation Johnson emphasized the need for more frequent top-level meetings. He said, "The more we meet, the better it will be for us all."

Despite our stalemate over Vietnam, Johnson had expressed his interest in concluding a range of agreements on such subjects as cultural exchanges, outer space, fishing, and air traffic.

In November 1966, an agreement was signed establishing direct air links between the United States and the Soviet Union. The inaugural flight direct from Moscow to New York was made by a Soviet crew headed by a well-known pilot, Boris Bugayev, who later became Brezhnev's personal pilot and then the Soviet minister of civil aviation. His navigator was believed to be proficient in English. As the plane approached Kennedy Airport the navigator contacted the American control tower and requested clearance to land. He was instructed to take his place in line along with the other planes.

The navigator could not figure out his instructions and cheerfully radioed, "O.K., I am landing." He was again told to wait in line, but again the instruction was lost on him. In a louder voice he repeated that he was quite all right and was coming in for a landing. The air controller, terrified, ordered all the planes in the traffic pattern to get out of the way "for the crazy Russian." The landing itself was performed brilliantly, and everybody on board was thoroughly pleased but totally unaware of the narrow escape.

That night a dinner was given to celebrate the flight. The guests exchanged speeches and toasts. The atmosphere was friendly, and hardly anyone had the slightest idea of what had happened. But the head of the U.S. air traffic service recounted the episode to me with a smile, and then in a more serious manner suggested that our pilots and navigators undergo a week of training in English-language radio communication.

At first the crew would not hear of any such thing. As excellent pilots and navigators, which indeed they were, they insisted they had no need for any extra training. I had to contact Moscow and suggest that the crew be ordered to undergo special language training. Moscow reacted promptly. I was instructed to thank the Americans for their offer, and the crew was directed to start training at once. All crews subsequently flying to New York received such training.

## Mixed Results in Disarmament

It has often been said that the interminable disarmament initiatives, discussions, and negotiations represented the most reliable barometer of the fundamental Soviet-American relationship; when times were fair, talks on arms control moved ahead, otherwise they were clouded by self-interest and suspicion. Consider the case of the long-standing proposal known as the Mansfield Amendment to bring home a sizable proportion of the American troops stationed in Western Europe, which at that time was potentially the most dangerous area of confrontation between the main forces of the North Atlantic Alliance and the Warsaw Pact. War here would not just be a conflict in some faraway jungle but could destroy all civilization, although the situation had stabilized since the tense days over Berlin early in the decade.

Senator Mansfield gained considerable support from his colleagues for withdrawing some American troops from Europe by citing budget constraints and other demands of the Vietnam War. The Johnson administration opposed reducing the American military presence in Europe. Like all U.S. administrations, it recognized this would also mean a diminution of American political influence in Europe, and in this it was supported first and foremost by Bonn but also by NATO in general. Yet in the United States public opinion was increasingly in favor of U.S. troop reductions in Europe, not just for budgetary reasons but because of the growing antiwar mood caused by American intervention in Vietnam.

Mansfield pointed all this out to me when he paid me a visit to explain his proposal and seek Moscow's support for it. If the Soviet Union would declare its readiness to withdraw some of the Soviet forces from Eastern Europe, the senator said, he was sure the Senate would pass his resolution, and that would actually help improve Soviet-American relations. Later on, Senators Edward Kennedy and Dick Clark called on me separately to make the same appeal.

Of course, I reported all this to the Soviet leadership, and the question was discussed by the Politburo. It finally decided not to make any announcement in support of Senator Mansfield's resolution, mainly because of its own fears that if some Soviet troops pulled out of Eastern Europe this might aggravate the unstable situation there, and in any case the U.S. government opposed it. Mansfield nevertheless reintroduced his amendment in later years, but it never was approved.

We also conducted regular exchanges in an attempt to check the arms race between the two great powers. The background can be found in the early days of Johnson's presidency, when as a symbolic unilateral gesture Rusk had asked me on December 9, 1963, to inform Moscow that the U.S.

government intended to cut its military budget by one billion dollars for the 1964–65 fiscal year, a reduction of 2 percent.

Three days later, on December 12, Moscow replied that the Soviet government was also planning to reduce its military expenditures for 1964 by 600 million rubles. This was comparable to the American reduction, but the real problem with any comparison was that both governments structured their military budgets differently and both had hidden military expenditures elsewhere in their national budgets, particularly the Soviet Union.

The same day Rusk reminded me of a proposal he had made to Gromyko, for both sides to scrap their B-47 class bomber fleets. He added that they were also ready to discuss the mutual destruction of other types of weapons at agreed sites. I replied that my government had instructed me to say that such mutual destruction would hardly represent a serious step toward mutual disarmament since each side would destroy its obsolete arms and immediately replace them with new and more sophisticated weapons. The Soviet Union still believed in an agreed program leading toward general and complete disarmament, with each side aware of its commitments and those of the other at every stage.

Frankly speaking, I did not share this all-or-nothing approach, and I told Gromyko so. Alas, for many years his favorite topic in this field was precisely this policy of "general and complete disarmament"—nothing more than a good piece of propaganda dating as far back as the League of Nations between the wars. So he would not at that moment even consider smaller and more discrete steps, let alone anything connected with verification through foreign inspections on our territory. This proved to be the stumbling block for many disarmament initiatives.

But the more fundamental reality was that the Soviet leaders, and Khrushchev in particular, strongly doubted the effectiveness of practical steps toward disarmament at that stage of the arms race. They did not believe that it was really possible, and their minds were not ready for it. Thus during the years Khrushchev was in power they kept wasting real chances to initiate a coordinated disarmament process. The only thing that was admissible at the time, they thought, was some mutual reduction in military budgets.

In October of 1966, the Soviet leadership decided to focus on the nonproliferation of nuclear weapons because NATO was canvassing the idea of a joint nuclear force among its members, with the aim of giving them a sense of sharing in their use lest they feel the United States alone controlled their destiny. However laudable may have been this self-denying constraint on American power, it frightened us to think of Europeans and especially Germans with their fingers anywhere near a nuclear trigger. So on behalf of my government I told Rusk this idea was the main obstacle in the way of a nonproliferation agreement: the Soviet Union was ready for negotiations to limit the spread of nuclear weapons, but the U.S. government must make its choice between a nonproliferation agreement or a NATO nuclear force.

Long negotiations on the nonproliferation treaty were completed at the end of 1967 and at last it was laid out for signing on July 1, 1968, in the capitals of the three depository states, the Soviet Union, the United States, and Great Britain. It was signed in Washington by Secretary of State Rusk, the Soviet and British ambassadors, and the ambassadors of fifty more countries. The solemn ceremony took place in the White House in the presence of the president, top administration officials, congressmen, and newsmen. The treaty was signed in Moscow and London on the same day.

By the end of 1968 it had been signed by eighty-three states, and the number continued to grow. The treaty helped to a large degree to check the spread of nuclear weapons, though there were some notable exceptions— India and Pakistan, Israel and the Arab countries, and North and South Korea. Nevertheless, the nuclear countries undertook to work out effective means of control over nuclear arms, and the treaty was and still remains one of the basic agreements of the nuclear age aimed at reducing the possibility of nuclear war.

After the signing ceremony was over, President Johnson made a solemn announcement. He said the governments of the Soviet Union and the United States had reached an agreement to begin discussions on reducing the delivery systems for strategic nuclear weapons and limiting antiballistic missile systems.

Unfortunately, because of Johnson's strong desire to combine the beginning of this discussion with a summit meeting with Soviet leaders, and because the diplomatic atmosphere was soured by the Soviet invasion of Czechoslovakia, strategic arms limitation was not seriously explored during the last period of the Johnson administration, and the Non-proliferation of Nuclear Weapons Treaty was not ratified by the United States in 1968. That had to wait until after the Nixon administration began the following year.

But the topic that engaged most of our energies in the field of disarmament during the Johnson administration and for several years afterward was whether to build a large and expensive antiballistic missile (ABM) system, the efficiency of which had not yet been ascertained. By the middle of the decade, Soviet researchers were working on the design of the first ABM networks around Moscow and in the western part of the country near Tallinn in Estonia. A defense against missiles, specifically for the protection of civilians, was considered in Moscow as a legitimate matter and was not supposed to arouse suspicion abroad.

The project began to attract the attention of the Pentagon. The American military insisted that the reported deployment of a Soviet ABM system be countered by a similar system in the United States. Yet the administration believed that rather than construct such a costly system in response to the Soviet challenge, it would be better to agree with Moscow and mutually refrain from building the systems at all, especially since no one was certain they would really stop incoming missiles. Furthermore, some officials argued that it would be much cheaper for the United States to improve and strengthen its offensive nuclear systems forces, thus making it easier to penetrate an antimissile defense. It is interesting to note that it was McNamara, the secretary of defense, and not Rusk, the diplomat, who turned out to favor abandoning the ABM program. Rusk never talked with me about ABM; his attention was mainly on Vietnam. McNamara deserves to be remembered as a pioneer in advancing in general the idea of strategic arms limitation in the United States.

The secret discussions about the ABM system took place within the administration, naturally without addressing us. But there were some private feelers from the American side. On January 16, 1964, less than two months after Johnson had taken office, William Foster, who was McNamara's soul mate and director of the Arms Control and Disarmament Agency, had a long conversation with me at lunch. He argued it would be feasible for both nations to renounce building a major ABM system, the cost of which he estimated at a minimum of $15 billion to $20 billion. Foster believed that some preliminary confidential arrangement between the heads of both governments would represent a significant step forward, the more so since President Johnson had not yet committed himself. There was no time to waste, Foster concluded, and he smiled as he warned me, "Don't talk about this in public, or I'll be called before the Un-American Activities Committee." From time to time through 1966 Foster privately raised this with me.

Early in December 1966, Llewellyn Thompson confided to me that the U.S. administration was alarmed at the reports of the Soviet ABM system. They stirred up old feelings in the Pentagon and in Congress in favor of creating a system in the United States. Even McNamara, although he made no official proposal to us, touched on the question during a conversation at a White House reception. By that time we already were on good personal terms. His arguments ran like this: promising achievements had been reported in the research and development of antimissile systems, and many of the Pentagon brass were sold on the idea. They had gone to their friends on Capitol Hill and won the support of some influential members of Congress. But after studying the project, McNamara found it would be costly and in the last analysis rather ineffective: ABM systems can be penetrated simply by increasing the number of incoming missiles. Therefore a mutual renunciation seemed the best solution.

I sent Moscow numerous reports on ABM systems but received no formal reaction, the pretext being that my contacts on the subject in Washington were unofficial and informal. In the meantime our embassy received solid intelligence reports confirming that the United States was going ahead with the development of an ABM system. I forwarded a detailed account to Moscow. Simultaneously I strongly advised the Politburo that we at least must determine our position lest we find ourselves in a serious new stage of the arms race.

In Moscow, there was no consensus within the government. Some ministers, led by Kosygin, believed that ABM systems were clearly designed to protect human life, and no negotiations were needed to prove it. How could one refuse to protect people against missiles? A different kind of argument favoring the ABM came from our military-industrial complex. The defense minister, Dmitri Ustinov, and the chairman of the Military and Industrial Commission, Lev Smirnov, argued that the first Soviet ABM designs looked promising and the Soviet Union could fall behind the Americans if it allowed itself to become entangled in prolonged preliminary discussions.

But Brezhnev, who was familiar with defense and industrial problems, pointed out that McNamara made sense when he argued that ABM systems could be overwhelmed by increasing the number of offensive missiles. He was not, however, willing to give up work on our ABM system entirely. In the meantime, he said we had to seek a balanced and a more conclusive response to meet "the American challenge" diplomatically and militarily. Gromyko suggested what would amount to stalling by sticking to our well-known concept of demanding the whole loaf or nothing, "universal and comprehensive disarmament."

In the course of further discussion within the government, Moscow came up with the more realistic idea of combined talks on offensive and defensive weapons. Underlying this was our principal objective of reaching parity with the United States in strategic weapons. As a result, on March 18, 1966, I was instructed to sound out this idea with Foster. I told him that ABM systems deserved our attention. The question could be discussed in a package with the problem of nuclear delivery vehicles.

To this, Foster reasonably observed that an agreement on ABM systems need not include any provisions for control or inspection, because it was impossible to conceal their huge supporting facilities of countermissiles, targeting equipment, and tracking radar. But that was not the case for offensive nuclear forces, which demanded closer surveillance. Foster also made it clear that for the Americans any agreement not to deploy ABM systems would not affect research and development.

Thus for the first time we touched on controlling missile and antimissile systems, an arms control process that would lock the two superpowers into a dialogue that lasted a generation. On June 27, 1966, a message from Johnson was delivered in Moscow suggesting a meeting in Geneva of "the highest-ranking" officials to discuss mutual restraints on deploying ABM systems. The idea was to establish a "mutually acceptable and stable balance of forces easily verifiable by national means of control" and thereby curb the strategic arms race. Llewellyn Thompson, back in Moscow for his second tour as ambassador, delivered the note and added that the U.S. government accepted the Soviet suggestion that the discussion should cover the earliest possible cessation of deploying additional strategic arms as well as antimissile defenses. The United States was ready to focus mainly on self-policing national systems of verification, although it did not rule out the possibility of on-site inspection. And during the negotiating period neither side would carry out any major modification of its strategic systems; otherwise the other side could do the same.

This represented an important step by the Johnson administration. But Washington was interested almost exclusively in ABM and Moscow in strategic arms, so further exchanges of views developed slowly until 1967, when the issue was directly discussed by Johnson and Kosygin at their Glassboro summit.

## McNamara, Nuclear Strategy, and the ABM

The ABM discussions helped me develop a personal friendship with Robert McNamara. He was a man of complex character, with a rare ability to adjust his views to changing circumstances, a pragmatist and realist who never became a slave to ideology. We used to meet from time to time. I remember in particular a private lunch at his home on April 11, 1967, a few months before the Glassboro summit meeting between Johnson and Kosygin. Nearly the whole of our conversation was devoted to strategic nuclear missiles and ways of controlling them.

McNamara explained that U.S. military doctrine was grounded in the idea that the United States should be ready to absorb a surprise nuclear missile strike while preserving its capability to hit back and cause irreparable damage to the enemy. As far as he could understand, McNamara said, the Soviet military doctrine was based on the same principle. He was convinced that both sides possessed such capability. It was precisely this factor that in a peculiar way provided for stability and adequately guaranteed that neither of the two great powers would attack the other, because each well knew that an attack on the other meant committing suicide. This doctrine was of course well established, and what impressed me was McNamara's firm conviction that this balance of terror, as some called it, actually kept the peace.

But McNamara admitted frankly that the U.S. nuclear arsenal exceeded what was necessary to support this doctrine, which was known to experts as "mutually assured destruction" and likewise by its quite appropriate acronym, MAD. It was, however, mere accident that the United States found itself with an excess of missiles to underwrite the doctrine. When president Kennedy took office, having campaigned on a charge that the Republicans had allowed a "missile gap" to develop that put the United States behind the Soviet Union, his administration decided to focus on a speedy buildup of the nation's nuclear missiles. The decision was based on the U.S. evaluation of Soviet missile potential. But that potential had been overestimated because the Soviet government, although it had decided on a major shift in resources from civilian to military needs, did not go as far in actually making the shift as it said it would. The 1961 Berlin crisis nevertheless accelerated the American missile program, while the Soviet Union was not building up its missile forces as fast as U.S. intelligence believed. This led to a situation in which the United States had a greater number of missiles than the Soviet Union, but the Soviet Union still had enough nuclear missiles to ensure its own security under this formula of mutual suicide.

Antiballistic missile systems would introduce an entirely new element. McNamara said that the data available to him utterly convinced him that it was impossible to create a reliable antimissile system. If the other side went ahead with the project, the United States would only have to decide on the number of new offensive weapons to be built (which would be much cheaper) in order to keep the same basic formula in effect for mutual suicide. That was the reason why the United States, in response to the establishment of an antiballistic missile system in the Soviet Union, increased its strategic nuclear missile potential before considering the deployment of its own ABM system.

McNamara emphasized that Washington fully realized the difficulties of mutual understanding or indeed of concrete agreements. They were inevitable in view of the difference in the two countries' main objectives and their lack of mutual trust, but he believed we nevertheless should try. In a nutshell, the United States was aware of the fact that reaching an agreement on antiballistic defense systems would not be quick or easy—but the United States hoped, in spite of all the difficulties, to reach a mutual understanding.

McNamara was ready to go to Moscow to meet his Soviet counterparts, but he realized perfectly well that, while the Vietnam War was going on, he was "not the best candidate for such a trip." But, if need be, McNamara would send his own assistants to join Ambassador Thompson for talks in Moscow, since they were quite at home with the problem. He also expressed his readiness to continue the dialogue on the subject with me in Washington. But in the meanwhile, the United States wanted at least a preliminary response from Moscow on the points he had raised at our luncheon conversation.

That was actually the first time that a high-ranking American official directly informed the Soviet ambassador, albeit informally, about his views on the important issues of limiting nuclear weapons. But there was no response from Moscow. Our conversation again engaged the Soviet leadership in an internal debate over antimissile systems, and it was still going on even when Johnson and Kosygin met a few months later in Glassboro. Both leaders were unable to reach an agreement. Nevertheless, these meetings laid the preliminary groundwork for what would become the Strategic Arms Limitation Talks, or SALT as this principal East-West conduit was known.

Looking back, I must admit that Moscow made a grave and costly mistake in refusing to agree with the United States on an early ban on ABM systems. Another serious and also very costly Soviet mistake was the decision to introduce our SS-20 missiles in Europe, which provoked a prolonged and angry dispute with the United States and NATO over Intermediate Range Nuclear Forces, or INF, in Europe. That problem was not resolved until the beginning of the 1990s in a treaty to destroy all these medium-range missiles.

It was certainly unfortunate that little attention was paid to that forced break in the SALT talks in 1968. Important qualitative changes in the nature and force of strategic arms were under way and might have been prevented by a mutual agreement at that time. They only came into public view much later—too late to prevent yet another stage in the arms race. These were the multiple independently targetable reentry vehicle warheads, the multiple warhead missiles, or just MIRV for short. One MIRVed missile could replace several strategic missiles, increasing the offensive potential of a nuclear arsenal without any way of detection by the other side.

It was during the Nixon administration that Moscow and Washington cautiously agreed to start SALT, with both sides finally recognizing that they had to do something to slow the expensive and dangerous nuclear arms race. The Joint Chiefs of Staff refused to limit the development of their technology and would only hear of limitations on numbers of weapons. They won over the president, and this military position formed the basis of the American approach to nuclear arms limitation. The United States began tests of its Poseidon and Minuteman MIRV missiles in 1968, and in the following year the Soviet Union tested its SS-9 triple warhead missile. That marked the advent of the MIRV era. Twenty-five years were to pass before the United

States and the Soviet Union declared in 1993 that the development of such arms was an absurdity destabilizing the strategic balance, and that large numbers of them should be scrapped. That was the end of the expensive and dangerous strategic arms spiral. We probably could have prevented, or at least decisively slowed, that dangerous turn if we had been able to make a start at Glassboro. Who can tell? At any rate the Kremlin leadership and Soviet diplomacy were unprepared for such bold initiatives at that time.

# IV. Soviet Policy Seeks
# a Steady Course

## *Kosygin Tries to Mediate in Vietnam*

Early in February of 1967 Prime Minister Kosygin visited London to discuss the essential issues between Britain and the Soviet Union—but not just that. Hanoi had secretly asked us to use the government of Prime Minister Harold Wilson, one of Johnson's few European supporters on Vietnam, to put pressure on Washington to reach a peaceful solution in Vietnam. The Soviet leadership also attached some importance to this. The Johnson administration, for its part, was anxious to take advantage of Kosygin's good offices in Vietnam. It had been searching avidly for any nation or individual who could reach the leadership in Hanoi and broker a settlement.

The U.S. ambassador in Moscow handed us a confidential message from Johnson to Ho Chi Minh containing a new proposal for the United States to halt its bombing and troop buildup in exchange for the Democratic Republic of Vietnam's pledge not to send its forces to the South. The proposal had been already passed to Hanoi, we were told, and Rusk complained that Washington had received no reply.

Johnson's suggestions were relayed via Moscow to Hanoi from Kosygin himself at Wilson's request, thus implying Wilson's own support. Kosygin sent a covering message on his own recommending that Ho Chi Minh join in the search for a compromise to end the war. For personal reasons of status, Brezhnev was not too happy about Kosygin's initiative, but he let him continue, however unwillingly, lest he be seen as impeding a settlement.

Pending Vietnam's response, Johnson declared another short-term moratorium on bombing North Vietnam. But when it expired without any reply, he declined Kosygin's suggestion that it be extended to continue awaiting a favorable response from Hanoi. Thus the Soviet premier's mediation efforts ended in failure, although there were moments of high drama before the world press in London with Wilson, backed by Kosygin, publicly inviting Johnson to extend the moratorium. Johnson meanwhile passed word to us that when Kosygin appeared at a televised press conference in London, he hoped the premier would find "the right wording" for his answers so as not to provoke the increasingly bellicose right in the United States. And Rusk tried to justify the resumption of American bombing with the unconvincing explanation that there had been a "misunderstanding."

Kosygin was vexed by the whole proceeding. He had expected a repetition of his successful mediation the previous year in Tashkent between the prime ministers of India and Pakistan. But this time he got nowhere, and it consolidated Moscow's conviction that it was fruitless to meddle in anything between Vietnam and the United States. It would do its duty in terms of "proletarian internationalism" by sending arms to Hanoi, and leave it at that. Shortly afterward Rusk conveyed another proposal to us on Vietnam: If the Soviet Union would consider a mutual "de-escalation" of arms supplies to Vietnam, the United States might consider halting its bombing of North Vietnam. Moscow did not respond at all.

## The Politburo Outlines the Basis of Soviet Foreign Policy

With worldwide criticism of U.S. escalation in Vietnam growing increasingly fierce, questions arising in Congress of the president's unchecked authority to commit troops, and the consequent bankruptcy of his Great Society programs, the stability of relations between Washington and Moscow seems paradoxical, inasmuch as the cause of most misfortunes between us was an adventure conceived as part of a global battle against communism. But the long-term interests of both countries prevented Soviet-American relations from swinging to extremes, a point that can be demonstrated here by publishing for the first time a remarkable confidential report that Gromyko presented to the Politburo at the start of 1967. It formed the basis of our foreign policy and shows how we attempted to navigate through very stormy diplomatic seas.

In Moscow, our leadership sought an assessment of Soviet-American relations and instructed the Foreign Ministry to present a detailed analysis which would form the basis of our future policy. Gromyko submitted it to the Politburo on January 13, 1967, on behalf of the Foreign Ministry. The significance of this is that it was not prepared for public consumption or propaganda but for the private eyes of the members of the Politburo, and for them only, to evaluate and approve, which they did. Students of Soviet policy will recognize—maybe with some surprise—much that is familiar in our policy as publicly enunciated.

But those who thought at the time that the Soviet Union was embarked on an aggressive program of world conquest, and those who still may think so, would have been confounded by this secret memorandum if they could have read it at the time.

Although in the West and the United States in particular, North Vietnam's attacks on the South were seen as the spearhead of some communist master plan of conquest, our official analysis offered no justification for this kind of aggressive military posture. It was mainly remarkable for its confidence in the eventual triumph of our social system—confidence that history proved was utterly misplaced. Those who might have sought evidence of war plans by the Soviet Union to advance its system or even its national interests would have found none at all.

It states unequivocally at the outset: "On the whole, international tension does not suit the state interests of the Soviet Union and its friends. The construction of socialism and the development of the economy call for the maintenance of peace. In the conditions of detente it is easier to consolidate and broaden the positions of the Soviet Union in the world."

The document covers all significant political and geopolitical areas of foreign policy. Its strong ideological tone illustrated our desire to advance socialist ideas in the context of the "struggle with imperialism." But it stressed the great importance of Soviet-American relations, stating that "the answer to the question of whether a global nuclear missile war should break out, without any doubt depends on the state of these relations."

Moreover, good relations with the United States were seen as a bulwark against the "adventurous schemes" of the leaders of China; it was they, not Moscow, who held the view that Washington wanted war. As for the Soviet Union, it said, "The concentration of our main efforts on domestic purposes is fully in line with Lenin's statement that the final victory of socialism over capitalism will be ensured by the creation of a new, much higher level of labor productivity."

And here was Moscow's stance toward the American role in Vietnam:

As regards the American aggression against Vietnam and its effect on bilateral relations, we should go on rendering comprehensive assistance to the DRV [Democratic Republic of Vietnam] in consolidating its defense capacity to repulse the aggression, without getting directly involved in the war. We must give the Americans to understand that further escalation in the military actions against the DRV will compel the Soviet Union to render its assistance to this country on an ever-growing scale, and that the only way out of the present situation is reaching a political solution on the basis of respecting the legitimate rights of the Vietnamese people. Nevertheless, putting an end to the Vietnam conflict would undoubtedly have a positive effect on Soviet-American relations and open up new possibilities for solving certain international problems.

We should not avoid agreements with the United States on questions of our interest if such agreements do not contradict our position of principle in regard to Vietnam. Needless to say, we should avoid a situation where we have to fight on two fronts—that is, against China and the United States. Maintaining Soviet-American relations on a certain level is one of the factors that will help us achieve this objective

This foreign ministry memorandum was approved by the Soviet leadership and served as the basis for Soviet foreign policy toward the United States during Johnson's presidency. Its principles guided me and our embassy in Washington, but it still was not easy for me to play a constructive role in sustaining our relations with the United States as well as calming our domestic hawks.

## The Six-Day War

The history of Soviet relations with Israel is dramatic and filled with deep feeling on both sides. Initially the attitude of the Soviet Union toward Israel was balanced. Russians and Jews had suffered greatly during the war against the Nazis, and mutual sympathy developed between us. In the United Nations Security Council, Moscow spoke out in 1947, even before the United States, in favor of recognizing Israel as an independent state. Full diplomatic relations were established between the two states shortly afterward. Embassies were opened in both capitals.

This huge reservoir of goodwill was emptied by a totally misguided Soviet policy that resisted Jewish emigration and viewed any demand for it as a reproof to our socialist paradise. That anyone should have the temerity to want to leave it was taken as a rank insult! Worse, the Soviet leadership failed to make a distinction between its problems with Soviet Jewry—many of whom merely wanted to flee the system and go to Israel—and dissidents like Andrei Sakharov, the great scientist, and Aleksander Solzhenitsyn, the wartime officer and gulag prisoner turned author who became the most profound critics of the Soviet system, above all on human rights. These and their allies were not connected with Jewish or Zionist groups, although in the minds of many in the Kremlin, all were lumped together as enemies of the Soviet state, a heavy heritage of Stalin.

The prohibitive policy of the Soviet authorities over Jewish emigration resulted in growing friction with Israel and contributed to a vigorous anti-Soviet campaign in the United States. This, in turn, made the Soviet government retaliate by toughening its stand against Jewish emigration: the Soviet leadership regarded any relaxation as a concession to the anti-Soviet Zionists.

Virtually no Soviet citizen, Jewish or otherwise, was permitted to emigrate or even to travel abroad on anything except officially sanctioned business or cultural exchanges.

As we shall see later, American anti-communist politicians, most notably Senator Henry Jackson of Washington, allied themselves with Jewish organizations in the United States to turn the issue of Jewish emigration into a political football and advance their own careers, doing much in the process to wreck detente between Moscow and Washington. Our biggest mistake was to stand on pride and not let as many Jews go as wanted to leave. It would have cost us little and gained us much. Instead, our leadership turned it into a test of wills that we eventually lost.

Anti-Semitism as such has a long history in Russia. During the revolution the situation began to change: a good half of the revolutionary leaders were Jews, and that included some of Lenin's close collaborators. It was not a problem in the interwar years or during the war with Hitler's Germany—until Stalin made it one after World War II by invoking "cosmopolitan plots" in his permanent search for enemies. Thereafter policy went consistently wrong. Anti-Jewish and particularly anti-Zionist trends in the Soviet Union developed in the mid-1960s in parallel to demonstrations and a propaganda campaign on behalf of Soviet Jews in the West and especially in the United States. The persistent and outspoken desire of some Jews, including political dissidents, to leave the Soviet Union for Israel and the publicity surrounding some of these "refusniks" made things even worse. Inside the Soviet Union there was considerable popular resentment about them.

In addition, the strategic ties between Israel and the United States gradually became quite evident and came under strong criticism on the part of the Soviet government and mass media, particularly after the Six-Day War between Israel and the Arabs in 1967, which evoked pride and strong passions among Jews around the world, including those in the Soviet Union. The Israeli victory provided a stronger impetus to demands for emigration by Soviet Jewry than anything since the founding of the state of Israel, since it reassured them about the security and continued existence of the homeland, the state of Israel. Only in the mid-1980s did the situation begin gradually to normalize, and now there are practically no restrictions on exit visas for anyone. With many business and cultural ties between Russia and Israel, it has become one of the most frequently visited countries by Russians.

The Six-Day War was the decisive event in the conduct of the Soviet Union in the Middle East. Although the Middle East remained tense during Kennedy's presidency and the Johnson administration's first years, it did not grow into a serious conflict involving the two great powers. There was no regular exchange of views between Moscow and Washington on regional affairs, and the Middle East was not prominent on the agenda of Soviet-American relations, as were Europe and Southeast Asia.

During the spring of 1967 the situation in the Middle East began to deteriorate. On May 27 Kosygin sent a message to Johnson calling on him to prevent a military conflict, indicating he thought this was within Johnson's power because, he said, any decision by Israel to attack the Arab states would depend solely on the United States. If Israel started military operations, he warned the Soviet government would render assistance to "the victims of aggression."

Israel began military operations on Monday, June 5, by destroying the Egyptian Air Force on the ground in a surprise attack after Egypt had effectively blockaded Israel's access to the sea from the south by demanding the withdrawal of UN forces from Sharm el-Sheikh. Jordan then joined the war, as did Syria. The Soviet government declared its support for the Arab states and, in an attempt to halt the fighting, instructed the Soviet ambassador to the United Nations to call for an urgent meeting of the Security Council. Simultaneously it called on President Johnson to exert pressure on Israel. The president replied on June 6 that the United States was using all its influence for the cessation of hostilities. On June 7 the Security Council unanimously adopted a resolution calling for an unconditional cease-fire as a first step, but military operations continued unchecked.

With Israel heading toward military success, Moscow on June 10 broke diplomatic relations with Jerusalem. It was an emotional step. In the long term this proved to be a grave miscalculation because it practically excluded the Soviet Union from any serious role in a Middle East settlement. On the same day, Kosygin used the hot line to call on President Johnson urgently to demand that Israel unconditionally and within hours cease its military operations in accordance with the UN Security Council resolution. The Soviet government declared that unless Israel complied with the resolution the Soviet side would apply necessary sanctions. Kosygin's appeal to the president hinted that the Soviet Union could even take military action. This did not fail to alarm the White House. The U.S. 6th Fleet in the Mediterranean was ordered to move speedily to the area of conflict.

As President Johnson later admitted in his memoirs, at that point the situation became rather heated, and there was a more vigorous exchange of hot-line messages between Johnson and Kosygin. This made it possible for the White House and the Kremlin to keep the dangerous developments under control and gradually ease tension. As long as the situation remained crucial, Johnson, together with Rusk, McNamara, and their principal aides remained in the White House Situation Room. In Moscow, the Politburo remained continually in session. The hot line played an invaluable role in maintaining uninterrupted contacts between Moscow and Washington, preventing each side's perception of the other's intentions from becoming dangerously uncertain to a point that might precipitate rash acts in support of either side. In fact, the Kremlin did not actually plan any definite military action against Israel. It only considered further airlifting of armed supplies to the Arab countries at their request, and we did it as the West began resupplying Israel, as early as the second day of the war.

Late on June 10 Israel ended its military operations on all fronts, and cease-fire agreements were signed. The Six-Day War dealt a crushing defeat to Egypt, Syria, and Jordan, which created some perplexity in the Kremlin. The Soviet Union had to devise a new Middle East policy, since its authority in the region had been considerably damaged by the defeat of its clients. The policy again favored the Arabs because the Soviet leadership wanted to restore its role in the Middle East and prevent the United States from dominating that strategic area. But this policy left us with little flexibility because we often blindly followed our Arab allies, who in turn used us to block many initiatives that were advanced for a peaceful settlement.

When the UN General Assembly convened on July 17 for an emergency session on the Middle East, Soviet and American delegations began by coordinating their work in reaching a compromise. Kosygin led the Soviet delegation and tried to persuade Mahmoud Fawzi, the Egyptian foreign minister, to accept a compromise that would officially recognize the existence of Israel in exchange for the return of the occupied territories, but Fawzi was adamant. With no acceptable solution in sight, the American position on Israeli withdrawal began to toughen, in no small measure because of the Israeli lobby and pro-Israeli officials in the U.S. government, including Ambassador Arthur Goldberg and the Rostow brothers. The assembly session was suspended, and as the conflict was passed to the Security Council, the United States spun out the negotiations. I met with Goldberg several times. Finally he proposed a draft that seemed reasonable to me and I recommended it to Moscow.

After long and complex talks with Arab governments, Moscow accepted his compromise, and I so informed Goldberg. But then strange things began to happen. He suddenly insisted he had not suggested any formula; it had all been an "unfortunate misunderstanding." I still had a piece of notebook paper with the text of the proposed compromise written in Goldberg's own hand, and I took it to Rusk, who recognized his own ambassador's handwriting. But Goldberg said he could not remember when he might have written it, and Rusk tacitly backed him.

Angered, Moscow moved the dialogue to a higher level with a message from Kosygin to Johnson, and we ultimately worked out Security Council Resolution No. 242 on November 22, 1967, under which Israel and the Arabs were supposed to trade the captured territories for security guarantees, or, as it was said afterward, "land for peace."

But none of this concealed the fact that in the years to come the Soviet Union had been effectively frozen out of Middle East diplomacy. Brezhnev gradually came to realize that our one-sided policy had swung too far. I spoke to him privately several times and tried to convince him that the Soviet Union had made a mistake in breaking relations with Israel in 1967. What is not widely known is that late in the 1970s Brezhnev proposed a gradual restoration of relations with Israel, starting with reopening our consulates. The Politburo agreed to instruct the Foreign Ministry to examine the question. But Gromyko and Suslov were on vacation and on their return strongly protested against any change in our policy until there was a complete peace settlement in the Middle East. Brezhnev had to give in. For some time, Gromyko was angry with me for my role. Only in the mid-1980s did the situation begin to normalize when diplomatic relations with Israel were restored, which essentially amounted to admitting that the Soviet Union made a mistake by breaking them in 1967.

## The Glassboro Summit

Kosygin's visit to the General Assembly provided the occasion for an unexpected summit meeting with Lyndon Johnson, who still hoped for leverage from Moscow that would help start negotiations with Hanoi. The president also very much wanted to impress upon the Soviet government the dangers of proceeding with an ABM system.

The Americans suggested holding the meeting as soon as they learned that Kosygin would be coming to New York. The venue was discussed for several days because it had some political undertones. President Johnson through Ambassador Thompson invited Kosygin to visit Washington. Kosygin, who was already in New York, immediately sought the Politburo's opinion. The Soviet leadership, especially his rival Brezhnev, reacted in a rather reserved way. While a meeting seemed a possibility, Moscow sent a cable saying that it had to take place "in New York or in any event in its environs, clearly indicating that Johnson would be coming to visit the Soviet prime minister rather than A.N. Kosygin going to the president for a meeting."

Johnson understood Kosygin's reluctance to go to Washington—"considering possible Arab reaction, let alone that of Beijing," as he told Thompson. But the president himself, likewise sensitive to protocol, refused to go to New York to meet Kosygin.

The American side then proposed that the meeting be held at McGuire Air Force Base in New Jersey, about an hour's drive from Manhattan. Kosygin flatly refused a meeting at any military base. After careful consideration, and with the help of the governor of New Jersey, Richard Hughes, they compromised on Glassboro, a small college town sixty miles from New York, as a halfway point.

Glassboro was a typical American town. The college president, Thomas Robinson, a very friendly and agreeable man, was certainly thrilled by the extraordinary event and the enormous attention of the press. I talked with him after the meeting was over. When I suggested that such a great invasion of people could have caused some damage to college buildings or property, he said that the case was just the opposite. He was immensely gratified at the fact that the Soviet-American meeting had taken place at his college. The president confessed that apart from enormous publicity, the government had carried out a complete renovation of the premises at its own expense and installed additional telephone lines. The college itself never would never been able to bear such expenses. In short, he welcomed the guests without reservation.

Kosygin, accompanied by Gromyko and me, arrived from New York at the president's house shortly after 11 A.M. on June 23. We were delayed by heavy traffic. It was a hot and humid summer day. There was a huge crowd of local residents, reporters, and other curious folks waiting for us outside the building. They had been waiting for several hours eager to see the event, with vendors selling hot dogs and cold drinks, a typically American picture our prime minister watched with great interest.

President Johnson welcomed Kosygin on the porch of the president's house. Rusk, McNamara, Bundy, and Walt Rostow arrived with the president. Just before the meeting, they were joined by the president's wife and Kosygin's daughter to pose for pictures. The crowd applauded enthusiastically as Johnson and Kosygin spoke. Pictures were taken again. At last, all participants to the meeting entered the house.

Johnson suggested beginning with a short face-to-face talk with only interpreters present. Kosygin agreed. The rest of us sat in another room, talking, waiting for the end of the conversation between the two leaders, in which they got so absorbed that what was scheduled as only a "short talk" lasted until lunch.

Kosygin started by questioning the direction of American policy, remarking that it was currently directed toward military objectives: considerable growth in military expenditures, broadening military operations in Vietnam, and the aggravation of the military situation in the Middle East.

He warned that the United States had begun an arms race that others must join, and all this could threaten the world with nuclear war.

Johnson disagreed. He said with some emotion the United States did not in the least want to create a situation leading to war, and that whatever his government had done, it had been forced by circumstances to build up defensive and not offensive capability. He added that he attached primary importance to relations with the Soviet Union, had taken concrete steps to develop them peacefully, and was as anxious as ever to prevent a military conflict with the Soviet Union.

Kosygin "took note" of Johnson's assurances. More concrete questions were then discussed during two days of talks. The major issues were Vietnam, the Middle East, and ABM systems, and there was little advance in any of them. Kosygin put special emphasis on the Middle East following the war and the efforts to settle it through the United Nations. Johnson did not try to justify Israel's policy but repeated that the United States favored Israel's withdrawal in exchange for a guarantee of the territorial integrity of all countries in the region.

Vietnam was the focus of Johnson's attention. Both sides rehearsed their positions once again on bombing North Vietnam and the withdrawal of U.S. troops, and then the president bluntly asked whether the Soviet Union could help the United States if negotiations could ever be started with the Vietnamese. He wanted us to stand as something of a third party in a Vietnam settlement so as to enable the United States to withdraw all its forces.

Kosygin made no promises, because he had no authority to do so. He simply said the United States and North Vietnam should negotiate directly. (When he reported to Moscow on this part of the conversation, Kosygin admitted that personally he was not confident that Hanoi would be prepared to negotiate even if the United States stopped bombing North Vietnam.)

On the second day of their meeting Johnson came back with a new proposal dropping his demands for guarantees of North Vietnamese military restraint in the south. He said the United States would stop its air raids if Hanoi would immediately start discussions with the United States.

Kosygin was anything but sure of the attitude of the North Vietnamese leadership, which was playing its own game and seldom let us know its real views on a possible compromise. So he stuck to the Soviet position that the conflict could not possibly be settled unless the United States stopped bombing the North and withdrew its forces from the South. (About a month later, Rusk asked whether we had received any reaction from Hanoi on Johnson's Glassboro proposal to start talks. I said that Hanoi had rejected it because of continued U.S. troop escalation in Vietnam. I was then told by Harriman that while Washington wanted negotiations, it would continue its buildup as long as Hanoi refused to talk.)

Thus both sides seemed locked in a tragic spiral, although I was able to encourage important military limits to it: I raised the issue of atomic warfare in Vietnam, and I was assured privately by Harriman and others in the president's entourage that Johnson had completely ruled out the use of tactical nuclear weapons or an invasion of North Vietnam. Moscow knew about these private assurances although they were never made officially.

During his talk with Kosygin, Johnson also displayed an active interest in the problem of an antiballistic missile system. He said unambiguously that he would prefer to delay its deployment. One way to send that message to the public would be to announce that an exchange of views with Soviet representatives on the subject would take place very soon, say, in a week. He was prepared to send McNamara anywhere we wanted, and McNamara would also be empowered to discuss cutting military budgets as a whole. The president said he had been delaying an ABM decision for the past three months, and an announcement of talks would help him continue to resist the heavy pressure from the military and their allies in Congress.

Kosygin replied by stating the principal Soviet thesis that, ideally, the best way to freeze defensive weapons would be to make cuts in offensive arms or to discuss the whole package of disarmament questions together. In defending his position on the ABM against Johnson, he came close to losing his temper (which was remarkable in itself). In a loud and resolute voice he said, "Defense is moral, aggression is immoral!" Nevertheless he gave Johnson no definite answer on the talks because he needed the approval of other Soviet leaders, and he knew that no final decision had been taken in Moscow.

It was not by chance that Johnson suggested McNamara as his principal representative to start talks. Two days before the Glassboro meeting McNamara told me it would be very helpful to let him speak in private to Johnson and Kosygin alone. He said he would come prepared with the latest American confidential scientific and military data demonstrating the essential futility of ABM systems. I asked Kosygin if he would listen to McNamara's presentation, and he said yes. Throughout the first day of the summit McNamara was nervously kept waiting in the reception hall. But Johnson never called him in. He gave a lunch in honor of Kosygin, inviting all the accompanying officials down to the protocol officers. The president spied McNamara and suddenly remembered his promise, so he suggested that his report be made right there. McNamara was not prepared for that, because many of those present did not have security clearance for the confidential information in his briefing. But more to the point, he had suggested a secret briefing of the two leaders so that his position would not become known in public. That surely would have opened him to criticism by those who were pressing the government to go ahead with the ABM system.

Confused, McNamara feverishly began to sort out his papers, trying to select the least secret charts and diagrams from his folder. His main thesis was that a defensive arms race would only speed up the development of offensive weapons to break through the more complex defenses, thus destabilizing the fragile nuclear deterrent balance between the two superpowers. But because of his last-minute reorganization, his report proved disjointed, unconvincing, and uninteresting, and in fact Kosygin told me that night he was disappointed by it. At dinner he commented on the report by pointing out that Soviet missile defense systems around Moscow and Tallinn were designed to save the lives of Soviet citizens and that instead of negotiating them away, we first ought to agree on reducing the offensive missiles in the strategic systems.

Although Johnson tried to undo his clumsy handling of the matter by proposing the McNamara talks the next day, Kosygin was not prepared to start ABM negotiations; Moscow at that time sought first of all to achieve nuclear parity in strategic offensive weapons.

In mid-September the American government announced its intention to deploy a partial ABM system. Rusk gave me three reasons: first, a limited system was designed to neutralize the Chinese threat but was of minor importance in our two countries' mutual deterrence; second, Congress and the Republicans were accusing Johnson of "inactivity"; and third, there had been no Soviet reaction to the American proposal for talks on the issue.

Thus the Soviet government did not recognize a historic opportunity and responded by continuing ABM construction around Moscow and Tallinn. It took some years for negotiations to start under the next administration, and they proved difficult. I am convinced that there was a possibility for us to have reached a comprehensive agreement with Johnson on the ABM, especially before he announced his decision not to run for another term. We could have avoided a controversy that clouded Soviet-American relations in this area for many years to come. Nevertheless the Glassboro discussion was the first to help start talks on strategic arms limitation, and these ultimately led to the conclusion of the treaty on the limitation of antiballistic missile systems in 1972. It also led to a 1968 UN resolution, cosponsored by the Soviet Union and the United States, which in its turn resulted in the Non-proliferation Treaty signed by the two superpowers and sixty other countries on July 1.

On the whole, the meeting in Glassboro was held in a favorable atmosphere. Johnson was a good host, expounded his views in detail and with ample argumentation, and when it was all over said he wanted to hold a

Soviet-American summit like this at least once a year. Kosygin spoke less, but in a clear and definite manner. He reported to the Politburo that "Johnson and his associates treated us in a friendly manner, paid us much attention, and tried to show their eagerness to find solutions to crucial problems."

The fact that the Glassboro meeting seemed to yield no concrete results can also be explained by its sudden genesis; having been arranged with so little preparation, it could hardly be expected to make significant advances. But the more fundamental reason was that there was no real potential for a breakthrough in any important direction, and Kosygin, a reluctant participant, lacked a mandate from the Politburo to conduct productive negotiations on major issues, especially on the ABM, where results were sought by Johnson and McNamara. Kosygin focused on having the United States put pressure on Israel to withdraw its conquests in the Six-Day War and on the United States to withdraw from Vietnam. Glassboro was also the only summit in which the general secretary of the Central Committee of the Communist Party did not participate, and Brezhnev was not all that eager to promote Kosygin's success. But the meeting did produce a more balanced approach to Johnson by the Politburo. Unfortunately, there were no more summits during his presidency.

# V. The Fall of Lyndon Johnson

*Vietnam Becomes "Johnson's War"*

As 1968 began, the war was the talk of Washington, and it was a major topic in every conceivable official meeting, diplomatic interview, and social occasion. The Kennedy holdovers were jumping ship. Robert McNamara, who looked depressed, had told me late in 1967 that he planned to resign and become president of the World Bank. He said that he was very tired and no longer willing to argue with his top generals who insisted on military solutions, when there were none. More and more presidential aides sought to dissociate themselves from the administration's disastrous course in Vietnam. The president alone was blamed for the gamble in Vietnam and the failure of American foreign policy, although he had never lacked support when he set it in motion.

Robert Kennedy, who originally had abjured a personal political challenge to a sitting president of his own party, told me he was having "agonizing thoughts" over whether to run against Johnson for president. He ran for the Senate from New York in 1966 and won, but on March 16, 1968, four days after Senator Eugene McCarthy humiliated the president politically by winning 42 percent of the vote in the New Hampshire Democratic presidential primary on an antiwar platform, Kennedy announced he was seeking the presidency, only to be assassinated three months later while campaigning in California. That made Vice President Hubert H. Humphrey the favorite for the nomination.

The foundations of intervention in Vietnam had in fact been laid long before, during the three previous administrations of Truman, Eisenhower, and Kennedy, although they probably had no idea of the eventual outcome of their political, military, and psychological moves in the region to "save it from communism." Johnson continued and developed the same course without heed to its consequences. At the start both major American political parties approved the policy of military escalation, although by 1968 many liberal Democrats had turned against it, and against Johnson himself. The Republicans, including Richard Nixon, who was to follow Johnson in the White House, and Gerald Ford, then the Republican minority leader in the House of Representatives, who was to follow Nixon, stood solidly behind escalation of the bombing, although they began to distance themselves from the painful consequences of American troop losses by proposing to limit the involvement of U.S. land forces in a policy that became known as "Vietnamization." For Johnson, the result of all this was personal and national tragedy: the Vietnam War became Johnson's war.

It was around that time that Harriman told me indignantly, "It is hard to believe, but after several years of war Johnson has no definite plan for getting out of it." Harriman added that Johnson also had no strategy for improving relations with the Soviet Union, and only three men close to the president knew something about Soviet-American affairs: Thompson, Harriman himself, and Ambassador Charles (Chip) Bohlen, who returned from abroad early in 1968 to become deputy undersecretary for political affairs.

Fulbright told me that some of Johnson's political advisers were trying to persuade him to seek a formal declaration of war against North Vietnam, and Fulbright was trying to talk Johnson out of it because it would have had difficulty passing Congress anyway. These advisers argued that a declaration would make it possible to turn the war into a patriotic matter and, consequently, help him win the presidential election. Johnson was undecided and kept asking his old friends for their advice. Fulbright called the plan adventurism. And he prevailed.

On January 5, I had a private meeting with Rusk for a general review. For the first time, he made a formal proposal for the two opposing alliances in Europe to reduce their troop strength, with the United States to reduce its troops in Western Europe considerably—he repeated the word twice—if the Soviet Union would do the same in Eastern Europe. Moreover, the United States would undertake not to send the troops withdrawn from Europe to Vietnam, so China would not be in a position to criticize the Soviet Union for the agreement. It was an important proposal. I immediately informed the Soviet leadership, which had proposed similar reductions in Germany during the Kennedy administration. But this time there was no response. As I was later informed, the Soviet government was not sure it could maintain stability in Eastern Europe with far fewer Soviet troops, and it suspected Rusk's proposal was made specifically with this in mind.

Our next meeting was in February. In response to our recent protests over several incidents of bombing Soviet vessels in the port of Haiphong, Rusk assured me they had been accidents. Once again he sought to use us as a middleman to obtain "at least a rough idea" of Hanoi's intentions; this might make it possible to stop the bombing entirely, which the president could not do "blindfolded." He recalled the Pueblo incident, when the North Koreans seized an American ship off their coast, and we helped to arrange for the release of the crew, which was no easy matter. He also mentioned Tashkent, where the Soviet Union acted as a mediator between India and Pakistan. Rusk concluded bluntly: "Why shouldn't Moscow arrange for another Tashkent, this time to settle the Vietnam conflict?"

How could I possibly tell him that the Vietnamese would not accept our mediation or anybody else's? So I just repeated our cliché that it was the business of the United States and the DRV to negotiate the matter between themselves. Moscow did not react to the conversation in any way. It had nothing new to say.

Moscow in fact had heard little about any possible divergence within the North Vietnamese leadership over its strategy for waging the war or ending it. On the face of it, they looked unanimous. But the Polish ambassador, Jerszy Mikhalovsky, told me a different story. Before his appointment to Washington, he had served on the International Commission for Vietnam and Laos, which was created under the Geneva agreements. Mikhalovsky still visited Hanoi often, and in February of 1968 he was sent with instructions from his government to obtain firsthand information from the many friends he had made there. Prime Minister Pham Van Dong made it clear to him in private conversation that because of the increasing hardships of the war, he was inclined to consider proclaiming South Vietnam a neutral state "like Cambodia," although so far that was just his "inner belief" and not a decision of the whole leadership. Other leaders with whom Mikhalovsky talked were still sticking to the view that the United States had to get out of South Vietnam, and that was the line the North Vietnamese reiterated in Moscow, urging us to support it in our contacts with the United States.

## The Resignation Gambit Fails

It was against this increasingly troubled background that I was summoned unexpectedly to a meeting with the president at the White House on March 31 at the rather unusual hour of 6 P.M. I was shown to the president's living quarters on the second floor, which was even more unusual. Mrs. Johnson offered me a cup of tea and said the president would be back shortly. Soon the president came in. He looked tired and nervous.

There were just two of us in the room. The president informed me that later in the evening he would address the nation on television about Vietnam. But before doing so, he wanted to give the Soviet government additional information about his personal intentions and the steps already being taken to limit bloodshed in Vietnam. He hoped they would start the peace process. In appealing to us, he proceeded, first of all, from the major role played by the Soviet Union in international affairs and, secondly, from its position as a cochairman of the Geneva accords. "We count on the USSR's good influence on this issue," he said.

The president then informed me that he was taking the first step to de-escalate the conflict by unilaterally and substantially reducing its military operations, including air and naval operations. The area to be free from bombing would spare 90 percent of the population of North Vietnam and most of its territory. Even the remaining bombing, which would proceed on a heavily reduced scale, could be canceled altogether within a very short time if Hanoi showed some restraint in response to Washington's restraint.

"I call upon the cochairmen of the Geneva Conference to do all they can to proceed from my unilateral action to genuine peace. I am prepared to send my representatives to any meeting. I appoint Harriman as my personal representative for such talks or discussions. I hope Ho Chi Minh will react positively," Johnson said. He was convinced that the Soviet government had an outstanding part to play in the settlement of the conflict, and the mediation it had conducted in Tashkent between India and Pakistan demonstrated its potential influence.

He said he had no intention of imposing a military solution on Vietnam, and furthermore he was aware of the enormous importance of the Soviet Union in averting a major military conflict on a global scale. Hence even in the present difficult times of Vietnam, which had alienated the two superpowers, he worked to maintain an adequate minimum of normal relations with the Soviet Union. "I will go on holding to that line in U.S.-Soviet relations," he said, "I hope the Soviet leadership holds the same view."

In conclusion, Johnson stressed that the Soviet Union had a special responsibility and a special role in Vietnam. "Our opponent wouldn't have lasted long if it were not for your support, which keeps him afloat. But we appreciate your position of principle. We are not going to raise this question now, one way or another, although we are not indifferent to it, not by a long shot. We, the United States, may have made and apparently have made certain mistakes in Vietnam. But we really are ready now for serious talks in order to find a way to settle the conflict peacefully. Please communicate that to Moscow. I earnestly hope the Soviet government will carefully consider my suggestions without delay."

This of course was an obvious appeal to the Soviet government to help end the military conflict in Vietnam, yet essentially on the president's conditions. I expressed regret that the measures he had mentioned did not include complete cessation of bombing raids. Johnson quickly and nervously said he could not leave U.S. garrisons and strongholds in South Vietnam, especially near the demilitarized zone, to the mercy of some five North Vietnamese divisions operating there. The destruction of the U.S. troops by those divisions would create so violent a reaction in the United States that it could become difficult to maintain restraint and not use the whole military might of the United States in Vietnam. The president said he did not want events to develop that way, so he had to keep the bombing just north of the demilitarized zone, although it would be at a minimum and for purely military purposes. "I have no alternative," he said wearily.

As we parted, he handed me the text of his television address. I was still unaware of how fateful an event it would be for the president and the country, and I then went over to the White House West Wing and called on Walt Rostow to discuss some routine business. We spent about an hour together.

As I left his room and walked along the passage, I ran into the president. The president stopped me. After a moment of hesitation, he said he wanted to tell me in strict confidence that at the end of his television address he intended to announce that he would not run for another term as president. He expressed the hope that this hard decision he had made to withdraw would help pacify the fierce controversy over Vietnam during the election campaign and help settle the entire Vietnam conflict.

"I want to show them that I have no obsessive lust for power, as many believe. I want to spend the rest of my time serving the country, not the party," Johnson said.

The president added that I was the first foreigner to learn about his decision, and so far only four or five Americans knew about it, including his wife. Johnson spoke with difficulty and could hardly hide his emotion. He did not look well. It was clear that he had thought long and hard before taking the decision. He could not but realize that as he was doing this almost a year before the end of his presidential term, his further ability to influence the events in the country and abroad would be considerably diminished during the remainder of his term in office. It looked like a desperate move, a last-ditch attempt to prove to those who accused him of relentlessly pursuing the war merely to save his own face and ensure his reelection that he was ready to sacrifice his second term in the nation's highest office to calm the public, and from that position try to conclude an honorable settlement in Vietnam.

Victory for Johnson in the next presidential election had in any case become ever more doubtful. In the final analysis, the Vietnam War proved a trap. By announcing his refusal to be a presidential candidate, Johnson in fact tried to relieve his own nervous strain, which seemed to become unbearable. He looked at last like a man who was free from the heavy burden of making a hard and important, yet painful decision.

Johnson made his dramatic renunciation at 9 P.M. speaking on national television from his White House study in the presence of his family members, who stood off screen. The first part of his speech offered no surprises for the nationwide audience of seventy-five million. Only a handful of people in the White House and I, who witnessed his personal drama, were waiting with great suspense for the conclusive part of his statement. He stopped for a moment, as if trying to summon up his will, and slowly but firmly told the American public that he would neither seek reelection nor accept his party's nomination for presidency for another term.

It was a sensation. Vietnam had proven fatal for Johnson the president. He could not convincingly justify his foreign policy. Moreover, speaking the next day to a meeting of the National Association of Broadcasters in Chicago, he nervously blamed its members for all American failures in Vietnam. The president declared that they had set the whole nation against him. Needless to say, this brought him no laurels.

Personally, I was surprised at the president's decision. Moscow did not expect anything like that either, as the decision rendered the prospective summit with Johnson almost valueless. On the other hand, it only consolidated the determination of the North Vietnamese leadership to fight to the end while still hoping that the United States would become more flexible if negotiations actually began. American business circles saw Johnson's statement as a declaration of bankruptcy, an admission of the failure of his foreign policy, especially in Vietnam. Stock and commodities markets boomed. Johnson even regained some of his former popularity for a time, even though the antiwar movement remained very strong.

The following day I was invited to a dinner at the Harrimans. We had a lively conversation which, quite naturally, centered on the president's surprise decision. Harriman argued that it was not a political stratagem, but a carefully considered and final decision, however painful it was. He had learned earlier that day that only the president's wife Lady Bird, Vice President Hubert Humphrey, Rusk, and the new secretary of defense Clark Clifford had been informed in advance. Even Rostow and Harriman had not known. Harriman lamented that Johnson would have made a great president but for his obsession with the Vietnam War.

Harriman was sure that Johnson's decision not to seek reelection would induce Humphrey to join the race. Not that he had much chance to be elected. He did not command broad support in the country and the party. Having supported Johnson on Vietnam "not just 100 percent, but 130 percent" ("That's his exaggerated idea of loyalty to the president," Harriman said), Humphrey had lost his backing among the party's liberal wing. At the same time he failed to win over the party's influential conservatives. Harriman doubted that Johnson would really fight for Humphrey, although he was likely to say some kind words in support of his vice president for the sake of appearances. Earlier in the day, Johnson himself had told Harriman that he would not involve himself in the struggle within the party, or in the election campaign, for that matter. The one positive factor Harriman descried out of all this was that regardless of who was elected in November, he was certain of the forced resignations of the "stubborn Rusk" and of Rostow, whom he described as "the American Rasputin."

A few days later Harriman informed me that Hanoi had agreed to start negotiations with the United States; he was to lead the American side, assisted by Cyrus Vance. Evidently, the North Vietnamese had decided to sound out the administration to determine the effect of Johnson's decision not to run for the presidency. But the negotiations in Paris were stuck from the start because neither side had changed its position.

When Moscow inquired about the situation, Hanoi replied that it was impossible to conduct talks successfully while the Americans were bombing Vietnam, but that its position could become more flexible if the bombing stopped. That misled Moscow once again, although the Soviet leaders knew perfectly well that there was no point in trying to mediate between Hanoi and Washington, a very ungrateful role indeed.

On July 5 I was instructed to pass a message from Kosygin to Johnson which said, "My colleagues and I believe, and our belief is well-grounded, that a complete cessation of bombing and other military actions by the United States could reverse the situation completely and open up new prospects for a peaceful settlement . . . at the Paris negotiations, where no progress has been achieved so far."

The message was the subject of a vigorous White House discussion in drafting Johnson's reply, the essence of which finally was that the U.S. government deemed it impossible to stop the bombing completely. Harriman told me that Clifford, Vance, and Harriman himself had insisted on a positive reply to Kosygin's message, with Rusk, Rostow, and Bundy dead against it. This response deflated any enthusiasm that might have remained in Moscow over serving as a mediator. The Paris talks made no progress.

## Humphrey Declines Moscow's Secret Offer to Help His Election

During a diplomatic reception in the White House on April 23 Hubert Humphrey told me privately that he was inclined to try his luck at the presidential election and was going to announce his candidacy soon. Humphrey said he had always considered U.S.-Soviet relations as a major factor influencing the prospects for war and peace and that he had always tried to improve them. He asked me to inform Moscow about it, adding his personal greetings to Brezhnev and Kosygin. Some days later the Soviet leadership instructed me to wish him success in his election campaign. Moscow believed that as far as its relations with Washington were concerned, Humphrey would make the best president at that time.

During our conversation Humphrey readily shared his amusing recollections of a trip to the Soviet Union that had turned into a hunting expedition. In Moscow he had mentioned to our defense minister, Marshal Andrei Grechko, that he was fond of hunting. Grechko, himself an eager hunter, suggested at once that they hunt wild boar together. Humphrey agreed. As Humphrey told me the story, when they arrived at the hunting lodge, Grechko treated him to a dinner. The marshal proposed toasts to President Johnson, to General Secretary Brezhnev, to both their ladies, to better Soviet-American relations, to the health of their ministers, to the health of their wives, to a successful hunt, and so on, with Grechko each time insisting that Humphrey drain his glass. In short, they prepared themselves thoroughly for the hunt.

The last Humphrey could remember was Grechko's entourage of generals carefully carrying him on their outstretched hands to the bedroom "to rest a bit before the hunt." When Humphrey awoke next morning they solemnly handed him a trophy, the head of the wild boar allegedly killed by Grechko and him. The trophy was then delivered to Humphrey's plane.

In his presidential campaign, Humphrey sought the support of the Kennedys. Ted Sorensen told me they would agree only on condition that he speak out against bombing North Vietnam and in favor of a coalition government in South Vietnam including the National Liberation Front. Humphrey replied that while he sympathized with the policy he could not possibly speak out publicly in favor of it while he was a member of the government, and furthermore such a shift in position would go down badly at the Democratic Party's nominating convention. Summing it all up, Sorensen said, Humphrey was in a rather miserable situation.

The paradox of all this was that North Vietnam probably could have guaranteed Humphrey's victory and made him a president if only it had helped to show some progress at the Paris talks. The situation was in many respects similar to that of Jimmy Carter, whose reelection depended largely on Iran's attitude toward the American hostages it held throughout his campaign for reelection.

After his nomination at a tumultuous Democratic convention, which painfully illustrated the wounds in American society that had been opened up by the war, Humphrey told me in August that Johnson was giving him no appreciable support; the president, adhering to his promise of neutrality, was sitting out the campaign. But Johnson's public statements about the war also did not allow Humphrey to take a more flexible stand on Vietnam. "I don't even know who Johnson would prefer as the next president, Nixon or me!"

Humphrey remarked sarcastically. Having been in the administration for four years, he was under no illusions that his connection with it, and Vietnam especially, would prove a dead weight on him throughout the campaign.

To Moscow, Humphrey certainly was preferable to Richard Nixon, who had founded and built his career on opposing communism and was considered profoundly anti-Soviet. Our leadership was growing seriously concerned that he might win the election. As a result the top Soviet leaders took an extraordinary step, unprecedented in the history of Soviet-American relations, by secretly offering Humphrey any conceivable help in his election campaign—including financial aid.

I received a top-secret instruction to that effect from Gromyko personally and did my utmost to dissuade him from embarking on such a dangerous venture, which if discovered certainly would have backfired and ensured Humphrey's defeat, to say nothing of the real trouble it would have caused for Soviet-American relations. Gromyko answered laconically, "There is a decision, you carry it out."

Shortly afterward, I happened to be at breakfast at Humphrey's home. Naturally, we talked about the election campaign, so I tried to take advantage of that to carry out my instructions as tactfully as possible. I asked him how his campaign was going, and then I moved the conversation diplomatically to the state of his campaign finances. Humphrey, I must say, was not only a very intelligent but also a very clever man. He knew at once what was going on. He told me it was more than enough for him to have Moscow's good wishes, which he highly appreciated. The matter was thus settled to our mutual relief, never to be discussed again.

This story has never been told before. The Politburo always watched American presidential elections closely for their potential effect on Soviet-American relations and usually had a preference but rarely expressed it or took sides by offering diplomatic or other help. To my knowledge this was the only time Moscow tried to intervene directly to help a favored candidate—and it got nowhere.

Ambassadors of course were expected to provide timely advice about which way an election might go. Although I tried to give reliable guidance, I thought it unwise to make firm predictions. A colleague of mine in London once did so in advising Moscow it would be safe to receive Prime Minister Harold Wilson for a preelection visit less than a month before he was turned out of office in a defeat widely regarded as an upset. For this imprudent piece of advice, the ambassador was relieved of his post.

## *Johnson Seeks a Summit to the Bitter End: It Dies in Prague*

After Johnson renounced another term in the White House he began a curious campaign for another summit meeting with Kosygin. On July 2, the day
after signing the nonproliferation treaty, Rusk asked me to inform Kosygin
of the president's interest in a meeting, not necessarily in the Soviet Union.

The problem for Moscow was that it did not believe it could achieve
any meaningful agreements with the outgoing president even though one of
Johnson's principal reasons for trying to place himself above politics was his
mistaken hope that he would thus be seen as a more valuable interlocutor.
Besides, not only was our leadership uncertain about the possibility of any
decisions on major questions, but Brezhnev did not want to give Kosygin
any additional exposure in world affairs. Johnson had conducted all his correspondence with Kosygin and not Brezhnev, which hardly made Brezhnev
receptive to Johnson's request for a meeting with his rival.

For all these reasons, Moscow tried to delay its answer but did not
want to decline the proposal directly. The situation remained undecided,
ambiguous, and rather embarrassing for me. Rusk repeatedly asked me if
a reply from Kosygin had arrived, and I repeatedly had to tell him it had
not.

To complicate matters even more, after the Republican convention in
July, Nixon sent an informal request to be received in Moscow, to which the
government consented. I was instructed to inform Johnson and Humphrey,
and I decided to ask Rusk to break the news. Rusk observed rather gloomily
that if Moscow was ready to receive Nixon, who he pointed out was "not yet
the president," it might yet agree to meet the man who was still president of
the United States. He added that he was joking but Johnson was really serious. The president was willing to travel to Geneva or even Leningrad, and
Rusk asked me to telephone him directly and in person "at any time at the
office or at home" with Moscow's reply to the president's proposal for a
meeting. Ten days later Rusk again asked if I had received a reply to "the
rather important and confidential message" of the president and then expressed his dissatisfaction over the absence of any reply during the past fortnight, when he had expected to receive one "at least out of courtesy," in the
course of two weeks.

Again I had nothing to report. I filled in Moscow about my conversation with Rusk, pointing out that it was necessary to reply somehow, because
it affected Johnson's personal relations with Moscow and he was going to be
in power for at least six more months.

When I handed Rusk a message from Kosygin on July 25 proposing
that nuclear arms talks could start within a month or six weeks, Rusk asked

again, "Well, what about the main question? Is there anything I can tell President Johnson?"

I replied I still had received no instructions from Moscow on a meeting with Johnson, which clearly annoyed Rusk. The secretary of state told me that during a recent meeting between Nixon and Johnson the Republican candidate had informed Johnson "in strict confidence" about his intention to visit Moscow, and Johnson had replied that he thought it was a good idea. Rusk added sarcastically that Johnson at least had the satisfaction of having previously learned about Nixon's trip to Moscow from us rather than having it sprung on him by Nixon himself.

Meanwhile I learned unofficially from the State Department that Johnson would like to head the U.S. delegation at the first stage of the bilateral strategic arms limitation talks. Although Johnson was clearly anxious to boost his international prestige, the State Department was cool about his personal participation in these technical talks.

On August 15 Rusk reminded me again that the president was still waiting for a reply to his confidential request for a summit meeting, and I sent yet another urgent telegram to Moscow seeking an answer. This time I ventured to the Politburo a personal observation that our silence was becoming embarrassing and was going beyond the standards of normal diplomatic relations.

Two days later a positive reply at last arrived inviting Johnson to Moscow. Rusk was pleased and then gave me his personal view on Nixon and his policies. He predicted that Nixon would carefully steer clear of any confrontation with the Soviet Union, although at the start he was very unlikely to take any initiative to improve relations. Nixon supported the buildup of the U.S. armed forces but, judging by what he had told Johnson during a visit to his Texas ranch, he would if elected continue the strategic nuclear arms talks with the Soviet Union. This was not a "new Nixon," as he was being widely characterized, Rusk said, because he was a born conservative by conviction. But he was beginning to realize the need for a new approach to world problems as the world changed. Just how profoundly Nixon could recognize those changes and adjust to them was a different matter and remained to be seen, Rusk said. Actually, Nixon and his chief foreign policy adviser and operative, Henry Kissinger, adapted to the changes better than Rusk and Johnson.

## The Invasion of Czechoslovakia

All these geopolitical insights and careful political calculations were to be upset by the invasion of Czechoslovakia. By 1967, with sentiment mounting against Stalinist rule in culture, politics, the economy, and much else, a group of reformers in Prague led by Alexander Duček tried to introduce their version of "socialism with a human face." Unfortunately, this "Prague spring" happened to coincide with a time when conservatives were consolidating their control over domestic policy in the Soviet Union.

By 1968, the reforms in Czechoslovakia led to major disagreements with other Warsaw Treaty members. But the idea of putting down the reformist regime in Prague through military action was by no means unanimously supported in the Kremlin. Brezhnev, who did not have a resolute character, was still unsure about it even as the troops were poised to strike. Kosygin also voiced his doubts, but most of the other members of the Politburo and the Central Committee Secretariat held to a tougher line against the Prague reformers. Pyotr Shelest, Dmitri Polyansky, Kyril Mazurov, Andrei Kyrilenko, and Arvid Pelshe, all of the Politburo; Central Committee secretaries Dmitri Ustinov, Konstantin Katushev, and Pyotr Demichev; and finally, almost all the marshals who were members of the Central Committee, spoke out in favor of an invasion. Aleksander Yakovlev, who later came to be one of Gorbachev's most trusted associates, then headed the Propaganda Department of the Central Committee, which provided rhetorical and ideological support for the whole Soviet operation that crushed the reformers. As ambassador to Washington, I was not informed in advance about our plans, but for me it was clear that the invasion would certainly destroy the summit with the United States and spoil our relations with the West in general.

The Warsaw Treaty invasion began at 11:00 P.M. on August 20, which was a Sunday. Early that morning I was surprised by an urgent instruction from Moscow to arrange a meeting with President Johnson to explain the reasons for our actions. (I was sent the text of our formal "explanation.") The situation was complicated by the fact that the invasion took place on a weekend, making it much more difficult to arrange a meeting with the president at such short notice on the same day. Besides, my instructions were to schedule my meeting with the president precisely between 6 and 8 P.M. Washington time, or just when the tanks would be rolling into Prague.

I considered the matter and decided not to make a formal request for a meeting through the usual channels, which especially on a Sunday could result in a delay, but to turn directly to the president himself. I remembered that a few years back during an encounter with Walt Rostow the president himself had given me his personal phone number "just in case," but I had never used it before. This matter was certainly urgent enough to call him directly. Without asking about the subject, Johnson immediately agreed to meet, suggesting that I come by noon. As I had to keep to a strict schedule laid down by Moscow, I asked him to receive me after 6 P.M. on the pretext that I had to translate the message I would be delivering. He agreed.

I arrived at the White House at 8 P.M. Johnson received me in the cabinet room. We sat at a long polished table, with his national security adviser, Walt Rostow, sitting in silently. The president began by recalling the Glassboro meeting. He had just been watching a documentary film about it and had been pleased to note the friendly welcome given by local population to the participants.

Then I read out the message from Moscow saying that there had been "a conspiracy of internal and external reaction against the social system" in Czechoslovakia, and the Soviet Union and its Warsaw Pact allies had replied to a request by the Prague government for help. "Accordingly," the message continued, "Soviet military units have been ordered to cross into Czechoslovakia. Needless to say, they will be immediately withdrawn from Czechoslovak territory once the existing threat to security is removed." The message concluded by saying that Moscow assumed there would be no damage to Soviet-American relations, "to which the Soviet government attaches great importance."

President Johnson listened carefully, but apparently he did not immediately appreciate the significance of the news. Much to my surprise he did not react to it at all, just thanked me for the information and said that he would probably discuss the statement with Rusk and others the next morning and give us a reply, if need be.

He proceeded to another subject, on which he seemed to be much more keen. He said he was awaiting our response to his plans to announce his visit to the Soviet Union. The announcement was scheduled for 10 o'clock the following morning. (Moscow had agreed in principle to his visit a couple of days before, but now, of course, there was slight hope that the visit would take place.)

The president added that he had already invited some of his friends to breakfast at the White House in order to break the news about his trip and then make a major announcement about it to the press. Still utterly oblivious of the impact of what was happening in Prague, Johnson asked us to give him a reply about his visit to Moscow in time for the next morning's meetings, or not later than between 8 and 9 A.M.

He looked cheerful and said he attached great importance to his forthcoming meeting with the Soviet leaders; he hoped to discuss a number of major topics, including Vietnam and the Middle East. Johnson pointed out that this time he "had more freedom of action," and that he expected the meeting to produce certain results.

Johnson then reverted to his meeting with Kosygin in Glassboro, going over the details in his memory and evaluating the whole thing positively. He offered me a whiskey (I would have agreed to drink anything at that moment!) and began to tell me various entertaining stories about Texas. He was good at it.

While the president was going on about his forthcoming trip, the Glassboro summit, and other things that pleased him, Rostow, the only witness to the conversation, sat with lowering face, trying not to interrupt the president. As we parted, Johnson was very friendly and once again reminded me that he was looking forward to our response so he could announce his visit to the Soviet Union.

I returned to the embassy and urgently reported the conversation to Moscow. I recommended strongly that we accept his proposal for an announcement of his visit to the Soviet Union because, as I explained, I was certain that Rusk and Rostow would now undoubtedly do everything they could to make the president reconsider the trip. The Politburo had hardly expected Johnson to react so placidly to the events in Prague and immediately issued the invitation he so earnestly sought. I received my reply in a matter of hours. But events marched faster still.

Rusk invited me to come to the State Department late that very night. He told me he was just back from a meeting in the White House and the president had asked him to pass on a message expressing ignorance of any involvement by non-communist countries or any public request for help from Prague. "And, finally," the message said, "we feel we should carefully reconsider the possibility of announcing a meeting between our leaders. We will keep in touch with you about this."

Rusk read out the statement from notes. He did not, however, show any change in the attitude of the American side toward the proposed meeting. On the whole, Rusk was composed and calm, yet it was clear enough that his attitude toward our action in Czechoslovakia represented anything but approval, and that he would spare no effort to make President Johnson disapprove of it just as strongly as he did. But the most remarkable thing about the statement and indeed the developments in Washington throughout the evening was that Johnson, in spite of everything, was still hoping for a meeting in Moscow!

Three days later I visited Rusk again at the State Department, where he remarked that in his previous discussions with the president he said he "could have bet that the Soviet Union would not invade Czechoslovakia." So he asked me to tell him privately what were the real reasons for going ahead. And then he added rather unexpectedly, "Will Romania be next? That would be too much, and we would hardly expect to be able to control public opinion." It was already tough enough for him because of Czechoslovakia: Johnson had met with about twenty congressional leaders earlier in the day and had "a hard time" there with sharp criticism of his mild reaction to the invasion.

After the events in Czechoslovakia, Rusk stressed, the United States was not certain about the prospects for our relations, and this greatly concerned the president. Johnson also had to take into account the present public mood, which was unlikely to understand or accept presidential initiatives now in East-West relations. So for the present there was nothing the president and the American government could do but to sit back and hope things would get better, and that left little time for accomplishment in the remaining months of the Johnson administration. I felt the conversation with Rusk demonstrated a certain measure of confusion in the administration over Czechoslovakia, and this was confirmed by what I learned over the next few days.

Five days after the invasion the columnist Drew Pearson told me about the president's private meeting with the leaders of Congress, where the legislative and executive tried to work out an appropriate reaction to the Soviet invasion in Czechoslovakia. Angered at congressional criticism for not opposing the invasion more vigorously, Johnson exclaimed, "Are you suggesting we send American troops there?" Military retaliation was "out of the question," and the president told the congressional leadership that little was possible beyond a propaganda campaign. The angry meeting brought no results.

Then Thompson told me about another presidential meeting, this one with the Joint Chiefs of Staff. It was agreed that the United States would not use force against the invasion. Furthermore, the president ordered, there would be no further public condemnation beyond the critical statements already made by Johnson and Rusk. Johnson even remarked half-jokingly to the military brass that "hopefully, Moscow will appreciate that we are not bully-boys here in the United States."

But nervousness persisted. On August 28 Rusk summoned me urgently to say he had learned of an unusually active movement of Soviet troops along the Romanian borders within twenty-four hours. There had already been speculation in the West about the possibility of a Soviet invasion of Romania, based largely on its refusal to take part in the joint action with other Warsaw Treaty states against Czechoslovakia. Indeed, Moscow was highly irritated with Romania's leader Nicolae Ceausescu, and Soviet troops engaged in demonstrative tactical movements near the Romanian border. But Moscow was not really thinking of invading Romania, because it never doubted the stability of the communist regime there.

Nevertheless the troop movements were fully tracked by Western intelligence and news of them quickly reached President Johnson. He was down at his ranch in Texas and called Rusk with some urgency. Rusk had a message for the Soviet government ready when I arrived. It proved quite emotional. "On behalf of mankind," he said, "we ask you not to invade Romania, because the consequences would be unpredictable. We also hope that no actions will be taken against West Berlin, which could cause a major international crisis, which we are anxious to avoid at any cost. All this would be disastrous for Soviet-American relations and for the whole world."

I urgently recommended that Moscow reply without delay to calm the situation, and soon I was back at the State Department with a reply.

"I am instructed to inform you," I said to Rusk, "that the reports about a forthcoming movement of Soviet forces into Romania are specially designed by certain circles to mislead the American government and do not correspond to reality. The same fully applies to West Berlin."

Rusk received the message with evident relief.

The Czechoslovak crisis gradually lost its intensity, but the invasion cost us dearly both politically and morally. The mood of the Czechoslovak public turned abruptly against us. A wave of protest swept the world. Even in the Soviet Union itself dissidents emerged in public for the first time to demonstrate their opposition to the government. Speculation also appeared in the Western press and among some Western officials about what they called "the Brezhnev doctrine." No such policy had ever been proclaimed or in fact even mentioned at Politburo meetings in Moscow, but the determination never to permit a socialist country to slip back into the orbit of the West was in essence a true reflection of the sentiments of those who ran the Soviet Union.

The Soviet government did not normally draw up a specific foreign policy doctrine, but the elements of policy would be considered rather closely when preparing for a Communist Party Congress or a Plenum of the party's Central Committee. Discussions would be held in the Politburo about the draft of the summary report to be delivered by the general secretary of the party and the draft resolution to be presented to the meeting, which always included a section on foreign policy. After their approval by the congress or the Plenum, these documents in effect constituted the "general line" or the doctrine of the Soviet Communist Party and automatically became the guidelines for the government.

However, the need would arise time and again to analyze the world situation at crucial moments between the party congresses, which were held only at five-year intervals. At such moments—and the aftermath of invasion of Czechoslovakia was one of them—the Foreign Ministry usually prepared a special confidential document to be discussed at the Politburo. Once approved, it served as foreign policy guidelines for the immediate future.

On September 16, 1968, Foreign Minister Gromyko presented the Politburo with a document entitled "An Assessment of the Course of Foreign Policy and the State of Soviet-American Relations," which in effect gave in detail the essence of the foreign policy doctrine of the Soviet Union. It was approved by the Politburo and determined the course of Soviet foreign policy and the scope of Soviet-American relations in the years to come. The document expressed such new ideas as the prospective creation of a confederation of socialist countries in Europe to match Western economic and security institutions such as the European Economic Community and NATO, and this goal was proclaimed here in a clear-cut manner for the first time by the Soviet leadership, although it was done behind closed doors, so to speak. It called for a combination of "firmness with flexibility" in dealing with the United States and said that the U.S. leadership is using the events in Czechoslovakia "to damage the international prestige of our country. . . . On the other hand, the determination with which the Soviet Union acted in relation to the Czechoslovak events made the leaders of the United States consider more soberly their potential in the region and see once again the determination of our country's leadership in defending the vital interests of the Soviet Union."

It is thus clear how the Soviet leadership judged the relatively weak Western reaction to the invasion of Czechoslovakia; it proved to Moscow that Western governments were not prepared to commit themselves militarily on the territory of the Warsaw Treaty powers. This weighed in the balance in the Kremlin when it decided on a new invasion, in Afghanistan, slightly more than a decade later.

The negative effect of these events on our foreign affairs was less strong than its domestic implications. One reason probably was that the Vietnam War was in full swing. Among the Western public, moral criteria were diminished in politics, in part because the American president was himself prevented by the Vietnam War from laying moral principles on the scales in judging the motives and actions of other nations.

## Johnson Presses for a Summit to the Bitter End

Certainly such and other considerations were left aside when the administration pressed its case for Johnson to visit Moscow, a project that our leadership had thought would be abandoned after the invasion. Yet, much to my surprise, Rostow raised it again at a private dinner with me on September 9. After a long discussion he told me bluntly that President Johnson wanted first of all to know whether the Soviet government believed a summit meeting could produce any results in three crucial areas—arms control, the

Middle East, and Vietnam. I pointed out that while these questions were undoubtedly of major importance, it looked like the American side was setting certain preconditions or trying to get assurances of success in advance, and that was hardly a very productive way of handling a summit, which would have had to be thoroughly prepared to ensure concrete results.

But Rostow did not engage my points. He merely repeated "the principal idea" of the president: Johnson wanted any meeting with Kosygin to make progress in order to create a major political response in the United States and thus prevent Nixon from attacking it as a Democratic election gimmick. Rostow added that no one, not even Rusk, knew about our conversation. However, the next day Rostow called to let me know that he was no longer handling the matter and that the president had entrusted it to Rusk. It appeared Johnson did not think too highly of Rostow's diplomacy.

Moscow's reply arrived on September 13. Rusk was not in Washington at the time, so I passed it to Rostow. The message said Moscow still favored a meeting with the president, was anxious for it to be productive, and was ready to discuss the three areas singled out by the president as well as other questions. The message even outlined a prospective agenda for the discussions.

As we talked the telephone rang. It was the president himself, who had learned I was there and wanted to know about Moscow's reply. I gave him a summary of the message, and the president asked me to relay his thanks for the prompt answer.

After that, I had no communication with Johnson for a month. Evidently the entire subject was still under discussion inside the administration, and on October 14 Rusk told me privately that President Johnson had not yet made a decision. Rusk believed that any summit was as good as ruled out until the election, and he did not even bother to hide his belief that it was too late altogether to hold a summit.

Throughout the month of October a vigorous exchange of views on Vietnam and a possible settlement was conducted through Rusk, Rostow, and me. The Soviet prime minister urged Johnson to stop bombing North Vietnam to give an impetus to the Paris negotiations between the United States and DRV. Johnson hesitated. He was unwilling to go down in history as the president who failed to find a way out of the deadlock of the Vietnam War. At last he decided to accept Hanoi's condition that bombing cease entirely and all combatants in South Vietnam including the Vietcong participate in the negotiations.

With the presidential election only days away and Humphrey trailing in the public opinion polls largely because of his identification with

Johnson's conduct of the war, Rusk telephoned on October 31 to inform me that the president would announce the complete cessation of bombing North Vietnam as of the following day. Later that night Rusk communicated Johnson's formal message to Kosygin: "Now that the bombardments of North Vietnam are halted, I hope and expect that the Soviet Union will use all its influence to exit the impasse and bring about a reliable and durable peace in Southeast Asia as soon as possible." The next day Kosygin expressed his satisfaction to Johnson.

But the shift in policy came too late to save Humphrey, and Nixon won the presidential election by a narrow margin.

On November 24 I was invited to a private dinner by Nixon's aide Robert Ellsworth. He announced to me rather solemnly that Nixon had asked him to communicate to me that he, Ellsworth, was authorized to maintain informal contacts with the Soviet ambassador on problems of mutual interest to Nixon and the Soviet leaders. Although Nixon was not yet president and was well aware of the sensitivities raised by the transition, he wanted to open up a ready channel for confidential contacts with Moscow "just in case" of a possible exchange of views on problems with which we would be confronted after his inauguration.

Ellsworth was obviously proud of his assignment but perhaps a bit in awe of the responsibility it implied. He went on to remind me of Nixon's statement at the Republican convention in Miami that it was time to proceed from the era of confrontation to the era of negotiations in Soviet-American relations. This was no piece of electioneering, Ellsworth declared, but reflected the core of the president's approach.

Since Nixon knew I was about to leave for Moscow for consultations about the incoming American administration, he had sent Ellsworth to ask me to sound out the views of the Soviet leadership, primarily about Vietnam and the Middle East, but also on disarmament and the situation in Czechoslovakia. On my return from Moscow, Ellsworth said, I could start discussions with the president-elect on concrete questions and initiate a confidential exchange of views between Nixon and the Soviet leaders through verbal messages and correspondence.

Rusk also wanted to talk with me about my trip to Moscow and again raised the question of the proposed summit, which, incredibly, still hung in Johnson's mind. Rusk said that if the meeting were to take place—in mid-December, only about a month before Johnson was to leave office—it would have to produce positive results, and the principal topic should be strategic arms limitation. "Is the Soviet government sure about positive results? What could Moscow do to promote progress on the Middle East and South East Asia?" Rusk was clearly skeptical about what he believed to be a belated meeting.

I told him the question had been repeatedly discussed by the leaders of both countries and there was no point in launching a new discussion. Rusk nodded and never raised the subject again.

Some days later Ellsworth asked me to visit him again to discuss rumors circulating in Washington about the possibility that the outgoing and incoming presidents could join in a summit meeting with the Soviet leadership. Nixon, he said, seriously objected because he believed Johnson really wanted to enhance his role in history rather than to promote U.S.-Soviet relations, and that could do nothing but harm. There was no time left to complete serious preparations for talks on strategic arms, Ellsworth said, yet the meeting would raise hopes. Nixon, with four years to go in the White House against Johnson's forty remaining days, would have to bear the brunt of people's anger if the summit flopped. As for Nixon himself, Ellsworth assured me that his approach was positive and serious, but not hasty, and he asked me to pass all this on to the Soviet government. (I learned much later from Johnson's memoirs that after the election he had actually tried to convince Nixon to join him at a summit with Soviet leaders or send his representative. Nixon declined.)

It was already clear to Moscow that a summit with Johnson would not take place. A week later I passed to Ellsworth Moscow's reply saying that Nixon might not have been aware that it was President Johnson who wanted a meeting, and that "it is up to the American side to form its attitude to such a summit. As to us, we do not adjust our views to momentary advantages." Thus Johnson's inconsistent and irresolute attempts to arrange a summit finally ended.

I could not help wondering at the paradoxical situation in the United States, where the president, rejected by the nation, remains in office under the Constitution for nearly three months after the presidential election. While he officially remains chief executive, his decisions and actions are restricted. No surprise that in America such officials are known as "lame ducks."

As the Johnson presidency drew to its end, the Vietnam War buried the president's hopes for a "Great Society," and the moral and political image of America underwent a grave trial even in the eyes of its own citizens. After Rusk left office I gave a private farewell dinner for him before he departed for Atlanta. He arrived in his old car and remarked rather bitterly that after eight years of service as secretary of state, with all means of modern transport at his disposal, he had to learn again how to drive his car and book airline flights himself. His pension was small and he had no family money so he could not afford to hire staff. But this difficult transition was not just a matter of money. He no longer was able to occupy himself with important and interesting affairs of the state, and he openly admitted it—even though he had previously told me that he was fed up with his long service as a secretary of state.

He was rather philosophical during our last conversation. Indeed, mistakes had been committed during the Kennedy and Johnson presidency, he conceded, and he was largely responsible for them. He would have to think them over for himself. But "what's done cannot be undone" and he was not going to search out excuses. That was why he would not write his memoirs. Let history pass its verdict. I walked him to the door. We parted outside the embassy and, as I stood watching the old car start and go, I could not help seeing it as a symbolic end of the Johnson administration. After Rusk settled in his native Georgia as a professor at the state university, his son finally persuaded him to cooperate in a memoir. He remained true to his convictions to the end, although he did not try to impose them on others or champion them in public. His personal integrity was never questioned by anyone.

Years later I visited the Johnson Memorial Library in Texas. The former president was no longer alive. I found myself seized with melancholy and sadness as I examined the exhibits, especially those depicting Johnson's presidency, period by period, with old and faded photographs and other materials illustrating Soviet-American relations, the rise and fall of Lyndon B. Johnson, all telling the story of frustrated hopes. There were few visitors. One of them remarked thoughtfully, "The man died broken-hearted."

In the Soviet Union Johnson was always associated with the American military intervention in Vietnam, which determined the Soviet attitude to him. Otherwise he was little known and of no great interest. In a sense Johnson still remains a half-forgotten and somewhat accidental political figure in Soviet-American relations. But he was by no means a bad president in dealing with us, and at least not much worse than John F. Kennedy, whose character and achievements are invariably described by both American and Soviet historians in flattering terms. Although there is no way of knowing for certain, had it not been for the Vietnam War, detente in Soviet-American relations could have come as early as Johnson's time, even before Nixon came to the White House.

Long before his vice presidency, especially in the 1950s, Johnson was widely known as anti-communist and a convinced champion of the position-of-strength policy toward the Soviet Union. But even during his election campaign against Goldwater, he pragmatically defended a policy to avert rather than reinforce the threat of a nuclear war and normalize rather than exacerbate relations with the Soviet Union. As president he tried to separate the relations between the two superpowers that were crucial for peace from other international problems which, however complex, did not pose the same awesome threats unless they happened to become linked to the fundamental East-West conflict.

Indeed, a more detailed comparison between the practical policies of Kennedy and Johnson shows an interesting contrast to the conventional wisdom: in Johnson's time we had no serious conflicts in Soviet-American relations, such as the confrontation over Berlin, the demonstrative buildup of the armed forces in Europe, or the Cuban crisis. Further, the potentially destabilizing events of 1968 in Czechoslovakia proceeded in a relatively quiet manner. It was with the Johnson administration that we reached agreement on the important treaty on nonproliferation of nuclear weapons and their ban in outer space, that we began talks on limiting antiballistic defenses and approached the SALT talks, and that attempts were made to broaden U.S. trade with East European countries, a program that was held hostage by Congress to our policies in other fields. In addition to a Soviet-American consular convention, our agreements also covered the opening of direct air travel, the rescue of astronauts, water desalination through the use of nuclear energy, and fishing.

As Johnson himself noted rather proudly in his memoirs, during his presidency from 1963 to 1969 the United States concluded more agreements in various fields with the Soviet Union than over the thirty preceding years from the establishment of diplomatic relations between our countries. As president, his own attitude toward promoting relations with the Soviet Union was positive, and he never gave way to outright anti-Sovietism, although the notions of the Cold War continued to dominate the foreign policy of the United States and accounted for the acceleration of the strategic arms race and, of course, the determination with which the United States pursued the Vietnam War as part of its global confrontation with communism.

As the inevitable defeat in Vietnam became increasingly evident, Johnson's primary objective became a withdrawal without losing face. He sought to induce the main socialist country, the Soviet Union, to exert pressure on another one, the Democratic Republic of Vietnam, in order to force it into accepting American conditions. He could not fully realize the depth of the Soviet leadership's blind ideological adherence to the idea of "international solidarity," which paralyzed any mediation efforts by Moscow itself. These half-hearted and impulsive efforts alternated between creating hopes that turned into illusions and frustrations that were very real for both sides, for when there was, so to speak, a war under way between capitalists and communists, leaders of both sides found themselves powerless to stop it. Clearly the impasse demonstrated that the time had come for a fresh look at the foreign policies of our two countries and the relations between us as we moved into the 1970s.

## I. Richard Nixon and Henry Kissinger

*Soviet-American Relations in the 1970s*

The 1970s hold a special place in the postwar history of Soviet-American relations because of the advent of detente, which reached its height during the middle of the decade with the summit agreement to begin limiting the growth of our strategic nuclear arsenals.

Soviet and American historians were not in accord about how to characterize the international environment that generated this relaxation of tensions during the years of Richard Nixon and Leonid Brezhnev. Policy experts differ over the basic question of who forced whom into detente. American political literature contains numerous interpretations ascribing detente to changes in the Soviet approach to the United States, supposedly the only reason that made detente possible. This is only partly true; there were changes on the American side as well. But let me first examine the evolution of the Soviet approach.

Soviet foreign policy was always closely connected to the philosophy and ideology of the Communist Party. Consequently and invariably, its international outlook was an important component of the whole political platform of the party. From the first days of the 1917 revolution there was a struggle among leaders of the state and party leadership over the direction of the country's development and its foreign policy. The two different approaches were personified by Lenin and Trotsky.

The extremists advocated the view that the Russian Revolution was only the beginning and therefore an inalienable part of the world revolution and that a victory of the proletariat over the world bourgeoisie—the final victory of socialism and communism—would justify revolutionary wars. Indeed, the path to this final victory could even require that short-term revolutionary gains be sacrificed for the sake of those supreme goals. Recall that a slogan of the party for many years was rendered into English as "Workers of the world, unite!"

The Leninists believed their primary task was to carry out a revolution in their own country, to transform it into a highly developed socialist state that by its very existence and successful progress would represent the highest form of the execution of Russia's international duty to the world proletariat. Capitalism was offered peaceful coexistence on the condition that history finally be allowed to pass judgment on both systems. But at the same time we declared our support for national liberation movements.

These two views were later curiously interlaced in the minds of the country's leadership and the members of the Communist Party. The Leninist approach became dominant, but the other view was never entirely abandoned because of a strong revolutionary character that appeared to be its primary emotional attraction.

After the Twentieth Congress of the Communist Party of the Soviet Union in 1956, the theory of Marxism-Leninism incorporated new and less bellicose concepts of war and peace. But the legacy of the past was still there, in the form of attempts to preserve continuity of ideology and demonstrate the party's revolutionary orthodoxy. Thus, the new thesis that wars were not fatally inevitable was made more acceptable by adding the old formulas declaring that the threat of wars still remained. In any case, the ideology said, should a war be unleashed it would inevitably lead to the overall victory of socialism, which would arise from the ashes of capitalism.

The thesis proclaiming peaceful coexistence was recognized as a basic principle of Soviet foreign policy, but it was made more palatable by an ideological compromise describing peaceful coexistence as a form of class struggle. The ideologists somehow had to reconcile "internationalism," which was defined as international solidarity with the struggle of working people abroad against capitalist oppression, and "peaceful coexistence" with the capitalist world where those same working people were waging their struggle. The new policy stressed that there was no intention of abolishing the worldwide struggle of ideologies, and the Soviet Union proclaimed for the all the world to hear that it by no means refused to give full support to national liberation movements.

The East-West confrontation was a practical result of the Soviet leadership's attempts to reconcile these two ideological principles and somehow strike a balance between them. But it also resulted in our unnecessary involvement in a superpower rivalry with the United States in the Third World. All this was also going on at a time of fierce ideological dispute with the Chinese.

Needless to say, any general secretary of the Central Committee of the Communist Party of the Soviet Union always played a crucial role in determining policy guidelines throughout the party's history. Brezhnev was not much of a theorist, but he had lived through a devastating war and knew beyond doubt that our people put peace before all other things. Having assumed his position, he spent a couple of years gingerly examining the intricate workings of international life. But even by the middle of Johnson's term and surely by the beginning of Nixon's presidency he had come to a rather strong conviction about the need to improve relations with the West and especially the United States, although he rendered appropriate homage to what then were considered ideologically sound Marxist-Leninist positions.

Several factors made Brezhnev and the highest officials of the party and state adjust their approach to foreign policy.

First, a nuclear war was utterly unacceptable, as the Cuban crisis had clearly demonstrated. Second, there was the enormous burden of military expenditures, which both sides unsuccessfully tried to reduce at the start of Johnson's presidency. Third, the process of improving relations between the Soviet Union and Western Europe, especially with the Federal Republic of Germany through the so-called Berlin Agreements, would become extremely complicated if the United States were to try to impede it, and the American position was largely determined by the prospects for strategic arms limitation talks. Fourth, there was a sharp aggravation in Soviet-Chinese relations in the late 1960s and early 1970s, and it was essential to avert or neutralize any collusion between Washington and Beijing. Fifth, the improvement of relations with the United States would undoubtedly consolidate the prestige of Brezhnev's leadership within the Soviet Union.

Admittedly, Soviet foreign policy was largely shaped by events in the world, often through improvisation rather than according to some permanent grand plan. Suffice it to recall the major crises of the era ranging from Cuba in 1962 to the wars in the Middle East and Southeast Asia.

For our diplomatic service at the time, the certain difficulty was a lack of practical grasp and adequate background knowledge for serious negotiations on arms reduction in this main area of our bilateral and international relations. The State Department and its staff were far better prepared than we were. Their diplomats and negotiators were closely in touch with the Pentagon. In both American departments, special divisions dealt with disarmament issues. But we had nothing of the kind. Soviet Foreign Ministry officials were left to their own devices and did not even have a group or special section to develop expertise or deploy its bureaucratic weight in disarmament questions. At first, the subject was entrusted to a small group of people in the American department of the Foreign Ministry. But they had virtually no access to any information about our nuclear weapons and their production. Whatever they knew, they got mostly from American publications. As ambassador, I was in a somewhat better position since I could communicate directly with my official American counterparts and with American scientists.

This led to incongruities. When serious negotiations began, our diplomats had to pick up the niceties of disarmament and its extremely complex concepts that had been in circulation in American military, diplomatic, and scientific quarters for years. For a long time our people used American abbreviations for both the American and Soviet strategic systems in public and between ourselves. The most striking fact was that in the course of the first years of negotiations on the SALT I agreement we volunteered virtually no Soviet military data, even though in due course data on our position would have to be part of any agreement. Quantitative data were suggested by the American side both for their armaments and our own, and we just agreed or corrected them. It took some time before we established due communication with our own military and created the appropriate good coordinating groups in Moscow to adequately prepare for the talks.

Simultaneously, although at a rather delayed pace, our highest political leadership was mastering details of military-industrial matters and relevant disarmament issues. Of the members of the Politburo, only our defense ministers—Georgi Zhukov, Rodion Malinovsky, and then Andrei Grechko, all of them military men with the rank of marshal of the Soviet Union—were familiar with these problems. But even their knowledge was far from complete, as a defense minister usually would know little about the details of military manufacture, to say nothing of how to apply them to the process of disarmament. This gap somehow was filled when Grechko was succeeded at the start of the Ford administration by Dimitri Ustinov, who dealt with the armaments industry as early as in Stalin's day. But he was not a champion of disarmament and he had to be prodded from time to time by Brezhnev, who was at home in the military-industrial complex.

For the United States, this period proved to be a time of painful reassessment of the political maxims of the Cold War. The United States also had a number of objective reasons for moving toward more normal relations with the Soviet Union: Soviet nuclear missile potential now was comparable with America's; major Western powers, led by West Germany and France, increasingly sought to pursue a more independent policy and improve their relations with Moscow; U.S. social and economic problems were seriously aggravated by the national gamble in Vietnam, and it became increasingly clear that the United States could not have both guns and butter. Furthermore, the Nixon administration was clearly anxious to play up its foreign policy achievements with Russia and China in order to play down its failure to end the war in Southeast Asia and thus consolidate the president's chances for reelection in 1972.

The Nixon-Kissinger administration sought to achieve several important short-term and long-term objectives of American foreign policy. They were: to find the least painful way to end the Vietnam war and an acceptable way to settle some of the more explosive postwar problems such as West Berlin; to reduce the threat of a nuclear war between the Soviet Union and the United States by limiting armaments and creating a Soviet-American system of consultation for mutual restraint in dealing with explosive regions; to re-align American and allied forces in order to preserve the status quo and sat-isfy American interests; to secure for the United States a greater freedom of maneuver in relations with its allies by normalizing Soviet-American relations and thus consolidate its own coordinating role in the global confrontation between East and West; and, finally, on the domestic front, to help prevent polarization and outspoken pacifism. All this, it was thought, would boost the prestige and authority of Nixon and his administration at home and abroad.

The principal American protagonists of this process were, of course, Richard Nixon and Henry Kissinger. Both are major figures in the history of American foreign policy. Their strength lay in their ability to approach prob-lems conceptually and not be distracted by minor questions or subordinate fragments. The global diplomatic game and the imperatives of *realpolitik* ap-pealed to both of them. In addition, Kissinger was a good tactician, as was particularly evident in both direct and behind-the-scenes negotiations (which I personally witnessed). On the whole, their administration did its share to improve Soviet-American relations during the Cold War without, of course, overlooking the interests of the United States.

But when I assess their activity in retrospect, taking into account my personal observations, their memoirs, and numerous books and essays by commentators, and then analyzing in the round what they accomplished, I cannot escape the conclusion that they were not really thinking in terms of bringing about a major breakthrough in Soviet-American relations, and of ending the Cold War and the arms race.

Underlying their policy toward the Soviet Union was a combination of deterrence and cooperation, a mosaic of short-term and long-term consider-ations. Both Nixon and Kissinger sought to create a more stable and pre-dictable strategic situation without reducing the high level of armaments, which remained the basis of a policy that was essentially based on military strength, and on the accommodation of national interests only when they found it desirable to do so. Their arms control efforts thus disguised this pol-icy of strength, but only slightly. Essentially, neither the president nor his closest aide proved able (or wanted) to break out of the orbit of the Cold War, although their attitude was more pragmatic and realistic than other Cold Warriors in the White House.

## Enter Nixon and Kissinger

Nixon's election in 1968 was received in the Soviet Union with a considerable measure of wariness. The Politburo was unanimous in believing that his classic anti-communism would mean hard times for Soviet-American relations. There is no concealing the fact that our embassy in Washington initially held similar views, and for solid reasons. Nixon arrived at the White House as a prominent political figure. Opportunism is deep-rooted in the American political world, and Nixon was no exception. His career was imbued with anti-Sovietism, anti-communism, and militarism, and he had skillfully used irresponsible and demagogic attacks on his political rivals and others he considered fair game to advance his political ambitions.

As a dominant feature of American political life, anti-communism emerged as an offspring of the Cold War, when the Soviet Union and its ideology were seen as a direct threat to the American and capitalist way of life. But what always surprised me was the scale and the fierce character the struggle against communism acquired in America, although it was starkly evident that this struggle amounted essentially to tilting at windmills. From the FBI, a powerful police organization with its extensive network of informers,* to a whole host of voluntary agents-provocateurs and genuine patriots who combed the country for subversive elements from Hollywood to Washington, from the top of the Time and Life Building to the unions of longshoremen up and down the East Coast, this mammoth and unprecedented hunt for communists failed to uncover anything but the most minuscule number of communists dreaming of overthrowing the American system.

But then they never were numerous in America, in contrast to Europe where Communist parties with a mass following in several countries were politically powerful. Even during the years of detente the Communist Party of the United States had no more than ten or fifteen thousand members, and even that figure, reported by the party leadership, was doubted in Moscow. We felt they may have been half that figure at most. During the postwar period the American Communist Party was never taken seriously in Moscow as a political force. Moscow contented itself with the fact that the leader of the American Communist Party made eloquent speeches in support of our policies and our fight with China in the world communist movements. As ambassador, I usually met him once or twice a year at lunch or dinner in New

---

* Once Kissinger jokingly said to me that the United States government financially keeps the Communist Party going, because 50 percent of its members are FBI informants who paid their party fees from FBI funds.

York at our United Nations mission for general discussion. But he was always evasive about the exact number of party members and about the situation within the party, and he tried to overemphasize its influence among working people. I did *not* give him any advice on party matters; it was not my business. Communications between the parties in New York and Moscow were carried out through the party apparatus.

No one in the Soviet leadership, including the most zealous supporters of communism, ever talked seriously about any concrete prospects for communism in the United States. Needless to say, I did not believe in any such prospect either, the more so because I had been living in the United States for so long. In my boldest thoughts I never looked beyond the idea of our two systems peacefully converging somehow in the distant future, a contemporary idea that gained some popular credence among some intellectuals, based in part on the organization of modern society, but it was also taboo in Moscow at the time.

But did Richard Nixon really believe in the communist threat in the United States, or was it just a convenient means to climb the political ladder? To my mind, the latter was more likely. As he made his way to the top, he increasingly regarded the communist threat not as a reality of American domestic life but as a factor related to the foreign policy struggle against the communist world, first of all with the Soviet Union and China. Thus the matter was increasingly translated from a domestic issue to the more rarefied plane of relations between nations. This did open up certain prospects, complex as they were, of beginning a dialogue with the new president and even reaching agreements with him.

Those were my thoughts on Nixon's inauguration in 1969. I had first met him in 1959 when I was chief of the Foreign Ministry's American Department and he visited Moscow as vice president to inaugurate an American household exhibit at which he engaged in his famous "kitchen debate" with Khrushchev on the relative merits of our two societies. At the time Khrushchev was infuriated by an anti-Soviet resolution referring to "captive peoples" of the nations of Eastern Europe just passed by the U.S. Congress, and the premier gave free vent to his emotions. After the debate, Khrushchev took Nixon for a ride on a motor launch down the picturesque Moscow River. It was a weekend, and the boat stopped at sandy beaches, where Khrushchev introduced Nixon to ordinary citizens enjoying themselves in the sun. He then would ask them loudly and in a joking manner if they felt enslaved. The answer was always a burst of laughter. Throughout the trip he persisted in lecturing and teasing Nixon, who was made quite uncomfortable by his hectoring host.

▪ ▪ ▪

Needless to say, when I first met Nixon in his exalted new position I did not remind him of our past meeting. On February 17, 1969, about four weeks after his inauguration, Nixon received me at the White House in the president's Oval Office. After Johnson's departure, the room had been completely redecorated and the carpet and curtains were done in golden colors. On the wall hung a beautiful embroidery of the American national emblem made by one of the president's daughters. Flags and standards of various colors framed the desk on both sides, symbolizing president's military and civil powers. The president said the desk was particularly dear to him because he had used it ever since he was first elected to public office.

Thanks to the president, we still keep a family remembrance of his Oval Office, a wonderful color photograph of my three-year-old granddaughter sitting with an important air at the president's desk. The picture bears the president's warm inscription. The most difficult thing about it was to make her sit still and distract her from opening and reaching into the desk drawers of the highest-ranking official of the United States.

I had been instructed to give Nixon our government's views on Soviet-American relations and the principal issues in international relations as a way of opening our relations with the new president. Moscow's attitude toward him remained guarded.

I told him the Soviet Union favored peaceful cooperation and if the United States would proceed from the same principle, broad possibilities would open for the solution of pressing international issues. The main goals, as we saw them, were to enforce the nuclear nonproliferation treaty; find a political settlement in Vietnam leading to the withdrawal of American troops, open a bilateral exchange to settle the conflict in the Middle East, base our actions and policies in Europe on the postwar status quo, and continue the Soviet-American exchanges on strategic weapons in order to curb the arms race between us.

Nixon said that in principle he agreed with these goals and attached major importance to the improvement of relations with the Soviet Union, although he was aware of serious differences which must be prevented from reaching a boiling point. He also wanted to avoid confrontation in regional and similar side issues outside the main thrust of Soviet-American relations—what we came to call "peripheral issues"—in the Third World and elsewhere.

Nixon proposed holding a summit meeting but said it needed thorough preparation and time for him to gain a more complete idea of world affairs and the details of the specific issues. On my part, I welcomed his suggestion

204 ■ IN CONFIDENCE

of a Soviet-American summit, although I knew Moscow would also take some time to get used to the idea. It took more than two years to hold the first meeting, but then in the following three years—1972, 1973, and 1974—an unprecedented three successive summits were held.

Then the president went on to establish a confidential channel through Henry Kissinger, his national security adviser, the extensive use of which turned out to be unprecedented in my experience and perhaps in the annals of diplomacy. Apart from my routine official contacts with William Rogers, his secretary of state, the president wanted to be able to exchange views urgently and privately with the Soviet leadership, and he wanted to do this through me via Kissinger, who would maintain direct contact with me and report to the president only.

As if trying to clarify the somewhat extraordinary nature of this two-tier arrangement, Nixon said that the disadvantage of communicating through Rogers—although he had "every confidence in the secretary of state"—was that an exchange of views would be open to an excessively broad range of officials. This might occasionally cause unpredictable leaks of information. But there were questions that needed to be restricted to a very narrow circle, and for some questions that circle should be limited to the president alone, who would receive information via the channel of Kissinger and Dobrynin, the more so because we both could talk in private without an interpreter.

I expressed my willingness to reopen this confidential channel, the existence of which under other presidents and in various forms, Nixon had been informed. He highly appreciated the fact that no information about the channel had ever leaked from the Soviet embassy. All in all, he was friendly and raised no controversial issues, and this first meeting consolidated my belief that we could develop a dialogue with him.

Four days later, on February 21, Kissinger suggested that we meet in his White House office. Like most of my meetings with Nixon, all my meetings with Kissinger were private, without interpreters and secretaries. This meant there was no official record of our meetings except what we kept ourselves. Although at times it could have led to differing versions of what was actually said and meant (for the participants might also yield to the temptation of presenting themselves in the best possible way, especially later, in their recollections and memoirs), no problems or arguments arose during the actual talks and negotiations over what had actually been said in previous conversations. There always was a clear understanding of what had been said in an official way, as distinct from what had been said during a more general *tour d'horizon,* when we would explore new ideas or approaches on a personal basis. This enabled us to keep our frank exchanges in strictest confidence and preserve secrecy in negotiations. That was why our channel was of a great value to both governments. Its importance should not be underestimated.

On Nixon's instructions, Kissinger stressed that the president wanted to promote better relations between our two governments, and that included the specific issues I had raised. As for the more immediate question of Vietnam, Kissinger said that the new American administration was ready to negotiate on the basis of two principles: first, the United States could not accept a settlement that would look like a military defeat, and second, the Nixon administration was not prepared to accept a settlement immediately followed by the change of government in South Vietnam which would also entail an abrupt shift in policy, although they had no objection to a gradual evolution.

He also said that Nixon agreed there should be no change in the postwar relationships in Europe and that the exchange of views on the Middle East should continue between Moscow and Washington.

The one omission I noted—and so did Moscow—was that Kissinger ignored our proposal to resume our exchange on limiting strategic arms, which had been suspended for months since the invasion of Czechoslovakia. When I pointed that out to Kissinger, he said the Nixon administration was prepared to discuss the subject a bit later but did not elaborate.

This first meeting left me with a good impression of Kissinger. He was businesslike and did not resort to ambiguities or avoid specific problems. When we later entered into serious negotiations, I learned that he could give you a big headache, but he was clever and highly professional, and never dull or bureaucratic. For the next years, the confidential channel between the leaders of both countries functioned continuously in the greatest secrecy. We used it by treating each other to breakfasts and lunches in private, but mostly I would visit Kissinger, entering the White House through the service gate. Our meetings there were usually held either in his office near the president's, or, when protracted negotiations on Vietnam and strategic arms limitation began, in the imposing and quiet ground floor Map Room from which Franklin Roosevelt used to address the nation by radio during the war. Later, as our contacts became more frequent and we met almost daily, the president ordered the installation of a direct and secure telephone line between the White House and the Soviet embassy for the exclusive use of Kissinger and me; we would just lift our receivers and talk, without dialing.

Thanks to this confidential channel the Soviet leadership had a sure and reliable connection with the president. Secrecy was further ensured by the absolute confidentiality of the proceedings and discussions within the Politburo itself. The channel also enabled Nixon and Kissinger to avoid the pressure of the Congress and public opinion on a number of occasions. Thus the White House not only shaped American policy, but also directly carried it out without the intrusion of Congress and the public, who were totally unaware of this secret channel of diplomacy.

Looking back, I can say with certainty that had it not been for that channel, many key agreements on complicated and controversial issues would have never been reached, and dangerous tension would not have been eased over Berlin, Cuba, or the Middle East. The basic agreements on the limitation of strategic arms, and, finally, the most sensitive negotiations on the preparation of summit meetings would all go through our confidential channel. That was the beginning of our unique relations with the administration of Nixon and Kissinger. We were on many issues both opponents and partners in the preservation of peace.

Good personal relations with Kissinger were founded on our mutual desire to listen to and understand each other, and to seek some agreeable solution or compromise to our differences, all of which helped overcome or minimize our difficulties during our official contacts or negotiations. Of course we had rather heated discussions on some issues, but they never turned into personal confrontations. One factor, which I always valued, was Henry's keen sense of humor, which I always did my best to answer in kind. After all, humor helps to reach the heart as well as the mind of your partner.

## Negotiating with the Nixon Administration

Judging by the memoirs of Nixon, Kissinger, and some other American negotiators, the strategic arms limitation talks, or SALT, were not regarded by Nixon as vital in the initial stages of his presidency. It was by no means accidental that in the memoranda prepared by the National Security Council in the spring of 1969, SALT was not at the top of America's priorities, which were Vietnam, the Middle East, and military policy, all approved by the president. It was only gradually that SALT shifted to a more prominent position until it became the key point in all agreements reached at the 1972 Moscow summit.

The Nixon administration's unhurried pace was prompted, among other things, by the impression that Moscow was more eager for an agreement than Washington. Pleading for time to organize their negotiating position, Nixon and Kissinger partly artificially delayed the beginning of the talks in the hope that linking them to other questions would force Moscow into concessions. At least that was my impression.

On July 10, Gromyko presented a foreign policy report to the Supreme Soviet stressing the desire of the Soviet Union to improve relations with the

United States. The foreign minister as usual spoke of the "deep class contradictions" between the two social systems but said that "when it comes to the preservation of peace, the Soviet Union and the United States can find a common language." Nevertheless the new administration remained silent on the matter, so Moscow decided to encourage a dialogue with Washington, the more so because there were certain indications that the Nixon administration was making overtures to China.

On October 20, I called on president Nixon and told him the Soviet government was prepared to open an official discussion on limiting our strategic arms. Simultaneously, I hinted in a disguised warning against any American attempts to capitalize on the differences between the Soviet Union and China, which by that time had become substantial. Nixon got the hint and assured me that American policy in relation to China "was not directed against the Soviet Union." This was not completely true, because the president's China policy, developed and vigorously pursued by Kissinger, provided for dynamic maneuvering within the strategic triangle formed by Moscow, Washington, and Beijing, and the China card was a major component of it. Personally, I believed that we were making a mistake from the start by displaying our anxiety over China to the new administration.

At the end of our conversation the president agreed to start discussion on strategic arms limitations. On October 25 both sides announced the SALT talks would start in Helsinki on November 17, 1969. Secretary of State Rogers publicly emphasized that the United States was not linking progress in SALT to political developments elsewhere. This was said under pressure from us, although in fact this policy of linkage, as it came to be called, would be an integral part of American strategy and tactics for some years, extending into the Ford and Carter administrations.

Why did Nixon agree to start the SALT talks? I think he had begun to realize that, aside from the inherent importance to the security of the United States in exploring this vital problem, the talks could be used as a serious tool in the diplomatic game with the Soviet Union in other areas. A whole year had passed since he had taken office, and his absence from the negotiating table had conferred no benefit on him. Moreover, time was pressing; he had already completed one-quarter of his first term while Soviet leaders could look forward to a much longer span in office.

Thus began the long process of negotiations between our two countries on limiting nuclear arms. For many years these talks became a barometer of our relations with the United States. They had their ups and downs and were often postponed, delayed, or in recess, but they were the one important area in which our two countries were directly and continuously engaged.

The structure of the SALT talks during the Nixon-Kissinger administration was unprecedented. They were two-tier talks, only one of them between the formal delegations of both sides as publicly announced in November. The preliminary Helsinki session lasted for five weeks, from November 17 to December 22, 1969. After a break, another seven rounds of SALT negotiations followed over a period of thirty months, held alternately in Helsinki and Vienna until the Nixon-Brezhnev summit in Moscow in 1972.

Negotiations in the confidential Kissinger-Dobrynin channel began after the SALT talks formally began in Europe. We negotiated simultaneously in Washington, and in far greater secrecy. Neither the general public, nor the diplomats in the U.S. State Department and Soviet Foreign Ministry, nor even the negotiators themselves meeting in Helsinki and Vienna had the slightest idea that these secret exchanges were going on. No one except senior members of the Politburo, Gromyko, and the head of the Soviet Foreign Ministry's American division knew about them. In the United States only the president and Kissinger were in the know.

Our exchanges through the channel made it possible for the leadership of both countries to override the negotiations, to interfere and untie the knots of many principal and delicate disputes. On the other hand, negotiating simultaneously at two levels at times produced some confusion and occasional misunderstanding in the process. The American delegation found it harder to deal with this than ours, since officially the negotiations were handled by the State Department but all the strings on their side were pulled by Kissinger, and, for all his diplomatic talents and bureaucratic skills, he was probably physically unable to embrace all the details and minor nuances that arose in the negotiations.

The Soviet delegation was not in too different a position, but we supervised and conducted negotiations in a very different way. A single team in Moscow backed up both our official negotiators and the confidential channel. But Kissinger single-handedly had to orchestrate the whole complex business, keeping all the diplomatic and military staff involved in the negotiations on a very short leash by rigorously rationing information from our channel. Gerard Smith, the head of the American delegation, wrote in his memoirs that he discovered the existence of the channel by accident. He and Raymond Garthoff, a member of the delegation responsible for close contact with the Soviet side at the talks, were certainly unhappy if not outraged at times by this parallel negotiation. Neither did everyone in the Soviet Foreign Ministry, or other ministries represented in the formal talks such as Defense, particularly like the idea that the channel was the main avenue of negotiations between the two governments. But while the highly centralized and confidential way of handling the talks was a Nixon-Kissinger idea, it was accepted and prevailed in Moscow, too.

■ ■ ■

By contrast, Kissinger was not active in the Middle East peace negotiations. He evidently did not consider the time ripe for real progress there and consequently avoided personal involvement. He tacitly yielded that honor from the start of the administration to Secretary of State Rogers. I suspect that Kissinger was certain that negotiations at that stage would bring credit to no one, whereupon his hour would come. The two-tier structure of managing foreign policy—Rogers's official level and the confidential channel between Kissinger and me—was fraught with permanent rivalry and friction between Kissinger, the Washington celebrity, and Rogers, the soft-spoken Establishment lawyer. More than once, when Kissinger knew I was going over to the State Department, he would ask me to bear in mind that Rogers had not been told about this, that, or some other aspect of the issue under discussion—and I was definitely not to tell Rogers about it.

In the Middle East, the administration had a dual purpose. While consolidating its support for Israel, it sought to curb the massive Soviet military supplies to Arab countries and prevent the expansion of Soviet influence on a future political settlement. We gave our main support to Egypt, whose army had lost nearly all its military equipment in the 1967 war, and sent advisers with our materiel, even including Soviet military pilots to fly our MiG fighters. They went at Nasser's request to protect Cairo and other major cities from Israeli raids, but they did not overfly the Suez Canal where Israeli and Egyptian troops confronted each other.

Nixon and Kosygin exchanged messages on all this. On March 25 Rogers suggested we resume confidential negotiations, which would take place at the working level between me and Joseph Sisco, the assistant secretary of state for the Middle East. They began on April 1, and as far as I know, no account of the talks has ever appeared. Our complicated work proceeded slowly, but in several weeks we managed to agree on a dozen clauses of a possible Arab-Israeli agreement. The work stopped abruptly when Israel via Sisco accused Egypt of using the talks to justify its military moves. (Nasser had unilaterally and unwisely moved his antiaircraft batteries a couple of kilometers into the demilitarized zone.)

On July 19 Sisco informed me that the United States was going to take a new initiative and propose that Arab and Israeli representatives meet "in one city or in one building" for indirect talks in which Swedish Ambassador Gunnar Jarring would be the go-between. I asked what would happen to the accomplishments of our previous talks; he hesitated and said the matter would be dealt with later. The next day Rogers appealed for support from Egypt, Syria, Jordan, and Israel, plus United Nations Secretary General U Thant and the Soviet Union. It was touted as "the Rogers Plan." The

Americans meanwhile delayed further secret Soviet-American negotiations on the Middle East.

When I was invited to Rogers's home for dinner, he said Moscow could not imagine the pressure exerted on Washington by the government of Israel's prime minister, Golda Meir, who believed that the presence of Soviet military pilots in Egypt meant the Soviet Union was bent on crushing Israel. She appealed to Washington not to leave Israel "face to face with the Soviet Union." The secretary was clearly anxious to obtain our assurance that our military would not come too close to the Suez Canal, and I told him our pilots had instructions not to overfly the Canal Zone.

The divided authority in Washington left Gromyko thoroughly unnerved. I was dealing with Sisco, who was shrewd, knowledgeable, and very stubborn. He took all his orders from Kissinger, who remained in the shadows, while officially working for Rogers and doing what he could to accommodate him. Gromyko arrived for his annual visit to the U.N. General Assembly, and I reported to him that Sisco and I were deadlocked on the text of a possible declaration on the Middle East. Gromyko decided he would speak directly to Rogers about it during a lunch arranged by U Thant for ministers of the five permanent members of the Security Council. Gromyko told me afterward that he found Rogers quite an agreeable person and that a compromise certainly could be reached. He wanted to report this favorable impression to the Politburo.

I asked him not to be in any hurry to cable Moscow but at least wait until the next day, when a lunch was scheduled for the four of us together—Rogers, Gromyko, Sisco, and me. He reluctantly agreed to postpone his report.

At the lunch Gromyko started to explain his position. Rogers said he "basically" agreed.

I knew very well what would happen next: I would have to sit down with Sisco alone and formally draft the agreement—and that would be when the disagreements would really begin.

So in front of Gromyko and Rogers I turned to Sisco and said, "Joe, our job will be very easy today. We'll just sit down and draft what our ministers have agreed." And I summarized what Gromyko had said.

Sisco quickly commented: "My impression is that Mr. Gromyko didn't quite understand Secretary Rogers."

I looked at Gromyko.

Gromyko became very angry: "I came here to negotiate with the secretary of state. I don't want to listen to you."

After the lunch broke up and Gromyko asked me: "What do we do now? What do we send to Moscow?"

"Nothing for the time being," I replied. "Let's wait for a meeting with the president."

Gromyko then became really angry. "What kind of secretary of state is this?" he said.

The next day Gromyko met with Nixon and of course discovered that what Rogers had confusingly told him reflected neither the president's nor Kissinger's policy. Afterward he told me: "It's good that you said not to send a telegram but I resent the whole thing. First I spoke to the secretary of state, and then to Kissinger and the president, and they had a completely different position from Rogers."

Needless to say no agreement was forthcoming on any Middle East declaration. When I spoke later with Kissinger, he smiled but said nothing. I was learning to navigate in these cross-currents within the administration, but Gromyko was not. He wanted to know: "Who am I going to write in Washington when I get home? Rogers or Kissinger?"

### Washington and Moscow in 1970: A Year of Drift and Doubt

The whole of 1970 proved to be a curious year of drift. Although the protracted SALT negotiations were under way, the administration took no major initiatives in international affairs or in Soviet-American relations. Its actions were either negative, in blocking a European security conference, or uncooperative, as in the Middle East. It was sending signals to China seeking normal relations. The president also received the prime ministers of Germany, France, and Britain to renew personal contact with them and hoping, among other things, to control their eagerness to open more cooperative relations with the Soviet Union, especially under Chancellor Willy Brandt's new *Ostpolitik* of improving relations with Germany's wartime enemies.

The need to end the Vietnam War, of course, was the prime focus of the Nixon administration's international activity. It virtually abandoned the idea of a political settlement. Starting with the American invasion of Cambodia in May 1970, the administration put its main emphasis on military solutions, including turning over the brunt of the battle to the South Vietnamese themselves under the label of "Vietnamization."

Nixon's policy toward the Soviet Union was characterized by two opposing yet closely intertwined strands. One was his traditionally hostile stance aimed at undermining Soviet international positions; the other was aimed at avoiding the risk of excessive aggravation in order to maintain the contacts to search for acceptable solutions, although on concrete issues they showed no evident desire to do so. This merely intensified the deadlock. But it also is noteworthy that 1970 did not see a single major crisis in Soviet-

American relations. Nixon realized that a grave worsening of relations with the Soviet Union and a policy of confrontation would contradict the interests of the United States and could alarm the nation. That was why he reiterated his motto as "the era of negotiations rather than confrontation"—but, in contrast to the year 1969, he made the meaning of this motto more transparent in 1970 by declaring that "negotiations do not necessarily imply agreements."

The Soviet leadership was prepared to wait Nixon out because the true direction of his administration was unclear. Moscow had taken the measure of it. On April 6, Gromyko submitted a secret memorandum to the Politburo summarizing our relations with the new administration. Its main thesis was: "It is to our benefit to maintain in the United States the awareness of the hopelessness and unprofitability of a policy of confrontation with the Soviet Union, as well as the understanding of our country's readiness to promote Soviet-American relations on a mutually acceptable basis. Our experience of one year of relations with the Nixon administration shows that such an approach is correct." The Politburo approved this policy.

The question of a summit cropped up time and again during my contacts with Kissinger during the administration's first two years, but it became a live issue only during the following year, in the middle of 1971. Kissinger in his memoirs claims that the Soviet side overplayed its hand by making its price for a summit during 1970 a de facto alliance by Moscow and Washington against China, a European security conference, and a SALT agreement on Soviet terms. He writes that Nixon would not agree to any of these demands and that the Soviet Union "achieved nothing."

I do not remember any such demands about an alliance against China or any solid grounds for his sensational conclusion that "collusion against China was to be the real Soviet price for a summit." The leadership of the Soviet Union was not that naive. We could not conceive of an alliance against China with the United States, especially under Richard Nixon whose anti-Soviet persuasions were well known. As for the SALT agreement, neither side was ready for it in 1970 or even in 1971; it was concluded only at the summit in 1972.

I also knew there could be no decision on a summit because it still was not clear who would represent the Soviet leadership—Brezhnev or Kosygin. The infighting between them continued for the first two years of Nixon's presidency until Brezhnev established his preeminence through his authority as general secretary of the party, a job Kosygin never wanted. Nor was he ready for a fight with Brezhnev for the right to handle our high-level foreign exchanges.

The Nixon administration, for its part, was ambivalent and confusing to its supporters. David Rockefeller told me the president struck his fellow bankers as "obsessed by the idea of a global contest with the Russians," and that Nixon believed we were challenging him "in all conceivable ways." Henry Ford II, whom I had first met when he escorted me along his Detroit assembly line in 1964, came to dinner en route to Moscow where he would discuss building a plant on the Kama River—only to discover upon his return that the project had been vetoed by the administration, probably because of the harsh Soviet reaction to the U.S. invasion of Cambodia.

I was also told by Harriman that Kissinger and Nixon felt ill-used by our military support of Egypt, worried by Soviet naval activity around Cuba, and persuaded in any case that a tough stand against Moscow would not harm the Republicans' prospects in the November congressional elections, even though they had no intention of provoking a direct confrontation. In sum, the administration was not yet genuinely interested in making Soviet-American relations a major foreign policy priority in 1970. The clear evidence of this was the fact that Kissinger was almost completely inactive in the area, except for SALT. Nor was the confidential channel fully in operation yet.

## II. Summit Foothills

*Gromyko and Andropov Want to Drive a Hard Bargain*

On the eve of the New Year of 1971, there was growing irritation and impatience with Nixon in Moscow. Two years of his presidency had already passed, but nothing was clear about his intentions toward the Soviet Union. Gromyko and Yuri Andropov, the head of the KGB, drafted a memorandum on Soviet-American relations for discussion by the Politburo. The authors did not then hold out much hope that our relations would improve soon, let alone turn friendly.

The memo warned that during its first two years Nixon's presidency had produced only idiosyncrasies and tactical delays in foreign policy, and no major changes from its Democratic predecessors. "The confrontation between the United States and the USSR will apparently cover a historically long period," the memo said. It emphasized that the Nixon administration "must realize the need for the West to reckon with the interests of the Soviet Union," and it enumerated the objectives of our foreign policy. These included maintaining Soviet military capabilities to convince "American ruling circles that it is in the most vital national interest of the United States" to conduct its foreign policy to avoid the dangers of a direct clash with the Soviet Union. At the same time Gromyko and Andropov proposed that we press for peaceful coexistence with the United States and emphasized the necessity of reaching agreements that served our interests.

The Soviet leadership approved the policy in the belief that Nixon wanted a summit meeting to enhance his political fortunes for his reelection campaign the following year. They also wanted one because, as the memo said, it was "in our long-term interest to demonstrate the possibility of a further development of Soviet-American relations in spite of their inherent fluctuations." Thus the Politburo had made a major decision to become more actively involved with Nixon.

As ambassador, I had already been thinking along these lines for several months and recommended that Moscow follow that same course toward the summit. Andropov, who also headed the powerful Soviet intelligence services abroad, had by that time become very active in foreign policy. Gradually he became a cosponsor with Gromyko of major foreign policy proposals introduced to the Politburo. Gromyko did not mind this at all, because it assured approval of his most important suggestions. Their personal relations were not bad, because Andropov was cautious enough not to interfere in Gromyko's everyday management of foreign policy, and Gromyko for his part respected Andropov's growing influence in the Politburo.

The Politburo's policy shift in a curious way coincided with Nixon's own political scenario for the campaign. He began to show a renewed interest in our relations and in the possibility of a summit meeting. Vietnam remained a burning problem, so improving relations with the Soviet Union was even more vital for the president.

Kissinger in turn became more active in our relations, especially in his exchanges with me on strategic arms limitations and the arrangements for the summit meeting. The confidential channel became increasingly busy. The Politburo thought that Nixon's desire to secure Moscow's consent for a summit would push the administration to search for new agreements on Berlin and take a more definite stand on the strategic arms talks. Gromyko and Andropov did not know for sure but guessed it was worth a try. I was also guessing, but to a lesser extent because I favored a summit, and probably more so than Gromyko.

In any case, their strategy not only helped secure an agreement on Berlin but also unfroze the restrictions that had so annoyed Henry Ford II on U.S. help for the construction of the Kama River automobile plant (although by that time Ford had lost interest). There were some formal steps promoting bilateral relations, a modernization of the Soviet-American hot line, and an agreement to limit the risks in case of nuclear accidents, both signed later by Gromyko and Rogers in Washington. And of course, the agreement to hold the summit in May of 1972, and in Moscow.

On January 9, 1971, I met with Kissinger who had flown specially from Nixon's vacation home at San Clemente on the Southern California coast. He wanted me to communicate the president's ideas to the Soviet leadership. Nixon, he said, shared the Soviet leadership's belief that our relations left a great deal to be desired, and he now felt he could work full force on improving them during the year of 1971, before turning his attention to the elections.

Kissinger then touched upon the major issues to be discussed: the Berlin problem (the president suggested a strictly confidential exchange of views through our direct channel), the Middle East (the president proposed to resume the bilateral dialogue to reach a settlement), and strategic arms limitations (the president suggested first to agree on defensive weapons and then prepare an agreement on offensive arms). Kissinger particularly emphasized the importance of a summit meeting for all these issues.

Then he came forth with a rather "delicate request": the American side strongly hoped that if the Soviet government had any major proposals on international issues, they would make them directly to the U.S. government and not through Senator Edmund Muskie, a Democrat from the state of Maine who was shortly to visit Moscow and was already planning to run against Nixon the following year.

I got the impression that Nixon and Kissinger had held an important discussion in San Clemente and they agreed on the need to resuscitate the Soviet-American dialogue and move toward the summit. At any rate, his message to me surely represented a serious first attempt to do so. I reported my conclusions to Moscow, recommending that we react positively. Electoral considerations were already at work!

The response arrived quite promptly. On January 23 I informed Kissinger that Moscow would agree to a summit and suggested the second half of that summer. The president's agenda was acceptable, with the understanding that it would include Europe, West Berlin, strategic arms limitation, a possible settlement in the Middle East, and the war in Indochina. In short, the Soviet response immediately put our relations for the year on a practical footing.

Five days later Kissinger told me the president agreed with the Soviet suggestions but said it was "physically difficult" for the two of them to handle simultaneous preliminary talks on three major problems: West Berlin, nuclear arms, and the Middle East. Kissinger then proposed that "for the time being" we concentrate our efforts in the confidential channel on the first two issues. He was generously leaving the Middle East to Rogers and the State Department, knowing perfectly well this was a hard nut to crack. We had no objection to this division of labor.

## SALT, ABM, and the Summit

From their very beginning in November of 1969 and during 1970, our delegations carried on lengthy and complicated discussions on SALT in Helsinki and Vienna without evident success. SALT negotiations involved two different types of strategic forces: offensive nuclear arms systems and defensive antiballistic missile systems. The Soviet side initially introduced—but Washington declined to discuss—the American aircraft based in Europe and on aircraft carriers in the Mediterranean and North Pacific. These were the so-called forward-based systems that could reach our territory on U.S. fighter-bombers. Eventually these were discussed in the later rounds of talks, which began after SALT I was signed in 1972.

The impasse developed over offensive arms, which involved a wide variety of weapons and was complicated by the different nuclear force structures of the two countries. Ours depended strongly on land-based heavy missiles, while the West had a "triad" of land, air, and submarine-based missiles. Moreover, more sophisticated types of missiles were being developed, so military technology was running ahead of the protracted negotiations. For example, the broad public discussion for some time left out of the count the important question of missiles with multiple warheads, or MIRVed missiles, which, once at the target area, could launch their warheads at a number of separate and more specific targets. This subject was not at first on the table for negotiations, although MIRV and ABM systems actually were two crucial issues in SALT I.

The American side was the first to achieve a technological breakthrough in MIRV and the Nixon administration tried to preserve its advantage for as long as possible. By 1970 the United States had MIRVs ready for deployment whereas the Soviet Union had not even begun testing them. So the Americans did not exert themselves to discuss MIRVs during the SALT talks and definitely were not eager to ban them. In a private talk Kissinger bantered with me, "Well, you are very smart indeed to suggest banning something you don't have and we already do."

So Moscow formally raised the question of MIRVs when the American side began to seek definite limitations on intercontinental ballistic missiles (ICBMs), including our heavy missiles, because a straightforward missile count without MIRVs would give them a clear advantage. The American agreement to count MIRVs was then rather skillfully hidden under the cover of a condition which the Nixon administration (and Kissinger especially) knew Moscow could not accept: a link between a ban on MIRVed missiles and on-site inspections to verify the ban. As expected, the proposal was immediately rejected by the Soviet side. Besides, the American proposal to reduce the number of ICBMs was couched in such terms that it would have significantly reduced the principal Soviet heavy missile systems but not those of the United States.

America's confidence in its technical superiority played a major role in the whole story of nuclear disarmament. From the MIRV controversy all the way to Ronald Reagan's favorite dream of a Star Wars defense, it is easy to trace an American desire to acquire some form of ultimate weapon guaranteeing superiority over the Soviet Union, however illusory that might have been. The whole history of the arms race showed that neither side would let the other pull ahead. MIRVed missiles lasted as an American advantage for only a couple of years, when the Soviet Union built its own.

The American refusal to ban such missiles was a major mistake throughout the SALT negotiations. The failure to realize the need to work for mutual renunciation of MIRV during Nixon's presidency proved to be yet another missed opportunity in curbing the Soviet-American strategic arms race at an early stage. No such effort was made by the Nixon administration. It was not until the early 1990s—twenty years later—that both governments came to realize this in their 1993 agreement, to scrap MIRVed missiles as part of the overall strategic arms reductions by both countries.

Because a limitation on MIRVed warheads or an outright ban would have been opposed by the Pentagon and its political supporters on the right, Nixon and Kissinger gradually decided to seek curbs on ABM systems only. At the same time, the White House was looking for some agreement symbolizing its readiness to continue seeking limitations on strategic arms. An impasse developed in the SALT negotiations in Helsinki and Vienna, and the confidential channel became correspondingly more active in preparing arms agreements for the summit.

On behalf of Moscow I proposed to Kissinger that we separate out the issue of antiballistic missiles and, as an initial step, concentrate our efforts on it in order to conclude an agreement that same year, meanwhile deferring the deadlocked issue of offensive arms control. But Kissinger wanted some kind of offensive missile agreement, and Llewllyn Thompson, who was a member of the American delegation to the SALT talks, told me that Nixon would not sign a separate ABM agreement without reaching at least a limited, even symbolic, SALT arrangement on offensive weapons. At least those were the instructions to the delegation.

The discussion about ABM systems also was not simple. Should they be outlawed completely or permitted to protect capitals, National Command authorities, and ICBM sites? The question became even more complex and confusing because of continuing disputes inside both governments. In Moscow, some members of the political leadership were prepared to discuss a zero option for ABM systems with the Americans. But most of the military brass opposed a total ban, arguing that a system was already under construction around our capital, although there was a technical argument against that: the system was imperfect and further construction would demand huge expenses. That left the Soviet leadership undecided.

The American side had its own disagreements and in any case misread the already confused Soviet intentions. As a result, after prolonged negotiations the zero option for ABM was dropped. What was finally worked out was an agreement giving each side the right to an ABM site protecting its capital and, if it wished, one of its ICBM bases. This was a grave mistake on both sides, because forswearing ABMs before they were built would have solved one of the most crucial disarmament problems. To understand what a major opportunity we had lost, suffice it to recall how the idea of an ABM system developed into Ronald Reagan's "Star Wars" program about a decade later.

In our private talks to construct a diplomatic framework for disarmament agreements politically acceptable to both sides, Kissinger and I reached "an understanding" that ultimately led to the idea of coupling ABMs to certain limitations on ICBMs, which then would be the subject of specific future negotiations. Both governments decided to formalize the results of our talks by exchanging confidential letters between Nixon and Kosygin, and during May Kissinger and I worked on the wording.

On May 20, 1971, the breakthrough was announced in Washington and Moscow. It was stated that the United States and the Soviet Union had agreed to seek to work out an ABM agreement and certain measures to limit offensive strategic weapons. Precisely what that agreement and those limitations would be remained to be determined during further negotiations prior to the summit.

Again Rogers knew nothing about the numerous meetings between Kissinger and me to negotiate the agreement. He was deeply hurt when he was informed about the forthcoming announcement, and according to the memoirs of H. R. Haldeman, the president's chief of staff, he asked Haldeman, "Why didn't you tell me you were doing this? There's no need for me to be involved, but I do have to be informed."

Kissinger's SALT negotiators also were furious at him. They later accused him of selling them out to obtain a quick agreement to dress up the summit which, in their opinion, Nixon wanted badly. I cannot speak for them or the American side, but my personal impression was that both sides wanted to have the summit without undue delay. It would be unfair to create the impression that everything was achieved through the confidential channel. Very important work was done by the delegations which, throughout many months of difficult negotiations, helped to analyze, clarify, and formulate concrete positions on both sides. But the confidential channel was a more convenient means for both governments to compromise a deadlock and reach a final decision at the crucial moments of negotiation. That was why the heads of both delegations angrily felt that they had been deprived of the fruits of their work by the participants in the private channel. I can understand their anger, especially since they had been working so hard at their job.

The complex nature of these two-level negotiations is illustrated by one episode. In mid-May, I received an unexpected telephone call from Kissinger concerning the arrival in Washington of Gerard Smith, the American SALT delegation leader. Smith had submitted a memorandum to Nixon on a lengthy conversation he had held with Vladimir Semenov, head of the Soviet delegation as they were out boating alone on the Lake of Geneva. The confidential memorandum summed up Semenov's suggestions which, according to Smith, finally opened the way for agreement.

To the great surprise of the president and Kissinger, Semenov's suggestions in the memo covered the very points on which the president himself had exchanged views with the Soviet government through the confidential channel, of which Smith and his delegation were not supposed to have the slightest idea. Kissinger vehemently accused the Soviet side of neglecting the confidential channel and ignoring the president's eagerness to keep in touch personally with the Soviet leadership. The Soviet side, he said, preferred routine diplomatic channels although it was perfectly aware it could spring leaks, which could make things difficult for both Nixon and Kissinger himself. "We can just stop using the channel," he warned.

I replied that it was up to either party whether to use the channel, but I was sure this incident was based on a kind of misunderstanding or misconduct that could never be excluded in the difficult conditions of two-tier talks.

It turned out that Semenov, who held the post of deputy foreign minister, had learned from his friends in Moscow about the confidential channel and its work, and decided to take an initiative along the same lines, without of course revealing to anyone that he knew about the channel. He hoped to give Moscow a pleasant surprise with his improvisation and obtain permission to continue negotiations along those lines. Nothing of the kind happened. Moreover, Gromyko launched a secret investigation in Moscow to find the source of his information but did not succeed in uncovering it. In any case, the SALT negotiations continued, with Semenov still in charge of our delegation but without information on what was passing through the confidential channel.

Evidently to encourage us to conduct negotiations on SALT, Kissinger informed me on May 24 about Nixon's decision to exempt wheat and other grain exported to the Soviet Union from the list of items requiring the Commerce Department's prior approval. At the same time they lifted another requirement, that half of all wheat supplies be carried by American ships (their shipping charges were higher than ours). In November the American government approved the sale of grain worth $136 million to the Soviet Union.

One final sensitive SALT question also needs clarification here, that of sea-launched or, more accurately, submarine-launched ballistic missiles. When Kissinger and I had first discussed the relationship between ABMs and a possible freeze on strategic missiles back in January of 1970, I asked him at once if sea-launched missiles were to be covered. He said the United States was prepared to accept both schemes. I stated, on my part, that the

Soviet Union preferred not to include the missiles in the freeze, and that was the end of our discussion, the outcome of which I reported to Moscow.

On February 4 I confirmed that the Politburo agreed to the idea of linking an ABM agreement with "a freeze in the deployment of offensive missiles." The issue of SLBMs was not mentioned separately because Moscow believed Kissinger had already accepted our position on them. Once again he did not raise the issue with me.

As a matter of fact, that understanding was still in effect on May 20, 1971, the day of the Soviet-American joint statement on our preliminary agreement on SALT. But, as it turned out later, only the Soviet side and Kissinger proceeded from this, because the Pentagon and other American negotiators at the official talks (not in the confidential channel) believed it important to cover SLBMs by an overall SALT agreement, since the United States had by that time achieved superiority in strategic submarines, while the Soviet Union was building its submarine fleet in a bid to catch up. In short, freezing submarine-launched missiles by official agreement would have benefited the United States rather than the Soviet Union, thus preserving American military superiority. That was why I first rejected the idea in my discussion of the subject with Kissinger.

I am not sure if Kissinger kept it all in his mind, which was burdened with so many other concerns, or if he just concentrated his main efforts on the limitation of land-based strategic missiles, which were believed to be the most dangerous weapons in the whole Soviet strategic arsenal. In any case, he did not attach due importance to sea-launched missiles at the initial stage. It was not until the end of 1971 that he realized it and tried, over our objections, to adjust his position. He managed to fill the gap to some degree only during his trip to Moscow in April 1972 during his talks with Brezhnev to prepare for the summit.

As a result of the visit, an agreement was reached to freeze the construction level of new missile-launching submarines. American historians regard that as Kissinger's major achievement. True enough, but one should not forget that in accepting the freeze, the Soviet side agreed to a ceiling that ensured it would also be able in due course to construct the number of submarine missile launchers it was already planning. Kissinger knew that, too. But both sides preferred not to publicize it.

## Maneuvering Toward the Summit: China in the Wings

As I was preparing to leave for the Twenty-Fourth Party Congress in Moscow as a delegate, Kissinger said he had a message from Nixon for me to convey to the Soviet leadership. It was one of their typically delicate maneuvers.

Frankly speaking, said Kissinger, the president wanted Moscow to know that he found it difficult to see much definition in Soviet-American relations. The Soviet government had been pressing for a settlement on West Berlin during the previous two months, and while Nixon understood the importance of the issue, Kissinger said, the Soviet side had been rather sluggish on strategic arms limitation, something the president regarded as no less important. There also had been no Soviet reaction to his message in mid-February expressing concern over the increased activity servicing Soviet submarines in Cuban ports.

The president had a vague feeling—and maybe, Kissinger said, it was wrong—that "a shade of uncertainty" had arisen about the proposed summit. Nixon was still sure it could be useful if both sides reached an agreement on West Berlin by, say, July, and also wrapped up an ABM agreement at about the same time for signature at the summit. Finally, Nixon also offered the possibility of a European Security Conference that could be convoked at the summit to meet in 1972, and he was also ready to discuss the Middle East.

However informal in its presentation, this was an important message. Nixon was making it clear that he was ready for a Soviet-American summit in 1971—even before his trip to China—although many American historians see things otherwise and believe he played the China card to strengthen his hand at Moscow. The message also was undoubtedly designed to influence the Soviet leadership prior to the party congress, which would be discussing our relations with America. In fact, it was received favorably in the Kremlin and consolidated Brezhnev's desire to improve relations with the United States. But it was not enough to hasten the summit, which did not take place until 1972, because Moscow tried to force the United States to move substantially on West Berlin and SALT before the meeting. This tactic only helped precipitate Nixon's visit to China, something we were of course unaware of at that time and did not in the least expect.

The party congress was held from March 30 to April 9, 1971, and was an important event for the country and the party. The Soviet leadership knew that the country was in a difficult situation. The Soviet economy and living standards were stagnant. Famous dissidents were emerging, such as the physicist Andrei Sakharov and the author Aleksandr Solzhenitsyn. Underground *samizdat* publications showed that discontent was growing among our educated classes. The sharp exacerbation of our relations with China and uncertainty in our relations with the United States led to greater military expenditures, which strained the national budget.

The party establishment gradually began to realize the need to satisfy the population's basic requirements more fully and to narrow the gap with the West in technology and the economy itself. But it was not yet prepared to set about solving the country's domestic problems by offering a measure of political or economic liberalization. Dissidents were considered enemies of the regime, and authors who published their works abroad were subjected to reprisals. Nonconformity was still frowned upon. In short, our dogmatic domestic ideology remained unchanged.

But the realities of the rest of the world and the strains on our economy prompted the Soviet leadership to improve relations with the nations of Europe and the United States. Our foreign policy pronouncements were increasingly based on the idea of peaceful coexistence with these countries despite their different system. Within the Kremlin, these sentiments were consolidated by the dialogue with Nixon about holding a summit meeting. The party congress therefore was designed essentially to proclaim the party's peace program, and that was favorably received in the country.

The improvement of our relations with the United States was among our major priorities, although it was balanced by the usual criticisms of American foreign policy in various regions and declarations about "the ever deepening crisis of capitalism." But for the first time, the summary report by the party's general secretary also emphasized the production of consumer goods as a priority in the new five-year plan. He also stressed that the Soviet Union would continue to favor better relations with the United States. Support from the party congress itself made him feel that he had more freedom of action in foreign policy, and particularly with respect to arranging his first meeting with Nixon.

After the Congress the Politburo met to hear me deliver Nixon's message and discuss our response. I expressed the view that Nixon's conditions could form a good basis for a summit meeting, and Kosygin supported me. Some other Politburo members began to lean toward the same view. But Gromyko rather surprised me by insisting that we should take advantage of Nixon's eagerness for a summit by first solving the problem of West Berlin which, no matter how important it was for the Soviet union, "is passed from one American administration to another." Led by Brezhnev, most of the Politburo members agreed with Gromyko that "a meeting with Nixon can wait," especially against a background of the war in Indochina and the approaching presidential election in the United States—which of course was exactly why Nixon wanted the meeting.

Except for the handful involved in foreign affairs—Brezhnev, Gromyko, Kosygin, Andropov, and the representatives of the military—very few members of the Politburo knew much about America. Their views were limited mainly to what they read in *Pravda* and *Izvestia,* and their discussions of the subject sounded very much as though they could have been lifted from their columns. They received my telegrams but stayed away from the complicated issues I raised unless they were actually discussed at their meetings. For most Politburo members, America and foreign policy were not part of their domain; each had his bureaucratic territory and would not welcome an invasion from another member, so they acted accordingly in foreign territories that were not their own. They usually held the most orthodox views and rarely made concrete proposals of interest on their own. As a rule, they could be counted on to support the general secretary's proposals in foreign affairs (which were usually prepared by Gromyko).

In the West many believed that the general secretary of the Communist Party was a true dictator accountable to no one, and this was of course true for Stalin, but not his successors. Brezhnev was no exception. True, he was number one among the leadership, but even as first among equals he could not always impose his views on the other members of the Politburo. Each of them had a right to express his opinion on any subject on the agenda of the regular weekly meeting, which was usually held on Thursdays. Meetings could be called at any time to discuss urgent matters.

All meetings were held in the Kremlin in what was called the Politburo Room, a rather spacious but simple room with no touch of Kremlin splendor. Members would sit on both sides of a long table in a predetermined order, as in White House Cabinet meetings. At the head of the table sat the secretary general who presided. After he announced the item to be discussed, the floor was given to the member who had proposed the item or prepared it on behalf of the general secretary. A general discussion would follow, at times rather lengthy and lively, as was the case with the question of whether to have a meeting with Nixon in Moscow while he continued to bomb North Vietnam. Discussions were concluded and summarized by the general secretary. As a rule decisions were taken by consensus, and voting was extremely rare. If there was a strong division of opinion, the general secretary usually postponed the decision for the next meeting, which was a signal for him to meet privately in the interim behind the scenes with each of his colleagues to work out a compromise. A general secretary of course had many ways of persuasion to carry his ideas through the Politburo, but he was always careful not to antagonize the other members unnecessarily. After all, they could always revolt and replace him, as they did with Khrushchev.

On all important international issues the foreign minister—Gromyko, during most of my career—had to present a draft of our position for discussion and approval by the Politburo. To gather support, he usually discussed his suggestions with the general secretary and some influential members of the Politburo beforehand. Sometimes, the Politburo invited ambassadors to report on the situation in their respective countries, which I did many times.

When Brezhnev planned a visit abroad or any negotiations with foreign leaders, he or the Foreign Ministry presented to the Politburo for its approval a written draft of basic instructions which he would follow. This draft was always drawn up with Gromyko's assistance. While Brezhnev had some room for maneuver, essentially he had to follow the guidelines approved by the Politburo. Afterward, the general secretary always presented, orally or in writing, his report to the Politburo for its deliberations. Other Politburo members receiving foreign visitors or negotiating abroad followed the same procedure.

American presidents had much more freedom in the conduct of foreign affairs. They were not obliged to tell anyone the details of their meetings with foreign leaders. Of course the general secretary of the party also had more than one way to pursue his policies, though no decision of substance could be taken without Politburo approval.

When the Politburo meeting was over, Brezhnev told me in private that although the decision of the majority not to agree right away on a summit had to be respected, I was on the right track toward a summit and should "proceed along these lines." He added, "The summit is most likely to be held next year." He confided to me that he would very much like to visit America and hoped to do so after Nixon's visit to the Soviet Union. He commanded me lightly and in our usual friendly exchange "to continue on the same course."

For me, the party congress marked a step in my career. With the increasing importance of our relations with the United States I had to conduct talks regularly with the highest officials in Washington; I was therefore advanced from alternate to full membership of the Central Committee.

On my return to Washington I met with Kissinger in the White House on April 23 to report on the events in Moscow. They had of course already heard of Brezhnev's public speech, and Kissinger said that the president welcomed his point about pursuing a constructive approach to our relations. I informed him that the Soviet government was ready to exchange letters with the president on limiting ABM systems, and Kissinger commented, "This is a serious step toward an agreement."

Then I proceeded to the question of a summit. On instructions from Moscow, I told him that President Nixon had already been advised of the Soviet government's essentially positive attitude, but I voiced "my serious personal doubts" about the meeting unless we could first reach an agreement on West Berlin. Kissinger was patently surprised and reacted rather nervously. He vehemently declared he could not possibly accept an ultimatum from the Soviet side making a Berlin agreement a price for the summit; that would leave the president no alternative but to give up the summit.

I told him he had no reason to be indignant. It was anything but an ultimatum. The public in many countries, including our own, would be puzzled at a Soviet-American summit if tension still persisted around West Berlin. I knew perfectly well why Kissinger was disgruntled, but I was bound by the Politburo decision. I was not surprised later that our tough response on Berlin made Nixon set his political sights on visiting China before he would visit the Soviet Union. That was a direct result of Gromyko's Politburo proposal.

Four days later I met again with Kissinger at his request. He said the president had instructed him to discuss three questions: the summit, West Berlin, and SALT.

On the summit, he said Nixon had long noted the hesitation of the Soviet leadership, and whatever Moscow's private reasons, he no longer felt entitled to raise the question of a definite date of a summit—nor could he accept any linkage between the summit and another problem (hinting at West Berlin), although he was prepared to discuss any other world issues. So he was leaving open the question of a summit indefinitely, although he was prepared to discuss it again when Moscow was ready.

As to West Berlin, Kissinger said that unfortunately, the pace of negotiations appeared to be much slower than expected but the president was prepared to continue his efforts to seek an agreement. Kissinger himself had discussed matters with Egon Bahr, West German Chancellor Willy Brandt's personal assistant for East-West questions, who wanted an agreement. (Bahr was particularly helpful in improving relations between Bonn and Moscow.)

It took Kissinger several days to cool down and deny, with Nixon's knowledge, speculation in the American media that the administration was improving its relations with Beijing for anti-Soviet motives. China and the United States were already warming up to each other through an unofficial process of exchanging delegations and sports teams, which was known as "ping-pong diplomacy" for the first such team to visit the United States. It looked like the White House was trying to dampen any negative effect of its overtures to Beijing on Soviet-American relations, but in no way did it refuse to stop playing the diplomatic game with us.

On June 10, Kissinger invited me to a very informal meeting with him alone at Camp David, the president's retreat in the mountains north of

Washington. It was a most unusual and friendly gesture toward a foreign ambassador. We two flew there by helicopter. Kissinger said that on the president's instruction—Nixon was not there at the time—he would like to
review our relations in specific areas without haste. We talked for six relaxed
hours and the conversation was marked by a positive attitude on almost all
issues. In conclusion Kissinger again raised the question of Nixon's prospective visit to the Soviet Union. I had felt all along that this whole *tour d'horizon* was designed to lead the conversation to its principal subject, the summit
meeting.

Kissinger said the president was ready to discuss concrete moves by
both sides in Europe in order to "start untying" European problems.
Kissinger went on to stress the importance attached by the president to the
Middle East and wanted it moved up on the agenda so he and Brezhnev
could discuss it without the presence of other Americans (he even preferred
to have only a Soviet interpreter). If such a frank conversation resulted in a
strictly confidential agreement with the Soviet leadership, Kissinger said, the
president would find ways and means to keep his side of the bargain without
accounting to anyone.

Unfortunately, Moscow failed to take advantage of Nixon's interest in
finding a mutually acceptable first step toward a solution. It was a time of
opportunity because Washington was concerned about Soviet arms supplies
to the Arabs. We had just signed a Treaty of Friendship with Egypt and continued to supply Syria with combat aircraft and surface-to-air missiles; we
also sent military advisers. But our excessive connection with the Arab countries prevented us from pursuing a more flexible policy in the Middle East
and acting in concert with Washington.

In conclusion Kissinger asked me to inform the Soviet leadership about
the projected date of Nixon's visit to Moscow, provided the Kremlin regarded
such a visit as acceptable in principle. He said September would be the most
suitable time (apparently, Nixon still hoped to arrange a summit in 1971,
probably before his trip to Beijing). Another acceptable period would be between March and May of 1972.

For my part, I gave him our detailed proposals on West Berlin, which
remained unsettled following negotiations in Berlin and an exchange in
Bonn in connection with Brandt's visit to Washington. Kissinger commented that the negotiations held by the Soviet Union and the United States
and Germany in Berlin were both crucial and confidential. Only three
Americans were immediately involved in the matter: the president, Kissinger,
and Kenneth Rush, the U.S. ambassador to Bonn who was trusted to be in
the loop because he had been Nixon's law professor at Duke University. The

State Department, including Secretary Rogers, had no idea about the confidential exchange and proceeded from the guidelines agreed upon by the four Western powers.

I then began hearing confidential reports of progress being made in negotiations with Willy Brandt on West Berlin from Kissinger and from the West German ambassador, Rolf Pauls, who informed me that Brandt had been told by Nixon that he was much more optimistic than on Brandt's last visit. The president based his optimism on the more positive foreign policy of the Soviet Union following the Communist Party Congress. But in all probability, progress in the Berlin talks was also the result of the implicit linkage with the summit that had been made at the secret meeting of the Politburo.

On the government's instructions, I visited President Nixon late in June to deliver the text and give him the details of a Soviet statement calling for a conference of the five nuclear powers to discuss the questions of nuclear disarmament. The president said he would carefully examine the proposal but said he wanted to make some frank but strictly confidential preliminary observations. He stressed that he wanted them brought to the notice of the Soviet government, but without their being recorded in the official exchange between the State Department and our Foreign Ministry.

"I don't want to appear cynical," Nixon said. "I am a realist as much as the Soviet leaders." But there were only two real nuclear powers in the world, he said, and they of course were the Soviet Union and the United States. The other three could bear no comparison in terms of nuclear potential, although they were going out of their way to boost their prestige and it would take them a long time to bridge the gap. Given this relationship, he suggested, wouldn't such a five-power conference turn out to focus on reducing the nuclear armaments of the two nuclear superpowers without seriously affecting the other three? Before even discussing a reduction of their own small nuclear arsenals, they could demand from the very outset that the nuclear potential of the Soviet Union and the United States be reduced to their level. Finally he suggested we continue the exchange through the confidential channel. To my mind, his arguments were sound.

The president then turned to Soviet-American relations. He believed there had been a certain improvement although not a very significant one. In a sense, our relations were entering a new important period of trials and opportunities, he said, and given good will on both sides, it would be possible to make headway before the United States focused on the election campaign in the middle of the next year.

NIXON: SUMMIT FOOTHILLS ■ 229

"At present," the president continued, "I see two main priorities in our relations in this particular period, that is, reaching agreements on West Berlin and SALT. There are other questions, like the Middle East, but this cannot be solved easily."

In the Middle East, he said Moscow and Washington should concentrate on preventing a new outbreak of armed hostilities. Then, with some visible hesitation, the president added that the Soviet leadership should know about his suggestions on "an important question" recently raised by Kissinger to the Soviet ambassador on his personal instructions (Nixon clearly meant the summit but avoided using the word). He hoped the Soviet leadership would devote as much attention to these suggestions as he devoted to Moscow's suggestions on other questions, including Berlin. On the whole, the president said in conclusion that he believed it would be possible "to achieve a breakthrough" in U.S.-Soviet relations during the months preceding the election campaign. I expressed my personal agreement.

We did not discuss relations with Beijing, which had begun to emerge as an important and newly vexing strand in geopolitics and a question of Washington's priorities between the Soviet Union and the People's Republic of China. The administration continued to hide its contacts with the Chinese. They were handled confidentially and at the highest level by Nixon and Kissinger. Only a limited circle of confidants was involved.

Nevertheless, a general discussion within the government was under way. Llewellyn Thompson, who had remained an adviser to the White House and the State Department, told me confidentially in mid-June that there had been a struggle within the American leadership, including the highest State Department officials, over American foreign policy priorities and their influence on American-Soviet relations.

There were basically two camps. He said one side leaned toward giving priority to agreements with the Soviet Union, arguing that this was justified by the role played by the Soviet Union and the United States in the world. The other view gave precedence to an opening to China—with which the United States had had little official contact and no formal relations at all since the Communists came to power in 1949. This camp believed China could help end the Vietnam war soon, partly by bringing pressure to bear upon the Soviet Union. They reasoned that Moscow would hardly choose to have tense relations with both Washington and Beijing. Thompson's impression, from his private conversations with the president, was that Nixon was trying to keep both opportunities open for the time being.

Kissinger went off to Asia shortly thereafter and on June 30 even called me in to talk about it. The trip was supposed to acquaint him with the rising tensions between India and Pakistan, and perhaps it did. But Pakistan turned out to be the jumping-off point for his secret visit to China, which was of course the principal goal of the journey. He kept silent about that.

While Kissinger was away, Moscow finally settled on a date for the summit in November or December, thus effectively postponing it until the end of the year. I delivered the message to Kissinger's deputy, Alexander Haig, who was demonstrably pleased by what he called "the good news" and said he would immediately report it to the president and Kissinger. The Soviet government, given the long history of unfriendly relations between the United States and China under the Communist government, had not even considered it a possibility of rapprochement between the two nations on the scale that was taking place in secret at that moment. No one was more surprised and confused than the Kremlin when it received the news of Nixon's plan to go to China even before, as it finally turned out, he would meet Brezhnev at the summit in Moscow.

# III. A Geopolitical Triangle

## *Enter China*

I was called to the White House at 9 A.M. on July 15, 1971, to talk on the secure telephone with Kissinger who, upon his return from Asia, was with the president at his vacation home in San Clemente, California. The call was urgent and quite unexpected.

Kissinger said that the president was to speak on national television later that day. He would announce that Kissinger had visited Beijing on July 9 to 11 and met with China's premier, Zhou Enlai, who on behalf of the Chinese government had invited Nixon, in accordance with the president's own wishes, to visit China before March 1972. The president accepted the invitation "with satisfaction."

Kissinger sounded noticeably pleased, clearly implying that our delays in responding to the president's requests about a Soviet-American summit played into the hands of the Chinese. In my heart of hearts, I could only agree with him. He went on to say that President Nixon had asked him to communicate an oral message to the Soviet government; it was an obvious attempt to offset the unfavorable impression made by the surprising news of his trip to China.

In his message the president said the Soviet government knew of the sequence of events preceding the announcement of his visit: the American government had repeatedly indicated its foreign policy priorities and the president was anxious to reiterate and reinforce the spirit of the statements made by Kissinger to Ambassador Dobrynin at Camp David on June 10 and in Washington on June 30. The announcement of the president's scheduled trip to China was not directed against any third country, and any reversal of the latest positive developments would undoubtedly have grave consequences for our two countries. The president hoped the Soviet government would not misinterpret the meaning of his trip to China. "You, Mr. Ambassador, know better than anybody else about the efforts made by us over two years to achieve progress and particularly give priority to the issue of a meeting of our countries' leaders," the president said through Kissinger.

He insisted that the recent decision of our leaders to postpone the summit meeting made Nixon advance his meeting with the Chinese but that this had no bearing whatsoever on American-Soviet relations. Both sides now had two alternatives. On the one hand, they could advance quickly on the many questions we had already discussed—and the American side hereby confirmed its readiness to do so. Or they could retreat to a painful reassessment of our relations. He was prepared for either alternative but "we would prefer to follow our present course."

Once back from San Clemente, Kissinger invited me to dine with him in the White House on July 19 and give me his views, fully approved by the president. He clearly sought to justify the arrangement on Nixon's trip to Beijing, although I took care not to raise the question on my own.

His remarks boiled down to the point that the American-Chinese agreement was not directed against the interests of the Soviet Union. He put the main emphasis on the fact that Nixon had repeatedly raised the question of his meeting with the Soviet leaders but they had never given a definite reply, which I could not deny. I felt we had allowed ourselves to be outplayed by the Americans and the Chinese, although I certainly did not let Kissinger know that.

Kissinger strongly complained about serious "psychological" difficulties in establishing an adequate personal understanding between President Nixon and the Soviet leaders and an unbiased assessment of both sides' motives. He said that relations between them were characterized by an "exaggerated mistrust" of each other's assurances, which harmed the whole enterprise, and both sides should overcome that "psychological barrier." The president, he said, wanted our relations to continue in the same positive direction, and his attitude to a summit meeting remained unchanged. He expected it to take place in April or May of 1972.

Kissinger also gave me some details of his trip, evidently hoping to calm our apprehensions. According to him, they talked little about the Soviet Union, and he even had the impression that the Chinese were actually more concerned about Japan than the Soviet Union. The Chinese leaders were nervous about the rapid growth of Japan's economic potential and its prospects of becoming a nuclear power. They also had an elaborate discussion about the war in Southeast Asia, but Kissinger avoided talking to me in detail about it. He merely said that a lengthy dialogue between the two governments lay ahead, and that despite considerable difficulties facing both sides in Southeast Asia, he still had the impression the problems could be solved by neutralizing the region and preventing any outside interference after a settlement there. The most serious problem in Chinese-American relations remained Taiwan and not Southeast Asia. He told me he was leaving it "to the

Soviet government's discretion" to use his information as best it could in its discussions with Hanoi.

In conclusion Kissinger generously said that if Moscow had any questions about his China trip, he had the president's instructions to answer them "frankly." Not that any questions from Moscow followed.

On July 27 Nixon made another goodwill gesture toward Moscow by proposing through Kissinger to conclude an agreement on reducing the risk of an unprovoked and accidental outbreak of nuclear war. During ten years of disarmament talks, the United States had rejected our idea, but now Nixon suggested that it be singled out for a separate agreement. This was signed on September 30 by Gromyko and Rogers during the Soviet foreign minister's visit to Washington.

## Nixon Opens a Dialogue with Brezhnev

After these goodwill gestures, Kissinger made a rather extraordinary request on behalf of the president. For the first time, Nixon wanted to send a message directly to Brezhnev as general secretary, in order to establish a closer personal contact. Up to that moment, Nixon and his predecessors had addressed their messages to the Soviet leadership through Kosygin as prime minister under traditional diplomatic protocol, since he officially outranked any party official. In Brezhnev's struggle within the Politburo to be the one to deal with foreign heads of state, Gromyko quietly helped him by sending Soviet ambassadors special instructions and instructing me, in particular, to talk with Kissinger privately and explain things. I was instructed to say "it is more appropriate" to address the president's letters to Brezhnev, and I did.

Kissinger said the letter did not directly bear on Nixon's proposed meeting with the Soviet leadership because he wished to avoid appearing too importunate. However, he said it would be expedient to announce a date and an agenda for a Soviet-American summit before Nixon actually went to China the following year. The letter therefore outlined "a number of ideas" on our relations and stressed their importance. These included Washington's understanding of the Soviet Union's special interests in Eastern Europe. The letter also explained the American policy in relation to China and confirmed that the United States was interested in promoting the Soviet-American dialogue on strategic arms limitations, West Berlin, the Middle East, and Southeast Asia.

One of the most important points of the message, Kissinger stressed, was Nixon's emphatic desire to discuss matters on a grand scale and not waste time on minor questions that could and should be dealt with in detail by appropriate departments once an agreement of principles was reached at the highest level. For all its appeal, this philosophy failed with the Soviet leadership of the time. Brezhnev was largely incapable of conceptual thinking in foreign policy. For that he put his entire faith in Gromyko, who by contrast preferred to deal with concrete problems and decisions, all the while adjusting them to internal politics. His approach was prompted by the fact that most Politburo members had only a poor knowledge of foreign affairs, which made it difficult to review the broad prospects on a conceptual level or to devise and then conduct complicated tactical maneuvers. All of Brezhnev's letters to foreign leaders required approval by the whole Politburo, so Gromyko found it hard to draft and put through far-reaching conceptual messages. Nixon by contrast wrote his messages himself or in consultation with Kissinger alone, which enabled him to work out his policy on both a strategic and tactical level.

For all the talk about the imperfections of American democracy—and it has some—I have to admit that in actual fact President Nixon was more independent in pursuing his policy and more free to conduct diplomatic business than Brezhnev, especially on major issues. This may sound surprising, but it was exactly so.

Some of the details about Nixon's daily routine in the White House further illuminate why it was difficult for him and the Soviet leadership to get on the same strategic wavelength. Kissinger explained that the president established a strict and basic rule from the very start that he was not to be burdened with minor matters and thus would have time to concentrate on major problems. Nixon, a pedantic man, followed the rule unswervingly. For two to three hours after dinner every day, he would retire to a small personal study without telephones to think over important questions. No one, not even his aides, was permitted to disturb him in his seclusion.

When minor questions or petty details were reported to him, they would give rise to irritation and scathing remarks about subordinates who supposedly could not solve them by themselves. This led to some dissatisfaction outside the White House at Nixon giving too much authority to his aides in various domains—including of course the same Henry Kissinger who was explaining this daily presidential routine to me.

Take Berlin as an example. The president knew the main lines of the talks, but no more than that. When the Soviet leadership turned to him on this issue, he took what is called in the White House a "principal decision": the United States should under the prevailing circumstances promote a positive solution outlining suitable deadlines. Whereupon the issue was "closed" for the president. All subsidiary matters that ensued were left to Kissinger's discretion, Kissinger said bluntly, "including the talks with Egon Bahr and the Soviet ambassador" in Bonn, Valentin Falin. Kissinger then would take

appropriate decisions on behalf of the president concerning the tripartite negotiations in Bonn. Only on individual occasions would he consult the president on questions of special importance.

As the Soviet leadership continued to turn to the president for details
on the Berlin talks and link them increasingly to the summit, the president
began to lose his temper. As far as he was concerned, the question had already been solved, and repeated inquiries from Moscow just showed him the
Soviet side would not depend on his word, on his promise to crown the
Berlin talks with a concrete agreement.

But according to Kissinger, Nixon was special "for better or for worse,"
in that he liked global questions and was always ready to take major decisions without involving a broad range of staff and advisers. If the president
was convinced of something, he was prepared to make a sharp turn in his
policy; China was of course the most celebrated case. On that occasion, the
president did not bring in the State Department at all or even consult it, because too many of its officials were likely to reduce his initiative to minor,
discrete steps which would have resulted in staying on the old course. But
the president took his decision independently, put it in practical terms, and
the State Department had no choice but to implement it.

The president would have liked to do business with the Soviet leadership in the same spirit, said Kissinger, but to no avail. Nixon repeatedly
called upon Moscow to arrange a discussion of the Middle East on a grand
scale. He also wanted Moscow to help arrange peace talks on Vietnam,
which was a Soviet ally. But there had never been a major discussion of either
issue. Every time it had ended up in long delays or petty details and tactics,
which, though important, did not determine the general course. The collective Soviet leadership could not rapidly rally the imagination and flexibility
among its members to conduct a foreign policy along lines that would be demanded by everyday diplomacy.

Kissinger observed that he had tried more than once to talk in more conceptual terms with Gromyko, but his Soviet partner always dodged. Remarkably, neither Nixon nor Kissinger understood the way Moscow shaped its
foreign policy. In fact, decisions of the magnitude they were seeking could not
be made by Gromyko or indeed Brezhnev himself without the consent of the
Politburo. That is why Gromyko could not talk completely freely about
Soviet-American affairs. His reticence was due neither to ignorance nor unwillingness but to lack of the necessary authority. Without it the cautious
Gromyko would never step onto the dangerous ground of improvisation.

Far from home, I enjoyed more freedom, because on some occasions I
was able to say that I was expressing my personal view. This enabled me to
sound out the Americans' views without simultaneously committing myself

or my government. In a way I was permitted to improvise within certain limits, which allowed Moscow to consider more options. Little by little Moscow got accustomed to a situation in which the ambassador sometimes went beyond his instructions in private explorations. It helped to introduce new ideas and some flexibility within the rigid constraints of the Politburo. This willingness to improvise was fairly rare in our diplomatic service and indeed in our bureaucracy in general, but I developed it gradually. Ultimately it probably helped to account for my longevity as ambassador in Washington. In a way I sometimes dared to speak the unspeakable to my bosses, and this helped Moscow take some new approaches because I could introduce fresh proposals and suggestions to the Politburo on the basis of my informal conversations with the top level of American officials.

My reports to Moscow thus had a dimension beyond those of ordinary diplomatic cables. Most of my cables (except for the strictly confidential ones) were circulated to members of the Politburo. When I made a suggestion, Gromyko had two alternatives: either to offer a draft reply to my proposal for the approval of the Politburo, or to wait until some other Politburo member raised the matter. I was fully aware of that, so I would include in my telegrams a passage saying that I would work along the lines of my proposal "unless instructed otherwise." Ambassadors normally concluded their cables by saying, "I await your directives," but with my formulation, if Gromyko agreed with what I was doing, all he had to do was keep silent while my telegram circulated. Other Politburo members rarely took the initiative in preparing their own comments if they wanted to raise doubts or controversy. Of course they could always question or object at the next Politburo meeting, but few did. Most hesitated to intrude in the sphere of foreign affairs and in any case were unaware of the details of our relations with Washington. This unorthodox procedure helped speed our business through the Politburo without seeking formal approval each time.

To return to Nixon's August 5 letter to Brezhnev, it was in a way provoked by Gromyko (besides his private instructions to me). In one of his rare conversations with U.S. Ambassador Jacob Beam in Moscow, Gromyko unusually emphasized Brezhnev's great personal interest in relations with Washington and gave some of his personal thoughts on the subject. According to Beam, Gromyko attached special significance to the role played by the general secretary in international relations. Nixon and the State Department could not miss this rather unusual declaration by Gromyko, and it was drawn to Nixon's attention.

Rogers gave the State Department instructions to prepare comments for Beam in replying to Gromyko, and the White House had no objection because they were fairly general. At the same time Nixon sent his own confidential message through Kissinger, who asked me to explain this "sensitive matter" to Moscow, lest Brezhnev become confused by two different messages from Washington, one via the confidential channel and one via the State Department. He asked me to stress that the only authoritative message was the one sent from Nixon on August 5 through Kissinger and me—the one advancing ideas for possible discussion with Brezhnev at the summit, of which both Beam and Rogers were unaware. But in addition to cutting the State Department out of the loop, the president and especially Kissinger also left Gromyko tied down because he could not discuss some of the most important questions in our relations with Ambassador Beam, who was out of the loop, too. The foreign minister could hardly hide his irritation because his own role as an interlocutor and negotiator was thus devalued. Of course Gromyko knew what was passing through the channel, but he himself could not use the American ambassador for this purpose as Kissinger did.

The message of August 5, addressed for the first time by Nixon or any American president to Brezhnev in person, had the expected impact. Brezhnev quickly agreed to the announcement of a summit. On August 10 I received specific instructions to tell Kissinger that in view of Nixon's wishes, his visit to Moscow could take place in May or June of 1972, and a definite date would be fixed shortly.

A week later Kissinger informed me that Nixon proposed to hold the summit on May 22, 1972, and that once the date was agreed, he and I should proceed in strict confidence to prepare the agenda. As for the secretary of state, Kissinger said the president would inform Rogers on September 7 upon Nixon's return from the Western White House in California. Keeping the secretary of state in the dark about such important matters was unprecedented, and it certainly sounded very strange to Moscow. Kissinger said he was going with Nixon to California by plane. We arranged to keep in touch, if need be, through the government communication line in the White House, and in the last resort I would be able to use the White House plane which would shuttle daily between Washington and the president's California residence.

Kissinger returned from California at the end of August. We discussed the text of the public announcement of the visit for several days because we could not at first agree whether to indicate that Nixon was visiting Moscow at the invitation of the Soviet government (as Nixon himself wished) or to give a neutral wording (and avoid any reference to an invitation as Moscow wished, since no invitation had been mentioned in the announcement of Nixon's trip to Beijing). We finally settled on a brief announcement referring to the unspecified progress in talks throughout the past year and saying that "an agreement has been reached that such a meeting will take place in Moscow in the second half of May 1972. President Nixon and the Soviet leaders will discuss all principal questions with a view to further improving bilateral relations between the two countries and consolidate the prospects of universal peace." It was issued simultaneously in both capitals on October 12.

I sighed with relief that the long negotiations at last were over. Two days later I delivered Brezhnev's reply to Nixon's message of August 5. The Soviet leader was in a philosophical mood. "If we put it bluntly," he wrote, "we should first of all make clear if we have similar views on the main questions of shaping the policy of nations, especially of those playing a major role in world affairs. What must be the ultimate objective?" He praised the desire of both sides for better relations, although he added that specific issues such as disarmament, the Middle East, Vietnam, and China "leave much to be desired, and something in the American position puzzles us." But he concluded by expressing the hope that the summit "may become an event of great significance" because Moscow had a feeling there was still enough positive material to make the summit worthwhile.

## Pre-Summit Maneuvers

Just before the announcement, the Soviet government on September 3 had signed the most important agreement of 1971, the so-called quadripartite agreement between the Soviet Union, United States, Britain, and France on West Berlin. Looking back, we could say that in a way the Politburo, under pressure from Gromyko, ultimately got this long-sought deal by delaying the meeting with Nixon. True, as a consequence, Nixon went to China first. Was the delay worth it? It is difficult to say. I still believe that it was very important to solve the Berlin question as soon as possible and remove its permanent threat of dangerous crisis. The agreement crowned the difficult talks that had been going on intermittently for many years since the days of Khrushchev and Kennedy. Final preparations had been completed during Nixon's stay in California in late August. There was a delay at the final stage of negotiations in Bonn when Rogers, who was ignorant of the arrangement reached via the confidential channel, interfered and confused matters. Nixon had to call Ambassador Rush to San Clemente and give him final instructions personally.

The agreement was a hard-won compromise. It guaranteed free passage of traffic between Berlin's western sectors and the Federal Republic of Germany, and better communications between West and East Berlin as well as with the German Democratic Republic. The agreement included a broad range of practical and legal arrangements; thus, the legal status of West Berlin was finally determined after many years of controversy.

When Gromyko arrived to attend the UN General Assembly session, he met with Nixon in the White House on September 29 in the presence of Rogers, Kissinger, and myself to discuss current issues. But first the president talked with Gromyko alone. Nixon said he would like to point out, first of all, that it would be wrong to describe him as a man who felt unfriendly toward the Soviet Union. He respected the Soviet Union and the Soviet people and proceeded from the assumption that stable peace could only be based on cooperation between the Soviet Union and the United States. Both countries should avoid confrontation and seek agreement on a maximum number of problems, he said, and it was necessary to act in such a manner as to ensure peace for at least twenty-five years. He then turned to a "question of special importance"—developing a good personal relationship with Brezhnev—and signaled that he was fully aware of the primacy of his position as general secretary and his role in determining foreign policy.

Then, in the presence of Rogers, Kissinger, and myself, Nixon and Gromyko discussed a number of issues—mainly the SALT negotiations but also European security, the Middle East, the conflict between India and Pakistan, and our own relations. As we were leaving, we saw a large number of cars arriving at the White House. Nixon explained there was to be a meeting with delegates to the International Monetary Fund and asked half-jokingly if the Soviet Union was going to join the IMF. Gromyko replied that it looked like the Fund best served the interest of the multimillionaires, "so we don't belong in there, after all." Little did he know that Russia would seek membership in this rich man's club twenty years later.

In mid-October, after Kissinger had returned from his second trip to China, I had dinner with him at my embassy and gave him a personal message from Brezhnev to Nixon expressing his satisfaction about the prospects of the summit. Meanwhile, Kissinger pointed out "in a friendly way" that a squadron of Soviet warships, including submarines, was steaming toward Cuba in the Atlantic, and the American press was playing it up. He hoped the Soviet side would try to avoid anything that could cast a shadow on the summit.

I must admit that Soviet naval exercises sometimes caused us diplomatic and political problems. The annual schedule of maneuvers was drawn up by the general staff of the armed forces and submitted to the Supreme Defense Council once a year. Only two members of the entire Politburo were also members of the council, the foreign minister and the head of the intelligence services. Council sessions were chaired by the party's general secretary—then Brezhnev—who also held the position of commander in chief of the armed forces.

When the schedule was submitted to the Defense Council for approval,

Gromyko would comment on whether the political situation in a given region might be affected by any particular exercise. But as the year went on, there inevitably would be developments in one area of the world or another, and Gromyko could easily forget the schedule; it was top secret, and for security reasons no copies were kept in the Foreign Ministry! Nevertheless the general staff would follow the schedule to the letter unless the general secretary intervened and overrode it at the recommendation of Gromyko or other members of the Defense Council. The difficulty of coordinating these matters did not make diplomatic life any easier since ambassadors were kept completely in the dark about the scheduled maneuvers.

We also discussed the Middle East, since Kissinger had told Gromyko he was moving into that area and was evidently quietly edging out Rogers. Later I had a long conversation with Sisco, whom Rogers had ordered to prepare materials for the Moscow summit. But Sisco himself expected instructions directly from Kissinger, the only one who could give a definite line as to exactly what the White House required from the State Department.

It was clear from what Sisco said that he did not know about the exchange with the White House about the Middle East, and when I had a private conversation in November with Rogers, matters began looking more charged. The secretary of state said he thought it would be a good idea for him to go to Moscow to prepare the way to the summit, although he sounded unsure because he had not talked with the president. The next day I had another private conversation, this one with Kissinger, who by contrast said bluntly that the president wanted *him* to go to Moscow for the preparations in January.

Some days later Moscow cabled that there was no objection to Kissinger's visit. He was obviously pleased with the Soviet reply but observed that his personal relations with Rogers were to become more complicated; he would have to talk about that with the president. Kissinger had outplayed Rogers again. Moscow also preferred to use "the Kissinger channel," especially for confidential questions of great import, because the Kremlin knew from experience this channel was far more effective than the State Department.

## War Between India and Pakistan

Henry Kissinger writes in his memoirs that one of his first exercises in the balance of power diplomacy he and Nixon had constructed to play Moscow off against Beijing took place in the quarrel between India and Pakistan in 1971. This resulted in Kissinger's famous "tilt" toward Pakistan. But this new strategic game did nothing to prevent West and East Pakistan from splitting into two separate nations in a brutal war.

Kissinger originally assumed a publicly neutral position of sorts. L. K. Jha, the Indian ambassador in Washington, told me that during Kissinger's stopover in Delhi (en route secretly to Beijing) he unexpectedly told the Indian leaders that the United States was interested in the preservation of a "necessary balance of forces" in Asia, and should China attack India, Delhi could count on all-round support from the United States. The Indian government found this surprising since it had never raised the question, but it guessed that the United States was anxious to neutralize unfavorable reaction in Delhi to some as yet unknown American move in Asia—the nature of which they only discovered when his mission to Beijing was disclosed. Delhi was also concerned about the increase in American arms supplies to Pakistan, which appeared to be Nixon's compensation to Pakistan for its services in maintaining informal contacts with Beijing as Kissinger arranged his secret visit to China.

Relations between India and Pakistan became more aggravated during the summer and autumn, gradually involving the Soviet Union on the one side and the United States and China on the other. In August Moscow and Delhi concluded a Treaty of Friendship, although not the mutual assistance pact Indira Gandhi was seeking. As long as India stayed outside the nuclear club, the Soviet leadership considered granting it protection against a nuclear threat by China, but caution prevailed. (Remember that Soviet-Chinese relations in that period were very tense. The number of Soviet divisions along the Mongolian border increased from fifteen to forty-five between 1968 and 1972, even more than in Central Europe.)

As relations between Pakistan and India worsened in October, we had vigorous exchanges in the confidential channel, but we failed to avert the conflict. The American government covertly supported Pakistan and, when its military position became precarious, urged the Soviet Union to intervene to restrain India, which was actively supporting the separatist movement in East Pakistan. Judging by Kissinger's conduct and statements, the White House was nervous because it lacked suitable pretexts for the effective military support of its ally, whose policy of reprisals and punitive actions in East Pakistan caused a great outcry in the United States. But the White House was also reluctant to burn its bridges with India.

From December 6 to 10 there was an active exchange of messages between Nixon and Brezhnev, with each side maneuvering to prevent a military conflict but at the same time eager to support its own ally. This was especially important to the White House because it felt Pakistan was militarily vulnerable. On December 10 Nixon asked us to join him in a joint appeal for a complete cease-fire. In a clear attempt to pressure both the Soviet Union and India, Nixon made an extraordinary disclosure to the Soviet leadership. In strict confidence, he had Kissinger inform us that there was a secret protocol in the agreement between the United States and Pakistan (drafted under the Kennedy administration and handed to then president, Ayub Khan, by the U.S. ambassador on November 5, 1962) saying that the American government would support Pakistan against Indian aggression.

To build American pressure, Kissinger told Yuli Vorontsov, our able chargé d'affaires during my absence in Moscow for consultations, that the American military had already been ordered to start preparations for assistance to Pakistan under the cover of tactical redeployment of its naval forces, including the dispatch of an aircraft carrier task force from Southeast Asia. In response, a number of warships from the Soviet Indian Ocean fleet were sent northward.

Kissinger made it clear to us that the United States was mostly concerned about the western section of the India–Pakistan front, which Washington feared would collapse after Pakistan's defeat in the East. As Kissinger later wrote, he believed Mrs. Gandhi was planning to attack the Pakistan-held portions of Kashmir, recover them for India, and thus precipitate through a humiliating defeat the disintegration of what remained of Pakistan in the West. (In the East the White House had to accept that the war was as good as won by India.) As part of his maneuver, Kissinger then asked Vorontsov to assure Moscow that the White House was not in contact with Beijing over the conflict even though Pakistan was close to China. He simultaneously proposed referring the matter to the United Nations.

The tension was broken upon my return on December 12. Moscow sent a particularly important message to Nixon: "Our contacts with Prime Minister Indira Gandhi suggest that the Indian government does not intend to take any military action against West Pakistan." With noticeable relief, Kissinger said that was good news. At the same time he complained that Indian assurances lacked clarity and called upon us to continue close consultations in the confidential channel. But what really mattered was that, after taking Pakistan's side as a payoff for helping open up China, Nixon and Kissinger had to rely on Moscow's word that India would not attack West Pakistan.

Thus the Soviet Union's diplomatic intervention helped prevent the military conflict from spreading to the point where it would have resulted in a total defeat and breakup of West Pakistan, not just an amputation of its eastern province fifteen hundred miles away. I suspect that Pakistan's arrogant behavior at the start of the conflict was probably to some degree fostered by manipulative American diplomacy, which left the impression that the United States would strongly be on Pakistan's side. But—if so—the

Nixon administration failed to fulfill the Pakistani military regime's great expectations. Pakistan, actually an American ally, lost half of its territory.

The final word came in January when we began work with Kissinger on the details of the summit. Admitting that he had been unduly nervous about Soviet intentions during the Indo-Pakistan War, he virtually admitted that he had taken some "unreasonable steps" at the time. He acknowledged that our assurance about India's intentions at the critical moment was a breakthrough in ending the war. For him, that was an extraordinary confession—but not one that he made in public.

# IV. To the Summit

*Kissinger and I Start Work on the Summit*

On January 17, 1972, Brezhnev sent Nixon a message proposing we begin practical work on the agenda for their summit meeting in Moscow. The most pressing issues, Brezhnev said, were Berlin, European security, Vietnam, the Middle East, SALT, and our economic relations—a very broad agenda indeed.

Vietnam played a special role. Nixon and Kissinger had been stressing its importance from their very first meeting with us. But the real dialogue developed slowly. Both sides shared a desire to end the war, but the terms that would be acceptable to each were completely different. More than that: they depended heavily on what Hanoi was prepared to do. Meanwhile, Washington and Moscow continued to stay in touch throughout the conflict. Both expected little from the discussion of the war during the summit but still wanted to continue their dialogue. Nixon hoped to use Moscow, whenever possible, as a mediator between Washington and Hanoi. Even as he announced the Moscow summit in October, he characteristically ordered an increase in the bombing of North Vietnam because he evidently feared being accused by the right of compromising with the communists. The North Vietnamese broke off their dialogue the next month, and in January Nixon asked me to send Brezhnev a message to pass to Hanoi that the American government was prepared to resume the dialogue.

It was only to be expected that the State Department and Secretary of State Rogers would become involved in preparations for the summit. Rogers therefore planned a number of meetings with me.

This prompted Kissinger to talk with me early in February about what he termed "a very sensitive subject." I was intrigued. He said he wanted to inform me in strict confidence exactly what the secretary of state knew about Soviet-American relations, especially the exchanges between the Soviet ambassador and the White House, because the secretary was "far from knowing all." He asked me to keep this in mind when talking with Rogers and avoid the issues with which he was not familiar. Even Brezhnev's personal messages to Nixon were edited before they were shown to Rogers, and any references to the confidential channel were cut out. Some messages were not shown to him at all. They included messages about some sensitive details of the summit agenda that had been discussed only in the exchange of personal letters between Nixon and the Soviet leadership. On the other hand, all the bilateral questions for the summit preparations were under the control of the State Department and Rogers in full measure.

This was quite a surprise to me and a unique situation in my diplomatic experience, in which the president's assistant secretly informed a foreign ambassador as to which high-level information on our relations with the president his secretary of state had access, and which he did not. When I met Rogers the next day, it was clear that he was indeed in the dark about my confidential talks with Kissinger. (We conducted more than 130 conversations during 1972.) Apparently, the White House was going to keep all major questions related to the summit to itself, without initiating the State Department into its secrets. While facing Rogers in this bizarre arrangement, I felt rather uneasy. Did it help or hinder Nixon's diplomacy? I don't know. But he preferred to maintain maximum secrecy and was especially concerned about leaks to the press and Congress.

There was also Nixon's classic anti-communism. This led to hostile outbursts by officials, whether actually encouraged by the White House, we never knew, but also not prevented by the president.

Brezhnev sent Nixon a message at the end of February expressing some irritation at the "double standards" applied by the United States to its relations with the Soviet Union. It pointed out that while a "lively, constructive dialogue" was under way in the confidential channel, members of Nixon's own administration such as Defense Secretary Melvin Laird were spouting anti-Soviet statements. "How shall we take it?" Brezhnev asked. "Surely, it is impossible to do business on two different planes. It is impractical. It is not realistic. There should be a uniform approach to the main issue."

When I passed this to Kissinger, I gave him some more illustrations. Kissinger did not dispute them but emphasized that we must depend only on the statements made by the president himself. A week later, Kissinger gave me a conciliatory response from Nixon to Brezhnev's message, promising to be careful.

## Tripartite Diplomacy

Nixon's visit to China was undoubtedly a major achievement of the personal diplomacy of the president and Kissinger. It marked the formal beginning of a tripartite diplomatic strategy involving the United States, the Soviet Union, and China that had surfaced for the first time to the public with the invitation of an American ping-pong team to compete in China in April of 1970. An agreement to receive Kissinger was concluded secretly in May of 1971, and Nixon's trip was announced in July. The president was in China from February 21 to 28, 1972. Needless to say, his visit did not "change the world," despite what Nixon said with his characteristic hyperbole at a Beijing banquet. Nor did it completely normalize diplomatic relations between the United States and China (the exchange of missions did not take place until 1973 and formal recognition not until 1979).

Yet it was even more than a breakthrough in Chinese-American relations. It had major international implications in the way Washington and Moscow dealt with each other. No longer would they regard themselves as the only two heavyweights at the opposite ends of a tug-of-war. A third force had been added to the equation, offering the other two the challenges and risks of greater maneuver. China was also altogether too willing to play this game. Nixon told congressional leaders in private after he returned from his trip that he believed the Chinese leadership was motivated by two factors: first, their eagerness to bring China to the level of a global power, and second, their unfriendly relations with the Soviet Union.

When he had returned from accompanying the president to China, Kissinger confessed to me that they had failed to agree with the Chinese on Vietnam. The president made it clear that if North Vietnam showed some flexibility and understanding, Hanoi would essentially get what it wanted over two or three years. Nixon implied the possibility of some changes in the political structure of South Vietnam sought by Hanoi, which could not be ceded now without loss of American prestige. He warned the Chinese that Hanoi could not win the war for all its military efforts, even though the North Vietnamese could prolong it indefinitely. History has shown that Nixon was wrong. He was ultimately forced to back down first under enormous pressure from the American people, who increasingly opposed the war.

After Nixon's return from China, Kissinger arranged for us to dine at the White House. When I arrived I had a pleasant surprise: the president himself was joining us to participate in the summit preparations. He began by observing that his principal political activity for the next two months would be preparation for what he hoped would be a successful Moscow summit. He stressed his satisfaction with the frankness of his exchanges with Brezhnev and said that, in contrast to his talks with the Chinese, his Moscow conversations would not have to start at the level of A-B-C's and could tackle important issues at once because Soviet-American relations were already well advanced.

I asked Nixon to give me his thoughts about the summit. The president agreed and then, pointing at Kissinger, who sat next to him and had so far been silent, "Here is Henry, whom I trust completely. Whatever he says comes directly from me. There is no man in the administration who can speak on my behalf with greater authority. It is true, Bill Rogers is an old friend of mine and has all necessary authority as secretary of state. But he is locked together with a great bureaucratic machine. His staff cannot be controlled, nor can it keep things in strict confidence. That is why I do this kind of thing through Kissinger."

Nixon said that there were two questions of great importance and complexity to be discussed with the Soviet leaders: SALT and the Middle East. The United States was yet to speak out on the second question, and would do so through Kissinger. But the strategic arms talks, like it or not, would be a measure of our future relations, especially in the judgment of American public opinion. If we could reach agreement on that, it would be taken as a good sign showing that our relations were on a new and sounder basis. But if we failed, people would regard the summit as a flop, the more so because the second important question of the Middle East could only be subject to a preliminary secret agreement between us: it was too emotional an issue inside the United States for public discussion. I agreed with him.

It was time to take political decisions, Nixon continued. He was ready to establish parity in strategic weapons, though this concept was not especially popular with some influential groups in the United States. So, he said, "let us approach the situation from political positions without neglecting the interests of our countries' defense." He wanted an agreement virtually immediately lest both sides decide to move ahead with the construction of new strategic systems that could determine the pattern of the arms race for the rest of the decade.

The conversation with the president made a favorable impression in Moscow, especially his readiness to agree to strategic parity with the Soviet Union, which had long been a goal of the Soviet leadership. Brezhnev replied with a message on the summit agenda in which he included Europe, West Berlin, the Middle East, and Vietnam. He said Moscow had considered the SALT question in detail. He noted that both sides had drawn closer on ABMs and land-based missile launchers, and that the Soviet Union was studying the American proposal for a freeze on submarine-launched missiles.

As I handed the message to Kissinger, he said the president was becoming increasingly aware that his meeting with the Soviet leaders would probably be one of the most significant events in his political career. That was of course in part a diplomatic nicety, but at the same time it represented a growing acknowledgment by the Nixon administration of the importance of

Soviet-American relations. As if to confirm this, Kissinger raised another "sensitive question." After the Moscow summit, the president was going on to Iran, and after that he had been invited to visit Poland. Considering that "Eastern Europe was within the sphere of special Soviet interests," Kissinger said, the president wanted to consult the general secretary in advance privately because his visit to Warsaw would follow hard upon the trip to Moscow. Brezhnev had nothing against the trip, especially as Nixon demonstrated his consideration for our sensitivities.

## Vietnam and the Summit

On April 3 Kissinger requested an urgent meeting. He was unusually agitated. On behalf of the president, he wanted to inform the Soviet leadership that North Vietnam had launched large-scale military operations across the demilitarized zone, penetrating ten to fifteen miles to the south. The president, Kissinger said, will therefore have to take military countermeasures, and he hoped that Moscow would not regard them as hostile to its own interests, nor would they affect our relations on the eve of the Moscow summit.

Kissinger added that the advancing North Vietnamese troops were "armed 90 percent with Soviet-made weapons," and the North Vietnamese command had gambled nearly all its regular troops on the offensive.

A few days later, on Sunday, April 9, I was invited to a White House showing of newsreels covering Kissinger's two secret visits to China that had been filmed by Chinese cameramen and sent as a gift by Zhou Enlai. Present also were Kissinger's father and mother, a nice couple who had specially come from New York, and Kissinger himself. My wife and I were the only guests. The film was shown in the Situation Room. After the show Kissinger and I had a brief conversation, face-to-face. He again raised the question of the latest developments in Vietnam and implied that the president would very much like to get "a word" from Hanoi through us, especially whether they would meet Kissinger privately, in which case the White House would show some restraint in retaliating for the North Vietnamese attack. Obviously, the president would not mind if we acted as mediator.

The evening left an odd, somewhat irrational impression: nice people in a nice room watching a nice newsreel against a background of bloody battles raging thousands of miles away in the jungles of Vietnam. Somehow, this implicated us all.

The next day we met again in the White House for a grand public ceremony to sign a treaty banning bacteriological weapons in the presence of the diplomatic corps, government officials, and reporters. I signed on behalf of the Soviet Union (I still have the pen). Afterward Nixon took me aside to say that he stood behind what Kissinger had told me about Vietnam the day before. He only wanted to add that in going through the crisis, he wanted our two governments to keep themselves under control so as to do the least possible damage to Soviet-American relations. Although the president was not specific, I came away with the feeling that the White House was preparing to launch dramatic new actions against North Vietnam.

Some days later Kissinger informed me that, in view of the dangerous aggravation of the situation in Vietnam, the president believed Kissinger should pay a short visit to Moscow to meet Gromyko and Brezhnev. Kissinger would then fly from Moscow to Paris for a private meeting with Hanoi's representatives. The Moscow visit would take place in complete secrecy, without even the knowledge of the American Embassy, and Kissinger would stay in Moscow wherever the Soviet side could accommodate him.

The Nixon administration was attempting to draw Moscow into the diplomatic game with Vietnam. Moscow apparently was willing to become engaged, hoping it could help settle the conflict. When I informed Kissinger on April 13 that we agreed to receive him on his secret mission, he said he was also willing to meet the North Vietnamese in Moscow if they wanted (they said they preferred Paris). He briefed me on the basic American position, but the leadership in Hanoi did not let us know where it stood.

Two days later Kissinger turned to me again on behalf of Nixon. He did not try to conceal his anger. Without explanation, he said, the North Vietnamese had just informed the Americans they had retracted their agreement to meet with him. Meanwhile they continued their military operations south of the demilitarized zone, which prompted the president to order bombing raids on military targets in the Hanoi-Haiphong area. The bombing would be halted if Hanoi agreed to a meeting on April 24 or 27. Kissinger warned that the United States would have to resort to "resolute measures" if Hanoi went on to seek a military solution and "tried to topple another American president" after chasing Lyndon Johnson from office. After several days of meetings and a feverish exchange between Hanoi and Washington via Moscow over the date of Kissinger's meeting with the North Vietnamese, he finally told me he was prepared to leave for Moscow to discuss the Vietnam crisis and prepare for the summit. I accompanied him.

Kissinger left for Moscow by plane on April 20. In deep secrecy, I drove in the dead of night in an embassy car to a prearranged place, where a station wagon from the White House was waiting for me. It took me to a military airfield near Washington. Kissinger also arrived secretly. On our way to Moscow we made a refueling stop at a NATO air base in Britain. Kissinger told me, half-joking, half-serious, not to get out of the plane for exercise because they would faint if they saw the Soviet ambassador walking around their super-secret base. To preserve the secrecy of our mission, he did not get out either.

In Moscow Kissinger met Brezhnev and Gromyko. The idea of meeting with Nixon in Moscow while American bombs were exploding incessantly in Vietnam did not appeal to the Soviet leadership in the least, and it strongly urged Nixon to show restraint and caution. Kissinger said the United States was trying to show restraint but the "superaggressive" actions of the Vietnamese might force the administration to "more drastic action."

On the summit itself, the discussion focused first on SALT; as I have already mentioned, an agreement also was reached to freeze the construction of new missile-launching submarines.

In accordance with Kissinger's request for total secrecy, he was accommodated at a separate mansion in the Lenin Hills and attended only by Soviet staff. Neither the American Embassy nor the ambassador himself knew about Kissinger's stay until the final day, when he chose to speak to the American ambassador, who was taken to the government guest house to find Kissinger there, much to his surprise.

The day after his return to Washington, Kissinger told me the president was "very satisfied" with the results of his Moscow discussions and wanted to continue narrowing our differences to ensure a successful summit. One more thing: the president wondered if he would be able to attend a Sunday church service in Moscow. Not that he was all that religious, but for domestic political reasons; his church attendance in Moscow would be nationally televised at home and would make a favorable impression while he was visiting the capital of what some Americans called "godless communism." I said we had absolutely no objections to Nixon going to any church in Moscow.

As the summit approached, it became clear that Vietnam could kill it. Early in May, three weeks before the date scheduled for the meeting, a lively exchange of messages was under way between Brezhnev and Nixon. On May 1 Brezhnev sent Nixon a message calling for restraint in Vietnam, especially in aerial bombardment, because of its explosive effect on Soviet-American relations. Kissinger replied that the president believed—and deep inside I shared that view—that Hanoi was out to take advantage of the summit for its own purposes: first of all its military goals, but also the diplomatic goal of simultaneously provoking both Moscow and Washington against each other. "One can only wish their efforts will not be crowned with success," Kissinger intoned.

The next day, the president let Brezhnev know that the talks with the North Vietnamese had been "highly disappointing." Kissinger said Le Duc

Tho, the chief North Vietnamese negotiator, had told him bluntly that Nixon should stop discussing Vietnam with Moscow and negotiate directly and exclusively with the Democratic Republic of Vietnam. "The man was as defiant as if he had won the war after all," Kissinger said.

Brezhnev sent another message about Vietnam on May 6 again appealing for restraint on the eve of the summit. Kissinger commented soberly: "It can be safely stated that our exchange on Vietnam has not advanced the matter by an inch. We have no claims on the Soviet side in that respect. The United States will do all it can for a summit to take place and produce good results. But we will have to act in Vietnam as required by the military and political situation."

Kissinger also confirmed that the United States had tried to obtain help on Vietnam from the Chinese, who turned aside the request with the observation that it was not Beijing but Moscow that had a stake in the military operations in Vietnam. The Soviet Union, they told Kissinger, wanted to put pressure on Washington for concessions on Europe and the Middle East as part of its bargaining at the summit. This of course was nonsense because we couldn't deliver Vietnam in the first place.

On May 8 Nixon went on nationwide television with a solemn announcement of grave military measures to cut off North Vietnam's arms supply. The approaches to North Vietnamese ports would be mined and blockaded, the rail network would be bombed, and air and sea strikes against military targets would continue. The address also devoted considerable attention to relations with the Soviet Union. Nixon pointed out that the North Vietnamese invasion was possible only because of military supplies from the Soviet Union and other countries, but he also enumerated recent advances in Soviet-American relations and concluded with something like an appeal to Moscow to put its relations with Washington ahead of those with Hanoi.

An hour before the address I was called to the White House, where Kissinger handed me a personal message to Brezhnev from Nixon. The president referred to North Vietnam's intransigence in negotiations and its military operations against South Vietnam and declared his determination "to deprive the aggressor of the means of perpetrating his aggression." He said the military measures he was about to announce would be abolished as soon as an internationally supervised cease-fire was established in all of Indochina. The message also contained a more detailed call for the preservation of our relations at that "moment of statesmanship," an appeal upon which Kissinger elaborated on the president's behalf.

I sharply criticized the military actions as a crude violation of international law, including freedom of the seas. Kissinger tried to justify them, adding that Soviet vessels would not be attacked. On the whole, the conversation was rather tense, especially when I insisted and managed to have one offensive passage deleted from the draft of Nixon's announcement. Frankly, I began worrying about the summit.

Two days later I was instructed to make a strong protest to Kissinger "against the criminal activity of the U.S. Air Force" that had killed some crewmen on Soviet vessels in North Vietnamese waters. We also demanded that the United States guarantee the safety of Soviet vessels and Soviet sailors' lives. The protest was communicated immediately to the president.

Kissinger was back ten minutes later. He said the president had asked me to deliver to Brezhnev his deep personal regret, especially for the casualties, an offer to pay damages, and his assurance that he was ordering the military command to prevent any recurrence.

The Politburo discussed the delicate situation in Vietnam several times, It was caught in a dilemma between wanting to stop the American bombing and wanting to go ahead with a summit meeting with the president who had ordered the attacks. It could not decide, so there were intense Soviet-American exchanges. On the next day I delivered Brezhnev's reply to Nixon's letter announcing the military escalation against North Vietnam. Brezhnev's letter was filled with criticism and entirely devoted to Vietnam and its perils for our relations. "Mr. President, at this dramatic moment for Soviet-American relations and for the world situation as a whole, I and my colleagues expect the American side to do all in its power to prevent irreparable damage to our relations in the present and the future."

Ominously, the letter avoided any mention of the summit, which Kissinger noticed at once.

"Now, what about the Moscow summit? The general secretary does not say anything about that." Kissinger repeatedly posed that question in various forms during our conversation. Finally he asked if we had any objections to the White House publishing the statement that it had received a reply from the Soviet leadership confirming that the summit meeting was still on.

I said there were no grounds for such a statement, as the summit had not been directly discussed in the exchange of letters.

Kissinger then asked if he could at least tell the president that the Soviet government confirmed its readiness to hold the summit as scheduled. I had to say again that, as was evident from the messages exchanged, we had not touched upon the question at all.

Kissinger assured me the president was really anxious to have the summit on the date we had already fixed. On Nixon's behalf he asked me to inform Brezhnev that most drastic measures would be taken to avoid any accidents to Soviet vessels in North Vietnamese ports or on the open sea.

Besides, the United States was prepared to reduce the bombing of North Vietnam during the meeting and completely halt the bombing of Hanoi. All these assurances did not allay our apprehensions about the summit, which we both felt.

In Moscow, the summit literally hung in the balance. The Politburo continued its crucial discussion about whether to receive Nixon in Moscow while the United States was bombing a de facto Soviet ally. The military leadership headed by Marshal Grechko opposed the meeting, and so did President Podgorny. Suslov, the chief ideologist, and many prominent party figures were undecided, while Kosygin and Gromyko favored a summit. Brezhnev hesitated, although for personal reasons he was eager to have his first meeting with an American president. Besides, he was well aware that if he refused to receive Nixon our relations would be adversely and profoundly affected.

The debate was decided finally by the following argument. The leadership in Hanoi, while our ideological allies, doggedly avoided informing us about their long-term plans in Southeast Asia or their policy toward the United States, notwithstanding our considerable military and economic aid. As a result, their actions often were a surprise to us and put us in difficult positions. Actually they did not pay much attention to how they affected our relations with Washington. On the contrary, they did not mind spoiling them. We learned much more from the Americans about their negotiations with Hanoi than we did from the Vietnamese. All that aroused irritation in Moscow. The final verdict of the Politburo was to go ahead with the summit, because its members recognized that the alternative would amount to handing Hanoi a veto over our relations with America.

There were also other factors contributing to the decision that had nothing to do with Vietnam. First of all, the agreements with the Federal Republic of Germany were to be ratified several days before Nixon's arrival, and a cancellation of the summit could exacerbate relations and block the ratification, giving weight to the arguments of the ultra right in West Germany who opposed the agreements. Moscow was fully aware of this. Moreover, it also realized that refusing to receive Nixon would complicate our relations with the American administration for a long period, putting off the summit indefinitely, jeopardizing the ABM and SALT agreements, and promoting another round of the arms race. And in any case our refusal to meet with Nixon would not help the Vietnamese people; on the contrary, the United States would increase its military pressure even more, including the bombing of North Vietnam.

Just to be on the safe side, the Soviet leaders secretly decided to place the question before the Plenum of the Party Central Committee, which met in May. That meeting of about two hundred members of the party and government leadership approved the decision to proceed with the summit, which turned out to be of major significance in the history of our diplomacy. It consolidated the policy of peaceful coexistence and opened the way to promoting our relations with the United States, notwithstanding our ideological differences with the West and our commitment to the dogma of "international solidarity" with the "victims of imperialism." That was probably the first time that ideological considerations gave way to common sense on so important a subject, although they did not vanish entirely and would be felt in other issues.

Both Nixon and Kissinger realized that it was not easy for Moscow, the leader of the socialist camp, to agree to a meeting while their forces were bombing our allies in the Democratic Republic of Vietnam, and had well-founded fears that the Soviet Union might scrap the summit. So, when I brought in the final reply to the White House, Kissinger, hiding his and Nixon's concern by a joke, proposed to bet a case of champagne that he would guess our answer.

I accepted. On a slip of paper, he wrote what he thought our answer was and covered it with his hand. I told him then that we were ready to proceed on the agreed date, with no amendments. His forecast read: "The summit is not canceled but postponed, with the date to be fixed and agreed on later." I still have this piece of paper as a souvenir of that remarkable moment. Of course, Henry never liked to lose a bet, but in this case we were both satisfied with the final outcome, having worked so hard to prepare for the summit. Detente in Soviet-American relations had stood a serious trial successfully, but Kissinger still owes me the champagne.

The crisis surmounted, Kissinger and I spent the following week almost entirely in businesslike meetings daily to agree on summit arrangements and complete as much as possible of the prepared agreements and texts. We made amicable private deals, too. He would tell me he was prepared to accept a certain wording proposed by Gromyko, but on condition that he would only make it official in Moscow when he met Gromyko—"just to please him." He kept his promise. Moreover, Kissinger made concessions to Gromyko on the wording of some agreements, shifting toward habitual Soviet phraseology in order to reach general agreement on major questions. He knew that phraseology would be important to Gromyko when he reported to the Politburo, but it was not crucial for the Americans as long as the essence of the matter was acceptable.

In the final stage of preparations for Nixon's Moscow visit, the president himself took the extraordinary step of inviting me to stay overnight at Camp

David on May 18 to discuss all details thoroughly. Nixon was relaxed. It was an important and pleasant meeting. We were completely alone. Moscow instructed me to point out to the president that we believed the summit offered real prospects for achieving tangible results that would help promote our relations and ameliorate the situation in the world. So I told the president: "Quite a lot has been done for the summit to be a success. But whether we are able to make the best use of today's opportunities will undoubtedly depend on the positions of both sides at the meeting, as well as on the atmosphere in which it will proceed."

This was not just the rhetoric of diplomacy. Moscow still harbored fears that Nixon would spring some new shock tactic against Vietnam, although the Soviet leaders recognized that he was just as interested in the success of the summit as they were. Besides, the very fact that Moscow had agreed to receive Nixon gave him a certain satisfaction because it put Hanoi in something like diplomatic isolation. But the Americans also feared that Hanoi might launch a major land operation during the summit, as Mrs. Nixon told my wife Irina while they were discussing the program for her visit.

At Camp David, Nixon showed me the cabins—I thought of them as "dachas"—where he expected to lodge the Soviet leaders "when they pay a return visit next year." Then he took me to his personal study. There were several thick files on the Soviet Union on the desk, with two folders marked "Brezhnev" on the top. One folder contained recorded conversations between Brezhnev and Kissinger, the other was a selection of Brezhnev's main public statements starting with the Twenty-Fourth Congress of the Communist Party, where he laid out his policies of economic growth and international accommodation.

In the course of our long conversation we discussed in detail the main issues for the summit. To do him justice, he formulated his approach to the issues and to possible agreements clearly and expertly.

Nixon told me he believed that the confidential contacts between the White House and the Soviet ambassador in Washington would become even more frequent after the agreements that we expected to be sealed in Moscow. He added that they were considering installing a direct secret telephone line between my office in the embassy and Kissinger's office in the White House. This second hot line, which required no dialing and was not dependent on the ordinary telephone network, was installed after Nixon's visit to Moscow, and Kissinger and myself used it all the time. Its very existence has been kept secret until now.

## The Summit in Moscow

The presidential plane landed at Vnukovo airport at 4 P.M. on May 22 for a state visit of eight days. Nixon was accompanied by Rogers, Kissinger, and other officials. It was drizzling when Nixon landed. Podgorny and Kosygin handled the official welcome properly, but the general atmosphere was rather half-hearted. The streets of Moscow were deserted, and no welcoming crowds had been turned out to cheer the president.

At the outset, the American delegation was not sure how Brezhnev was going to treat them. They apparently feared that he would start lecturing them, especially Nixon, for bombing Vietnam. That could put Nixon in an embarrassing position, and indeed the whole meeting in jeopardy—which was what happened in 1960 when Khrushchev wrecked the Paris summit by lecturing Eisenhower about spy planes overflying the Soviet Union. The American concern was palpable during the first face-to-face meeting between Nixon and Brezhnev in the Kremlin, which lasted over an hour. Only a Soviet interpreter was present. Both delegations waited apprehensively out- side. Rogers was on his guard and so was Kissinger, albeit less so. They anx- iously asked the Soviet participants in the neighboring hall just what Brezhnev was telling Nixon. But the widespread fears proved unfounded. The conversation went off very well. It opened the way for further successful negotiations in Moscow, which were also joined by Podgorny and Kosygin. Nixon also made short trips to Kiev and Leningrad.

The meeting turned out to be a significant event in Soviet-American re- lations, demonstrating the desire of both sides to start a process of detente. The talks covered political, economic, scientific, and technical ties, and strategic arms limitation. A communiqué marking a solid advance in our re- lations was published May 31, the day after Nixon's departure. Of all the documents produced at the summit, I would emphasize two: one on the conduct of our relations and the other on arms control.

On May 29, in the solemn atmosphere of the Grand Kremlin Palace on the final day of the summit, Brezhnev and Nixon signed a joint document entitled "The Basic Principles of Relations between the Soviet Union and the United States of America." It was adopted at Soviet initiative and was an important political declaration laying the foundations of the new political process of detente in our relations. The Soviet leadership attached special significance to the document because it set forth publicly and jointly the main principles of international conduct we had long been striving to have recognized. First of all, it noted that there was no basis for mutual relations in the nuclear age other than peaceful coexistence. It also acknowl- edged the "principle of equality as a basis for the security of both countries."

Broadly speaking, the summit and its documents symbolized the mutual recognition of parity between the Soviet Union and the United States as two great powers.

That mattered to the Kremlin leaders not only in terms of their prestige, but also in putting Soviet-American relations on a more stable basis. The document was widely publicized in the Soviet Union where it was often cited even when the new Cold War returned under Ronald Reagan. Although the principles proclaimed in Moscow were sound, the main weakness was that of many such declarations of principle no matter how important: it did not provide for any control of its observance and had no safeguards to ensure compliance. Nor was anything done about that in later years.

The document did not get much publicity in the United States. The administration did not give it much prominence, probably because it was a product of Soviet perseverance, and the administration itself was not sure that American public opinion was prepared for it. In any case the document came into being essentially because of Kissinger's conciliatory attitude. He was the only American negotiator to participate in its drafting, while Rogers was ignorant of its very existence until the last moment. In public Kissinger later defended it as a philosophical concept but not as a guide to concrete situations.

I am inclined to agree with Kissinger. The administration did not give away much by signing the document. True, it recognized our equality, but practically only in the field of mutual security and armaments. As for other locutions such as "peaceful coexistence," these did not do any special harm to the American side but were very dear to the hearts of the Soviet leaders, primarily for domestic reasons. The declaration thus created the impression among the Soviet population that its government at last had prevailed over the United States on this important principle, which had long been reluctant to accept it even though we had presented it as a fundamental issue of war or peace. And Nixon himself was seen in a more favorable light by the Soviet public.

The overall importance of the joint document lay in creating a friendlier atmosphere in our relations, an atmosphere of cooperation as opposed to pure confrontation, which soon became known as the era of detente. It created the basis and cleared the way for a number of agreements during the Nixon administration.

Another basic achievement of the Moscow summit was the signing of the SALT I agreements, including the agreement to limit ABM systems of both sides and a provisional agreement on certain steps toward limiting strategic offensive weapons for the first time, the result of many months of talks. The provisional agreement provided for a period of five years to continue the negotiations on far-reaching arms *reductions*. The SALT I agreements were an unprecedented step toward arms control, providing an agreed and concrete basis for the SALT process: first limitation, then reductions of nuclear armaments under international control. That was the concrete foundation of detente.

Several specific bilateral agreements were signed during Nixon's visit: on the peaceful use of space; on cooperation in science, technology, medicine, and public health; on prevention of incidents at sea; on cooperation in environmental protection. Nixon was right. The first summit allowed both sides to overcome strong mutual suspicions and become engaged in more constructive relationships, though they continued to pursue their own goals in the international arena.

There were some difficulties in trade and economic questions, mostly caused by the Americans. Negotiations on liquidating the Soviet Union's unpaid lend-lease debt for American supplies during World War II were conducted in conjunction with talks on a bilateral trade agreement. Nixon promised to take steps to create more normal conditions for Soviet-American trade and business and to remove commercial and financial discrimination. Details were turned over to a special Soviet-American commission, which later put together a package in which both countries would eliminate special tariffs and grant each other what is known as most favored nation trading status, and the United States would offer long-term credits to the Soviet Union through the Export-Import Bank. Lend-lease debt was resolved more quickly and directly.

The gap between the two countries' estimates of the debt was huge, nearly one billion dollars. The United States insisted on a sum of $1.2 billion, while the Soviet side suggested $200 million, arguing that the country had already paid in blood with its catastrophic wartime losses. Kosygin, who handled the issue for the Soviet side, proposed to settle in a businesslike manner and said the Soviet Union was prepared to offer another $100 million. Nixon immediately agreed to bargain, reducing the American claim by a corresponding $100 million. Then, with complete silence in the room, they began as if they were at an auction, with Kosygin raising the amount in bids of $100 million while Nixon cut it by the same figure. It took them half a minute to reach a compromise for a dispute that had lasted for a generation. They met each other about halfway and settled for a payment of $722 million.

Although hardly as dramatic as this settlement, the atmosphere of our negotiations on other matters was constructive and there were no sharp, discordant outbursts. Nixon would open for the American side on each issue, stating the essence of the American position clearly and tersely. Then Kissinger would take over for discussions with the Soviet side and do the bulk of the negotiating. Nixon would join the discussion at key moments, but on the whole, Kissinger seemed to enjoy genuine freedom at the negotiating table. The two of course coordinated their tactics, although it was not always easy for him in Moscow because Nixon had been accorded the rare privilege for a foreign visitor of staying in the Kremlin Palace. For fear of listening devices, the president felt unable to consult with Kissinger in his Kremlin apartment. Instead, they locked themselves in the president's own limousine, which had been flown to Moscow and parked inside the Kremlin.

The Soviet side practiced its own division of labor. Kosygin led on economic questions. Brezhnev was in charge of military and political questions, with Gromyko actively supporting him in diplomatic details. Negotiations thus were often reduced to a two-way discussion between Gromyko and Kissinger in the presence of their bosses, who periodically interfered.

When the negotiations on strategic arms limitation reached an impasse, Brezhnev instructed Leonid Smirnov, deputy prime minister for military industry, to help Gromyko. Smirnov was thoroughly familiar with strategic arms and conducted negotiations with Kissinger, who could not help noticing that Gromyko usually stated the Soviet official position but Smirnov was entrusted with concrete bargaining. Smirnov knew all about weapons but had no experience in diplomatic negotiations, the complete opposite of Gromyko. To finalize the SALT agreement, it took an additional, closed meeting of the Politburo during the negotiations with Nixon.

Both sides paid much attention to international issues although few specific questions were resolved in wide-ranging discussions on the Middle East, Korea, Cuba, and security and detente in Europe. We came one step closer toward a European security conference with Nixon's agreement on timing; he agreed that it could be held the following year.

Brezhnev pointedly told Nixon that the Chinese leadership was out to sow discord in international relations and exploit the differences between the Soviet Union and the United States, and other countries as well. Nixon confined himself to just a few phrases about China's positions on individual issues. The Soviet side pointed out that it was important to reiterate that both sides continued to recognize and observe their 1962 agreement on Cuba. Nixon had no objection, and it was so reported to Fidel Castro. In the communiqué, both sides restated their positions on war in Vietnam, but it was hardly discussed at plenary sessions.

So as not to spoil the good, businesslike atmosphere of the negotiations, the Politburo decided to give one unpublicized dinner for Nixon at a state dacha outside Moscow to discuss Vietnam with him in private. They tried to make Nixon change or adjust his attitude to the Vietnamese, but since they had nothing new to offer, needless to say they had no success. But it was nev-ertheless important for them to be able to report their efforts to Hanoi and other socialist countries, thus clearing their conscience before the Vietnamese.

Nixon was to spend one day seeing the sights of Leningrad. He arrived at Moscow airport, where a special Soviet plane was waiting for him and Kosygin, who came to see him off. They got into the plane and chatted for ten to fifteen minutes waiting in vain for the pilot to appear. Kosygin or-dered him summoned. He finally appeared, red with embarrassment, and re-ported that one of the engines was out of order; they had to change planes. Kosygin, highly embarrassed, began swearing at the pilot.

Nixon asked him what was going on. Kosygin explained and said the pilot would be punished for failing to prepare the plane for the flight. Nixon appealed to him to calm down, saying the pilot should be rewarded rather than disciplined. The puzzled prime minister wondered just what he was to be rewarded for. The president recounted a similar situation in Africa. The American pilot noticed that one of the engines was not working well but did not report the trouble, hoping it would make it through the short flight. But the engine failed and the plane had to make an emergency landing in the desert, a narrow escape for Nixon. "That is why," Nixon said, "I suggest your pilot be rewarded for his courage in speaking the truth." The pilot was clearly thankful for the intercession. Kosygin tempered justice with mercy and ordered a reserve plane.

In Leningrad Nixon was deeply moved when he lay a wreath at the Piscarev cemetery, where about a million Leningrad residents had been buried during the German siege of the city for almost three terrible years of shelling and starvation during World War II. He was especially shaken by the diary of a little girl who recorded the deaths of her family members, one by one, of starvation. She entered the death of her mother, then died herself.

Kissinger also had his share of personal attention. Since his stay in Moscow coincided with his birthday, the Kremlin confectioners prepared a big birthday cake. When he emerged from his room in the morning, he was handed the cake by the KGB general in command of the Kremlin security guard. Soviet and American officials wished him many happy returns. Brezhnev congratulated him personally. Back in Washington, his staff mem-bers handed him their gift, a wooden bear playing soccer (Kissinger was one of the few fans in America and perhaps the most celebrated one). Presents were also exchanged at the highest level. Brezhnev gave Nixon a hydrofoil. The president took his wife, daughter, and son-in-law for his first ride in this Soviet boat the day after his reelection in the waters near his Florida home in Key Biscayne, and it was so safe and seaworthy that the Secret Service made an exception to its presidential safety rules and allowed him to drive it himself. Nixon had been informed in advance that Brezhnev liked to drive big, fast cars at top speed, so he gave his host a new Cadillac.

After Nixon's departure for Iran on May 30 the Politburo held a special session to discuss the visit. Its assessments were positive, and the Soviet leadership found itself far less biased against Nixon, whom they had long regarded as a Cold War crusader with deep-rooted anti-Soviet views, with whom any agreement on major questions seemed practically impossible. But the agreements reached in Moscow showed him as businesslike and pragmatic and marked a serious turn in our relations.

"You can do business with Nixon," was how Brezhnev summed up his impressions. "It is time to prepare for a return visit to the United States."

Brezhnev also formed a good opinion of Kissinger, who had managed with his characteristic style and charm to find the right approach to him during the negotiations in Moscow. Gromyko did not share Brezhnev's admiration for "the smart Henry." He appreciated Kissinger as a professional diplomat but disliked him as a person, partly because Kissinger was popular with the world press and basked too often and easily in its attention to suit the dour Gromyko.

I personally regarded the summit as a major success for changing our relations and installing detente as policy. It was a policy, I must confess, with which we linked many high hopes. But not having entirely shaken off the shackles of the Cold War, I must confess that I could not help wondering just exactly what had happened in Moscow. Was it the beginning of a real relaxation of tensions between the two most powerful nations in the world? Or just another episode in the confrontation that had locked them together in mutual suspicion and animosity for a generation? Did it mean that the Nixon administration was in earnest about more pragmatic relations and mutually beneficial cooperation? The answers were crucially important at the time, but things had not yet taken a definite shape. Still, I was optimistic somehow, although I must say I had no real foundation beyond what I suppose was simply professional intuition.

Indeed, after the summit, such Soviet-American meetings became an important consolidating link in our relations and prevented them from going out of control. When I returned to Washington on June 8, Kissinger handed me a personal message from Nixon to Brezhnev in which the president, like Brezhnev himself, indicated he was already thinking about the next meeting. After discussing a number of questions left unresolved at Moscow, Nixon wrote, "With so many important differences remaining between us, the road to the next summit will undoubtedly not be easy. But now we know how to prepare for it and we can accelerate the process." In his reply, Brezhnev fully shared the president's positive assessment and wrote, "A sound basis has been laid for a radical improvement in Soviet-American relations. Our principal aim now is to implement our agreements consistently."

But Kissinger told me that from then until November, Nixon would have to focus on his campaign for reelection. His foreign policy positions were solid enough, except of course for Vietnam, which no doubt would lie at the center of the election debate. Kissinger gave me to understand that in order to move toward a solution for Vietnam, the president would not mind playing his game with the Chinese, using the successful Moscow summit as his trump card to exercise more pressure on the Vietnamese.

Shortly afterward Kissinger returned to Beijing at the invitation of the Chinese. We were also informed of the president's specific instruction halting the bombing of Hanoi and its port of Haiphong, and of a reduction of U.S. air activity over North Vietnam in conjunction with the forthcoming visit of Soviet President Podgorny to Hanoi, about which we had informed Washington. Podgorny tried to search for a compromise solution to the war. But our attempt to act as a go-between had little effect. Brezhnev soon wrote to Nixon that Podgorny had outlined the American position on ending the war to the Vietnamese leadership. But it continued to focus on the direct talks with the Americans in Paris and told Podgorny to inform Washington that Hanoi's chief negotiator, Le Duc Tho would soon return to the negotiating table in Paris.

Kissinger fared no better in Beijing. He briefed me after his return. It was clear that he had failed to reach an agreement with the Chinese on Vietnam. The Americans had to resume their direct negotiations with North Vietnam without having any clear idea of their prospects as the November presidential elections were nearing.

## Basking in Detente

I was on a business trip at our consulate in San Francisco when Kissinger telephoned me on July 12 and told me that Nixon would like to invite me and my wife to stay at the Western White House in San Clemente to rest for a few days. We drove down the Pacific Coast along the picturesque California Highway 1, which passed through a number of small towns. It was a pleasant journey. Like so many Americans, we were especially charmed by the town of Carmel, with its writers and artists. We stopped there for half a day.

When we arrived at San Clemente, Nixon showed us around his picturesque Mexican-style house, Casa Pacifica, set on the shore and overlooking the sea, and the offices where he and his White House staff worked. He showed me his direct communications links with Washington, the U.S. military command in the United States, and vital regions of the world and with the most important embassies. Nixon could contact anyone by phone within two to three minutes and could receive facsimiles of documents. At that time it was all very new and impressive. Mrs. Nixon also showed my wife around the house. My wife and I both liked it, and I thought the place would be fine for private talks between Nixon and Brezhnev the next year.

In this informal atmosphere, I had a long conversation with the president and Kissinger. We started with a review of the results of the Moscow summit, whereupon Nixon proceeded to the main subject. He said our governments now should focus their attention on preparations for another important step, the next summit in Washington. Of course, he had to win the election first, and he said, "I'd rather not look an irresponsible braggart, but I think I'll manage to defeat McGovern." (Senator George McGovern of South Dakota, running as a peace candidate with strong liberal support, was his Democratic opponent and proved even easier to defeat than Nixon's modest claim indicated.)

After that, Nixon spoke confidentially about the next summit. He proposed a meeting in May or June 1973, with the date announced well in advance. He expressed the opinion that this would have a positive effect on international developments later on. With advance preparation, important agreements would be signed by the United States and the Soviet Union, although hardly as many as the record number at the Moscow summit. As part of the summit, he proposed that Brezhnev come to the United States on an extensive tour for a first-hand look at the country. Finally, success in Moscow had demonstrated to the president that a whole series of summits would be feasible. He suggested that they be held regularly and said that if reelected he would not mind continuing the exchange of visits on an annual basis after the meeting in the United States for 1973.

Work could start, Nixon said, in September with a visit to Moscow by Kissinger, and this was Nixon's immediate agenda: Europe presented no major difficulties, and he agreed to an East-West conference on European security, which was sought by many European countries and supported by Moscow. Confident that the SALT treaty would be ratified, he suggested we start exchanging ideas through our private channel on the second stage. The United States was also sounding out its allies on limiting conventional weapons. The trade and economic discussions begun in Moscow should be continued because they showed promise, he said, but they might encounter difficulties in the Congress. He also wanted to consider further joint steps on the Middle East and Vietnam, the latter especially because of its paramount importance in view of the election campaign just starting.

Nixon also asked me to communicate a personal invitation for Marshal Grechko, our defense minister, to visit the United States at his convenience and meet the U.S. military. Nixon believed it was important to establish links between the two defense departments, but Moscow proved unprepared for that, mostly because of the conservative attitude of Grechko himself.

I vividly remember the conversations with Nixon in the informal setting of San Clemente on the Pacific shore. The atmosphere was quite different from our official meetings in the White House. Personal interaction was much easier. The president himself was at ease. He spoke freely, joked, and was prepared to share his personal views on foreign policy with unusual candor. His scenario for future Soviet-American relations was vast and imaginative. His critics claim he was thinking of something very close to a Soviet-American condominium. I do not know anything about that, but his program of annual summits and regular interaction at the highest levels of our governments not only would have charted the relations between us but would have profoundly affected all international relations whenever the two superpowers threw their weight on the same side of any issue.

The whole idea never got very far because of the scandal over the Watergate burglary, which at that moment was no more than an offshore cloud on our horizon. But it was also too much to swallow for his domestic opposition, which was already accusing him of trying to create an imperial presidency.

Business apart, Kissinger and I arranged for a short vacation of a day and a half. We lay on the beach and even managed to get a couple of hours sleep right on the sand under the warm California sun. The sight would have shocked the Washington diplomatic corps, to say nothing of Nixon's right-wing political opponents: the president's assistant for national security and the Soviet Ambassador, wearing nothing but bathing trunks, sleeping side by side, with a security guard keeping a watchful eye on their papers and personal effects.

Kissinger took us to Hollywood where we visited some of the movie studios, watched film-making and stunts. Kissinger seemed to be popular with the stars, and my wife and I, who were fascinated by this unknown world, were presented with folding chairs as if we were famous directors. They are still in our Moscow apartment to remind us of our Hollywood adventure.

At one studio we were invited to lunch by Alfred Hitchcock, the celebrated master of suspense, who proposed doing a suspense film set in the Kremlin. He argued that the picture would be a formidable success. I did not question its potential for success, but I voiced doubts that the Moscow leadership would fully appreciate the depth and originality of the idea. "The time is not ripe yet," I intoned. Not that I could tell him exactly how long it would take for that to happen. But we understood each other.

That night we had dinner with a number of well-known movie actors led by Bob Hope, the great comedian. Most of them turned out to be very agreeable and intelligent people, far removed from their media stereotypes. Hope, a witty man with a great number of anecdotes and funny stories up his sleeve, could not possibly be as clever when encountering a new and unfamiliar subject, and his edge over other guests would become less conspicuous; indeed he confessed to me that he had a whole team of writers working up his funny stories for him.

Kissinger also invited my wife and me to a small, neighborhood Mexican restaurant, where we tried our first margaritas, which they made with thirteen ingredients. The three of us consumed two sizable pitchers of this formidable cocktail. It was a nice party, especially because not a single word was said about politics.

On my return to Washington I received a letter from Nixon for Brezhnev summing up the ideas he had advanced at the San Clemente meeting with me and expressing thanks to the Soviet leadership for helping restart the Paris talks between the United States and Vietnam following Podgorny's trip to Hanoi. The letter emphasized the role of the confidential channel in the creation of "a new spirit of cooperation, now characteristic of our relations and promising further progress in the forthcoming period."

## Moscow, Washington, and the End of the Vietnam War

A thaw also seemed to be developing when negotiations resumed with the Vietnamese in Paris. Kissinger told me Le Duc Tho had been less harsh and reckless in his attacks on the United States, which Kissinger attributed in part to the favorable effect of Podgorny's trip to Hanoi. By mid-October he told me the negotiations had advanced considerably and there was a real chance of reaching a final agreement even before November 7, election day in the United States. He told me in strict confidence that he and Le Duc Tho had agreed on the preliminary text of an arrangement to end the war. Nixon instructed Kissinger to send the fourteen-page confidential draft with his comments to Brezhnev for information. The Vietnamese had not even informed us of its existence.

On October 15, Kissinger handed me an urgent letter to Brezhnev from Nixon asking about Soviet arms-supply policies "in view of the fact that the Vietnam negotiations have entered a crucial phase." Nixon wanted to know whether the Soviet Union would continue to send military supplies to North Vietnam if the United States concluded a peace settlement that restricted American military aid to South Vietnam.

I voiced my personal view that it would be premature to link the negotiations between the United States and the Democratic Republic of Vietnam to any unilateral commitments by the Soviet Union as if they were the only crucial prerequisite for an accord. We were not participating in the negotiations. We could not consider ourselves bound by any pledges to the White House about its negotiations with the Vietnamese. "But it does not mean," I stressed, "that we are unwilling to promote an early settlement in Vietnam. Quite the reverse, we are doing our utmost." Kissinger confined himself to the observation that the president appreciated our efforts.

Between October 19 and 23 there was a busy exchange of messages between Moscow and Washington about Vietnam. Kissinger meanwhile conducted intensive negotiations with the North Vietnamese in Paris. The American side was keeping us informed confidentially and in detail about the talks, thus depriving the North Vietnamese of the opportunity of manipulating the scarce data they actually did give us.

On the eve of the election in the United States Hanoi assumed a tough posture. Kissinger returned to Washington on October 23 and told Moscow that Hanoi's final response sounded very threatening—but Kissinger offered "guarantees to Hanoi and its friend, the Soviet Union, that even after the election the president would keep his word and honor the Paris agreements."

Then came messages between Nixon and Brezhnev on Vietnam. Brezhnev's attitude was: "There is conclusive evidence that a final settlement on Vietnam is nearer today than at any moment in the past. We cannot have minor considerations of procedure or prestige gaining the upper hand and ruining the whole business."

This was all happening around the time of Kissinger's famous and probably ill-advised statement in the month before the election over nationwide television saying, "We believe that peace is at hand." Many believed it was duplicitously designed to help Nixon get reelected, and this was probably so. But at the same time, an agreement really seemed close—although exactly how close was really part of the negotiating endgame. The Americans insisted that their Saigon ally should approve the peace terms, and that implied a delay of at least until the end of November since Saigon was trying to stall an agreement in hope of derailing it. Hanoi wanted to reach an agreement before the presidential election to avoid further difficulties if a new president were elected.

After the election Kissinger flew to Paris for a new meeting with Le Duc Tho. Nixon had already told me when I called to congratulate him on his reelection that he felt the primary task facing him was to conclude an agreement finally ending the Vietnam War, and he hoped it would be signed not later than the next month. He also expressed his appreciation for the role played by the Soviet leadership in exchanging information and applying diplomatic pressure for settlement. But peace was still not at hand.

The next month saw difficult negotiations and disputes between Washington and Hanoi, accompanied by frequent appeals by Nixon and Kissinger to the Soviet Union, urging us to influence the North Vietnamese. Kissinger would even show me shorthand records of his conversations with Le Duc Tho. Information given by the Americans did not always coincide with that provided by the Vietnamese and vice versa; both sides did not always give us important details. But the Americans informed us far more fully and confidentially, which allowed us to talk more candidly with the Vietnamese about concrete questions and advise them to reach a settlement without undue delay. This they did not like, and kept urging us to press the American side. Both sides were dissatisfied with our intercession. Each wanted much more pressure to be applied to the other side, which made our role neither easy nor especially effective, because we had no desire to become deeply involved and take sides in the controversial negotiations.

At 10 A.M. on December 1, I received a call from Nixon in person. He said he wanted to inform Brezhnev and his colleagues of his assessment of the Paris talks, which were now entering a crucial stage. He began by thanking the Soviet leadership for their close attention and informal assistance. Speaking with emotion, he implied that he hoped the Soviet Union would help him overcome "the last impasse" in the talks with Hanoi. Two weeks later Kissinger told me that Nixon had instructed him to suspend his meetings with Le Duc Tho until they could determine whether Hanoi was ready to agree or was still demanding new concessions. Kissinger handed me a paper giving the American view of the negotiations and a document entitled "The Outstanding Questions at the Paris Talks." He also gave me a complete draft of the proposed peace agreement that had been discussed with Le Duc Tho and some records of his meetings with the North Vietnamese negotiator. He asked me not to inform the Vietnamese that he had given me the documents.

Three days later, just before my departure for Moscow to celebrate the fiftieth anniversary of the founding of the Soviet Union, Kissinger handed me a private message from Nixon to Brezhnev. Optimistic about our relations and especially about Brezhnev's trip to the United States in the coming year, the message obviously was intended to encourage Brezhnev to exercise more pressure on Hanoi. But the timing was bad: all the leaders of the socialist countries were present at the festivities in Moscow, and there was already much talk about "fraternal solidarity with Vietnam." The Vietnamese were extremely clever at exploiting it. Ho Chi Minh understood that we were in ideological bondage—not just Suslov but all the others—and he continued to use it during the war's final stages. They told every leader in Moscow that the Americans were bargaining for too much and thus prolonging the war. They hinted that Brezhnev as leader of the socialist community should put pressure on Washington to settle. On our own, we wanted the war to end as soon as possible, because it affected our relations with the United States.

While I was in Moscow Nixon ordered the most intensive bombing campaign of the war. We understood the political nature of the bombing; the administration had already turned over all ground combat to the South Vietnamese, and now it needed to end the war and bring home its prisoners. After four years in office and two years of negotiations, it did not really care very much which regime would end up in control. Kissinger and Nixon were making it very clear that they wanted a political solution to get out of Vietnam because they needed peace for domestic reasons.

Immediately on my return to Washington on December 28, I had a phone call from Kissinger, who was staying in California with the president on a short vacation. The conversation was entirely devoted to Vietnam, and I told Kissinger that the Soviet leadership believed that the United States should show more flexibility at the final stage of the conflict, first of all by ceasing the bombing of North Vietnam immediately. This would help overcome stalling tactics on both sides and lead to a speedy conclusion of a peace agreement.

Kissinger remarked, rather angrily, that it was difficult to deal with the stubborn Vietnamese who were unreasonable at the conference table. "Is the American side more reasonable when it tries to make its arguments more convincing to the accompaniment of bombs?" I asked him in turn. But we agreed on one thing—that we did not need unnecessary tensions between our two countries at the end of the war.

A couple of hours later he called back and said he had informed the president about Moscow's attitude. Nixon decided to agree to a proposal by Hanoi for Le Duc Tho to meet with Kissinger in Paris on January 8. Simultaneously, he had ordered a halt to bombing north of the twentieth parallel starting the next day, December 29. Hanoi had not yet been informed, so they asked us not to tell them. The United States would do that directly. Kissinger read me the text of the message that had been prepared for Hanoi. Negotiations were on again.

On January 27, 1973, a peace treaty was signed in Paris by the United States, the South Vietnamese, the North Vietnamese, and the Vietcong. A cease-fire took effect the following day, and on that day I delivered a letter from Brezhnev to Nixon saying, "Peace in Vietnam opens up new possibilities for the strengthening of Soviet-American relations and general improvement of the international situation."

Kissinger was jubilant. He said the president felt it now was time to fix the date of Brezhnev's visit to the United States. He said also that Nixon had privately offered the post of American ambassador to the Soviet Union to former Secretary of State Dean Rusk in order to put the relations with Moscow on a solid basis. But Rusk unfortunately had refused to return to public life and preferred to remain a lecturer at his state university in Georgia.

In his reply Nixon agreed with Brezhnev that an end to the war would benefit Soviet-American relations and stressed that the process of detente would now be accelerated. He asked Brezhnev to tell him the most convenient date for his visit to the United States and the next summit meeting.

Undeniably, both Brezhnev's and Nixon's letters reflected genuine feelings of relief and satisfaction at the end of the Vietnam War, although perhaps for different reasons. But they both believed the end of the war opened up new prospects for promoting relations between the two countries. As for me, having lived through three difficult presidencies with their permanent irritation in our relations over Vietnam, I was really happy in my own professional way, for more constructive work lay ahead. Both governments were now set on a firm course toward the next summit.

# V. To the Summit Again, in America

*Detente and Its Problems*

Soviet-American relations reached a level of amity in 1973 never before achieved in the postwar era. Events demonstrated the viability of the policy of detente, although there were some relapses, mainly on the American side. Indeed, the very idea of detente in terms of its practical implementation came to Americans out of the blue and caught many completely unaware. The shift also created new and strange domestic alliances, the most aggressive linking right-wingers, liberal anti-communists, and Jewish groups working together for free emigration and other human rights in the Soviet Union. It was their campaign that prompted Congress to endorse the Jackson-Vanik amendment, linking trade concessions to the Soviet Union to a relaxation of its domestic policies. Thus it was not yet time to talk about a serious change in the American mood in favor of a stable improvement of our relations, in contrast to the sentiments in the Soviet Union.

But by far the most remarkable influence on the developments in the United States was made by Watergate, which provoked a crisis of American constitutional democracy. At first the break-in on May 28, 1972, at the Democratic Party's headquarters in Washington's Watergate apartment building, had seemed only a minor event. The burglars were later discovered to have been acting on behalf of Nixon's inner circle of political operatives, but even then I did not pay much attention to the first reports of the trail leading toward the White House. I thought it inconceivable that Nixon, a man of great political experience, would permit his office to become involved in such a petty venture.

The Soviet Union and its government had great difficulty understanding how public opinion in the United States could have gotten rid of President Nixon, surely one of the most able leaders of his time in foreign affairs even if he was also one of the most reckless in his climb to the top. Here was the president, elected for the second term by a significant majority, threatened by impeachment for what was seen as a minor affair. His use of the CIA, the FBI, and the considerable powers of his own office to remain in the White House was considered in the Soviet Union at that time a fairly natural thing for the chief of state to do. Who cared if it was a breach of the Constitution? So our inclination was to think that Watergate was some kind of intrigue organized by his political enemies to overthrow him. And in Moscow, most of those enemies were considered anyway to be the opponents of better relations with the Soviet Union. Although in the short run all this had no serious effect on the process of detente, it was eventually recognized as capable of exploding the process at any time. It was of course the time bomb that finally destroyed the presidency of the man who in our minds was the principal force in the United States behind the policy of detente.

## Jewish Emigration and the Coalition Against Detente

After the first summit an anti-Soviet coalition had begun to take shape from opposite sides of the U.S. political spectrum. It is perhaps not surprising that conservative forces became more active in their opposition to detente, a policy that flew in the face of their traditional hostility to the Soviet Union and communist countries and their determination to prolong the arms race. But they were joined by those who decided the time had come to challenge Soviet policy on emigration, especially Jewish emigration, and by liberals who supported the dissident movement.

Perhaps we should have been forewarned of the emotional content of the issue by the activities of Jewish extremist groups who began picketing our embassy almost daily in 1970. They set off explosions outside Soviet offices in Washington. Rifles were fired at the windows of the Soviet Mission to the United Nations in New York City and its residential compound in the suburbs, which Secretary of State Rogers publicly condemned as "a barbarous act." Hooliganism against individual Soviet citizens in the streets and stores became common. The most violent were performed by militants of the Jewish Defense League, led by Rabbi Meir Kahane, later the founder of an extremist political party in Israel and victim of an Arab assassin in the United States. He made it abundantly clear that his campaign was to designed to "provoke a crisis in Soviet-American relations."

The irony of the situation was that our embassy and other Soviet officials in the United States were, as a rule, in favor of improving our relations and lifting the unreasonable restrictions on Jewish emigration from the Soviet Union, and that was what we recommended to Moscow. But the outrages vexed Soviet diplomats emotionally and discouraged them from continuing their efforts to persuade our leadership.

Many Jewish leaders as well as officials of the administration condemned the attacks in their private conversations with us. The State Department deployed its own security service to help protect us, but we were officially urged to advise all Soviet diplomats and their families living in the Washington area to be careful, which did not make a Soviet diplomat's life easy in Washington in that period. When Gromyko was about to fly home after attending a General Assembly session, there came a call warning of an attempt on his life at the airport. His plane was moved to a far corner of the airport and he remained in the airport hangars until the alarm was lifted.

As our preparations advanced for the second summit and Brezhnev's visit, so did a vitriolic but politically sophisticated campaign to promote free emigration from the Soviet Union that was actively supported by a number of American members of Congress and led by Senator Henry (Scoop) Jackson, a conservative Democrat from the state of Washington with strong presidential ambitions and a long record as an opponent of the Soviet Union.

The opposition coalesced around a request by Nixon in the spring of 1973 for Congress to grant the Soviet Union "most favored nation" trading status, which meant that we would essentially be on the same commercial footing as America's other trading partners. Liberals wanted to make our MFN status dependent on Moscow lifting all restrictions on emigration from the Soviet Union. Conservatives were against granting MFN status simply because they were against detente as such. All this prompted a debate that blighted U.S.-Soviet relations ever after.

Let me explain the background of the notorious subject of this debate: Jewish emigration from the Soviet Union. Nowadays it is difficult to believe, but during the period of Stalin's tyranny anyone who wanted to emigrate was considered a "traitor to the Motherland" and was imprisoned or sent into exile. After Stalin's death the situation began to change gradually, but the government was still very reluctant to permit Soviet citizens to leave. It was not much easier to emigrate than qualify for cosmonaut training.

I never understood why we did not allow Jews to emigrate. What harm could it have brought to the country? On the contrary, by solving this question we could have ridden ourselves of a serious and permanent source of irritation between us and the West, particularly the United States. Even the members of the Politburo under Khrushchev and Brezhnev could not provide a clear and convincing answer when asked in private to explain their views on emigration. Some were still under the influence of Stalin's view that emigrants were traitors. Others would claim that many Jews in the Soviet Union knew state secrets because of their work on military projects using science and technology or other sensitive work, or that Jewish emigrants would join noisy anti-Soviet campaigns abroad. Then there was our Middle East policy: the Arab countries were in permanent protest against Jewish emigration, which they thought would strengthen Israel by augmenting its population and skills.

Those reasons were often heard in Moscow. But the most important one was not often heard. In the closed society of the Soviet Union, the Kremlin was afraid of emigration in general (irrespective of nationality or religion) lest an escape hatch from the happy land of socialism seem to offer a degree of liberalization that might destabilize the domestic situation. So the crucial difference in the Soviet and American approaches to the issue was that while the Americans wanted to export to the Soviet Union its free humanitarian and commercial values, the Soviet government simply wanted the commercial benefits of trade, but not the political values.

Nevertheless, the Soviet government could not completely ignore the growing foreign and domestic pressure because it sought an improvement of Soviet-American relations, to be fixed by summits in Moscow and Washington. Thus the issue of Jewish emigration was cautiously discussed through the confidential channel between Kissinger and myself.

The Nixon administration understood that it was better to proceed without publicity, rightly assuming that Moscow was more likely to change its practices if not openly challenged. Indeed, in planning for the first summit in 1972, Kissinger had delivered an assurance from Nixon to the Soviet leadership that the president would not make any appeals on behalf of Jewish and Zionist organizations during his Moscow visit. Quietly though reluctantly, Moscow began to change its emigration policy. Whereas only 400 Soviet Jews had been allowed to emigrate in 1968, the number rose to nearly 35,000 in 1973.

This process was marred by the administrative decree of the Presidium of the Supreme Soviet of August 3, 1972, imposing an exit tax on emigrants, ostensibly to "refund" the state for the cost of their free education in the Soviet Union. I was both surprised and disturbed by this decree, and not only because of its petty justifications but because of the fact that it was issued so soon after the Soviet-American summit in Moscow, which both sides had proclaimed a big success. I sent a telegram to the Foreign Ministry saying that the step would provoke adverse reaction in the United States and asked them to explain to me the meaning of this decision. I never received an explanation.

Later on, while in Moscow for consultation, I found out about this bizarre affair. It was our Ministry of Education that originated the idea of seeking a refund. At the moment the tax was imposed, Brezhnev and Gromyko were on vacation at the Black Sea. Mikhail Suslov, number two in the Communist Party and its chief ideologist, was left in charge in the Kremlin. He had always been reluctant to accept the new, more liberal, emigration policy and found the new tax quite a reasonable idea, so the tax went on the books. When Gromyko returned from vacation, he realized what a stupid political move it was. Gradually we convinced Brezhnev and the Politburo to annul it. But the harm had been done, and it only helped stir up the debate in the United States linking Jewish emigration to trade with the Soviet Union.

On March 15, Senator Jackson, with the support of seventy-three senators, introduced an amendment to the Nixon trade reform bill known as the Jackson-Vanik amendment for its cosponsor, Representative Charles Vanik. The amendment barred the Soviet Union from receiving most favored nation status and trade credits until it had lifted restrictions on emigration.

The Soviet rulers gradually became alarmed by the scale of the campaign. On March 30, Brezhnev instructed me to give Nixon—at the president's own request—confidential data on Jewish emigration. It stated that 95.5 percent of applications for emigration to Israel had been authorized in 1972. It also said that from 1971 to 1973 a total of 60,000 Soviet Jews had left for Israel. In the same message Brezhnev informed Nixon that the Soviet Union had lifted the exit tax.

Both Nixon and Kissinger asked me whether they could use all this information in their discussions with Congress on the trade bill. Moscow's reply showed how much importance it attached to U.S.-Soviet relations on the eve of the second summit. It authorized Nixon to communicate Brezhnev's message to Congress as an official Soviet statement.

On April 18, Nixon briefed the congressional leaders. Senator Mike Mansfield, the majority leader, and some leading Republicans, including Hugh Scott of Illinois and George Aiken of Vermont, expressed their satisfaction with the news. Senator Jackson, however, was unconvinced. The report, he said, gave no guarantees for the future. He demanded that the Soviet Union commit itself publicly to a large and fixed number of emigrés, which implied that there was an unlimited number of people eager to emigrate from the Soviet Union. He was supported by Senator Abraham Ribicoff of Connecticut and some other senators who could not risk accusations of being soft on the issue of Soviet emigration.

The administration and its Soviet counterparts were still trying to work out some compromise. I thought that the threat of the Jackson-Vanik amendment helped keep the Soviet government focused on the question of Jewish emigration, but Jackson kept escalating his demands in an appeal to the Jewish constituency for his presidential aspirations. I am convinced that had it not been for him and his disruptive tactics, we could have found a way out. Nixon even instructed Kissinger to ask Israeli Prime Minister Golda Meir not to incite the American Jewish community against the Soviet Union and the U.S.-Soviet emigration agreement. This had no appreciable effect.

The summit, when it took place in Washington in May 1973, left unsettled the future of trade and economic relations between the two countries. The Congress had linked them too tightly to the freedom of emigration. Nixon explained all this to Brezhnev during the summit and promised to help solve the problem, but he warned that Congress would have the last word. Brezhnev could not accept the Jackson bill because of the organized public campaign that supported it. In the eyes of the Soviet leaders, that would have been tantamount to yielding to open American interference in the internal affairs of the Soviet Union. A lack of political courage and foresight prevented them from crossing this threshold.

Still, both sides recognized that the issue had become a sore spot in our relations. Several additional attempts were made to untie the knot through the confidential channel. The emigration statistics showed a continued increase, but this only spurred Senator Jackson to exploit the issue even more to advance his political career. He and his supporters were not satisfied with the administration's quiet diplomacy; they wanted Moscow to capitulate to their demands. Characteristically, about a week before Brezhnev's arrival for the summit, Jackson demanded that the visit be canceled. The senator needed confrontation, not agreements or detente. The Jackson-Vanik amendment continued on the statute books until after the end of the Cold War.

## Nixon Reshapes His Government

At the start of the year Kissinger told me that, in preparation for a meeting with Brezhnev expected in May or June, Nixon proposed to conduct an intensive review of all questions through the confidential channel in February. He wanted to start preparing the texts of the joint documents so that they would be almost completely agreed even before the summit began. Once again, the State Department would play the lesser role in the preparations. Kissinger had already told me before the New Year that Nixon had decided to reshuffle the government, particularly the State Department. Rogers was to stay for about six months, and Kenneth Rush, the ambassador to West Germany and Nixon's friend and former law professor, would probably replace him. Elliot Richardson, who had earlier served as deputy secretary of state, would become secretary of defense. Kissinger explained that "it will be easier for the president and me to manage the Pentagon, because Richardson is flexible enough and knows military and political affairs." Nixon was also planning to replace Commerce Secretary Peter Peterson.

In the White House itself, the shake-up sent Alexander Haig back to the Pentagon. Haig was moving from the position of deputy national security adviser to deputy chief of staff of the army and was to be replaced by

Brent Scowcroft, a forty-seven-year-old air force brigadier general who was serving as the president's senior military assistant. Kissinger observed that Scowcroft lacked Haig's political skills and experience—an opinion he later changed—so he had decided to split his deputy's duties. Scowcroft would handle military affairs while diplomatic questions would go to Helmut Sonnenfeldt, although he did not like Sonnenfeldt's "arrogance." Sonnenfeldt, like Kissinger of German origin, invariably accompanied Kissinger on his Moscow visits and so shadowed his boss's steps elsewhere that he became known as "Kissinger's Kissinger."

Kissinger also said the president told him he would remain as his principal foreign policy assistant for another four years, that is, to the end of his second term. Kissinger said he was pleased to accept it. By that time Kissinger had reached his highest point in terms of political popularity. In the opinion polls, he was the most popular person in America, followed by Billy Graham, with Nixon, already under suspicion because of Watergate, ranking third. His lifelike dummy was on display in the waxworks museum in London, and even the participants of the Miss Universe beauty pageant enthusiastically chose him as "the most outstanding world figure."

In his memoirs, Kissinger records his reluctance to move up to the position of secretary of state because he had no political constituency of his own. He writes that he had been planning to retire from his White House post after the end of the Vietnam War because his celebrity had made his position untenable as a supposedly anonymous White House adviser dependent entirely on the president's favor. He indicates that he was the reluctant choice of a president who had little alternative but to select him since the source of his power was a presidential mandate and now, weakened by Watergate, Nixon needed him in a public position to ensure the continuance of their policies.

Let me add my own observation. Kissinger told me in May in strict confidence that the president was prepared to let him decide who should replace Rogers as secretary of state: Rush or Kissinger himself. Rogers's resignation was to be announced in July after he attended the NATO Council in Brussels. Kissinger was evidently flattered that the president had left the matter to him, although it implied certain inconveniences such as the heavy burden of protocol and the regular demands of explaining himself to congressional committees.

Nixon had been prepared to offer Rogers the position of ambassador to any country or any other government position in the United States, but Kissinger thought that Rogers would rather return to the legal profession where he had earned large sums representing corporations. By August, however, Watergate was beginning to dominate Nixon's decisions, and Kissinger said Nixon wanted Rogers as his attorney general to organize his defense. To Nixon's annoyance, Rogers refused, and the president finally decided to get rid of him.

On August 22, Kissinger called me from San Clemente to tell me that the president had finally decided to appoint him secretary of state. The appointment would be announced that evening. Kissinger was also to continue as national security adviser, and our confidential contacts, including lunches and dinners, were to continue. Rogers would leave as of September 3.

Thus, the protracted period of speculation was over, and I was not surprised that Kissinger had emerged victorious from the behind-the-scenes rivalry. It would mean an improvement in managing Soviet-American relations, if only because it would end the confused and uncertain situation in which the White House kept the secretary of state and indeed his entire department in the dark. The agreements reached through the confidential channel would become easier to put into practice through the State Department's diplomatic staff, thus eliminating many of our earlier difficulties. I therefore welcomed Kissinger's appointment and sincerely congratulated him.

Kissinger explained how he would rearrange his schedule as secretary of state. Since his work could only be successful if he kept in close touch with the president, he would continue to begin his working day by meeting the president in the White House between 8 and 9 A.M. to discuss fundamental as well as urgent foreign policy problems. He would also continue attending the daily morning meetings of the White House staff to keep in touch with its views and with domestic issues.

He planned then to go to the State Department, remaining there from 11 A.M. until late in the evening, although he would still spend some evenings in the White House. Needless to say, he was to be present at all National Security Council meetings in the White House chaired by the president. Kissinger remained the NSC executive secretary in his capacity as the president's assistant for national security, and as such he would continue to conduct meetings with the secretary of defense and the director of the CIA. These meetings would continue to be held at the White House rather than being shifted to the State Department to emphasize White House control of foreign policy. Kissinger hoped that his appointment as secretary of state would consolidate the White House control over the huge diplomatic and national security machinery of the United States, making it more workable and reliable. This he managed to achieve.

## Brezhnev Makes Kissinger "Sign for It"

Early in May Kissinger visited Moscow, and as usual I accompanied him.

Kissinger's talks involved not only Gromyko, but Brezhnev himself, who participated actively, especially on military and political issues. They were held at Brezhnev's favorite hunting preserve in Zavidovo, about eighty miles from Moscow, where they devoted much time to discussing the draft of an agreement on the prevention of a nuclear war, which Brezhnev believed to be of special importance.

There was an extraordinary episode, totally characteristic of Brezhnev's and, indeed, the whole Soviet leadership's attitude to Nixon and his administration. When the working draft was finally prepared, Brezhnev suggested that Kissinger initial it. But he declined, saying that he lacked the authority. At the same time he expressed confidence that the president would approve it entirely.

Brezhnev gave vent to his emotions (which I think were somewhat artificial), declaring that surely he had not spent two days with Kissinger just to find his work had ended up in noncommittal talk. The upshot was that Brezhnev finally made Kissinger take a piece of paper and write "a pledge" that the American government was ready to sign the agreement as drafted. While it had little legal force, the pledge nevertheless gave Brezhnev a sense of satisfaction. He acted as if he regarded it as a great personal diplomatic achievement and told members of the Politburo how he "forced Kissinger's hand and made him sign for it." But the whole scene was reminiscent of the famous bargaining scene in Gogol's comedy *Dead Souls* between Chichikov and Sobakevich, the two characters who did not trust each other.

When I spoke with Nixon after my return to Washington, the president told me he was rather surprised that the Soviet leadership would not trust his word as given through Kissinger. And in any case, he said, even Kissinger's written undertaking would not have helped if as president he had finally decided against it. I did my best to play down the episode, and frankly I did not much like Brezhnev's behavior myself.

Brezhnev liked to play jokes whenever he met with Kissinger and his advisers. During one break in the talks, they were chatting about their wristwatches. Kissinger's aide Helmut Sonnenfeldt proudly showed off his Swiss watch. Brezhnev suddenly covered his watch with his hand so Sonnenfeldt could not see it and suggested a swap. Sonnenfeldt hesitated, but then changed his mind, apparently thinking that the general secretary of the Communist Party certainly would have a luxurious watch. After he accepted he discovered that Brezhnev wore a common Soviet watch, a gift from the workers of the Moscow clock-making factory. It was of good quality, but steel rather than gold, which is what Sonnenfeldt had expected. His only comfort was the fact that he had received a souvenir watch from the leader of the Soviet Union.

The talks over, Brezhnev invited Kissinger for an automobile ride around the picturesque countryside of Zavidovo. Kissinger said he would love it. Little did he know that they were in for an adventure with Brezhnev, a reckless driver. They sped along a winding narrow road for about half an hour with the security guards in another car behind them. Traffic militiamen did not dare to stop the general secretary. Who would have? The daredevil ride was a harrowing experience. After the drive came another dashing ride on a powerful motorboat in the upper reaches of the Volga that totally shook Kissinger and temporarily took away his habitual sense of humor.

At the beginning of May Kissinger also talked to me confidentially about Watergate, evidently to show he was not involved and that it would not affect his position in the White House. On the contrary, he claimed it had consolidated his position with the dismissal of two of the president's closest aides, H. R. Haldeman and John Erlichman. Because of Watergate, Kissinger had never gotten on well with them.

Kissinger stressed that the president would not "even think of resigning" because of Watergate but, still, it was a very unpleasant affair for Nixon. At the same time Nixon believed his political opponents would play it up for some months but eventually the matter would settle down. According to Kissinger, Nixon was angry and upset that his major foreign policy achievements were ignored by his compatriots, while "a trifling matter by American standards" was being exaggerated by his adversaries.

Kissinger remarked in passing that the president had a long memory and he would certainly repay the harm done to him during the remaining three and one-half years of his presidency. He also said that the demands by opposition newspapers that he postpone his meeting with Brezhnev had no influence on the president. Quite the reverse, he was increasingly convinced that the summit should be held as scheduled and was bound to be a success. "The president just cannot let it be otherwise," Kissinger said.

It may be difficult to believe, but Moscow did not try to exploit its knowledge that Nixon badly wanted the summit to be a success for domestic reasons. It had practically no effect on our bargaining before the new summit, and Moscow did not push harder to obtain more from him. First, Moscow was not interested in creating additional difficulties for the president who had just begun to improve Soviet-American relations. But the main reason was that in the middle of 1973 the Soviet leaders (and I should confess, our embassy in Washington as well) still did not believe that

Watergate was a political crisis of major proportions. To my knowledge, that issue was not discussed in the Politburo seriously until the beginning of 1974.

At the end of May Nixon sent Brezhnev a detailed program of his visit to the United States for his approval. He had already decided that the summit would be held at the White House, Camp David, and San Clemente in violation of all the established diplomatic norms in order to emphasize the importance of the visit. Nixon proposed to sign two principal agreements (on the prevention of nuclear war and on "fundamental principles" of SALT) on two days, to accentuate their specific importance. But then early in June our agreement on the SALT stalled. At the last moment Nixon made some categorical amendments to the text which Brezhnev had to accept, though reluctantly.

This angered Brezhnev and he declined Nixon's invitation to visit his private residence in San Clemente. He excused himself by saying that his doctors advised him against too much flying. (This was one result of the initial signs of disturbed cerebral blood circulation, but it had not gone too far and few knew about it in even in the top leadership.) On June 11, Kissinger and I conducted a thorough review of all documents to be signed during the summit and continued our elaboration of the communiqué. At the end of the meeting Kissinger told me "without beating about the bush" that Nixon was deeply hurt by Brezhnev's refusal to visit San Clemente. I was convinced that the place was a good location for informal talks, and I therefore cabled my recommendations to Moscow for Brezhnev to reconsider.

The next day Brezhnev informed Nixon about his decision "to defy his doctors' advice" and go to California. Around midnight Nixon himself telephoned and asked me to forward his thanks to Brezhnev. He had invited Brezhnev to stay in his house because he was confident that the time they would spend under the same roof would promote a closer personal relationship; he was convinced that together the two could largely determine matters of war and peace.

"That is not vanity or presumptuousness of any kind," Nixon went on, "that is a historical reality. My house in California is called Casa Pacifica, Spanish for 'House of Peace.' This is an old name, quite unpretentious, but now it acquires great symbolic importance." Nixon sometimes liked grandiose language.

All draft agreements were prepared beforehand, to be signed during Brezhnev's visit. Thus, the forthcoming talks between Nixon and Brezhnev would not involve any negotiations or the elaboration of the agreements, leaving plenty of time for a free exchange of views on a broad range of questions.

## Brezhnev in America

Brezhnev arrived at Andrews Air Force Base aboard our special plane on June 18 with an entourage that included Gromyko. They were met by Secretary of State Rogers. I accompanied Brezhnev and Gromyko as we were flown by helicopter to Camp David, where they stayed the night. Brezhnev liked the rustic place (it reminded him of his hunting lodge), and he immediately shared his good impressions with some Politburo members via the specially installed radiotelephone.

The next day he flew to Washington for his meeting with President Nixon. I still remember the ceremonial reception of June 19 on the well-groomed South Lawn of the White House, with Brezhnev and the American president standing on a special platform. For Brezhnev, it seemed the moment of his highest triumph. What could be greater than his being placed on a footing equal to the American president, with the Soviet Union equal to the United States—of all powers—in its nuclear might, its missiles, and their warheads? Even the brilliant sunshine seemed to accentuate the importance of the event.

The solemn ceremony, with both countries' national anthems and a guard of honor, the leader of the Soviet Communist Party standing side by side with the American president for the whole world to see—all this was for the Soviet leadership the supreme act of recognition by the international community of their power and influence. I must confess that for all of us who accompanied Brezhnev, it was a proud moment. The irony of all this was that the influence and authority of Nixon, the president of the greatest country of the West, was in decline. The televised Watergate hearings were under way, although they had been suspended for a week during Brezhnev's visit.

The visit resulted in two important agreements, one on the prevention of nuclear war, and the other outlining the "fundamental principles" for limitations on strategic weapons. There also were the agreements on scientific and technical cooperation in the peaceful use of nuclear energy; cooperation in farming, transport, ocean research; and a tax treaty. At the insistence of Brezhnev, who wanted detente to sound like an irreversible policy, the communiqué formally declared the promotion of Soviet-American friendship as a permanent factor in world peace. It also included an agreement to hold regular summits; Brezhnev invited Nixon to visit the Soviet Union in 1974, and Nixon accepted.

The summit also helped to advance other issues. The month following the summit, NATO and Warsaw Treaty member states finally agreed to begin talks in Vienna on October 30 on mutual reductions of their armed forces in Europe. And thirty-five foreign ministers began preparations for the

Conference on Security and Cooperation in Europe, which was convened in Geneva September 18. Thus, by mutual concessions, the Soviet Union and its allies obtained a European conference they had sought, while the United States and its allies obtained negotiations on troop reductions in Central Europe.

The Soviet leadership regarded the agreement known as the Prevention of Nuclear War (the PNW agreement) as the main result of Brezhnev's visit to the United States, and so it was loudly acclaimed in the Soviet media. The American critics of the agreement, however, did not see it that way. They regarded it as a threat to NATO's basic military strategy of launching a nuclear counterstrike to defend Western Europe against conventional attack. In his memoirs, Kissinger wrote that he saw the agreement as a Soviet attempt to establish a Soviet-American condominium directed at supporting a potential Soviet attack on China. Even in their dreams, the Soviet leaders of the time never went that far.

Our main political and ideological doctrine provided for peaceful coexistence not condominium with the capitalist United States, and the Kremlin publicly and angrily denounced "fabrications concerning superpower condominium." For Moscow, the PNW agreement marked a further step in the process of detente, or as it was rightly put by the American writer Raymond Garthoff, a step toward some sort of crisis management and prevention by defusing tension before a crisis arose. But it was still only a step because the agreement was never institutionalized. As for China, the Kremlin was not so naive as to ally itself with Washington against Beijing, knowing only too well that Washington would not agree and that its sympathies lay on China's side anyway. Many years later Kissinger admitted to me that he had been wrong in basing his concepts on the inevitability of a Soviet attack against China.

In his memoirs, Kissinger recounted how during Brezhnev's visit to the United States he managed to stall Moscow's supposed gambit of a "nuclear condominium" and finally persuaded Brezhnev to accept a watered-down version of his original goals in the PNW agreement. But he ignored the fact that the original and longstanding Soviet goal was a *mutual pledge not to use nuclear weapons first.* So, instead of saying that the administration, and he as secretary of state, were against nonuse of nuclear weapons (which was not a very popular thing to say), he skillfully put into circulation the phrase about him and Nixon being against "nuclear condominium" with the Soviet Union. This was not exactly the same thing, to put it frankly. This should have been obvious simply from a quick examination of the history of the PNW agreement.

Starting in the 1960s, the Soviet Union in various forums repeatedly proposed a joint pledge not to use nuclear weapons first. Anxious to keep their nuclear deterrence in case of a conventional attack, the United States and its allies repeatedly rejected the idea. Brezhnev pursued the subject at his meetings with Kissinger and his first summit with Nixon, and Nixon essentially dodged the subject, although he okayed discussion of a noncommittal draft through the Kissinger-Dobrynin channel. The Soviet side continued to press Nixon and Kissinger. But our American partners kept procrastinating, something I palpably felt with Kissinger.

This turned out to be the most difficult part of the preparations for the Washington summit. The Americans finally decided to accept an agreement but tried to shift the emphasis from nuclear weapons to the broader concept of the nonuse of force. After hard bargaining, we agreed on a compromise: the agreement did not contain a joint pledge adjuring the first use of nuclear weapons, which was what Moscow initially wanted, but it recognized our military parity and declared it unsuitable to threaten or use military force to serve political objectives. What that really did was to expand our general policy of avoiding confrontation and the risk of war, including nuclear war, by engaging in urgent consultations to defuse political tensions in times of crisis or when one loomed. In general this represented an advance in our relations. But since both sides were not yet ready to commit themselves fully to crisis consultations, the document was vague and nonbinding.

Of course, the chief disadvantage of the agreement, as well as the 1972 statement of basic principles in Soviet-American relations concluded at the previous summit, was that neither contained workable measures to put their principles into operation. It soon became clear during the Arab-Israeli war less than six months later that the idea of working together did not operate too well without mutual trust and firm commitments. Nevertheless one could not underestimate the moral and political effect of the agreement on the international atmosphere and on Soviet-American relations. In their communiqué Brezhnev and Nixon declared that the agreement marked a historic turn in bilateral relations. In a confidential summary by our Foreign Ministry for Soviet ambassadors, Brezhnev's visit was proclaimed an important milestone in the removal of the threat of nuclear war.

Some details of the organization of Brezhnev's visit to the United States were unique. Brezhnev himself had instructed the Soviet security service to organize his trip in such a way that he would in no way appear to the Americans inferior to the president of the United States. Sometimes this led to curious situations. First of all, there were stringent requirements for Brezhnev's telephone service to match Nixon's. Apart from an individual local telephone, he was connected by a special Soviet network with Soviet operators to any point in the city of Washington where members of the Soviet delegation might be. He also had a direct and instant connection with Moscow, something extraordinary for us at the time. The Americans sensed his mood and went as far as to permit us to install some of our intercom network devices even in the White House, in case Brezhnev should feel the need for urgent consultations by phone while visiting there. (Predictably, there were no such cases.)

Brezhnev was remarkably pleased at the signs of Soviet technical progress that accompanied his journey and began to call other members of the Soviet delegation in Washington, his wife in Moscow, and friends back home in the Moscow leadership to give them his highly favorable first impressions about America immediately on his arrival at Camp David. While in Washington he stayed opposite the White House in the principal government guest house, Blair House, which gave rise to still another request of ours: traffic on Pennsylvania Avenue, one of the capital's principal streets, was closed off near the White House for security reasons so Brezhnev could cross on foot. It was the first closing of that central avenue in the American capital's history.

At Camp David, Nixon gave him a Lincoln Continental of the latest model, knowing his passion for collecting foreign cars (Brezhnev had broadly hinted at this through the confidential channel in advance). Brezhnev was very pleased with the new gift and eager to try it immediately to show Nixon his driving prowess (I accompanied them to interpret). The general secretary was a good driver, but he was unfamiliar with the Lincoln and its powerful engine. I warned him about it but he was itching to start. He put his foot down hard on the gas pedal at once. The car jerked violently. Both Brezhnev and Nixon (the president was in the front seat, I was in the rear) nearly hit their heads against the windshield when Brezhnev had to hit the brake because of a sharp curve in the road. The winding roads of Camp David are clearly not suitable for auto racing and usually only carry small, battery-driven cars. Nixon was shocked, but still managed to say tactfully, "Mr. General Secretary, you drive very well." Brezhnev took this at face value. Among the gifts also was an eagle in Steuben glass, and Brezhnev, not fully acquainted with traditional American symbols or the famous maker of this token, wondered why Nixon had given it to him. "I don't need it," he said to me. "You take it." I said that would be just fine but told him it was quite an expensive gift. How much? Thirty to fifty thousand dollars, I said. "Really?" he said in amazement. "Give it back."

Among the most impressive events of formal protocol was the ceremony to sign the joint documents, followed by an official dinner in honor of the Soviet leader. The functions were arranged with impeccable taste and tact, especially in view of the fact that events of this particular nature were new to the White House and the Cold War was still not over. I remember the solemn moment when the master of ceremonies loudly announced Brezhnev's entrance inviting everybody to stand up: "Ladies and gentlemen! The general secretary of the Communist Party of the Soviet Union." Certainly that was the first time in history such an announcement had been heard in the White House. Brezhnev and his associates, as well as all others present, recognized that this was extraordinary. Little could anyone even imagine that twenty years later the Soviet Union would no longer have any such party, which for so long—and even then—symbolized an evil empire to many Americans.

Brezhnev gave a return dinner in Nixon's honor at the embassy. All the food was delivered by special plane from Moscow for a lavish display of Russian cuisine. There was Russian vodka and wines from the Caucasus, and the dinner went off in the embassy's Golden Hall in an informal and friendly atmosphere. There were about one hundred guests, including the president and his wife. Kissinger, who was still unmarried at the time, brought a starlet with him and asked without embarrassment for her to be seated next to him in a breach of protocol; his request was granted. Nixon, by the way, was well aware of this habit; as early as 1971 Haldeman sent their protocol officials a jocular memorandum saying that Kissinger "is not necessarily to be seated next to the most gorgeous woman at state dinners."

Brezhnev was satisfied with the dinner and after it he wanted "to see where the ambassador and his wife live." We went up to our apartment on the third floor. Sitting cozily and buoyed by the dinner that put him in good humor, Brezhnev began to question us about our life in Washington. The lively conversation was interrupted by the security service chief, who beckoned me to follow him. Brezhnev noticed the signs and snapped: "You don't have to whisper into his ear. We know each other quite well. Come on, tell us."

After a moment's hesitation the security officer said there had just been an anonymous call saying a bomb had been planted at the embassy; he suggested that Brezhnev return to Blair House urgently. I also urged the general secretary to play it safe.

"Well, what are you going to do?" Brezhnev asked. My wife said such calls were rather common, and normally we would just go on with our business because we had nowhere else to go anyway.

Brezhnev declared he "would not be panicky, either" and, despite efforts to persuade him otherwise, stayed with us for another half-hour until about midnight. All ended well, though I felt uneasy, conscious of my responsibility.

The other unusual stage of Brezhnev's visit was his trip with Nixon aboard the president's plane to Nixon's private California residence at San Clemente. On arrival at the local airport the telephone game was on again. Since no official ceremony was planned, there were only a few people there, mostly the Security Service and attending staff. But there was our secure telephone on a table nearby, just in case the general secretary might happen to need to make an urgent call to Moscow. It had been installed at Soviet insistence for prestige rather than business. Brezhnev did not use it.

I should add that before leaving for home, Brezhnev magnanimously offered to let me maintain the embassy's direct telephone link—via satellite—with Moscow despite the expense of operating it. I thanked him but declined his offer, referring to the cost of its maintenance and of the additional personnel that would be needed to service the line. Besides, I said, we now had continuous cable communication with Moscow. But the real reason behind my refusal was much simpler. I had already had my fill of that telephone, which had been installed a week before Brezhnev's arrival. During that whole week preceding the summit, I hardly had any sleep. Brezhnev, Gromyko, and other leaders happily experimented with the new line to call me from Moscow on every conceivable pretext, or without any at all, to ask questions like, "What kind of weather are you having there in Washington?" It did not matter to them that because of the time difference of eight hours, their calls would arrive in Washington in the middle of the night. I came to hate that telephone and refused to keep it. As for Brezhnev, he appreciated what he thought was my desire to save state funds.

In San Clemente Brezhnev stayed in the same compound as the president. We arrived there late in the day on June 22. Since it had been a long flight from Washington, Brezhnev decided to retire early, around 6 P.M., after exchanging short greetings with Nixon. But two hours later he still could not sleep. So he went out onto the patio to have some fresh air. I happened to be there (all other members of our party had gone to their apartments to rest). Brezhnev started telling me that he liked the Spanish style of Nixon's house. Suddenly Nixon appeared on the patio. He was alone, so I had to act as an interpreter. After a brief discussion of the architecture of Casa Pacifica, the president invited Brezhnev inside and offered him tea, wine, and whiskey. Leonid Ilyitch preferred straight whiskey—he did not want "to spoil it with water"—and before long he was tight. The conversation shifted its focus from international issues to effusive outpourings. Brezhnev complained it was not easy being a general secretary. He had to listen to "all kinds of silly things" from other Politburo members whose opinions he still had to take into account. Some of his colleagues, he volunteered, were trying to undermine his authority, so he had to be on his guard all the time. He gave names, too.

Nixon was evidently uneasy listening to Brezhnev's revelations, although he seemed interested. As for me, the scene was most awkward. In fact, it was the most bizarre situation in all my years of diplomacy; he was especially critical of Kosygin and Podgorny. I did my best to avoid translating the most sensitive details of these behind-the-scenes Kremlin relationships, some of which were not known even to me.

I finally managed to assist the drunken Brezhnev to his room, which, fortunately, was close by. Nixon lent a hand. The next day Brezhnev asked me: "Anatoly, did I talk too much yesterday?" I told him he had talked too much, but I had been careful not to translate everything. "Well done," he said. "Damn that whiskey, I am not used to it. I did not know I could not hold that much."

During that night there was another highly unusual event. Around 2 A.M., Brezhnev's bodyguard, standing watch near his bedroom in the courtyard just across from Nixon's apartment, saw the door of the president's quarters open. His wife Pat appeared in a long nightgown, her hands stretched forward and her eyes fixed in the distance, apparently in some kind of trance. She reached our bodyguard and stopped, saying nothing. The guard attempted to turn Mrs. Nixon around, but she refused to move and stood stiffly. After some hesitation the Soviet guard, an officer of the KGB, took Mrs. Nixon in his arms and carried her back to the room from which she had just emerged; it was her bedroom. He put her back in bed, and at just that moment the Secret Service arrived. They waved, smiled, and said to our man, "Okay, okay, thanks." They did not seem all that surprised. Our bodyguard left, wondering what had happened. Carrying the American first lady in his arms had been a real adventure to him! His chief told him to keep the story to himself. Only I was informed—just in case.

The next day, June 23, Brezhnev and Nixon had a tête-à-tête meeting at noon, devoted to China mainly on Brezhnev's initiative. The Soviet leadership was worried that American cooperation with China would lead to sales of military equipment and wanted to prevent it. Brezhnev was vigorous, persistent, and indeed emotional in warning the Americans against concluding any military agreement with Beijing. Nixon assured him that the involvement of relations was by no means directed against the Soviet Union. But Brezhnev complained of China's "perfidious attempts to bring about a clash between the Soviet Union and the United States." He asked for stronger assurances. Nixon again assured him, though in such a guarded way as to keep Moscow still guessing about the future course of the United States.

At 4 P.M. Nixon held a poolside reception in Brezhnev's honor for some of the Hollywood and California elite, including Ronald Reagan, the future president. But Brezhnev, who liked westerns, paid more attention to the cowboy stars than to other performers present at the reception, which somewhat hurt their feelings. He especially liked Chuck Connors, who gave him a cowboy belt with two guns. (Brezhnev would proudly demonstrate the pistols to his colleagues later. Flying home to Moscow from the United States, he buckled on the gunbelt and like a boy dexterously manipulated the pistols, imitating the movie cowboys and amusing his staff.)

The reception was followed by Nixon's dinner for a close circle, including Brezhnev, Kissinger, Rogers, Gromyko, and me. During the day Gromyko and Kissinger had held a separate and fruitless discussion on the Middle East. On the next morning we were to leave San Clemente, so after dinner Brezhnev suddenly decided to take the issue personally to Nixon. After hasty and embarrassing last-minute arrangements, the meeting took place in Nixon's study around 11 P.M., attended by Kissinger, Gromyko, and me. It lasted for several hours, well into the night. Brezhnev, having had a nap of one hour, was in good shape. By contrast Nixon, accustomed to being in bed by then, was inactive, tired, and by the end of the meeting was propping up his head with pillows. Nor was he interested in the subject. It was clear that no Middle East settlement would be reached there. Clear to all, that is, except Brezhnev himself, who apparently believed he was defending a just cause and that his eloquence would convince Nixon. On the contrary, his perseverance created the impression that the Soviet leadership was keen on reaching a secret agreement with Nixon on the Middle East, and that put the president on his guard. Actually it was Brezhnev's favorite Mideast theme: employing joint U.S. and Soviet diplomacy to impose a Mideast peace on Arab terms, based on total Israeli withdrawal in return for security guarantees—which were not yet spelled out. All this was definitely unacceptable to Nixon.

We parted at about 2 or 3 A.M., with the usual reference—in such cases—that the issue would be further discussed at ministerial levels.

But there was still one important new element in Brezhnev's presentation on the Middle East that Nixon should not have overlooked. From my observations, neither he nor Kissinger, evidently tired of the whole conversation, took it seriously. The point was that Brezhnev had been specifically instructed by the Politburo to draw the president's attention to the mounting threat of a new Arab-Israeli war. The Soviet Union was finding it increasingly difficult to keep its Arab allies in check. In Moscow's view, this should lead to closer cooperation between the United States and the Soviet Union to find a solution and to prevent the war. Brezhnev did tell Nixon that in as many words, although in a very obtrusive and clumsy manner that hardly convinced the president of the need for stronger cooperation in this delicate and explosive area. Nixon and Kissinger, judging from their memoirs, thought Brezhnev was simply using the threat of war to press them for tactical purposes during the negotiations. But they were proved wrong. A new Arab-Israeli war broke out in October.

After the late-night meeting Gromyko and I saw Brezhnev to his room.

As we entered, he suddenly remembered that the Politburo had instructed him to make an agreement with Nixon to purchase several million tons of grain. Since no more meetings were scheduled and we were to leave early that morning, it was not clear how we could discuss a grain deal since Nixon was staying behind.

Gromyko immediately suggested that I go to Kissinger, who was billeted in a separate cottage to which he had already retired. Gromyko assured Brezhnev that Kissinger would find a way to get in touch with Nixon, even in the dead of night, and obtain his consent for the grain sale.

I pointed out to Gromyko that Kissinger would be already in bed and my intrusion would be rather awkward. But Brezhnev gladly supported Gromyko. He said I could say I was relaying the general secretary's personal request, and "Henry will certainly understand us and help." Brezhnev did not want to leave without carrying out the Politburo's important instruction. He believed that I could find a common language with Kissinger.

Kissinger was surprised, to put it mildly, when I entered his cottage bearing Brezhnev's belated request. He said that awakening the president at this hour was out of the question; but thinking aloud, he said he would rather not reject Brezhnev's request out of hand. Yes, he said, they had grain for sale, and the president would most likely agree to sell it to the Soviet Union.

Kissinger suggested the following course: he would report the matter to the president in the early morning and, he hoped, obtain his approval. But if the president did not agree, Kissinger would immediately call me with some explanation for Brezhnev. Fortunately, all ended well and we did not have to explain anything to Brezhnev. In the morning Kissinger informed me that the president had sanctioned the grain deal in principle, and Brezhnev was grateful to Nixon for it.

Early in the morning of June 24, Brezhnev and Nixon said goodbye to each other on the lawn in front of the San Clemente residence. Then they took a short helicopter ride to the local Marine Corps Air Station. Both were in a good mood. Brezhnev warmly thanked Nixon for his hospitality and invited the president to visit the Soviet Union next year.

## Aftermath of the Summit

Brezhnev's visit to the United States served to advance the process of improving Soviet-American relations that was set in motion by Nixon's first presidential visit to Moscow. I still believe that both leaders were sincerely prepared for an extensive period of stability and further cooperation. Their personal relations were consolidating. They exchanged a series of messages. Kissinger told me in mid-August that Nixon had remarked to him an exchange on such a confidential level was inconceivable even with some of America's allies. To some extent this could have been a diplomatic nicety, but I believe the two leaders grew even closer when Watergate intensified Nixon's political and personal isolation. I got this impression from my personal conversations with Nixon a few months later.

Of course, no opportunity for strategic gains would be left unexplored indefinitely by both governments. The process of detente not only improved Soviet-American relations, it affected all major powers by easing global diplomacy.

Brezhnev's visit did not take long to arouse equal suspicions on the other pole of this new, trilateral world. Soon after the visit the Chinese ambassador urgently handed Nixon in San Clemente a message from Beijing (Kissinger, who was with the president, called me on July 6 to let me know about it). The message complained about what the Chinese leadership saw as the pro-Soviet behavior of the United States by signing the Prevention of Nuclear War Agreement. It attacked the agreement as a step toward "a world hegemony by the two powers" and warned that "it is impossible to rely on the words of the Soviet Union." With this stick, the ambassador also carried a carrot—an invitation from Zhou Enlai for Kissinger to visit Beijing during the first half of August.

Later, in the process of discussing another Kissinger trip to Beijing, the Chinese hinted to him that they would be prepared to consider a similar agreement with the United States. The president, mindful of his animated conversation with Brezhnev on that subject, displayed no interest. At least that was what Kissinger told me. The play within this geopolitical triangle continued.

The improvement of our relations also had a favorable effect on SALT. On July 17 I informed Kissinger Moscow was ready to discuss MIRV limitations, which Washington had begun seeking after it learned we had successfully tested our own MIRVs. Kissinger expressed satisfaction but observed that verification could be the main difficulty. I cannot help noting the historical irony of arms control; as each side made technical advances, our respective positions would change diametrically. In 1967, it was ABM systems, and now it was MIRVed missiles, which were to destabilize the strategic balance when both sides had them. Only then did Moscow and Washington begin looking for a compromise, in which Kissinger and I were actively involved through the confidential channel.

At the end of July Kissinger raised with me the subject of Watergate, on Nixon's instructions. Kissinger said that "under no circumstances" (he repeated the phrase twice) would Nixon resign and that Moscow should not trust any such speculations, including those about impeachment. The president, he said, was determined to serve out his term, continuing his activities vigorously, particularly in foreign policy. That would be the best answer to his critics. In the meantime, he was looking forward to next year's summit in Moscow.

Kissinger concluded that because of the special relations that had been developed with the Soviet leadership, Brezhnev was the only foreign leader to whom the president deemed it necessary to give such frank and confidential clarification of a purely domestic American affair. I must admit it was a curious goodwill gesture; rather than demonstrating the security of Nixon's position, it disclosed his growing awareness of domestic pressure and, simultaneously, his eagerness to reassure Brezhnev (and himself) of his determination to continue his course in Soviet-American relations. The Soviet government began to understand his serious difficulties but still believed that he would overcome them, and that the process of consolidating our relations would develop further. But the events in the Congress, courts, media, and a number of disputes in international areas were to show how ephemeral were our hopes of making detente irreversible.

# VI. The October War

*Moscow, Washington, and the Middle East*

The October 1973 Arab-Israeli War engaged the superpowers in a competition that bordered on confrontation, but also in a collaboration that meant close day-to-day contact, mainly through the confidential channel between Moscow and Washington. The two countries found themselves deeply involved both as partners seeking the earliest possible end to the war, and as rivals supplying their traditional clients with arms. At the same time, the crisis demonstrated that tension could be localized and prevented from disrupting relations between Washington and Moscow. This was the first serious international conflict under the conditions of detente, which was strongly affected by it.

While both powers cooperated in bringing the war to an end, they sought to manipulate events to serve their own ends and to extend their own influence in the Middle East. Both shared the objective of preventing the war from engulfing them while preserving their relationship. But as it became clear later on from Kissinger's memoirs, he was at the same time prepared to use and even sacrifice this relationship to reduce and if possible eliminate Soviet influence in the Middle East under the cover of detente. He made it clear that the United States was not willing to sacrifice its geopolitical position for detente. He wrote in his memoirs that it was often forgotten that "detente defined not friendship but a strategy for a relationship between adversaries. After all, a principal purpose of our Mideast policy was to reduce the role and influence of the Soviet Union, just as the Soviets sought to reduce ours." *

American policy during the war seemed to be designed almost exclusively by Kissinger, while Nixon was preoccupied with Watergate and its ramifications. In a way, one could say it was Kissinger's war as far as the American side was concerned. Thus an important part of American diplomacy was to play the Arab-Israeli rivalry in such a way that both sides would

---

* Henry Kissinger, *Years of Upheaval* (Boston: Little, Brown, 1982), p. 600.

become dependent only on the United States and the Soviet Union would be rendered irrelevant to the peace process.

That was the key difference in the American approach to the Middle East, especially Kissinger's view of a settlement. While Brezhnev and the Politburo as a whole, in the best tradition of detente, were trying to organize a joint Soviet-American effort while advancing Arab and their own interests, Washington was actually seeking to exclude the Soviet Union, as was evident in the period at the end of and just after the war. Meanwhile Washington remained in constant communication with Moscow, especially at the start of the war, maneuvering to bring joint sponsorship of a cease-fire at the time most convenient for Israel.

The Soviet goals during the war were rather simple: to win back Arab confidence, prevent their military rout, and to bank on our hopes that the new collaborative relationship with the Nixon administration would allow us to share in the peace process.

Even before the war broke out in October of 1973, the Soviet government had warned Nixon and Kissinger several times of the rising danger of an Arab-Israeli military conflict. Moscow argued that the only way to head off the war was for the Soviet Union and the United States to agree on principles for a peaceful settlement of the Middle East conflict. This was first said to Kissinger in May when he arrived in Moscow to prepare for the summit meting. At the summit itself in June, Brezhnev personally emphasized the same warning during his heated discussions with Nixon in San Clemente. And in September, Gromyko repeated all this once again to Nixon and Kissinger when they held their regular meeting during the UN General Assembly.

Later on Kissinger would admit that they had dismissed these Soviet warnings "as psychological warfare because we did not see any rational military option that would not worsen the Soviet and Arab position." In other words, Nixon and Kissinger actually refused to join the Soviet Union in sharing responsibility to defuse a critical situation. Who knows? perhaps both governments could have jointly prevented the outbreak of war by more energetically engaging Israel and the Arabs in the process of a peace settlement.

The war forced Washington and Moscow to reestablish close contacts to deal with crises. But cooperation was not a smooth process. From the beginning of the war on October 6 until the cease-fire on October 20, the two powers alternated between urging a prompt cease-fire and using delaying tactics to postpone one, depending on the tide of battle and their reckoning of the course of hostilities. Both resumed supplying their warring clients with arms and munitions, using this leverage to press for a cease-fire when they believed the time was ripe.

At the crucial stage of the conflict, when Israel broke the cease-fire, Washington put its armed forces on alert. This was supposedly done in response to a Soviet threat of unilateral interference, but in reality it was prompted both by insufficient trust between Washington and Moscow and by Israel's desire to gain additional territorial advantage at the last moment with the support of American diplomacy. Ultimately we worked out a cease-fire agreement and cosponsored the negotiations on a peace settlement in the Middle East, although Washington was doing everything to put them under its exclusive control.

During the war, practically all high-level messages between Washington and Moscow went through the Kissinger-Dobrynin confidential channel. Personally, I was in a rather difficult position. Because of the military secrecy and probably out of concern that the Americans could be decoding our cables, Moscow reduced the flow of information to our embassy in Washington about battlefield and diplomatic events connected with the war. The lack of information made me unusually restrained in my comments to Kissinger. Later I was amused when reading in his memoirs how skillfully he spoke during our conversations, saying one thing but actually being guided by a different motive. Once again he proved himself a versatile diplomat, especially when stalling to gain time for himself and Israel. In spite of this, I believe, we understood each other well enough.

The account here does not pretend to be a comprehensive diplomatic history of the Arab-Israeli War, but only a review of the Soviet-American exchanges in which I participated. It contains detail that has never before been published and will enrich the historical record of events, which themselves were matters of high drama.

## The War Begins

For me, the war began early in the morning of October 6, when I was awakened at 6:40 A.M. by Kissinger telephoning from New York. He asked me to pass on to Moscow immediately the information he would give me about the threat of an attack on Israel. On behalf of the president he assured the Soviet leadership that the United States was just as concerned as the Soviet Union in preventing another major military outbreak in the Middle East. The Americans were not playing games, he stressed, but proceeded from the need for drastic action to prevent events in the Middle East from spinning out of control.

Kissinger's call was a complete surprise. After Brezhnev's talk with Nixon in San Clemente in June concerning a growing threat of a military conflict between Arabs and Israelis, I received no telegrams from Moscow on the subject. I knew that the Middle East was tense, but I did not know the war was so close. Our embassy was not informed of the conversation Anwar Sadat had with our ambassador in Cairo on the eve of the war, when the Egyptian president rather clearly hinted at hostilities but did not name an exact date. Neither were we informed about evacuation of Soviet families from Egypt and Syria.

Some hours later Kissinger told me that Egypt and Syria had launched military operations against Israel all along the Suez Canal and Golan Heights cease-fire lines established following the Israeli occupation of Arab territories during the previous Arab-Israeli war, the Six-Day War of 1967. Kissinger was already in New York for the annual session of the United Nations General Assembly, and he wanted to convoke the Security Council. He wanted both the Soviet and American representatives to be instructed to take a measured position without siding entirely with their traditional clients. The United States, he said, intended to propose a resolution calling for a cease-fire and return to the previous position and setting up a special committee to deal with the conflict.

Moscow replied promptly: "The Soviet government received reports about the beginning of hostilities in the Middle East simultaneously with you. We are taking all reasonable measures to clarify the real situation in the region, because the reports coming to us are highly contradictory. . . . We are considering, like you, possible steps to be taken to remedy the situation. We hope to communicate with you soon to coordinate our actions."

From October 6 to 8 an intensive exchange went on through the confidential channel between Moscow and Washington. Brezhnev tried to avoid a Security Council meeting on the grounds that Israel had long been an aggressor by holding onto the Arab lands it had occupied for years. He opposed an Arab withdrawal from their latest gains because they had, in essence, just won back what was theirs. "In this connection," Brezhnev wrote to Nixon on October 7, "it would be very important, to our mind, if Israel stated its readiness to withdraw from the occupied Arab territories without any reservations on the understanding that security would be guaranteed for Israel as well as for other countries in the region. What in this proposal can be unacceptable to Israel?"

During the first days of the conflict, Moscow was under strong pressure from Cairo and Damascus to keep the whole thing out of the United Nations while they thought they were winning on the battlefield. Brezhnev initially agreed with them, although reluctantly because we were against the war in general, and besides, we did not believe that the Arabs would finally win. It was then that Nixon voiced his hope to Brezhnev that the Middle

East war would not damage the achievements in Soviet-American relations. At that precise point, he was not sure Israel would win a rapid and final victory and wanted to keep open his lines to the Arabs via Moscow if they were needed.

The lively exchange continued between Moscow and Washington from October 10 through 13 in the confidential channel, which also carried an intense discussion about the Security Council resolution. Moscow sought to broaden it by providing for the phased withdrawal, within a strictly limited period, of Israeli troops from all the Arab territories occupied in 1967. Washington opposed mentioning any Israeli withdrawal at all.

Kissinger told me on October 12 to inform Moscow that the United States would not send its troops to the Middle East unless the Soviet Union did likewise. I asked him about reports of a sharp increase in U.S. military supplies to Israel, and he denied them. But on October 13, Kissinger informed me of his reports that Sadat strongly opposed a cease-fire resolution. Nixon therefore no longer supported our mutual efforts in the Security Council: let things take their course—by that time Israel had begun regaining its strength. Kissinger said the president therefore would be forced to revise his pledge to exercise restraint in resupplying Israel and adjust the U.S. supply line to the level at which the Soviet Union was resupplying the Arabs. By spurning a cease-fire earlier, it was obvious that Sadat had made a gross political and strategic blunder, because it brought military disaster some days later.

Late on the night of October 13 Kissinger called me on the confidential phone and said the White House still believed there should be a cease-fire in place (the Israelis had regained some territory by then). We were still pressing the Arabs' demand that Israel withdraw to the borders it held before the 1967 war, but Kissinger said the very best he could do would be to agree to a reference to Security Council Resolution 242, the postwar resolution prescribing a policy of an Israeli pullback in exchange for peace with its Arab neighbors. Kissinger said the United States would accept nothing more "even if it meant a clash with the Arabs and the Soviet Union."

Earlier in the day I had attended the swearing in of Gerald Ford as vice president to succeed Spiro Agnew, who had to resign in a financial scandal, and the president took me aside. He said he wanted me to inform Brezhnev that both leaders were being provoked on all sides in order to frustrate the process of detente. Many would like to see it flop, Nixon said, "but we should not fall for that because the destinies of our peoples depend on it. Tell the general secretary that I will not give in to pressure and will keep my side of the bargain with the Soviet leadership." While the president was speaking about "provocations from all sides" his secretary of state was more one-sided.

On October 15 I was visited by Senator Fulbright who favored good relations with the Soviet Union as well as supporting the Arabs. He said the Pentagon's secret assessment, given at a White House briefing for the leaders of Congress, was that the Arab military success had peaked, and it would not be long before Israel, heavily resupplied with American arms, mounted a counteroffensive and threw the Arabs back to the other side of the Suez Canal. Fulbright believed it necessary to convince "the short-sighted Sadat" that the best way out for him would be to accept the Security Council resolution for a cease-fire and enter into negotiations. That would enable the United States and the Soviet Union to act jointly which, in turn, would help confirm the policy of detente between us rather than undermine it; pro-Israeli and anti-Soviet elements were already combining against the policy to wreck it if they could.

I believed it was a good assessment, and so I reported to Moscow. Meanwhile both the Soviet Union and the United States began to heavily resupply their respective protégés with arms and munitions.

On October 16, Kissinger informed us that the United States was starting an airlift to deliver supplies to Israel, and the deliveries would increase as the war continued. The White House would call off the operation once a cease-fire came into force, and the Soviet side followed suit. Actually the U.S. airlift had begun on October 12, and ours two days before that. The United States airlifted $2.2 billion worth of military equipment to Israel, and I believe the Soviet Union sent no less to the Arabs.

### Kissinger's Maneuvers

The private U.S.-Soviet dialogue on the wording of a draft UN resolution meanwhile continued. Since the negotiations and the situation as a whole were entering a crucial stage, Kissinger hinted to me it might be useful if he were to fly to Moscow to discuss the text of a joint resolution calling for a cease-fire. Brezhnev replied on the next day with an invitation to the secretary of state, and Nixon sent a formal notice that Kissinger would have his full authority.

More than that, while Kissinger was already in Moscow (he arrived there on October 20; I accompanied him), he received another secret message from Nixon, to be conveyed orally to Brezhnev. It was a remarkable change in the American approach. Nixon said he agreed with Brezhnev's view, as expressed in San Clemente in June, that the two leaders representing the two great powers "must step in, determine the proper course of action to a just settlement, and then bring the necessary pressure on our respective friends for a settlement which will at last bring peace to this troubled area." This very important message, if implemented thoroughly, could have changed significantly the future course of the Middle East peace settlement. But Kissinger never delivered it to Brezhnev because it would undercut his own diplomatic tactics.

Before Kissinger left for Moscow, he appeared to be stalling the negotiations on a UN resolution for a day or two in order to gain time for the advance of Israeli troops; they had already established a bridgehead on the western side of the Suez Canal and thus started to outflank the Egyptian force stranded on the East Bank in the Sinai. A completion of this flanking maneuver on the battlefield would have added to his bargaining leverage during the negotiations. But Nixon's new, broader, instruction to cooperate with Moscow in imposing a settlement could only interfere with Kissinger's strategy. "It will totally wreck what little bargaining leverage I still have," he cabled to his deputy Scowcroft. Then he complained by telephone to Haig, who had been transferred back from the Pentagon to replace Haldeman as chief of staff. But Haig refused to interfere; he told Kissinger he had troubles of his own. Under way right around the newly promoted General Haig was the Saturday night massacre; Nixon fired his attorney general and lesser officials from the Department of Justice for refusing to dismiss the Watergate prosecutor, Archibald Cox.

Kissinger virtually ignored the president's instruction, though he did not admit it directly. In his memoirs he states that he adhered to the earlier plan concerning the UN resolution approved by Nixon before his departure for Moscow, but he does not say anything about outlining the new American position to Brezhnev. I do not recall his doing so during the discussion of a few hours he had with Brezhnev and Gromyko.

To Kissinger's surprise, the Soviet leaders rather quickly agreed to a compromise draft resolution. It called for an immediate cease-fire and compliance with Resolution 242 (the latter part was basically the American draft). Moscow accepted it, believing it to be a balanced document and knowing that the military situation was irreversibly changing in favor of Israel (Sadat at that moment was pleading with us to hurry with a cease-fire resolution). That was why Brezhnev proposed to Kissinger that our two countries immediately and jointly introduce the resolution in the Security Council.

But Kissinger, it seemed, wanted to wait a bit longer. He said he needed time for consultations with Israel to persuade it to agree to a cease-fire. The Israelis quickly realized that they could take advantage of a few hours' confusion at the beginning of the cease-fire and encircle the Egyptian Third Army on the East Bank of the Suez Canal. Actually, it was a premeditated violation of the agreement from the start. Later, Kissinger wrote about the Israeli action with evident approval. The only thing that remains unclear is whether Nixon knew about this at the time.

Late at night on October 22, the Security Council adopted an important resolution, No. 338, declaring an agreement on the cease-fire. For all their intense rivalry, the two superpowers jointly sponsored it.

## A New Crisis

Although the crisis appeared to draw to a peaceful end, its peak had not in fact been passed. After just a few hours of the cease-fire, the agreement suddenly collapsed. Israeli troops broke the pledge by advancing to the Suez Canal in an attempt to encircle and crush the Egyptian Third Army Corps of some 25,000 men, which still was on the eastern side of the canal.

The next day Nixon received an angry message from Brezhnev on the hot line: "Mr. President, Israel has grossly violated the Security Council decision on the cease-fire in the Middle East. We are shocked that the agreement reached just two days ago has been virtually blown up by this action of the Israeli leaders. You are in a better position to know why Israel has committed this perfidious action. We can see only one possibility to remedy the situation and implement the agreement. The only way to do that is to force Israel to comply immediately with the Security Council decision. Too much is at stake, not only as regards the situation in the Middle East, but also in our relations."

Nixon replied that the United States "was assuming full responsibility for ensuring the termination of military operations by Israel." But he replied that information available to him indicated that the Egyptians were to blame for breaking the cease-fire. "A historic settlement was reached by you and me," he wrote, "and we should not let it be broken."

Through the day there were active contacts between the White House and the Soviet Embassy to align our positions at another meeting of the Security Council called to discuss the cease-fire. Brezhnev addressed Nixon once again on the hot line: "I would like to inform you that the Egyptian side is ready to cease fire immediately if the Israeli armed forces do the same. You can inform the Israeli government categorically." The message stressed the need for a joint U.S.-Soviet position before the Security Council.

I was then in Moscow attending Politburo sessions on the crisis and heard Anwar Sadat's calls to Brezhnev on a special phone, with the Egyptian president begging "to save me and the Egyptian capital encircled by Israeli tanks." When Brezhnev called our chief military representative in Cairo, he replied that there was no immediate threat to Cairo but said that "Sadat completely lost his head" when he learned that several Israeli tanks had crossed the Suez Canal and were heading toward Cairo. This turned out to be a reconnaissance by three or four tanks, which soon withdrew.

But it was the Egyptian Third Army Corps that was the real focus of developments, surrounded as it was by the Israelis in the Suez area. Unless the cease-fire took effect immediately, it would be crushed. Another Security Council resolution, No. 339 of October 23, also cosponsored by the Soviet Union and the United States, was quickly passed. It called on both sides to return to their cease-fire positions and provided for UN observers.

On the morning of the next day, Brezhnev indignantly informed Nixon that the Israeli forces were engaged in fierce fighting on the west and east side of the Suez Canal "just several hours after the second Security Council resolution calling for an immediate cease-fire." He expressed confidence that the president would be able to influence Israel to stop violating the new resolution. The Soviet leadership itself hardly had at that time the means to influence developments on the ground, which angered the Kremlin. There was a lot of harsh criticism of Israel and the American administration, because the Kremlin strongly believed that Israel could not act without at least tacit knowledge of the White House.

The Soviet government issued a public statement concerning "Israel's perfidious attack" on the Egyptian forces and population centers. "The Soviet government warns the Israeli government about the most grave consequences of the continuation of its aggressive actions against Egypt and Syria," it said. Moscow then received another urgent message from our chief military adviser in Egypt reporting that the Israelis were continuing their offensive, and that the Egyptian Third Army Corps was surrounded and would be annihilated unless the cease-fire came into effect immediately. Our embassy in Cairo reported that Sadat's rule was about to collapse.

The same night Brezhnev called an urgent meeting of the Politburo. Vasily Grubjakov, an assistant to Gromyko who was with him at that important meeting, told me later that the most aggressive stand was taken by Defense Minister Grechko. He insisted on an impressive "demonstration of our military presence in Egypt and Syria" and was supported by Podgorny. Kosygin was flatly opposed, and Gromyko supported him. Brezhnev, following a cautious line and trying to maneuver between the Arabs and the United States, also came out against any involvement of our troops in the conflict.

So after an argumentative meeting they finally approved a message to Nixon which was strongly worded but did not contain any threat to act unilaterally. However, a stronger phrase about our possible involvement appeared in the text of the message as it reached Washington. It is anybody's guess how and when it was inserted, since the main participants of the meeting are no longer alive. The final decision could have been influenced by a last-minute telephone appeal from Sadat.

As a result the message warned Nixon that in breaking the cease-fire Israel was "flagrantly challenging both the Soviet Union and the United States, since the Security Council decision rests on our agreement." Brezhnev proposed that Soviet and American military contingents be dispatched to Egypt and he warned "bluntly that if you do not deem it possible to cooperate with us in this respect," he was ready to act alone. Brezhnev concluded: "Let us implement that agreement in this concrete case and in this complicated situation. This will be a good example of our coordinated action in the interests of peace." As appears from the last phrase, the Soviet leaders were still hoping for some cooperation with the American administration.

To add to their pressure, the Soviet Air Force mounted several symbolic exercises in Transcaucasia, and one or two Soviet transports flew to Cairo. But as I learned later from Moscow, Washington never had any real cause for alarm because the Politburo did not have any intention of intervening in the Middle East. It would have been reckless both politically and militarily, for at that time the Soviet Union was not prepared to mount immediately a large-scale intervention in the region. And even if we could have done so, it would have transformed the Arab-Israeli War into a direct clash between the Soviet Union and the United States. Nobody in Moscow wanted that.

In his memoirs Kissinger claims that Washington feared Soviet intervention. Maybe so. But it appears more likely that a major factor in American behavior was its determination not to accept a joint Soviet-American military presence to supervise or observe the cease-fire under UN auspices. For the administration that would have been tantamount to Soviet military penetration in the Middle East, which Kissinger would have found unacceptable.

Kissinger sounded nervous as I read to him Brezhnev's message over our confidential telephone line on the evening of October 24. He read it back to me to be sure he had understood it correctly and promised to report it promptly to the president.

He telephoned back at 10:15 P.M. to say that Nixon had ordered a meeting of presidential advisers and assistants at the White House. The president hoped that the general secretary would await the outcome of that meeting and that in the interim the Soviet Union would not act by itself and create a grave situation.

In his reply, Nixon agreed with Brezhnev that our accord to act jointly to preserve peace was of the highest value. He nevertheless declined Brezhnev's proposal for joint action by dispatching Soviet and American military contingents to Egypt, saying that it "was unsuitable under the circumstances." Nixon said that Washington had no information about Israeli cease-fire violations on any appreciable scale. Therefore, he stressed, the

Soviet warning of unilateral actions caused grave concern and could have incalculable consequences. Nixon expressed his readiness to strengthen the UN supervisory forces with additional manpower and equipment and declared himself ready to include some American and Soviet noncombat personnel, if that was what Brezhnev meant by the joint dispatch of contingents to the Middle East.

## The Superpower Stakes Rise: A U.S. Combat Alert Is Declared

Shortly after receiving Nixon's message, our embassy heard news flashes on the radio that the U.S. armed forces were being put on combat alert. There was no official confirmation, and initially the Soviet Union was not mentioned in the reports. But then we heard about a purported Soviet threat to send forces to the Middle East to impose a cease-fire even if the United States did not join in. Broadcasts reported Soviet aircraft moving closer to the region and stressed the White House's refusal to give in to Soviet pressure. The firm stand "taken by the White House"—it was said—was designed to "prevent Soviet military interference" in the Middle East.

Frankly speaking, I was not unduly alarmed at these reports, in contrast to the Cuban crisis of 1962. But I was rather angry. I called Kissinger on our special telephone and demanded an explanation in a tone that was highly unusual in our personal relationship—the more so because in our private conversations he had never as much as hinted at the possibility of an alert. I stressed that it was clearly contrary to the spirit of his recent negotiations in Moscow, and I did not see why the U.S. government was trying to create the impression of a dangerous crisis.

Kissinger excused himself by saying that the White House instructions for limited combat readiness should not be taken by Moscow as a hostile act on the part of the U.S. government and were mostly determined by "domestic considerations." He assured me that the order would be revoked the next day, and that in the meanwhile I could urgently inform Brezhnev about it in strict confidence. Indeed, the order was revoked on October 26.

Kissinger did not specify what he meant by domestic considerations. For my part, I stressed the total incompatibility of the American alert with the general level of relations we had been trying to promote between our countries. That evening, we had a similar tense conversation when we met accidentally at the Kennedy Center, which we both attended for the opening of a new opera (during a "grave crisis"!). Donald Kendall happened to be there and wondered what was going on. I told him, "Oh, it's just Henry playing his diplomatic game."

## The End of the War: Nixon Becomes Apologetic

I was not of course present at the important White House meeting on the night of October 24 that ordered the alert, but I received a fairly detailed account two days later from Deputy Secretary of State Rush at lunch in his apartment, which had been scheduled two weeks before. (Rush had obviously been hurt by the fact that Nixon, who had repeatedly hinted at the chance of his appointment as secretary of state, finally appointed Kissinger with Rush as his deputy.) Nixon was not at the meeting, for reasons not clear to Rush. The later, official explanation was that the president was tied up with Watergate, but I found it hardly tenable. If the White House regarded the threat of Soviet interference in the Middle East—and a possible conflict—as seriously as Kissinger later wrote it did, then surely the president's participation in the meeting would have been essential. But why was he not there? Was he less worried than some of his assistants? And why did he later become apologetic about his message to Brezhnev?

According to Rush, those who participated in the meeting included Secretary of Defense James Schlesinger; the chairman of the Joint Chiefs of Staff, Admiral Thomas Moorer; and CIA Director William Colby. They had information about Soviet air maneuvers and discussed the possibility of a confrontation, but there was no unanimity, and some doubts, about whether the Soviet Union really wanted to stage one with the United States. At the same time, they understood that Israel had violated the Sunday resolution of the Security Council and took advantage of the cease-fire to occupy as much Egyptian territory as possible.

Kissinger was, according to Rush, very agitated throughout the meeting, which he chaired. He declared that it was important to understand the Russians' real intentions, which were to send their troops to the Middle East to consolidate Soviet influence in the region. That was why Kissinger strongly objected to dispatching a joint Soviet-American military contingent to the Middle East: the Russians would surely take advantage of it to reestablish their physical presence in Egypt and elsewhere in the area. He then proposed placing the U.S. armed forces immediately on a temporary combat alert to demonstrate Washington's firm opposition to any introduction of Soviet troops in the Middle East.

Not all the participants agreed at once with this plan. Some proposed warning Moscow if necessary that the United States would put its troops on alert if the Soviet Union began planning the unilateral dispatch of its troops to the Middle East. But Kissinger finally gained the upper hand, and that decision was approved by the president several hours later. Rush was convinced that Kissinger's profound pro-Israeli bias showed up at the meeting even at the expense of Soviet-American detente and their relations.

But I think that Kissinger, as usual, was pursuing his strategic goal of securing American influence and dominance in the Middle East. It was a continuation of his global "realpolitik" toward the Soviet Union, with detente only as a part of this policy.

On the very same day, the UN Security Council adopted still another resolution, which finally put an end to the war by sending a UN peacekeeping force to the Middle East, pointedly excluding contingents from any of the five permanent members of the Security Council. The next day, October 26, both Nixon and Brezhnev spoke out in favor of the creation of a UN supervisory peacekeeping force. The war was over.

Nixon also held a press conference claiming credit for Middle East peacemaking—a credit he really needed to offset the rising Watergate scandal. He attributed the administration's success in avoiding a confrontation to his good personal relations with Brezhnev and likened the whole thing to the Cuban crisis. I called Kissinger next day and told him this comparison was hardly relevant and essentially incorrect. He called me back in a couple of hours to tell me that the president agreed that it had been a lame comparison.

Brezhnev, spurred by the latest developments, sent an angry message to Nixon the next day, October 28. It said that "as I and my comrades see it, there is a credibility crisis." All the assurances given to Moscow and Cairo for more than a week about compliance with the cease-fire and the resolutions of the Security Council, he said, had served only to demonstrate direct American support for the Israeli military, which continues to behave "provocatively with a clear, or, I should say, naked aim." The situation, he said, was the result of misleading and even deceptive information reaching the president "aimed at encouraging the aggression and worsening relations between the United States and the Soviet Union, and . . . at undermining our personal mutual trust."

Brezhnev did not hide his own and his colleagues' suspicions about Kissinger's behavior. Clearly impressed by Brezhnev's message, Nixon invited me to come to Camp David October 30 to discuss the matter in private. He spoke in a conciliatory and even apologetic manner, stressing his intention to continue his policy of improving Soviet-American relations. He said he saw the previous week as just an unpleasant episode in our relations and asked me to inform Brezhnev personally that he would not permit the Israelis to crush the encircled Egyptian Third Army Corps. He also expressed his readiness to cooperate with us through the United Nations to settle the crisis.

"Please inform the general secretary," he concluded, "that as long as I live and hold the office of president I will never allow a real confrontation with the Soviet Union." He conceded that he might have lost his cool a bit during the crisis, but that could be explained partly by the siege of his political opposition and personal enemies who were using the pretext of Watergate to undermine his authority. To tell it in plain human words, he said, it was very hard for him at times. That was the first time I heard Nixon admitting to the depth of his domestic troubles because of Watergate. Kissinger was not present at the conversation, and Nixon may have wanted to disassociate himself from some of his secretary of state's behavior during the crisis. I do not know for sure.

Kissinger himself in due course found it necessary, for his own private reasons, to express his regrets for the alert. Early in November he conceded to me that "the White House had made a mistake putting its forces on high combat alert. The general secretary proved to have more nerve than the president. We could see now we had made a rash move damaging American-Soviet relations. That is undeniable. But the main thing for all of us is not to worsen that damage by further mutual recriminations and offenses, just because we have admitted what could have been a gross miscalculation on our part."

Many American historians describe the Middle East War as the deadliest crisis in our postwar relations, comparable to the Cuban crisis. While it was indeed a serious political crisis, which made a rather unpleasant impact on our relations, there was no threat of a direct military clash between us. At least that was and is Moscow's assessment. We took no measures to put our armed forces on high combat alert even in response to the American move, and we certainly did not alert our strategic nuclear forces as the Americans did. One cannot help but think that the myth of the Middle East being saved from a Soviet armed invasion was consequently put into circulation by the high American participants in the events in order to justify their rather unseemly role in the course of the crisis.

The protracted Arab-Israeli conflict nevertheless ended with the active behind-the-scenes involvement of Washington and Moscow. The involvement was characterized by an intricate pattern of cooperation and rivalry. Both countries worked to settle the conflict between the Arabs and Israel and arrange a truce through the UN Security Council. Detente notwithstanding, the conflict clearly showed that both countries did not necessarily have parallel objectives and interests. The Middle East War never grew into a direct military confrontation between the Soviet Union and the United States—in contrast to the Cuban crisis—precisely because of the remarkable new level of Soviet-American relations. Moreover, the conflict ended in an agreement between the Arabs and Israel to begin direct negotiations in Geneva in December, cochaired by the Soviet Union and the United States. All that represented a certain success for the policy of detente. Characteristically, neither government called the process into question or denied its usefulness during the conflict or afterward. At the same time, the conduct of the Middle East War showed that the process was very delicate and fragile; it definitely damaged the trust between the leadership of both countries.

The October crisis and the American role were discussed soon after the war by the Politburo. Did the Middle East policy of Nixon and Kissinger indeed demonstrate that they had no interest in cooperating with the Soviet Union when it really mattered? Had they really considered a military clash with us? And if so, what about detente between us? All these were legitimate questions. And they somewhat cooled the excitement about detente that had reigned in Moscow after the summits. Yet the ultimate result of this comprehensive and animated review was once again our reaffirmation of detente as a useful and important policy, while recognizing that in some areas such as the Middle East it would be very difficult to reconcile our different approaches. The rivalry would remain. Detente had its limits.

# VII. The Fall of Richard Nixon

## Nixon's Last Friend

The Soviet leadership could not help noticing that the Arab-Israeli War was being waged against the background of Nixon's growing domestic difficulties over Watergate. I got an inside view from Senator Fulbright at the end of October, after the firing of Archibald Cox as Watergate special prosecutor. He remarked that Nixon was in a state of permanent agitation, which he explained by the unprecedented attacks on the president's character in the mass media.

We began receiving more and more information about the president's Watergate troubles, not least from Nixon himself, who communicated them to Brezhnev via the conversation I had with him at Camp David. But many Soviet leaders including Brezhnev believed that the scandal was being used against Nixon by opponents of detente. Nixon's conversation and message opened a unique personal exchange with Brezhnev that has never before been chronicled. As Watergate turned against the president, Brezhnev proved himself Nixon's staunch friend and supporter, probably the last he had among the leaders of great nations, including his own. Alone and under siege, Nixon reciprocated.

A man of impulsive sentimentality, Brezhnev was impressed by what Nixon had conveyed through me, and on November 10 he sent a sympathetic private reply. It concluded: "I should like from the depths of my heart to wish you energy and success in overcoming all kinds of difficulties, the causes of which are not easily seen at a distance. Understandably, our wishes of success are essentially concerned with the sphere of developing Soviet-American relations. Our determination to proceed with the radical improvement of Soviet-American relations has not diminished on account of the Middle East developments."

Four days later I met the president at his invitation. He was in good spirits, but looked rather haggard, clearly affected by the Watergate scandal. He said he had read Brezhnev's letter carefully and was preparing a reply, but meanwhile he asked me to relay his thanks to the general secretary for being the only foreign leader—including America's own allies—who had been able to find human words of cheer amidst his difficulties. He told me such kindness would not easily be forgotten and would I, please, inform Brezhnev that he was full of determination, in spite of their recent disagreements, to continue developing and consolidating our relations.

Nixon continued these themes when I visited him again in the White House on December 13 at his invitation. The private conversation was unusual both in content and form in that he was extraordinarily frank about domestic questions. He said he attached much importance to developments in the "troubled Middle East" and the prospects of the forthcoming Geneva peace conference. He explained that he thought much about the region, not only for its international implications, but since Israel and its supporters were very influential in American political life.

Surprisingly, Nixon then went on to criticize Israel's policy. He argued that Israel actually did not want to end the state of war with the Arabs and indeed the Cold War in general. He said Israel and the American Jewish community were anxious to prevent any improvement in Soviet-American relations and wanted to take advantage of permanent confrontation between the United States and the Soviet Union. Nixon said he had come to these conclusions only recently, because he had not even imagined at first that Israel could have such long-term aspirations. But the result, he said was "Israel's intransigence" about a Middle East settlement, which was encouraged in every way by the politically influential Jewish lobby in America, which in turn helped shape American foreign policy. As a result, the United States found itself gradually in a situation where its course ran counter to the whole world: the Arabs, the Soviet Union, and nearly all its allies in Western Europe as well as Japan.

The president went on to say that was one reason he was determined to seek a settlement in the Middle East. He knew he would inevitably face trouble with Israel and its champions in the United States. But he said he was ready to embark on that road, since he had done quite a bit for Israel and still believed that as a small state surrounded by its enemies, it needed help. He stressed that he did not owe anything to the Jewish vote, as he said most Jews had always voted against him. Therefore he could afford to take a more balanced stand in the forthcoming negotiations. He was also clearly vexed by the hostile campaign against him over Watergate by the mass media. The president said that the American media were run "essentially by the same Jewish circles," which, he insisted, were against him and showed no gratitude for all he had done for Israel. In fact he used even stronger language than that.

He then made a curious remark about Kissinger. He paid deserved tribute to his intelligence and service and pointed out that his Jewish origin made him less vulnerable to the attacks of the American Jewish community, which would be an asset at the coming Middle East negotiations. Nixon observed that Kissinger had at times strongly indulged Israel's nationalist sentiments, for which he had to be corrected, but on the whole, the president was convinced that Kissinger was working along the right lines.

Nixon told me rather emotionally that he considered addressing the nation frankly to turn the tables on Israel and its American lobby (something he never did). He also complained that the lobby, represented in its congressional fight against the Soviet Union by Senator Jackson, was hampering his government's efforts to grant the Soviet Union equal trade status. Finally he told me to give no credence to the hue and cry in the American media about his possible resignation or impeachment. He said he would stay in the White House until the end of his term, he was a persistent person, and he would be as good as his word—make no mistake about it.

My overall impression was that his criticism of Israel and the Jewish community grew out of his identifying them with the mass media, whose attacks on Watergate and issues of policy he resented strongly and emotionally as the end approached.

On December 26 I visited President Nixon again with a response from Brezhnev. By then our meetings with the president were becoming almost a regular fixture; through me both leaders carried on what amounted to a confidential correspondence that has never before been disclosed.

Brezhnev thanked Nixon "for the spirit of sincerity and straightforwardness, absolutely necessary for our contacts." He stressed that much in what the president had said about the Middle East and his policy toward Israel coincided with the view of the Soviet leadership and that both countries had to search jointly for a solution in order to avert a new outbreak of hostilities. As to the deadlock over trade in Congress, Brezhnev pointed out that "we are no beggars; this is a mutual affair." In conclusion, Brezhnev referred to Nixon's remarks about Watergate by stating: "Thank you for your firm decision to stay."

When I turned the conversation to ideas for improving Soviet-American relations, Nixon responded that he would do all in his power during the remaining three and one-half years of his presidency "to make the course worked out at the two summits remain irreversible." He conceded that he faced many American critics: pro-Israeli organizations, the mass media, the liberals, the congressional opposition, among others. They had various ambitions and goals of their own, but were acting jointly as a coalition to launch fierce attacks on his policies of detente.

"Paradoxically, many of them opposed the Cold War and favored better relations with the Soviet Union," he said, and the same turnabout applied to the America's West European allies, who had previously pressed the United States to minimize the risks of Soviet-American confrontation. But now that all this had been largely achieved, they have made a U-turn criticizing the White House for "collusion with the Russians" and supposed attempts to establish "a hegemony of the two superpowers."

As far as I know, Nixon did not inform anybody about the substance of our two last conversations and kept his entourage in the dark. Nor did he mention them in his memoirs. But I reported them to Moscow. They were unique in the entire history of Soviet-American relations.

The irony of the situation was that during this period Nixon seemed to be as frank, direct, and even cynical in conversations with his old communist enemies as he was with friends, if not more so. I think the old cold warrior finally became friendlier toward the Soviet Union in the deepening Watergate isolation. The good personal contacts and deepening relationship he developed with Brezhnev also helped. After all, we are all human.

## Rumblings in the White House

On January 17, I invited Vice President Gerald Ford to dinner at my embassy. He conceded that Nixon was in a difficult position, but seemed likely in the end to hold his ground. Ford, who had served as Republican leader in the House, told me that Nixon had asked him to use his connections to help push through the administration's programs and meanwhile monitor congressional sentiment about Watergate. The vice president did not beat around the bush about his own political ambitions; he told me he liked the idea of running for president some day, but it was too soon to talk about that.

Nevertheless, he was already thinking about presidential prerogatives in foreign policy and told me that if he were to be president "by the chance of fate" Kissinger would be his secretary of state. Ford had a high opinion of Kissinger who was careful to keep him personally informed about foreign policy. The vice president said he fully supported the policy of negotiation rather than confrontation with the Soviet Union, and he believed a considerable part of the American people did, too. He kept referring to "Kissinger's policy" rather than Nixon's when talking about foreign affairs, although he spoke quite respectfully about the president.

The closest members of Nixon's entourage, including Kissinger himself, persistently echoed the president's own words that he would not resign. Kissinger writes in his memoirs that up until July of 1974—one month before Nixon actually resigned—he had "sought to banish the hitherto unthinkable idea" of the president's resignation. But I first heard him talk about it more than six months earlier, at the end of January 1974. He confirmed that in several private conversations, Ford had already asked him to continue as secretary of state if he succeeded Nixon as president. Kissinger therefore could not foresee any serious changes in American foreign policy under Ford, especially with respect to the Soviet Union.

Kissinger told me the situation was already very grave, and he was beginning to reckon with the probability of the president's departure, something he would not have previously believed. The secretary of state was losing confidence in the ability of the White House to defend the president against the array of charges facing him. His main handicap was the lack of one resolute individual to shape a strategic plan of defense and subordinate all the actions of the administration to it without the distractions of new developments, which came daily. Six or seven lawyers and several aides consulted with the president regularly, and their activity was directed by Nixon himself, who Kissinger said was prone to emotion, leading him to take rash decisions out of irritation.

Congress sensed this collapse of White House morale and consequent weakness and became more headstrong in foreign policy, which added to the factors impeding Soviet-American relations. This was particularly reflected by legislation to continue trade discrimination against us; the sapping of administration strength made it impossible to change this policy. Meanwhile the country's anti-Soviet forces gained in cohesion and increased their activities.

Kissinger's own position and influence were undermined as his leader's position weakened, and he directed much effort toward single-handedly trying to untangle the problems of the Middle East by shuttling back and forth among the capitals of that region. This placed him far from Washington and Watergate. He refused to bring in the Soviet Union through the framework of the Geneva peace conference, taking advantage of Egypt's new pro-American orientation and our own inflexible policies in the region.

All this annoyed Moscow and exacerbated Soviet-American relations, although Moscow should also be blamed for insisting on its counterproductive policy of refusing to restore diplomatic relations with Israel and categorically refusing to have any direct contacts with the Israeli side. If we had an even-handed policy, we could have played a more active and successful role. Far from helping to improve relations was the stubborn, doctrinaire, and even foolish position of the Soviet leadership concerning human rights, and especially emigration, which permitted our opponents to turn the Congress into the principal American forum and bulwark of sentiment against us.

Inside the Nixon administration itself, those who had long been suspicious of detente were emboldened to carve out their own positions. On

January 10, Secretary of Defense James Schlesinger, long a personal critic of Kissinger's ideas and methods, advanced a new doctrine of limited nuclear war to redirect American strategic weapons from civilian to military targets in the Soviet Union. The Soviet military command greeted the decision with concern. Ostensibly designed to spare the civilian population, it was actually meant to legitimize a knockout blow to the other side's military potential on the first strike. With one side thus deprived of the capacity to retaliate against enemy missiles and bombers before they had been launched—a return blow against empty missile silos and airfields would of course be purposeless—the strategic balance would vanish. This military balance helped underpin the diplomatic balance implied by detente. But the new doctrine was actually meant to legitimize a strategic nuclear war and, indeed, to increase the strategic nuclear threat to the Soviet Union, since the United States had more MIRVed missiles.

Schlesinger insisted that his plan for retargeting the U.S. strategic triad of missiles, bombers, and nuclear submarines was not meant to gain a first-strike advantage. But that was exactly how it was received in the Kremlin, to say nothing of the way it contradicted the recently concluded agreement on the prevention of nuclear war. The very discussion of the question of strategic nuclear exchanges was timed by the Pentagon to coincide with the beginning of the SALT II negotiations and the preparations for the third summit in Moscow in June. We regarded it as nothing less that an attempt to chill detente and to demonstrate that the influential people in the administration were not excessively interested in further restricting nuclear arms and improving Soviet-American relations.

Some American historians believe that in the period before and during the third summit, the Soviet leadership began to consider seriously whether Nixon was worth negotiating with any longer because of his domestic troubles. This is wrong. Of course, Moscow knew about the growing Watergate scandal and the attacks on detente. But the Politburo in the final analysis preferred to deal with a president who happened to favor better Soviet-American relations, and who still had the authority and will to negotiate and conclude agreements with foreign countries. Nothing could be gained by waiting for a new president with a less known character and views. "Strike while the iron is hot" says the old proverb, in Russian as well as English. Although communist doctrine does not recognize that policy is based on personalities, there was a curious personal chemistry between Brezhnev and Nixon that was felt until the end of the administration.

## Summit Preparations Again

At the end of January, Kissinger and I started to discuss preparations for Nixon's next visit to the Soviet Union. He summarized the president's approach to the summit with Brezhnev. Nixon believed there was not enough time to prepare a full-fledged agreement on limiting strategic weapons. But he still wanted that agreement to be the main topic of the Moscow summit. Therefore, the president suggested preparing a more limited document that would extend the period of the 1972 interim agreement for several years and limit the number of MIRV warheads on both sides. Meanwhile negotiations on a comprehensive SALT agreement would go on, and Kissinger provided some estimates to illustrate the American proposals. Of course, some international and bilateral issues were to be discussed too, as usual.

I found Nixon's approach reasonable, so I promised to recommend it to Moscow. As we prepared through the confidential channel for Kissinger's presummit visit (which by now had become almost routine), Nixon followed it up in March with a letter to Brezhnev, the highlight of which was the president's pledge to commit himself to detente as an irreversible policy. He commented on the agenda—SALT, the Conference on Security and Cooperation in Europe, the Middle East, and bilateral cooperation—and added a handwritten postscript: only the day before he had met with Soviet space experts in Houston and found them "excellent people." He noted that one result of the first summit had been plans for a joint (Nixon underlined the word) space flight, and "that might be our purpose in other fields, too." When Brezhnev replied two days later agreeing to the agenda, what pleased him most was Nixon's support of the irreversibility of detente, a Brezhnev thesis. To my mind, Nixon was playing a bit on Brezhnev's own hopes, because Watergate was already casting its shadow on everything. His close colleagues were being sentenced to prison, Judge John Sirica declared there was ample evidence of Nixon's involvement, and congressional hearings began May 6.

In his personal dealings with Moscow Kissinger used a negotiating technique that usually worked well for both sides. Kissinger knew full well that neither Brezhnev nor Gromyko would be able to react immediately to any of his proposals during a meeting with him because they had to refer them to the Politburo. This of course would make for protracted negotiations, and his time in Moscow was limited. Well before his departure from Washington he would normally outline some of the basic American positions to me, so Moscow had time to discuss them. By informing us privately in advance he knew he was giving us a basis for discussion, which then would usually have taken place within the Soviet leadership by the time he arrived. That enabled Brezhnev and Gromyko to start negotiating with him without losing much time and to prepare beforehand their own counterproposals and eventual compromise.

Gromyko employed quite a different method. A man with a mania for secrecy, he never showed his hand (even to our delegation) until the beginning of negotiations. He would always prepare for a thorough dialogue in an unhurried way. He did not like the far-flung and mobile diplomacy to which the secretary of state was committed. Besides, having been ceded great negotiating powers by Nixon, Kissinger could work in a faster and more flexible way, and that made it easier for him to outwit Gromyko tactically. Apart from deep differences in their diverse characters, Kissinger had to clear his moves with only one man, Nixon. Gromyko on the contrary had to check with the entire Politburo; Brezhnev alone would not assume responsibility for decisions about our relations with the United States. Hence Gromyko's great caution in his negotiations with American officials.

But this time, because of the administration's concentration on Watergate, Kissinger was not as well prepared as usual for his presummit visit to Moscow. Kissinger also had devoted much energy and time to his Middle East "shuttle diplomacy," to the neglect of his brief on SALT. At home he faced a rising campaign against any agreements with the Soviets whatever, orchestrated largely by Senator Jackson and James Schlesinger.

Kissinger was in Moscow from March 24 to 28 and devoted a considerable part of his meetings with Brezhnev and Gromyko to SALT, which was still a provisional agreement expiring in 1977. Kissinger wanted it extended a few years, and we had no objection to extending it to the end of the decade; this new agreement could be signed at the summit. But Brezhnev rejected the essential part of the American proposal on limiting missile throwweights which, if accepted, would deprive the Soviet Union of the main advantage of our biggest missiles, the SS-18s, and inevitably lead to overall American missile superiority. I think Kissinger understood this quite well. As a result no compromise was reached, but both sides agreed that there still was a chance to come to terms at the working meeting of high-level officials at the end of the year.

The conversation in Moscow with Kissinger about a Middle East settlement was difficult, even sharp, and produced no results. "The United States," said Gromyko in his summary for the Politburo, "is 100 percent behind Israel, and the influence and dominance of Zionism are evident at every step." On other issues, there was a more constructive and businesslike dialogue.

## Watergate, the White House, and the Kremlin

Following Kissinger's visit to Moscow there was an intensive exchange during April between Kissinger and me and then, on April 29 in Geneva, between Kissinger and Gromyko on the limitations of strategic arms. The talks were very complicated. The debate was essentially over the quantitative levels and types of missiles, including MIRVed missiles.

Moscow, meanwhile, cautiously watched the deterioration of Nixon's domestic position. It became increasingly evident that Nixon was becoming oblivious to matters of foreign policy, and that Watergate was taking an ugly turn. But the Kremlin still believed that the real source was some conspiracy by anti-Soviet and pro-Zionist groups trying to scuttle Nixon's policy of good relations with Moscow. Even Gromyko held that opinion. Our embassy tried to explain to our leaders that Nixon was being accused of violating American laws and the Constitution. But Moscow did not (or would not) understand how the president of the United States could be prosecuted for what it viewed as such a "small matter." The minds of the Soviet rulers simply could not grasp the situation, because they never even thought possible such a thing as the criminal prosecution of the highest authority. In any case, Moscow did not believe until the last moment that Nixon could be forced to resign. The embassy, I should admit, was cautious in its predictions concerning Nixon's resignation, but it recognized the general possibility.

With their summit meeting only about a month away, Brezhnev decided to boost Nixon's morale. On May 28, I met President Nixon in the White House to convey Brezhnev's message. We talked in private, without interpreters, and I read out the cable from Moscow. The message began with ritual optimism about the results of the summit, then turned to its real purpose, which was to share his thoughts and those of his colleagues with Nixon, "man to man." The cable admitted that the Kremlin did not really understand what Watergate meant, but "we still can see that there are forces that are apparently rather powerful and that they are up in arms against you." It lauded him for nevertheless giving his attention to foreign affairs and Soviet-American relations in particular and concluded:

> This is the only way to act for a statesman confident in the correctness of his chosen course and well aware of the weakness of those who, for their narrow purposes or for reasons of shortsightedness, come out against his policy. In such cases you really need stamina and spiritual strength. Surely there are people in the United States and elsewhere who expect Richard Nixon to give way and break down. But, as we note with satisfaction, you are not going to please them in that respect. We are stating this on the basis of our good

relations and our confidence in the success of the new meeting. Meanwhile, we are looking forward to the arrival of your secretary of state at the end of May to complete preparations for our June summit as arranged.

Such an extraordinary message from a Soviet leader to an American president was unprecedented in the history of our relations, and it has never been published before. It was nothing short of a gesture of moral support for President Nixon in his hour of need—and the gesture came from Moscow, of all places.

Nixon was clearly moved by the message. After a moment's silence he asked me to relay his thanks to Brezhnev for his kind words, which he regarded as entirely sincere. He also told me to inform the general secretary that he was "completely healthy, both physically and emotionally," ready to rebuff all attacks by his adversaries, and certain of a favorable outcome.

Nixon went on to say that in his view, historians might yet start talking about a "Brezhnev-Nixon doctrine" as the basis for Soviet-American relations. Although never officially formalized or proclaimed, he said that such a doctrine did in fact exist, and it meant that the leaders of the Soviet Union and the United States, rather than stand in confrontation to each other, sought to do their utmost for their two great peoples to work jointly for one great goal, the cause of peace on earth. That was the main legacy the president hoped to leave upon his departure from the White House in 1976, Nixon stressed, and it would be produced in close cooperation with the Soviet leadership and Brezhnev personally. The president seemed palpably buoyed by the fact that in the clouds of Watergate there was a chink of light broadening in foreign policy, particularly in American-Soviet relations. He even cheered up.

On June 4, some three weeks before the summit, I had a long conversation with Kissinger to prepare for Nixon's visit to Moscow. We expected to complete a rather broad range of agreements that had been set in motion at the preceding two summits, but the shadow of Watergate nevertheless fell over our conversations. The White House badly wanted to minimize any criticism of the president from the right in connection with the summit. Kissinger was reluctant to involve himself too deeply and publicly so as not to expose himself to criticism and be drawn, one way or another, into the political whirlpool of Watergate.

By weakening Nixon, Watergate had strengthened the forces opposed to detente. They made it virtually impossible for Nixon and Kissinger to conduct serious negotiations in Moscow on a new SALT agreement. Besides, inside the administration itself there was a heated debate on how to compare

Soviet and American nuclear arsenals, as their structure was asymmetrical. The Pentagon remained the main obstacle.

On June 8, Kissinger told me that he had held private meetings about our emigration policy and its links to liberalized Soviet-American trade with Senators Jackson, Jacob Javits of New York, and Abraham Ribicoff of Connecticut—both Javits and Ribicoff were Jews with important constituencies of Jewish voters. He showed me a draft of a letter to Jackson explaining the administration's position on the link and seeking a compromise in order to push through congressional approval of most favored nation treatment for us. What leapt to my eye was a passage saying that the Nixon administration had "reason to believe that at least 45,000 people will be allowed to emigrate from the Soviet Union every year." I voiced my doubts over the advisability of giving a precise figure in the letter. But Kissinger said that Gromyko had raised no objections to the figure when he cited it at their recent meeting in Cyprus and asked me to check back urgently with Gromyko. He added that he managed to beat Jackson down to 45,000 from his excessive demand of 100,000 emigrants a year. But Jackson was still dissatisfied. It was obvious that this question would vex our relations for a long time.

## The Last Summit

President Nixon flew to Moscow on June 27. As on the previous occasion, the negotiations were held mostly in the Kremlin where the official documents were signed. Then Brezhnev and Nixon flew to the Crimea for a couple of days of informal conversations in Oreanda, near Yalta, where Brezhnev had his summer residence. The Oreanda meeting was arranged like the San Clemente meeting.

My own trip to the Crimea had a touch of adventure to it. Our official departure was scheduled for 4 P.M., one hour after the Kremlin talks were supposed to end. So I decided to take advantage of the break and pick up some personal effects from home. But Brezhnev did not keep to the schedule and called for Nixon at his Kremlin apartment right after the talks. They proceeded directly to Vnukovo airport. By the time I reached the airport, all the participants in the negotiations had already flown to the Crimea on board our plane. I was left out in the cold, while Brezhnev, as I was told, was aloft wondering where I was.

Fortunately, Nixon's own plane was still at the airport awaiting takeoff to follow the president and his entourage to the Crimea. The American crew knew me and agreed to give me a lift. Thus, I was flown comfortably from Moscow to Simferopol in the presidential plane, which I had all to myself. Since the president's Boeing 707 flew faster than Brezhnev's TU-104, we got to the Crimea first, and both Brezhnev and Gromyko were quite surprised to find me welcoming them at the airport. Their mystification ended only when I explained. Such things happen to diplomats whose life is open to adventure, as long as they maintain the presence of mind to seize opportunities when they arise.

The Yalta discussions focused on SALT in the presence of Gromyko and Kissinger, as well as the two ambassadors, Walter Stoessel of the United States and myself. The conversations between Brezhnev and Nixon took place on the shore of a warm and calm sea, where two government dachas stood. In this sense, the meetings consolidated the personal relationship established between the two leaders over the preceding years, which unfortunately was not to last much longer.

At the summit meeting proper in Moscow, most of the questions and especially the formal agreements were discussed by Gromyko and Kissinger, who was the driving force of the American delegation. As we proceeded through the agenda, Brezhnev would read out introductory statements on the issues and then interject comments during the ensuing discussion between the foreign minister and the secretary of state. SALT was the sole issue Brezhnev discussed actively, because he was quite familiar with it. But the general secretary did not know the details of other matters, though he sought to impress us otherwise by pretending to be actively interested. Kosygin conducted the discussion on economic matters for our side with his usual expertise.

There is no escaping the fact that the shadow of Watergate dominated Nixon's conduct; the scandal was to drive him from office in slightly more than a month. He was reserved. Once he cited incorrect figures during the SALT discussion and had to be corrected by Brezhnev. In general he let Kissinger conduct the major portion of the talks and discussions, although he would tersely state the American position at crucial moments. But most of the time he appeared brooding, absorbed in his thoughts.

But in contrast to the view of some American historians and officials—including Kissinger himself who later wrote that the Soviet leadership cut Nixon loose to "cut their losses"—I can testify that neither Watergate nor the prospect of impeachment had any appreciable effect on the conduct of our leaders, including Brezhnev. They were as interested as before in developing and promoting the process of detente and arms control, although they were conscious of the president's dwindling power. They supported Nixon because he continued to endorse detente, even though they were worried about the implications of his political decline. Nixon was right when he wrote in his memoirs: "In my judgment my Watergate problems and the impeachment hearings did not play a major part at Summit III. Our intelligence . . . beforehand—and my distinct impression while in the Soviet Union—was that

Brezhnev had decided to go all out for detente and place all his chips on my survival and my ultimate ability to deliver on what I promised."*

It is true that the Kremlin still could not believe in the possibility of Nixon's precipitous departure from the political scene. Brezhnev even told him in private he was confident that the president would stay in office until the end of his term. He did not exclude the possibility of another meeting with Nixon in that same year. I do not know what made Brezhnev so sure. In all probability, he was trying to boost Nixon's morale. My personal view was that Nixon would have to step down in several months, while Gromyko believed that he would hold out for about a year. In any case, neither Brezhnev nor Gromyko tried to distance themselves from Nixon, and they sought to demonstrate the Soviet leadership's invariable commitment to detente, no matter who might be president of the United States.

The summit's principal although predictable failure was the lack of appreciable progress on strategic arms limitation. Watergate not only undid Nixon's presidency but also destroyed any chances during the visit of a breakthrough on SALT II. But despite Watergate Nixon proposed and Brezhnev accepted an interim summit meeting in a third country late in the same year in order to make another attempt at reaching an agreement on SALT. (And all this was done only one month before Nixon's resignation!)

Several useful agreements were signed in Moscow: on limiting the number of underground nuclear tests and their power to 150 kilotons; reducing the number of antiballistic missile defense systems from two to one for each country; banning environmental warfare such as changing the weather; setting out rules for the replacement, dismantling, or destruction of strategic weapons.

As a whole the summit was successful enough in continuing the constructive development of relations between the two countries, and we discussed a host of problems including foreign policy issues such as Europe, the Middle East, Indochina, and the role of the United Nations. Agreements were concluded in bilateral areas such as energy, construction, artificial heart and transplant research, space cooperation, transport, environmental protection, cultural exchange, and opening new consulates in New York and Kiev.

During the official dinner given by Nixon in honor of Brezhnev in the American Embassy, they sat at the same table, and Brezhnev raised the sensitive issue of China. He warned that China was a threat to peace and urged the conclusion of a nonaggression treaty between the Soviet Union and the United States to dissuade the Chinese from any attempts to embroil the two

---

* Richard Nixon, *The Memoirs of Richard Nixon* (New York: Grosset and Dunlap, 1978), p. 1036.

powers in conflict. Brezhnev had repeatedly raised this since 1970, but Nixon was always evasive. Surprisingly, this time Nixon told Kissinger on the spot to pursue the idea in confidential negotiations with me for the planned interim summit. But Kissinger later on quietly killed the idea. Our diplomacy did not pursue it either.

The joint communiqué, signed in Moscow on July 3, declared that both leaders would "continue active contact and consultation." Brezhnev accepted Nixon's invitation to visit the United States in 1975. The communiqué stressed the need for a new SALT agreement covering quantitative and qualitative strategic arms limitations. There was an agreement on signing a world convention on chemical weapons and the earliest possible convocation of the Conference on Security and Cooperation in Europe.

These documents were useful during the next administration of Gerald Ford, helping it to chart our relations during its first year. The third summit as a whole further institutionalized the process of detente and sustained its momentum, however modestly. And even though Nixon was under heavy fire at home and was about to leave, the Soviet leadership communicated a rather optimistic confidential summary to the socialist countries' leaders assessing the results of his visit. Sounding as if the Soviet leadership was anticipating a long period of cooperation, the message said: "We see the main political result of this summit and talks held with the president of the United States in the further consolidation of the United States on the course of peaceful coexistence. Nixon has confirmed the desire of the American side to maintain its course toward better U.S.-Soviet relations and global detente."

## Nixon's Last Days

After the Moscow meeting our relationship with official Washington continued on its regular routine as if nothing were about to happen. Almost to his final day in the White House, Nixon was occupying himself with Soviet-American relations. It is hard to say whether it was a kind of a psychological opening, a last ray of light in the gloom that was closing in on him, or whether he was still hoping for a favorable outcome.

On July 9, Scowcroft asked me to convey Nixon's thanks to Brezhnev for his hospitality and their frank discussions in the Soviet Union. Following up one aspect of the talks in Oreanda, he asked for more data on Jewish emigration for Nixon's use in discussing Soviet trade with congressional leaders. We provided it, but by that time the administration was in no position to have any meaningful dialogue with Congress.

On July 15, I discussed with Kissinger the steps we would take to implement the summit decisions and drew up a detailed schedule as if

Watergate had never existed. We concentrated mostly on arranging the next stage of the SALT talks in Geneva in September. He hoped to come to Moscow to discuss the package around October.

In our *tour d'horizon* that followed, I expressed the opinion that the most recent period of Soviet-American relations had been damaged by the lack of any purposeful, thought-out program on the part of the administration. This evidently was a principal result of Watergate, which had come to be a national disaster of sorts, and of the general public confusion over U.S.-Soviet relations resulting from the lack of a clearly articulated set of goals.

Kissinger agreed that indeed all these factors combined to paralyze the administration and the effective implementation of its foreign policy. He remarked that there were some lessons to be drawn from the past year: idealistic approaches and gross public pressure had not improved Jewish emigration from the Soviet Union, which had dwindled abruptly and only aggravated our relations still more. The fierce attacks by conservatives on the nuclear arms talks, far from strengthening America's security, had mainly led to greater military expenditures. This crusade against detente had serious international implications and created a domestic debate that not only had failed to clarify the purposes of U.S. policy but produced greater confusion nationwide. Indeed, we agreed that policy could not be founded only on a negative basis, without struggling for something positive; and the country was entangled in contradictions, while the administration's authority had been collapsing disastrously.

On this sad note we concluded our rather pessimistic conversation, which proved to be my last meeting with any high-ranking official of the Nixon administration. The White House was almost totally absorbed by the Watergate crisis, which was speedily coming to its climax.

Nixon's final appearance on national television on August 8, when he announced his resignation, and the farewell meeting with his White House staff before his helicopter took off from the White House lawn was, undoubtedly, one of the most dramatic moments in the postwar history of America.

To the Soviet leadership such a precipitous collapse after Nixon's visit to Moscow still came as an unpleasant surprise. While such an outcome was evident from the course of events, there was perplexity in the minds of the Kremlin leaders, who were at a loss to understand the mechanics of how a powerful president could be forced into resignation by public pressure and an intricate judicial procedure based on the American Constitution—all because of what they saw as a minor breach of conduct. Soviet history knew no parallel.

Brezhnev reacted to the events by sending a private message on to the outgoing president:

On behalf of myself and my colleagues I should like to express kind feelings with regard to the fruitful cooperation and the spirit of mutual understanding that marked our joint efforts aimed at improving Soviet-American relations and normalizing the international situation. All that has been done over the last year in relations between the Soviet Union and the United States is highly appreciated in our country, in the USA, and the whole world. These truly great achievements cannot be regarded otherwise by all those who really care for peace and the future of mankind. I would also like you to know that we have received with satisfaction President Ford's statement of his intention to continue the course in our relations aimed at their further broadening and deepening.

As to the Soviet Union, we are determined to further the cause of developing the relations of peace and cooperation between the Soviet Union and the United States, the cause we have started together with you. We have also communicated that to President Ford.

Our best wishes to you, your wife and the whole family.

Sincerely,

L. Brezhnev

August 10, 1974

Nixon sent a return message to Brezhnev. [Reverse translation from the Russian.]

Leaving my Presidential position, I am sending you my personal farewell. I am going with a feeling of pride at how much you and I have done to transform relations between our countries, thus winning great achievements for the cause of world peace.

I know that President Ford believes as much as I do that nothing is more important in foreign policy than further consolidation of the growing ties of friendship between the United States and the Soviet Union. He will do all in his power to achieve that goal.

I am sending you my best wishes for a prosperous future for you personally and for the great people of the Soviet Union.

Yours sincerely,

Richard Nixon

August 12, 1974

So ended a unique correspondence between the heads of two different worlds.

Another president had left the White House, but under conditions unprecedented in American history. He was a man of contradictory views, convictions, and actions. His attitude toward the Soviet Union was mixed, but, together with his resourceful assistant, Henry Kissinger, he played a positive role in stabilizing and developing Soviet-American relations. But the direction they tried to set for American foreign policy in the Cold War lacked consistency and was subject to changes and collisions, which, together with the conservatism and inflexibility of the Soviet leadership, led to a new upsurge in the opposition to detente.

## I. Searching for the Real Gerald Ford

*Starting Out with the New President*

Despite the constitutional upheavals caused by Watergate, the transition from Richard Nixon to Gerald Ford was successful, and with it the continuation of the policy of Soviet-American detente. This reached its high point under Ford at his first summit with Leonid Brezhnev at Vladivostok four months after Ford assumed the presidency. There in a snowbound setting they settled on the outlines of an agreement to limit the growth of strategic nuclear weapons. But a zenith also implies a nadir, and thereafter detente went into an inexorable decline for reasons ranging from Brezhnev's health to Ford's domestic political difficulties.

Only hours after Ford took the oath of office on August 9, 1974, Henry Kissinger invited me to the White House and showed me directly to the Oval Office. It was the new president's first official communication with a foreign representative. Ford seemed elated although somewhat unaccustomed to his new situation. But as we had met before and knew each other pretty well, our conversation was not too formal.

Ford sent a personal message to Brezhnev unequivocally stating his determination to continue Nixon's policy of improving relations with the Soviet Union. Nixon had given him a long farewell talk on foreign affairs the previous day, minutely informing the incoming president about his discussions with Brezhnev in Moscow and the commitments they implied. The new president reaffirmed his invitation for Brezhnev to visit the United States the following year and was also prepared to meet him before then on "neutral territory" if the meeting was well prepared. The idea had already been raised in Moscow, and Kissinger had christened it a "mini-summit." Ford turned for corroboration to Kissinger, who confirmed Ford's words with a smile.

The president said he had known Kissinger for many years, ever since this Harvard professor had invited "a rank-and-file Congressman Ford" to speak to his students on the role of Congress in foreign policy. They understood each other well, Ford continued, and he appreciated Kissinger's views on the primary importance for the United States of its relations with the Soviet Union. Therefore he wanted us to know that he and Kissinger were going to be just "as effective a team" as Nixon and Kissinger in dealing with Moscow. Kissinger of course was listening to all this with evident pleasure.

As we were about to leave the office, Ford stopped for a moment and said that he wanted to let Moscow know one more thing on the first day of his presidency. He was well known in the country for his sharply uncompromising statements as a congressman about the Soviet Union. He could not find the "accurate and elegant wording" for what he wanted to say, but speaking straightforwardly, he said that as president he now would be much more discreet in his public statements: he had now to approach foreign policy with greater responsibility.

I told the president that my government would undoubtedly welcome his intention to continue improving our relations. All in all, I came away with a favorable impression of the new president. Although he was a novice at foreign policy, I felt he already possessed some knowledge in that field. I reported to Moscow that Ford seemed ready for a sensible dialogue.

After the meeting, Kissinger invited me into his office and gave me his own personal letter to Gromyko reassuring him about Ford. Whatever Gromyko "might hear or read" during the weeks to come, he said, President Ford intended to follow and expand the policy that had determined relations with the Soviet Union under Nixon. Ford had asked him to stay on and pay special attention to relations with the Soviet Union. He would be a strong president, Kissinger wrote, and would continue to pursue and implement the policies they had formulated last time in Moscow.

I could not help but notice Ford's personal warmth toward Kissinger and his appreciation of Kissinger's talents, a feeling that continued much later even through the president's memoirs. Kissinger remained the incontestable captain of American diplomacy, yet his potential was restricted. Under Ford, domestic policy and campaign strategy—the president faced reelection within two years—prevailed over foreign policy, including Soviet-American relations.

Kissinger also let me in on the rather complicated White House transition. It appeared that Ford was going to replace nearly all his cabinet members, apart from Kissinger himself. Not entirely in jest, Kissinger remarked that for the time being he would suspend his Middle East shuttle diplomacy in order to stay close to Washington for at least two months. Kissinger said Ford was now surrounded by many of his old friends from Congress and the Republican Party leadership. They might be nice people he said, but they had no experience whatsoever in international affairs and concealed this behind "patriotic phraseology" borrowed mainly from the lexicon of the postwar period when the relations with the Soviet Union had been far from normal. As an intelligent person, Ford understood this quite well, and as president he was trying hard to escape from the limited outlook of his friends. Yet their influence was not to be underestimated.

Frankly speaking, at the beginning of the Ford administration my principal hopes were set on Henry Kissinger and his views. By contrast Ford was known to me for his consistently conservative convictions first as a member and then as Republican leader of the House of Representatives. He had been a superhawk on Vietnam. He generally avoided meeting Soviet representatives, made no secret of his highly negative attitude toward the Soviet Union, and on the few occasions when he spoke out, his statements about us usually were openly hostile.

In short, Ford was a typical American congressman-patriot of the Cold War era, and this could not but worry us when he came to power. But as vice president under Nixon his record gave rise to some hope that he might have acquired a better idea of the policy of detente shaped by Nixon and Kissinger. I had spoken with him twice when it began to become obvious that he might succeed Nixon. He told me he believed Congress was mainly ignorant about the Soviet Union and would easily fall victim to the well-organized anti-Soviet campaigns of the sort led by Senator Jackson, which could only be broken by perseverance. He also said he fully supported a policy of negotiation with the Soviet Union, which he had insisted on referring to as "Kissinger's policy" and not Nixon's.

Alas, the experience of a vice president is not in itself a guarantee of continuity in policy, and the most enduring proof of this was provided by the complete shift in policy toward the Soviet Union after Harry Truman succeeded Franklin D. Roosevelt. Nevertheless many in the Soviet Union (and in other countries as well) were of the opinion that it was the secretary of state who directed the American foreign policy. In real life, this was not always true. President Kennedy had Dean Rusk as his secretary of state. Yet, in the issues of Vietnam, Cuba, and arms control Kennedy listened more to his defense secretary, Robert McNamara. The same was essentially true in the case of President Johnson. Nixon's secretary of state was William Rogers, whose role was insignificant. Henry Kissinger, the president's national security adviser, was entrusted by Nixon with directing his foreign policy. Finally appointed secretary of state, Kissinger like John Foster Dulles in his time, played first fiddle in foreign affairs.

I had an impression, and even a subconscious conviction, that the new president was going to let Kissinger direct American foreign policy. This would ensure some stability in our relations, or at least make them more predictable. However, the matter was not that simple. Soviet leaders overestimated America's readiness to accept detente as a norm in bilateral relations, while the American administration, Kissinger included, was growing dissatisfied with the Soviet conception of detente, particularly with regard to the countries of the Third World, where rivalry between the United States and the Soviet Union was becoming overt. I feared that the increasing contradiction between the Soviet and American approaches to detente could in the end undermine it, although this did not yet worry Moscow, which was firmly convinced of the rightness of its policy.

In the very first days of the new administration both governments deemed it necessary to reaffirm privately to the other their loyalty to the preceding course in their relations. Brezhnev welcomed Ford's first message. Just two days later he asked me to pass to the president his own message expressing his appreciation for Ford's determination to follow the policy of further developing our relations and coming out for a working meeting in the current year. Kissinger told me Ford agreed, and once again a summit was becoming an important reference point in our relations. Ford planned a visit to Japan to chart his own course there, and Kissinger remarked that it would be a good idea to link the president's first meeting with Brezhnev with this trip so it would appear less deliberately staged. This was also important for protocol reasons since the next of the alternating summits had already been scheduled for the following year in the United States.

Ford invited me to the White House once again on August 14. While photos were being taken, the president recalled our relaxed meeting a couple of months before, when my wife and I had invited him as vice president along with Mrs. Ford to an informal dinner at our embassy. We had shown some films about the Soviet Union, including a rather interesting documentary about tigers in the Ussuri taiga in Siberia. Ford later joked that it had been an unplanned introduction to what would be his first encounter with Brezhnev.

After the photographers left, Ford asked, "What do you think about my meeting Brezhnev in that region, say, in Vladivostok?" I replied that the idea deserved serious attention but I had to report it to the general secretary, and Ford remarked he wanted Brezhnev's opinion anyway before things went any further.

How far was it from Moscow to Vladivostok? he wanted to know. When I answered that New York was closer to Moscow than Moscow was to Vladivostok, Ford was amazed by the size of my country and said few Americans could comprehend this. Kissinger, never forgetting his triangular diplomacy, observed that a Soviet-American meeting in Vladivostok would "delight" the Soviet Union's nearest neighbors—the Chinese.

Ford kept to the point: in his view, the first meeting between him and Brezhnev should be devoted to a practical, friendly, but essentially introductory review of the international situation as well as of principal questions of Soviet-American relations, which would not necessarily have to be decided immediately. At the same time he wanted to discuss specific proposals in the field of strategic arms limitation, which would be worked out by officials before the meeting, so they could agree on how to instruct their own delegations for further negotiations. I answered that Brezhnev had already minutely informed Nixon in Moscow of the Soviet side's ideas, and now it was the Americans' turn. Ford was aware of this, but he still wanted Brezhnev to instruct his experts to continue looking for a compromise.

As we parted, Ford said he would like to be invited to another informal dinner at the embassy with his wife, even if it breached presidential protocol, so they could see more documentaries about the Soviet Union and gain a better picture of the country. On a second thought, he pointed to Kissinger, who had married for a second time earlier in the year, and said, "Maybe you could arrange a dinner for six, in honor of the newlyweds."

I passed by the cabinet room on the way out and noticed some changes among the portraits on the walls. Eisenhower's portrait was still there, but Roosevelt and Wilson had been replaced by Lincoln and one Democrat—Harry Truman.

## My Dinner with Nelson Rockefeller: The Middle East

Late in August Ford announced his decision to appoint Nelson Rockefeller as his vice president, the post which Ford himself had occupied and which still remained vacant. Kissinger made no secret of his satisfaction with this choice, for Nelson Rockefeller had long been his patron, and he joked that if he ever had to leave his job as secretary of state, he could always count on a position as a secretary to one of the Rockefellers, and anyway, "The pay will be no less."

The congressional hearing on the nomination aroused huge interest, for it provided a unique opportunity to throw some light on a matter of great curiosity to many Americans: How much is a Rockefeller really worth? According to Kissinger, Nelson Rockefeller himself did not know exactly how large his fortune was. His wealth consisted mainly of multitudinous stocks and bonds; enormous real estate holdings in the United States and abroad, the value of which was steadily growing; and a huge art collection, one of a kind and really priceless.

On September 6 I went to meet Rockefeller at a dinner for three, arranged by Kissinger. But Kissinger was delayed at the White House, so Rockefeller and I were left tête-à-tête. As I was ushered in, Rockefeller was talking on the phone with his wife, Happy, asking her in which banks she kept her money and how much was in each account. He explained to me that when he married her, he never bothered to find out how much money she had, but now he had to provide the information for Congress. About four hundred FBI agents were checking him out by interviewing virtually all of his known acquaintances on the instruction of Congress, because for the first time in American history both the president and vice president had not been elected but appointed following the departure of their predecessors in clouds of scandal.

Rockefeller remarked that this whole "X-ray procedure" was rather unpleasant yet unavoidable in view of nation's post-Watergate mood with its suspicions of power and the establishment. It could be worse, he added. In 1964, for instance, when he was competing with Barry Goldwater for the Republican presidential nomination, some of the senator's ardent followers had put something in the drinks at a Rockefeller cocktail party—without Goldwater's knowledge, he hastened to add. It upset the stomachs of some guests, but fortunately a wave of serious illness was avoided. "Our political customs are sometimes brutish, but you have to be ready for them when you start out on a political career." Rockefeller told me these and other stories with visible pleasure, as though demonstrating what an old hand he was in American politics.

He admitted having made some anti-Soviet statements, principally as governor of New York State, where he had to reckon with New York City's big Jewish vote. But he said Moscow could rest assured that he would support President Ford and his old friend Henry Kissinger in developing relations with the Soviet Union. Some of the "more practical" members of his family—hinting at his brother David Rockefeller, president of Chase Manhattan Bank—had already begun doing business with the Soviet Union, he reminded me, so he would "take this good experience into account." But he said he had asked Kissinger to arrange this meeting with the Soviet ambassador to start off his own relations with the Soviet Union. We briefly touched upon some specific aspects of Soviet-American relations, and it was obvious that his knowledge of them was rather superficial and somewhat stereotyped, although he did his best to sound friendly, trying to demonstrate that as a vice president we would see a "new Rockefeller."

At this point Kissinger joined us and dinner started. Kissinger began the conversation with a statement that the president and vice president attached great importance to establishing personal contact with representatives of the Soviet government. The new administration, he said, was interested in achieving positive results in Soviet-American relations in order to enter the presidential campaign of 1976 with accomplishments in foreign policy—it did not regard itself as just a "transitional stage" between two presidencies and intended to stay in the White House for at least six years.

Kissinger asked me to brief Rockefeller on Soviet foreign policy and quickly added that I could touch upon the most confidential details of our relations, for he had already briefed Rockefeller himself. I succinctly outlined our approach without any interference from Kissinger until I touched upon the desirability of coordination between the United States and the Soviet Union in the Middle East. Rockefeller looked inquiringly at Kissinger, who promptly remarked that "Washington's freedom of action in this field has its limits."

Kissinger did not elaborate on this in Rockefeller's presence. But when we lingered after dinner, he returned to the question on his own initiative. He said he wanted to explain his viewpoint strictly off the record, and not just with regard to the Middle East, but in a broader context. In Kissinger's words, the "limited nature" of Washington's room for maneuver was largely accounted for by the "jealous and sensitive" reaction of the NATO allies to joint Soviet-American moves. Detente, he said, was undoubtedly influencing the solidity of both alliances, NATO and the Warsaw Pact, and Washington found it much more difficult to control its allies than Moscow. "In this sense detente damages NATO a lot more than it hurts the Socialist bloc headed by the Soviet Union," the secretary of state observed. It was one of his first open indications of the limits to detente.

Here I must admit that the Soviet Union at the time did not have a clear and independent strategy of its own for reaching a Middle East settlement. Our Arab allies abused our readiness to protect their interests and often used us diplomatically to block any emerging peacemaking initiatives, American or otherwise. All this made constructive cooperation between the Soviet Union and the United States in the Middle East very difficult. Basically we both were in favor of the same formula: peace in exchange for the return of the occupied territories. But in this case American diplomacy had the more realistic option of step-by-step accommodation. We followed the Arabs in demanding immediate withdrawal of the Israeli troops while the Arab countries remained vague about recognizing Israel after withdrawal. That was an unrealistic approach.

## My Granddaughter and Ford Divide the Globe

On September 7 Ford received three Soviet cosmonauts and three American astronauts who had been training for a docking mission in orbit the following year. Models of the two spacecraft were displayed in the White House, and Colonel Alexey Leonov volunteered to explain the docking procedure to the president. He did it in decent English.

Wives and children of both space crews were present at the reception. Ford asked to be photographed with them. My five-year-old granddaughter Katia was also there, standing to one side with my wife and myself but dying to pose for the cameras, so her grandmother had to hold her back. Ford nevertheless noticed the little girl and asked if she wanted to be photographed with him. Katia bravely answered, "Yes, I want." The president then invited her to choose a place to be photographed in his office. The child walked up to a large colorful globe, as tall as Katia herself, which was standing on the floor. She embraced half of it with her arms and said, "Let's do it here." The president laughed and encompassed the other half saying that they had divided the globe between them. This picture still hangs on the wall of my study, signed by the president of the United States, showing him and a little Russian girl reaching for each other across oceans and continents. I had always hoped the appealing scene would be a symbolic forerunner of future Russian-American cooperation, but that was not to happen for almost twenty years.

After the pictures were taken, Ford invited the cosmonauts, the astronauts, and myself to fly with him in the presidential helicopter to Alexandria, just across the Potomac River from Washington, where he had been living as a congressman for the past quarter-century before moving to the White House.

The town community, firefighters, and police organized a so-called crabnic—a picnic of beer and crabs, a local delicacy. The inhabitants greeted the president and his Soviet guests with loud cheers. All this was televised nationwide.

While flying back to Washington, Ford inquired about my impression of his first days in the White House. I replied that the first thing I noticed was that the American public had clearly calmed down from the agitation and concentration on Watergate and was returning to its everyday life and its problems. I told Ford that, as a president, he had played an important role in this process and expressed my hope that he would soon start playing the same positive role in foreign policy, including Soviet-American relations. Ford observed that my assessment coincided with the objectives he had set for himself as he took office; he confided that as part of clearing the air one of his first acts as a president had been to order the Oval Office cleaned of all listening devices.

Now he said it was time for him to concentrate on foreign affairs. He was looking forward to his working meeting with Brezhnev as a starting point for businesslike cooperation. He emphasized the importance he attached to an agreement on limiting strategic arms, which was essential both for bilateral relations and for his presidential campaign.

## On to Vladivostok with Ford

Just as he had with Nixon, Henry Kissinger made a presummit visit to Moscow to prepare for the summit. He was there from October 23 to 27; the summit had been formally set for the following month in Vladivostok. In the middle of his talks with Brezhnev and Gromyko, Ford sent a message to Brezhnev saying, like Nixon before him, that Kissinger had his complete personal trust and was empowered to discuss all summit issues.

The issues of strategic arms limitation were central to the Moscow negotiations with Kissinger, which were based on the understanding reached during Nixon's last visit only a few months before. Both sides exchanged exact figures for their armaments, which permitted an in-depth discussion on an agreement lasting to 1985.

After Kissinger returned, he told the president that at first he had been afraid that no progress was likely on disarmament because of Brezhnev's tough stand. However, on the last day of the meting Brezhnev advanced a number of suggestions which, in Kissinger's view, deserved thorough study, for those could pave the way to an agreement even if further hard negotiations were needed.

Kissinger and I had detailed discussions on November 13 to 16 to prepare for the meeting. The latest American proposals to prepare the outlines for the SALT II negotiations showed some toughening; the Pentagon had managed to influence the new president, who was not quite familiar with the intricate history of past negotiations on the subject. Kissinger and I also continued discussing the text of the communiqué and of a separate declaration on strategic arms limitation, upon which Ford insisted. We managed to prepare the principal documents for the summit even though some points remained at issue.

Ford was to visit Japan on November 18 to 22 before going on to Vladivostok. The objective of the visit was to bring Japan closer to the United States and rebuild relations after the turn toward China in order to avoid what Kissinger saw as the principal danger, a revival of militant Japanese nationalism. He confided that the U.S. government's own secret analysis showed that Japan could become a leading military power within three to five years by building up a civilian production base that could be converted to military uses—especially in alliance with China—that could also be turned not only against the Soviet Union, but also against the United

States. In Moscow this was quickly recognized as a sign that Kissinger could not resist the temptation to play the China card on the eve of the summit and even strengthen it by invoking the specter of the Japanese; but in general Kissinger expressed his conviction that in the long run, the United States and Russia would cooperate against any combined Chinese-Japanese pressure.

The departure ceremony for the president took place on the White House lawn. Ford said good-bye to each of those present, and when he approached me, I noticed he was not wearing a hat; Americans rarely do, even in winter. I told him he had better take a fur hat to Siberia, where even the locals never go out hatless in a climate that is not to be trifled with. Somewhat flustered, Ford said he had no hat and had never worn one in his life. So I took off my fur hat, a classic Russian shapka made of beaver that I had bought in Moscow, and gave it to him as my "Siberian gift." The president tried it on, and it fit. Whenever he went outside in the Soviet Union, he wore that hat and was photographed in it.

The same day I flew to Moscow to catch the government plane taking Brezhnev and Gromyko to Vladivostok. For the first time in my life I perceived the immensity of my own country. While we were airborne, we learned that a snowstorm was raging in the Vladivostok region and landing there was out of question. We had to spend the night in Khabarovsk while a Soviet division in Vladivostok was urgently ordered to clear the local airfield of huge snowdrifts. We landed the next day without incident.

To accommodate the Soviet and the American delegations, a number of cottages had been set aside in a rural community some twenty kilometers from Vladivostok, where the local party leadership used to spend their days off. Brezhnev asked me to go ahead to Ford's cottage and ascertain if everything was "on a proper level." The president's American staff was already there examining the facilities when I arrived. A marine had already been posted to guard the president's bedroom. I decided I had better test his bedroom phone and did so by calling my wife in Washington. It was a very long distance call indeed—halfway round the globe. My wife was pleasantly surprised. Everything in the cottage seemed fine.

On the next day our group, headed by Brezhnev, took a suburban electric train to the military base where Air Force One was to land; normally it served as a base for our interceptor aircraft. Cars then took us to the airfield, where we saw a surreal sight: a vast, treeless field of snow with just a few scattered buildings (all military facilities and hangars were underground). Everything was deep in snow, with only one landing strip cleared during the night. As Ford was getting off the plane, he, too, looked overwhelmed by this white stillness, which brought to mind Jack London's Alaska.

After greetings were exchanged (there were no protocol formalities), everybody got into cars and went to the train waiting for us in a glen. As soon as the train started off, Brezhnev invited Ford to his coach "for a cup of tea" accompanied by some cognac. Both leaders recalled their achievements in sports. Speaking of the weather, Ford complained that in Washington even a light snowfall caused major tieups. The smiling Brezhnev promised him to send Russian snowplows there. Then they retired to their compartments for some rest.

At that moment Brezhnev suffered a seizure. Professor Evgeny Chazov and other doctors managed to control it, but insisted Brezhnev postpone his negotiations with Ford, which were to begin the next day. Brezhnev categorically refused and demanded that nothing be said to anyone, and indeed nothing ever was, in contrast with the way even the minor ailments of a U.S. president are closely monitored and broadly publicized. The negotiations were to get under way the next day as planned. I should add that Brezhnev had been under severe stress: he had flown more than seven thousand miles across Russia to conduct complicated negotiations with the president of the United States, whom he was to meet for the first time. The issues of strategic arms limitation were not entirely agreed on beforehand, which demanded concentration and difficult decisions during the talks. Although no one but his attending physicians knew it, by that time the first signs of Brezhnev's ateriosclerosis of the brain also made themselves felt. When Brezhnev left Vladivostok by train en route to Mongolia, he suffered another seizure, lost consciousness, regained it, and continued his trip. Shortly thereafter he made a state visit to France, but the long countdown to his fatal illness had begun.

History rarely has definable turning points but this was one of them. If there was any point at which it could be said that detente had reached its height and then begun its decline, it probably would have been at the very moment of Brezhnev's seizure, for from that moment the summit process was inevitably slowed.

But there were also important political reasons on both sides: an unelected American president operating under political constraints, the problem of Jewish emigration, our confrontations with America in the Third World, and the essentially different views and expectations that Moscow and Washington entertained about detente. All of this accumulated and laid Ford open to political attack. The policy of detente steadily eroded into the following administration of Jimmy Carter, when we will revisit all these factors in detail. But Vladivostok was its high point, and for that Ford deserves credit as well as Brezhnev.

The working meetings at Vladivostok were held in the community's small local clubhouse on November 23–24, 1974. Ford had with him

Kissinger; the U.S. ambassador to the Soviet Union, Walter Stoessel; Presidential Aide Donald Rumsfeld; General Brent Scowcroft; and some other advisers. Brezhnev had on his side Gromyko; Georgi Kornienko, the head of the American department of the Foreign Ministry; myself; and some of his aides.

The meetings lasted for two days and were intense and heated but genuinely businesslike, and without any of the usual protocol formalities. The whole of the first day was devoted to working out a long-term agreement limiting strategic arms. The discussion was far from easy. Not only were the issues extremely complex, but the American position was greatly influenced by domestic considerations. Several times the American delegation left the negotiation table to refine its position. Kissinger played the leading role in the deliberations because Ford did not yet know all the details. The president, on the other hand, was better able to anticipate the likely problems of defending before Congress the agreements he made. The president preferred not to get involved in long arguments with Brezhnev or Gromyko; he had Kissinger for that. And Ford was not a man with a high sense of humor. He was a solid and decent American who meant business when he understood it. Otherwise he listened to the disputes and quietly smoked his pipe, relying on his common sense to decide.

The Soviet delegation had its problems, too. The American position had toughened somewhat under pressure from the Pentagon during the month since Kissinger's visit to Moscow, and we had to seek new compromises at the negotiating table. Brezhnev made repeated telephone calls to Moscow to coordinate his position with the other leaders. At one point he had a serious dispute with Grechko, the defense minister, who opposed any further concessions and insisted on counting the nuclear arsenals of Britain and France in any SALT agreement, while Brezhnev became convinced during the negotiations that Ford would never concede to this. Military man that he was, Grechko made other excessive demands; they were rejected by Brezhnev with Gromyko's support. Both believed that the excessive claims of the military, if pressed, could ruin the agreement and the summit as a whole. Grechko yielded only after Brezhnev angrily employed his authority as a general secretary, and did so in strong words.

On the first day the meeting dragged on until midnight. Both sides refused the prearranged dinner and called for sandwiches. There were only two short breaks during the day, used by the Americans to discuss matters between themselves. Despite the cold winter, they would go outside for fear of being overheard by listening devices. During one of these breaks, Brezhnev gave Ford his portrait in wood by a local amateur artist who had never seen the president and used a poor newspaper photo as a model. The portrait hardly resembled Ford—one of the Americans said it looked more like Frank Sinatra—but the artist had put his heart and soul into it, and the president showed his appreciation.

To understand the SALT debate without burdening it with technical detail, it is necessary to understand the fundamental task faced by both governments during the protracted negotiations. They had to agree on limiting their strategic armaments that were from the beginning completely different in both structure and deployment. Since the Eisenhower and the Kennedy administrations, the Americans developed their strategic arsenal on the basis of a so-called strategic triad of nuclear armaments delivered via land, sea, and air. As a continental country without bases abroad, the Soviet Union initially concentrated on developing large land-based missiles. In 1974 the discussion centered on finding a tricky balance between the larger number of Soviet land-based missiles, which were also heavier in terms of throwweight, and the greater quantity of superior American MIRVed missiles, of which the Soviet Union had very few at the time.

Kissinger had worked out a preliminary compromise in Moscow that would have permitted each side to have up to 2,400 units of strategic arms carriers—strategic bombers and ballistic missiles launched from land and undersea, or ICBMs and SLBMs for short. Each side would be entitled to the same number of missiles capable of carrying MIRVed warheads. The number would not exceed 1,300 on each side as of the end of 1985. There remained considerable dispute—which was not solved at Vladivostok—over how to count submarine missiles and launcher aircraft (especially our new TU-22M bomber known in the West as the Backfire), as well as the fighter-bombers assigned to forward positions in Europe and therefore capable of delivering atomic weapons to Soviet soil.

At Vladivostok, Brezhnev proposed the idea of a "framework agreement" for ten years, specifying equal upper levels which neither country could exceed. But each side would have a certain degree of freedom in defining the land, sea, and air structure of its strategic armaments within these numerical limits. Such an agreement would not decrease the level of already existing armaments, but at least it would provide a ceiling. To reach it, each side would be able to choose the mix of missiles that suited its own strategy. On receiving the proposal, the American delegation asked for a recess. The substance and intensity of the talks were increasing.

In the end, a compromise was worked out on the most complex points. It was agreed to fix a ceiling for strategic armaments until 1995: each would be permitted 2,400 strategic arms carriers based on land, sea, or air. Each side could MIRV a maximum of 1,320 of its missiles. This eliminated what in our view had been the principal deficiency of the SALT I agreement we had concluded with Nixon after four years of negotiations—an inequality in the total numbers of missile carriers. There was also compromise on some other elements, for example, strategic aircraft. This explicitly acknowledged a shift to the principle of numerical equality and equal security, which was of profound diplomatic and military importance to the Soviet Union. At the same time this principle carried potential domestic political trouble for the Ford administration, as some members of the American delegation privately warned us. The American public was not used to the notion of strategic military equality with the Soviet Union.

The discussion of other international issues began at 10 A.M. on the second day of the meeting, which was less tense than the first. There was a useful exchange on the Conference on Security and Cooperation in Europe. The Americans were palpably reluctant to assume definite obligations that could put them at loggerheads with their European allies. The talks also covered the Middle East but produced nothing new. The Americans harped on the complexity of their relations with Israel and their domestic problems.

Only reluctantly did they agree to incorporate into the communiqué some useful phrases on the Middle East about a resumption of the Geneva conference. The communiqué reemphasized the "practical value of Soviet-American summit meetings." The end of the summit was toasted with a local ginseng vodka with Amur River caviar.

After the meeting was over, Brezhnev drove Ford and Kissinger through Vladivostok to the airport and showed them the sights. The American guests were surprised at the absence of Chinese houses with their distinctive roofs; the style of the domestic architecture was European. The Americans seemed to be under the influence of an active propaganda campaign waged by the Chinese, who then laid claims to extensive parts of the Soviet Far East. The Americans expected to see some characteristic Chinese architecture in the city as a sign of its Chinese past, but nothing could be further from the truth, since the city had been founded by Russians and settled by us for more than a century. Ford admitted that he had believed Vladivostok to be more Asian than Russian, and Kissinger joked that he would be the last man to tell the Chinese about what he had actually seen in the city when he met them next lest he annoy them.

On parting at the airport, Ford gave Brezhnev a wolf skin coat he had received during a stopover in Alaska. He simply took it off before boarding his plane and handed it to Brezhnev, who promptly put it on, to the delight of press photographers. It seemed they parted friends.

Both sides were satisfied with the results of the meeting, even though it was short. On arrival at Andrews Air Force Base near Washington Ford described his meeting with Brezhnev as "very, very good," and he later would write in his memoirs that the results surpassed all his expectations. Brezhnev, in his report to the Politburo, also assessed the meeting as a success, especially in the terms of understanding reached on strategic arms limitation. He said he believed that his personal contact with President Ford was good and "one could do business with him in the future."

On December 10, on instruction by our governments, Kissinger and I exchanged confidential memoranda with details of the limitations on strategic arms agreed at Vladivostok. The agreement would be in force from October, 1977, to December, 1985.* Simultaneously Kissinger formally confirmed the president's confidential pledge in Vladivostok that the United States would discontinue using the Rota naval base on the Atlantic coast of Spain as a base for its nuclear submarines after 1983. The existence of this agreement was long suspected in Madrid, but it was never published.

The Vladivostok agreement became a significant starting point for all subsequent nuclear disarmament talks. Ford and Brezhnev succeeded in reaching agreement on the framework for limitation of strategic offensive missiles, which was a notable achievement considering the turmoil that had been created by Nixon's resignation only four months earlier. Regardless of its technical merits or deficiencies, the Vladivostok summit provided a sense of continuity to the SALT process.

But President Ford soon was caught between strong criticism from both left and right. Opponents of detente accused him of yielding to Soviet pressure and especially attacked the principle of equality in strategic arms and the limits on them. Among those who most actively opposed the results of the summit were Republican right-wingers headed by Ronald Reagan, and Democratic Senator Jackson with his followers. Unfortunately Ford was per-

---

* The key provision read:

The new agreement, based on the principle of equality and equal security of the parties, will incorporate, in particular, the following limitations which will remain in force for the duration of the agreement:

a) For the duration of the new agreement each party will be entitled to the total amount of strategic arms carriers not exceeding 2,400 units. This number includes land-based intercontinental ballistic missiles launchers (ICBM launchers), submarine-launched ballistic missile launchers (SLBM launchers) and heavy bombers if those are armed with bombs or air-to-surface ballistic missiles (ASBM) with a range not exceeding 600 km. If a bomber carries ASBMs with a range exceeding 600 km, each of these missiles shall be counted as one unit and shall be included in the total amount of strategic arms carriers (2,400).

b) Within this limit, each party will be free to determine the composition of the total amount provided for this party's abiding by the agreed ban on building new underground silos.

c) Each party will be limited to not more than 1320 IBMs and SLBMs armed with MIRVs within this total amount each party is free to determine types and numbers of its MIRV'd missiles.

suaded that as the election year got under way, the SALT process should be shelved. But I believe it was not the Vladivostok meeting that brought down Ford's popularity ratings; it was his pardon of Richard Nixon on September 8, which started speculation that he had made a deal with Nixon to promise a pardon in exchange for the presidency. The media then lifted their truce with the new president. All his unfortunate or erroneous remarks were widely publicized, and photographers competed to film him in the most awkward situations and poses, in stumbling and accidental falls even though he was a good athlete. Some opposition newspapers began unfairly calling him an accidental president. All this impaired the president's self-esteem and confidence in his own policy, including detente.

But the boisterous debate about the SALT talks did not help, either. For decades Americans had been told they had nuclear superiority over us, so word that their president had agreed to nuclear parity raised puzzling questions and even worry. Most people could not figure out the new abbreviations used in complex technical discussions, which only added to the confusion. The French word "detente" provoked still more argument. It stands for two quite different things: one is "relaxation of tension," the other is "trigger." In Russian we never used this elegant but confusing foreign word. Some Americans even tended to think of detente as *entente,* which was far from the real situation in Soviet-American relations. All this confusion (real or deliberate) came from differences and contradictions between the Soviet and American concepts of detente. The euphoria surrounding the idea of detente in Nixon's years had faded away.

## Jewish Emigration and Detente

Probably no other single question did more to sour the atmosphere of detente than the question of Jewish emigration from the Soviet Union. Even the Kremlin began to understand it and tried—though inconsistently and hesitantly—to correct the situation right after Ford took office. At our August 14 meeting in the Oval Office, I raised the issue of the legislation to prevent trade discrimination against the Soviet Union. I told the president in confidence that the Soviet government was prepared to give him an unwritten guarantee that it would allow 50,000 Jews to leave the Soviet Union each year—the actual rate of Jewish emigration reached 35,000 in 1973—but Moscow would not sign any official promise lest it be used by Sen. Jackson for his own political ends. Ford promised to examine the offer although he was unable to guarantee it would be acceptable to the Jewish lobby.

The very next day he met with Senators Jackson, Javits, and Ribicoff to relay this to them, also in confidence. Ford declared the meeting a success despite Jackson's customary stubbornness. His interlocutors expressed their readiness to modify the Jackson amendment if they received a letter from the administration clarifying matters. The difference between Jackson and his two Senate colleagues was that they were prepared to accept an oral assurance and Jackson wanted it in writing.

Kissinger informed me he was preparing a letter to the senators. I told him that the correspondence between the White House and the members of Congress was of course the internal business of his government. But under instruction, I had to warn him again that we could not accept any reference in this letter to any Soviet official guarantees on the number of emigrants, although in fact we would not prevent an increase to the level of 50,000 and were prepared to give our word to President Ford. But Kissinger went ahead and wrote a letter which Senator Jackson released with great fanfare to the press. He declared that the letter implied that the Soviet Union had pledged to permit not just 50,000 but even 60,000 emigrants a year (a figure of his own upon which he insisted). The Kremlin became angry: with great difficulties it had made secret concessions that then were widely publicized.

The next day I told Kissinger he had violated his own confidential understanding with Gromyko that no exact emigration figures would be cited in official correspondence—not to mention the increase in the number. I stressed that in claiming that the Soviet Union had agreed to a yearly quota of 60,000 emigrants Jackson had violated the confidential understanding between us. Now we had the right to explain our position in public. Kissinger was definitely feeling ill at ease, for the understanding had certainly taken place.

A day later he informed me that he had talked with the president, and Ford was indignant at Jackson's conduct and believed that the Senator had "behaved like a swine." He wanted that passed to Brezhnev and Gromyko. When Ford had talked to Jackson in person on October 18 they had agreed that the Senator could only tell the media of a basic agreement between Congress and the White House on lifting trade discrimination against the Soviet Union by granting it most favored nation status. The senator was to say that the agreement had been reached on the basis of a compromise on the Soviet approach to emigration—and that was all. Jackson had not been granted permission to publish the correspondence.

But as soon as the senator had left the president's office, he held a press conference right in the White House and passed the texts of the letters themselves to the press. The White House distributed its own explanatory statement saying that the Soviet side had never mentioned any figure and Jackson's declaration only represented his own opinion. Kissinger left shortly thereafter for his summit preparatory meetings, whereupon Gromyko handed him a formal letter stressing that his interpretation as relayed to Jackson was "categorically rejected." This killed our compromise with the administration. But Kissinger told no one outside his closest aides about the letter, hoping to finesse the matter at the summit.

All this merely consolidated my personal conviction that Senator Jackson was not seeking a compromise but preferred to keep the problem unresolved for publicity and his own political future. The administration, although seeking a compromise, still had to take into account pro-Jewish opposition in Congress, so it resorted to all kinds of maneuvers. We were also more or less prepared for a practical compromise but without public acknowledgment which would create the impression that we had yielded under pressure to Senator Jackson and his followers. Emigration continued to aggravate our relations.

On December 18, after the summit, Kissinger and I were having breakfast at the State Department when an aide rushed in and gave him a copy of a censorious Tass statement that had just come over the wires. The article published Gromyko's letter concerning a "Kissinger-Jackson accord." Alluding to the Jackson-Vanik amendment to the trade bill, which would link our emigration policy to trade privileges in the United States, the statement said: "The Soviet ruling circles categorically reject as inadmissible all attempts, whomever those might come from, at interfering in matters which are the exclusive responsibility of the Soviet state."

At first, Kissinger was indignant that Moscow had not notified him it was planning to publish Gromyko's letter and told me that would only complicate the problem of passing the trade bill. I felt I had to interrupt him. I said the trade bill before Congress appeared to be even more discriminatory toward the Soviet Union than the law that was on the books in 1972 when the two governments started their policy of detente. The new law would discriminate against us not only in trade, but in export credits (the Senate passed the Stevenson amendment doing so on September 19). At no point, I continued, had the president or the secretary of state protested against this openly discriminatory legislation, which Nixon had promised to veto.

Kissinger cooled down and dialed Scowcroft, who confirmed everything I had just said. The secretary swore at his being left out of the loop and slammed down the receiver. Then he called the president and recounted our conversation. As far as I could judge by what Kissinger was saying, Ford admitted that the situation in the Congress had indeed grown unfavorable for Soviet-American trade relations and it was high time for the administration to step in. Only two days remained before Congress would recess for the Christmas holiday. Ford told Kissinger to call a meeting in the White House that same day to discuss what could be done. The president said Congress should not be allowed to continue "tripping up the administration" in the field of Soviet-American relations, and something had to be done when the new Congress convened in the new year.

But it was clear that the administration was unable to do anything in the closing days of the outgoing Congress, which on December 20 passed the trade reform bill with the amendments holding Soviet-American commerce and credits hostage to our emigration policy. The Soviet Union was to be granted most favored nation status only on condition that it changed its emigration policy. That policy would come up for review in eighteen months (or just when Senator Jackson hoped to be running for president). Credits by the U.S. Export-Import Bank and Commodity Credit Corporation were limited to $300 million for four years, and the Soviet Union was refused credits for mineral extraction—which principally affected oil and natural gas development. The law effectively blocked the development of trade and economic relations between our countries for a long time.

The congressional vote was an unpleasant surprise for the leaders of the Soviet Union. They had always underestimated the influence of American public opinion on U.S. foreign policy because they were free from such pressure at home. They could not imagine an American president who was not exactly a supreme ruler. They were shocked, and their reaction was swift and angry. On December 25 Brezhnev sent Ford an indignant letter declaring the trade and credit legislation "fundamentally unacceptable." He added: "It goes without saying that this relieves the Soviet side of its commitments assumed within a package of agreements on trade and credit questions (including an agreement on the repayment of the Lend-Lease debt). Grave damage has thus been inflicted to our trade and economic relations, which by no means encourages Soviet-American relations in other spheres."

Ford signed the bill on January 3, 1975, having little choice to do otherwise because he needed its general authority to conduct trade negotiations with other countries. Moscow made good on its threats to suspend Lend-Lease repayments, a deal that had been reached so amicably between Nixon and Kosygin in that bargaining session three years before. Both sides tried to put the best face on things by declaring publicly that detente would not be affected, but it was.

A footnote to all this was written the following summer when Senator Jackson invited me to breakfast at his home. It was a hot July day. Jackson lived in a small two-story house with deliberately modest furnishings, although it was situated in a prestigious neighborhood. The senator proudly told me that his children were attending an integrated public school, while his neighbors' children had been sent to expensive and almost entirely white private schools. He summoned his young children to say hello to the Soviet ambassador. Then we had breakfast for two.

Jackson remarked in jest that the Soviet people probably were frightened by the mention of his name, as if he were some sort of devil with horns. I replied in the same light manner, but I had to tell him that the Soviet people were not easily scared, for they had passed through a very hard school of life, and feared neither devils nor witches wherever they might be found. Our people read his statements on Soviet-American relations and their impression was, frankly speaking, most disapproving.

The senator said he appreciated my frankness, and that was precisely the reason he wanted to talk with me. Then, with some ardor, he started to develop his views. What underlay all his statements was the idea that his approach toward the Soviet Union was not all that different from Presidents Nixon and Ford. But both presidents had to play at politics, while he was more candid in saying things with which both administrations would essentially agree, although their viewpoint would come out in actions rather than words.

Jackson claimed he did not basically oppose a strategic arms agreement with the Soviet Union. His criticisms were based on his contention that the Nixon administration "was not honest with Congress" about the 1972 SALT I agreement and had concealed secret arrangements it had made with the Soviet Union. When I asked him to tell me what those secret arrangements supposedly were, he avoided a direct answer. He found the same untruthfulness in Kissinger's initial concealment of the October 26 letter from Gromyko killing the emigration compromise. Leaders of Congress, including himself, had developed a false impression that Moscow would eventually concede on Soviet emigration if they kept pressing. Eventually, their mistake became obvious, but by then the matter had become so clouded by emotion that it was too late to compromise. The resulting impasse did not benefit anybody. As for Kissinger, Jackson felt that although guided by the best of intentions, he had outmaneuvered himself.

Jackson complained that the word "detente," used by Moscow to describe its policy toward the United States, was unknown to many Americans, so it was interpreted quite differently, at times even in a negative sense. I told him that we never used this word which was a French translation—launched by someone in the United States—of our word *razryadka*, meaning "relaxation of tension." The senator remarked that if it had been formulated that clearly at the very beginning, there would have been hardly a politician in the

United States who would have dared to oppose it. I responded by saying that now he knew the precise meaning of what was said in Moscow, he could fearlessly support detente. He smiled but said nothing.

As we parted, he asked me to tell Brezhnev that he was not and never would be guided by hostility toward the Soviet Union. He said he supported the improvement of Soviet-American relations, yet as a member of the opposition, he sometimes had to criticize the administration as a matter of tactics rather than strategy.

Although I could have been wrong, Jackson left me with the impression that he was beginning to see the futility of campaigning for the presidency with only an anti-Soviet plank for his foreign policy platform.

## Ford versus Nixon

Nixon's forced departure inflicted severe damage on the Republican Party. Senator Hugh Scott, the Republican Senate leader, privately admitted to me that the party found itself in a difficult situation. Unless measures were taken to improve domestic conditions, especially the economy, the Republicans would suffer serious losses during the next elections, including the struggle for the White House.

As his party's Senate leader, Scott met with Ford practically every day. Unfortunately, he went on, in spite of his extensive presidential powers, Ford had not yet displayed sufficient will, courage, and other qualities of a strong national leader for his party and his nation. The Republican leadership and Ford himself, Scott said, had counted on Vice President Rockefeller to bring in "the brightest Wall Street minds" to serve the administration, the more so as Ford's own attempts to get hold of these people had failed.

Somehow, Ford had not gotten rid of his congressman's mentality; that is, he had not perceived his extensive opportunities and privileges as a president. To some extent, he even avoided using the power of the presidency in full measure, fearing that his inexperience or some inappropriate application of his powers might damage his political future. All this made Ford excessively cautious in taking important decisions, especially the unpopular ones, which were unavoidable in dealing with the economy. The conflicting opinions of his old friends from Congress would only disorient Ford and delay his decisions.

Late in the year, during a private dinner with Kissinger, we made a comparative analysis of the performance of the two presidents, one of whom had passed the presidential baton to the other under unprecedented circumstances.

Kissinger said that, as odd as this might seem, he found it easier to work with Ford during the past few months than with Nixon, with whom he had worked for more than six years. Nixon was much more proficient in foreign policy, and Nixon would offer his own ideas in this area, which Ford could not. But Nixon's ideas were not easy to decline if they appeared unacceptable, for he would stubbornly defend them anyway. At times, it would take two to three weeks of delicate maneuvering to bring him to give up some idea.

Unlike Ford, Nixon would not limit himself to considering just one option on an issue, invariably demanding additional data. For example, how might a decision influence other aspects of foreign policy—relations with the Soviet Union, China, India, and so on. In other words, an issue had to be approached from all possible angles, which consumed a lot of time and energy. Ford did not raise side issues or ask questions about complicated interrelationships. He preferred the issue to be clearly formulated and submitted to him with definite recommendations for action. But Ford looked at issues through the prism of domestic policy: How would his decision be received in Congress, in the party, in the nation? Only then would he consider its international implications.

Kissinger said he was trying to induce the president to approach his decisions from both domestic and international viewpoints; that is, Kissinger tried to avoid having domestic considerations determine his actions on each and every foreign policy issue. But the president was much more expert than Kissinger on domestic questions, and in such cases he had the last word, especially in view of impending presidential elections.

In one sense, Ford's inner convictions made him more conservative than Nixon. Nixon was not essentially a die-hard, although he was known to the public as a conservative anti-communist, Kissinger said. Rather, he had posed as such in order to attain his goals. But when he deemed it necessary, he was ready to depart from his classic line, for example, in his policy toward the Soviet Union and China. But Ford had spent a quarter-century in the House of Representatives, which was much more reactionary and domestically oriented than the Senate. Regrettably, this disposition was supported by his old friends from Congress, who still saw him regularly. Among these was Melvin Laird, who had served Nixon as defense secretary and retained his close ties with military circles.

President Ford was not predisposed against the Soviet Union, but he was apprehensive about "Soviet intentions," Kissinger said. He did not purposely promote the arms race, but he was devoted to the patriotic idea of a "strong America" and all his convictions sprang from his "internally rather than externally oriented political upbringing." Lately, however, he had become attracted to foreign affairs and started to display greater interest in its details, although his overall competence was still much lower than Nixon's.

The secretary of state also noted a significant difference in the character of the two presidents. For all his reputation of a man of decision in a crisis, Nixon was essentially rather irresolute and would make up his mind only after agonizing hesitations and sleepless nights. Ford was not like this. He preferred simplified "clear combinations," tended to take quick decisions and was difficult to dissuade from them afterward. At times, he was even more impulsive than Nixon, although in everyday dealings with people Ford was simpler, more compassionate, and approachable, and was always prepared to listen to his assistants. In general, personal relations played a much greater role for Ford than for Nixon. In this sense, the fact that he had evidently established a good contact with the Soviet leaders in Vladivostok became especially significant.

I realized that however full of dramatic events the past half year had been for the United States, Soviet-American relations had almost miraculously not undergone any serious change. Throughout this unprecedented period of transition, we had somehow managed to navigate a comparatively steady course. Rougher weather was soon to come.

## II. The Erosion of Detente

*Thunder on the Right*

Gerald Ford's first full year in office was a troubled one. The recession was part of the most severe economic crisis of the postwar world, a direct result of the quadrupling of oil prices after the Middle East War of 1973. In the United States it was exacerbated by the weakening of political institutions, by the Watergate scandal, and the erosion of public trust in government. Not least was the impact of the final defeat of American arms in Indochina, which delivered a severe blow to the militaristic cult of America as a country that "had never lost a war," even though the withdrawal from Vietnam to some extent untied its hands to act in other areas.

But Ford failed to boost his political prestige in the country significantly, although he managed to free himself and his administration from Nixon's shadow. Electoral politics caught him in a cross fire between Democratic opposition and the right wing of his own Republican Party and its principal standard-bearer, Ronald Reagan, who publicly claimed that the United States was getting a raw deal out of detente while the Soviet Union reaped all the dividends.

Soviet-American relations were by this time based on a broad foundation of compromise during three years of summit meetings. Previously concluded bilateral treaties, agreements, and exchanges were still in force and functioning rather smoothly. Congress sent its first official delegation to the Soviet Union. The docking of a Soviet Soyuz and American Apollo spacecraft, broadcast live on television by agreement between our two governments, clearly demonstrated the potential for Soviet-American cooperation in science and technology—and much more.

Nothing like the live Soyuz launching had ever been shown before by our television to the Soviet public—let alone the rest of the world. I must admit that I was in a state of nervous excitement as the broadcast was beamed into the State Department conference hall on July 17 before a large American audience. There was the president, the secretary of state, other cabinet members, members of Congress, media, and all the rest. "What if something goes wrong?" I thought. But nothing went wrong, and everybody in the hall relaxed.

The Ford administration was basically following the course of detente it had inherited, although Ford supplemented it with his own thesis of a "strong America" and with the Kissinger doctrine of maintaining a balance of forces as a keystone of American international strategy, especially within the triangle of Washington-Moscow-Beijing. But the pressure on Ford's right, to say nothing of the ideological habits developed during a generation of the Cold War, proved too overwhelming against what was essentially a weak administration that had to struggle to maintain its legitimacy until it could be elected by popular mandate. And that very electoral process opened the way to unite the disparate forces opposing detente: the Jewish vote, the trade union leadership, conservatives of every stripe, and the media connected with all of them.

The White House soon found itself restrained in any major new agreements with the Soviet Union that might cause controversy in the election campaign. The president, as yet unelected, suffered from a virtual inferiority complex. He had to reckon with Congress and pressure from the Pentagon and CIA, which did not favor compromises with the Soviet Union, especially on strategic weapons. He gradually swung to the right as the Republican convention drew closer and took up the Reagan line by introducing into the administration's lexicon the thesis of "the inadmissibility of one-sided detente." In a speech to Congress April 11 he vowed that he was not going to allow detente to turn into "a license for fishing in troubled waters. . . . Detente must be a two-way process."

## The Fall of Saigon

From the very start, the Ford administration was confronted by the abrupt deterioration of its position and that of its allies in Southeast Asia. Soon after Ford took office, he sent the South Vietnamese dictator Nguyen Van Thieu a confidential message promising him adequate American support. Until the very last moment the Republican administration tried to maintain the pro-American regimes in Saigon and Phnom Penh. But this ended in fiasco. America's protégés in Cambodia capitulated on April 17, and on April 30 Saigon surrendered.

In the critical days of Saigon's downfall, which was turning into a flight by the Americans, Ford turned to Moscow for help. On April 19 Kissinger passed me a "highly urgent message" to Brezhnev appealing to the Soviet government to help obtain a temporary cease-fire to save lives through "an uninterrupted evacuation" of the remaining Americans and their remaining loyal South Vietnamese protégés. He confirmed that all the Americans were at last getting out, explained that this was essentially a request for Brezhnev's good offices in "finally ending the whole Vietnam tragedy," and that the president was not asking anyone else's help, including that of the Chinese.

On April 24 Brezhnev replied that the Vietnamese had informed him they would not impede the speedy evacuation of American citizens from Saigon and had no intention of damaging the prestige of the United States. They would proceed from the Paris agreement. Ford received this reply with relief.

Two days passed without event, and on April 26 I received another urgent message from Ford for Moscow: the North Vietnamese had resumed shelling Saigon Airport and the buildings around the American Embassy in Saigon. Contrary to Hanoi's assurances, Kissinger said excitedly, its actions constituted a direct, premeditated blow to the prestige of the administration and to the president himself, for they were aimed at demonstrating that the Americans were leaving under direct North Vietnamese pressure. I drew Kissinger's attention to the criticism in the Congress and in the media of the too prolonged withdrawal of the Americans from Saigon. The North Vietnamese advanced to the city, but they did not prevent the final evacuation from the American Embassy by helicopters.

Later there was a final exchange of messages through Moscow between Washington and Hanoi. On May 28 I gave Brent Scowcroft an oral confidential message from Hanoi saying that "the leadership of Vietnam favors the establishment of good relations with the United States." On Moscow's recommendation, the message from Hanoi said: "There is no animosity toward the United States in Vietnam and they seek the same from the American side." A few weeks later, Scowcroft gave me the American reply saying Washington also favored good relations, that there was no hostility in principle toward Vietnam, and that the United States proposed to proceed on this basis in all relations between the two nations.

This exchange, which has never been published before, was the last official page of the Vietnam tragedy.

One can only guess how frustrated Kissinger must have felt at that moment. After all, it was he who had negotiated the Paris peace accords that were supposed to permit the United States to end the war in Vietnam without at least the appearance of defeat. When we met at a reception just after Ford had announced the final U.S. departure from Vietnam, he was in a dismal mood. He declared with obvious regret that "the North Vietnamese are very lucky indeed" that Congress had formally legislated against any American military interference in Indochina, and that there was currently widespread disagreement in the United States on many issues, which "prevents the country from displaying its will." Had it not been for Watergate and the consequent sharp decline in Ford's popularity, he said, North Vietnam would not have gotten away so easily with violating its agreement with the United States.

It was obvious that Kissinger still looked back on Nixon's time with nostalgia, especially the initial period when American foreign policy had been planned and implemented by the White House without any particular regard to public opinion about Vietnam.

## The Helsinki Conference and Its Aftermath

The final stage of the Conference on Security and Cooperation in Europe took place on July 30 and August 1, 1975, in Helsinki, Finland. It was the most representative meeting of the heads of European states since the Congress of Vienna in 1815, only this time the United States and Canada were also there. Thirty-five countries took part in the conference. The United States had initially been demonstratively indifferent in the belief that it had nothing to gain. But then an East-West agreement on the status of West Berlin was signed, and the Soviet Union expressed its readiness to start talks in Vienna about a mutual reduction of our European forces. With this favorable turn of events, preparations for the Helsinki conference had begun in 1973.

The fundamental documents signed in Helsinki contained the participants' commitments in three key areas, or "three baskets," as they were called in the Helsinki jargon: security, economic cooperation, and humanitarian cooperation. The third basket included the important issues of human rights, freedom of movement, and the exchange of ideas. From the very outset of the negotiations, the Soviet leadership was interested only in the first two baskets and laid principal stress on recognition of the postwar boundaries of Europe dividing it into East and West. At the same time the Soviet Union did all it could to diminish the significance of the third basket, for it still believed humanitarian issues to be domestic matters. The West, on the contrary, rightfully considered them to be important international issues on which Moscow had to assume certain obligations. Otherwise, the Western states would refuse to agree on the rest. This dispute continued until the very opening of the conference.

The Kremlin's attitude toward the third basket had been affected by the psychology of the negotiations. The proposed text was prepared during several months of heated debates among the delegations—word by word, phrase by phrase. The Soviet foreign ministry could not have asked the Politburo's approval for every one of them. Gromyko from time to time informed Brezhnev and others in the Politburo of the progress of the negotiations, but they paid little attention to the complex phraseology. To them, it all looked like the routine work of diplomacy.

But when the treaty was ready and the third basket emerged in its entirety before the members of Politburo, they were stunned. As opening day drew closer, the Politburo engaged in heated debates over the documents Brezhnev was to sign on behalf of the Soviet government—not much about the first or second baskets, but about the third. Many in the Politburo (Podgorny, Suslov, Kosygin, and Andropov) had grave doubts about assuming international commitments that could open the way to foreign interference in our political life. Many Soviet ambassadors expressed doubts because they correctly anticipated difficult international disputes later on. Moscow had to take a fundamental decision with serious domestic consequences because of the liberalization process implied by Helsinki.

Gromyko had to become the main defender of the agreement that his ministry had worked out, and eventually his compromise viewpoint prevailed. He argued that the main goal for the Soviet Union for many years had been the general recognition of the postwar boundaries and the existing political map of Europe, which would amount to a major political and propaganda victory for Moscow. Furthermore, the second basket, he argued, would open up prospects for economic cooperation with the West. As for putting the humanitarian commitments into force, Gromyko argued that would still be up to the Soviet government, and it alone would decide what did and did not constitute interference in our domestic affairs. "We are masters in our own house," Gromyko said. The majority of the Politburo bought this argument. Thus, from the very start, the Politburo's acceptance of the Helsinki humanitarian principles implied some noncompliance.

Brezhnev played the decisive role in supporting Gromyko. His principal personal motive was his ambitious desire to participate in signing important international acts before such a broad, representative forum as the Helsinki Conference. He could easily assess the potential publicity he would gain—above all, in his own country—when the Soviet public learned of the final settlement of the postwar boundaries for which they had sacrificed so much. As to the humanitarian issues, these could be mentioned at home just vaguely, without much publicity. He thought this would not bring much trouble inside our country. But he was wrong. The condition of Soviet dissidents certainly did not change overnight, but they were definitely encouraged by this historic document. Its very publication in *Pravda* gave it the weight of an official document. It gradually became a manifesto of the dissident and liberal movement, a development totally beyond the imagination of the Soviet leadership.

President Ford's situation was different. Not a single one of his visits abroad as a president, he would admit later in his memoirs, had created such broad misunderstanding in the United States as his trip to Helsinki. In signing the Helsinki documents he counted on support in his country, mainly because the Soviet government actually was forced at last to assume important obligations for human rights. In addition, in exchange for the recognition of the frontiers established after the war, the Soviet Union recognized the lawfulness of changing national boundaries in Europe "by peaceful means," which preserved the possibility of reunifying Germany. The Ford administration never made all this clear to the American people, and his opponents exploited the resulting ambiguity in the public mind.

The Helsinki Final Act was signed on August 1, 1975, and its ultimate reality was that it played a significant role in bringing about the long and difficult process of liberalization inside the Soviet Union and the nations of Eastern Europe. This in the end caused the fundamental changes in all these countries that helped end the Cold War.

During the conference Brezhnev and Ford met twice, primarily to discuss SALT, an agreement on which the Soviet side regarded as essential before fixing the date for a summit and Brezhnev's visit to the United States. As they were about to leave Helsinki, Brezhnev took Ford aside on the spur of the moment and expressed the hope that Ford would run for president and win.

That was why two attempts on the president's life in September in California caused concern in Moscow. Not only did Brezhnev send an urgent personal message expressing his satisfaction at their failure, but the Soviet leader's security system was tightened and Brezhnev's limousine was reinforced to withstand not only gunfire but antitank missiles.

## The Difficult Road to the Summit

Kissinger and the president had foreseen that the Final Act would cause trouble in conservative circles but after weighing all the pros and cons, they decided that the advantage to domestic policy and Ford's election campaign lay in going ahead. So the White House and Kissinger were taken unawares when conservatives and liberals, supported by the media, fell upon the Helsinki Act and upon Ford personally for signing it. Right-wing groups in the United States, especially the Eastern European emigré organizations, criticized Ford mercilessly. Ronald Reagan and Senator Jackson issued harsh statements. Congress also expressed its dissatisfaction. In the press some saw Kissinger's hand in the Helsinki conference, although he was not all that enthusiastic about it. Essentially, the criticism came down to the allegation that through Ford the United States was formally agreeing to a division of Europe yielding the East to the Soviet Union, the shorthand for which was "the Yalta partition" of Europe supposedly agreed in the closing stages of World War II among Stalin, Roosevelt, and Churchill.

The administration was accused of excessive tolerance toward Moscow—and international communism, for that matter. Detente, they charged, had benefited the Soviet Union and not the United States because it had settled Europe's postwar borders and confirmed Soviet dominance over Eastern Europe. Conservatives also found nothing good in the SALT talks, so they accused the administration of being "too submissive to the Russians" there. Liberals blamed the administration for being too weak in defending the humanitarian issues, especially Jewish emigration and the plight of Soviet dissidents. And both groups raised a great outcry over Ford's refusal to receive the author Aleksandr Solzhenitsyn after he was expelled from the Soviet Union and emigrated to the United States. Even grain sales to the Soviet Union became the object of an anti-Soviet campaign on the ground that they would raise prices for American consumers by limiting domestic supplies, even as they were profitable for American farmers.

This outcry so concerned the White House that the president held a special meeting about it. Kissinger said the majority attributed it to electoral politics but the president was still convinced that detente was supported by the general public and would be worth the struggle sure to take place in the election campaign. I thought Kissinger gave a good assessment of a complex domestic situation, but for us the principal question was whether the Ford administration would really be able to resist the temptation of a turn to the right in Soviet-American relations as the pressure mounted—and not only from the conservatives—when the campaign got tougher.

When I reported this to Moscow, I urged them to decide on the date for a new summit meeting, because our failure to do so was beginning to irritate the White House and the president. Furthermore, it was time for us to consider how we wanted to steer our relations with Washington during the always difficult period of a presidential campaign.

My report was discussed at the Politburo and prompted a more definite answer about the date of the summit. They took into account the fact that a new party congress in the Soviet Union was scheduled for the next February, in 1976, and it was important for the Politburo and Brezhnev personally to have achieved significant progress by then in relations with the United States. A meeting with Ford, the Politburo hoped, would produce a SALT agreement. So on August 13 I conveyed Brezhnev's message suggesting a visit late in November or during the first half of December. Ford immediately suggested November 15 or December 16.

But the road to the summit presented serious difficulties. The Middle East remained an apple of discord between Moscow and Washington; Brezhnev and Gromyko were furious that the United States had ignored the Soviet Union in mediating an agreement between Israel and Egypt on partial withdrawal of Israeli troops from Sinai. Negotiations on SALT were running into additional trouble over the definition of a "heavy ICBM" such as our SS-18.

Military technology was outpacing diplomacy, and new, complex problems kept emerging in the negotiations. In the United States, cruise missiles were being developed fast. Under certain conditions, these missiles could represent a new kind of offensive strategic weapon, carrying nuclear weapons by swooping in low under radar and cruising to their target with extraordinary accuracy. Right-wingers and military men were hoping that the massive deployment of these cruise missiles would regain superiority for the United States in strategic arms. Consequently, the Soviet side began demanding that their production be limited and they be taken into account in the numbers agreed at Vladivostok.

In the Soviet Union, a new bomber was being built (nicknamed by NATO as "Backfire"). The Soviet side claimed it was a middle-range aircraft because it could not reach American territory. The Americans argued that when refueled in the air it became a long-range bomber capable of striking the United States and therefore should be included in the Vladivostok limits. Naturally, this long-range potential was deliberately played up by American opponents of disarmament, as Kissinger admitted to me much later. The fact remained that the Soviet Union did not have any aerial tankers, and building them would be a costly affair.

Since a SALT treaty was meant to crown the summit, the latter was not really possible without the former. Although Ford believed that the very fact of holding a summit would help his electoral prospects, for Brezhnev it would not do just to have a meeting. His previous two summits had been productive. He needed a serious agreement with the United States to present to our next year's party congress, and a SALT agreement was the obvious one—but the Americans were throwing up an additional obstacle.

By the start of October Kissinger was applying additional pressure by telling me that the administration had come to the conclusion that for some "unaccountable reason" Brezhnev seemed inclined toward postponing his visit until after the Communist Party Congress, or maybe even until after the U.S. elections in November of the following year. I replied that our position had always been clear: a new SALT agreement had to be signed during Brezhnev's visit and that understanding dated back to the Vladivostok meeting almost a year ago.

On October 7 at a White House reception for the members of U.S.-Soviet Trade and Economic Council, the president took me aside and continued the conversation Kissinger had begun. He observed that Soviet-American relations had been subject to periodic swings and now were heading into a "time of troubles" before the elections. The mass media, dominated by the anti-Soviet lobby, were whipping up public interest in emigration and human rights in the Soviet Union. Ford remarked that even he himself as president sometimes received far less publicity than Andrei Sakharov and some of his dissident Soviet colleagues, and the dissident movement was being used by those in the United States who opposed better relations. They were highly influential and had both the money and the opportunity to orchestrate the mass media. He knew from his own experience as president and candidate that they could not be ignored, and that meant he had to maneuver carefully.

Ford said he hoped Moscow understood this. The SALT agreement had many enemies, the Pentagon included, and he said that was why it was so important that the Soviet reaction to the latest American proposals not be downright negative. "Let Brezhnev give me anything, at least something of a positive nature, to be able to continue the dialogue on a constructive, not totally pessimistic note," the president said.

But Moscow was in no mood to oblige. The Soviet leadership was under strong pressure from our own military, which sought restrictions on America's cruise missiles. At the same time it underestimated the importance of domestic factors for American presidents. Moscow believed that all requests of this kind from Washington had only one objective—to wring some further concession from the Soviet side. Nor did the leadership heed our reports about the serious differences of opinion among factions inside the cabinet, which the president could not disregard. The Kremlin was convinced that a president was the boss and had the power to decide unilaterally, especially given his desire and need to reach an agreement. So, instead of attempting some goodwill gesture toward the president, we fell into our habit of stubbornly prolonging the argument. Usually we would make some concession at the end, but often only at a time when the moment for doing so had passed, and the only thing we would get in exchange was the enmity that arose from a deepening of the rift between the leaders of our countries. The history of the Soviet diplomacy was marked by such wasted opportunities.

Then Ford suddenly announced a radical reorganization of his cabinet early in November. Schlesinger was dismissed as secretary of defense, as was William Colby as director of the CIA. George Bush was recalled from Beijing to replace Colby. Donald Rumsfeld, the White House chief of staff, was appointed defense secretary. Rockefeller was given to understand that he would be dropped from the ticket in the next elections because of opposition from the right. His protégé Kissinger lost one of his two posts, as assistant to the president for national security affairs, and was replaced with his deputy Brent Scowcroft.

From the point of view of Soviet-American relations and especially SALT, this shake-up did not look promising. Kissinger lost his daily access to the president and his chairmanship of a number of influential interdepartmental committees where policies are usually hammered out. This significantly limited his influence on the White House decision-making process in foreign policy, although he remained the leading figure. Electoral politics also touched him: the right accused him of being too accommodating to Moscow, and the liberals of excessive pragmatism that ignored human rights and the moral aspects of foreign policy. In Congress, the Democrats tried to weaken what it considered "the monopoly of the executive branch" in foreign policy by putting obstacles in the way of Kissinger's diplomacy. Inside the cabinet, the members of Ford's immediate circle ("the Grand Rapids' Mafia," as some papers called it) used every opportunity to trip him up. This could not but affect Kissinger. I noticed that he was growing nervous and that his actions were more hectic and controversial than before. He nevertheless remained the principal advocate of detente within the administration.

Scowcroft, while close to Kissinger, held more conservative views on military matters. Rumsfeld supported the Pentagon's policies and strongly opposed any agreements with the Soviet Union unless the United States could demonstrate it had come away with clear advantages. Moreover, he had convinced Ford that this was the right line for his election campaign.

When I next met Scowcroft in mid-November I congratulated him on his new post. During our previous meetings, he had usually been rather reserved, but this time I found him more open, perhaps as a result of his release from Kissinger's constant control. Scowcroft remarked that he was rather troubled by the weakening of contacts between our two governments and of the mutual understanding between our leaders as well. Scowcroft conceded that a number of circumstances had forced the full range of Soviet-American relations to focus on just one issue—the SALT agreement—which was complicated for a number of domestic and foreign policy reasons. Consequently, the dialogue between our two leaders regrettably focused on this one issue, however important it was. Moreover, Scowcroft cautiously admitted that SALT issues were still causing serious disagreements inside the administration, and the cabinet reshuffle had not settled but only amplified them.

I must also note here that I had already privately drawn Gromyko's attention to the danger of concentrating almost exclusively on SALT in our relations with Washington. He answered in his customary dry and decisive manner that our main objective at this time was the conclusion of a SALT agreement before the Communist Party Congress the following February.

Thus in both of our countries the most important issues of our foreign policy—SALT and the summit—had become hostage to domestic politics, and for this we were both soon to pay the price. On December 9 I was invited to the White House for a meeting with President Ford. Kissinger and Scowcroft were also present. The president handed me a message to Brezhnev requesting a postponement of Kissinger's visit until January. That certainly put Brezhnev's visit to the United States into the indefinite future, if any doubt remained on that question.

The president, seeking to forestall accusations from the right that he and Kissinger were in too much of a hurry to conclude a SALT agreement explained to me that he had decided to wait until his new secretary of defense returned from a trip to Europe in order to hold a full-dress meeting of the National Security Council to hammer out the American position for further SALT talks. The difficult issues were the same, but Ford's apologetic manner did not inspire me with hopes for a close agreement. The president went on to say that he wanted Brezhnev to know that he intended to maintain his commitment to detente despite U.S. domestic politics and the attacks against him over detente. Frankly, his reassurances did not sound very convincing.

## Intelligence Wars

A few months after Ford became president, someone slipped a note under the door of our embassy saying, "Certain authorities of the United States are taking measures to raise the Soviet submarine sunk in the Pacific Ocean. Wellwisher." I reported the this Moscow, but our navy did not believe it possible to raise a submarine from such a depth. Later on March 29 I told Kissinger that Moscow was concerned about press reports of work under way off Hawaii to raise a Soviet submarine armed with missiles that had sunk in 1968. The reports also said some of the crew's bodies had been dumped into the sea. The Soviet Union, I said, could not be indifferent to this; the law of the sea provides that a sunken warship remains the property of the nation whose flag it flew. I demanded an explanation and said all salvage work must stop.

"My information is without doubt no news to you," I told Kissinger, and asked if he could explain. After some hesitation, he replied, "This whole problem has already caused extensive debate inside the government." He declined to elaborate because he needed more information. Several days later he formally assured me that no work on the Soviet submarine was under way at the time, nor would it be in similar cases in the future. More information would be coming from Scowcroft, he said. Later Scowcroft gave me a written message saying six bodies had been found, three identified, and that in accordance with established American practice in such cases they were buried with full military honors. We asked for further information. But the American side never gave us a complete explanation.

Years later we learned that the CIA had ordered the construction of a special ship, ostensibly for mineral extraction on the seabed. It was called the *Glomar Challenger,* cost more than $300 million, and the real purpose of its huge underwater tongs was to lift our submarine with its missiles and technical documentation from a depth of more than 16,000 feet and bring it right inside the ship. That was a violation of maritime law: a man-of-war cannot be raised without the permission or knowledge of its government, which is its owner.

The White House, of course, knew all about this when we raised the question. Ford recalls in his memoirs that on the second day of his presidency he was visited by Kissinger, Scowcroft, Defense Secretary James Schlesinger, and CIA Director William Colby, who asked permission to proceed even though a Soviet trawler lay nearby. Ford ordered the operation to proceed, but as the submarine was being lifted, its hull broke in two, and only one part could be pulled into the hold. The White House also knew that the bodies had been buried at sea with full military honors in a ceremony that was fully recorded on film. It was turned over to our government only after the end of the Cold War.

In April Kissinger raised "a highly confidential and delicate question" about what came to be called political disinformation. While they had no objections to my meetings as ambassador with different people in Washington, including the representatives of the opposition, he said it was quite a different matter when Moscow dispatched special and unofficial emissaries to criticize the administration in talks with Americans, especially with the members of the opposition, and then proposed establishing closer contacts with them to discuss the state of Soviet-American relations under the present administration. This only played into the hands of the president's opponents, Kissinger said, and the president wanted this brought to Brezhnev's personal attention.

What was the real situation? Basically, two kinds of people were involved. First there was the normal run of scientists, academics, journalists, and others who came to America, contacted different people, and expressed their own views on the Soviet-American relations, sometimes critical. After they returned home they shared their impressions and information with their official sponsors in Moscow or the Foreign Ministry. Lacking real experience in diplomacy and knowing no details of our negotiations, they often improvised in their conversations with Americans—just to leave an impression of their own importance. This was often the case with academicians and professors specializing in foreign relations. Their dilettantish activities in diplomacy were not always helpful.

But others were directly used by Soviet intelligence, such as the journalist Victor Louis, who was of dubious character and had been specifically named by Kissinger. When Louis visited Washington he did not contact our embassy, and I never saw him in the United States or at home. In their own search for political information in the West, Louis and people like him presented themselves as more knowledgeable than Soviet diplomats about the inner secrets of the Kremlin and more suitable for finding "compromises" in our relations. They were trying to establish contacts outside of official channels with some influential people in the administration as well as those in opposition. But they were doing more harm than good by their free and incompetent performance in Washington.

During one of my trips to Moscow I drew Gromyko's attention to this. He got annoyed: "You ought to know that I am not a partisan of such silly improvisations." I realized he did not want to quarrel with the intelligence services. So I went myself to talk to Yuri Andropov, then the chairman of the KGB, and explained the situation to him. The practice of sending the most objectionable people to the United States was discontinued, and Soviet citizens were advised to steer clear of domestic disputes or outright criticism of foreign governments, above all when they visited the United States.

Ambassadors like other human beings have their share of personal opponents, enemies, and plain envious people at home, and I was no exception. My post in Washington carried great prestige with the people in our government and bureaucracy, and they knew me as an active ambassador with a wide circle of friends and acquaintances in the United States. My wife and I also traveled widely. All this was rather unusual for a Soviet ambassador. Most preferred to stay within the walls of their embassies, which promised them a more quiet life. So the word occasionally spread in the Central Committee of the Communist Party, the KGB, and the Foreign Ministry that I had become too "Americanized," which to say the least was not a flattering term in the Soviet Union. That reminded me to be a bit cautious. But my main advantage in this was that I was a member of the Central Committee and that as the ambassador to Washington I was personally well acquainted at home with all members of the Politburo, the general secretary of the party, the premier, and many ministers, including those in charge of the KGB and Defense and of course the foreign minister.

The KGB residents in Washington often had only rumors and hearsay, while they knew I was getting information through the confidential channel.

I might tell the resident that his information was simply wrong. I had no need to drop the names of my sources and say I had heard this or that from the president or the secretary of state. They knew who my contacts were. I also showed or informed them of the contents of certain summary telegrams from me to Moscow, so the political assessments coming from the same embassy would not differ too much. We would from time to time jointly discuss foreign and domestic problems bearing on our relations with the United States.

In too many Soviet embassies, normal personal relations between ambassadors and the KGB resident were the exception rather than the rule. Not only did the residents have their own separate coded communication network with Moscow, but keen local rivalries not infrequently developed over supplying Moscow with information. There were also cases of personal incompatibility, presumptuous boasting, and attempts to show who really was boss in the embassy. On the whole, such behavior did not testify to the great intellect of those involved in these primitive quarrels. Time and again the Central Committee of the party had to interfere in local squabbles and even recall either the ambassador or the resident.

I saw quite a few KGB residents pass through our embassy—six altogether during my term as ambassador—and normally I got on with them. There were no clashes or collisions, and only partly because I was a high-ranking ambassador and Moscow knew me well enough. No less important was the fact that our spheres of competence were clearly defined and never overlapped. When KGB residents obtained important political information through their channels in Washington, they reported to me or often consulted me as to whether it seemed trustworthy. For my part, I did not interfere in the everyday business of their intelligence work, nor was I either informed or interested in their concrete operations and their agents; that was beyond the range of my duties. I dealt with their intelligence operations only if they surfaced at the intergovernmental level or threatened to do so. Then the resident was obliged to report to me because the government or Politburo became involved. For instance, during the exchanges of visits at the highest levels I would recommend that Moscow order a temporary halt to intelligence activities to prevent any possibilities of public scandal. As far as I know, they complied.

But there was one problem we did have with our intelligence officers, and it was so egregious that it reached the notice of no less than Yuri Andropov when he headed the KGB. He wondered how the Americans managed so often to identify which embassy officials were KGB officers. I told him frankly that there were several unmistakable signs of their real identity.

"What are they?" Andropov wondered immediately.

First, KGB officers had more expensive apartments in Washington than foreign ministry employees, who were not supposed to stage official receptions at home because they simply were not allocated the funds. Second, all the KGB workers, even of the lowest diplomatic rank, had personal automobiles supplied and paid for by the KGB. Foreign Ministry employees up to the highest-ranking officials used embassy cars on call because the Foreign Ministry had no funds for individual cars. Third, whenever embassy officials invited a foreigner to dine in a restaurant, their expenses were limited to twenty to twenty-five dollars for the whole meal, which was the maximum amount that the embassy would reimburse. The rest of the bill had to be paid out of their own pockets. Accordingly, an embassy official who was a real diplomat would be careful about the restaurant and the menu he chose, but not an employee of the KGB, whose expenses would be covered when he presented the bill. Fourth, diplomatic staff would normally attend to their business in the embassy during working hours, while KGB officers would spend much time around town. Fifth, the members of the diplomatic staff were known to the State Department through routine working contacts on specific problems, so everybody's line of work was clear. But KGB operatives showed no special knowledge of any subject and were interested in everything.

There were other reasons—and there was one more by which we in the diplomatic service also knew who was who. At embassy staff meetings those on the KGB payroll mostly kept silent and took no part in general discussion, which distinguished them from the rest of the diplomatic staff.

Andropov clearly was interested and said he would think about all this without fail. I don't know what he really did, but changes were introduced before long. No one referred to any orders from him, but I had no doubt that he had insisted on them. Diplomats were in many respects raised to the level of KGB officers in terms of private cars, more convenient apartments, restaurant bills, and similar business expenses. Our ambassadors had long raised many of these points with Gromyko, but he just waved them aside and said the Foreign Ministry had to save hard currency. But Andropov apparently managed to convince the Politburo that such questions deserved serious attention.

Mutual accusations of espionage were widely publicized, which was a permanent source of irritation. Kissinger and I discussed this delicate question privately, and he said he was authorized to propose that both sides agree not to disclose cases of spying. The United States, he said, was prepared to handle proven espionage as well as simple misunderstandings through private representations and, if necessary, by quietly recalling the suspects. To avoid leaks to the press, he would personally discuss the cases with the Soviet ambassador. I confirmed that the Soviet side fully agreed, and a few days later Kissinger informed me that the president had issued written instructions to the director of the FBI stipulating prior approval by the president or the secretary of state for all of the director's public statements concerning relations with the Soviet Union. Kissinger said discipline was deteriorating among civil servants, many of whom did not consider Ford a legitimate president because he had not been elected, and the administration had to tighten up. Moscow took similar measures, which ensured that both sides adhered fairly strictly to this confidential and sound arrangement for a long time during that administration.

Interception was a venerable activity of the secret services. In 1962 Khrushchev inadvertently and with characteristic indiscretion and bluster made it clear to Ambassador Foy Kohler during a heated discussion that we had tapped his coded cables. He wanted to confront the ambassador with the fact that we knew he had personally opposed the delivery of steel tubing from the West for natural gas pipelines. Thus alerted, American intelligence presumably acted, and our information from the U.S. Embassy in Moscow was much reduced.

For many years both our intelligence services were engaged in active competition over the installation of very sophisticated eavesdropping devices that were hidden in each other's embassies. To realize the scale of these operations it is enough to say that when the buildings for our new embassy and the housing for its personnel were completed in Washington in 1979 by an American contractor, we found more than two hundred listening devices secreted inside. We showed them to Secretary of State Cyrus Vance. But what could he say? Of course, our services were not idle either. When the new American Embassy was built in Moscow, U.S. officials, in their turn, refused to move in for the same reason. A more alarming aspect of the war conducted by both of our intelligence services appeared late in November 1975, when Kissinger told me that the American ambassador in Moscow, Walter Stoessel, was suspected of having developed leukemia, possibly as a result of extended electromagnetic exposure in the embassy in Moscow. American specialists assumed it had something to do with intercepting, decoding, or jamming the embassy's messages. Kissinger said that if the ambassador's illness became known, it could lead to a major scandal. The U.S. government therefore was asking the Soviet government to stop the radiation.

Moscow instructed me to deny Kissinger's charge that the American

Embassy was being deliberately subjected to radiation. I said we had conducted a thorough investigation and determined that the electromagnetic field around the embassy did not exceed Soviet health standards, which were considerably lower than American standards.

Many years later I learned the real reason for the radiation. The KGB was trying to jam electronic espionage by the American secret service, which used the American Embassy in Moscow as a base to intercept important official telephone and radio conversations, which were mostly unscrambled. Both secret services therefore tried to cancel out each other's efforts; hence the diplomatic representations and counterrepresentations under different pretexts. They reached the presidential level, with Ford, under pressure from American intelligence, demanding that the Soviet side stop immediately, and Brezhnev replying that the electromagnetic field around the embassy was of industrial origin carrying no risk to health. A joint study was proposed but the Americans refused; for two years a special American medical team from Johns Hopkins University had been studying the medical histories of nearly five thousand officials and their families who had been stationed in Moscow from 1954 to 1976 and found no influence of the electromagnetic field on their health. We were privately informed about this by the State Department during the Carter administration. Meanwhile some precautionary measures were quietly taken by both sides.

In fairness, I should add that our embassy in Washington was in the same situation, but once we were told by our doctors that, in their opinion, our health was not in danger, we did not complain. I myself repeatedly suffered from throat and respiratory ailments. Our doctors suspected them to be the result of many years of work in an enclosed electronic space; my embassy office more than any other had insufficient ventilation because it was enclosed in double walls with a magnetic field permanently between them. Of course all these medical assurances and reassurances were fine, but who really can say with certainty that in the long run the health of diplomats in embassies of both countries was not compromised for the sake of the Cold War?

Secret services of both our countries cooperated quietly but very expertly in protecting leaders and officials when they visited the United States or the Soviet Union. Fortunately this protection never failed. More than that, they occasionally exchanged intelligence information about possible attempts on some high officials traveling in third countries. I have personal knowledge of at least two warnings I passed on from Moscow in total confidence, one report about preparations for an attempt on the life of the director of the CIA, and another on the life of Henry Kissinger during the Paris peace talks on Vietnam.

Even in his own country Kissinger was not safe enough. During one of our conversations he told me about a kidnapping plot that, on Nixon's instructions, had not been made public. The whole thing was rather characteristic of American ways. A terrorist group had plotted to kidnap several of the president's principal aides, Kissinger included, and hold them hostage to secure radical changes in policy on issues ranging from the Vietnam War to the Black Panther movement. They also planned to demand the release of some radicals from prison. The group consisted of trained professionals who would not have stopped short of murder had they met with resistance at the decisive stage.

The president had issued secret instructions to provide three of his principal aides, including Kissinger, with bodyguards around the clock. Kissinger himself hired two private detectives to ensure the safety of his two children, who were living in Boston with their mother. The Secret Service gave Kissinger the code name Woodcutter, which was hardly appropriate to this eminent intellectual, and whenever he visited our embassy he was accompanied by his security guards. The president himself received fewer threats than Johnson, but nevertheless his presidential car and helicopter were given new bulletproofing.

Mutual suspicion and mistrust never fully cleared away among the intelligence services. The eighth floor of the U.S. State Department building leads from the office of the secretary and a magnificent suite of reception rooms to a large balcony that he often uses for summer cocktail parties. It has a panoramic view of Washington, looking across the Potomac River. After I ended my service as ambassador in Washington in 1986, I asked George Shultz, who was then secretary, to send me a photograph of the view as a souvenir of my many pleasant visits there. In due course it arrived with a cordial and humorous inscription. He later told me that obtaining the photo had not been easy. The American secret services opposed sending it to the Soviet ambassador because it supposedly depicted strategic points at the center of Washington, although the photograph showed neither the White House nor other important government buildings. Picture postcards of more strategic buildings could be bought in any shop. Shultz refused to take the argument seriously and sent the photo, which I hung in my Moscow office.

# III. How Appeasing the Right Helped Ford Lose the Presidency

## Angola

If any one point of controversy over regional conflicts soured Americans on detente, it was Angola, a country on the Atlantic coast just under the bulge of Africa that few Americans, and probably fewer Russians, had ever heard of before. A sleepy colony of Portugal that had the mixed blessing of oil, it broke free after Lisbon's own revolution shook off the Salazar dictatorship in April of 1974. Various Angolan factions had already been fighting colonial rule, whereupon they turned on each other in a civil war. Such ideological or other fundamental differences as may have existed among them had to be left to the trained observer, a point that might easily be discerned from the similarity of their names, the Movement for the Liberation of Angola (MPLA), the Front for the National Liberation of Angola (FNLA), and the National Union for the Total Liberation of Angola (UNITA).

The MPLA, whose leaders professed a Marxist ideology, had been receiving our assistance during the liberation struggle against the Portuguese, and this was withdrawn when the movement became locked in its own internal struggles. But soon the different factions began receiving assistance variously from Cuba and the Soviet Union, South Africa, the United States, and China. Angola became a cockpit of international ambition far beyond its importance to anyone, not least the unfortunate people of Angola itself. The conflict gradually became one of the most acute regional points of the confrontation between Moscow and Washington, although it was very far removed from the genuine national interests of either country. Moreover, it seriously aggravated the central problems of Soviet-American relations and raised the question of whether detente had any general rules outside our mutual behavior toward each other, and if so, what they were.

President Ford addressed all this at a meeting with me in his office on December 9, 1975. He said he had no real concern about the strategic interests of the United States in Angola, but the events there were increasingly being perceived by Americans and played up by the media as a test for the policy of detente; he had been accused of yielding to the Russians on still another issue. Ford said American intelligence had reported that the Soviet Union had established an impressive arms airlift to Angola, and it was also being used to transport Cuban troops who now constituted the principal striking force of the MPLA. The United States had established a similar airlift, and it was not all that difficult to recruit foreign mercenaries for the FNLA, he said. But was it really necessary for both our countries to challenge each other in such a faraway place which was of no particular value to either of them? (This was, I admit, a very good question.)

Accordingly, Ford proposed: first, that we appeal jointly to the parties in Angola to stop their internecine war and agree to a peaceful settlement, and second, that we call on all interested states to stop interfering in Angola by sending arms there. Kissinger carried a similar message to the NATO foreign ministers in Brussels but he sounded more belligerent, warning that relations between Washington and Moscow would suffer if the Soviet Union went on participating in military operations or supporting them thousands of miles from Soviet territory in a place where there were no Soviet interests.

Brezhnev replied to Ford on December 18 that what was happening in Angola was not a civil war but direct foreign military intervention, and on the part of South Africa in particular. He said peacemaking had to be focused on jointly stopping foreign intervention, and the Soviet Union was not interested in viewing the events in Angola through the prism of "confrontation between Moscow and Washington" or "as a test of the detente policy."

But it was exactly in this light that events in Angola were seen not only by the Ford administration but by the American public, and they had the effect of worsening Soviet-American relations. Our embassy in Washington repeatedly warned Moscow of this. Our reports and arguments fell on the deaf ears of the morally self-righteous.

On December 23 Kissinger again questioned the Soviet role and linked it to detente. He proposed a face-saving exit by referring the whole thing to the Organization of African Unity, which was already involved in mediation without success. What really mattered to Kissinger was not who won, but that none of the combatants themselves should achieve victory with the outside help of a superpower.

But by this time Angola had become a superpower issue with a dynamic of its own. The MPLA, which we were supporting, formed a transitional government in the capital of Luanda. It looked like they were on the winning side. So we felt that our clients in Angola had more legitimate grounds then America's. Moscow instructed me to reject Kissinger's charges against the Soviet Union and accuse the United States and its special services of wrecking the normal functioning of the transitional government in Angola. Moscow and Washington were thus drawn deeper and deeper into a vicious circle in Angola, which was to last for many years.

Considerations of superpower image only increased the obstinacy of both sides, since neither felt it could afford to "lose Angola." During one of our conversations, Kissinger rightly said that it was essential not to let our two countries be guided by the iron laws of superpower competition, which had caused unpredictable catastrophes in the past. I felt the same way, especially about Angola, but it was too late for that.

A leading if not decisive role in the Soviet involvement in the Angola adventure was played by the International Department of the Central Committee of our party, which for many years was headed by a secretary of the party, Boris Ponomarev. He was a protégé of our principal ideologist, Mikhail Suslov. Through the Portuguese Communist Party, the International Department had long before established contacts with some leaders of the liberation movement in Angola and supported them ever since. The Soviet Foreign Ministry had nothing to do with our initial involvement in Angola and looked at it with some skepticism. But the decision had been taken by the top party leadership, and the diplomats followed the decision of the party.

When I spoke with Ponomarev he advanced his set of arguments: the United States was involved in many civil wars around the globe, it was busy consolidating its positions in Egypt and elsewhere, and had actively overthrown a socialist government in Chile that came to power legally. So how could the Americans see our support for the newly formed government in Angola as a violation of detente? Must we yield to American arrogance and their double standard? This viewpoint came to dominate the Politburo. Furthermore, the Politburo felt we had to show the flag against China in Africa so as not to be seen by international communist and democratic movements as being idle in postcolonial areas.

Although the Kremlin saw Angola primarily as an ideological conflict with the United States, the Soviet leadership clearly underestimated the psychological effect of the Cuban factor in Angola on American public opinion and on the administration. The myth of Cuba as a Soviet proxy was especially damaging for us in America, where the Cuban crisis of 1962 had fixed the idea firmly. But it was the Cubans and not us who had initially interfered by sending their own military forces to back the MPLA, on their own initiative and without consulting us. The Cubans had connections with the political groups, and of course Fidel Castro liked to make things difficult for the Americans. As evidence of this, let me cite a visit I made to Cuba in 1986 as representative of the Soviet government when we were trying to restrain

Castro in order to help improve our relations with the Americans. Castro made it clear to me that what was happening in Angola was a Cuban show. "It is my command," he said. He wanted to be a player on the world scene, and that was one way he could do it.

The Soviet leadership never contemplated using the Cuban troops in any third country, but the Cubans quickly managed to involve us there on the pretext of international solidarity. It was not difficult to do because of the mood of the party leadership. But by supporting the Cubans in Angola (all their arms were of Soviet origin) we played right into the hands of our opponents in the United States, and the Soviet-American dialogue over Angola became a dialogue of the deaf, which hardly improved our relations.

When Kissinger went to Moscow in January to discuss the SALT impasse, he also raised Angola in vain. "If Kissinger wants to talk about Angola, he has Sonnenfeldt to talk with," Brezhnev snapped to an American journalist who asked him about the agenda of his talks. Kissinger's assistant Helmut Sonnenfeldt, for his part, had relayed ahead Kissinger's "hope that there is not going to be a massive offensive in Angola during his stay in Moscow." They were under the understandable misapprehension that military operations in Angola were directed from Moscow.

When Kissinger returned, he began advancing a twofold policy toward the Soviet Union, supposedly to combine firmness and reconciliation, as well as strong defense and arms limitation. He also devised a so-called concept of historic interests—according to which the Soviet Union never had any interests outside Europe and Asia and therefore had none now. In March the administration canceled three Soviet-American government-level meetings on trade, energy, and construction. It also decided not to ask Congress for legislation to normalize trade and economic relations with the Soviet Union. The spirit of cooperation was disappearing, and this surfaced with a vengeance in the next round of talks on SALT.

In his Moscow talks on SALT, Kissinger found the outstanding issues unchanged—cruise missiles and the Backfire bomber. Brezhnev accepted Kissinger's main condition setting the maximum range for air-launched cruise missiles at 2,500 kilometers but refused to accept the same range for ground and sea-launched cruises. He wanted a shorter range for them as a matter of equality; American cruises could reach Soviet territory from their land or naval platforms, while American territory was out of our cruise range. Brezhnev made more concessions guaranteeing that the plane would not be adapted to intercontinental range and handed over all of its performance data. Kissinger seemed satisfied. Limitations on cruise missiles also moved toward compromise, but Kissinger warned that his position had been agreed with Ford but had not passed the Pentagon, an unusual proviso for him.

Sure enough, when he returned to Washington, the military leadership rejected his deal on the Backfire bomber. Donald Rumsfeld, the new defense secretary, was becoming a leader of the opposition to a new SALT agreement. On January 21 an angry meeting of the National Security Council took place in the White House. William Hyland, Scowcroft's deputy, told me in confidence that as the result of fresh wrangling everything just fell apart, and once again there was no consistent American position on SALT. The president faced the task of putting it back together anew, a task he was unlikely to complete because of the gulf between his principal advisers, Kissinger and Rumsfeld. Since the opening of the election season, Ford had increasingly tended to listen to Rumsfeld, who like the president was a former Republican congressman from the Midwest and held the same conservative views on many things.

It was therefore growing more evident that Ford was turning away from the Vladivostok agreements, or at least putting them aside until after the elections. With the Republican right continuously attacking Kissinger, it was not hard to understand why the secretary of state lost interest in SALT, which was taking so much of his energy to such little effect. Kissinger was demolished on some other international issues and even gave Ford a draft of a resignation statement in January, but Ford talked him out of it. Nevertheless his position was hardly auspicious. He was under public pressure from the right on at least the two principal issues with the Soviet Union: Angola and SALT.

In Moscow positions also were hardening. Brezhnev told the Twenty-Fifth Congress of the Communist Party that a base had been created for Soviet-American cooperation but refused to accept any connection between the events in Angola and current difficulties with Washington. The congress closed without adopting any measures that might have neutralized the first indications of trouble for Soviet foreign policy. Brezhnev was named chairman of the Defense Council soon afterward and raised to the rank of marshal of the Soviet Union, attaining the peak of his domestic political power precisely at the time that detente started to lose momentum. But no one in the Soviet leadership worried very much about that because they thought it was a temporary trend.

It is interesting to draw a comparison between the Soviet and American attitudes. On March 1, when the Communist Party Congress in Moscow was in full swing, Ford succumbed to pressure from Reagan and his allies and publicly refused to employ the term "detente," replacing it with the phrase "peace based on force." Things were gradually changing, and not for the better.

## Turmoil in the White House over Detente

It was clear that there was no hope for progress in Soviet-American relations during the election year. There were other complications beside Angola and SALT. Emigration and dissidents in the Soviet Union continued to be a politically charged issue. Loud and abusive picketing, hostile demonstrations, telephoned threats to Soviet diplomats and their families, rifle shots at the Soviet mission in New York, and a bomb explosion outside the Aeroflot office in Washington prompted President Ford publicly to condemn "these outrageous actions." But all this only caused further tension and anxiety among diplomats of both countries, which hardly helped our negotiations on any issue, and that may have been just what the provocateurs and political terrorists in the United States such as Rabbi Kahane wanted to achieve. An especially destructive role was played by the American mass media, which was increasingly used by politicians hostile to the Soviet Union including Jackson, Reagan, and others. For the first time, an assignment to the United States was no longer a prize among Soviet diplomats. Living in the United States became unpleasant and even dangerous for them.

I was returning to Washington from Moscow aboard our government plane, and we scheduled a stop at Kennedy airport in New York. Air traffic was heavy. Planes had to wait in line, each at an altitude assigned by the control tower. Suddenly we lost communication with the American control tower. For a minute or two our pilots had to descend by peering through the clouds. As the airspace was crowded with other planes, there could have been a catastrophe at any moment. Later we learned that the controller who handled our plane was a member of an anti-Soviet organization. For a moment, he had let his emotions gain control over him and stopped guiding our plane. The officer was fired. We decided to let the matter drop, even though some American friends suggested we bring suit against him. We refrained, partly because of the generally unfavorable feelings toward the Soviet Union in the country.

Both Brezhnev and Ford could not help noticing the deterioration. They exchanged letters. On April 16 Brezhnev wrote that the American leadership "says and does a lot of things which can only be viewed as the opposite" of building good relations, especially its new policy of peace through military strength. He warned that election considerations "do not constitute grounds for endangering everything of significance and value that was so hard to achieve in Soviet-American relations." Ford replied that despite the different voices in an election campaign, he wanted Brezhnev to remember that only the president or the secretary of state had authority to make official statements on foreign policy, and he remained a partisan of improving

Arriving with my wife Irina at
Idlewild (now John F. Kennedy)
Airport in New York en route to
Washington in March 1962
to assume the post of Soviet
ambassador.

Presenting credentials to President John F. Kennedy in the Oval Office
of the White House in April 1962.

At the Glassboro summit, June 1967, with Premier Alexei Kosygin at the microphone.
Front row, from the left: Victor Syhodrev, official Soviet interpreter; Foreign Minister
Andrei Gromyko; Alexei Kosygin; the American interpreter, Akolovsky;
Lyndon Johnson; and Secretary of State Dean Rusk. I am standing behind Kosygin.
To the left of me in the picture are W. Averell Harriman and
Defense Secretary Robert McNamara.

Discussing ABMs with President
Johnson and Dean Rusk in the
Oval Office, 1967.

Trying out a snowmobile in Washington
in 1971 (with no snow). It was a gift
from a company in the home state of
Senator Hubert H. Humphrey, the
back-seat driver.

Meeting with Harry Truman.

A moment of relaxation at the Western White House
in San Clemente, July 1972, with Richard Nixon and Henry Kissinger.

On the same visit. President Nixon takes the wheel of a golf cart,
with my wife in front, and Henry Kissinger and me in the back.

The "chief's" family. The headdress was presented to me by the chief of a Native American tribe from Nebraska in 1973.

My granddaughter embracing the globe with President Ford in the Oval Office of the White House.

On the Johnny Carson set. Guess who is interviewing whom.

On a Siberian train to the Vladivostok summit. At left, Henry Kissinger, Gerald Ford, Walter Stoessel; at right, Leonid Brezhnev, Andrei Gromyko, and me.

With the Carters at the White House, January 1977.

*To Toly — for better or for worse, this is the way to negotiate — Zbig.    July, '77.*

Hoisting a glass of the real thing with Zbigniew Brzezinski, President Carter's national security adviser, in his White House office. His inscription reads: "To Toly—for better or worse, this is *the* way to negotiate—Zbig. July '77." (Carter's reaction was somewhat different. He memoed Brzezinski, "Now I know why we lose.")

Enjoying a Western barbecue and some animated conversation with Ronald Reagan, July 1984.

Coming to an agreement is a long process. I am meeting with President Reagan and Secretary Shultz with staffers in the White House in 1986.

With our great-grandson, Peter, in April 1991.

My parents, Moscow, 1975.

Soviet-American relations. But he added that in all candor he was concerned about their relations because of events in Angola and because of his responsibility—like Brezhnev's in his own country—for the security of the United States, which demanded increased military appropriations. This exchange clearly demonstrated the increasing interference of the election campaign in Soviet-American relations.

Our embassy in Washington made sure that the Soviet leadership was well aware of the widespread anti-Soviet campaign in the United States, but Moscow did little to neutralize it. Moscow was strangely convinced that such campaigns were inevitable as a direct result of the ideological struggle between the different social systems. They therefore believed it was hardly possible to stop it without grave concessions. American pressure over humanitarian issues caused particular indignation in Moscow, where the leadership continued to believe that this was purely our own business.

In local American politics international questions were often used for political gain. Congressman Charles Vanik, full of favorable impressions after a visit to Moscow, called on me, mentioned his Slavic origins, and said he was not predisposed against the Soviet Union. But he frankly explained his cosponsorship of the discriminatory Jackson-Vanik amendment principally by his desire to be reelected in his Cleveland district with its many East European voters. His constituents now were lobbying against the grain deal with the Soviet Union but were making no progress against the twelve grain states.

Lou Harris, the pollster, told me of a confidential poll commissioned by the White House disclosing that a majority of the population supported the detente mainly out of fear of a nuclear confrontation. He concluded that an important agreement with the Soviet Union in 1976, say, on SALT, would persuade millions of Americans to support detente notwithstanding the opposition's attacks. This in turn would benefit President Ford. If, on the other hand, relations with the Soviet Union deteriorated, this would mean the end of the Ford administration. His prognosis proved correct.

Donald Kendall, chairman of Pepsi-Cola, a prominent Republican, and an early proponent of trade and investment in the Soviet Union, said he had spoken to Ford about election strategy and criticized him for his anti-Soviet remarks and for overestimating the role of Reagan and his conservative supporters who constituted, he said, only "a minority in the party of the minority." Hugh Scott, the Republican leader in the Senate, told me that a conference of Republican leaders pressed similar advice and told Ford to ignore Reagan and consistently urge the positive aspects of his program: peace without the threat of war. The president, he said, promised to take this advice into account, but he insisted that he could not ignore Reagan.

Less surprisingly but with no less concern, Ford's attempt to walk a political tightrope also produced critical reactions among Democrats in the Senate. Senator Edward Kennedy was concerned about the threat of the arms race. He recalled that his brother had exploited the infamous "missile gap" with the Soviet Union and discovered a new "gold mine" of political propaganda during the 1960 presidential campaign against Nixon. His own propaganda was immediately exploited by the military-industrial complex and its conservative political allies for an arms buildup further exacerbated by the Cuban crisis and lasting for a decade. Edward Kennedy believed his brother had made a "tragic mistake" by allowing himself to be carried away by a strong-America theme that was largely responsible for the lack of progress in Soviet-American relations. He feared the same tragic mistake would be repeated without a new SALT agreement.

Kissinger himself complained to me that the president was surrounded by petty politicians and campaign experts who saw their main task as forestalling attacks by Reagan instead of devising an offensive strategy based on the issues of war and peace. This internal turmoil surfaced after Kissinger passed to me on May 10 a proposal by Ford for simultaneous ceremonies in Washington and Moscow to sign a treaty on the peaceful use of nuclear explosions. Brezhnev agreed. But the next day Scowcroft urgently asked for a postponement on Ford's behalf. Scowcroft said the president was embarrassed to have to admit "without too much diplomacy" that the political timing was bad. Reagan had just won the Republican primary in Nebraska, and another victory for him in Ford's home state of Michigan could be fatal. Ford's domestic policy advisers pleaded with him to postpone signing the agreement, while his foreign policy advisers, headed by Kissinger, believed that the agreement might enhance his chances. Scowcroft reported that Ford had given in to the domestic advisers "after some painful vacillation." Apologizing once again for the "embarrassing situation," Ford asked for another postponement on May 20. As Scowcroft remarked, "It seems that our foreign policy and our relations with you won't amount to anything worthwhile until August"— after the Republican Convention. The treaty was finally signed May 28.

## Henry Kissinger's Swan Song

In mid-June Kissinger invited me for a conversation. He had no specific issue to discuss but just wanted to talk informally "about the past, the present, and the future." This was one of several talks during the year reviewing our long relationship. I already knew that he was feeling somewhat gloomy, partly because of enforced idleness, which was not his natural state. A fortnight before he had complained to me that Ford had discouraged him from attacking

Reagan on issues of war and peace and, under pressure from his conservative advisers, forced his secretary of state to cancel two important speeches in California. Kissinger then decided to disengage himself from the president's election. "Let them do what they want," he said.

Now he was in a philosophical state of mind. No matter who came to power next year, he said, his policy of negotiation would remain at the basis of our relations, even if some problems remained hard to solve. The first year under Jimmy Carter might seem more difficult than it had been under Ford, not because of any bias against the Soviet Union but because Carter lacked experience in international affairs and tended to oversimplify them. He figured it would take Carter four to six months to get a grip on foreign policy in general and Soviet relations in particular.

Kissinger noted that Carter had the disposition of a Baptist preacher, which meant he might indulge himself in "moralizing" over human rights without realizing how this would be seen as interference by the Soviet Union. Nevertheless, Kissinger could not foresee any significant differences in Carter's policy, although he would seem more dynamic and self-directing than Ford. (Carter, by the way, consulted Kissinger privately even before the election for advice on choosing his own successor if the Democrats won. Kissinger told me one thing he tried to do was to talk Carter out of appointing one of his advisers, Zbigniew Brzezinski of Columbia University, as secretary of state because he found the Polish-born professor excessively emotional and not able to think impassively in the long term.)

A few days before the elections, on October 29, Kissinger invited me to come see him "to cast a look" at the general state of our relations and the philosophy underlying them since he had started playing a major role in them in 1969. He called it a "time of great achievement" which now was at its lowest point because of the election campaign. The decline had begun, he said, in 1974 when Congress refused to grant MFN status to the Soviet Union. Since then, the issue of Jewish emigration from the Soviet Union had prompted strong opposition to the Soviet Union by the American Jewish leadership on practically all issues of Soviet-American relations. And these events in turn influenced the mass media and public opinion in both countries. I agreed with him that Moscow's handling of the issue had not only been unfair but also very clumsy.

He cited other factors accounting for the degradation of our relations. Massive military deliveries to North Vietnam which "the Soviet Union and not China" carried out during the preparation and immediately after the conclusion of the Paris agreements on Vietnam allowed the North Vietnamese to launch a major offensive in the South and destroy the agreements he had negotiated. Then there were the events in Angola, which

Kissinger interpreted as a deliberate violation by the Soviet Union of the global balance with the United States which predisposed American public opinion against the detente. He claimed that our policy was designed to hurt America—even hurt Kissinger himself (which was not true).

I answered that in some respects he was probably right, but it was unwise to link Soviet-American relations almost mechanically to all the failures in American foreign policy, some of which arose from Kissinger's own mistakes. I said, "We are no saints, but neither are the Americans."

In a pacifying tone Kissinger said that his remarks should be interpreted just as "a short historic excursus," and he was merely voicing his thoughts candidly and not for polemics, although they were shared with many Americans.

I felt that this man of exceptional intelligence was in a state of confusion and worry: the outcome of the election and what lay beyond it were obscure.

When we met again on the day after Ford's defeat, he seemed above the battle for the first time and had a rather other-worldly look. He told me that in his heart he had for quite some time known that Ford would most probably lose, but he kept subconsciously pushing the thought aside and nevertheless hoping for the best, "as happens in the face of imminent disaster."

Kissinger strongly criticized Ford for failing to use the real assets of American foreign policy, especially relations with the Soviet Union. Most of all, Kissinger blamed Ford for lack of foresight and vacillation, which prevented a new SALT agreement. He was sure, he said, that if Ford had made a firm decision after Kissinger's return from Moscow in January with a compromise, and if he had then made the Pentagon respect his opinion, the agreement could have been signed as early as March. While it certainly would have been the subject of heated debate during the campaign, Kissinger was sure it would have been supported by most Americans if Ford had presented it as a war-or-peace issue, which really was a principal determinant in the American public's attitude toward foreign policy.

Now it was time to decide what to do next. Up to then he had not seriously thought about what he would do when he left office and he still did not know. He had plenty of options, but they seemed boring and shallow after his long term as secretary of state. Money was no problem, he said; he could earn it with publicity. The problem was to find a job which would satisfy his spirit.

Henry Kissinger, for all his zigzags and political maneuvers in our relations in a framework of his "realpolitik," played a significant part in the general improvement of Soviet-American relations during the Nixon and the Ford administrations and in establishing the policy of detente. This was his indisputable personal achievement as a statesman, and his international reputation endured. After leaving the government, he remained as controversial as ever, but he never lost his political stature and most of all, his role as a leading analyst of international events.

## Ford versus Carter, as Moscow Saw Them

Well before the election, Moscow had to decide whether to take a position for or against Ford or Carter, or to remain neutral. On August 22 a special Politburo meeting was held in Moscow to discuss Soviet-American relations after the Republican convention in Kansas City had nominated Ford by the narrow margin of only 1,187 votes over 1,070 votes for Ronald Reagan. I reported to the Politburo on the electoral campaign in the United States. There were many questions for me about the outcome, the candidates' positions, and what I thought our attitude should be.

There was not much interest during the meeting in what American domestic policy would be under Ford or Carter. Nobody asked about their positions toward workers or members of the American Communist Party inside the country. The main points were: What kind of policy would both candidates have toward the Soviet Union? Who would have more ideological and military overtones in his policy? Who would rely more on competition and even outright confrontation than on cooperation, and who was more in favor of detente?

Ford was already known in Moscow. He left a rather mixed impression after three years in office. He looked like a decent man who would like to have more stable relations with the Soviet Union. But at the same time he had predominately conservative views, tended to yield to pressure from the right, and therefore could not be predictable in relations with us.

Carter's reputation in the United States was of a man who was more liberal than Ford. There was some unofficial information from different sources that he was interested in the SALT process and had some ideas of his own in this field that included radical reductions of strategic arms. But on the other side he was well known as a strong advocate of human rights and other humanitarian issues and his readiness to be involved in disputes with us about them could only bring trouble. Moral crusaders often make dangerous statesmen.

It was difficult to lean toward either candidate and better to remain evenhanded during the election campaign. In any case foreign interference or even expressing our preference would not do any good. That was the essence of my report to the Politburo.

Vivid discussion of both candidates followed along these lines. It was inconclusive, though with slight preference of Ford as a known quantity. The Politburo decided to remain neutral. Its formal directive said we would "continue business as usual with the Ford administration" and simultaneously, "maintain contacts with Carter's associates and establish direct contact with Carter if he displays readiness." The Soviet press was instructed to interpret the election campaign "in a calm tone and balanced manner."

What worried us was Ronald Reagan's success in shifting the political debate to the right even though he had not won the Republican nomination. A Foreign Ministry analysis of October 12, which was approved by the Politburo, remarked that the campaign debate had "produced a number of points unfavorable for us . . . in particular . . . the general tone of statements by both candidates who insist upon maintaining military might of the United States as a basic prerequisite for dealing with the Soviet side." Noting that the foreign policy statements of Ford and Carter were "obviously a reflection of certain rightist tendencies in U.S. public opinion on issues of Soviet-American relations," the analysis recommended that we continue trying for constructive cooperation with Washington while reacting firmly against any hostile American actions.

During my stay in Moscow I had my traditional one-on-one meeting with Brezhnev, who was greatly interested in the election campaign but tended to oversimplify it. He was indignant at Ford and accused him of failing to take the position of peace candidate against "this obscurantist Reagan." Brezhnev was sure that would have won over "all honest Americans." He was also indignant that Angola was being used against us, for he was convinced that "our cause is just." I tried again to explain things as Americans saw them, but I failed to impress the general secretary, who believed that "the imperialists in the United States" simply would not accept that his intentions were fair in Angola. He was not attempting to establish in Angola any Soviet military bases, as Americans were doing around the globe, but was only "helping local patriots and internationalists." In short, he was still held captive by his own ideology. And there were limits to my ability to change his mind.

At the same time, it was curious that he remained firmly convinced of the necessity of improving our relations with Washington, in part because he actually admired and almost even envied America's living standards and the achievements of its economy, science, and technology. He would tell me about this in private, but he still believed that the future belonged to socialism, which he was certain would ultimately gain the upper hand in the historic competition with capitalism. Even then, he completely excluded any possibility of a war with the United States, for this would amount to "the end of the world."

That is why I can testify that all allegations in the United States that the Soviet leadership may have been planning a "preventive strike" were completely groundless. The Kremlin was afraid of war with the United States. Detente in Soviet-American relations was Brezhnev's true objective, although he failed to comprehend fully what it entailed. His credo was based on the traditional Marxist-Leninist "class approach" to foreign policy, which cast even peaceful relations into a mold of confrontation although not necessarily on the battlefield—a point those on the right in the United States had just as much difficulty understanding as he did when trying to view international relations as a fruitful compromise of interests. The United States thus remained for Brezhnev the principal opponent, which strove to undermine the socialist order inside the Soviet Union and the socialist camp as a whole. Detente, therefore, had to have its limits.

## Ford Loses the Election

The election was close, and political maneuvering by both candidates lasted until the very last moment. Late on the night of October 30 I got a phone call from Scowcroft. A group of Jewish leaders had sent Ford a request that amounted to an ultimatum to express his public support for the right of Jews to emigrate from the Soviet Union. They said that Carter had already committed himself by sending a telegram expressing his sympathy to a group of Jews in Moscow. Scowcroft was calling to tell me, apologetically, that Ford had yielded to their demands. He asked us for "patience and understanding for another forty-eight hours, until this madhouse is over." After the election on November 2, he promised, everything was going to be "back to normal."

That never happened. Carter received 40.8 million votes to 39 million for Ford, or 51 to 48 percent, hardly an impressive majority, and close enough for Ford and some of his supporters to feel bitter. I believe that Ford's tactics of appeasing the right had failed him. They only destabilized his domestic policy, which ran counter to the nation's post-Vietnam mood of cutting military expenditures and staying out of remote quarrels in places like Angola. But he still did not succeed in gaining the support of ultraconservative groups which had staked their all on Reagan, and the public was left confused by his foreign policy. Not only did he fail to use the issues of war and peace to his advantage, but he created a very harmful perception of detente: in spite of public support for detente, the administration had proposed the largest military budget in American history, along with drastic cuts in health care, education, and other social programs.

In my opinion, Ford's hour of triumph in Soviet-American relations was the Vladivostok agreement. After that, he had a choice between turning it into a formal SALT II treaty notwithstanding the rightist opposition, or rejecting this course and thus his own highest achievement in foreign policy.

But Ford hesitated. His decision during the election campaign to appease the right probably cost him the presidency.

As the Ford presidency was nearing its end, Brezhnev, at the age of seventy, was at the height of his political power. A sick old man, the Soviet leader came to believe (not without the help of his immediate circle in the Politburo) in the infallibility of Soviet domestic and foreign policy and saw no need of any major corrections at the time when reality demanded changes that should have broadly implemented detente. Stagnation of thought, ideological inertia, and lack of flexibility could not but lead to serious failures and an ultimate deadlock in Soviet policy.

Diplomacy and negotiations always played an important role in Soviet-American relations. But their quality depended on many domestic and foreign factors. The highest diplomacy does not consist of trying to drown differences in champagne and vodka toasts at feel-good summit meetings, nor of papering over unresolvable issues with communiqués written in gobbledygook, but in finding ways to disagree without doing profound damage to an important strategic relationship. Ford and Brezhnev failed in this because they were confused over their interpretations of detente and lacked a clear vision of a common goal.

## I. The Contradictions of Jimmy Carter

*Jimmy Who?*

J immy Carter came into the White House with a relatively unimpressive political background and a lackluster record, with little national experience or recognition when he started his quest for the presidency. Political humorists called the governor of Georgia "Jimmy Who?" A couple of months before the election, Gerald Ford still believed he would beat Carter hands down. The diplomatic corps in Washington, very much the same as most American voters, was mystified by Carter's relatively unorthodox style and his original views and judgments. He seemed to have no definite program, and ordinary Americans would find in his speeches just what they were eager to hear. He clearly did not belong to the Washington Establishment, nor did he enjoy solid support within his own party. He was a political phenomenon, and his conduct in public defied all standards. A devout Baptist, he gave a straightforward interview to *Playboy* magazine admitting that he had moments of "lust in my heart," all of which acquired broad and controversial publicity. In short, he cut quite a fresh and rather unusual figure on the American political horizon.

When Carter was elected I found it difficult to forecast his future actions, as there were too many unknowns. Deep down I hoped that Carter, with his military and technical background—he had graduated from the U.S. Naval Academy and trained for the elite nuclear submarine service—could prove a more reliable and stable partner than his predecessors in the White House, especially in the talks on limiting nuclear weapons. Life proved more complex than that, and Carter and his presidency turned out even more contradictory than they appeared at the start. Many also regarded him as naive. That is clearly wrong. Personally, I respect Carter and his high spiritual and moral convictions. He was ahead of some other presidents in his public stress on such values common to all mankind as genuine disarmament, human rights, famine relief, environmental protection, and the need to preserve and use properly the resources of the whole planet.

American historians describe his presidency as erratic, and in my country it is considered one of the unfortunate pages in Soviet-American relations, an assessment with which I am inclined to agree, although at the start he had good intentions and wanted to develop stable relations with the Soviet Union. One of the main reasons for his failure was the incompatibility between his ideas, some of which were very good, and his ability to put them into practice. He lacked flexibility. Seeking to achieve the best, he would underestimate tangible assets. The most egregious example was in the field of disarmament. As he pursued the wonderful bird of his dream—a drastic reduction in nuclear weapons—he let go of the bird in his hand, the ratification of the SALT II treaty.

Sometimes Carter behaved as if he were deliberately trying to disprove the truth of the aphorism that politics is the art of the possible. Occasionally he was just unlucky. But more often he failed to find the most important goal by which to chart the policies of his government and then implement them steadfastly. His failure to pick his priorities and stick with them was in no small measure due to great disagreements among his principal aides. Since he had to depend on an unstable and heterogeneous coalition, he picked a cabinet which helped create contradictory foreign and domestic policies. Along with time-tested Cold War soldiers like Zbigniew Brzezinski as national security adviser, James Schlesinger as energy secretary, and Admiral Stansfield Turner as director of central intelligence, more moderate circles were represented in the government by Secretary of State Cyrus Vance, Chief Arms Negotiator Paul Warnke, Treasury Secretary W. Michael Blumenthal, and Health, Education, and Welfare Secretary Joseph Califano.

These contradictions plagued Carter's presidency with crises and minicrises, particularly in its relations with the Soviet Union. But his own character was also contradictory, composed of interwoven conservative and moderate views on affairs of state and personal matters. Foreign policy was focused on restoring the international position of the United States, which had been seriously undermined by the loss of the nation's gamble in Vietnam. Thus the administration proclaimed the need for more solid relations with its military and political allies in the triangle of North America, Western Europe, and Japan, as well as the strengthening the military force of NATO. Carter built up the U.S. armed forces in keeping with the Pentagon's military and political doctrine, making the Soviet Union its main opponent and rival. Military force was considered one of the crucial tools to influence international affairs. When Carter spoke on foreign affairs, we tended to hear echoes of the anti-Sovietism of Brzezinski.

The policy of human rights, aimed against the Soviet Union and the socialist community, was launched by Carter from his very first days in office to cement the West's foreign policy under the leadership of the United States.

Carter saw it as a continuation of his role in the American civil rights movement and presented it as establishing new moral standards in America's foreign policy, in contrast to what he viewed as the immoral period of Nixon, Kissinger, and Ford. The ideological campaign had the auxiliary role of mobilizing domestic support for the administration's foreign policy and helping to overcome the deep split left by the Vietnam war and Watergate. But it was carried out mainly at the expense of Soviet-American relations.

All this took place while the elders of the Soviet leadership persisted in pursuing their conservative domestic policy and allowed the country to sink gradually into economic and political stagnation. It was a dramatic part of the history of our relations with the United States: two nations and their leaders, each of which seemed in early 1977 to desire better bilateral relations and a reduction of the nuclear danger, had by early 1980 arrived at a situation in which relations were terrible, detente had collapsed, a nuclear arms reduction treaty lay unratified in the United States, and the groundwork was laid for a revival of intense Cold War rhetoric and confrontation after the election of Ronald Reagan. The detailed history of Soviet-American relations during this period, which I will try to set down here with its principal characters, resembles a complicated and tricky game of chess, with only one essential difference: in reality it ended with both rivals losing the game and the policy of detente in ruins.

## Friendly First Soundings

Even before Carter's election, I began learning from his supporters and intimates how he planned to govern. Late in July I was invited to dinner by J. Paul Austin, a financial backer and chairman of Coca-Cola, the most powerful company in Carter's home state of Georgia. He said Carter wanted to appoint Dean Rusk, whom he held in great respect, as his secretary of state, but Rusk refused categorically, preferring to remain a university professor in Georgia. His next potential candidate was Brzezinski, with whom Carter had become close during their meetings as members of the Trilateral Commission, an organization of notables in many fields which concentrates on the relations among the United States, Western Europe, and Japan. But Carter had grown apprehensive about one aspect of Brzezinski's personality: he took too much pleasure from personal publicity, so Austin said Carter wanted to use Brzezinski in the White House, where his vanity would be more controllable, as assistant to the president for national security affairs.

Shortly afterward I attended a dinner given by David Rockefeller at which Brzezinski was also a guest, probably with the express purpose of displaying him to the Soviets in the most favorable light. We already knew of his position as one of the leading Western experts on communism, of his origins in the old Polish nobility, of his father's refusal to return to Poland with his family after World War II, and of the son's marriage to a niece of the prewar president of Czechoslovakia, Edvard Benes. All this to some extent influenced his views, which were notoriously anti-communist, although in recent years he had moved toward the center. When the possibility opened up of joining Carter's team, he even started talking about progress in some areas of Soviet-American relations.

During the conversation at dinner Brzezinski visibly tried to refrain from extreme statements, and his attitude was quite friendly. After listening to a philosophical monologue about foreign policy, I remarked that it would be nice to hear something more practical, for example, an explanation of the real differences between the foreign policy of the Ford administration and the Democrats, especially on Soviet-American relations. Brzezinski made a special point of arguing that Carter would find it easier to implement his foreign policy because Congress would be dominated by members of his own party. But he failed to outline any essential distinctions, at which point Rockefeller interrupted our conversation and said, pointing to Brzezinski, "I have already told him that I don't see any particular differences."

I came away with a strong impression of the Rockefellers: they were running a virtually no-risk political game. Irrespective of which candidate won, they would be able to have their views known to him through the people they supplied. Nelson Rockefeller, the vice president, was well known as Kissinger's patron, and here was his brother David, the famous banker, sponsoring Brzezinski for a high position in the Carter administration.

Some days later I attended another dinner at the house of Averell Harriman, the Democratic Party elder who had become one of Carter's advisers. Harriman attached great importance to the fact that Carter, if elected, would be the first American president with an advanced technical education, moreover in the field of nuclear technology. In Harriman's view, this accounted for Carter's special interest in "the central issue of the modern times, that is, the prevention of nuclear war." He stressed that Carter did not consider it essential to pursue American superiority in any type of strategic arms, but was prepared to negotiate an agreement with the Soviet Union limiting them to "approximate equality."

Harriman wanted to visit Moscow in September, meet with Brezhnev and Gromyko, and report back to Carter. I arranged this visit quickly, and he made his trip on September 16–22. Brezhnev received Harriman as a statesman identified with American goodwill, and they agreed on the need for further strategic arms limitation talks. Brezhnev expressed the hope that summit meetings would continue their useful role.

Harriman became an unofficial channel between Carter and Brezhnev during the transition period. He briefed Carter, who pronounced himself satisfied with the trip to Moscow, and relayed to me Carter's reaction that his first priority in negotiations with the Soviet Union was curbing the arms race, hopefully by even lowering the strategic arms ceilings fixed in Vladivostok. Carter was interested in agreeing with the Soviet Union on reducing troops and weapons in Central Europe; Pentagon briefings left him with the impression that the Soviet Union had started building up its forces in the region, and that worried him.

In Moscow meanwhile, the Politburo reacted quickly to Carter's victory. Two days after the election, on November 4, Gromyko sent the Politburo a memorandum proposing that I be authorized to open a direct dialogue with the president-elect even before his inauguration. Gromyko argued that it was especially necessary for us to reach the new president of a different party because "during the period of elaborating his policy toward the Soviet Union, Carter may be influenced by the general rightist trend in American public opinion which has been taking shape lately and which became so evident in the election campaign." He also proposed that if Carter "displays an interest in entering into a businesslike dialogue with us even prior to assuming office," he should be handed a confidential message from Brezhnev.

The Politburo immediately approved this plan, and I was sent instructions on the same day to establish contact with Carter. I did so through Harriman at his home in Georgetown, calling on him as soon as the instructions arrived that very day, which happened to be his eighty-fifth birthday. Harriman looked good and was alert and ready to act. A few days later he told me Carter's reaction. Carter attached great importance to Soviet-American relations and to SALT and had instructed Harriman to tell me that he deemed it important for the cause of peace to meet Brezhnev; he believed summits could be useful on a regular basis, probably once a year. But before that he wanted to respond to requests for meetings from the leaders of America's European allies, who were responding to his campaign statements suggesting closer contacts. It was clear that Carter wanted first of all to restore America's influence in NATO. But Moscow did not want to wait too long and decided to continue to develop a dialogue, encouraged by Carter's readiness for an exchange of views.

Next I heard from Henry Kissinger, who had talked for six hours with Carter at his home in Plains, Georgia, on November 20 en route to a short vacation in Mexico. A large part of the conversation was devoted to Soviet-American relations, and Kissinger said he was somewhat surprised when Carter started off by asking the outgoing secretary of state to tell him in detail about "the Soviet-American showdown" in Vienna in 1961, when the newly elected President Kennedy had met Khrushchev for the first time. Carter's questions left Kissinger with the impression that the president-elect was apprehensive of the prospect of meeting his Soviet counterpart, although Carter did not say anything like that directly. (It turned out that someone in Carter's circle had been spreading stories that Moscow would try to throw the new president off balance by an early test. These had even reached Brezhnev, and he went out of his way to dismiss them as "evil fabrications" during a visit by outgoing Treasury Secretary William Simon early in December.)

Harriman came back to me on December 1 with a message from Carter to Brezhnev saying that as soon as he was inaugurated, he promised to act quickly to conclude a SALT agreement, and even though he was not bound by previous negotiations, he would take full account of all the work accomplished during the last two years. Carter hoped that the talks would be crowned with a summit meeting.

I became a little alarmed and remarked that I did not understand Carter's statement about not being bound by previous SALT negotiations, which had been officially conducted on behalf of the United States. Harriman replied that he, too, had asked Carter about this. Carter explained that he only wanted to reserve the right to suggest some possible new considerations or make corrections, especially if it would help to untie outstanding issues. Nevertheless, Moscow was put somewhat on guard.

Later, a grand dinner was organized in Washington to celebrate Harriman's eighty-fifth birthday. I was the only foreigner there. The American Establishment since the times of Franklin D. Roosevelt was amply represented, and there were many speeches. Harriman thanked the guests and recalled the most important moments of his life. Quite unexpectedly, he then delivered an emotional appeal for developing favorable relations with Moscow. "The Soviet leaders," he said, "also want peace with the United States. Only schizophrenics believe that the Soviets are preparing for a first nuclear strike. They, too, have children, grandchildren, and great-grandchildren whom they love as much as we love ours."

The Soviet leadership, still uncertain about Carter, wanted to be sure that we started off with no misunderstandings. To give detente a second wind through the SALT process, Brezhnev made a speech in Tula on January 18, two days before Carter's inauguration. He renounced the pursuit of military superiority and said the Soviet Union did not even approve of it as a matter of doctrine, because our policy was simply to maintain a capability strong enough to deter any aggressor from launching an attack on the Soviet Union (it was our first formulation of the principle of military sufficiency). He also defined detente in our terms: "Detente is above all an overcoming of the Cold War, a transition to normal, equal relations between states. Detente is a readiness to resolve differences and conflicts not by force, not by threats and sabre-rattling, but by peaceful means, at the negotiating table. Detente is a certain trust and ability to take into account the legitimate interests of the other." This speech was made as a signal of goodwill from Moscow to the new president.

## Carter's New Team

On January 4, 1977, Kissinger arranged a breakfast in the private room of his State Department office, which was so familiar to me, to meet his successor, Cyrus Vance. Only the three of us were there. This meeting of the outgoing and incoming secretaries of state with the Soviet ambassador was unprecedented, a point noted in the press.

The mood was light and friendly, and Kissinger began in a jocular tone by saying that he wanted to pass his responsibilities in the field of Soviet-American relations to the new secretary of state in the presence of the Soviet ambassador and make a few valedictory recommendations.

Kissinger stressed the importance of the confidential channel between the secretary of state and the Soviet ambassador in the maintenance of a direct dialogue. He informed Vance of our established system of off-the-record contacts, our periodic private meetings, our special direct telephone, and so on. Vance was conspicuously interested in these details and said immediately that he would like to preserve them. Needless to say, I accepted at once. It was Vance who suggested that we call each other by our first names as was customary in my relationship with Kissinger. "Henry" was to be replaced by "Cy."

Kissinger stressed the special role played by summit meetings in our relations. Vance commented that he and Carter shared that view and told me in strict confidence that they had even discussed possible dates, partly dependent on a new SALT agreement, which he declared was a crucial element in Carter's foreign policy.

Then Vance turned to a subject we all knew would be an irritant in our relations, human rights. He said he had been committed to the humanitarian ideas of human rights for many years, according to his conscience and religious convictions. I replied that Vance undoubtedly had every right to his personal convictions, but it was quite a different matter if his views or beliefs were brought to bear on relations between countries, especially when these beliefs led to direct interference in our domestic affairs. Kissinger cut in on the conversation to say that he would not carry such matters to the point of public confrontation and urged Vance to take care to avoid doing so. Vance dropped the subject, but it was clear he would raise it again.

President Carter received the diplomatic corps in the White House on January 22, two days after his inauguration, but the function was arranged in a somewhat unusual way. Ambassadors together with their wives entered the hall where the president stood with his wife to receive them. White House photographers took photographs of each group of four, for inscription later by the president. Each ambassador received a picture, which made a pleasant souvenir. But the procedure took up nearly all the time for the reception, since there were 130 ambassadors and chargés d'affaires in Washington.

As we were getting ready for the picture, the president asked me to give his personal thanks to Brezhnev for congratulations on his election sent through the unofficial channel. "I am looking forward to fruitful personal cooperation with the general secretary," he said, adding that he hoped to talk to me in private, but first he had authorized Vance to present some of his views to me two days later.

I could not help remembering my first conversations with four of Carter's predecessors in the White House. They would invariably start by mutual assurances of top-level cooperation. But as time passed, each of these assurances developed and transformed in different ways. Needless to say, I wondered how things would proceed with the new president, who was not a part of the Washington Establishment, which I knew rather well and was completely unknown in my country.

Vance and I had lunch on January 24 at my apartment in the embassy. As a first step in our relations he proposed to visit Moscow in March to explain to Brezhnev and Gromyko in person the policies of the new administration. The central topic would be SALT and other measures to curb the arms race. I welcomed the idea and said I would report it to Brezhnev with a recommendation that he accept it, which he did and set aside the dates of March 28–31.

Vance stressed that Carter was deeply convinced it was indispensable to limit and considerably reduce nuclear stockpiles. He said Carter considered really serious reductions in that area; for example, the Vladivostok figure of 2,400 carriers could be cut by half, or more. I immediately made a mental note that this would represent a really new approach to SALT; however, it was not yet in the form of a concrete proposal, although when the proposal eventually came it threw the arms talks into confusion.

This was the start of my long relationship with Vance. He was highly professional, methodical, consistent, and industrious. He prepared himself elaborately on each individual question. Unlike Kissinger, he avoided publicity and preferred to work without much ostentation. His attitude to the Soviet Union and his negotiations with it were unbiased. You could depend on his word, which was of no small importance during that complicated period. Vance coordinated all his moves with the president and carried out his wishes punctiliously. In this sense he had less room for maneuver than Kissinger.

At the same time Vance had an unshakable confidence in the correctness of his position, which led to his voluntary resignation in 1980 on a point of principle about the disastrous raid on Iran to retrieve the American hostages there. This only enhanced his authority and respect in the United States and abroad, but it also permitted his opponents within the administration to take advantage of his integrity and conscientiousness. He also commanded the deserved respect of his Soviet counterparts. During our meetings, whether private or official, his behavior was impeccably correct, even if the Soviet and American positions were poles apart. He never used sharp words, especially in public, for rhetorical effect. As a person, he was optimistic, lively, intelligent, and sociable, and I remember with pleasure my contacts with him, both official and informal. We still meet from time to time.

I also met with Brzezinski on January 24 to get to know the main protagonists of the new administration. It would be a serious mistake to claim that the administration's uneven course was only due to the different personalities of Vance and Brzezinski; in themselves they represented and reflected the mood and opinion of some of the main currents in American political life. Brzezinski praised Carter's political courage for telling the press on the second day of his presidency he was going to seek an agreement on SALT and take other measures to check the nuclear race in spite of the anti-Soviet campaign mounted by the American military. He then admitted that there was indeed too much noise over the Soviet military threat, which contributed to public support for the arms race.

In this connection he singled out, not without reason, the undue secretiveness of the Soviet Union about its armed forces, because it prevented the president from convincing the leaders of Congress, the military, and their supporters that there was no need for exorbitant military expenditures, especially in the field of strategic weapons. But the military proceeded from the argument of "the highest risk"; that is, they would always seek to maintain Soviet military potential at its maximum.

Brzezinski remarked with some amusement that when Carter began examining the background of SALT negotiations, he was amazed to discover that the entire discussion had for years been almost exclusively based on the American data covering both sides' strategic forces, and the Soviet side had furnished only a few figures on its own initiative because of the Kremlin's mania for secrecy. It would be a good idea, he suggested, if we made it a practice to exchange military data.

That was how I started out with Brzezinski (we called each other by our first names: Zbig and Tolya). It was less systematic than my relationship with Kissinger, although we met fairly frequently. He impressed me as an interesting, emotional, and highly intelligent interlocutor, although his outlook was markedly ideological. He preferred to discuss concepts and sometimes failed to take account of the concrete realities of international relations. He did not dwell on the details of Soviet-American negotiations and did not as a rule participate directly in them, although he was well informed. He did not go to Moscow, like Kissinger; that was Vance's job as secretary of state. I got the impression that Brzezinski also decided he would be unsuitable as a negotiator because he was so well known to Moscow as a long-standing critic of the Soviet Union and an anti-communist ideologist. Nevertheless that did not by any means diminish his influence on Soviet-American relations, in which he could have played a more positive role if Carter, rather than employ him as a principal opponent of the Soviet Union, had given him responsibilities for conducting concrete negotiations with the Soviet side on individual issues, as he did with China. Brzezinski and I followed the useful practice of informal conversations at breakfast in his office or our embassy. My wife and I, together with our granddaughter, visited his house several times, and we met his wife, who was an original sculptress, and his children. We also played chess, although our scores must remain a state secret.

## Face to Face with Carter

Two days after my meetings with Vance and Brzezinski, on January 26, Vance handed me the president's first private letter to Brezhnev, which outlined the main lines of his foreign policy toward the Soviet Union. Carter endorsed Brezhnev's Tula speech on disarmament and proclaimed that "my solid objective is to liquidate nuclear weapons completely." He named three areas in which progress toward that objective could be achieved: an immediate SALT agreement as the most important first step, another agreement on a duly verifiable and complete nuclear test ban, and a redoubling of efforts for progress on negotiations on the balanced reduction of conventional forces in Central Europe.

Carter also noted the need for the joint prevention of crisis in the troubled regions of the world, making particular mention of the Middle East. But he warned that he could not be indifferent to the freedoms and rights of man. In conclusion he wrote that he was looking forward to meeting Brezhnev in the spring to discuss both "our divergences and our common interests."

On the whole Carter's message was well received in Moscow because it seemed to open good prospects for negotiations on disarmament. At the same time his statement on human rights indicated that this question could become a constant subject of controversy.

On February 1, President Carter invited me to the White House. As usual, I entered the familiar Oval Office alone. Carter was somewhat surprised that I had not brought anybody to record our conversation, but I assured him that all his statements would be reported to Moscow accurately, just as I had done with other presidents. Joining us for the conversation were Vance, Brzezinski, and Reginald Bartholomew, a State Department official.

Since I was the only one on the Soviet side, I started out by remarking lightly that the American side had clear numerical superiority. I congratulated Carter on his election as president, and he was pleased to point out that he came from the very heart of America, and only in this country could an ordinary man become an "emperor," that is, the president.

In this connection I told him a historical anecdote. One of Napoleon's marshals, Bernadotte, was elected King of Sweden. The court physicians found it strange that he would never take off his shirt when they examined him. The whole court was mystified. It was not until his death that they discovered the reason. On his chest, dating from his days as a revolutionary soldier in France, they found a tattoo saying "Death to kings." Carter and his aides burst out laughing, and the atmosphere of the meeting became more informal.

Carter got down to business by saying he wanted me to tell the general secretary that he was sincere in his wish to ameliorate Soviet-American relations. Moscow probably had learned from previous presidential campaigns that Carter would forget many of his pledges. But the President said, "I want to stress that this will not happen"—especially with SALT. Above all he believed that the main thing we could do to reduce tension drastically, and therefore be able to cut military expenditures, would be to build mutual trust by agreeing to a minimal level of strategic weapons—just enough to be sure that each country had a sufficient number to deter an attack but not big enough to inspire fear that its arsenal could annihilate the opposite side in a first strike.

What would those approximate levels be? I was struck by this because the statement of a new president could mean a radical departure from his predecessor—and that is exactly what this turned out to be.

Carter replied that we could agree on a level of "some hundreds of carriers" instead of the existing 2,400, and we could reduce the number of MIRVed missiles proportionately within that limit. He said he had entrusted Paul Warnke, former undersecretary of defense under Johnson and now director of the Arms Control and Disarmament Agency, with working out the American position on SALT. Carter suggested that we exclude the Backfire bomber and the cruise missiles from the count, but I reminded him of our long-standing opposition. .

Then I raised the main question: What were we to do with the Vladivostok agreement? Did the president reject it? Carter did not give a direct answer, saying only that "a fresh look" could be useful. This turned out to be a radical position. He favored a quick and simple SALT agreement excluding cruise and Backfire bombers. Then he wanted to move to a SALT II treaty with major reductions in strategic forces, cutting the number of missles to several hundred—especially the heavy missiles that were the backbone of our forces. I made it clear to the president that any departure from the Vladivostok agreement would create serious problems in further arms limitations talks with the Soviet Union.

Looking back, I must admit that while Carter was far ahead of his time in proposing such reductions, they could not then have been realistically accomplished. Moscow felt Carter had taken a shallow approach to SALT negotiations and relations with the Soviet Union in general. We favored a gradual, stage-by-stage process of nuclear arms limitations and we were not yet ready to discuss more drastic cuts. It took us more than a dozen years and a radical change in the international political situation to accept this approach.

Carter himself had been advised of the Pentagon's opposition to his approach two days before his meeting with me. His secretary of defense, Harold Brown, had forwarded an analysis of cuts to 200 or 250 missiles for each country that had been drafted in conjunction with the joint chiefs of staff. The paper argued that such a low level would require a fundamental change in U.S. policy and could incur significant risk to U.S. national security; it would require almost total reliance on retaliation against population and industry to deter attack, and at these low aggregate levels, undue international influence could be exerted by one or several small "members of the nuclear community." Carter nevertheless decided to proceed.

He made a similarly sweeping proposal for banning all nuclear tests; even if Britain, France, and China demurred, the Soviet Union and the United States would conclude an agreement for two or three years and use it to bring pressure on the others to accede.

The president also took the initiative in raising the subject of human rights, assuring me that he had been as sincere about it in his campaign as he was about disarmament. So he asked for our understanding if he, unlike previous presidents, were to receive, say, the Russian writer Aleksandr Solzhenitsyn in the White House or issue a statement in support of some Soviet individual, which he gave us to understand could be about Andrei Sakharov, the dissident physicist who had been awarded the Nobel Peace Prize for his stand on human rights inside the Soviet Union. He promised not to abuse the right to make such declarations because he realized they might complicate our relations, but still he would do it from time to time according to his convictions.

I reminded him of Brezhnev's promise not "to test the new American president." I concluded, "You, Mr. President, have reacted to it favorably. Now let us not test Moscow, either. That will certainly benefit Soviet-American relations."

The president exchanged glances with Vance and Brzezinski and said he did not want to force a confrontation with us on that subject. It was dropped at that point but evidently would remain on the agenda and indeed was likely to become a major sore spot in our relations—as I reported to Moscow. Carter obviously believed he could harmlessly separate his public statements about human rights from the whole package of the U.S.-Soviet problems.

Throughout the conversation Carter was at ease and friendly. I was for the first time exposed to his famous smile, said to have the broadest grin of all the American presidents after Theodore Roosevelt. His expertise in all questions, his ability to grasp their essence at once, and his evident desire to understand the most crucial issues in detail were superior to those of President Ford. Just as evident was his desire to produce new original ideas of his own, though they were not always properly thought out. That put his interlocutors on their guard because it could affect the continuity of the American position in negotiations that had long been under way.

I reported the conversation to Moscow and recommended that we lose no time in developing good relations with Carter, although I warned of trouble ahead with SALT and human rights. Carter himself wrote in his diary favorably about our meeting.

## The Carter Crusade

The coming of every new American administration inevitably implies a certain change in the conduct of American foreign policy, and the Carter administration was no exception. But under Carter there probably was more controversy and heated debate among top officials than under any modern American president. That applied, first and foremost, to his principal lieutenants, Vance and Brzezinski, one a practical and balanced lawyer, the other a rather vigorous and pushy academic. Carter himself proved unable to give solid and consistent direction, reminiscent of the fable by the Russian poet Ivan Krylov about the incongruous team composed of a swan, a pike, and a crayfish.

Hence the constant struggle of Carter's main advisers to gain the president's ear. The Washington diplomatic corps followed closely that continuous tug-of-war with Brzezinski pulling ever more vigorously on his end of the rope. Hence also the zigzags in foreign policy, particularly in relation to the Soviet Union. While there was a consensus inside the administration that detente was a combination of "rivalry and cooperation," there was practical disagreement over which of the two elements was to be emphasized at any one time. Brzezinski regarded the global strategic struggle as paramount, but Vance thought it should not overshadow important areas of prospective cooperation.

The main handicap of the Carter administration was, if anything, its failure to see the long-term implications of all major problems taken as a whole. Both Carter and his advisers not infrequently sought to solve such problems spontaneously by snatching "hot questions" to be tackled separately and at once. Sometimes they turned to what they hoped would be quick fixes to buffer political and other pressures within the country, or to placate influential groups. Needless to say, this lack of clear priority did not often serve their own or the country's long-term interests.

At first Moscow was somewhat puzzled about what Carter was driving at in his relations with the Soviet Union. Judging by his vigorous correspondence with Brezhnev at the initial stage, his intentions seemed positive and constructive. But some surprise invariably seemed to interfere, leading to quite unexpected results and puzzling many supporters of normalization. The administration demonstrated that, except for SALT, it did not intend to treat relations with the Soviet Union as a priority, and even with SALT Carter's departure from the Vladivostok accords made matters more difficult.

Washington's relations with Moscow were greatly damaged by Carter's moralizing approach, which seemed ostentatiously calculated to enlist mass support in his country, meanwhile caring little for the damage it inflicted upon our relations. At the initial stage Carter probably did not mean to make human rights one of the most controversial issues of his policy toward Moscow. But his position was propagated through the mass media rather than traditional diplomatic channels. I came to the conclusion that Carter believed, erroneously as it turned out, that a formidable campaign against the Soviet Union would yield major gains in public relations without essentially damaging relations with Moscow because of our overriding aspirations for a SALT agreement.

But Moscow believed Carter was deliberately interfering in the Soviet Union's internal affairs in order to undermine the existing regimes in the Soviet Union and Eastern Europe. Carter proved incapable of seeing that, and his insensitivity to our concerns was responsible for the disagreements that followed. Whether or not Carter meant it, his policy was based on linking detente to the domestic situation in the Soviet Union. This represented an abrupt departure from the policy followed by preceding administrations, thus inevitably making his relations with Moscow tense. The Soviet leadership tried to reason with Carter through diplomatic channels and high-level exchanges of letters, all in vain. Public criticism of Carter by the Soviet Union did not help, either.

In a show of stubbornness and irritation, Carter rejected appeals from American public figures who became concerned about the aggravation of Soviet-American relations. He told one member of Congress that he saw no need to be concerned every time Brezhnev sneezed. Of course, Carter could also sneeze at Brezhnev whenever he chose. But then how could he expect to build long-term relations with Moscow? The two nations were sliding right past each other.

## SALT and Human Rights

SALT remained the centerpiece of Soviet-American relations as it had been under Ford and Kissinger, but the new president and his team were determined to come up with a better treaty than their predecessors. Carter did not like Kissinger's 1976 proposal to trade reductions in American cruise missiles for Russian Backfire bombers and thought the former secretary of state had struck a bad bargain; it provided for too many restrictions on cruise missiles (somehow counting air-to-surface cruise missiles within the totals of strategic arms) and too few on Backfire bombers. He also thought that the agreement set the overall ceilings for strategic arms too high. Hence he thought, as a temporary measure, we might consent to a quick agreement based on Vladivostok but excluding cruise and Backfire while negotiations proceeded on his bold approach. He knew that we categorically opposed excluding cruise missiles—where the United States had a big advantage—but when Vance went to Moscow that was exactly the proposal he brought.

On March 4 Carter sent Brezhnev a message to this effect via the hot line in order to bypass the Soviet Foreign Ministry, which Brzezinski thought was the main opponent of the president's new ideas. Carter meanwhile ordered a new "comprehensive proposal" with substantial reductions that in fact changed the structure of the Vladivostok agreement, including total overhaul of strategic bombers and multiple warhead launchers. The Soviet heavy missile force would also be cut in half from about 300 to 150. The basic line actually was that the United States was seeking substantial reductions in *existing* Soviet systems in exchange for marginal cuts in *future* American systems.

The White House brushed aside objections from some experts within the administration that new American proposals would not be negotiable with the Soviets. Negotiability with the Soviet Union was at that moment clearly not the criterion that interested President Carter and his key advisers (Vance probably excepted). They were looking for good publicity and for new negotiations with the Soviet Union on their terms. Moscow bluntly rejected these proposals and indeed their entire underlying concept. It took an additional two years of protracted negotiations to reach the SALT II compromise signed in 1979.

Brzezinski supported Carter's approach. Paul Warnke, the chief American negotiator at the SALT talks, criticized Carter in a private conversation with me; he said the president was too rash and eager to get too much done in too short a time without considering the interests of the other side. Vance and Warnke both favored a step-by-step approach, but they had to follow Carter's instructions. It was this controversy, between the two main parties, as well as within the American administration itself, that doomed a quick agreement on disarmament and damaged our long-term relations with Carter.

The other major irritant in our relations was the question of Soviet dissidents and human rights. After Andrei Sakharov wrote Carter to compliment his human rights policies, he replied with a personal letter and then received individual immigrant dissidents at the White House, causing growing indignation in the Kremlin. I came to the conclusion that while Carter really believed it was morally justified to defend human rights (and he deserves credit for that), he saw the question as a convenient propaganda weapon to keep on wielding in public at the expense of agreements on other major issues in Soviet-American relations, whether by design or not. There are good arguments for and against this policy, both moral and political. In the final analysis I believe it did more harm than good to our relations and even to the course of human rights in our country. These would have been more successfully enhanced through a combination of permanent and strong but essentially private pressure through the confidential channel, along with negotiations on issues of interest to the Soviet leadership.

In the middle of February I delivered a special oral note on the basis of a Politburo text angrily protesting State Department interference in the case of a leading Soviet dissident, Aleksandr Ginzburg, who was later arrested for currency offenses for receiving funds from abroad to support the Moscow group monitoring human rights under the Helsinki accords. The presentation was made to Arthur Hartman, who was acting as secretary of state during Vance's absence from Washington. Hartman said to me he had nothing to add to Carter's official position but remarked privately that, as a professional diplomat, he anticipated major difficulties in our relations on account of the new, activist administration policy supporting Soviet dissidents.

Then Vance privately voiced his growing apprehensions about the effect the official focus on dissidents could have on our relations, even the SALT negotiations. After I reaffirmed our position to Vance, he asked me rather unhappily what could be done to escape from the vicious circle. I replied officially and tersely: "Stop your interference in our internal affairs." What else could I say? The conversation produced no results.

Two days later I had a conversation with Brzezinski on the same subject. He did his utmost to justify Carter's posture on Soviet dissidents and human rights. As he wrote later in his memoirs, not without pride, from the very outset he had seen this issue as a splendid "opportunity to put the Soviet Union on the defensive ideologically."

But Carter himself failed to realize that the Soviet leaders would regard his position as a direct challenge to their internal political authority and even as an attempt to change their regime. Thus what was seen by the Soviet leadership as strictly a domestic issue spilled over to our relations with a new administration.

## Moscow Stands Firm

Inside the Kremlin, the reaction was indignation, irritation, and concern. At the end of February, the most influential members of the Politburo—Gromyko, the foreign minister; Ustinov, the defense minister; and Andropov, the head of the KGB—circulated a joint memorandum to their colleagues. With Vance due on a visit in March, the memo assessed Carter's latest messages and public statements as designed "to try to impose on us his own approach to the basic questions of Soviet-American relations even before we set about negotiating." It suggested that the Kremlin should signal the new president that pressure would be "unacceptable and futile." The three ministers were also skeptical about drastic cuts in nuclear missiles and accused Carter of raising the question for "political demagoguery and propaganda" to force Soviet concessions. In short, the memo suggested a tougher stance toward the new administration at the very beginning of its term, something very unusual in our relations with the United States for many years.

After a detailed discussion—and every one at the meeting was highly critical about Carter's human rights and SALT positions—the Politburo decided to send Carter another personal message from Brezhnev, which I handed to Vance on February 27.

This important letter largely determined the development of our relations with the new American administration, especially about SALT, and was marked by a hard and sometimes sharp tone. It warned him that progress in arms control would be hampered by abandoning the "balanced, realistic approach to new concrete steps by advancing utterly unacceptable proposals." It called Carter's stance "unconstructive" and asked flat out: "What is the meaning of the idea of drastic cuts in nuclear missile forces on both sides? . . . We hope to see a more balanced approach when Secretary of State Vance comes to Moscow."

On human rights, it was even more dismissive, accusing Carter of corresponding simultaneously with Brezhnev and "an apostate [Sakharov] who has proclaimed himself the enemy of the Soviet state and is against normal, good relations between the Soviet Union and the United States. We do not recommend taxing our patience in any area of international politics, including the sphere of Soviet-American relations. There is no dealing with the Soviet Union that way."

Vance read the letter twice. After a while he noted that the letter was a tough one but personally he welcomed plain language by a general secretary who "does not beat around the bush." Indeed, Vance admitted that he had told his president more than once that he treated certain international problems too lightly. He had warned Carter against believing that he could reach a SALT agreement without long negotiations.

"I tell him it can't happen, but . . ." Vance made a helpless gesture. He regretted this turn of events, especially when policy in the public eye was focused on human rights. "I hope that Brezhnev's straightforward letter will make the president look at things somewhat differently. Needless to say, I am not completely in agreement with the letter, but I think it is important that the president should receive exactly such a letter now."

Vance and I understood each other; after all, we were professionals.

Brzezinski reacted completely differently. In his memoirs, he calls the letter "brutal, cynical, sneering, and even patronizing" and, according to him, found that Carter agreed with him. The angry debate continued through a high-level exchange of letters. Carter replied to Brezhnev on March 4, showing little change in his agenda in a letter delivered to me not by Vance but Brzezinski, who insisted it was positive.

"Now, what do you think?" he asked me.

I remarked that it did not advance us much toward a solution of the

THE CONTRADICTIONS OF JIMMY CARTER ■ 397

main question, which we saw as preparing a new SALT agreement on the basis of the Vladivostok meeting. On March 16, I handed Vance another letter from Brezhnev to Carter, which reemphasized our disarmament positions and rejected "the attempts to raise questions going beyond the scope of relations between states" such as human rights. On that question, we had quickly reached an impasse.

These conversations offered no real possibility of compromise before I left for Moscow to prepare for Vance's talks. Brzezinski relayed to me the president's opinion that his first year in office offered the maximum political opportunity to reach a SALT agreement; I certainly agreed—but on what terms?

Vance meanwhile outlined to me in a very private way new approaches to SALT, which he most probably would carry to Moscow. They had two alternatives: either a comprehensive agreement, which the administration of course preferred, or a more limited version. Both these proposals would mean serious reductions, essentially at the expense of Soviet missiles, because all substantive cuts would come from the Soviet side. I warned Vance that they would most certainly would be rejected. The very fact of publicizing the basic content of American proposals before Vance presented them to the Soviet leadership was taken in Moscow as an indication that Carter's intentions were not serious, and that he was merely trying to achieve a propaganda victory. It was obvious that his mission to Moscow was doomed even before he left if he were to persist in these huge cuts, and my impression was that he himself was not sure of his own position but had to follow Carter's instructions.

It is exceedingly rare for an ambassador to tell a secretary of state so bluntly that his trip will be a failure if the president is going to insist on his proposals, but I also knew too well what he faced in Moscow. I reported our conversation to Moscow, so the Politburo had time to consider Carter's proposals properly and prepare our reply.

## The Price for Trying Too Much

Vance's visit to Moscow took place on March 28–30 and was a predictable failure on SALT.

"If the United States wants to reopen questions that have already been solved," Brezhnev told the secretary of state, "then the Soviet Union will again raise such problems as the American Forward-Based Systems in Europe and the transfer of American strategic weapons to its allies. The principal demand of the American administration is for half of Soviet heavy land-based missiles to be liquidated, and that is utterly unacceptable."

Vance had a third option—essentially splitting the difference between the other two—but when he cabled back to Washington proposing to submit it, Carter approved a message prepared by Brzezinski instructing him not to. Vance was completely discouraged, while Carter was hurt and angry that both his options had been so quickly turned down. Disapproving public statements and press conferences followed on both sides. The failure of Vance's mission drew much public attention and introduced distrust on both sides. What was the explanation for such a diplomatic disaster?

Some historians believe this was a case of a missed opportunity. Maybe so. But the Carter proposals, which suggested in a effect a wrenching departure from the long-established course of the talks, were not properly and patiently explained to Moscow through diplomatic or confidential channels before Vance's visit, although the White House had mounted a publicity campaign for them. The Soviet leadership had already staked its prestige on the Vladivostok accord as the basis for SALT II. Any attempt to change that understanding invited an explosion in Soviet-American relations, especially when Moscow was not yet ready to accept the idea of a practical reduction in its nuclear arsenal rather than an agreed set of limits.

I think the best possible scenario would have been for Vance to have brought to Moscow Carter's consent to conclude SALT II on the basis of the Vladivostok agreements, and for the Soviet side then to declare its readiness to discuss Carter's comprehensive proposal immediately afterward. With such a package we could have had an early summit, reopened the high-level direct dialogue, and cleared the air. That might also have opened the possibility of another and earlier SALT agreement than the one we finally did get at the 1979 summit in Vienna.

But bad strategy sinks good ideas. All these practical possibilities turned into lost opportunities at an early stage of the Carter administration and put Soviet-American relations on a more difficult path of mutual suspicion and mistrust. More than that, the new administration's comprehensive but not very well conceived proposals on SALT became a sort of yardstick which enabled the critics to condemn any reasonable, negotiable compromise as a capitulation to the Soviets. The president's evidently sincere but impulsive and radical proposals created additional difficulties in subsequent disarmament negotiations. Carter himself publicly and unnecessarily staked his personal prestige. His tactic was to reach for too much too soon, and it proved unsuccessful.

Carter's plan disrupted the Kremlin's hopes for continuity in Soviet-American relations, which were based on consolidating the gains of the Nixon and Ford administrations by the earliest possible signing of a SALT II treaty on the basis of the Vladivostok arrangements. Carter's rejection of those accords was a serious psychological shock for Brezhnev, who would have found it politically impossible to reassemble an arms control package even if he had agreed with Carter's ideas. Remember that the Vladivostok agreement had caused a debate within the Soviet leadership that Brezhnev won only by warning Marshal Grechko, the defense minister, that he was prepared to confront him before the Politburo. With this behind him, Brezhnev certainly could not deliver the Soviet military establishment again for Carter's even more radical proposals.

The collapse of Vance's mission did not surprise the Soviet leaders. I don't think it completely surprised Carter either. According to his diary, Carter already knew before Vance's departure for Moscow that Brezhnev found his latest SALT proposals "deliberately unacceptable." Why then did he nevertheless send them to Moscow with Vance?

## Trying to Pick Up the Pieces

On the day after Vance's departure from Moscow, with angry statements flying around from both sides, Brezhnev convened a meeting of the Politburo. What had happened was in a way the deliberate application of an angry shock treatment to the Carter administration. On the agenda for the meeting was only one question: How were we to deal now with the Carter administration. After the lesson, what next? The main line of our policy remained the restoration of good relations and the atmosphere of detente as best we could—first of all by putting the SALT negotiations back on the right track. But it was very important not to waste much time lest hostile feelings harden in Washington. So it was decided to let Brezhnev write Carter a conciliatory letter with an appeal for joint efforts to solve our complex problems.

On April 4 I called on Vance with a letter from Brezhnev to Carter welcoming his concrete suggestions and stating his "strong conviction that there cannot possibly be any insurmountable obstacles in solving even the most complex problems in relations between our two countries." As we talked, I saw that Vance was still deeply affected by his failure in Moscow. Because of my experience with other administrations in Washington, he asked for my private views on the present state of Soviet-American relations. I told him that, frankly speaking, they were the most unsatisfactory in the last ten years. In less than three months, I remarked that the Carter administration had contrived to impair relations with the leadership of the Soviet Union, which had from the very outset been trying to establish good relations with the new president. I asked Vance if the president really believed that the

Soviet leadership would have accepted the SALT proposals he brought to Moscow.

Vance made an attempt to justify Carter's approach by saying that the president had been eager for a dialogue and perhaps a compromise on the two options. But once the Soviet side rejected both of them, the president and Vance himself were utterly surprised, and his delegation was "shocked." All had been expecting a critical examination of their proposals by the Soviet side, rather than a short and quite unexpected rejection by the general secretary with hardly any explanation. Vance noted that Carter had lost his cool under the shock of the rejection and called congressional leaders together to make an emotional statement even before Vance had left Moscow. By the time Vance returned he had calmed down.

At the end of our conversation Vance reaffirmed that he would continue discussing SALT with Gromyko in Geneva in May (as was agreed during his visit to Moscow) and expressed the hope that he would also be able to discuss the Middle East. On the whole, it looked like the administration was looking for a way out of a blind alley into which it had driven—or at least that was the way Vance himself saw it.

More than that, meetings with president and some other officials during the next few days showed that a certain change in the administration's handling of SALT was under way. I felt a growing interest in a return to confidential diplomacy—to the "back channel"—regular, informal, unpublicized contacts. It looked as if a tacit recognition had taken place that Carter's public approach to SALT had not worked and it was worthwhile trying it Kissinger's way instead.

The president invited me to the White House on April 12 to discuss SALT. Evidently trying to avoid the subject of Vance's mission, he wanted to discuss ways of reaching a SALT agreement within several months. He wondered if we should resume the negotiations in Geneva. I replied that as long as there was no mutual understanding in principle on the highest level, delegations of disarmament specialists were unlikely to remedy the situation. Then why had Brezhnev and Gromyko rejected the American proposals without even so much as discussing them? asked the president. I replied that the Soviet leadership was profoundly convinced that the American proposals could not provide any basis whatever for agreement because they had been prepared without reckoning on the Vladivostok accord and carried a definite advantage to the United States. Carter asked me to assure Brezhnev he had not tried to cheat in order to obtain advantages for the United States. His sole idea was to start an exchange of views on a broad range of problems—first of all on really deep cuts in nuclear arsenals, which was his sincere aspiration.

The following day I met with Brzezinski in the White House, and we had a rather tense conversation. He appeared to have been one of the main sponsors of the proposals Vance brought to Moscow, and he argued heatedly that it was difficult to conduct negotiations when the American proposals were flatly rejected without detailed explanation. We circled around the well-worn arguments surrounding the proposals, and then I asked him what he thought was the most important thing to do for the future of Soviet-American relations. He rapped out a highly characteristic response: "Learn to live in conditions of continued disagreement."

But the public reaction toward the failure of Vance mission did not favor the administration. Carter himself was under pressure from America's allies to be more forthcoming. One way to resume contacts with Moscow was through an early Carter-Brezhnev summit. In his private correspondence with Brezhnev the president repeatedly referred to the possibility of a summit. The other way would have been to activate the confidential channel.

That is why, after the unsuccessful Vance visit, I had several confidential meetings with Vance and Warnke on instructions from Moscow. These were in fact negotiations and led us to a compromise, to a new, three-part SALT package late in April, which was finally approved by Gromyko and Vance after meetings in Geneva and again in Washington with Carter himself taking part.

What kept these arduous negotiations alive was a constant exchange of views among Vance, Brzezinski, Warnke, and myself through the confidential channel, although it was not as efficient as before. The negotiations were accompanied by active debate in the United States and on both sides of the Atlantic. Apart from the balance between our two central strategic systems, America's allies raised the question of the nuclear balance in Europe. Generally speaking, the conduct of the Europeans was rather uneven. Whenever the Soviet-American negotiations slowed down, they would criticize Moscow and Washington, but when prospects for agreement emerged, they would get nervous about being left out.

The United States did not remain heedless of its allies' appeals. The Joint Chiefs of Staff were developing plans to deploy land-based cruise missiles in a number of West European countries, including West Germany. That posed additional difficulties for the Soviet-American SALT negotiations. Shortly after that, the United States successfully conducted the initial flight tests of Pershing II, a new medium-range missile. If deployed in Europe, it could reach Soviet targets in eight to ten minutes, compared to twenty-five to thirty-five minutes for an intercontinental ballistic missile to hit the Soviet Union from the United States.

The arms race was taking another dangerous turn.

■ ■ ■

After the Moscow meeting I was visited by Henry Kissinger. I could almost feel his personal satisfaction at the Carter's disarmament failures. "For all his sincere desire for disarmament," said Kissinger, the trouble with Carter was that he tried to be different from all other administrations in every respect. In fact, he was so bent on doing things his own way that he would not even repeat the good moves made by his predecessors.

Kissinger believed that Brzezinski had also played a negative role, although he insisted he was in no way envious of his fellow academic and successor in the government. It was just that Brzezinski was a theoretician of anti-communism without practical experience in international relations. He prevailed on the president and his entourage by broad citations from the works of Marx and Lenin to encourage the human rights campaign and other ideas. In Kissinger's opinion all this was aggravating Soviet-American relations.

## Sounding Out a Summit

After Vance's failed visit to Moscow, the Carter administration seemed to start contemplating a summit to repair relations.

On June 3 Vance in confidence sounded us out about a meeting between Carter and Brezhnev, which both he and the president felt was the key to improving things. The question was when and where to hold it. The autumn seemed right, and if SALT negotiations were complete, the president would be pleased to receive Brezhnev in Washington to sign the agreement and conduct a broad exchange of views. If not, a summit could be held perhaps outside the United States. Vance emphasized that he was voicing these ideas with the president's knowledge, but not a single soul in the administration knew, or would ever know, about our conversation. He and the president were looking ahead rather than back and wanted Brezhnev's opinion completely off the record.

I welcomed the idea of a summit in principle, but stressed the need for a SALT treaty before the end of the year, which now was within our grasp. Brezhnev confirmed this in his reply of June 11, saying the way to the summit led through a SALT agreement in the fall or at least by the end of this year.

But Carter's response a week later did not include a SALT agreement. The president believed that the sooner his meeting with Brezhnev took place, the better it would be for Soviet-American relations. At that moment they were deteriorating, and the only way to reverse that and promote an early SALT agreement would be a high-level meeting in September or

October. I personally believed a summit could help retrieve the situation, and in my report to Moscow I recommended it.

Carter's request was discussed at length by the Politburo, which stuck to our SALT-first principle but decided to take a more flexible approach and watch for developments. Gromyko was the main supporter of this line; he would feel out Vance at their meeting in September, and that would also determine where we stood with SALT. In the meanwhile, Brezhnev replaced Nikolai Podgorny as chairman of the Presidium of the Supreme Soviet, removing another of his principal opponents of detente.

I continued to believe we were making a serious mistake in delaying the summit and linking it to a SALT agreement. But there was another major factor, as Gromyko explained later when I argued with him: Brezhnev, whose health was already poor, realized that without a guarantee in the form of a SALT agreement ready to be signed, it would be difficult for him to go through a long and complicated discussion with Carter on a broad range of issues. Gromyko believed likewise; in fact it was probably he who suggested it to Brezhnev himself.

Carter intervened personally on July 8, when I accompanied a prominent member of the Soviet Academy of Sciences, Vladimir Kyrillin, to the White House. He drew me aside to ask me to tell Brezhnev "that I really want to meet him. It is very important. I will be prepared to do so at any time we can quickly agree upon. Just let me know what time Brezhnev sees as convenient, and I will immediately renew my official invitation for him to come to the United States."

In late September Gromyko came to Washington for his traditional talks in conjunction with his annual visit to the United Nations General Assembly in New York. Both sides were in a mood to proceed toward the summit soon. At the same time they agreed to prepare a joint statement on the principles of a Middle East settlement. I participated in its preparation.

On October 1 Vance and Gromyko, acting in a closer spirit of cooperation in this area than at any previous time, issued a statement in New York calling for an international conference in Geneva under the joint chairmanship of the two countries. This surprise declaration was received with immediate hostility by Israel, backed by its powerful lobby in the United States, which rejected it because it would involve the Palestine Liberation Organization. Vance was attacked in the American press to his great discomfort, and I was told later by his adviser Marshall Shulman that there was "an angry call of dissatisfaction from the White House" (presumably from Brzezinski).

Carter retreated under the pressure and a few weeks later initiated separate negotiations between Sadat and Begin at Camp David but without

Moscow. Brezhnev wrote to the president protesting the exclusion of the Soviet Union from the Middle East peace process. I believe it was one of the missed opportunities for joint action during the Carter administration, and it grew out of American domestic controversies and the inconsistency of the administration itself. In general, I should note, the Americans wanted to talk with us about the Middle East only when they had problems in the region.

In Washington, important meetings took place at the White House with Carter on September 23 and 27, attended by Vance, Brzezinski, and others. Deputy foreign minister Georgi Kornienko and I backed up Gromyko on the Soviet side. After difficult discussions on SALT, Carter agreed after all not to insist on reducing Soviet heavy missiles and to limit them to the existing level of 308, with none for the United States. The Soviet side, in its turn, agreed to the major concession of a fixed limit for its MIRVed missiles program. Both sides agreed to limit the range of the air-to-surface cruise missiles by 2,500 kilometers. The Soviet Union agreed not to develop the Backfire into a strategic bomber. Restrictions were introduced on American cruise missiles carried aboard strategic bombers by including them in the number of MIRVed carriers. Since the SALT I treaty was to expire in October, Carter and Gromyko agreed to honor it until the SALT II Treaty came into force. Carter's radical plans had been quietly shelved in favor of more realistic progress.

Carter predicted an agreement on SALT within "a few weeks," but difficult negotiations lay ahead on the details, and they lasted well into 1979. From a purely technical point of view the talks were complex and time-consuming, but the main reason for the delay was that political forces in the United States, and even inside the administration itself, demanded more concessions from the Soviet side. The spokesman for these forces became Senator Jackson, who also made himself the champion of human rights.

During the meeting at the White House on September 23, Carter started a discussion of human rights in the Soviet Union that turned into a sharp exchange. Gromyko adamantly demanded that the United States stay out of Soviet internal affairs. Carter took up the defense of the dissident Anatoly Shcharansky, whose attacks on Soviet human rights policies had received wide publicity in the United States and were well known in Moscow, too.

"Who is Shcharansky?" Gromyko asked nonchalantly. Carter looked bewildered.

"Haven't you heard about Shcharansky?" he asked, amazed.

"No," Gromyko replied, as unperturbed as before.

Carter was at a loss and dropped the subject.

I must confess that at that moment I remarked to myself that Gromyko had shown great diplomatic skill in handling such a sensitive subject by feigning ignorance of it.

But as we got into the car to return to the embassy, Gromyko asked me in a low voice, "Who really is Shcharansky? Tell me more about him."

It was my turn to be amazed. It emerged that he knew little indeed about the Shcharansky case, because he had instructed his subordinates in Moscow not to bother him with what he called such "absurd" matters.

As Gromyko was about to leave Carter's office, the president gave him a surprise souvenir, a wooden set of toy Soviet and American missiles made to scale. Gromyko seemed somewhat unhappy at the gift, which graphically demonstrated that Soviet missiles were bigger in size and came in more varieties than the compact arsenal of American strategic missiles. Later he handed the set to me, saying he did not "play with toys." Carter's souvenir is still in my apartment.

The key figure in the battle for the eventual Senate ratification of SALT II turned out to be none other than our old adversary, Senator Jackson. We made one last try to win him over at the personal suggestion of no less than President Carter, who reminded me during a meeting with our visiting trade minister that the senator was also the key to the passage of trade legislation to expand Soviet commercial opportunities in the United States. The Chinese had already invited Jackson to visit, and Carter recommended Brezhnev approve an invitation for the senator to visit the Soviet Union. Brezhnev gave his consent.

In mid-November I visited the senator to convey the invitation in the name of a number of members of the Supreme Soviet. He was unmistakably pleased and asked if he could count on being received by Brezhnev. I replied that I believed he would have the opportunity to do so.

Jackson thanked me for the invitation saying he would by all means visit the Soviet Union the following March when the press of congressional business would be less. He insisted that he was seeking to improve relations with our country even if he did not agree with all Soviet policies. The main thing was to start a positive dialogue.

But the devil is in the details. The following March the senator invited me to his office, and I first saw his assistant, Richard Perle, a die-hard opponent of the Soviet Union who had drafted many of his critical statements about us. The previous day Perle had run into one of my associates at a diplomatic reception and told him the Soviet ambassador had made a smart move by inviting Jackson to Moscow. The senator was very pleased. But still, Perle himself strongly believed something would happen to thwart the visit.

As Perle saw me, he smiled and expressed the hope that the senator and

I would be able to arrange everything. But he said it rather sarcastically. On entering Jackson's office, I immediately felt the senator was somewhat embarrassed. It turned out that he was demanding permission from the Soviet government to hold a meeting with prominent dissidents in Moscow, which would be covered by the Western press. He conceded that he was setting complex conditions, but he justified his demand by saying he was a known defender of the dissidents and it would be strange if he did not meet them on a visit to Moscow.

I asked the senator who exactly he wanted to meet with in Moscow: Brezhnev or the dissidents. He said he would like to talk with them all. When asked if he realized that his new demands might make his visit difficult after all, Jackson said he well understood "Brezhnev's difficulties," but those remained his conditions.

Later I delivered Moscow's reply to Jackson: "In inviting the senator we proceeded from the need for constructive development in relations between our countries. Even mere considerations of tact seem to show the irrelevance of a situation where the senator makes his trip to the Soviet Union dependent on our agreeing to his meeting with a group of persons defiantly opposed to our system."

Jackson's visit never took place.

# II. Carter's Muddled Priorities

## Hung Up on the Horn of Africa

Linkage reasserted itself strongly in our relations with the Carter administration in 1978 under the influence of the president's moralistic views on human rights and Brzezinski's insistence on opposing communism wherever he found it. It represented a major effort by the United States to strengthen the restraints on the Soviet Union and thus on the scope of detente. Soviet conduct, at home and abroad, was thus held hostage to Moscow's hopes of a summit and the general pace of our negotiations on SALT, as ever the barometer of our relations. They fell to a low point during the first half of 1978 before recovering, although to nowhere near the level of the Nixon-Kissinger detente. But the principle of a controlled and selective detente did remain the governing force in holding the threat of a nuclear war at bay. Local conflicts were exploited by both sides at a much lower level of danger, but at a level of considerable diplomatic and political discord.

Conflict in the Horn of Africa between Ethiopia and Somalia was the focus of Soviet-American rivalry by early 1978. Somalia had long claimed Ogaden, an Ethiopian province populated by about two million Somali nomads. In 1974 the Ethiopian emperor Haile Selassie was overthrown by a military coup in Addis Ababa. After several years of internal struggle and maneuvers, Lieutenant Colonel Mengistu Haile Mariam emerged in February of 1977 not only as the leader but as a professed Marxist-Leninist. Somalia, to which the Soviet Union had supplied arms, meanwhile took advantage of Ethiopia's domestic instability and occupied Ogaden province.

Initially Moscow had maintained friendly relations with Somalia, signing the Treaty of Friendship and Cooperation in 1974; we supplied arms and they permitted Soviet vessels to use the port of Berbera on the Gulf of Aden and the southern approaches to the Red Sea. The United States had been Ethiopia's traditional ally until the overthrow of the emperor.

Fidel Castro and the Soviet president, Nikolai Podgorny, visited the region and tried to organize a progressive front or a federation incorporating Somalia, Ethiopia, and South Yemen, which faced the two nations across the

Gulf of Aden. But the attempt failed because Somalia stubbornly refused to return the occupied Ogaden province. A further advance of Somalian troops into Ethiopia was halted with Soviet and Cuban support for Colonel Mengistu's regime in Ethiopia. All of this led to a paradoxical reversal in the positions of the superpowers; in effect they exchanged clients.

As the Soviet Union shifted its support toward Ethiopia, the United States, in its turn, accelerated the process by stopping its military assistance and accusing Mengistu's new Ethiopian government of human rights violations. (The real reason, of course, was the overthrow of the emperor and a clear left-wing takeover.) Washington then turned its attention to Somalia, the more so because Somalia canceled its treaty with the Soviet Union at the end of 1977 after Moscow had refused to provide more arms. The Soviet Union then signed a similar treaty with Ethiopia. By the end of 1977 about two thousand Cuban troops and one thousand Soviet military advisers were sent to Addis Ababa. Somali troops were forced to retreat in Ogaden province but still held a considerable part of it.

From the long-term geopolitical point of view, the developments in that part of Africa were unmistakably of local importance, and the political leadership in Moscow regarded them as such. Nevertheless, the Soviet and Cuban interference and the deployment of a Cuban task force in yet another African country just two years after they had gone into Angola, plus Soviet transports and other logistic support, caused an uproar in the West, especially the United States. Suspicions were aroused that the Soviet Union had adopted a new strategy of challenging and outflanking the West in the Third World. This quickly became a priority in relations between the Carter administration and Moscow for much of the year, further complicating our relations and provoking serious discord within the administration itself. The most aggressive member in pressing his suspicions was Brzezinski, and his principal opponent was Vance. In his memoirs Vance explained that he did not see Soviet activity in Africa as part of some huge scheme but simply an attempt to take advantage of a local opportunity—but domestic political pressure to counter Soviet and Cuban intervention prevented the administration from dealing with them as local conflicts.

Linkage nevertheless demanded slowing down the SALT and other disarmament talks and imposing restrictions on trade and high-level visits. Vance opposed it as counterproductive, but linkage was constantly increased.

In my capacity as ambassador I was fairly familiar with the sentiments of the Kremlin leadership concerning the developments in that part of Africa. I can say with confidence that Vance was right in the sense that the Kremlin had no far-reaching global plans in that region. But having suffered no major international complications because of its interference in Angola,

Moscow had no scruples about escalating its activities in other countries, first Ethiopia, then Yemen, a number of African and Middle Eastern states, and, to crown it all, in Afghanistan.

Each of these situations of course had its own local peculiarities. But underlying them all was a simple but primitive idea of international solidarity, which meant doing our duty in the anti-imperialist struggle. It made no difference that often it had nothing to do with genuine national liberation movements but amounted to interference on an ideological basis in the internal affairs of countries where domestic factions were struggling for power. Some in the Kremlin were flattered at our country's involvement in faraway conflicts because they believed it put the Soviet Union on an equal footing with the United States as a superpower. But that was a hare-brained thought.

In order to understand our sometimes bizarre policy in the Third World, it is important to know how the decision-making mechanism in foreign affairs operated in the Kremlin. On a day-to-day basis it was the Foreign Ministry who gave recommendations for dealing with current problems. In practice that mainly meant Gromyko himself, and as a rule all his suggestions were accepted. He was a recognized authority, especially in dealing with the West and the United States in particular, and he stubbornly defended his position in this field during Politburo meetings. Overall he was a cautious man who opposed any serious confrontation with the United States if the vital interests of the Soviet Union were not involved.

But the Third World was not his prime domain. He believed that events there could not in the final analysis decisively influence our fundamental relations with the United States; that turned out to be a factor he definitely underestimated. More than that, our Foreign Ministry traditionally was not really involved with the leaders of the liberation movements in the Third World, who were dealt with through the International Department of the party, headed by Secretary Boris Ponomarev. He despised Gromyko; the feeling was mutual.

All this work in the Third World, especially with liberation movements, was coordinated by the very influential second man in the Politburo, Mikhail Suslov, who for many years was in charge of the party's ideological work and its international activity. He was convinced that all struggle in the Third World had an ideological basis: imperialism against communism and socialism. Under the slogan of solidarity, he and his zealous followers in the party managed to involve the Politburo in many Third World adventures. The KGB supported him in this because many of the party contacts in that area were handled through their agents. The military was prepared to send arms and advisers but not Soviet troops.

Many professional Soviet diplomats opposed our deep involvement in these remote areas, but who would openly object when all this was done in the name of the party? Some diplomats, myself included, tried on their own in informal conversations to minimize the damage in the West. We explained to our Western colleagues that all these actions were spontaneous and not necessarily part of any Soviet grand plan to deliberately undermine the world positions of the West. But this was hardly persuasive when viewed against our adventurous involvement in remote regions, and it raised a very negative reaction in the United States.

I tried to explain to Brezhnev, Suslov, Andropov, Ponomarev, and others how our Third World adventures undermined our relations with Washington. Their own reaction was always the same: Why does the United States raise such complaints about us when they are themselves so active around the globe?

I happened to be present at several meetings of the Politburo dealing with Angola, Somalia, and Ethiopia, and I can report that American complaints were not even seriously considered. The Politburo simply did not see them as a legitimate American concern and not a major factor in our relations with Washington. Nor was the strategic military value of those Third World countries actively discussed at the Politburo; they were too far from the Soviet Union. But some of our top generals headed by the Defense Minister Grechko and Ustinov toyed with the idea: they were emotionally pleased by the defiance of America implied by our showing the flag in remote areas. I also suspect that they privately played on Brezhnev's vanity on the theory that all this somehow demonstrated the Soviet Union was already a world power to be reckoned with. That helped explain why Brezhnev occasionally supported some of our adventures for which the ideological justification was provided by Suslov, but only when Brezhnev felt he could be sure that they would not lead to direct confrontation with the United States.

Vance raised the subject of the conflict between Ethiopia and Somalia during private conversation with me on January 14. I told him Moscow rejected the American thesis of Soviet involvement and that for a peace settlement, Somali troops must withdraw from Ethiopia. Anti-Soviet groups and the press in the United States meanwhile were increasingly anxious to link our activities in the Horn of Africa with SALT and other issues. Asked about this linkage at a press conference on March 2, President Carter denied that it existed but said it was Soviet behavior that caused the link to other policies. On March 17 Carter spoke at Wake Forest University about "an important reassessment" of American military strategy caused by the Soviet Union's "sinister propensity" to interfere in local conflicts.

Our embassy warned Moscow that Washington saw such things in global terms even when not justified, and that events in the Horn of Africa were beginning to look like those in Angola in 1975, "providing all kinds of opponents of our good relations with ammunition to keep these relations under fire." The report also pointed out that Cuban investment in the region remained a very troubling aspect for the Americans. The embassy recommended that Moscow try to view Africa through the prism of its potential to damage Soviet-American relations. But Moscow continued to dismiss American reaction as just another series of propaganda attacks in the framework of the continuous "natural" ideological struggle between us.

This different approach became especially evident during an important conversation I held with Vance on January 31. He said nervously that some Soviet combat and landing ships were concentrated in the Red Sea, and that undermined his own arguments for maintaining good relations with Moscow. He added: "Let me tell you straight that there are people close to the president telling him that the latest Soviet actions are a direct personal challenge to the president, a test of his firmness, and he should show the Russians he is not to be trifled with."

I understood that Vance's sense of alarm about public opinion in the United States was well-founded. But the only thing I could honestly do was explain to him that Moscow was not out to test the president's will. During 1977 the Politburo tried several times to mediate unilaterally between Ethiopia and Somalia but failed. It was clear that our countries were involved in a real conflict in the area, and maybe our mutual involvement could be used to help obtain a settlement. But how should we go about it?

One attempt was made by Moscow. In January of 1978 Gromyko officially proposed joint U.S.-Soviet mediation for the Horn of Africa. But the Carter administration dismissed this proposal because, as Brzezinski explained in his memoirs, it would have "legitimized the Soviet presence" there and "pointed to a condominium" between the U.S. and USSR. Here he sounds very much like Henry Kissinger who used the same slogan against Soviet participation in a Middle East settlement. The Carter administration also turned down another Soviet suggestion to resume our suspended talks on limiting arms in the Indian Ocean area. More missed opportunities to act together in cooperation in the Third World.

A month after meeting with Vance I discussed African problems with Brzezinski. All his pronouncements were focused on just one thing, Carter's growing concern. He repeatedly stressed that Soviet and Cuban military presence in Ethiopia posed a threat to the interests of the West and endangered the safety of the transport links for oil between the Middle East and the United States and Western Europe. He said they could be "cut off."

I asked him how he thought the Soviet Union could actually cut the oil routes. Would it attack and sink American tankers? That would constitute a direct act of war. Did the White House really have such absurd ideas? Brzezinski admitted that the White House did not give much credence to such a scenario, but such oversimplified concepts were widespread in the Congress and the American media. But he made it clear anyway that our presence in that area was not welcomed.

Overall anxiety was mounting. At a press conference on March 24, Vance said Soviet-American relations had "entered a stage of instability." Carter decided to try to get in touch with Fidel Castro secretly. Paul Austin of Coca-Cola confided to me that he had flown to Cuba on a secret mission for Carter to meet the Cuban leader and tell him in the name of the president that Cuban activity abroad prevented the United States from continuing the process of normalization between Washington and Havana, which Carter insisted was one of his goals. Carter's message was that the main stumbling block to normalization was Cuban military activity in Africa, particularly in Ethiopia. Castro had asked him to tell President Carter that not a single Cuban soldier would cross the Somalian border. But at the same time Fidel had refused to make any promises in general about Africa to the Americans, declaring he would support revolutions and national liberation movements everywhere.

In retrospect, I cannot help being surprised at the amount of energy and effort spent almost entirely in vain by Moscow and Washington on these so-called African affairs. Twenty years later no one (except historians) could as much as remember them. Even when American marines were sent to Somalia in 1992 by George Bush to join United Nations forces to help feed the starving there, no one in the U.S. government and only a very few in the press remarked that the seeds of the anarchy then prevailing in Somalia had most probably been planted by the great powers' engagement there fifteen years before. Somalia was only one of a number of countries whose local quarrels became enmeshed in the Cold War—Angola, Ethiopia, Afghanistan, among them, and all of them worse off for their involvement with the two superpowers.

We made a serious mistake in involving ourselves in the conflict between Somalia and Ethiopia and in the war in Angola. Our supply of military equipment to these areas, the activities there of Cuban troops, and especially our airlift to get them there, persuaded Americans that Moscow had undertaken a broad offensive against them for control over Africa. Although that was not really the case, these events strongly affected detente.

## Confusion Grows about Detente: Cooperation or Confrontation?

The Kremlin began to worry about the threats to detente, but still underestimated them. At the beginning of May the Politburo held a special session to discuss the mounting American attacks. I joined the discussion and tried to paint an objective picture of Soviet-American relations, especially how Soviet actions were viewed in America. It was not easy to convince the Politburo, as ideological prejudices remained very strong.

Members of the Politburo lived in the certainty that a historical process was under way: the collapse of the old colonial empires and general weakening of the capitalist system. These were not of our making, declared Suslov with Brezhnev's support, because they were "historically inevitable." For ideological reasons we should support this process whenever possible, but this did not mean that we deliberately were trying to undermine or even infringe on American interests: it had nothing to do with the state relations between two governments and two countries. Such was the abracadabra of the official reasoning at the top of Soviet leadership. Of course, some of them who dealt with the outside world, such as Gromyko, Andropov, and Kosygin, understood that the situation was not that simple, but when confronted with the heart of our party ideology they often preferred not to argue too strongly against it.

In this connection it is interesting to note that the final decision of that meeting was not to adjust or correct our actions in the Third World or in the field of human rights but "to improve the explanation" of our views and actions and "to defend our positions more actively." That is, there was nothing wrong with our policy, only our propaganda.

Brezhnev, in a bid to protect detente from growing Western criticism, publicly denied accusations about Soviet intervention in the Third World, arguing that there was no contradiction between detente and the Soviet Union's relations with the "countries freed from colonialism." Simultaneously, he defended detente as the basis of relations between the Soviet Union and the United States. While there was no doubt that Brezhnev was confident in the soundness of his own views, our disputes with the United States were really grounded in the contradictions between Soviet and American approaches to the notion of detente, and these led to even more divergent interpretations of Soviet activity in local conflicts. To the Kremlin leadership, detente was also part of the inevitable course of history, especially now that Moscow had been accepted as an equal nuclear superpower with a global role. But to the American public, Soviet policy in the Third World and toward dissidents was seen simply as unjustified and aggressive. It was an angry view whose force was still evidently underestimated by the Kremlin.

The administration also had a view of detente, but it was more clouded. Oversimplifying somewhat, for the Carter administration detente was based on a formula comprising cooperation and rivalry; Vance leaned toward seeking new fields of cooperation, while Brzezinski paid more attention to the points of rivalry. The secretary of state believed there should be no overestimating Washington's differences with Moscow over Angola and the conflict in Ethiopia and Somalia lest they overshadow the principal questions of Soviet-American relations, above all the limitation of strategic arms. By contrast, the national security adviser saw nearly all Soviet political actions as intrigues directed against American interests and therefore was more inclined for struggle than cooperation.

These disagreements were an open secret among my fellow diplomats. Multiple information leaks came from the White House itself, mostly from Brzezinski's supporters. Foreign ambassadors therefore could not help wondering how President Carter could possibly use the services and recommendations of persons so different in their character and views. Could that explain the zigzags and lack of definite priorities in Carter's foreign policy? What was his own position, after all?

Clarity was not enhanced as Carter also revived his relations with China, playing this card in the hope of bringing some pressure on the Soviet Union. This was actively promoted by Brzezinski, who was sent to Beijing on a diplomatic mission hoping to impress Moscow and consolidate its suspicions. That was precisely what Vance did not want to do.

Brzezinski's visit on May 21–23 came at a critical juncture in Soviet-Chinese relations. Beijing had just rejected Soviet attempts to start negotiations about our border dispute. There had been clashes along the Soviet-Chinese border. Brezhnev and Ustinov had journeyed to the Far Eastern districts of the Soviet Union to inspect our defense capabilities and strengthen them. Brzezinski was clearly enthusiastic about his talks in Beijing about American strategic plans, technological aid, and plans to counter Soviet policy by cooperating in Africa and elsewhere. He went as far as to make direct public attacks on "the Polar bear."*

Although Brezhnev publicly attacked the "cynical" use of the China

---

* According to a recently released State Department document, Carter gave Brzezinski secret instructions for talks with the Chinese leaders. Among other things he was to tell them that "I [Carter] take seriously the Soviet action in Africa and this is why I am concerned about the Soviet military buildup in Central Europe. I also see some Soviet designs pointing toward the Indian Ocean through South Asia, and perhaps to the encirclement of China through Vietnam (and even perhaps someday through Taiwan)." I do not know whether Carter himself believed in all these scenarios or he was just trying to impress the Chinese, but this perfectly showed his state of mind at that time.

card against us as "a short-sighted and dangerous policy," it was also decided to improve relations with Washington. Gromyko met with Carter in Washington on May 27 and proposed a number of major Soviet concessions on SALT, agreeing to freeze the number of warheads carried by Soviet heavy missiles (no more than ten warheads on each SS-18, rather than the twenty or thirty they could carry). They reviewed the draft agreement on SALT. Some progress was achieved, yet they failed to finish the draft.

Unfortunately, an acerbic and fruitless discussion was initiated by the president on human rights in the Soviet Union and Cuba's involvement in Africa. On his return to the embassy, Gromyko, who was famous for his reserve, tersely but strongly cursed Carter for his persistence in pursuing questions that we regarded as the internal affairs of the Soviet Union.

Gromyko had a separate long meeting with Vance on May 27. Both agreed frankly, confidentially, and without exchanging propaganda that relations were reaching a dangerous impasse. Two days later, as I learned afterward, Vance then wrote a confidential memorandum personally urging Carter to review Soviet-American relations because his administration actually held two different viewpoints on the subject. He warned that the advice the president was receiving from some senior officials (Brzezinski) could provoke tough Soviet countermoves if taken too far. For example, the human rights campaign could push the Soviet Union into cracking down on dissidents even more harshly—and what would the administration do then? He criticized the use of the China card against us, but he insisted that in the Third World the United States held "nearly all the cards," and the administration should be more self-confident.* He opposed linking Soviet behavior there to matters of "fundamental interest to ourselves," such as SALT. This memorandum represented, in my opinion, an important attempt to forestall the negative shift in American foreign policy that he foresaw if Brzezinski's views prevailed. But the national security adviser, taking advantage of his daily briefing of Carter, continued to press for a tougher policy, using our bilateral relations to step up pressure against the Soviet Union.

Fourteen members of the House Committee on Foreign Affairs wrote Carter asking him to end the confusion arising from the disagreements within the government. Carter decided to make a policy statement about Soviet-American relations. He privately asked Brzezinski and Vance for

---

* In all fairness the image of Soviet expansion of influence in the Third World in the 1970s was blown out of proportion in the United States. Soviet gains were more than offset by a chain of geopolitical losses. (Soviet influence was replaced by American in Egypt, Sudan, Somalia, North Yemen, Guinea, Zaire, and Chile, to say nothing of the growing American politico-military tie with China.)

drafts of his speech separately. The final version was prepared by Carter himself and delivered on June 7 at his alma mater, the U.S. Naval Academy at Annapolis. It represented an odd mixture of detente and confrontation, of common sense and bellicose rhetoric, of views held by both Vance and Brzezinski.

Carter began by stating that detente between our two countries was the basic element of peace and should be clearly defined and made really reciprocal. Praising America's democratic aspirations and principles, Carter in the same breath challenged the whole Soviet system and sharply criticized Soviet policy on human rights. "We want to increase our collaboration with the Soviet Union," he said, "but also with the emerging nations, with the nations of Eastern Europe, and with the People's Republic of China. We are particularly dedicated to genuine self-determination and majority rule in those areas of the world where these goals have not yet been attained." And he concluded his speech with his main thesis: "The Soviet Union can choose either confrontation or cooperation. The United States is adequately prepared to meet either choice."

It was not quite clear just exactly what the president had in mind. The American press described it as a challenge to the leaders of the Soviet Union. The Soviet Union and many in the United States had the impression that Carter was leaning toward a policy of confrontation rather than detente. In an article approved by the Politburo, the Soviet newspaper *Pravda* said the president's speech showed the aggressive hand of Brzezinski and threatened the return of the Cold War.

On the very next day after the president's speech Vance told me hesitantly that the president hoped Moscow would find it well balanced. I bluntly told him that in my personal opinion the speech could be described as anything but balanced. In the very frank conversation that followed Vance said that there was a psychological underlay to the whole debate and the president's public approach to the Soviet Union during the past weeks—Carter's anxiety about not being regarded as a firm and resolute president, and not just in Moscow but in his own country. His anxiety was partly based on the sharp decline in the opinion polls and the generally negative public reaction to his presidential performance. The image of an irresolute and vacillating politician, Vance said, was largely created through his failure to persuade Congress to pass a number of his important bills, his acceptance of much lower reductions in the strategic arms ceilings, and his waffling about whether to deploy the neutron bomb, a new invention that would kill people but not destroy property. This was all in sharp contrast to the highly trumpeted declarations at the start of his presidency. His domestic reputation was also severely damaged by the struggle to ratify the Panama Canal Treaty at the cost of a great deal of his personal political capital. Moreover, Vance said Carter believed that the image of a weak and ill-starred president was the reason behind "Moscow's tough challenges." Suspicions therefore were mounting that Moscow was scheming to gain advantage.

In Moscow the Politburo was meeting at about the same time to hear a speech by Brezhnev warning of a serious deterioration in the international situation, which he blamed on "the growing aggression of the foreign policy" of the Carter administration, including the sharp anti-Soviet statements by the president himself and his close colleagues, above all Brzezinski. He said Carter seemed to be falling under the usual combination of anti-Soviet types and the military-industrial complex, but was also intent upon struggling for election to a second term as president under the banner of a return to the Cold War. This line was also influencing U.S. policy toward the NATO, Africa, and China, Brezhnev declared, and he proposed to publish throughout the Soviet press a long and serious article along these lines, and arrange for a declaration of Warsaw Pact governments accusing the latest NATO Council meeting of intensifying the arms' race. The Politburo agreed.

New and alarming signals meanwhile came from Congress. Senator Frank Church, a powerful member of the Senate Foreign Relations Committee who would later become its chairman, told me that there had been "virtually no political question over the past two or three months on which the administration has tried to overcome congressional opposition without playing the anti-Soviet trump." Church said the administration's arguments all rested on the hackneyed claim of Soviet expansionism, pointing out that for once it was not Congress but the White House that depended, voluntarily or not, on primitive anti-communism.

"I am telling you this," Church said, "because the atmosphere created by the White House in Congress leads to growing suspicions and jingoism among senators concerning the Soviet Union. Clouds are gathering in the Senate over the SALT agreement. Unless the administration takes urgent steps the Senate may not ratify the agreement." He said it would be best to postpone the vote on the SALT treaty until after the 1978 congressional elections to allow Soviet-American relations to settle down. Indeed, in July Senate Republican Leader Howard Baker publicly called for a suspension of all negotiations with the Soviet Union. Soviet interference in Africa, he said, was more important strategically than the limitation of strategic nuclear weapons.

## Downhill into Deadlock

For the remainder of the year our relations became increasingly aggravated. Virtually every issue, whether it was the dissidents in the Soviet Union, the

Middle East, a scare over Cuba, or playing off China against us, grew more entangled in a web of misunderstanding and suspicion, with matters made worse by the rivalries within the Carter administration, whose effects we could not escape.

Our discussions became more clouded by Soviet human rights abuses. I had several uncomfortable conversations with Vance and Brzezinski on the administration's attempts to trade imprisoned Soviet dissidents for two Soviet employees of the United Nations who were arrested in May on charges of espionage and sentenced to fifty years in prison six months later. The discussions took a great deal of time and exacerbated the working relations between the embassy and the State Department and, worst of all, relations between our governments. As a goodwill gesture, Vance proposed trading the two UN employees for Shcharansky, who was charged with spying. All would then be spared trials. I personally supported this idea and recommended it to Moscow. Marshall Shulman, Vance's adviser on Soviet affairs, told me that the trade was President Carter's idea. But Moscow quickly rejected it. This intransigence puzzled me because the deal seemed a reasonable way for both sides out of the deadlock. It could only be explained by a strong sense of irritation among the Soviet leadership about Carter as a person.

With the trials of Shcharansky and Ginzburg approaching, Vance turned to me again on July 7 to express deep concern over their implications for our bilateral relations. He also expressed his deep personal regret that Moscow planned to stage the trials just as he would be meeting with Gromyko in Geneva on July 12–13. If the trials were not postponed for a week or so, he would be placed in a delicate domestic position and Carter might not let him meet with Gromyko under the circumstances. The next day he issued a statement saying the trials "could not but affect the climate of our relations."

Two days later Shulman told me Carter had consented to that meeting but planned a strong statement about the trials. Simultaneously it would be announced that his science assistant, Frank Press, would cancel a planned visit to the Soviet Union. Press had already warned me that a "high-level decision" had already been made for him to refuse an invitation from our Committee on Science and Technology if Shcharansky went to trial. Shulman said Ambassador Toon had sent a cable from Moscow insisting on canceling the Vance-Gromyko meeting. This cable had touched off a debate right in the president's office. Most of those present were ready to support Toon. Vance was dead against a cancellation, while Brzezinski suggested a postponement. Carter was of two minds. The matter was decided after Vance declared that if the president canceled the meeting, the summit between Carter and Brezhnev might be indefinitely postponed.

A series of other, lesser official and scientific visits and contacts were canceled, however, and late in July President Carter's mother visited the Vatican and handed Pope Paul VI a personal letter from her son calling upon the Roman Catholic Church to take a more active part in the struggle for human rights in the Soviet Union and other socialist countries. In short, our relations entered even deeper into deadlock amidst the growing hostility between Carter and the Kremlin leaders, to say nothing of the disagreements and struggles for power among Carter's own entourage.

When Gromyko and Vance met in Geneva on December 21–23, new questions emerged to delay the conclusion of the SALT agreement. Vance came with instructions from Carter to take a tougher position on the monitoring of telemetric information from missile tests to help verify compliance with the agreement. After discussing the matter with Gromyko, Vance tried to adjust the American position to a compromise proposed by Gromyko. He then cabled to Washington. The next day he received a phone call from Brzezinski while actually meeting Gromyko at our mission. Using an ordinary open telephone line so we could hardly help but know the full details, Brzezinski told Vance that Carter was determined to stick by his decision and would reiterate it to Brezhnev at the summit. He added that he had the support of Defense Secretary Harold Brown and CIA Director Stansfield Turner. Twice Vance attempted to defend his compromise, but to no avail. The whole scene was rather embarrassing to us, as if Brzezinski was giving the secretary of state strict instructions.

# III. The Summit with Carter

*Reviving the Arms Race*

An intractable domestic economy, the decline of America's international prestige, and a president who appeared increasingly unable to deal effectively with either contributed to the rise of a sense of frustration within the United States during the latter part of President Carter's term in office. Nationalist, ultra-conservative, and extremist views, concepts, and recipes were widely propagated for the United States to escape from its problems, mostly by stepping up the militarization of its policies and the tempo of the arms race. This led to chauvinism and pronounced anti-Soviet pressures on foreign policy. Every single event that took place throughout the year was used for those ends: the Iranian revolution and the seizure of the American hostages, the Panama Canal Treaty, Vietnam's troops in Cambodia, the revolution in Nicaragua, oil problems and the weakening of the dollar, the situation in the Middle East, the SALT II Treaty, a Soviet brigade in Cuba, nuclear missiles in Europe, and finally the upheaval in Afghanistan. One way or another, many American foreign policy difficulties and setbacks were blamed on the Soviet Union in a new version of an old-fashioned Red scare.

There also arose a thesis that the United States had fallen behind the Soviet Union militarily, which was simply not true. From the administration there appeared widespread geopolitical schemes or what Brzezinski termed "geostrategic" concepts and theories about the so-called "vital spheres" of American interests threatened by the Soviet Union, such as the region extending from the Hindu Kush through Iran, the Middle East, Turkey, and ending at the Bosporus in what he grandiosely drew as an "arc of crisis" that cut a swath from Pakistan to Ethiopia, encircling the oil states of the Middle East. It made for excellent propaganda and ended up in the vocabulary of numerous commentators and on the cover of *Time* magazine.

The peculiarity of the political situation in the United States was that the ultra-right appealed to mass sentiments more skillfully and vigorously than other political forces, and this damaged the process of detente. The Carter administration responded by continuing its buildup of the armed forces, and this assumed new proportions because of commitments to increase military spending for years to come and at a rate unprecedented in peacetime, which was only accelerated even more after the election of Ronald Reagan.

The Soviet leadership increasingly regarded Carter as a hostile president and contributed its own share to the reviving arms race. The Soviet military-industrial complex gladly stepped up its arms program. The Soviet military presence in Africa and other local conflicts ultimately grew into direct military intervention in Afghanistan. The trials of dissidents in the Soviet Union also contributed to the growing anti-Soviet sentiments in the United States.

The instability of the general political climate in Soviet-American relations had a negative effect on disarmament talks apart from SALT. Trade, economic, cultural, and other links between the two countries suffered after they had become an important aspect of our intergovernmental relations following great effort on both sides for a number of years. The climax was reached with extensive sanctions announced by Carter on January 4, 1980, in response to the introduction of Soviet combat troops in Afghanistan. The sanctions included suspending the Senate debate on the SALT II Treaty and curtailing or canceling a number of agreements in many fields of our bilateral relations. The Carter administration declared that Soviet-American relations had entered a long period of confrontation that would last until the withdrawal of Soviet troops from Afghanistan.

Early in 1979 Vance invited me for a general review of the diplomatic horizon. Our conversation took place on January 5 and began with the president's reply to our recent complaints about remarks by leading American officials who systematically described the Soviet Union as an enemy or a potential enemy. Vance said the president had taken the message very seriously, admitting that he himself was not without fault.

I said that Moscow would of course watch Carter but I nevertheless drew Vance's attention to a new line of comment by Brzezinski and Secretary of Defense Harold Brown; their thesis was that one principal focus of future challenges to U.S.-Soviet relations lay in a confrontation in the Third World over raw materials, which the Soviet Union allegedly was trying to snatch from the United States when it had more than enough of its own natural resources. Vance agreed and said too many fancy theories had been presented to the public of late without any critical analysis.

Vance told me that he and the president had gone through a detailed examination of the administration's foreign policy priorities for the remaining two years of Carter's term, and they had agreed on three areas of prime concern:

- East-West relations, with Soviet-American relations as the key, and completion of SALT II negotiations and the start of SALT III as a matter of paramount importance.

- The consolidation of the dollar (it had fallen to a record low and had to be underpinned by huge lines of credit from Germany and Japan) and the solution of serious economic disagreements among the major industrial nations.

- The further development of relations with China.

Vance referred to Iran, Turkey, and Pakistan, as well as Southeast Asia and South Africa as regions of relatively less importance, yet capable of affecting the general atmosphere of international relations and the administration's priorities, among which was of course a meeting with Brezhnev. We agreed that the earliest possible conclusion of the SALT negotiations was to take precedence over other things. But in fact it was these supposedly lower priority regions that pushed themselves to the front rank in world affairs and ruined the aspirations of the United States and the Soviet Union during the second half of Carter's term, and none more than Iran for him and Afghanistan for us.

## Carter Pushes for a Summit

The president invited me for a discussion in his office February 27 to reassure us about his interest in maintaining good relations (a matter of some concern to him, since he was facing reelection in the following year). The unstable condition of Soviet-American relations and delayed negotiations on SALT II had begun to worry him, so he decided to intervene personally in the march of events. Vance and Brzezinski were also there, so I could see we were in for a serious conversation. One topic was SALT and its connection to the preparations for the Vienna summit; the other was China. But equally important was Carter's tone.

In his diary, Carter recalls that he wanted to stress to me the fundamental importance of relations with the Soviet Union, his concern over their recent aggravation, and the need for us to remedy it together. Actually he said much more than that.

The president began by telling me he wanted Brezhnev to know that he felt that his greatest responsibility as president was the maintenance and development of good relations between our two countries, and that he regretted that we had failed to make progress during the first two years of his administration. He sincerely hoped for an early summit; the important thing, he said, was to meet and exchange views, and he understood Brezhnev's view that a summit should be marked by signing a strategic arms limitations agreement, even if negotiations had already delayed the summit for more than two years. But in Carter's opinion the SALT negotiations were nearing an end so the summit appeared near at hand, and he was looking forward to it.

The president hoped that the summit would take place in the United States, but if doctors did not recommend long flights to Brezhnev, a meeting could be arranged in a neutral country. "I would like to assure the Soviet president," Carter said in conclusion, "that right after the signing of the SALT agreement, I intend to use every means in my power, including direct appeals to the people, to convince the Senate to ratify this important agreement, although it will not be easy considering the sentiments of our senators today." (It was a historical irony that just one year later, Carter himself asked the Senate to postpone the ratification of that agreement because of the Soviet invasion of Afghanistan.)

Then President Carter turned to relations with China. After China invaded Vietnam on February 17, Brezhnev and Carter exchanged messages on the hot line, Brezhnev branding the Chinese as aggressors while Carter appealed for restraint in what he viewed as a Chinese response to Vietnam's aggression against Cambodia. Each side suspected the other's strategy in dealing with China. Carter asked me to assure Brezhnev that, first, there were no secret agreements between the United States and China, and second, the American government had not been informed in advance about Chinese preparations to attack Vietnam less than a month after Deng Xaioping had visited the United States. The president said he himself had strongly warned the Chinese leader against military action in Vietnam and had demanded a quick withdrawal of Chinese troops after the attack—just as the Soviet Union wanted.

I told the president his assurances would be reported to Moscow. "We regard them as positive," I remarked. "But our wariness is well understandable. The fact remains that the Chinese aggression against Vietnam came hard on the heels of Deng Xiaoping's visit to the United States. That was not just noted by the Soviet public but in the United States." I reminded Carter of Brezhnev's question in his latest hot-line message about the invasion: "Is it a mere coincidence?"

Carter replied that he well understood Brezhnev's question, and that was a principal reason he had called me in.

I left the White House with the impression that Carter was beginning to show real interest in a shift in our relations. Remarkably, it was the first time that he did not touch on his favorite subject of human rights. Moreover, during the next month an exchange of personal messages between Carter and Brezhnev finally solved one of the remaining SALT controversies over telemetric information about strategic missile tests. And when Vance informed me confidentially on March 5 that the Chinese ambassador had officially notified the United States that it was withdrawing all its troops from Vietnam, he also passed on to me Carter's appreciation of the restraint shown by the Soviet leadership—which was not exactly what the administration had been saying at the height of the crisis. Moscow and Washington managed to survive that difficult period without serious damage to their relations, and that, said the secretary of state, was a matter of no small significance.

## The Ascent to Vienna

Following Carter's professed turn in sentiment, Vance called me to talk informally on March 29 in a small cozy room adjoining the office of the secretary of state where we usually held such private conversations. Vance began by saying that the administration and he in particular had the impression that Moscow regarded our relations as clearly worse than under other presidents and that we felt the American side was primarily to blame.

"Is that right?" Vance asked me. I replied that I certainly would not question his assessment and had ample evidence to support it.

He said Carter was worried about our deep-rooted lack of trust and understanding and wanted to overcome it at the summit with Brezhnev "as the last remaining possibility" to put our relations on a more constructive basis. This had been exactly the subject of a private conversation with the president in his living quarters early that morning.

Vance said Carter told him he often pondered the problem of Soviet-American relations late at night and felt sure that Brezhnev did, too. Each apparently believed that what the other did in Europe, China, and the Middle East was largely prompted by hostile intentions. But neither side should necessarily regard the actions of the other as directed against it, even though that was the way Washington and Moscow tended to interpret them. In short, the concept of confrontation colored all elements in our relations. But Carter thought that we could have parallel interests in a number of regions, which would be important for one side and of subordinate concern to the other rather than resting on a common denominator of enmity everywhere.

I told Vance that I could well agree with much of what the president had said, but in politics statesmen are judged by their deeds and not their private sentiments, which are little known to Moscow.

Vance said that Carter was somehow sure that during his personal meeting with Brezhnev they would be able to remedy the situation. Carter had repeatedly tried to state his ideas in letters to Brezhnev, but with little success. He believed in talking face to face. Vance himself apparently hoped Brezhnev personally would be able to influence Carter and dispel some of the misleading concepts his boss held about the Soviet Union and its foreign policy.

I appreciated his frank desire to improve our relations and his hope that Brezhnev could influence Carter at a summit. But I knew that Brezhnev's physical and mental condition was too poor to justify such hopes and the main emphasis therefore should be put on thorough preparation of the documents for the meeting itself. Sometimes we expect too much from our leaders' personal contacts when they are not capable of making independent conceptualizations and bold, original decisions on the spot.

We thus pursued an intensive diplomatic dialogue through the confidential channel during the first part of 1979. There were exchanges between Carter and Brezhnev as well as Vance, Brzezinski, and me. The discussion was focused on remaining unsolved questions about SALT. I had two dozen or so private meetings with Vance to find solutions for such problems as missile telemetry and how to count new types of missiles. But the military establishments of both countries were in no hurry to compromise. They relied on the highly complicated, technical nature of the issues to obtain concessions or block the whole agreement. Vance was in an even more difficult position because he had to argue not only with the Pentagon but also with his opponents in the White House who were trying to use our talks for leverage—that is, linkage—on our political disagreements in Africa, Vietnam, Cuba, and elsewhere. But Vance and I knew that this time the political will of both top leaders of our countries was on our side; they wanted a SALT agreement and a summit.

We finally came to terms. On May 7 at 3:15 P.M., as Brzezinski recalled in his memoirs, Vance reported to Carter about his talks with me: "Mr. President, the basic negotiations for SALT have been completed." I must be frank: it was a moment of great relief and satisfaction for me. It had taken years to reach that summit, and I had participated in the difficult construction of the road that led to it. On May 9, 1979, agreement on a SALT treaty was announced. Instead of the large cuts originally sought by Carter, the agreement basically affirmed the Vladivostok limits.

The next question was the choice of the venue for the summit. Carter suggested it was Washington's turn, since the last summit had been held with Ford on Soviet soil at Vladivostok. Brezhnev, on doctors' orders, suggested Moscow. Carter replied he could not go to Moscow because some in Congress might accuse him of yielding another point to the Russians, which could affect ratification. Brzezinski favored neither. At long last we agreed on Vienna.

▪ ▪ ▪

On May 20, I met with Hamilton Jordan, Carter's closest official confidant
and the person most likely to know his motives as his principal domestic political strategist. The conversation took place at our embassy, and it was his
first visit there. Concentrating on the domestic implications of aspects of the
Vienna meeting, he began by saying frankly that the president was fully
aware of the worldwide importance of the summit and was determined to
ensure its success, but his principal task was to be reelected president. That
also meant another important objective was to have the SALT II Treaty ratified by the Senate.

Carter was anxious to establish a good and businesslike relationship
with Brezhnev, Jordan said, but he also sought to avoid looking like a leader
who flung himself carelessly into the embrace of the Russians. This, he said,
would only repeat the mistake of Richard Nixon and create the illusory impression of an unreasonably abrupt turn toward detente. But the political reality now, in the year 1979, was one of great controversy over relations with
the Soviet Union, a situation that differed considerably from Nixon's best
years.

President Carter was not going to blame anybody for the present low
state of our relations. He admitted there might have been some faults during
the first years of his presidency, but the Soviet side also could have done a
better job. "But let bygones be bygones. Our main goal now is the Vienna
meeting," Jordan said. It looked like Carter had forgotten—or was trying
to—the three-year record of troubled relations between his administration
and Moscow.

Three days later Brzezinski and I agreed on the agenda for the Vienna
meeting with only few disagreements. On human rights we worked out a
formula of agreeing to disagree in that either side could raise any subject outside the agreed agenda, but that the other would be entitled to avoid discussing what it regarded as irrelevant. The two leaders were to arrive on June
15 and follow a relatively light schedule of mainly two-hour sessions to spare
Brezhnev, with early dinners starting at 7 or 7:30 P.M. The summit would
close with a three-hour morning meeting on June 18 and a signing ceremony
for the SALT II Treaty. Other agreements would be signed at working sessions without the strain of special ceremonies with reporters.

As I met Vance and Brzezinski on June 11 to finish off the draft of
the communiqué to be issued in Vienna I informed them of the composition
of our delegation at the Vienna summit. It impressed the Americans and
included, apart from the general secretary, three additional members of
the Politburo—Gromyko, the defense minister Ustinov, and Konstantin
Chernenko, newly elected Politburo member and a Brezhnev protégé
who would eventually serve as general secretary. Brezhnev was clearly anxious

to be on the safe side by making the delegation so representative. The American delegation, headed by Carter, included Vance, Brzezinski, Defense Secretary Brown, and General David Jones, chairman of the Joint Chiefs of Staff.

The tactical approaches advocated by Vance and Brzezinski differed considerably. Vance favored looking for positive common points without accentuating controversial issues that would be difficult to settle, but Brzezinski believed it feasible to speak straightforwardly to Brezhnev about aspects of Soviet policy that did not suit the White House, "in order to avoid misunderstanding in the future."

When Jordan cautiously sounded me out about this tactical difference, I reminded him of the positive outcome of the first meeting between Brezhnev and Nixon, where the discussions were not unduly confrontational. Jordan promised to recommend the same approach to Carter. In his diary Carter tells about Harriman's briefing to him on how negotiate with Brezhnev. The Soviet leader, he said, would do everything possible to avoid failure on SALT. His deepest commitment was to keep war far from his own people, and it was very important not to surprise or embarrass him because Brezhnev was old, human, and emotional. A good recommendation by Harriman.

## The Summit in Vienna

The Vienna summit of June 15–18 turned out to be the only meeting of the leaders of both countries during Carter's presidency. As had been carefully planned, its principal concrete result was the signing of the SALT II Treaty on June 18. The very fact of their personal meeting was of no small political and psychological significance, but unfortunately, the meeting came too late. It was the middle of the third year of Carter's term, and by that time the negative momentum of the past was too strong. The best it could do was to arrest the erosion of detente for a short time. Carter had to overcome the growing opposition not only to the SALT treaty but to his very meeting with Brezhnev. Senator Jackson compared his trip to Vienna to Chamberlain's meeting in Munich in 1938 to appease Hitler. Jordan later told me that Carter was so hurt by this comparison that he refused to use an umbrella against the rain when he arrived in Vienna lest it recall Chamberlain's symbol.

The SALT II Treaty and its accompanying protocols were a major achievement, the culmination of many years of talks, vital for Soviet-American relations, a sizable deterrent to the arms race, and even though never ratified, the foundation for important agreements on substantial nuclear arms reduction in following decades.

However complex the details, the essence of SALT II was plain enough. Both sides for the first time agreed to specific, quantitative levels restricting armaments and their replacement and modification. There was even a small reduction. They also agreed to comply with a rather detailed verification schedule; this represented a major breakthrough in the traditional Soviet way of thinking, which had never allowed for any verification measures at all. For the first time in the long course of strategic arms negotiations, the SALT II Treaty established a numerical ceiling on the total nuclear weapons of all types, and it was equal for both parties, including MIRVed missiles. The number was not to exceed the Vladivostok limit of 2,400 units. As of January 1, 1981, both sides were to reduce that number to 2,240, and the treaty was to remain in effect until 1985. They also agreed to a ceiling of 1,200 MIRVed intercontinental and submarine-launched missiles, with the overall total on land, sea, and air not to exceed 1,320. The Soviet Union could keep its modern heavy missiles, the United States none. Both leaders also compromised on such controversial problems as cruise missiles and the Backfire bomber (their production was limited to 30 planes a year), and they agreed that test launches for missiles were not to be coded so each side could monitor the other.

The treaty was a marked improvement over the Vladivostok agreements. But the improvements, which were worked out with great difficulty during the protracted negotiations from 1977 to 1979, came at a high price. Precious time was lost, during which the political and public support for the treaty was badly eroded in the United States, and as a result it was not put for approval by the U.S. Congress.

One of its disadvantages was that it simply regulated rather than banned the build-up of MIRVed warheads. The SALT process also excluded medium-range nuclear missiles deployed in Europe, which ultimately led to our sharp conflict with the United States and its NATO allies over what were called Euromissiles.

But even these negative implications could have been overcome if the treaty had been ratified quickly and both sides had proceeded to the next stage agreed at Vienna, which would have been bilateral negotiations to achieve further radical cuts in nuclear arms and an eventual SALT III agreement. There was no doubt that the potential existed to move forward to the next stage, and this was illustrated by a curious episode at the Vienna summit.

On June 17, the second day of the meeting, Carter presented some new ideas about disarmament that were actually proposals for SALT III, but they were conveyed to Brezhnev in a rather unusual way. He handed them to the Soviet leader in the elevator in the American Embassy at lunchtime. Carter gave Brezhnev a piece of paper with the ideas he had jotted down on a yellow pad. He might have had it with him after discussions with the members of his delegation, but he apparently decided at the last moment to sound out Brezhnev's preliminary reaction. Had he handed them over without preparation in an official meeting, they would have run the risk of their being immediately rejected by Brezhnev, which is what happened to Vance in Moscow in March 1977.

Carter's proposals could have provided a solid base for further strategic arms limitations talks even though they contained a number of serious gaps. For instance, they ignored any limitations on the aircraft component of the strategic triad, which was traditionally stronger on the American side. But on the whole, in some respects they were rather close to the important initiatives on stage-by-stage disarmament advanced by the Soviet Union itself during the second half of the 1980s.

But the Soviet leadership under Brezhnev was not prepared for such a broad approach in 1979, and its desire to fix the balance of strategic forces prevailed over the search for a genuine balance of interests. Nor was it clear whether the Pentagon and the Congress would agree with Carter's new approach.

In any case, Brezhnev called the Soviet delegation into an urgent conference that same night to discuss "Carter's paper." Defense Minister Ustinov was dead against the proposals as too far-reaching. Chernenko seconded him at once. The wary Gromyko said such questions should not be decided overnight; there was time to consult the comrades from the rest of the Politburo and no need to commit ourselves immediately to Carter. As for Brezhnev, he did not find it appealing to engage himself even in a preliminary way with new and difficult problems like this right in the middle of the summit meeting. Once he had left Moscow, he was disposed only to sign the SALT II Treaty and not to tackle new difficult questions. Therefore, he agreed with Gromyko, and the semiofficial proposals made by Carter were mothballed. Thus another opportunity for a further breakthrough on SALT was missed.

Carter's American critics, as well as the Soviet leadership, generally dismissed his radical proposals in the disarmament field as typical idealism or an unserious approach to a serious problem. But as I look back to 1979, it seems to me that his actions were guided by impatience and growing apprehension of how dangerous the nuclear arsenals were becoming and how quickly technological advances make agreements and treaties obsolete. The treaty-making process was too slow. It had taken three administrations six years to work out SALT II; meanwhile, weapons laboratories had given the world new generations of missiles, bombers, and the neutron bomb. The only real answer was for the heads of both countries to streamline arms negotiations by taking an active, continuous, and direct role themselves. I confess that I myself had some of these thoughts before and during the summit in Vienna.

Carter's cherished hopes for personal diplomacy with Brezhnev did not come alive because of the delay in holding the summit meeting. During those two or three years Brezhnev had grown physically and mentally more decrepit—he dozed off at the gala performance in the Vienna Opera House—and at the same time the Soviet leadership began to write off Carter because of the unstable condition of Soviet-American relations, which they blamed on him. Besides, there was no way of knowing what Carter's political fortunes would be in the following year's presidential election. In short, the meeting of the two leaders came too late for personal diplomacy.

During the joint sessions both Carter and Brezhnev outlined their positions on a large number of questions—Europe, the Middle East, the role played by Cuba and the Soviet Union in Africa, Sino-American relations, human rights, trade, and so on. On most issues there was no agreement, but the review itself was useful for both leaders' awareness. Regional conflicts and human rights remained among the most controversial issues. Ideology clearly prevailed on both sides. The summit did not lead to improved understanding by the two sides of their differences, much less to ways of bridging them.

As I observed the main protagonists up close at the meeting, I found that Carter was at ease when discussing different subjects without the help of his advisers. Somehow, he resembled Kennedy during the summit with Khrushchev in Vienna. Brezhnev knew our principal positions on the major issues, but he was not prepared for a complex discussion. In most cases he confined himself to reading out the papers prepared by his aides on specific questions. He did not go into details. His interpreter had copies of all the papers and translated them faultlessly, even when Brezhnev went wrong in reading them. If a detailed reaction to a statement by Carter was required, it would be prepared by the Soviet delegation for presentation by Brezhnev at the following session. If this was not sufficient, Gromyko would intervene and state our position.

Although Brezhnev had mastered the indispensable minimum of material, especially on SALT, his dependence on prepared papers in this declining period of his life was a source of amusement. In one paper a paragraph had been deleted by our delegation at the last moment. When Brezhnev reached the passage, he turned to his interpreter and in a loud voice asked him if it was supposed to be read out. The interpreter said no—we always made sure to keep him fully informed about all statements to be made by the general secretary—whereupon Brezhnev proceeded with his reading. The interpreters themselves were experienced diplomats from the Foreign Ministry, and when they translated for Brezhnev in his one-on-one meetings with

Carter, they were armed with several versions of his possible reply and helped him pick the right one at the moment it was needed. This arrangement was a major state secret, although I guess the American delegation understood quite well what was going on.

China was discussed at the final tête-à-tête between the two leaders. As usual Brezhnev was very emotional on this issue and spoke without his notes. He tried to convince Carter it would be dangerous to put his faith in the assurances of the Chinese leadership and use the Chinese against the Soviet Union. Carter thus had the chance to see that Brezhnev took this subject very much to heart. But his very failure to keep his emotions in check only increased the temptation of the American leadership to use that trump against the Soviet Union.

Both leaders nevertheless established a good personal relationship in the course of the Vienna meeting. Indeed, it came to the point where they kissed each other at the final ceremony, much to the surprise of all those present— and to Carter's political embarrassment when he got home. As the two heads of state were about to rise after signing the SALT II agreement, I heard Gromyko, who was standing behind them, whispering to Ustinov:

"Do you think they are going to kiss each other?"

"I don't think so," Ustinov replied. "Why should they?"

"Well, I am not so sure," Gromyko observed.

Gromyko knew Brezhnev better than his colleague. Later in the evening, Brezhnev remarked to his associates that Carter was "quite a nice guy, after all."

Gromyko and Ustinov played the principal roles within the Soviet delegation, while Chernenko echoed their words or those of Brezhnev or just kept silent. As for Ustinov, Carter suggested during the opening session that both defense ministers should meet separately in parallel session. That would enable them to establish a personal relationship and explore allied questions, such as troop reductions in Central Europe. In general it was a good idea. That afternoon when our delegation caucused Brezhnev urged "Dmitri" (Ustinov's first name) to join his opposite number, Harold Brown, in a meeting. But Ustinov was clearly unwilling to negotiate with the Americans since he believed it was "Gromyko's business." This gave rise to a debate.

Gromyko said the Soviet delegation at the negotiations on disarmament in Central Europe had an unused card up its sleeve: We were ready to reduce our troops in the region by another ten thousand and make certain other concessions. Gromyko suggested that Ustinov use this card in his conversation with Brown to show that the Soviet defense minister had the goodwill to handle a meeting with a compromise proposal. This, he thought, might help Brown reciprocate.

Yielding to Brezhnev, Ustinov agreed reluctantly. The meeting took place the following day. No diplomatic representatives attended lest the presence of such professionals make the defense ministers uneasy. Ustinov was back at the embassy after a couple of hours, angry and irritated. Ustinov had long been loath to meet Americans in person at a high level; he avoided them and managed to convince Brezhnev it would be fruitless, and this experience only confirmed him in his opinions.

"I cannot imagine," he told Brezhnev in disgust, "how Gromyko or Dobrynin can endure negotiating with the Americans at all. I tried to approach Brown from all sides, told him about future prospects, and stated our concession. But he was very reserved and did not promise anything in return. Why, he just swallowed our concession and kept repeating the well-known American positions. I've had enough of that."

Gromyko did not try to persuade Ustinov to change his ways because he regarded negotiations with the Americans as his job. And so, by the end of the 1970s and the beginning of the 1980s Andrei Andreyevich Gromyko, in cooperation with Andropov and Ustinov, became almost an omnipotent figure in shaping the country's foreign policy, particularly in relation to the United States.

## Down from the Summit into the SALT Marshes

On his return from Vienna Brzezinski handed me a present from Carter, a specially made pen as a souvenir of signing the SALT Treaty. Brzezinski described Carter's state of mind after meeting in Vienna as "outwardly paradoxical but essentially understandable" because the president had experienced a psychological relaxation of tension that led him to believe in the possibility of a reasonable dialogue and further agreements with the Soviet Union. But there were ominous signs of the fate of the treaty itself. The White House was clearly worried by the opposition's bitter campaign against ratification, which Vance remarked was "supported by the mass media solely because the treaty was signed with the Soviet Union." David Rockefeller told me that while business was pleased with the results of the summit, he asked us as a leader of the foreign affairs establishment to be indulgent with the "senatorial prima donnas" in pressing our case for the treaty. Part of the problem, Rockefeller said, was that Carter was already in a difficult domestic political position, and Teddy Kennedy was taking advantage of it by trying to win over Democrats to support him in a possible primary campaign to unseat the president (Kennedy did not, however, oppose the treaty). Rockefeller said the senator really had no definite political line of his own yet and was only trying to impress the public and find its feelings.

The president meanwhile placed George Seignious, a retired general, at the head of the Arms Control and Disarmament Agency to calm somehow the opposition during the process of ratification with the presence of a military man. In conversation with me, Seignious acknowledged he faced no easy task. The public's attention was entirely focused on the energy crisis in the country and gasoline shortage brought on by the Iranian revolution. Administration officials trying to champion the cause of the SALT were being asked instead by the public why they had to wait in long lines at the gas pumps.

In Moscow, the Politburo, the government, and the Presidium of the Supreme Soviet published a joint resolution on June 22 approving the summit results as "an important stride ahead toward normalizing Soviet-American relations and the international climate on the whole." Several days later, Gromyko held an extensive press conference on the results of the summit; his assessments were balanced and restrained. He must have known that the summit had met with a mixed response in the United States. He therefore issued a warning that Moscow would refuse to consider further amendments or renegotiate the treaty. Events bore this out. Senate Republicans proposed dozens of amendments, and although the treaty just made it past the Senate Foreign Relations Committee after lengthy and controversial hearings by a vote of 9 to 6, the Senate Armed Services Committee sent it to the Senate floor with a virtual kiss of death—10 votes against ratification, 7 abstentions, and not a single vote in favor.

## The Cuban Mini-Crisis

Matters were made even worse by a new Soviet-American crisis over Cuba which, for once, was not directly initiated by either of the two governments. It was caused by the belated discovery, or more likely the premeditated leak by American intelligence, of the existence of a Soviet military detachment of between 2,000 to 2,600 men in Cuba. This detachment—or "brigade" as it was proclaimed in the United States—had in fact been there ever since 1962 training Cubans to handle Soviet military equipment, and President Kennedy knew of its existence, as his national security adviser McGeorge Bundy later confirmed. But when it became public knowledge in 1979 it created a huge political furor that further impaired the ratification of SALT. Senator Frank Church, the chairman of the Senate Foreign Relations Committee, was having trouble with his reelection, and to improve his chances he ordered a halt to the SALT ratification hearings.

At the time I was in Moscow, where my parents were dying. Vance had to ask Gromyko to send me back to Washington to help him straighten things out. Having buried my father, I left my mother's deathbed and missed her funeral for what was at best a stupid mixup and at worst a political ploy based on false or distorted information. My feelings were a mixture of anger and sorrow. I arrived to tell Vance about what the Americans were call-ing the Soviet Brigade in Cuba. "Cy," I said, "it's still the old stuff. I've just come from Moscow, and I checked it all again. Nothing has changed from 1962. It's the same situation as during the Kennedy, Johnson, Nixon, and Ford administrations." Vance was visibly relieved. Nevertheless it took several weeks of meetings by foreign ministers, members of Congress, the White House staff, and myself to untangle this Cuban mini-crisis. Vance later dis-missed the whole uproar sarcastically as a "memory lapse" by the intelligence services of the United States. As Marx said, history repeats itself, first as tragedy and then as farce. But this farce cost the ratification of the treaty. And our relations further deteriorated.

Other real and imaginary difficulties over the ratification were used by administration officials, members of Congress, and the media to bring pres-sure to bear on the Soviet Union, which either looked like attempts at politi-cal blackmail or at least were perceived to be so by Moscow. What the Americans did not know was that Gromyko and Andropov sent a memoran-dum to the Politburo on August 6 urging the government to stand firm. It cited American demands ranging from the approval of individual applica-tions for emigration to Moscow's relations with third countries and accused Washington of trying to cash in on the Soviet Union's desire for the ratifica-tion of the treaty and equalization of commercial relations in order to bully us into concessions on other, unrelated points. Gromyko and Andropov then warned: "Any concessions on our part will lead to new brazen demands. Proceeding from this, we should react to any new claims of that kind by con-firming our positions, or just leave them unanswered."

The Politburo endorsed their recommendations, which of course stiff-ened them in resisting the solution of the very problems Carter had hoped to solve in the improved atmosphere he sensed at Vienna. In the end, the exces-sive demands, devalued by the administration's failure to deliver on SALT, produced the exact opposite of what Carter had intended. Overall the United States overreacted with respect to a pseudo-crisis over Cuba in 1979. Detente was in danger.

## Europe as an Arena of Confrontation

Administration policy in Europe was directed toward vigorously strengthen-ing NATO to achieve military superiority over the Warsaw Pact powers, a policy adopted by the NATO Council meeting in Washington in May 1978.

The centerpiece was a program of so-called modernization of NATO's nuclear forces, which essentially amounted to the deployment in Europe of American medium-range nuclear missiles capable of hitting the European part of the Soviet territory. In December of 1979 the NATO Council accepted a U.S. plan to deploy 108 Pershing II missiles capable of striking Moscow from Europe in less than ten minutes and 464 Tomahawk land-based cruise missiles, which were more accurate and had a longer range of 2,500 kilometers (1,500 miles). The deployment, scheduled for 1983, was a response to the hasty deployment in the Western Soviet Union of our new SS-20 missiles, which were highly mobile and very accurate.

The Soviet leadership had taken a mistaken decision to deploy the SS-20s under pressure from our military, who were mesmerized by their high performance. As we secretly deployed our SS-20s unilaterally, the Soviet supreme leadership was pleased by the strengthening of Soviet nuclear potential in the European theater. But when similar plans were announced by the American side, Moscow was seriously alarmed. It cost us dearly politically, economically, and militarily by provoking the deployment of the American medium-range missiles in Europe.

The NATO deployment also was part of a new American military, political, and strategic concept. The concept implied that conditions of parity in "central strategic systems" between the Soviet Union and the United States grew out of the SALT negotiations. That was extended to mean that the United States should achieve the same equality with the Soviet Union in regional as in intercontinental nuclear delivery systems. But in reality that would shift the overall nuclear missile balance in America's favor. The point was, our medium-range missiles could not reach American territory, while the American missiles based in Europe could hit targets almost everywhere in the European part of the Soviet Union and thus were tantamount to strategic missiles.

Our decision to deploy the SS-20s therefore turned out to be particularly disastrous. It not only cost us enormous sums but provoked military countermeasures from the West in the form of its own medium-range missiles, which were deployed in Western Europe in 1983. As a result, military tensions rose in Europe, and the overall strategic nuclear balance shifted in favor of the United States. Major efforts had to be made much later to relieve tension by mutually renouncing such missiles and scrapping them. This was a belated and reluctant admission of the fact that the initial deployment of the SS-20s had been a gross miscalculation.

Many in the United States believed the Soviet Union could attack Western Europe with the confidence that the United States would not risk its own cities in an intercontinental missile duel merely to protect the

Europeans. Harriman had spotted the danger of this spiral in 1978 and through me advised Brezhnev to make a major public statement that the Soviet Union had ceased its military buildup in Europe. He would then be able to mount a vigorous and successful propaganda offensive—just as the Soviet campaign had undercut American plans to deploy in Europe a new kind of nuclear weapon, the neutron bomb. It killed people by radiation but preserved property, and thus was seen as a first-strike weapon to start a war and not as a defense against attack.

But our European policy in that period was torn between conflicting trends. We had some success in reducing tension and developing all-round relations with West European countries through accepting the German policy of reconciliation known as *Ostpolitik*. But we were also feverishly building up our nuclear and conventional arms in Europe beyond any reasonable measure, and this was being done secretly, away from the public eye and the Vienna multilateral talks, which only consolidated the suspicions of the West and provoked it to strengthen its conventional NATO forces and then its missiles in Europe.

Late in September of 1979, Vance and I discussed the American plans to deploy the medium-range missiles in Western Europe. It was, as far as I remember, the first time we broached the subject in detail at an official level. He was evidently anxious to prepare us and did not disguise the fact that the Carter administration expected to obtain the necessary support from its NATO allies at a special meeting in December. Without beating about the bush, Vance said the NATO decision was being pushed through by the American government in response to our deployment of SS-20s, about which he expressed his personal regret.

Moscow launched a major public campaign against deployment of the Pershings. In a speech in East Berlin on October 6, Brezhnev sharply criticized the deployment plans as breaking the balance of forces in Europe. Only then did he propose cuts in Soviet missile forces if NATO did not deploy the new missiles. He also proposed to withdraw 20,000 troops and 1,000 armored vehicles from Germany the following year. But it was too late. We should have done it earlier when it was being recommended by Harriman as well as Senators Mansfield, Fulbright, and Kennedy.

Carter rejected Brezhnev's offer on October 9 and came out strongly in favor of the program to strengthen the NATO forces. He also rejected Brezhnev's next proposal to start negotiations on the deployment of missiles in Europe before the NATO session scheduled for December. Determined to secure its European allies' support first, he would then, and only then, be prepared to deal with us.

On November 19, I met Brzezinski. He relayed the president's assurances that the United States was not seeking military superiority in Europe—but it could not acquiesce in Soviet superiority either, so it would not sit back and watch us build up our nuclear missile potential there. Brzezinski frankly admitted that American stubbornness was grounded in both political and military considerations, and the former were even more important than the latter. Underlying the administration's policy, he said, was the American desire to preserve a strong influence in NATO. Brzezinski said that Europeans knew powerful medium-range weapons were being aimed at them from the Soviet Union, and thus Moscow was capable of delivering a crushing blow to the countries of Western Europe while doubting that the United States would run the risk of retaliating with its intercontinental missile forces.

"Thus we can imagine a situation where the Soviet Union, taking advantage of its superiority in the region, may be able to exert strong pressure on Western Europe, confronting it with the dilemma of either being annihilated or accepting the status of, say, Finland, and breaking off its alliance with the United States," Brzezinski said. The Americans feared that the West Europeans would sooner opt for the neutral road of what was then called "Finlandization," which was against the interests of the United States.

Purely in terms of logic, Brzezinski's statement was sound. Of course, this scenario did not reflect any of the real plans or intentions of the Soviet government. But how could people in the West know for sure that Moscow would not be tempted to use the new leverage of its SS-20 missiles?

On my trips to Moscow for consultations during that period I never heard any member of the Politburo or our top generals discuss or even mention such political considerations. I did not see any Politburo or Foreign Ministry paper on the possible political opportunities or consequences of deploying our SS-20s. Military justifications were the only ones ever advanced. The Foreign Ministry barely participated in this Defense Ministry project until we faced a diplomatic confrontation with the United States and the European members of NATO over the Pershings.

This may be difficult to believe, but it was exactly what happened. The Politburo, still mentally engaged in the arms race, accepted with satisfaction the assessment of our military leadership that our new weapons system could provide us with a nuclear balance in Europe in medium-range delivery systems against the American forward-based systems in Western Europe. That was the decisive factor, together with the thought that it might also put us on a more equal level with Americans in the strategic balance: In Moscow's eyes NATO's nuclear weaponry in Europe was seen as a strategic threat to the USSR that ought to be offset by Soviet nuclear weapons. But the Kremlin did not expect that the European countries of NATO—

with the eager assistance of the United States—would so quickly agree to deploy American missiles on their own territory against our SS-20s to withstand any possible political blackmail from Moscow. That was exactly Brzezinski's theme, and it was very successfully used by American and pro-American propaganda in Europe while Brezhnev and his colleagues continued by pure inertia to underestimate the role of public opinion in the West.

On December 12, 1979, NATO approved the deployment of 108 Pershing II ballistic missiles and 464 cruise missiles on the soil of Western Europe. The NATO decision was part of what it called the "two-track" approach to deploy the missiles while at the same time seeking negotiations that would, if successful, slow or cancel the emplacement of the Pershing and cruise missiles. This reinforced Moscow's hostility toward Carter and his administration because the Soviet leadership regarded it, first of all, as a deliberate departure from the strategic limits specified in the SALT II Treaty. American medium-range missiles in Europe capable of hitting targets on the Soviet territory were after all a substantial addition to the American strategic nuclear potential. Moscow responded to NATO's proposal for negotiations by saying that the very basis of negotiations had been destroyed by the fact that NATO was attempting to conduct them from a position of strength. Moscow would go to the negotiating table only if the NATO decision was canceled or its implementation publicly suspended.

The stalemate continued, and the decisions of both sides on nuclear missiles stationed in Europe further aggravated their political relations without in any way reducing the threat to their national security.

# IV. Afghanistan

On the eve of 1980 I was in a Moscow hospital for my annual medical checkup. On the morning on December 28, I was awakened by a loud radio announcement. Soviet troops had entered Afghanistan "at the request of its government." For me it was a complete surprise. I called my friends in the Foreign Ministry. They confirmed the news but few could give me any details or explanation: the whole operation had been organized by the Politburo in deep secrecy. That was the beginning of the long and bloody Afghan tragedy, the sad consequences of which the world and especially my country feel years later, as I write this.

## The Background of Intervention

For many years Afghanistan lay far outside the mainstream of global events. It maintained equally good relations with the United States and the Soviet Union, satisfied with its neutral status and content in its isolation from the modern world. From time to time, the king of Afghanistan would visit the Soviet Union, even taking vacations there. He also traveled to meet Western leaders. The neutrality of Afghanistan continued after his overthrow by his cousin, Mohammed Daoud, in 1973, while the king was on a visit to Rome. The country was not involved in any serious international disputes and was respected by many nations for a policy of nonalignment that kept it out of great power conflicts even though it shared a border of almost a thousand miles with the Soviet Union. Even the great powers themselves reached a modus vivendi within the country; all aid projects south of Kabul, the capital, were run by the United Nations or Western aid specialists, all those to the north by Soviet aid specialists. In Moscow, the Afghan department of our foreign ministry was one of the quietest places in the Soviet diplomatic service.

The small Afghan Communist Party was split along ideological and tribal lines into factions known "Khalq" (Masses) and "Parcham" (Banner), with the former more radical and the latter closer to Moscow and operating within the local political hierarchy. Some Parchamites even served in the government, although Daoud began removing them during the 1970s as he attempted to tilt somewhat away from the Soviet Union, partly under the influence of the Shah of Iran, who was going to underwrite construction of Afghanistan's first railroad as a link with Iran.

In April 1978, there was a coup, the cause of which is still disputed by historians. Feuding between the communist factions, including the murder of a prominent Parchamite, probably played a role, and half a dozen communist leaders were arrested. On April 27, Afghan armored and air force units attacked Daoud's palace, killing him and most of his ministers and clan. As far as I know, the diplomatic staff of the Soviet Embassy was stunned at first. The involvement of the KGB, if any, was unclear.

Then began a period of rapidly escalating instability. The coup installed a government of both the Khalq and Parcham factions but the Parchamites were pushed out within two months, and the power passed to the Khalq through the new president, Nur Mohammed Taraki and his ruthless colleague Hafizullah Amin. The Parcham leader, Babrak Karmal, was exiled to Prague as Afghan ambassador. Mainly through our KGB agents, we gradually became involved in the fight between various domestic factions. The new Afghan government attempted to impose on a virtually medieval peasantry radical reforms in land tenure, education, and even dowries, which played an important role in rural areas. This was done without proper knowledge of the countryside and inflamed the local mullahs. Armed rebellion broke out in the eastern portion of the country by early autumn and spread to most provinces through the winter. Moscow became worried, but rebuffed Taraki's request in March 1979 for direct military support by sending troops to Afghanistan.*

In February of 1979, there was a tragic incident in Kabul resulting in the murder of the U.S. ambassador, Adolph Dubs, a highly professional diplomat whom I knew very well because he had served in Moscow as deputy chief of the embassy and in Washington as deputy assistant secretary of state for Soviet affairs. He had been pulled from his car in Kabul by terrorists while being driven to the embassy and taken as a hostage to the main hotel downtown, where his captors barricaded themselves in a hotel room and tried to bargain with the Afghan government. After about two hours, Afghan security forces stormed the room and Dubs was shot in the melee.

---

* The Politburo believed that such a move would wreck the preparations for the Brezhnev-Carter summit. And that was unacceptable for the Soviet leadership at that time (but in less than a year they changed their mind after our relations with Carter became worse and the pro-Soviet regime in Kabul demonstrated its fatal weakness).

Moscow expressed deep regret over the tragedy. At the same time, it denied any responsibility for the Afghan authorities' actions, which it said had been designed to free the U.S. ambassador from the terrorists. But we continued our own secret investigation and established that the Soviet advisers to the Afghan police failed to control them properly when they tried to free Dubs as quickly as possible. For the Afghan regime, this was a matter of prestige, but the poorly organized operation resulted in tragedy.

For the remainder of the year 1979, similar events, although few as spectacular, raised the tension in Afghanistan and increased Moscow's concern about instability on our southern border. The Soviet Union provided widespread political, economic, and military assistance in an attempt to stabilize the Afghan regime. Meanwhile, a bloody rivalry developed between Afghan leaders. The prime minister, Hafizullah Amin, ordered President Nur Mohammed Taraki put to death on October 8 after a plot to get rid of Amin backfired. The KGB became more and more deeply involved. Our secret service did not trust Amin and considered him a CIA agent who might turn to the Americans for help (he had studied at Columbia University). That was the essence of the KGB reports to the Politburo.

On December 27, 1979, Amin was overthrown and killed in a coup carried out with the support and participation of the Soviet secret services, which had contributed so much to Moscow's involvement and played a major role in the fateful decision to send in Soviet troops. The KGB had the strong support of the international department of the Central Committee of our party. The Soviet Embassy in Kabul cautiously opposed strife in Afghanistan, let alone the full-scale invasion that finally took place.

From my embassy in Washington, where I returned in early January of 1980, I at first viewed these events in distant Afghanistan as not yet central to our already deteriorating relations with the United States, although the U.S. government already viewed things there with increasing concern because of the growing instability in the region and Soviet involvement in the events. From time to time Washington communicated its concern to Moscow. But the Soviet leadership did not want to enter this dialogue actively because it considered Afghanistan its own sphere of interest. It did not want to legitimize any American interest in that area any more than the Americans were eager to legitimize any Soviet presence in Africa or in the Middle East.

A few words about the situation in Iran, which lies on the southwest borders of Afghanistan. In 1978 the United States increased the flow of arms and advisers to Iran to bolster the Shah, a move which could only alarm Moscow. On November 17, Brezhnev sent Carter a message stressing Soviet concern over U.S. attempts to influence developments in Iran, a neighboring country with which, as he pointed out, we maintained normal relations. He asked both governments to declare publicly that they would not interfere in Iran's internal affairs.

The next day, the State Department made such a statement, pointing out that the Soviet Union had, too, and also saying that the United States firmly supported the Shah in his efforts to restore tranquility in Iran and would maintain relations with Iran in foreign policy, economics, and security. But violent developments followed—the flight of the Shah and an eruption of anti-American sentiments. On November 4, 1979, the American Embassy in Teheran was seized by a fanatic mob and its diplomatic personnel taken hostage and held for many months. It was a severe blow to the prestige of the Carter administration.

With angry demands mounting in the United States for a military operation against Iran, Moscow again became alarmed. I visited Brzezinski on November 7 and privately told him, on instructions from Moscow, that we could not remain indifferent if the United States interfered militarily in our southern neighbor. He assured me there were no such plans. Later the same day Vance told me military action had been ruled out because it would endanger the lives of the hostages. At the United Nations, the Soviet Union supported the United States in demanding the release of the hostages, and Moscow also sought their release in a confidential diplomatic message to the new government of Ayatollah Khomeni. Brzezinski expressed Carter's appreciation to me on December 5.

## The Die Is Cast

From early December 1979, the Afghan situation had been intensely discussed in the Kremlin by a narrow circle consisting of Gromyko, KGB chief Andropov, and Defense Minister Ustinov. Amin was strongly suspected of tilting toward the United States. Then they went to Brezhnev and insisted that resolute steps should be taken in order "not to lose Afghanistan." They convinced him. But what proved decisive was an alarming private letter at the beginning of December from Andropov warning Brezhnev that the Soviet position in Afghanistan would deteriorate rapidly if our troops did not intervene against the opposition. Otherwise the United States would fill the vacuum, he wrote, stressing that Amin was already exploring openings toward the West. By mid-December Brezhnev decided to present the case to the whole Politburo. The other three participants in the inner discussion were instructed to prepare a special report giving an analysis and recommendations for Soviet military intervention in Afghanistan.

Late in the evening on December 12, 1979, a secret meeting was held in the Kremlin. Again the major decision was planned to be made not by the entire Politburo but only by a group of its most influential members. In addition to Andropov, Gromyko, and Ustinov, also present were Mikhail Suslov, the chief ideologist; Victor Grishin, secretary of Moscow party organization; Kyrilenko, close associate of Brezhnev; and Ponomarev, head of the party's international department. Brezhnev chaired the meeting.

The meeting discussed the proposals outlined by Andropov, Gromyko, and Ustinov. The main theme of this report was brief and clear: the situation in Afghanistan seriously threatened the security of the southern borders of the Soviet Union. All this could be used against us by the United States, China, or Iran through the creation and support of an unfriendly Afghan regime. So it was necessary to stop this dangerous development by sending our troops into Afghanistan without delay. Ustinov was sure that the whole military operation could be accomplished comparatively quickly. Andropov spoke about the good contacts his people in Kabul had with key members of the regime. Gromyko spoke about the possibility of international criticism of an invasion but agreed that security reasons outweighed it, just as they had when Soviet troops intervened in Czechoslovakia in 1968. Suslov and Ponomarev as usual supported with enthusiasm the policy "of international solidarity" with the people of the Third World. Brezhnev did not care to go into long explanations or discussion. He briefly proposed approving the plan for the dispatch of Soviet troops to Afghanistan. The same top troika was charged with making arrangements for troop deployment, which in fact was already under way, and with supervising further steps.

Thus, the final decision was taken without objection—a decision that had a disastrous effect on international relations for years. The United States was quick to spot by satellite that something was up and asked us about it. Shulman called in the Soviet chargé, Vladlen Vasev on December 15 and said the United States noted with concern "the continuing deployment of large contingents of Soviet troops beyond the national territory of the Soviet Union," that is, in Afghanistan. In this connection, Washington asked for an explanation in the context of the agreement between the United States and the Soviet Union—signed at the height of detente in 1972—providing for "consultations and mutual information concerning national conflicts that may threaten peace and our mutual relations." Moscow essentially ignored the American request.

Because of Brezhnev's lack of decisiveness and the poor state of his health, his doctors ordered him to avoid excessive anxiety and emotion, which was convenient for the most active members of the Politburo. The principal roles in the fatal decision on Afghanistan were played by Ustinov and Andropov, as their special services were already actively involved in Afghanistan. Vladimir Kryuchkov, the senior KGB official who rose to be its head under Gorbachev, personally directed that activity. They convinced Brezhnev that it was going to be an easy victory.

Gromyko, who was cautious and experienced in diplomatic affairs but not in military matters, apparently decided to rely on the knowledge of the more resolute fellow members of the Politburo in clandestine operations and the general mood in the Politburo. Characteristically, there is no trace of any objections or warnings by him about the possibility of a strong reaction in the West, especially in the United States.

Gromyko underestimated the strength of the reaction and must have believed that the already hostile relations between Moscow and the Carter administration could hardly be made any worse by what they planned to do in Afghanistan. No one in our embassy in Washington was asked about possible repercussions, and I was not consulted by Gromyko even though I was in Moscow at the time: he believed that the American reaction, whatever it might be, was not a major factor to be taken into consideration. Besides he like others in the Politburo was angry with the decision just made by NATO to deploy American missiles in Europe.

After Aleksandr Bessmertnykh replaced Gromyko as Soviet foreign minister, he told me he discovered a sealed envelope in Gromyko's personal safe. The envelope contained propaganda materials supporting the Soviet invasion. No other documents concerning Afghanistan were found. Even if Gromyko was of two minds at first, he always vigorously supported the action afterward.

Another important detail was that while defense minister Ustinov and other brass without any combat experience favored the use of troops, the plan was opposed by our general staff and by military officers who knew Afghanistan firsthand. Generals Nikolai Ogarkov, Sergei Akhromeyev, and Valentin Varennikov, charged with preparing a plan of invasion, filed a report to Ustinov warning of the dangers of inserting Soviet regular troops into a protracted civil war; and that it would serve no purpose in the difficult and mountainous terrain inhabited by warring tribes. They were immediately summoned before the defense minister, who made them stand to attention while reprimanding them strongly. "Since when are our military to determine foreign policy?" Ustinov demanded. He commanded them to "stop reasoning" and urgently prepare the plan for military operations.

Another conference attended by Brezhnev, Andropov, Ustinov, Gromyko, and Chernenko was held at Brezhnev's dacha December 26. The troika reported on the implementation of the decision taken at the December 12 meeting. Brezhnev approved the preparations, which apparently included the KGB plan to overthrow Amin, although there is no written record of this.

The next day, the entire Politburo discussed our next moves in Afghanistan and decided to start sending in our main force. The Politburo approved instructions for all Soviet ambassadors "to clarify" the decision and defend it abroad. It also sent messages to the leaders of a number of Communist parties abroad explaining our version of events in Afghanistan.

The Politburo also approved the official Tass explanation. It was to say that Soviet military contingents had been sent to Afghanistan "to carry out the missions *requested* [my italics] by the leadership of Afghanistan and exclusively aimed at repulsing the outside aggression." This did not sound convincing, so another secret decision was adopted on the spot. It was entitled "On the Propaganda Support for Our Action in Afghanistan." Information under the name of the CPSU Central Committee was approved for publication across the country, giving our interpretation of the Afghan events. Additional information then was sent secretly to all party organizations and committees of the Soviet Union. The Politburo sought to justify what was clearly to become an unpopular war.

On December 27 Amin was overthrown, with the help of our elite military units in Kabul. On December 28, a massive invasion began. It was announced that Soviet troops had entered Afghanistan "at the request of the new government" headed by our protégé Babrak Karmal, although the government itself had just been formed and Karmal was still outside the country. At its session of January 2, 1980, the Politburo put the strength of the Soviet troops in Afghanistan at 50,000.

"It'll be over in three to four weeks," Brezhnev told me with assurance early in January when I expressed to him my concern about our relations with the United States just before returning to my post. Indeed, Karmal seemed quickly established in authority in Kabul and in the major Afghan cities where Soviet troops were stationed with Afghan military units. Early in 1980, Brezhnev therefore raised at a Politburo meeting the question of a partial Soviet withdrawal. The troika of Andropov, Ustinov, and Gromyko, supported by Ponomarev, argued that Karmal was not strong enough and would be overthrown without the support of our troops. That would have sent bad signals to Soviet allies across the world that we could not be relied upon.

Brezhnev did not object, but being an old and experienced politician he understood that a major decision to send our troops abroad could not be made by him or the Politburo alone. He suggested that the Politburo seek the approval of the Central Committee of the party, a larger body of which the Politburo was in effect the powerful steering committee. A Central

Committee plenum of about two hundred party members was called shortly afterward in the Kremlin and unanimously supported the Politburo. Nobody spoke against it.

From then on, Afghan affairs were entrusted to the Andropov-Ustinov-Gromyko troika, which usually operated through a working group of their deputies consisting of Vladimir Kryuchkov for the KGB, Akhromyev for the Defense Ministry, and Georgi Kornienko for the Foreign Ministry. The last two opposed the military intervention but acted under orders of their superiors; later they played an active role in the withdrawal. The troika reported to Brezhnev from time to time with its recommendations, which he and the Politburo normally adopted. As their bosses changed, so did those who served on the troika. They included Eduard Shevardnadze, who later became Gorbachev's foreign minister; Victor Chebrikov of the KGB; and Dmitri Yazov, as minister of defense. Brezhnev so liked the way the troika worked that he set up a number of new troikas for Poland, Cuba, disarmament, and other important issues. In that way, Brezhnev moved away from day-to-day control as he grew more decrepit. He chose to rely on his fellow members of the Politburo who directed the work of the troikas.

What prompted the Kremlin to decide on the invasion of Afghanistan? No documentary evidence has been discovered so far to illuminate the initial motives with certainty, but circumstantial evidence and the testimony of those closely involved in the events make it clear that, in contrast to the claims of the most stubborn American opponents of the Soviet Union, including those in the Carter White House itself, there was no grand strategic plan designed by Moscow to seize a new footing on the way to the oil riches of the Middle East and thus gain global superiority over the United States. Had the Soviet leadership possessed such a plan, it would have paid far more attention to Washington's possible reaction and would have taken preemptive diplomatic measures. But there is no factual evidence in the Soviet archives to prove this theory of strategy of conquest.

It was a Soviet reaction to a local situation in which the security of our southern borders was threatened by the growing instability inside Afghanistan itself and the obvious ineptitude of the Amin government (as well as by troubles in neighboring Iran). Some months later in a private conversation Vance said to me that while he agreed with us that Amin certainly was a villain, I could take his word that Amin was not an American agent. In any case Ustinov believed that unless some measures were taken by us Afghanistan could become in future another U.S. forward base against the Soviet Union lying right against our "soft underbelly" in our Central Asian republics. Ideological reasons also played a serious role—the desire to pre-

serve the pro-Soviet regime to counter the growing challenge of Islamic fun-
damentalism near our border where our Moslem population lived. This
point was actively pressed by Suslov and Ponomarev, secretary of the Central
Committee and head of its international department. They were oppor-
tunists who wanted to grasp the opportunity to enlarge the sphere of Marxist
ideology.

In any case, it can be unambiguously stated that the appearance of
Soviet troops in Afghanistan was not the result of a conscious choice between
expansionism and detente made by the Kremlin leadership. To my knowledge the Kremlin was not even considering this kind of choice in any discussion, and the records I have seen give no evidence that they even thought in
those terms.

It was nevertheless a gross miscalculation. None of the Soviet leaders
ever supposed that a war in a small neighboring state was going to last for ten
years because of the rise of guerrilla resistance, or that the Soviet people
would have to pay dearly for their gamble no matter how hard Moscow tried
to settle Afghanistan's internal affairs by its continued and high-handed interference in the affairs of its own creature, the Kabul government.

During one short stay in Moscow I happened to attend a Politburo
meeting on October 17, 1985, which was the decisive one in determining
our withdrawal. It was a sober and restrained session. For the first time, at
least as far as I know, Gorbachev proposed "a solution for Afghanistan"—it
was time to end our involvement and withdraw. He gave a description of the
situation, the politics, the economics, and what it had meant for our foreign
policy with the United States. Then he said, "We have our boys there, and it's
not quite clear what they're doing there. It's time to leave." He did not dare
to describe the earlier Politburo decision to invade Afghanistan as a gross
blunder because he was addressing essentially the same Politburo that had
voted to go in five years before. But his summary was clear enough: "With
Karmal or without Karmal, we should firmly adopt a course leading to our
earliest withdrawal from Afghanistan." There was no objection and no
strong endorsement, but rather reluctant silent agreement. That was the crucial session that decided in principle our withdrawal from Afghanistan, although it did not yet fix any concrete dates.

The legacy of the past, viewing Afghanistan as a field of struggle between the United States and the Soviet Union for the Third World, had its
lasting effect. Besides, hanging in the air and slowly poisoning it was a growing dilemma that eventually became our own version of the "Vietnam syndrome"—the fear of leaving the battlefield in disgrace in the eyes of the
whole world, thus impairing the image of a great power.

In May of 1986—when Gorbachev gradually succeeded in cleansing the membership of the Politburo—he decided to get rid of Karmal, who had been installed by the Soviet occupation authorities and had proven completely inept. Gorbachev wanted to replace him with a "a strong man," Najibullah, who had been recommended by our security services. Karmal was summoned to Gorbachev's office in the Central Committee building. I remember it vividly because as party secretary for international affairs I happened to be the only witness to their meeting. Gorbachev told Karmal point-blank that he should cede his position to Najibullah and take up residence in Moscow, where his family was already living.

Karmal was dazed. He obsequiously begged Gorbachev to change his mind, promising to perform his duties in a more correct and active way. But Gorbachev was inexorable, because he did not believe any more that Karmal could find a way out of the deadlock that had in fact been created by the Soviet Union itself. The whole scene left a painful impression.

The question of Afghanistan was discussed increasingly inside the Politburo, which finally decided on withdrawal during 1987–1988. On November 3, 1986, my department was put in charge of the withdrawal, operating under the direction of the Politburo. Gorbachev's strategic aim and hope was that Afghanistan would be neutral and that the United States would play a useful role together with us in the future settlement. This turned out to be an illusion.

The withdrawal was completed by February 15, 1989. In December of the same year the Soviet Parliament condemned the invasion retrospectively, declaring that the decision to invade had been taken by a narrow circle in the former leadership, namely Brezhnev, Ustinov, Andropov, and Gromyko. This popular act of repentance was adopted by the new Soviet leadership along with a new approach to foreign and domestic policy. But the decade of tragedy had left a deep scar in the hearts of our people, ended in ignominious failure, and shook the whole Soviet regime.

## Afghanistan and Soviet-American Relations

History has unconditionally condemned the Soviet invasion of Afghanistan, and that verdict is completely accepted by the Russian Federation. But looking back, it is important to understand the motives of the Carter administration's feverish reaction. Carter reacted vehemently, declaring repeatedly, in a hyperbole the leadership of the Soviet Union found incredible, that the invasion was "the greatest threat to peace since World War II." This somewhat unreasonable exaggeration perfectly characterized the agitated state of the president's mind.

Was this, as some believe, the emotional outburst of a scorned and weak leader who was only more determined to react with everything at his command? Or it was a strong, considered decision of the president in the best interests of the country? What was the justification for Carter's outraged and, as some historians see it, overblown reaction that put back Soviet-American relations to the level of the Cold War? Not even the Reagan administration with its active policy of confrontation repeated Carter's most extreme claims that the withdrawal of Soviet troops was the precondition—a highly unrealistic one at that moment—for agreement on arms control and on a broad range of other issues. And why was the American reaction to the introduction of Soviet troops in faraway Afghanistan so disproportionately strong when compared, for example, to the reaction in Europe in 1968 to the Warsaw Pact's invasion of Czechoslovakia, where much more vital interests were involved?

I do not raise these questions to exonerate the Soviet Union in any way for its gross mistakes. I find no easy explanation for them. But it is important to draw lessons from mistakes that both sides made and the opportunities they missed. The Soviet intervention and the sharp response of the United States proved a final turning point in Soviet-American relations. It was the hinge that turned a decade of detente under Nixon and Ford to the years of confrontation under Reagan. Moscow tried to keep the rest of the detente policy afloat, convinced of the need to separate regional conflicts from the central issues of its relations with the United States. Still clinging to its illusions, the Politburo adopted a special policy to that effect on January 20, 1980. But Carter's entourage in the White House was handed a rare opportunity to convince the president of their thesis that the Soviet Union posed a global threat to the United States. The intransigence of both sides over the Afghan question opened a new Cold War.

The deeply erroneous Soviet action provided the American right with a solid political pretext for another spiral of the arms race and renewed attacks on detente, and of course helped the standard-bearer of those attacks, Ronald Reagan, defeat Jimmy Carter for reelection. As for Carter himself, he deliberately and vehemently reduced the whole scope of U.S.-Soviet relations, including nuclear issues, to the Afghan question, thus blocking progress anywhere else. Carter's set of retaliatory moves had a negative effect on the whole complex of Soviet-American relations across the board in politics, trade, economy, culture, science, and technology. The most prominent was his decision to postpone indefinitely the ratification of SALT II, even though the treaty was as much in America's interest as ours. Taken together, these actions constituted all of the administration's policy toward the Soviet Union, and consequently the policy of detente was practically doomed by making it dependent on the withdrawal of Soviet troops from Afghanistan.

Faced with a new situation, the Kremlin went for a reappraisal of Soviet foreign policy, with its main task that of cushioning and finally neutralizing the effect of its invasion of Afghanistan. That helped produce a conspicuous turn in our policy, with its priorities shifted from Washington toward more vigorous contacts with Western Europe. It was not accidental that in the middle of the year Carter chose to warn his European allies against their "illusory hopes" for detente as long as Soviet troops were in Afghanistan. And the Soviet leadership was preparing to take a tough line against the United States.

Finally, what was both remarkable and tragic after the withdrawal of Soviet troops and the end of the Cold War was that both Moscow and Washington lost interest in Afghanistan, which ceased to be an apple of discord. It was gradually forgotten, its civil war dismissed as its own business even though murderous fighting was still under way with weapons left from the supplies of the great powers. Had the long Soviet-American confrontation over Afghanistan been replaced by active Soviet-American cooperation to establish peace and stability, conditions in that war-devastated country might have been very different indeed.

Let me review from largely personal experience what actually happened in our relations during the Afghan crisis. The first rhetorical thrusts were traded almost immediately by Washington and Moscow at the highest level. On December 28, 1979, Carter sent a message to Brezhnev demanding that the invasion force be pulled out, and in a press conference the same day he called the Soviet intervention "a grave threat to peace" and "a blatant violation of accepted international rules of behavior." Later that afternoon, Brezhnev and Carter communicated on the hot line.

In his reply, Brezhnev claimed the Soviet action was temporary but in the same breath informed Carter that the limited contingent of Soviet troops would stay in Afghanistan until their mission was accomplished. A few hours after receiving this message on December 31, Carter gave a television interview accusing Brezhnev of falsifying the facts by claiming that the Soviet Union acted on the Afghan government's request. But he was remembered mostly for his remark that the invasion "has made a more dramatic change in my own opinion of what the Soviets' ultimate goals are than anything they've done in the previous time I've been in office." This was the phrase fastened upon by his domestic opponents as the naive and emotional reaction of a weak leader.

On January 4 the new year began with the president's dramatic television statement requesting a postponement of the Senate debate on the ratification of SALT. He also postponed the opening of new American and Soviet consulates, canceled a whole range of economic and cultural exchanges extending from wheat exports to an opening of paintings from our great collection in the Hermitage at the Metropolitan Museum in New York. He also announced that the United States and its allies would supply munitions, food, and other support to Pakistan, Afghanistan's neighbor, and was prepared to render similar assistance to other countries in the region.

I returned from Moscow on January 20. The Soviet leadership was consumed by strong resentment against Carter and his program of retaliation. Even Brezhnev, who felt rather friendly about Carter after the Vienna summit, cursed Carter heartily because of his hostile campaign. Gromyko was the only one to recommend to me (in his characteristically cautious and laconic way) that I try to learn in Washington whether anything could be done to prevent our relations with America from collapsing altogether. He added that Carter was acting like an elephant in a china shop—that is the Russian version of the well-known English phrase.

For all my experience of anti-Soviet campaigns in the United States, I had never encountered anything like the intensity and scale of this one. What particularly caught my attention was the president's personal obsession with Afghanistan. He repeatedly characterized the Soviet intervention as a direct threat to the security of the United States. Those who favored better relations with the Soviet Union had been largely silenced. I was also surprised by the thesis, widespread in American political circles, that the invasion of Afghanistan marked the start of some broad strategic plan aimed against America, going far beyond Afghanistan itself. Quite a few speculations were produced by all kinds of policy experts. Geostrategic concepts, mostly developed by Brzezinski, obviously prevailed in Washington over other political and diplomatic considerations.*

Vance asked me to come to the State Department for a frank conversation with him a few days after my return. He was noticeably excited and very straightforward. Pointing out that he had always been among those few in the administration who sought to protect our relations against "all kinds of extremists, of whom there are quite a few in Washington," he said the timing of events in Afghanistan could not have been worse because this was an election year. They had dealt a hard blow to Soviet-American relations and to those in the United States who consistently defended them. Vance said it was

---

*At an international seminar on Afghanistan held in Oslo, Norway, in September 1995, newly declassified National Security Council documents were presented that showed Carter and Brzezinski considered the crisis in global and not local terms from the start. In January 1980, within days of our intervention, the president and his national security adviser were discussing the possibility of two broad, opposing axes. One would run through Moscow, Kabul, and New Delhi. The other would run through Pakistan from Washington to Rawalpindi and Beijing—and might eventually take in Teheran!

important to avert a complete break in relations, especially in the heat of the election campaign, and we had to preserve a bridge until things stabilized. That could be accomplished by resuming negotiations on arms control. Given the locus of events in Afghanistan, however, he said talks on demilitarizing the Indian Ocean, which had long been discussed, would have to be off the agenda for now. He added that he had discussed all this with the president, and Carter was ready to continue negotiations, but privately and without any publicity.

I agreed that we certainly were at a low point and should seek a way out together. But I said the Soviet Union could not possibly ignore the anti-Soviet hysteria in the United States when it was being inspired and sponsored by the administration and, putting it bluntly, by President Carter himself. He was going beyond every reasonable limit, and instead of behaving like a responsible statesman was acting like a man overwhelmed by his emotions. I pointed out that in the president's numerous speeches embargoing the export of agricultural products, he persisted in his hope that they would lead to food, meat, and bread shortages in the Soviet Union and this would be felt by the Soviet people. This did not, to put it mildly, contribute to the growth of sympathy for and friendliness toward his administration among the Soviet people. Now, what kind of a bridge was the secretary of state talking about?

All of this was expressed by me rather heatedly, sometimes going beyond the limits of diplomatic courtesy. But I really took very much to heart the disintegration of our relations, which had demanded so much personal effort to build over so many years, although I fully realized that our invasion of Afghanistan had played a disastrous role.

Vance raised a question that seemed to be of particular interest. After a moment's hesitation he asked if the United States could assume that the Soviet Union did not plan to attack Iran or Pakistan from Afghanistan. He compared this to a hypothetical attack on Yugoslavia in case of Tito's death, which would put our relations on the verge of catastrophe. He assured me the United States had no such intentions and did not believe the Soviet Union did either—but the introduction of Soviet troops in Afghanistan, which was not a Warsaw Pact member, had shaken the administration's confidence in the prudent intentions of the Kremlin leadership.

I could feel here the influence of Brzezinski's "arc of crisis" theory. I told Vance I could assure him officially right then and there that the Soviet Union had no plans for expansion into Pakistan, Iran, or any other country of the region.

"Is it also true for Yugoslavia?" Vance asked.

I replied firmly that we harbored no such schemes, adding that I had just returned from Moscow and could speak on the basis of expert knowledge.

Vance observed with noticeable relief that both our countries needed mutual understanding. But the conversation showed me that it was at the secretary of state's initiative rather than the president's that we had an opportunity to talk things over. It was Vance who sought to prevent our relations from collapsing completely in the overheated atmosphere of the White House, and by all appearances, it had not been easy for him to persuade Carter to agree to such a conversation with me. On the other hand, Carter was certainly interested in sounding out our intentions toward Pakistan, Iran, and Yugoslavia, which showed that after all, he did suspect that some "grandiose Soviet scheme" was behind our policy.

Brzezinski had his hour of triumph in Carter's State of the Union address on January 23, when the president unveiled a policy later dubbed the Carter Doctrine, declaring that any attempt by outside forces to gain control over the Persian Gulf would be regarded as an attack on American vital interests and rebuffed by any necessary means, including military force. It sounded like the Truman Doctrine of 1947, which was the first step in the American policy of containing communism. He pledged to conduct an active diplomacy and "make any aggressor pay dearly for his aggression."

This marked a turn in Carter's thinking toward military might as the principal way of dealing with the Soviet Union. Such a radical reaction by the administration to Afghanistan only strengthened feelings against Carter in Moscow. The Soviet leadership had proceeded in Afghanistan from the assumption that it was not vital to American interests and moreover did not threaten American interests in the Gulf, which we knew were vital. Nevertheless, the administration reaction was so violent that it appeared Afghanistan was really regarded as crucial by Washington. This seemed farfetched, because they found it hard to attach much weight to the reasons provided by the administration for the Carter Doctrine and the anti-Soviet sanctions.

At a meeting of the Politburo after Carter's speech, the leadership came to the conclusion that the events in Afghanistan, which the Kremlin still saw as a local conflict, were therefore just a pretext for the Carter administration to resume the arms race on a still greater scale, strengthen American military positions in the Persian Gulf, and launch an overall anti-Soviet offensive. All this threatened to destroy the process of detente irreparably.

The Kremlin leadership continued its intervention in Afghanistan. The fateful chain of events took its course, with both sides losing confidence in each other completely. Brezhnev and his fellow members of the Politburo believed that Carter had consciously made a choice between cooperation and confrontation and decided for the latter. At the same time Carter was convinced that the Afghanistan invasion had been deliberately chosen by Moscow as a test of will. Both were on a collision course.

## Diplomacy and Presidential Emotion

Throughout the late winter and spring Vance and I tried to ease the tension over Afghanistan, although that may have been too much to hope for in an emotionally charged election year. Anti-Soviet feelings were being stoked up in the country, the exploitation of which few politicians could resist. Carter was no exception.

Vance and I held an informal conversation on February 2 during which we discussed the possibility of a meeting of foreign ministers to help clear the air. We both agreed that if he could meet with Gromyko they might try to shift the emphasis from mutual recriminations to calming the political atmosphere slowly and solving some problems. Vance asked me to sound out Moscow. I agreed, but an hour after I left he called me and withdrew his request. He had just talked by telephone with the president in Camp David and was told not to stick his neck out. But Vance kept trying, and on February 8 he told me the president approved the idea in principle. He handed me a private letter to Gromyko, expressing his hopes for their meeting in March, which he viewed as the only opening for the present.

We also discussed the administration's decision, disclosed by Defense Secretary Brown on a visit to China, to supply the Chinese with certain "nonlethal" military equipment, such as trucks and an American satellite terminal station, which Moscow viewed as a departure from the U.S. policy of denying military supplies to China and the Soviet Union. Vance admitted that we had a point: the decision to supply China had been a largely emotional departure made by the president himself because of Afghanistan.

On February 16 Gromyko replied to Vance's suggestion of a meeting with a negative letter very critical of present U.S. policy toward the Soviet Union. "The choice lies with the United States," was the last phrase in Gromyko's letter, echoing Carter's own belligerent statement in Annapolis in 1978.

Vance was rather discouraged by the reply. "Well, we'll have to see how it turns out," he sighed.

Brzezinski then made a speech to a closed White House meeting of the heads of major American corporations in which he accused the Soviet leadership of all mortal sins. It was reported to me by C. William Verity of Armco, cochairman of the U.S.-USSR Trade and Economic Council. Brzezinski said our relations would remain aggravated at least until the end of the election campaign and probably into 1981. Carter, he said, was determined to "punish the Soviet Union" for its activity in Afghanistan, but any military confrontation with the Soviet Union was out of question. The essence of his speech was a warning that the Soviet Union could mount a broad peace offensive with a partial withdrawal of its troops, and it was important not to fall into a Soviet trap and return to the status quo characterized by lack of vigilance in American public opinion about Soviet-American relations.

Two weeks later Vance told me that in his latest discussion with Carter he warned that if things continued as they were, our relations would be so badly damaged that a second Carter administration, if he were reelected, would not last long enough to repair them, and a second term would be a period of confrontation. He told the president that the only way out was to start a reasonable dialogue without giving vent to emotion. But Carter was extremely wrought up—and there were people around him only too eager to keep him in that way.

After some days' reflection, Carter had come to a rather original conclusion: he was asking Brezhnev to receive Marshall Shulman as his personal envoy with a confidential message. When I talked with Brzezinski the next day, he disclosed he had been one of the potential candidates for the trip but—he frankly added—he had been eliminated because of his hard-line reputation. When asked if Shulman had anything new to tell Moscow, Brzezinski said there would be no big surprises but rather a quest for common points for the immediate future. He added that he was not sure Shulman—who had been his own academic colleague at Columbia University—was the right man to conduct such an important exchange of views since he was not "close enough to the president." He evidently disapproved of the trip.

Deep down I was not sure of it, either. What agreement could Shulman produce when a complete deadlock already existed at far more exalted levels? In any event the whole idea proved poorly thought out and just as poorly organized by the American Embassy in Moscow. Shulman himself did not display the necessary perseverance in demanding to deliver his message to Brezhnev directly and returned to Washington without a reply. All that added more bitterness to our relations.

On March 18 Brzezinski invited me to dinner at his country house. He said Carter knew what we would be discussing. First of all, he assured me that the president was not planning to conduct his election campaign on an anti-Soviet platform—unlike some of his Republican rivals. The president wanted our relations normalized because he knew that if they were not, it would mean a lost decade with huge military spending on both sides, but relations would have to return to normal sooner or later because the two superpowers would hardly choose to fight it out in a direct military conflict.

We discussed Afghanistan for two hours, trying to find a mutually acceptable solution. Brzezinski's statements were of some interest because they apparently reflected some of Carter's ideas. At the same time he may just have been sounding me out on his personal ideas, but I had never heard anything of this kind from Vance. Brzezinski proposed that Afghanistan observe strict neutrality to answer Soviet concerns about its southern border. If Moscow tried to convert Afghanistan into an outright communist state and preserve Karmal as its head although he enjoyed no popular support, the United States would continue to oppose it.

Brzezinski stated the position clearly enough. The United States was for a neutral Afghanistan, friendly to the Soviet Union like Finland, but not another vassal state like Mongolia. The United States was also prepared to guarantee noninterference in Afghan affairs as suggested by the Soviet Union, but it would like to know how long Soviet troops would remain. Only a month or two, perhaps, or would it be a matter of years? How about replacing Soviet troops with Moscow's Moslem friends, such as Algeria or Syria? In the last resort, the Soviet Union might retain the right to reintroduce its troops if a threat arose from Afghan territory.

Brzezinski's suggestions could have provided a basis for negotiations if the Soviet leadership had not supported the Karmal regime so doggedly. By the time Gorbachev at last abandoned him, it was too late to negotiate.

Brzezinski also advanced some proposals for other trouble spots in his notorious "arc of crisis" and in China. I liked his straightforward ways, although it sometimes made for agitated conversations. If Iran and Pakistan were prepared to declare their neutrality, he said, the United States was ready to respect it under a secret U.S.-Soviet agreement but not give official guarantees lest they create the impression that the Soviet Union's reach had extended to the Persian Gulf with American consent.

On China, Brzezinski said the even-handed policy had been abandoned in favor of rapprochement for an original but straightforward reason: the administration had repeatedly drawn Moscow's attention to the use of Cuban troops against American interests in various parts of the world, but Moscow had turned a deaf ear; now it chose to use the Chinese in the same way.

I got the impression that Brzezinski had arranged the conversation as part of a definite scheme to emphasize concrete ideas on Afghanistan for the first time. The White House also seemed to have come alive to the apprehensions that Carter had carried his anti-Soviet policy too far. Hence the desire to keep the channel of communication with Moscow serviceable; it probably was no accident that Vance and Brzezinski alternately used it so they could blow hot and cold as it suited them. But the general impression left by the administration's ambiguous approach was rather queer. When contacting me privately to communicate their ideas to Moscow, Carter's people appeared genuinely concerned about the aggravation of our relations, but all the administration's public actions went in precisely the opposite direction.

This could not have been clearer when on March 13 Carter publicly called for a boycott of the summer Olympic Games in Moscow, an appeal that a number of American companies who had committed themselves to supporting the athletes told us privately they could not challenge. A week later a very pessimistic Vance told me Carter seemed to be obsessed with the vengeful idea of "punishing the Soviet Union for Afghanistan." That conversation showed that the Carter-Brzezinski team had substantially clipped Vance's wings. But the Soviet Union shared the blame for that, as it had rejected Vance's proposal for a ministerial meeting that might have helped unblock our relations.

Early in April I was summoned by the Politburo to Moscow for consultations about the sharp aggravation of Soviet-American relations. The Soviet leadership could not accept that Afghanistan was so vital to the interests of the United States and thus found it difficult to comprehend Carter's extreme reactions to Soviet troops in Afghanistan. There were two different explanations. Some thought that the American overreaction resulted, first and foremost, from the emotional instability of Carter himself; after all, he had been ready to allow relations to worsen by defending dissidents and human rights in the Soviet Union. Others believed that Brzezinski's strong anti-Soviet line had gained the upper hand in the administration and led the president along. Afghanistan was a mere pretext.

I told the members of the Politburo that the crux of the problem now was neither Carter himself nor his intellectual mentor Brzezinski. They acted in complete unison. The important point was that they had succeeded in convincing people in America that we were the aggressors in Afghanistan; more than that—that we were trying to expand throughout the Middle East, against American interests there. And there could be no detente with an aggressor. Anti-Soviet campaigns had put in a difficult position even such supporters of good Soviet-American relations as Senators Fulbright and Kennedy, Harriman, Donald Kendall, and many others, especially when nobody could see how detente could be restored in our relations.

I recommended that our foreign policy not concentrate on Washington alone, but find some other countries where constructive dialogue was possible. I felt that a political rapprochement with Carter was for the time being beyond our reach.

There was no serious disagreement among Politburo members. Practically unanimously it was decided to persist in making detente work wherever possible, especially in Europe, while trying to expose the American administration's motives for undermining it. They also found it unrealistic to expect the United States to play any constructive role in the future Afghan settlement. Brzezinski's ideas for neutralization were dismissed because they did not trust him and Carter, and therefore bet all their chips on Karmal as "our man in Kabul." So I had been told by Gromyko and then by Andropov upon arrival in Moscow. In general I found in the Kremlin a stubborn determination to continue its course in Afghanistan and stand fast against Carter.

While not in the least justifying the interventionist policy of the Soviet leadership in Afghanistan, I must note that by linking practically all the questions of our relations to Afghanistan, the administration essentially reduced its policy toward the Soviet Union to just this question alone, although it was hardly realistic to expect then an immediate withdrawal of Soviet troops once we had publicly committed them in an unstable country on our southern border. Did Carter himself believe in the possibility of such a sudden reversal of our policy? I rather think that he did not. But he assumed a tough anti-communist attitude in public, apparently out of electoral considerations, which, I thought, suited him perfectly.

Shortly after I returned, Vance invited me to his office to have coffee and an informal chat. He said he was leaving for Florida for a short rest, but before that, he wanted to hear about my visit to Moscow. I told him there was no anti-American sentiment, but, frankly speaking, resentment against Carter was mounting. People remarked to me with a mixture of incredulity and irony that Carter seemed to be channeling all his official energies into the boycott of the Moscow Olympic Games. (The Japanese ambassador had told me Carter was pressing for "punitive actions" against Moscow with an intensity unparalleled in his diplomatic career and was acting like a man possessed about the Olympic Games.) Vance remarked that Carter's agitation could be traced to the election campaign in general and two foreign policy conundrums in particular, Afghanistan and the American hostages in Iran.

With no further elaboration and after a moment's pause, Vance made then a surprising observation about how politically corrupt Washington had become. No longer were there any human relationships; everyone was eager to cut the ground from under others in a merciless struggle for power—or what seemed to be power. After this bitter reflection, Vance paused and sighed. Then he said he expected to meet Gromyko in Vienna at the celebrations of the twenty-fifth anniversary of Austria's State Treaty in May. His voice was uncharacteristically dull and he expressed no hopes or wishes for the meeting. When we met again on April 20 he told me that Carter was too busy seeking reelection to obtain the ratification of the SALT treaty, and it would have been a miracle to have obtained it anyway while he was continuously attacking the Soviet Union for electoral purposes. As if absorbed in painful reflection, he also admitted, with regret, that his personal struggle for better relations with Moscow had produced no positive results. For the first time he frankly admitted that other forces were gaining the upper hand. He was uncharacteristically sad, as if absorbed in painful reflection, and our conversation was anything but official and routine.

I did not know then that Vance was about to hand in his resignation. The proximate cause was his opposition to the commando operation to rescue the American hostages in Iran. He feared that even a successful outcome would produce casualties among hostages and aggravate U.S. diplomacy. His resignation was kept secret until the catastrophic failure of the operation on April 25, but it really represented the culmination of his dissatisfaction with administration policy. Besides, he did not fit well into the tough political struggle and domestic intrigue characteristic of Washington.

On April 29, the next day after the announcement about his resignation, Vance invited me for a farewell talk. He looked rather gloomy, which was only natural. He warned me to expect bellicose administration statements and threats to use force against Iran in the coming weeks though there were no real plans anymore to do so. Finally Vance looked beyond the elections with some trepidation. He had come to realize that Carter was abandoning the policy of dialogue with the Soviet Union to proceed to a long-term policy of confrontation. That policy would persist even after Carter's reelection, at least as long as Soviet troops stayed in Afghanistan. And that, said Vance, was the unambiguous way the president stated his position on the Soviet Union to his entourage.

In thinking of Vance's personal qualities of fairness and equanimity, I thought of the brief diplomatic career of Thomas Watson, the chairman of IBM. He was known to be a broad-minded businessman and well-disposed toward the Soviet Union, where he had ferried American planes as a World War II pilot. He had been appointed ambassador to Moscow at the time of the Vienna summit to succeed Malcolm Toon, a belligerent career diplomat. Watson did not have an easy time of it in Moscow because of Afghanistan and Iran. After Vance resigned, Watson cabled him to say he planned to make a quick visit to Washington to find out what was going on. Tensions were high, and Vance told me he hoped Watson would not follow him in resigning because it would be a disservice to the president during the election campaign, and it was especially important to have "a man of good will in Moscow who was eager to improve relations."

The problem with Watson, he said, was that as a businessman he "takes it all very much to heart. He is not a man to restructure his life easily. When he was at the head of one of the biggest corporations in the world, he did not know what a deadlock was. He could always find a compromise. Now our relations are at an impasse. A professional diplomat can see that and will bide his time. But Watson cannot remain inactive, he is nervous and at a loss about what to do."

On June 8, Vance invited me and my wife to a farewell dinner with his wife in his home. Only the four of us were present. We had a private conversation that was a mutual acknowledgment of personal friendship, itself a remarkable experience during such tense times. I was sorry indeed that a man of such caliber had to leave during such troubled times.

# V. Carter's Defeat:
# An Epitaph for Detente

## Deadlock on the Eve of the Elections

By now it should be clear that the principal weight in Moscow's judgment of an American president, whether in office or as a candidate, lay in the degree to which the leadership in the Kremlin felt he would advance and deepen Soviet-American relations and thus prevent them from being thrown back into another cold war. In the 1960s there was no question that Lyndon Johnson was the preferred candidate over Barry Goldwater for just that reason, and the reader will recall that Moscow misguidedly offered to help the campaign of Hubert Humphrey because of its profound worries about Richard Nixon, who had advanced his political career as an anti-communist. When Nixon in office surprised everyone, he and his diplomatic costar Henry Kissinger were preferred by Moscow over the liberal George McGovern of the Democrats in 1972 for reasons of continuity in our relations if nothing else, and that was also the case with Gerald Ford.

Jimmy Carter's presidency was also a surprise to Moscow but an unpleasant one. If we had misread him at the beginning, so had the voters of the United States. In his reelection campaign Moscow so distrusted Carter that it could not bring itself to support him even against Ronald Reagan.

But that also grew from a misreading of Reagan; the Kremlin found it impossible to believe that Americans would want to turn their backs on detente and return to the suspicions, the warlike behavior, and the huge military spending of the Cold War. But because of Carter's obsession with Afghanistan, that was already happening.

Our first opportunity to determine whether Carter would ever manage to cool down about Afghanistan and redirect his administration toward broader issues came with the appointment of a new secretary of state, Edmund Muskie, a senator from Maine who had tried to win the presidential nomination in 1972 and was generally respected in his party. I knew him as a steady person but one who did not know much about Soviet-American relations. I discussed Muskie with Ambassador Watson, who called on me the day after Muskie's nomination was announced. He said Muskie remained a man of liberal views, that he of course wanted to leave a record as a good secretary of state, but he had no clear ideas about what exactly to do.

Muskie and Gromyko met for the first time in Vienna at the celebrations for the twenty-fifth anniversary of the signing of the Austrian State Treaty and discussed the principal international issues. The administration's hostility toward the Soviet Union was starkly evident, especially during the discussion of Afghanistan. Muskie was calm and reserved, his sound judgment contrasting with most other administration officials, but his balanced views were drowned out by Washington's generally negative policy toward the Soviet Union. Gromyko spoke in favor of relaxing international tension, which hardly sounded convincing in the context of our actions in Afghanistan. In his report to the Politburo, Gromyko said the meeting was further proof that the Carter administration was shifting its policy toward making Soviet-American relations worse.

I was invited to meet Muskie at the State Department on June 16. He said he had thought about his Vienna meeting with Gromyko and had dispatched a letter through Watson which he hoped would restart our relations, but he was disappointed by Gromyko's reply, which he found half-hearted. I asked him whether his letter had contained any shifts in the American position. He replied after some reflection that the letter should be regarded as a summary of the American position. Not surprisingly, our conversation produced no results on Afghanistan or other questions. It was all a repetition of the past, and there was evidently no hope for a positive shift in relations with the Carter administration so sharply focused on Afghanistan. Although Muskie's views and sentiments were closer to those of Vance than of Brzezinski, he brought no changes.

The administration meanwhile was taking further steps "to deter the enemy," that is, the Soviet Union. In August the White House leaked that the Carter administration had adopted "a new nuclear strategy" envisioning the possibility of a protracted nuclear war with preemptive strikes against military targets in the Soviet Union as well as a nuclear war of mass destruction by strikes at enemy cities. Other directives signed by Carter provided for enabling military and government leaders to conduct hostilities from reinforced bunkers with secure communications after nuclear war had broken out and for mobilizing the economy to survive a nuclear war. Press reports on these directives, which were never officially made public, described them as part of the campaign of nuclear deterrence to demonstrate to the Soviet Union that the United States was capable of enduring a protracted nuclear conflict. Special command exercises had been conducted in simulated wartime conditions with President Carter participating. The United States government was stepping up the level of military hysteria. Twice the signal of Soviet nuclear attacks was mistakenly sounded because of electronic mal-functions.

So, the dominant theme of the last period of the Carter administration was to increase the sense of military preparedness against the Soviet Union instead of seeking accord. Carter's proclaimed choice between cooperation or confrontation had turned into nuclear deterrence and confrontation, and this was reinforced by the rapid growth of the military budget. Such was the metamorphosis or, if you like, the evolution of Carter as a president. In other words, Democrat Jimmy Carter left to Republican President Ronald Reagan a solid legacy of nuclear war plans and prepared the basis for Reagan's nuclear strategy. Moscow took its own countermeasures, and our military expendi-tures reached a record level. As a result, genuine security and common sense were the losers in this power play.

## Courting Moscow Before the Election

In the middle of June Harriman visited me, and he sounded very pessimistic. For the first time he talked about his advanced age and his death (he was about to turn eighty-nine), but he was anxious to make one last endeavor to put Soviet-American relations back on a more constructive track. His urgent suggestion was for the Soviet Union to make a prominent and dramatic ges-ture in Afghanistan, for example, an announcement of the start of a troop re-duction. Better than most Soviet leaders of that period, Harriman realized that the Afghan war was hopeless and damaged our relations enormously. He felt desperately helpless to remedy the situation and blamed Brzezinski and Carter—who appeared "hypnotized" by his loquacious aide.

"When I heard about Vance's resignation," Harriman said, "my first im-pulse was to take the earliest flight to Fiji or somewhere far away from Washington, if only to avoid making the painful choice between voting for Carter and Brzezinski, or for Reagan in the November election." He said that only when he learned that Vance was to be replaced by Muskie did he decide he could vote for Carter, after all, but he had refused a White House appeal to support the president in his campaign for reelection.

Then I had a visit from the other side. General Brent Scowcroft, who had served as Kissinger's deputy at the National Security Council and then as na-tional security adviser to Ford, had just been included in the list of Reagan's foreign policy advisers. He dined with me on July 2 and said that if Moscow gave Carter an opportunity to help resolve Afghanistan, Carter would very likely be reelected. But if the Soviet Union sat on the fence till the end of the election campaign and gave no trumps to Carter, Reagan had a good chance of winning. He was sounding me out on what I thought would happen. I pointed out to Scowcroft that given the hostile statements made by both contenders, the Soviet Union would find it hard to show its preference for either.

"What do you think?" I asked.

Scowcroft said he knew Carter well enough: the president had the vehement nature of a missionary, leaning toward exaggerations and overstatements while having no underlying belief in the correctness of his course. At first he had favored disarmament, but then he switched to a feverish arms buildup. He had believed in the possibility of reaching an agreement with the Soviet Union, but then became all but obsessed with the idea of a crusade on all fronts against the Soviet Union. Besides, his passion for seeking "various options" from different advisers led to zigzags in foreign and domestic policy, sowing antagonism among the advisers themselves.

By contrast, Scowcroft said, Reagan was like Eisenhower in that he preferred to receive an agreed and coordinated recommendation from his principal advisers so as not to be confused by conflicting options. If he did not like what he got, he would ask them to go back and think it over again. Hence Reagan's desire to select experts for positions of importance to whom he would delegate considerable powers. He characterized Reagan as pragmatic and not as incorrigibly anti-Soviet as his public statements made him appear.

I pointed out to Scowcroft that American voters that year appeared less eager to support one candidate than to oppose the other. He agreed. "So let us wait to see who the American people dislikes more," I said.

I should add that this was not the first approach by a Reagan emissary. Earlier, on March 3, 1979, I was visited by Richard Allen as Reagan's personal representative. I had known him since he had served on Nixon's White House staff. Allen conveyed a personal request from Reagan, who had not yet formally announced his candidacy but would soon do so, for a meeting with Brezhnev and Kosygin in Moscow or, failing that, with one of a number of Soviet leaders. I told Allen that Reagan was well known to us as an extreme right-wing political figure—and what was he hoping to gain? Was it just an election gimmick on his part? Would he redouble his efforts to attack the Soviet Union on his return under the pretext that his visit had made him more expert?

Allen denied that. He drew a parallel between Reagan and Nixon, reminding me of the latter's attitude to the Soviet Union before and after becoming president. Reagan had already traveled much, meeting many leaders of European countries, he said. He had recently been invited by the Chinese. But Reagan believed it was more important to go to the Soviet Union since

Soviet-American relations were more crucial than Chinese-American relations. Reagan had to fight his own political image in order to broaden his election base, Allen said, and was trying to shift to the center on both domestic and foreign policy.

I recommended to Moscow that Reagan be invited in April, the month he had proposed, and after some hesitation Moscow consented. The trip was postponed and never took place, since Reagan had decided by that time to conduct his election campaign in an anti-Soviet spirit.

Then it was Brzezinski's turn. On July 12 we had lunch in my apartment. We discussed Afghanistan, China, SALT, and the Middle East without advancing matters very much. He stated at the outset that he and Carter both recognized that if the deterioration in our relations continued we risked a return in the 1980s to the Cold War period between 1947 and 1955, but it would be far more dangerous, since the military might of the two countries had grown immensely. The question, he said, was whether the two governments would be able to summon up the courage and strength to overcome their differences. I responded that he had posed a very good question, but I would like him to put it first to the administration.

As if addressing Moscow on Carter's behalf—but without saying so directly—he came to his main point, that Soviet-American relations would be better if Carter remained president instead of handing over to Reagan. I asked him to prove it. Brzezinski evidenced Carter's readiness to continue negotiations on arms control and to the "unreasonable demands" for military appropriations made by Reagan, as well as Reagan's long history of opposing the Soviet Union. But simultaneously, Brzezinski insisted that Afghanistan was still the main problem in our relations, summarized the proposals he had outlined before, and repeated the official position on SALT and China. All this would hardly persuade Moscow to support Carter against Reagan.

In the middle of August the Politburo cast its vote. Fed up with Carter and uneasy about Reagan, it decided to stay on the fence. That was in effect what had been proposed by our embassy in Washington. After a special meeting to consider the Foreign Ministry's recommendation—I personally participated in its formulation—the Politburo realized that in a close race it would be wise to keep lines open to both sides. A directive stated "not to break the dialogue at our own initiative, and try to prevent Soviet-American relations from worsening further, keeping some positive assets for future use without prejudice to our interests or positions. If Reagan or his entourage show an interest in contacts with us, we should not avoid them." The Soviet press was told to give both candidates equal coverage and show no preference for either one.

Brezhnev commented: "Even the devil himself could not tell who is better—Carter or Reagan."

Early in October, I was visited by the industrialist Armand Hammer. He told me he had breakfasted in Carter's office with the president and a group of businessmen, most of them Jewish. Also at the breakfast was Robert Strauss, Carter's campaign manager, also Jewish and one of Washington's most important power brokers.

Carter, said Hammer, was clearly alarmed at the way things stood in the election campaign. Reagan had scored many points. The personal attacks launched by the White House against Reagan had not worked. Indeed they had boomeranged and undercut Carter's reputation as a decent man. Admitting that his campaign had stalled and he was at a crossroads, he called upon the businessmen for contributions to buy broadcast time. He especially stressed the importance of the Jewish community. By virtue of their organization, Jews could tip the outcome in his favor in the crucial states of New York, California, Florida, Pennsylvania, and others. Carter complained that the American Jewish community did not sufficiently appreciate his service to Israel in promoting the Camp David agreement and allocating huge official military and economic support to Israel. In conclusion, Carter asked the businessmen, Hammer first of all, to influence the Jewish community in his favor.

Hammer therefore came to me inquiring whether the Soviet leadership could expand Jewish emigration, which had been sharply reduced during recent months, mainly because of Carter's attacks on human rights in the USSR.

"Carter won't forget that service if he is reelected," Hammer said, implying that he gave the assurance with Carter's knowledge.

It goes without saying that Moscow did not react to his request. I believed that one important reason Carter was in trouble during the election was that he had no reliable support in his own party. He campaigned for the presidency as an outsider and not as one of the party's leaders. At the end of his presidency he remained an outsider to most of the leading Democrats in Washington, particularly the members of his own party in Congress.

Let me say a word here about the late Armand Hammer. It was no secret that, as with many leading American businessmen, I maintained periodic contact with him. But because of his connections with the Soviet Union—he was born in Russia, came to the United States as a young man, was one of the first Americans to do business with the new Bolshevik government— he was always a favorite American in Moscow. But he never shook off the rumors abroad that he had a special relationship with the KGB. Of this I have no personal knowledge. Hammer himself told me that Ronald Reagan's wife, Nancy, with whom he was on friendly terms, had shown him a private memo from Richard Allen, the president's assistant for national security affairs, warning Reagan against maintaining close ties with Hammer. Allen was convinced that Hammer was a secret KGB agent, although he had no evidence to prove it. According to Nancy Reagan, her husband had a good laugh at Allen's suspicions and left it at that. Moreover, he appointed Hammer White House coordinator of medical institutions engaged in cancer research, a largely honorary charitable position, as a reward for Hammer's campaign contributions.

While in Moscow Hammer liked to discuss politics but usually he would come up with rather primitive ideas, for example, on how to improve Soviet-American relations. This was his favorite and I suppose sincerely felt theme. He even tried to appoint himself a confidential go-between and organize a high-level dialogue. He was eager to impress us with tales of his conversations with presidents, many of whom had received his generous campaign contributions. But as far as I know he was never used by the American government as its representative, and we acted accordingly. Gromyko especially did not like this type of amateur diplomacy; as foreign minister he had to explain to Brezhnev that many of Hammer's ideas were either impractical or worthless. And we certainly never asked Hammer to carry any messages to the U.S. government on our behalf.

Respect for Hammer in the Soviet Union arose from an entirely different source—the legacy of his acquaintance with Lenin. In Moscow he would always be introduced as a man who knew Lenin, and this opened doors for him. To some of our leaders he proved an interesting conversationalist. Brezhnev liked to talk with him about life in America and political gossip in Washington, including his conversations with presidents and other prominent Americans. He usually exaggerated his political influence and flattered his Soviet listeners.

Prime Minister Kosygin respected Hammer as a businessman and liked his way of dealing. Once I witnessed negotiations between Hammer and Kosygin for a chemical project worth several billion dollars, which was discussed for several months by our representatives without success. Then Hammer asked for a direct meeting with Kosygin. When they met Hammer made concrete proposals, stated exactly how much money he was prepared to invest and what kind of money he expected both sides to earn. After some lively discussion, Hammer took a piece of paper and drafted a "framework of understanding" containing several key figures. Kosygin corrected one or two figures. Hammer agreed and the deal was done. All the details were left to their assistants, whose work was guided by the handwritten framework. Hammer understood his business of dealing with our important people quite well, and I suppose he made good money in our country and got a lot of publicity, too.

Two weeks before the election, Brzezinski visited me at our embassy and surprised me by talking about improving our relations if Carter remained in power. It was hard to say whether it was aimed at obtaining some positive gestures from Moscow on the eve of the poll, or whether it was Brzezinski's way of acknowledging that the policy of confrontation was reaching an impasse. In any case, it was remarkable enough to hear what he, of all people, had to offer.

Brzezinski assured me that a second Carter administration would be interested in making a good start "to the process of gradual normalization" in what they believed were the three most important directions. First, SALT: negotiations would resume and the arms race would be slowed by decreasing the pace of military spending. Second, Brzezinski said the war between Iran and Iraq threatened to turn into a war of attrition, and he suggested that we agree that if either of the two nations collapsed, neither Moscow nor Washington would yield to the temptation to exploit the vacuum. The third important change would be in Afghanistan: the administration would no longer link a Soviet withdrawal to SALT, and Carter would no longer insist on replacing Babrak Karmal, although his transfer to some respectable position and replacement by a new prime minister could contribute to a settlement.

Brzezinski also had a surprise. He claimed the administration had revised the American diplomatic theory that the Soviet Union was behind many of the Third World developments adverse to the United States. He cited Nicaragua and El Salvador as examples. I welcomed this conversion and said both sides should have had to admit it sooner or later, so better late than never. After the election, when passions subsided in the United States, he said the administration planned to broaden contacts and perhaps even establish diplomatic relations with Angola, Vietnam, and Cuba. And finally, although he said Washington would continue developing mutually advantageous contacts with China, it was not going to sell military equipment to Beijing and a Sino-American military alliance was "absolutely out of the question."

Brzezinski did not draw a direct comparison between Reagan and Carter, but his statements strongly implied that, if reelected, Carter would still be able to put Soviet-American relations on the right track even though the process was unlikely to be easy. His message was clear: Moscow should not do anything to diminish Carter's chances in the election race and might even help a bit.

That meeting took place on October 16. Brzezinski called on me again on October 31, only days before the November 4 election. He admitted that Carter was losing momentum and that the race would be close enough so it might even be decided by the weather on election day, which affects the turnout. Rather unexpectedly, Brzezinski began to talk about the Soviet attitude to him personally. He said that many prominent American political figures brought back critical assessments of him from Soviet officials, who in private conversations explained his animosity by the fact that he was Polish. He added that even the great Russian poet, Aleksandr Pushkin, had held the same kind of anti-Polish views!

Brzezinski enlarged on his theme by saying that history had indeed complicated relations between the Poles and the Russians and the tragic past was not completely over. He admitted to some subconscious prejudice as well. But he insisted that his conscious conviction was different: he was well aware of the fact that the national destiny of the Poles was unbreakably connected to the Soviet Union, to Russia. Against a background of the Germans' struggle for reunification, Poland had no other alternative but to ally itself with Moscow. Otherwise, the Germans would crush Poland, and "as a former Pole" he saw no other choice for Poland.

"Of course," he said, "I am a long way from liking everything about the Soviet Union and its policy. But I am not all that anti-Soviet as Moscow believes I am. For that matter, I am not any worse than Kissinger. He was lucky, though. From the very outset, Nixon sent him to Moscow to negotiate with Brezhnev, Gromyko, and other leaders. So Kissinger managed to establish a personal relationship with the Soviet leadership, although they could hardly have any illusions about his personality or his views. But I was put by force of circumstance in the position of being an *éminence grise* with the hard reputation of being one hundred percent anti-Soviet. None of the Soviet leaders would even talk with me."

I pointed out that it was not us but the president of the United States who selected American negotiators, and we would have accepted any choice made by Carter. It was clear from my conversation that if Carter were reelected, Brzezinski would be more than willing to occupy a loftier position and have more direct contacts with high-ranking Soviet officials, which I believed would be better for our relations than the continued behind-the-scenes maneuvers by a resentful and energetic presidential assistant. But that was my last meeting with him in his official capacity.

Finally, Henry Kissinger himself came to see me. I must preface the account of our conversation by telling of our last meeting, which had taken place almost one year before in November of 1979. I criticized him then for

opportunist behavior in moving toward the right with anti-Soviet statements in public and abandoning the policy he himself had pursued in office.
I asked him what he hoped to gain from it. Kissinger argued that his essential
views on Soviet-American relations remained unchanged, but he had to take
into account the mood of the public, especially as it moved toward the election. He was busy working with the Republican Party and seemed to be expecting to return as secretary of state if the Republicans returned to office;
then he could resume his policies of focusing on Soviet-American relations.
He was therefore anxious to remain on friendly terms with every potential
Republican candidate and not antagonize any of them. Although he would
not come out against Reagan, he was sure that Reagan would be the only one
who would not bring him into his administration under any circumstances.

Now it was almost a year later. Kissinger called on me again on October
22. He surprised me with the statement that he was making his visit with the
personal knowledge of no less than Reagan, with whom he had had a long
conversation in private the day before. Kissinger said the Reagan camp was
fairly confident of victory (absent some last-minute surprise from the Carter
camp) and was looking ahead. Kissinger had made some suggestions to
Reagan about developing relations with the Soviet Union, and Reagan had
authorized him to communicate them to Moscow in confidence.

Kissinger proceeded to tell me that if Reagan were elected, his best
course would not be to follow the scenario in his belligerent election
speeches because it would lead to continuous tension with Moscow and also
inflame America's relations with its allies. Kissinger explained that he knew
the Soviet leadership could not be browbeaten in matters it believed to be of
vital importance, and the Soviets were aware of the vital interests of the
United States, though they might not acknowledge them in public. It was
therefore important for the new president to recognize his limits and for
Moscow to know the boundaries of the really important interests of the
United States.

If Reagan won the election, Kissinger continued, it would be expedient
to clarify all this to the Kremlin by sending his personal envoy to Moscow
before the inauguration to outline the areas where the two governments
could immediately start searching for agreement, including SALT, and to establish a continuously operating private channel between Reagan and
Brezhnev. Kissinger added that he had not proposed any candidates for such
a mission, although he remarked nonchalantly that if Reagan were to choose
him he would most probably agree to go. He told me I could inform
Moscow of all this with Reagan's direct consent. But he cautioned me against
interpreting it as the start of an immediate dialogue with Reagan, which
would have to await the outcome of the election, and even then Kissinger

would still have to be sure that Reagan would agree. He promised to contact me after the election.

This remarkable talk left a strange impression. It was difficult to believe that Reagan suddenly was prepared to undergo a postelection conversion. But was he trying to use Kissinger to reassure Moscow that he was not the mad anti-Soviet right-winger we might have thought he was, perhaps in hope of forestalling any last-minute Soviet move that might support Carter and undermine his own candidacy? Rather doubtful. I believe that Kissinger, hoping for a comeback to high politics, was fully capable of developing some scenario or grand scheme about superpower relations in conversation with Reagan, just as he had done during his years with Nixon. Reagan on the eve of the crucial election evidently did not mind Kissinger having a talk with us about ideas of his own making, perhaps to gauge the Soviet reactions about first contacts with the possible new president. After all, they were Kissinger's suggestions, not Reagan's. In any case Kissinger was too smart to believe that Reagan would be favorably disposed toward him and his ideas. That is why he suggested we await the outcome of the election to see what Reagan would do. My recommendation to Moscow was not to react in any way for the time being and wait for the result of the election. Kissinger never became an adviser to Reagan.

## Carter's Defeat

Reagan won a decisive victory over Carter which swept out many liberal internationalists, Senator Frank Church among them. Soon afterward we received sound advice about how to deal with the new president, and it came from no less than Richard Nixon. The former president came down from New York unexpectedly to attend the embassy's National Day reception, which was held just two days after the election on November 6. He said his visit had a special purpose: he had decided to talk with me about Reagan and asked me to bring his views to Brezhnev's notice.

Nixon said he had known Reagan well, and for a long time. (Both were Californians.) While it was true that his views were conservative and indeed anti-communist, and it was also true that he wanted America to be strong, he was a fairly reasonable and, most important, a pragmatic political figure. Nixon was sure that the Soviet leadership would establish good relations with Reagan in the long run, the same way it had with him. But it would take some time, maybe a long time. It was important that the Soviet leadership keep that prospect in mind and not engage him prematurely in any dispute over Cuba or some other sore point, because Reagan would only become more stubborn.

Nixon went on to say that he maintained private contacts with Reagan, who consulted him on various questions time and again. He hoped they would keep in touch, and that he would be able to make a positive contribution by drawing on his own long experience to help Reagan get a better idea of the Soviet Union and its policies. Nixon said he would like to meet with me again after Reagan had picked his cabinet to offer some practical advice about doing business with the Reagan administration.

The former president looked good. He was clearly buoyed by Reagan's coming to power. It was still uncertain just how strong his influence was, although Reagan had confirmed in public that he consulted Nixon on certain matters. But I must admit that Nixon's predictions about how Reagan would act over the long term proved fairly correct.

In Moscow, our initial policy toward Reagan became the subject of active debate among the Soviet leadership. We were still uncertain of his future stance toward the Soviet Union. Reagan would be inaugurated the following January 20, and on November 17 the leadership instructed the embassy in Washington to contact Reagan's entourage to "take a closer look at these officials and obtain a clear idea of them," especially their views on foreign policy and of course, Soviet-American relations. "It goes without saying," the instructions read, "that this should be done discreetly, without haste, and unobtrusively, allowing for their readiness to make contacts." But Reagan's associates, busy preparing for the inauguration and enjoying their publicity, showed no such readiness.

In Washington I was surprised how quickly most of the American press had changed its attitude toward the presidency. Many in the news media, cynical and jaded since the death of Jack Kennedy, embraced Reagan as a new hero. They had seen Johnson as crude, Nixon as a liar, Ford as a bumbler, and Carter as an incompetent. But they were certainly rooting for the new president.

# VI. The Dismantling of Detente

When Ronald Reagan was inaugurated as president on January 20, 1981, he inherited a legacy of ruined detente in Soviet-American relations and a new era of the cold war. I was an eyewitness to these changes, or rather to the considerable evolution undergone by the foreign policy of the United States during the past two decades—from the enormous vitality, drama, and even danger of the era of Kennedy and Khrushchev; to the time of Johnson, dominated by Vietnam and, on our side, by the invasion of Czechoslovakia; to the era of detente and summits under Nixon and Ford. The pendulum of the American policy had swung sharply to the extreme right from the period of relaxation of international tension and the normalization of Soviet-American relations.

But I also see the decade of detente as a decade of missed opportunities, with blame enough for everyone. There was always one question that remained unanswered after Nixon and Carter. What was the historic nature of Soviet-American relations? Was it detente or confrontation? What were the principal reasons behind the change in our relations? More than ever, we should understand it now, in the 1990s.

Although detente proved short-lived, the importance of this failed experiment in partnership should not be underestimated. First of all, it showed the world that continuous confrontation between two social and political systems was not fatally inevitable and that detente could reduce considerably the risk of a nuclear confrontation. Serious agreements were reached on military matters, and arms control was placed increasingly higher on the agenda of our relations, although progress was impeded by hesitation and sheer delay. The policy was undoubtedly a success for both American and Soviet foreign policy as long as it lasted, but it unfortunately proved short-lived, incomplete, and not durable.

Who should be held responsible for the failure of detente? The Soviet Union or the United States? American historians blame the expansionist foreign and conservative domestic policies of the Soviet Union. Soviet historians during communist times almost unanimously blamed it on the aggressive policy followed by the United States. The new historical researchers of the

Russian Federation have jumped to the other extreme and paid their own tribute to a new process of radical revision about the former Soviet establishment by zealously laying practically all the blame on the former regimes of the Soviet Union, though a few, like Georgi Arbatov in his latest works, have sought a more balanced picture in the history of our relations.

But the matter is much more complex, and when the Cold War ended, few were left from our own era to answer the questions with personal, first-hand knowledge of events. I will try to summarize and analyze them from my own experience.

The principal reason for the failure was the existence of contradictory concepts of detente in the Soviet Union and the United States. They proved difficult to reconcile, and the final inability of both elites to do so is what ultimately destroyed the policy. The Soviet elite, as well as the administrations of Nixon, Ford, or Carter, never really examined and thoroughly questioned their respective philosophical and political assumptions about the policy.

The Soviet leaders after Stalin were content to see detente as a form of class struggle. They regarded as it a natural condition of political life but not as an inevitable and dangerous war with the capitalist world, which must be prevented. Thus they pursued it while simultaneously engaging in military and diplomatic activity in the Third World, proud to be assisting the struggles of subject peoples toward their liberation and trying to direct them along a familiar road to socialism. They thought that this would ultimately bring triumph over capitalism, and without a devastating nuclear war.

The American administrations saw the principal achievement of detente quite differently. For them it was a way of managing the emergence of Soviet power on the global scene. Washington and Moscow were equally anxious to accomplish this. But the United States, taking quite a different view of the class struggle as it affected other countries, pursued its global confrontation with the Soviet Union through the containment of communism and continued its pressure on the socialist part of the world community, counting on detente eventually to destabilize Eastern Europe and the USSR.

An important factor that strongly influenced detente and its mirror image, the arms control process, was the military misconceptions of both countries in dealing with the possibilities of nuclear war. They based their military planning on the worst possible scenario—a nuclear first strike with maximum devastation on the enemy. But lack of any real perception of the motives and intentions of the other side created an unstable situation grounded in mutual suspicion and mistrust. This slowed the SALT negotiations while technological advances in weaponry made agreements obsolete even as they were being negotiated.

Our nuclear strategies were also kept shrouded in ambiguity. Years later, the truth emerged at a conference sponsored by the Brown University Center for Foreign Policy Development, which I attended with veterans of those times at St. Simon Island, Georgia, in May 1994. On the American side, Vance, Brzezinski, and Harold Brown assured the Russian participants that the Carter administration did not work under a first-strike doctrine against the Soviet Union (though Carter—like his predecessors—considered the possibility of using nuclear weapons first in case of a mass Soviet attack by conventional forces in Europe). Two high-ranking Russian generals, Nikolai Detinov and Viktor Starodubov, both of them participants in nuclear war planning during the Cold War, also confirmed that the Soviet government and general staff never followed a first-strike doctrine because, contrary to its public statements in the 1960s, they were convinced that nuclear war would cause unacceptable damage to both countries. As Khrushchev had said, "the living will envy the dead."

Nevertheless hundreds of billions were spent to counterbalance the mutual fear of a sudden nuclear attack when—as we now know—neither side even conceived of such a strategy because it knew what horrors it would visit on both. Detente was a welcome relief from these fears, but these contradictory views could not be codified into a concept acceptable to the two superpowers. Each actually followed its own vision of detente. Each applied a double standard that favored its own motives when judging the behavior of the other. At the same time the leaders of both sides failed to explain to the public the limits of detente as well as its promises.

For the United States, detente began with the arrival in office of Nixon and Kissinger. The question of the time was whether the old politician had become, in his own campaign phrase, a "new" Nixon. It was the wrong question. While remaining a conservative, he undoubtedly started to consider new approaches to the existing relations with the Soviet Union. Nevertheless, for all the unquestionable contribution made by Nixon and Kissinger to the establishment and promotion of detente, I formed the conviction based on my frequent and close contacts with them, that when they came to power they had not thought through their concept of detente, let alone devised a way to end the Cold War. I believe they did not even consider it at that time as their final objective because they simply had not thought that far ahead.

During their first year or so, Nixon and Kissinger took no appreciable initiatives in Soviet-American relations because their most urgent foreign policy priority was to end the war in Vietnam. That, and not some abstract diplomatic notion of detente, was the main motivation for their desire to improve relations with the Soviet Union. In short, the concept of detente came to be linked to a much more urgent and short-term task, ending the Vietnam war.

But it would be an unacceptable simplification to link everything to Vietnam. Long-term factors finally came into play when Nixon and Kissinger came to consider the strategic parity and stability of relations between the United States and the Soviet Union, which of course was an essential matter for America's security. Hence the goal of trying to fix through negotiations the most favorable correlation of strategic and conventional armed forces. Another significant reason was the desire of the American administration to control, by strengthening its contacts with Moscow, the behavior of its West European allies, which were independently seeking to develop their relations with the Soviet Union. And I have already described occasions on which electoral considerations affected the idea of improving Soviet-American relations, but they were a matter of tactics rather than strategy.

The successive administrations of Nixon, Ford, and especially Carter did not pursue a consistent course of detente. Their very concept of detente was contradictory and ambiguous. It is sufficient to recall that the White House put its forces on combat alert against the Soviet Union at the height of the Arab-Israeli war in the fall of 1973. This quite bluntly and forcefully demonstrated that the American leadership was not really prepared to recognize the Soviet Union as an equal partner in such areas as the Middle East no matter how often the word "partnership" was used in the agreements we signed.

In domestic terms, it is also important that the movement in support of detente, although rather strong in business, church organizations, and many public policy and foreign relations councils, did not function in the United States as a united coalition. The deeper political foundations for detente were never laid in broad contacts between the legislature and public of both countries. Inadequate cooperation in business, culture, and science impeded the formation of a material and sociopolitical underpinning. This prevented us from finding solutions in the highly emotional domain of human rights and obstructed the process of neutralizing the stereotypes of the Cold War.

Meanwhile the opponents of detente were well organized and vigorously active. The Committee for the Present Danger, formed by influential circles to pressure the government about Soviet-American relations played a particularly negative part. So did Jewish and neoconservative groups and their publicists. Eventually the representatives of the most conservative, chauvinist, and bellicose part of American politics came gradually to the fore under Ronald Reagan, pressing for the restoration of American world leadership after the defeat in Vietnam.

Events in the Third World also caused considerable damage to the cause of detente—Angola, Ethiopia, Somalia, Yemen, Afghanistan—and this strongly undermined the concept developed by Kissinger and Nixon when they and their successors discovered that detente by no means ensured a freeze on the social and political status quo in the world. Moscow also proceeded from an erroneous assumption: that Soviet-American relations could develop independent of events in other parts of the globe.

In response, the United States developed a doctrine of coordinating different aspects of its relations with Moscow to bring pressure on the Soviet Union in areas that Washington believed to be of vital importance to us, for example, in the way it used the SALT process. This doctrine of "linkage" was advocated by Kissinger even though it contradicted his goal of reaching Soviet-American agreements limiting nuclear arms. Kissinger thus clashed with Kissinger, and this froze the strategic arms negotiations at the start of the 1976 election. The result was Ford's decision to replace the word detente with the slogan of peace through strength. "Soviet expansionism" became a new term of alert. With Carter and Brzezinski, SALT became an even greater hostage to linkage.

Watergate of course had sharply reduced the ability of both Nixon and Ford to pursue a consistent course in Soviet-American relations, but restrictive Soviet policy on Jewish emigration and the persecution of dissidents inflicted increasing damage during the Carter administration. The policy of linking detente to Soviet internal developments marked a sharp departure from the Nixon and Ford administrations. The Soviet leadership considered it an attempt to weaken if not change its regime. Soviet-American relations concentrated increasingly on one subject and thus depended on too narrow a foundation, limiting the growth of strategic weapons. In one sense this was inevitable. Up to 1972 relations between the two superpowers had been almost exclusively focused on nuclear questions through the treaties banning nuclear tests, limiting the spread of nuclear weapons, and restricting antimissile defenses.

But between 1972 and 1974 these areas were purposely broadened by the two governments to include another three areas, none particularly successful. First, the governments expanded into other forms of arms control, especially the Vienna talks on reducing conventional armed forces in Europe. Little progress was achieved there. Second, Congress inflicted a major blow to our attempts to expand economic relations in January of 1975, and further attempts by both sides to find a compromise that would remove trade discrimination from the Soviet Union came to nothing. Third, we tried to write rules for our behavior and relations at times of crisis, but on various occasions from 1972 through 1974 the two superpowers acted as if they had never signed a document entitled "Basic Principles of Relations between the

Soviet Union and the United States" at the 1972 Moscow summit. While Moscow was responsible for ignoring the rules in Africa, Washington was to blame in the Middle East.

Then Moscow followed with its own version of linkage, the Soviet strategy in 1977 of tying a summit meeting to successful negotiations on SALT. This strategy proved erroneous. Early discussions at top-level meetings of the whole range of the Soviet-American relations could have helped pave the way to a SALT agreement and better understanding. As the nuclear arms limitation talks—the principal remaining channel for our bilateral relations—entered a dead end because of the overall deterioration of the political situation, detente was doomed. And the absence of a solid political consensus in the United States in favor of detente contributed to its failure. Hence there emerged a general conclusion: military detente was impossible without political detente.

In the Soviet Union, the main elements of Brezhnev's foreign policy had all been in place at least since the late 1960s, and some traced back to the Khrushchev period: detente toward the West; defense of the East European status quo; containment of China; support of the liberation movements in the Third World. During the Carter administration a key objective of the Soviet leaders was to get back on track with a detente policy which had been partly derailed by an accumulation of difficulties after detente's first great success, the Nixon-Brezhnev summit of 1972.

For all the persistent efforts of our diplomats to relax international tension, to limit and reduce arms stockpiles, there were also domestic political, ideological, or military obstacles. Our foreign policy was unreasonably dominated by ideology, and this produced continued confrontation especially through our involvement in regional conflicts "to perform our international duty to other peoples." Moscow believed that it thus assisted the transition toward socialism in the Third World. This was complicated by the Soviet leadership's great-power aspirations and fraught with inevitable, but unnecessary, conflicts with the United States, though our diplomacy for years was trying to establish at least a minimum of trust between our countries. A dangerous precedent was set first in Cuba and then Africa, undermining the foundations of detente even as we tried to build them.

When leaders tried to reconcile detente with what they saw as the continuing class struggle in the world, they misjudged Washington's reaction, believing such regional conflicts were only side issues which Moscow somehow would be able to isolate from such basic issues as arms control. In all fairness, the same criticism could be leveled at Washington and applied to the policy pursued by the Nixon, Ford, and Carter administrations in the

Middle East, to name just one region, where American diplomacy persistently sought to undermine our influence and to exclude the Soviet Union. By the time Carter left office, the United States was also fighting proxy wars on three continents in Afghanistan, in Somalia and Angola, and in El Salvador and Nicaragua.

All in all one could say that detente was to a certain extent buried in the fields of Soviet-American rivalry in the Third World.

As for the human rights violations in the Soviet Union, this intensely complex issue was a picture of total confusion in which the separate issues of Jewish emigration, the rough treatment of dissidents, Soviet policy toward Israel and the Middle East, and finally, the totally unconnected issue of U.S.-Soviet trade relations became thoroughly entangled.

I am still convinced that if we had thought it through in a broad manner, a settlement of the conflict with the Jewish community of the United States could have helped considerably in promoting the process of detente. I tried from time to time to raise the issue with Brezhnev and Gromyko. But their position was irrational; their answers were vague and beside the point, accompanied by such comments as "There is no giving in to pressure from Zionists and letting them interfere in our domestic affairs." It was not easy to explain to them that our human rights policy was widely resented by the American public, and that the staff of our embassy was becoming resentful of the terrorist tactics of extremist groups.

The Soviet leadership also underestimated the role played by the U.S. Congress in American foreign policy. This first of all grew out of their own disrespect for our own parliament, the Supreme Soviet of People's Deputies, which obediently endorsed all decisions made by the party leadership. Accordingly, it was believed in Moscow that an agreement with the American president was of primary and indeed crucial importance, and Congress's sentiments were not to be taken much into account. As a result, the Congress sprang some surprises, and these turned out to be hard blows to Soviet-American relations.

The ideological bondage of Brezhnev's generation was aggravated by the country's isolation from the world, probably Stalin's gravest legacy. The mirror image of that was the projection of our inexperience and our ignorant notions onto American policy. The Soviet leadership and people did not understand America and its sources of political power, mistaking, say, Nixon for a American general secretary of sorts. It was not until 1973 that people in our country began to realize that the American Congress was at least as powerful as the American president. The Kremlin clearly underestimated the influence of American public opinion. Another grave result of this isolation is that it ultimately gave birth to a feeling of suspicion and apprehension of this obscure outside world, and of the United States above all. America was therefore perceived as having solely evil or expansionist intentions. True, Americans paid us back in the same coin. They also knew very little about our country.

Members of the Soviet political leadership often spoke in the language of ideology even when conversing between themselves, falling into the language of the official newspapers, *Pravda* and *Izvestia*. The way and form in which they expressed their thoughts inevitably affected its content. They used political jargon particular to their political philosophy. For some of them it was a convenient way to cover sheer incompetence in foreign affairs.

The growing influence of the Soviet military-industrial complex was among the major factors gradually undermining detente, and not just because of its growing demands for technological sophistication, as in the United States. The main reason for the inability of the Soviet parliament and public opinion to control the country's military policy and defense programs was that all the activities in the security sector were top secret in a way that could not be imagined in the West. Not even most Politburo members were fully informed because the Defense Ministry and the Defense Industry Ministry were only accountable to the general secretary, who was also commander in chief and chairman of the Defense Council. Brezhnev had long and close ties with the military-industrial complex, which he had formerly headed. He generally favored the military and, by virtue of his participation (not all that conspicuous) in World War II, counted himself among the greatest authorities on military affairs.

In short, the military brass and the captains of military industry, who were Brezhnev's reliable supporters in the party and the government, had free access to him with their projects, but they had little knowledge and less responsibility in the field of foreign policy. These military projects were not subject to any serious examination by the public or by civilian control outside the offices of the general secretary: neither in the Supreme Soviet, nor in the government, nor even in the Politburo, which even though it was the highest decision-making body in the land would sometimes merely be informed but not consulted.

All this led to an uncontrollable arms race that was not linked to specific objectives of foreign policy or general concepts such as detente. Even the principle of military parity adopted by both countries during the Nixon administration was interpreted by the top Soviet military as an entitlement to all types of weapons possessed by their American counterparts, and sometimes in much greater quantities. The old slogan of "catch up with America and leave it behind," which Khrushchev had coined for the nation as a whole and the civilian economy in particular, was adapted by the military for its own aggrandizement. Such a concept of parity actually deprived us of the possibility of determining our own military policy because it meant we had to follow the path determined by the United States for its own purposes—and not our own. As a result, the Soviet Union set off another sharp spiral in the strategic and conventional arms race, even though we were already well ahead of the United States in the number of armored vehicles, artillery pieces, and self-propelled launchers but behind in some strategic weaponry.

The shroud of secrecy caused bitter suspicion abroad. Except for Gromyko himself, even the very top Soviet diplomats including myself were completely ignorant of the Soviet military's expansion programs and discussed such matters with their foreign counterparts on the basis of figures that sometimes were long out of date. On some occasions we actually did not tell the truth on Moscow's instructions without knowing it, as in the case of the Krasnoyarsk surveillance radar designed for tracking space missions. We repeated the official line insisting that the project remained within the guidelines of the missile defense agreement with the United States, although it was actually a violation and was admitted as such in a secret memorandum to Brezhnev from the Army Chiefs of Staff when the radar system was built. I should also note—not to justify the Soviet leaders, but to state a fact—that for their part they did not always believe that the United States was playing fair in its observance of arms control agreements.

All this compounded the negative publicity about Soviet intentions in the eyes of the Western public. In so doing we involuntarily played into the hands of those in the United States who were vigorously creating the image of an enemy "evil empire," the fight against which demanded national unity and high combat readiness, notwithstanding the enormous expenditure.

But this escalation in military spending began to gnaw away at the Soviet Union. Signs of stagnation appeared at the end of the 1970s and in the early 1980s, gradually affecting the country's economic and social development. This in turn increasingly tempted the American leadership to bring the highest possible economic, political, psychological, and military pressure to bear, thus retarding the general development of the Soviet Union and weakening our international position. As if to compound its position, the Kremlin also allowed Soviet foreign policy to get caught up in patterns of imperial overextension like those that had begun to afflict the United States a generation earlier.

Last but not least, there was Leonid Brezhnev himself. Western political figures described Brezhnev in the years 1970 through 1974 in a relatively favorable light, as a man able to handle international affairs and negotiations, eager for peace and accords—and this was true. But the Western leaders who met Brezhnev in the latter half of the decade saw a different man. This was also clear to us as Soviet diplomats during our trips to Moscow. His health declining, he grew less interested in world developments. Gradually he became only indirectly involved in the process of shaping our position at even the most vital talks, including those on strategic arms limitations, although he chaired the meetings that gave the final approval to our positions, if in a rather perfunctory way. Brezhnev was no longer in a position to give any personal impulse to detente, which also contributed to its collapse. Detente, never forget, was in no small measure prompted by the personal ambition and drive of both the Soviet general secretary and his American counterparts. That was one reason personal summit meetings were so important. They were also the last, highest authority to take the most important decisions. Unfortunately, apart from the Nixon period, both capitals underestimated the essential role of these meetings for the open exchange of opinions and mutual assessment of the other's views so they could then be integrated into policy.

The tragic aspect of this was that both Brezhnev and Carter personally favored the principles of detente and slowing the arms race. But things developed in a such way that the Kremlin failed to see in Carter a potential American counterpart who shared that goal. Instead they viewed the administration's contradictory course in foreign affairs as a plot against Soviet interests. And Carter himself was no great help in the unpredictable and emotional way he conducted foreign policy.

The unreasonable delay in completing the SALT Treaty, which has never been ratified by the American side; the arms race; rivalry over Africa, the Middle East, and Cuba; the public confrontation over human rights; the rapprochement between China and the United States on an anti-Soviet basis—all pushed Soviet-American relations down the scale of American foreign policy priorities while the Carter administration was professing its ideological and political pressure for changes in Soviet foreign and especially domestic policy. It is no surprise that Carter's actions were particularly resented by Moscow while both sides were not trying to understand and accommodate their views on the most controversial issues.

All these factors, combined with the upheavals in the changing world of 1977–79, placed both superpowers in a bitter confrontation. Finally, the Soviet intervention in Afghanistan marked the dismantling of the policy of detente, bringing back the Cold War.

# I. The Paradox of Ronald Reagan

*The Cold War Returns*

Ronald Reagan's presidency revived the worst days of the Cold War and then brought about the most significant improvement in Soviet-American relations since the end of World War II. This paradox preoccupies many, from scholars to ordinary people. It is still difficult to say with certainty to what extent it was the product of an accidental chain of events or of the conscious if sometimes vacillating design of the leaders of both countries. But Ronald Reagan himself was far from a figurehead in this historic turn. The Reagan I observed may have been no master of detail, but he had a clear sense of what he wanted and was deeply involved in diplomatic events. He became a principal protagonist in ending the Cold War.

After this striking new leader came to power in the United States in a conclusive electoral victory, three ailing Soviet leaders, Leonid Brezhnev, Yuri Andropov, and Konstantin Chernenko replaced one another in rapid succession during Reagan's first term. Continuity was their policy. They all proceeded from the conviction that nuclear war was to be avoided at all costs and that the interests of the Soviet Union and the United States were served by at least a minimum of cooperation. For all their revolutionary rhetoric, they hated change, yet they displayed an interest in negotiations on arms limitations—in other words, they wanted to establish a measure of military detente. The restoration of the political detente seemed hopeless for the time being.

From 1981 to 1983 the Soviet government continued to favor a dialogue with the American administration, not only in its public statements but also by means of private diplomatic contacts, of which I was an immediate participant. But the main result of the first years of Reagan's presidency, and of our contacts with him, was his refusal to pursue a constructive dialogue while he aimed for military superiority and launched an uncompromising new ideological offensive against the Soviet Union. The campaign incorporated the fierce crusade declared by Reagan against us as the "evil empire" and the feverish buildup of weapons using advanced technology, crowned by the "Star Wars" program, which would have ended the nuclear standoff between the superpowers if it had worked. The Pentagon budget doubled within the first five years of Reagan's presidency, and so did the national debt. All these sacrifices were made for the sake of a strategy of global and regional confrontation with the Soviet Union to repulse communism.

As we in the Soviet Union saw it, Reagan was embarked on a path of breaking the military and strategic parity between the two nations. With characteristically reactive behavior, the Soviet leadership, having spent so much money and effort over the years to attain parity, viewed Reagan with great indignation and suspicion. They regarded his policies as a kind of betrayal of the agreements they had laboriously reached with previous administrations. But Moscow was determined to retain global equilibrium at all costs and to fight Reagan's policy even though they preferred to deal in terms of mutual agreements. They regarded his actions as adventurism.

The outlook was hopelessly gloomy. Tension in international relations grew. Diplomacy became more than ever an exercise in public relations, and the American-Soviet dialogue an exercise in propaganda. I remained the Soviet ambassador during the initial five years of Reagan's presidency before returning home to serve as the secretary of the Communist Party for international relations. Those early Reagan years in Washington were the most difficult and unpleasant I experienced in my long tenure as ambassador. We had practically no room for really constructive diplomatic work. The useful and direct contacts I had long established with the White House were broken.

The principal efforts of the diplomatic services were focused on cushioning the conflicts and preventing the tensions of the revived Cold War from turning into a hot one, but I must say that despite the level of acrimony and rhetorical abuse, I never really felt a sense of dread. Our relations sank about as low as they could after a Soviet fighter plane shot down a South Korean airliner on September 1, 1983, with the loss of 269 civilian lives, and Reagan used this tragic incident to full advantage, almost completely paralyzing diplomatic activity.

I was so depressed that around that time I was thinking of giving up and transferring back to Moscow, but at the same time, Reagan and Brezhnev were exchanging personal letters and trying to reach each other in some inchoate way on a personal level. This was the Reagan paradox.

The hesitant signs of a turn came gradually in the middle of Reagan's first term as president. The first was a characteristically personal gesture by the president when he visited the Soviet Embassy in Washington in November of 1982 to offer condolences on Brezhnev's death. This was followed by the deployment of missiles in Europe over huge popular protests, which strengthened the confidence of both Washington and the Europeans in dealing with Moscow. But there was a hard and bumpy road ahead. There was the president's own behavior, with his vacillations and sporadic anti-Soviet outbreaks in public, and the unsteady situation in the Kremlin caused by frequent changes in its leadership.

From the summer of 1984, the Politburo was increasingly dominated by Mikhail Gorbachev, who often chaired its meetings because of the illness of Chernenko. Without much publicity it took two important decisions, first to renew the disarmament dialogue with the American administration (which was broken off by Andropov later as a protest against Reagan's anti-Soviet behavior), and second to move toward a summit with Reagan. Not that we managed to establish a real dialogue with Washington at once. Moscow still harbored a strong suspicion that the Reagan administration's hesitant turn was prompted exclusively by the forthcoming presidential elections. The administration had no well-developed scheme of promoting relations with the Soviet Union, and strong differences persisted between George Shultz, the taciturn secretary of state, and Defense Secretary Caspar Weinberger, who never seemed to tire of leading the Pentagon charge. True, when the large-scale rearmament of the United States had been successfully completed, the president himself showed signs, however inconsistent, of a desire for agreement with the Soviet Union to reduce the nuclear threat.

Reagan had also undergone an evolution as president from opposing contacts with the Soviet Union to using them for domestic political purposes and specific foreign policy goals. He grew increasingly interested in acquiring a favorable political image as a strong president and a peacemaker. More than that, consciously or subconsciously, he began to think about the possibility of some kind of accommodation with Moscow.

After Reagan's reelection in 1984 and Gorbachev's ascension as general secretary in March of 1985, the idea of the first U.S.-Soviet summit in six years began to advance much faster. Gorbachev saw the summit as an important tool for boosting his personal political prestige and normalizing relations with the United States. It would also allow him more room for maneuver in preparing the next Soviet five-year plan, which was to devote fewer resources to the military and develop the civilian economy. Without such a shift, raising living standards would become increasingly difficult.

The first Reagan-Gorbachev summit was held in Geneva on November 19–25, 1985. To the satisfaction of both sides, it turned out that the two were able to talk, and not as irreconcilable antagonists, but as leaders looking for practical solutions. This meeting opened a new epoch, which eventually led to a drastic change in relations between the two countries and elsewhere. My long-cherished hopes for the restoration and development of cooperation in the spirit of detente appeared to come true. I was personally involved in these dramatic events, and I am going to tell my story of what happened.

## A Break with the Past

When he assumed the presidency, Ronald Reagan deliberately and persistently set about breaking with the past. The president and his entourage of radical conservatives lost little time in carrying out the pledges, nay, the threats, they had made during the election campaign. They scrapped detente, directly confronted the Soviet Union by all means possible, and emphasized the strengthening of military force, which meant the redirection of funds to the military budget at the expense of social programs that had built up during the previous half-century.

The hasty military buildup blocked prospects for businesslike negotiations on controlling the arms race. The new leadership dismissed the Soviet-American achievements in arms control as disadvantageous to the United States and turned the whole idea of arms limitation on its head, converting it into additional efforts to build up American military potential and change the strategic balance. Any negotiations with the Soviet Union were to be conducted from a position of strength and conditioned on Moscow's behavior in world affairs. At least that was the practical conclusion of the Soviet leadership after high-level exchanges and my own numerous unsuccessful attempts as ambassador to launch a dialogue with the new secretary of state, Alexander Haig.

In addition to Haig, a military man by formation and demeanor, the top echelon charged with American disarmament policy consisted mostly of those essentially opposed to what they were supposed to be doing. The director of the Arms Control and Disarmament Agency was Eugene V. Rostow, a hard-liner like his brother, Walt. The ambassador to the arms limitation talks was General Edward Rowny, an opponent of the SALT II treaty and formerly the Pentagon's representative at the Geneva disarmament talks. The assistant secretary of defense for international policy, who served as the Pentagon's representative on interagency disarmament and other groups, was Richard Perle, who as Senator Henry Jackson's principal foreign policy aide had accumulated vast experience in blocking agreements with the Soviet Union.

The administration's arms control proposals seemed designed to subvert rather than advance the process. The proposed "zero option" for intermediate-range missiles would have eliminated all of our SS-20 missiles in return for NATO's agreement not to deploy its own, ignoring the point that the Soviet Union would be trading actual missiles for nonexistent ones. The

Reagan policy of deep cuts in land-based ballistic missiles under START—the new acronym for Strategic Arms Reduction Talks that replaced SALT to emphasize a shift from limitation to reduction—would have required the Soviet Union to make disproportionate cuts; seven out of every ten of our ICBMs were land-based, as opposed to two out of ten for the United States. Moscow, as well as many in the West, regarded these proposals as an effort to stake out public positions rather than sincere attempts to reduce nuclear arms.

The United States continued its drive to separate the East European countries from the Soviet Union, pursuing its goals in a more straightforward and blatant way, as it did in Poland. American relations with China included military cooperation. American policy in the Middle East and the Persian Gulf took a geopolitical view of the region as a link in a broad front of resistance to Soviet influence and moved toward an active policy from the reactive policy of Carter. The United States displayed no interest in a political settlement of the Afghan conflict, which drew the Soviet Union into a protracted war of attrition. American political and psychological pressure increased on Havana to restrain itself in Latin America and Africa. When Reagan and Haig threatened to "get at the source of instability" in Central America, they meant Cuba. A separate Caribbean command was established for the armed forces, regular military maneuvers were conducted, and counterrevolutionary Cuban groups expanded their activities.

Relations with Moscow rapidly deteriorated. The Soviet leadership had hoped that Reagan would abandon his anti-Soviet attitudes of the election campaign and take a more sober approach when confronted with power, but these hopes proved groundless. The White House sought to damage the Soviet Union at every opportunity and obsessively viewed all international events in terms of confrontation with the Soviet Union, restricting American foreign policy to a gross and even primitive anti-Sovietism. In any case, that was the impression in Moscow.

Of course the administration could not completely ignore the realities of the strategic nuclear balance, nor the apprehensions of its allies and of the American population about the dangerous possibility that the new policy would explode into military confrontation with the Soviet Union. This contributed to a half-hearted and generally unproductive dialogue with the Soviet Union through personal correspondence between Reagan and Brezhnev, occasionally handwritten by the president himself in an attempt to vent his fraternal feelings, which he somehow believed would override and cancel out his aggressive public stand. These were passed through formal diplomatic channels. Unlike the previous administrations, the Reagan team refused any private channel.

Moscow had no illusions about Ronald Reagan. Still, somewhere at the back of the leadership's collective mind remained a subconscious, weak hope that the tough-talking politician would eventually turn out to be a realist with whom they could establish contact. Their disappointment turned to genuine worry when they realized they had to deal with a dangerous confrontational figure unwilling to reach any agreement whatever with the Soviet Union. At least, that was how it appeared to Moscow during the first years of Reagan's presidency.

The impact of Reagan's hard-line policy on the internal debates in the Kremlin and on the evolution of the Soviet leadership was exactly the opposite from the one intended by Washington. It strengthened those in the Politburo, the Central Committee, and the security apparatus who had been pressing for a mirror-image of Reagan's own policy. Ronald Reagan managed to create a solid front of hostility among our leaders. Nobody trusted him. His proposals were almost automatically considered with suspicion. This unique situation in our relations threatened dangerous consequences.

I had known Alexander Haig since his work in the White House under Nixon and did not believe he was the best choice for secretary of state. He was a typical bully, his manner of speaking was confrontational, and his reluctance to seek mutual agreement was well known. He saw everything in black and white and did not admit to anything in between. The categorical nature of his judgment seemed to reflect his military background. He was more used to the atmosphere of confrontation rather than one of uncertainty, which he connected with the relaxation of tension and vague prospects for protracted negotiations.

The one-man-in-command scheme he tried to introduce with himself as the "vicar" of American foreign policy making led to numerous skirmishes with the president's close entourage and Secretary of Defense Weinberger. None of them recognized any right of the new secretary of state to monopolize foreign policy and bit by bit set the president against him. He soon came to be regarded as a controversial figure both inside and outside the administration, although his views did not differ much from those of the president himself.

A problem with the new administration, as I shortly discovered, lay in the fact that another person was also responsible for Soviet affairs, and he was the president's national security assistant Richard Allen. He chose to avoid contacts with our embassy because he did not want to provoke an open battle with Haig, who insisted that those contacts were his own prerogative. This made little difference in the field of policy, because Allen was unfriendly toward the Soviet Union in any case.

Among Haig's first appointments were two good career diplomats with experience in Eastern Europe whom I knew quite well. Walter Stoessel, former ambassador to West Germany, Poland, and the Soviet Union, whom Haig had befriended during his service in NATO, was to become undersecretary of state for political affairs, the third-ranking position in the State Department. Lawrence Eagleburger, ambassador to Yugoslavia and formerly Henry Kissinger's assistant, was to be appointed assistant secretary of state for European affairs. Haig decided against having a specialist adviser on Soviet affairs.

My first conversation with Haig took place before he was confirmed by the Senate, at the reception in honor of the new president. We exchanged recollections about our numerous private contacts during his service with Nixon. I pointed out that our relations had seen better times, but Moscow was ready to cooperate. Haig noted that our relations were unfortunately going through a difficult period, and we would have to work hard to solve problems of real importance and dispel strong mutual suspicions about each other's intentions in various parts of the world—which to him represented one of the main reasons for tension between us. That, he said, could prove a worthy subject for discussion after his confirmation by the Senate.

At the reception, I also had a short conversation with Weinberger, whom I also knew fairly well from the Nixon years when he was secretary of health, education and welfare. Our own public health minister, an academician named Petrovsky, had met Weinberger earlier and was charmed by him; having learned about his appointment as secretary of defense, Petrovsky repeated to everybody in Moscow that there would be "a friend of his" in the Reagan administration. I regarded Weinberger as a balanced man, judging by his past record. But it was not long before we all were strongly disillusioned.

I congratulated Weinberger on his appointment and joked that he had already shown himself as an able diplomat by taking what I described as an "overflexible stand" in public. He opposed the SALT II Treaty and even the ABM agreement while declaring in the next breath that it would take him at least six months before he could speak with sufficient expertise to develop the right approach to arms negotiations with the Soviet Union. The two statements could not possibly go together, so I suggested we meet in private and discuss the subject. I said I was ready to outline the Soviet position and explain the motives behind it.

Weinberger admitted that he was new to such matters and therefore rather ignorant of them, so even an introductory talk with me would be rather immaterial for the present although it would be a different matter later. As for his public statements, in fairness to him he admitted frankly that they were merely repetitions of Reagan's own. It was to become characteristic of Weinberger's behavior in the government that he supported all of Reagan's statements on foreign policy without reservation, except that he tended to make them sound even tougher.

The first official exchange between Haig and Gromyko took place in a similar tone. On January 24, Haig wrote—through the American Embassy in Moscow—to warn about Soviet behavior in Poland and Africa and criticize our policy in Afghanistan. But about disarmament, his letter was completely silent. Several days later I delivered Gromyko's cool reply remarking that a number of outstanding questions deserved attention but expressing "regret that, judging by your letter, important questions have escaped the new administration's attention." Haig looked over the letter and said that on reflection, we could "call it quits" with this first exchange.

Then Haig asked me for my personal opinion of the new administration. We happened to be meeting on the very day of Reagan's first press conference, where he had just made the notorious remark that the leaders of the Soviet Union "reserve unto themselves the right to commit any crime, to lie, to cheat" in order to promote world revolution. I told Haig that, frankly speaking, I failed to see any basic difference from the arrogant moralizing of the departed Carter administration; even though its successors trumpeted the idea of "a new start," they were walking in Carter's footsteps and could end up in the same way.

"You can't compare us with the Carter administration," Haig snapped.

"Unfortunately, such a comparison suggests itself," I insisted. "If the administration is really anxious to improve our relations and not just looking for a pretext for public confrontation, that is not the best way to go about it. This is especially true for today's press conference and Reagan's extremely hostile statement concerning the Soviet Union, which we see as a declaration of his program. I can only express my regret and surprise. How is he going to do business with us? Reagan's unprecedented and unprovoked statement will undoubtedly make a most unfavorable impression on the Soviet leadership, and I believe it will arouse its strong indignation. What is the purpose of all that? Why should he set such a tone for the new administration from the very beginning?"

I confess that I was genuinely puzzled by the new president's fierce anti-Soviet attack. In retrospect I realize that it had been quite impossible for me at that moment to imagine anything much worse than Carter. But it soon became clear that in ideology and propaganda Reagan turned out to be far worse and far more threatening.

Haig said that the president had telephoned him about the press conference, particularly stressing that his statement about the Soviet Union was not meant to offend anyone in Moscow but was just an expression of his deep convictions.

I told Haig that this clarification only made things worse.

That was the end of my first formal meeting with the new secretary of state. In contrast to his predecessors, who preferred to talk with me alone, Haig arranged for our conversation to be attended by two assistant secretaries of state. Although Haig suggested we would be seeing each other at Senator Percy's house for dinner on February 5 and could talk informally then, it was clear that the confidential channel, as it had operated before, had ceased to exist. Instead, our first official encounter, like the first exchange with Gromyko, focused on such disputatious questions as Iran, Afghanistan, and Poland, ignoring areas of potential compromise such as disarmament. That was the course chosen by the new administration, and this first official conversation convinced me that we were in for hard times.

Furthermore, the propaganda aspect of all this was confirmed by the way the exchange became public. Evidently acting on Haig's and perhaps even the president's orders, the White House first leaked the substance of Haig's letter to Gromyko, although diplomatic practice generally prescribes confidentiality in any exchange of letters between foreign ministers. Gromyko angrily replied in the same vein and had his letter released, too. Thus from the very first, the new administration's diplomacy featured recriminations between the two governments conducted in public.

During my first call on Haig there was one incident that received wide publicity as a symbol of the new administration's uncompromising posture toward the Soviet Union. For almost twelve years, when Kissinger and Vance were the secretaries of state and our confidential channel was in full operation, my visits to them at the State Department were either official, when I came through the main entrance publicly like any other ambassador; or private, when I was driven in through the State Department's basement garage. Each time it was up to the secretary to decide which way I should arrive. That also determined whether he wanted our meeting known to the press or kept private, as often was the case. Before each visit, my aide would call the secretary's personal assistant and be told whether I was to enter through the main lobby or the garage.

My aide made his habitual call to ask which entrance to take for my first call on Haig. The State Department assistant answered, "As usual." My last several visits to the State Department had been through the garage, so my aide and driver decided to do the usual without bothering to inform me of what seemed a routine procedure. When we arrived at the garage, we were directed to the main entrance. Frankly I did not pay much attention to this change, because in the past there had been changes of this kind. I did not ask

Haig about it, nor did he mention it. But next day this "incident" was deliberately leaked to the press and blown up as an inspired gesture that aptly conveyed the change in America's attitude toward Moscow. When I saw Haig next time and explained to him how all this happened, he apologized for the "misunderstanding," as he termed it, and said his assistant should have told us beforehand of a new procedure. It was by then clear to me that all this had been a staged political show. It did not increase my confidence in the new secretary of state.

The Politburo discussed the whole situation on February 11 at an angry and emotional meeting. President Reagan was roundly and unanimously denounced because of the tone set at his initial press conference, which was fully reflected in the American media. During my long career as ambassador the collective mood of the Soviet leadership had never been so suddenly and deeply set against an American president. It was a catastrophe in personal relations at the highest level, though Reagan probably had not yet fully realized it.

As we had agreed, I met Haig on February 5 at a dinner given by Senator Percy in his home. It was a cold and windy evening, as if the weather were accommodating the political climate. Our conversation lasted well into the night. Haig remained true to his principles, but he behaved like an old friend. Although more articulate and self-confident than he was under Nixon, he spoke without subtlety. He was evidently anxious to assert himself as the main foreign policy-maker in the administration.

Haig made it absolutely clear in the course of the conversation that Reagan was unconditionally committed to sharp increases in military expenditures "to catch up with the Soviet Union." I noted that the Carter administration's final presentation to Congress had held that the United States and the Soviet Union already were at approximate parity in strategic weapons. Haig admitted reluctantly that parity did exist, but in the next breath he said that in the opinion of American military experts, the Soviet arms drive had grown in such scale and momentum that the Soviets were likely to surpass U.S. military potential by the end of Reagan's presidency unless urgent countermeasures were taken. He cited no data or figures.

Then what about arms talks to allay these fears? Haig made it quite clear that they were not on the administration's agenda. The priority was to launch a broad rearmament program—"Then we'll see."

Haig was also straightforward enough in stating that hostile public statements were an integral part of the administration's new approach to Soviet-American relations although "personally I wish the president had found more appropriate words in his press conference. But he did not do that by design. Anyway, what he feels and what he wanted to say were expressed clearly enough: the administration cannot deal with the Soviet Union as if nothing had happened." What this meant, he explained, was that Reagan would not put up with the Soviet Union's use of proxies such as Cubans in Africa and Latin America. Reagan was particularly outraged at Cuba's stirring up civil war in El Salvador and Nicaragua.

Haig drew an emphatic parallel between Moscow's concern about the events in Poland and Washington's concern about Central America. If Moscow wanted to risk a world crisis by putting down the Solidarity movement in Poland, "I'd like to tell you that, if need be, the United States will be ready to act with determination in our region. Cuba, of all countries, must realize this."

I asked him straight out if his words meant that the Reagan administration was not interested in any constructive dialogue with us at all. Would it ignore any diplomatic means and pin its hopes solely on the arms race? Could they really believe such a belligerent approach would get anywhere? Haig replied that they did not oppose a dialogue, but it would take time to prepare. At the same time he linked the possibility of agreements to "the Soviet Union's general conduct," of which the administration would remain the judge. I rejected this approach and explained that a history of our relations showed it could not produce anything but permanent confrontation.

Haig's statements were clearly designed to pressure us. There was not a trace of any search for agreement. The administration still believed that positive changes in our relations, especially in disarmament issues, did not meet its interests. It was unwilling, as Haig put it, to send "false signals" to the American people while they were being asked to make considerable sacrifices for the sake of a sharp increase in military spending.

I decided to explore the situation further with Stoessel, whom I had already invited for diner at my house. We had been on friendly terms since 1952, when I was counselor of the Soviet Embassy in Washington and he was the chief of the Soviet division in the State Department. Now he was there as undersecretary of state. Our conversation was frank, facilitated by the trust we had built up through years of contacts, talks, and discussions as friends and professionals, even though we were on opposing sides.

Some of his statements were remarkable. According to Stoessel, Reagan had a very special idea of the Soviet Union. He was sincerely convinced that he owed his political power to the American people's support for his anti-Soviet stand and for his determination to rearm vigorously, which he believed would regain the respect of the world for the United States. All that made it difficult for professionals like himself to take the initiative and make expert recommendations. They were confined to following instructions from on high. No one in the State Department knew exactly what to do with the SALT II Treaty: whether to work out a completely new agreement, alter the wording, or amend it. So on this or other questions of Soviet-American relations, they were just temporizing.

He felt there would be a pause of at least six to eight months in relations between our governments while Reagan sent his military programs to Congress. We professionals, he said, could use the time to start a dialogue between the two governments little by little, through regular diplomatic channels, with a view to preparing a ministerial meeting in the long term. I agreed with this suggestion. But for the present Reagan's anti-Soviet rhetoric would carry the day as if he were still campaigning. Only now his subjects would be Cuba, the leftist threat to El Salvador, and the struggle "for a free Poland."

## Brezhnev Tries a Breakthrough and Fails

The Communist Party of the Soviet Union held its Twenty-Sixth Congress in Moscow during the second half of February. Before the Congress the Politburo discussed foreign policy issues, especially our relations with the new administration in Washington. I reported about my first personal contacts with its high representatives. Gromyko made a very critical report. There was in the Politburo no lack of concern, indeed consternation, about the new president and his policies. What were we to do?

It was decided to follow a course for detente in the hope that Reagan little by little would become "more reasonable." During the party congress the leadership advanced new foreign policy initiatives in the hope of ameliorating the situation and reversing the rising sense of tension. Then, after the Congress, since there was no confidential channel through which to explore these ideas, the Politburo decided to start a personal correspondence with Reagan through Brezhnev.

On March 6 Brezhnev sent an informal letter that was actually an invitation for Reagan to begin a dialogue on a number of concrete suggestions. They started from the confidence-building measures against surprise attack devised at the Helsinki Conference on Security and Cooperation in Europe. Brezhnev proposed extending advance notification of maneuvers and similar measures more deeply into Soviet territory and Western Europe, and then taking in the Far East. He also suggested reopening negotiations on nuclear arms reduction, discussing a Middle East settlement and the Iran-Iraq war, and holding a summit-level session of the UN Security Council. The tone of the letter may be gauged from its opening assumption that "the military-strategic balance objectively serves to preserve world peace," to its conclusion suggesting that the new administration examine the Soviet ideas and explore them in "various forms of dialogue." Although some proposals may have been carried too far, and not every suggestion would be acceptable to the American administration, the letter contained enough positive material to feed further dialogue between Moscow and Washington—if Washington wanted it.

The program was also outlined at our party congress and therefore publicized in the West. Reaction in the United States was decidedly mixed. Richard Nixon commented on it favorably when he invited me to lunch in New York, saying Brezhnev was right to refuse to engage in a public wrangle with Reagan. Reagan was in a fighting mood and had been prepared for criticism from Moscow, so he was poised to hit back, and the proposal for a summit was the last thing he expected. Nixon thought the proposal could play a positive role in the long term but he warned us not to push it: "I should venture to give you some personal advice. I don't recommend that you press Reagan too persistently for a summit in your further dialogue with him, whether public or private. Don't overdo it!"

Reagan had talked with Nixon on the phone right after Brezhnev's speech. Much to Nixon's surprise, one of Reagan's people had already convinced him that the conciliatory Soviet proposals were the result of the president's own firm stance. Reagan himself suspected that Brezhnev had proposed a summit meeting because he was far more experienced and would be able to outplay the president, the more so because Reagan still did not know the particulars of many issues. But Nixon tried to convince Reagan on the basis of his own three summits with Brezhnev. But Reagan nevertheless seemed to have been persuaded by his own entourage of the correctness of his policies. Nixon recommended that we continue "reeducating Reagan" but that we make no haste because he was not yet prepared for it.

Several days later I met Weinberger at dinner at Kendall's house for the businessman's sixtieth birthday celebration. I asked the secretary of defense what he thought about Brezhnev's proposals, and he replied that the State Department was examining them. "But," he added, "frankly and in strict confidence, I don't anticipate any rapid improvement of our relations under the Reagan administration."

When asked what made him think so, Weinberger hesitated for a moment and then blurted out: "Moscow believes it can treat Reagan the way it treated Carter. Now, Reagan will prove the opposite."

I asked him to be more specific about those who suggested that extraordinary idea to Reagan and the reason behind it. Weinberger muddled along trying to explain. He began by repeating the old theory about the Soviet Union testing Reagan the same way it had tested Carter. However, he could not give any definite reply, but proceeded instead to argue that the Soviet leadership had outsmarted Carter at the summit by making him conclude the SALT II Treaty to its advantage.

Weinberger's further arguments boiled down to a simple statement that if Reagan did agree to hold a summit, he wanted to be sure that Soviet troops would not invade Poland following the summit, which is what happened in Afghanistan only months after Carter met Brezhnev in Vienna. Reagan would not allow himself to become the object of ridicule in the way people had laughed at his predecessor's naivete.

I told Weinberger his reasoning did not hold water. "Let's take the SALT II Treaty, for instance. Neither side outwitted the other. Just tell me what is wrong with it, exactly?"

Weinberger said he had not yet examined it in detail but the administration was reviewing it. I observed that it was odd, to say the least, to declare the treaty inadequate or unsatisfactory before examining it, and then to examine it with only one purpose in mind: to find it unacceptable. I also said that I could assure him that nobody had any intention of invading Poland.

On the whole, the conversation with Weinberger impressed me sadly with his primitive approach to our relations and his incompetence, something characteristic of the whole Reagan administration of that time. The president's image-makers liked him making provocative public statements against the Soviet Union, for example, on Poland. Donald Kendall told me Haig did not think much of this, although the secretary of state still believed the warnings could create the useful impression at home that the administration was able to deter the Soviet Union from doing some things (especially when the Soviet Union had no intention of doing them anyway). Weinberger followed the White House in this rhetoric designed to create a tough presidential aura. Besides, Weinberger himself very much liked being in public eye, and the numerous anti-Soviet statements he made to reporters helped keep him there. They also annoyed Haig, who resented his trespasses into what he considered to be the State Department's sphere of competence.

My next meeting with Reagan occurred, of all places, at Washington's famous annual Gridiron Dinner, to which I was among the few foreign ambassadors invited. There were as usual about five hundred representatives of the American elite from the administration, Congress, the State Department, the Pentagon, business, and the media. At these dinners prominent political figures including the president are the traditional butt of jokes—that is, they are "grilled" on the gridiron. The president spoke, exchanging jocular remarks with the opposition leader and others, and the first lady, Nancy Reagan, made a surprise appearance with a chorus of costumed reporters poking fun at her extensive wardrobe. That was unusual even for an American audience but it helped neutralize the initially critical attitude of the press toward the first lady. There were quite a few parodies and other entertaining performances. It was a curiously and characteristically American political show, something unfamiliar to a foreigner.

I had a short conversation with the president during the intermission. We exchanged greetings, and he expressed the hope that he would be able to have a more detailed conversation with me. He said Nixon had recommended that, too. I replied that I was willing to meet with him at his convenience. He assured me he would do that by all means, but a bit later, so as to make the conversation really productive after examining relations with the Soviet Union. He added jokingly that it would be hard for him to compete on an equal footing with the ambassador who had survived several American presidents and was thoroughly familiar with all the details.

## Reagan Writes to Brezhnev from the Hospital

I had Walter Annenberg and his wife Lenore to dinner. They were the closest California friends of the Reagans. He was a former American ambassador to Britain; she was the chief of protocol, an attractive woman who had come under attack in the press for making a curtsy to Queen Elizabeth II at the airport. She was accused of bowing to royalty although the American press and its readers could never get enough news of the visits of foreign monarchs, especially from Great Britain.

Annenberg said he believed that ultimately Reagan would be able to realize, probably even before some of his aides, that he had to adjust his policies toward the Soviet Union. "Reagan is not hopeless in this respect," he claimed. But he added that it would take time, especially after the president's narrow escape from death in an assassination attempt late in March had created a wave of sympathy that Reagan had turned into political capital, enabling him to ride high in Washington and the nation. (Brezhnev sent him a personal telegram of sympathy, for which Haig later thanked me.) Thus, Annenberg said in his characteristically formal language, the wound was likely to delay the president's "process of cognition" of the outside world.

More remarkable was the private conversation I had with Senator Paul Laxalt, a close friend and ideological soul mate of the president's who had been governor of the neighboring state of Nevada when Reagan was governor of California. Laxalt warned that we might forget that it was no easy thing to reform Reagan, a seventy-year-old man with ingrained suspicions about the Soviet Union. But he said the president's views had been slowly changing, and he was coming to realize that a dialogue with Moscow would be indispensable; he had even gone as far as to begin writing a personal letter to Brezhnev, something quite uncharacteristic of him. It was not of immense importance in itself and unlikely to impress Moscow greatly, but Laxalt said it was a real psychological stride for Reagan in his understanding of world realities. It should be kept in mind that he was writing the letter with his arm in a sling, not fully recovered, and his aides sought to talk him out of it. "But I supported Reagan," he said. Laxalt added that the Soviet leaders should not be surprised if they eventually found Reagan a partner ready for agreement.

While convalescing, the president had indeed taken up his pen. On April 25, Haig brought me not one but two letters from Reagan. The first was a formal reply to Brezhnev's letter of March 6, drafted, as Haig told me, by the State Department. But the other was written in Reagan's own hand, rather than typed, and was designed, the American president wrote, "to share some ideas with the Soviet president." Haig had received it from Reagan himself at the same time he was handed the formal reply. He believed that Reagan wanted to avoid the specific problems he had inherited from the previous administration and was trying to examine Soviet-American relations in a broader, philosophical, sense.

The letter was kept top secret by the administration as the president's intimates regarded it as naive, but it is of special interest because it is one of the few foreign policy documents personally composed by him in the early years of his presidency without the assistance of his aides or formal position papers from the State Department. In later years he would cite this letter as evidence of consistency in promoting favorable relations with the Soviet Union, and an answer to those who accused him of transforming his attitude toward the Soviet Union.

The letter recalled their first meeting when Brezhnev visited Nixon in San Clemente and said that at the time, "Never had peace and goodwill among men seemed closer at hand"—not least when Brezhnev took Reagan's hand in his and assured him of his dedication to peace. Evoking the hopes of ordinary people for personal autonomy and security, Reagan wondered whether governments had "permitted ideology, political and economic philosophies, and governmental policies to keep us from considering the very real, everyday problems of people."

As I read the president's letter I found that it was animated by the classic idea of America's invariable goodwill in international affairs. He invoked history, particularly the period immediately after World War II when the Soviet Union did not possess the atomic bomb and was completely devastated by the war. The United States then did not take advantage of its superiority, although no one would have been able to prevent it from doing so. But the subsequent policy of the Soviet Union, as the president stated it, looked different. If we could change that, both countries would be able to cooperate.

Brezhnev's reply was sent a month later. He, too recalled their meeting at Nixon's Casa Pacifica but also recalled the policy of detente and its companion policy of arms control. "Now, why did the process begin to malfunction, why has it stopped and even reversed?" Brezhnev wrote. Disagreeing with Reagan, he said the Soviet Union had kept its wartime commitments while the United States had achieved what "the American leaders themselves called Pax Americana," and in recent years relations had grown worse. "But the main message I would like to get across to you is that we are not seeking any standoff, and are making no attempt at your country's legitimate interests," Brezhnev wrote. "We are after something else, namely, peace, cooperation, a feeling of mutual trust and goodwill between the Soviet Union and the United States."

This was one of the key messages at the beginning of their exchange. Haig read the text carefully but declined to comment before the president saw it.

Reagan failed in his attempt to start a personal dialogue with Brezhnev, if that is what he really was trying to accomplish. Perhaps the Soviet leadership underestimated the psychological aspects of Reagan's behavior: while lying wounded, Reagan for the first time in his life addressed a personal letter to the leader of the Soviet Union and its Communist Party in his own hand. Brezhnev's letter (dismissed in Reagan's memoirs as an "icy reply") was cast in the standard polemical form stressing their differences, without any attempt to emphasize the necessity of developing their personal relations. The tone could not possibly have built a personal bridge. But Reagan's letter was not much practical help either, although he seemed to be revealing his personal convictions frankly. The main reason that both failed to tune into the same wavelength for further dialogue was, I believe, that the time was not yet ripe, and Reagan himself wrote the letter on the spur of the moment without really considering how to make concrete changes in his policy toward the Soviet Union. Further letters were again prepared by their diplomatic departments within the expected ideological framework, but the personal correspondence in effect lapsed. The breakthrough launched at the highest level was not accomplished. Moreover, as time passed, the White House would leak to the press biased information from Reagan's letters, which rendered their confidentiality meaningless.

In an ironic turn during this difficult period, I became dean of the diplomatic corps in Washington, succeeding Guillermo Sevilla-Sacasa, who had been Nicaragua's ambassador to the United States since 1943—when

Gromyko was our ambassador in Washington. A cheerful man, he was friendly to everybody and was not overburdened with routine business or concern for advancement since he was the son-in-law of the Nicaraguan dictator, Anastasio Somoza, with whom the United States had long had excellent relations because he was essentially Washington's political creature. Sevilla-Sacasa gladly attended all events at Washington's embassies demanded by protocol, until the revolution in Nicaragua deprived him of his ambassadorial post. The same revolution, which was of course anathema to the Reagan administration, made me dean of the diplomatic corps, since I was second only to Sevilla-Sacasa in my length of service in Washington.

I was immediately faced with two problems. First, I simply did not have the time to attend the numerous receptions at all of Washington's embassies, of which there were about 150 at the time. Each staged at least one reception annually to celebrate its national holiday, and there were other occasions demanding the attendance of the dean of the diplomatic corps—plus official ceremonies at the White House when heads of state arrived. That led to the second problem. Some of these countries had unfriendly relations with the Soviet Union or no diplomatic relations at all. That did not formally affect my status as dean of the diplomatic corps, but I sometimes felt out of my element at the ceremonies. Worst of all, President Reagan in his welcoming speeches could almost never forbear from criticizing the Soviet Union, its policies, and its ideology. It became something of a ritual with him. But there was absolutely no point in making the Soviet ambassador listen to it again and again.

The professional diplomats in the State Department were fully aware of the sensitivity of the situation, so we arranged that every time Washington was visited by heads of states unfriendly to the Soviet Union, or the State Department knew that Reagan would lash out at the Soviet Union in his welcoming speech, the Swedish ambassador, Wilhelm Wachtmeister, who was next to me in seniority, would attend in my place. We cooperated very well in this way.

I still witnessed many interesting events, not least the visit of Pope John Paul II to Washington. The papal nuncio gave a reception for diplomats, and the ambassadors, gathered in the grand hall, were invited one by one to enter a smaller reception room, where they were received by the Pope.

As dean, I was the first to enter. I knew that this Polish Pope understood Russian quite well, so I asked him in English in what language he would prefer to converse. The Pope suggested that he speak Polish and I speak Russian. After a while he asked me rather unexpectedly whether I would mind if he blessed me as the ambassador of a great country, so that he might wish us success in striving for world peace. (He knew that all Soviet ambassadors were supposed to be Communist Party members and therefore officially atheists.) I replied that I would be pleased to receive his blessing, especially in the great cause he mentioned. Thus I believe I am the only Soviet ambassador throughout the history of our diplomatic service to have received a blessing from the Pope.

## Moscow's Annoyance Mounts

It is important to understand the state of mind of the then Soviet leadership. Detente had become an integral part of Soviet policy under Brezhnev and it was personally identified with him. Most Politburo members had arrived at their supreme power during detente. There were no debates in the Soviet Union about the value of detente, either present or future. To Moscow, it not only meant a decrease of tension between two powers but made the Soviet leaders feel that they had achieved the permanent and internationally acknowledged status of a superpower equal to the United States. They wanted this process to be irreversible.

And then, suddenly, the Kremlin leaders were faced with a new American president, Ronald Reagan, who wanted all this swept away. Two features of Reagan's policy toward the Soviet Union upset them most. One was his apparent determination to regain military superiority; the other, his determination to launch an ideological offensive against the Soviet Union and foment trouble inside the country and among Soviet allies. American public opinion was on the whole willing to give Reagan the benefit of the doubt and even to support him.

Brezhnev and his colleagues found themselves dealing with something truly new, a deeply disturbing figure who tenaciously advanced a course that profoundly offended and alarmed them. Once they reluctantly came to the conclusion detente could not be recovered as long as Reagan remained in power, the inclination grew inside the Kremlin not to pacify him but to fight back.

When Gromyko and Haig met in New York at the United Nations in September, both sides restated their positions at their two meetings, though they agreed on the idea of negotiating the Euromissile dispute and on holding another meeting in January. Gromyko was hurt and angry that he had not received an invitation to the White House, especially since he carried special instructions from the Politburo to outline our views to the new president in person.

Instead, Reagan's latest message to Brezhnev, which had been sent on September 22 and restated the White House position on Soviet-American relations, was made public by the American side as soon as it was sent. By lifting phrases out of context, the White House and American embassies attempted to show that Washington was trying to promote good relations with Moscow, rather than the reverse. Furious, the Politburo publicized Brezhnev's own message, but it was particularly outraged by the Reagan administration's use of high-level correspondence for propaganda.

The Politburo nevertheless decided that Brezhnev should answer Reagan's letter as if no such leaks had taken place, and I handed Brezhnev's response to Haig on October 16. The message welcomed Reagan's ostensible readiness to maintain stable and solid relations with the Soviet Union, but it rebuffed the president's principal accusation that Soviet policies in places like Cuba, Angola, Kampuchea, or elsewhere represented the main obstacle to good relations. Linking that to better relations, Brezhnev said, would only produce "deliberate deadlock." He also rejected Reagan's claim that the anti-American campaign in the Soviet press was one of the factors poisoning the atmosphere of our relations.

> If anyone is entitled to complain about a campaign of rampant hostility, it is the Soviet side. Just look at the incessant campaign over the so-called Soviet threat. Now, what made you, Mr. President, declare in public the other day that the Soviet Union was founding its policy on the belief that it would win a nuclear war? Surely you know, unless somebody deliberately keeps you in the dark, about my statement that a nuclear war would be a catastrophe for the whole of humanity.

Brezhnev's letter tried to salvage the situation by approving the decision of Haig and Gromyko to start negotiations on limiting nuclear weapons in Europe. Haig made no comment, but promised to hand the letter to Reagan, who on October 2 had already announced a new long-term military buildup providing for the biggest increase in powerful strategic weapons ever planned or funded by any American president. It included one hundred B-1G bombers, development of the "invisible" Stealth bomber and larger Trident nuclear submarines and another 100 MX ICBMs, and improved systems of command, control, and communications. Some of these had been discussed under Carter, but it was Reagan who actually ordered them put into production, and with great fanfare. The buildup was part of an important modification of American military and political doctrines to include the possibility of limited nuclear war, endorsed by Reagan himself before the press.

The Soviet leadership felt itself under increasing attack by the administration's campaign, which it tried to justify with the false accusation that the

Soviet Union believed a nuclear war could be fought and won. On October 20, the Politburo once again met to discuss how to react to these continued charges of aggressive intent. Furious, the Kremlin decided to publish its position in the form of an answer by Brezhnev to a question by a *Pravda* correspondent. The Politburo approved the following text:

QUESTION: President Reagan said recently that the Soviet Union, judging by its leaders' private conversations, believes a nuclear war to be winnable. He used this to justify his course for a speedy nuclear buildup. What can you say about this statement by the American president?

ANSWER: I leave it to Mr. Reagan's conscience his statement that he allegedly knows what Soviet leaders say in private. . . . As to the point in question, I can say that . . . it is only a suicidal maniac who could begin a nuclear war in the hope of emerging victorious. However great his military power might be, and whatever way of unleashing a nuclear war he might choose, he will not achieve his aims. Retribution will inevitably follow. This is our stand of principle. It would be a good thing if the American president, too, made a clear and unambiguous statement rejecting the very idea of a nuclear attack as criminal.

President Reagan, of course, did no such thing. His bellicose approach caused increasing concern in a number of countries, especially American neighbors. President José Lopez Portillo of Mexico secretly offered to mediate the disputes between Washington and Havana. Reagan turned him down. After several attempts, the Mexicans arranged a secret meeting in Mexico City on November 23 for Haig with Carlos Rafael Rodriguez, a deputy prime minister and a long-time colleague of Castro's. Both sides kept the meeting secret and told neither us nor the Mexicans anything about it. I was kept informed only by the Mexican ambassador to Washington, Hugo Margain. A few days after the meeting Rodriguez informed our ambassador.

The issue of dissidents also continued to irritate our relations. In mid-November Haig told me that Reagan was personally interested in Shcharansky and Sakharov, whose cases if decided positively, he said, might have a constructive effect on our relations. But frankly neither Reagan nor Haig were especially committed to the rights of Soviet dissidents (in contrast to, say, Carter), although they would play that card from time to time for propaganda purposes. The embassy received calls from Carter, Vance, and other public figures inquiring about reports that Sakharov and his wife had been hospitalized. We informed Moscow and were told—"for our own information"—that they were not seriously ill. That was all.

Our embassy nevertheless regularly warned Moscow about the extremely negative effect the trials of Soviet dissidents were having on American public opinion and on Soviet-American relations, but Moscow ignored it all. Brezhnev's regime remained convinced that the Western campaign for the dissidents was a matter of ideological warfare aimed at undermining Soviet society. Personal anger against Reagan was an additional factor in their stubbornness.

On December 13 I had Billy Graham to dinner at our embassy. The famous preacher had sought an invitation to an interreligious conference on peace and disarmament in Moscow the following spring, which I helped him to obtain; he delivered a speech that was warmly welcomed. Graham told me he had just spent a night at the White House at the president's invitation and had a long conversation with Reagan and his wife, whom he had known for about fifteen years. During the conversation, he reminded the president that Nixon had gone down in history for achieving a major breakthrough toward normalizing relations with the Soviet Union and China, and he suggested that Reagan, too, could go down in history as a great president who had carried out a turn toward normalization of Soviet-American relations on an even greater scale. Graham particularly favored an agreement on nuclear disarmament and pointed out that the growing nuclear threat was promoting a surge in religious sentiment in America.

I asked him about Reagan's reaction. After some reflection, he replied, "I believe the president is on the right track." It was evident that Reagan had not been too enthusiastic about Graham's ideas but had not objected to them directly. I asked him who, in his opinion, had the most influence on the president. Without a moment's hesitation, he said it was Reagan's wife, Nancy. He characterized her as an intelligent yet rather conservative woman who seemed to be anxious for her husband to make a prominent mark in American history, including Soviet-American relations.

I would have liked that, too, but this was certainly not the figure Reagan had cut during his first year in office.

## II. The Reagan Crusade

*Impervious to Diplomacy*

No matter what diplomatic tack Moscow examined or actually took, the Reagan administration proved impervious to it. We came to realize that in contrast to most presidents who shift from their electoral rhetoric to more centrist, pragmatic positions by the middle of their presidential term, Reagan displayed an active immunity to the traditional forces, both internal and external, that normally produce a classic adjustment. After two years in power Reagan showed no signs of moving beyond the bellicose ideological approach that had characterized his career long before he entered electoral politics and dominated his 1980 campaign. The Soviet Union remained his number one enemy.

Haig and Gromyko met in Geneva on January 26 in the first major diplomatic encounter of 1982. They discussed nuclear arms limitation, the Middle East, South Africa, Angola, and other areas of conflict, but each held to his own views without any real attempt at compromise. The discussion on Poland was especially sharp, with each side demanding that the other stop interfering. There was no progress, but that did not seem to be the object for the Americans. At the end of the meeting Haig declared to the press: "I don't think the aim of these talks was to improve Soviet-American relations or East-West relations as a whole; on the contrary, they were designed to enable the American side to state its view on a number of pressing problems, first of all, to express concern over the situation in Poland. I think that our talks were more than useful in that sense."

What that did accomplish was to cause further mutual estrangement between Moscow and Washington, and this intensified when matters turned to arms control. Before the Senate Foreign Relations Committee, Haig justified himself by the events in Poland for failing to resume disarmament talks. Another deadlock.

In Poland, strikes and demonstrations by intellectuals and trade unions demanding democratic reforms had been shaking loose the government's control until martial law was imposed by the president, General Wojciech

Jaruzelski. The Politburo in Moscow was watching events very closely. The essential point about our position was that for many years Soviet troops had been stationed in Poland under the Warsaw Pact but had never intervened in Poland's domestic disturbances. But this time some of our Warsaw Pact allies insisted on military intervention. What was the Politburo to do?

Several urgent Politburo meetings were held. Leaders of the Soviet armed forces were prepared to repeat the invasion they had staged in Czechoslovakia, but this time the Politburo decided almost unanimously against it, the principal holdouts being the military members. Brezhnev declared, "Poland is not Czechoslovakia or Afghanistan." In a surprising argument from Suslov as the keeper of the party's ideology, even he said it would be preferable to admit a few social democrats into Poland's communist government than to use our troops. In short, the generals wanted to go, but the politicians did not.

Strict orders therefore were issued to Soviet troops in Poland confining them to their bases and keeping them off the streets. At the same time the Politburo decided to give all possible assistance to General Jaruzelski and his martial law regime. At several top-level meetings the Poles were offered money, food, and equipment to help them cope.

The Reagan administration retaliated with an angry campaign and an array of sanctions against the Soviet Union while supporting the Solidarity movement. What we did not know at the time was that the Reagan administration was in the process of redefining American goals in Eastern Europe in the light of events in Poland. The secret Presidential Directive-32 that emerged in the spring of 1982 was radical: the stated goal of U.S. policy would be to "neutralize the efforts of the Soviet Union" to maintain its hold on Eastern Europe. It authorized activities—both overt and covert—in that direction.

At the Geneva talks on Euromissiles, the American delegation had instructions to pursue the so-called zero option of total withdrawal of our SS-20s in exchange for NATO not deploying the new Pershing and cruise missiles. Even these Reagan proposals leaving the nuclear advantage to NATO caused heated debates inside the administration. Those who seriously wanted an agreement believed the proposals were so clearly one-sided that the Soviet Union was sure to find them utterly unacceptable, as indeed we did. Others, including apparently Reagan himself, proceeded from the assumption that simply proposing this zero option was a winner either way—if accepted, which seemed unlikely, and if rejected, which would give Washington the propaganda profit and still permit the installation of new missiles in Europe.

SALT was also stalled; the administration said it was developing new positions but the process was delayed by sharp internecine debates and an essential lack of interest at the top. This worried Americans who were concerned about the escalating arms race. Senators Alan Cranston, a Democrat from California, and Charles M. Mathias, a Republican from Maryland, both prominent liberal figures in their parties, visited me. They said ordinary Americans were confused by questions of nuclear arms, the more so because the president and the secretary of state deliberately mixed the balance of medium-range weapons in Europe with the balance of strategic forces. Both wanted Brezhnev to make a clear-cut statement that a rough parity existed between our two countries for all strategic forces and support it with concrete figures. They urged the Soviet Union to declare itself ready to freeze strategic weapons as well as missiles in Europe, too. Otherwise the administration would be left with room for maneuver to pursue the arms race.

I supported the senators' sound recommendation. Unfortunately, Moscow did not pay much attention. A mania for secrecy ruled all our thinking about nuclear weapons, and the Kremlin refused to publish the figures. Moscow was convinced that the Reagan administration was well aware of the rough nuclear parity but—to the indignation of the Soviet government—continued basing its defense and arms control policies on the public premise that the United States had fallen behind. Reagan told a news conference in March of 1982 that the Soviet Union had "a definite margin of superiority."

I do not know whether the president and his associates really believed what they were saying, or if it was mostly for public consumption. But Brezhnev and the Politburo firmly believed that the American leadership had fallen into the hands of those who had never liked detente, never accepted parity, and tried to regain superiority, dreaming of the revival of Pax Americana. They could not ignore the real situation: U.S. defense procurement budgets rose by 25 percent in each of early Reagan years. Once the Reagan administration had literally declared an arms race, the Kremlin saw no reason why it should pay some kind of penalty for having taken some advantage of the United States by developing such land-based nuclear weapons as SS-18 intercontinental and SS-20 intermediate-range missiles when American nuclear forces had advantages in air and submarine delivery systems.

After a long delay, the White House completed its proposals on strategic arms reduction early in May 1982. They were to be unveiled by the president in a speech at Eureka College in Illinois, from which Reagan had graduated. Haig invited me for a briefing and said the president wanted me pass on the gist of his proposals directly to Brezhnev. He stressed they were serious and resulted from a long debate within the administration between the two camps known as the "maximalists" and the "realists." Haig was among the latter and was happy that the State Department's suggestions had been approved by Reagan as the basis of the proposals, while "less realistic ideas" produced by other departments were rejected. He was evidently proud of his department. The president meant to propose starting talks in Geneva in the summer with the goal of a sizable reduction of strategic weapons to equal levels. But Haig gave me no details.

At Eureka on May 9 Reagan devoted a large portion of his speech to U.S.-Soviet relations and spoke in a more moderate tone, evidently as a concession to the mass movement against nuclear weapons. But there were virtually no major changes in the American position. His strategic arms proposals were openly directed at a sharply disproportionate reduction of the Soviet Union's strategic forces by cutting the land-based ICBMs of the two superpowers by equal proportions. We had been through all this before: because our missiles were largely land-based and theirs dispersed along the land, sea, and air triad, Reagan's plan was seen by Moscow as a crude effort to extend (or establish) U.S. nuclear superiority. If counted carefully, the proposals would have ultimately led to American strategic forces having one and one-half times as many strategic nuclear weapons as the Soviet Union and a threefold superiority in the number of warheads. The far-reaching U.S. nuclear rearmament program would not be affected.

But the most amazing fact was—according to Lou Cannon in his book, *President Reagan*—Reagan did not understand that the Soviet objections had a basis in fact and that these objections were not a sign of Moscow's unwillingness to negotiate. As Scowcroft would learn to his surprise nearly a year later, Reagan simply did not know that the Soviet strategic forces were heavily concentrated in land-based missiles! It was very difficult to believe but it probably was true. In any case, ignorance has its consequences. Reagan's lack of knowledge of the substance of arms control gave a great opportunity to those in his entourage who opposed the improvement of U.S.-Soviet relations and nuclear arms reduction. It enabled them to advance impossible but superficially appealing proposals that made the president look like a man of peace ready to negotiate.

Reagan's speech, of course, attracted the immediate attention of the Soviet leadership and caused an extremely negative reaction. On May 12, only three days after the speech, Gromyko, Ustinov, and Andropov sent the Politburo a joint memorandum vividly illustrating the real feelings of the core of the Kremlin toward Reagan's proposals and his presidency. It angrily accused him of creating "a propaganda cover-up for the aggressive militarist policy of the United States" and trying to break the detente agreements of nuclear parity. The speech as a whole, they said, "is saturated with gross, unadulterated hostility toward the Soviet Union" and was aimed at splitting the socialist countries and liquidating our system.

This unique document frankly revealed the mood and emotions of the Soviet leaders toward Reagan. His name became a synonym for all the evils in the "capitalist world." The Politburo discussed the memorandum and took a special decision to confirm it as the formal Soviet position on Reagan's speech. But when it replied through diplomatic channels, it decided to damp down its anger and coolly answered on May 25 that it agreed with the proposal for a full-scale, detailed summit, thoroughly prepared in advance. At the same time Moscow emphasized that it could not accept the president's arms control proposals as a realistic and practicable basis for negotiations.

## At the White House

When President Reagan gave a dinner for the diplomatic corps on February 13, I found myself seated next to his wife Nancy by virtue of my diplomatic seniority. My wife was likewise seated next to the president. The Reagans, like the Kennedys, knew how to stage such formal public events in the White House and enjoyed them. It was a splendid social evening. For most diplomats it was a rare opportunity to meet the president.

Mrs. Reagan complained to me during dinner about the almost complete restriction that the Secret Service had imposed on her own movements as well as her husband's after the attempt on his life the year before.

"We are regular prisoners here in the White House," she said, "especially after the thing that happened to my husband. Security guards watch us at every step. I can't even get out to visit my favorite museums and shops. Our sole safety valve is going to the ranch in California in the mountains where you can walk freely without running into our bodyguards. On the other hand, you have to put up with it. There are quite a few madmen around the country, prepared to make another attempt on his life. There are numerous threats."

Nancy Reagan complained that she had never had a chance to visit Moscow or Leningrad, nor would she ever have such an opportunity before the end of her husband's term of office, considering the current state of Soviet-American relations. But she would very much like to see our country. She confessed that neither she nor her husband knew much about the Soviet Union (which was clear from our conversation).

I remarked that it was important to judge other countries impartially and try to understand them, and that it was dangerous to employ stereotypes lest an attitude be constructed on the wrong basis. She repeated her idea that people should visit other countries and see them with their own eyes. She was evidently eager to learn things firsthand.

She criticized the American press for finding fault with her husband's statements, expressed interest and curiosity in Washington society, and all in all impressed me as a woman who knew her own worth.

After dinner I had a short conversation with the president, who knew I had just returned from Moscow and wondered how our relations were assessed there. I told him frankly that our relations were, if anything, at their lowest point since the end of World War II. I added that I could give him a more detailed report if he cared to hear it. Reagan hesitated, then pointed to the ambassadors crowding around us and said we could discuss Moscow's assessment of our relations some time later. I said I was ready for such a discussion at any time, but it was evident that Reagan himself still was not.

The president made a curious entry that day in his diary, later published in his autobiography. Noting that my wife and I had come to the White House for dinner, Reagan wrote the following: "Everything we've heard is true: They are a most likable couple. In fact, so much so you wonder how they can stick with the Soviet system. Truth is, he and his wife are most likable and very much in love with each other after forty years of marriage." *

I am not quoting this just because I am pleased (although I confess I am). What caught my attention was Reagan's earnest surprise that two people he found so likable could live in the Soviet system—that is, in "the evil empire"—and, indeed, represent it abroad. To me the directness and insouciance of his remarks confirms once again my belief that personal conviction underwrote Reagan's approach to the Soviets and everything associated with us, and not just some political pose.

On February 21, I had an introductory conversation with William Clark, the new national security adviser, whom I visited at the White House. He had replaced Richard Allen, who had to resign in a scandal over gifts from the Japanese. Clark, another California associate of Reagan's, expressed surprise that, apart from very rare ministerial meetings, there had been no particularly detailed discussion of major international issues between our countries during the past year. I replied that the administration avoided it, but we had been ready and still were. But my attempts to start at least a general conversation with Clark on some world issues were not successful, since he was poorly acquainted with them. But he fully shared his boss's ideological approaches. I thought to myself that Clark would hardly be the best partner in

---

* Ronald Reagan, *An American Life* (New York: Simon and Schuster, 1990), p. 822.

a confidential channel in the unlikely event that President Reagan decided to revive it. But in any event Clark preferred the security of the White House and was unwilling to maintain direct contacts with us. He was definitely neither a Kissinger nor a Brzezinski.

Early in April, Reagan, whether deliberately or merely in his characteristically light patter, said he was ready to meet Brezhnev if he attended a UN General Assembly session on disarmament in June. "We could have a talk," Reagan said while posing for photographers at the White House.

This caused quite a stir in the United States. But I had to tell Moscow that the administration had not contacted me and we had heard nothing more than the remark itself. The embassy was under instructions to follow this carefully, but we were also warned against taking any initiative. The Soviet leaders did not want to display any special interest in meeting with Reagan unless the Americans decided to talk about summits through official channels. But no American official from Haig on down ever mentioned the subject. Moscow then decided that complete silence from our side might be misinterpreted, and two weeks later, on April 18, *Pravda* published a remark by Brezhnev (in response to a correspondent's planted question) saying that the president's utterances about a summit "left a rather vague impression" but he favored an active dialogue with the United States at all levels, particularly at the summit, which he said should be well-prepared and could be held in a third country, probably by autumn.

A White House statement published on the same day said the administration would study Brezhnev's suggestions carefully, but nothing further was heard from the American side. Haig raised it again with me in May and said Reagan needed time to prepare. When I suggested October, for instance, Haig was evasive, but at least the question had gotten into official channels.

I must note that the Reagan Crusade against Godless Communism did have its limits, and these were defined by the direct financial interests of his supporters. The administration did not ignore their complaints. One such group was the grain farmers of the Midwest, who were smarting under the embargo on grain sales to the Soviet Union imposed by the administration after Poland declared martial law. On March 19, two Republican farm-state senators, Bob Dole of Kansas and Roger Jepsen of Ohio, visited me to remind me that America had enormous stocks of grain—82 million tons. Low grain prices and insufficient Soviet purchases, they said, combined with the possibility of a complete Soviet withdrawal from the American grain market to cause serious concern among businessmen and farmers in the Midwest. The senators wanted to strengthen our trade cooperation.

I had to tell them that the United States was not a reliable trading partner, which was clear from a number of arbitrary decisions taken by the administration, and they should address themselves to the White House. The senators said they understood that and meant to raise the subject with the president. Indeed, a meeting followed between Reagan and farm-state congressmen. Speaking afterward, Reagan admitted that the embargo had hardly any effect on the Soviet Union. "It turns out that we harmed ourselves without any damage to those whom this measure was meant to affect," he said, and promised that the administration would no longer use agricultural exports as a tool in pursuit of foreign policy.

## Haig Is Replaced by the Sphinx

On Friday, June 25, I received instructions from Moscow to deliver a message from Brezhnev demanding that the United States restrain Israel, whose forces just then were invading Lebanon and closing on Beirut in defiance of UN Security Council resolutions. I contacted Haig and we arranged to meet later in the day. The meeting was quite extraordinary, for it took place three hours after Reagan announced that he had accepted Haig's resignation and one hour after Haig himself had told a press conference he had quit. However, Haig did not cancel our appointment.

When I arrived, I found him agitated. We dispensed quickly with the matter at hand, for Haig clearly was not disposed to discuss official business, and I was certainly not going to insist. Instead, we had a long conversation about the reasons behind his decision to resign. I wondered how it had come about—by now the conversation had turned private—and he told me his story.

First, an increasing divergence had emerged on a number of foreign policy issues between him and Reagan with his California entourage in the White House. The points of disagreement included East-West relations, North-South relations, the strategic arms limitation talks, and certain aspects of Middle East policy. He said the imminent talks on strategic arms had forced him into a long battle with "ignoramuses and saboteurs" who championed an utterly unpromising position, and it had become more realistic thanks to his efforts, or at least more realistic than the one advocated by many of the president's assistants and advisers. (I tried to imagine what kind of a position they had advanced if even Haig had found it unacceptable!)

Second, Haig was fed up with the unending intrigues and odious leaks to the press constantly aimed against him by the president's closest associates. He dismissed them as "political pygmies skilled in behind-the-scenes machinations." Besides, they played up the stories of Haig's attempts to pose as the only genuine leader of American foreign policy, in a bid to eclipse the president's role in policy making. They kept whispering into the president's ear that Haig would take advantage of his position as secretary of state to run for president in 1984 against Reagan.

Haig told me he had no such idea, but Reagan seemed to take that slander at its face value. In short, it became hard to maintain a good personal relationship with the president, which was indispensable to a secretary of state if he wished to steer foreign policy with confidence. He said he had taken the decision to resign on his own initiative and it had long been maturing. He had told the president only that day and the president accepted—something Haig did not seem to have expected.

Presidential aides, he said, now were suggesting Caspar Weinberger or Jeane Kirkpatrick, the American ambassador to the United Nations, and even Eugene Rostow, head of the Disarmament Agency, as candidates for secretary of state. With gusto, Haig exclaimed, "You would have to be out of your mind to suggest them as candidates!" However, Reagan had made a good choice in the end by offering the job to George Shultz, whom Haig described as an old friend with experience in international affairs. (Both had served Nixon, Haig as chief of staff and Shultz as secretary of labor, treasury, and director of the budget.) Haig said Shultz was "alien to fantasy and hasty improvisation" and "something of a slow coach, but that's just as well."

Before I left for vacation I had a long talk with Stoessel, who gave me to understand, discreetly yet clearly, that no considerable changes for the better were to be expected in the foreseeable future. He said that the Reagan administration was not interested in agreements, even for the sake of improving the atmosphere. Theoretically they might be possible although that seemed unlikely given Moscow's stand on principle and its own intransigence, but there were some in the president's entourage who argued that the Soviet Union would be forced into concessions by difficulties in its economy and technological backwardness.

Stoessel said Reagan was not readily influenced by diplomatic experience and proceeded from the notion that the United States should gain advantages at all costs and not necessarily yield anything in return to its opponent. The president believed, for instance, that the Soviet Union had to make far greater sacrifices in reducing nuclear arms wherever it had an edge in order to put the two at equal levels, and he was convinced that the Soviet Union would be interested in such an agreement. This tendency to have it the "American way," disregarding foreign interests, was characteristic of Reagan throughout.

Stoessel gave me a fairly positive assessment of the new secretary of state as a conservative man not excessively burdened with bellicose ideology, and guarded and taciturn in character, which was probably just as well since he would not exploit anti-Soviet rhetoric. He proceeded from the possibility of coming to terms with the Soviet Union, but Stoessel warned me that he was unlikely to make haste in trying to improve relations and would in all probability bide his time until Reagan himself was ripe for it. The main question about Shultz's influence on American foreign policy was whether he would manage to become a member of Reagan's essentially impenetrable inner entourage, which resisted alien and unfamiliar ideas.

I did not meet Shultz in his new position of secretary of state until September 23, after his confirmation and my return from vacation. He opened the conversation by discussing his forthcoming talks with Gromyko at the UN General Assembly. He thought the best way to approach them would be to avoid covering too broad a range of questions, especially those smacking too much of propaganda, and try an approach that would ensure more favorable results. But what exactly? He did not know yet, but he would think about it as long as his Soviet counterpart had no objections. I told him I would report his ideas to Gromyko, who was to arrive in New York the next day, but I was sure he would join Shultz in avoiding propaganda.

Shultz recalled his trip to Moscow during the Nixon administration, his meetings with Brezhnev and our foreign trade minister, which I had arranged. He told me jokingly about fishing near Sochi on the Black Sea. They did not catch any fish but had very nice picnic at the shore with a good wine and many Georgian toasts.

On the whole, Shultz was at ease and did not use the sharp expressions characteristic of Haig. He conducted the conversation in a more businesslike manner, although he avoided talking to the point and in effect bypassed pressing issues, preferring to engage in general matters without discussing anything definite. He carried on in this distinctive style at his first meetings with Gromyko at the United Nations in New York on September 28 and October 4. They first discussed regional problems, such as the Middle East, Afghanistan, the Caribbean basin, and South Africa, then broader questions, including the observance of the Helsinki agreements, nuclear nonproliferation, curbing the arms race, and human rights. There was no appreciable progress, but the talks proceeded calmly, and both agreed to exchange views on a more regular basis. But the ice was far from broken. Once again, Gromyko did not get an invitation to meet with Reagan in the White House.

During the first Gromyko-Schultz meetings I was struck by a certain similarity between the two. Both were by nature guarded individuals and born functionaries, they were splendid representatives of high-level Soviet and American bureaucracy—cautious, close-mouthed, loyal, and technocratic. At the end of the month, on October 26, we sent a small, friendly signal, which was returned in kind. I was instructed to inform the U.S. government that the Soviet Union had launched a new type of light intercontinental ballistic missile code-named the RS-22. I passed the information to Eagleburger at the State Department and stressed that we were furnishing it as a goodwill gesture. Eagleburger thanked me, remarked that the Soviet Union was under no obligation to tell the United States about the launch, and expressed his appreciation.

A day later, as I attended a small reception at the State Department, Shultz took me aside and said he wanted me to convey to Moscow his personal appreciation of our gesture. As if demonstrating a response, he said he had just sanctioned the resumption of negotiations with the Soviet Union on consular matters, and had fixed the dates for consultations on nuclear nonproliferation and for a further exchange of views on South Africa. These had been discussed with Gromyko, and now they were implementing their agreement to resume official discussions.

Shultz said he had reported to the president about his conversations with Gromyko and described them to Reagan as detailed and serious. "I think serious is the word, isn't it?" Shultz asked. I agreed.

Shultz was a friend of Donald Kendall, who filled me in on the new secretary's troubles with Reagan's anti-Soviet ideologues. "You can hardly imagine what is going on within the administration," Shultz had told Kendall. He said Weinberger actively interfered in foreign policy by suggesting simplified initiatives for each international crisis by invoking military strength without much use of diplomacy. This appealed to the president and had caused enmity between Haig and Weinberger, finally leading to Haig's resignation.

"I am not going to repeat Haig's mistake," Shultz told Kendall, "but I will work patiently with the president." Shultz saw Reagan as "not hopeless," especially now that he had been in power for two years and was beginning to realize that huge military programs were no substitute for a genuine foreign policy. But he was stubborn and ideologically unprepared for agreements with the Russians. "We'll have to bide our time," Shultz said, and this became his motto.

This conversation, which I reported to Moscow, confirmed my own impression of Shultz: that he would act extremely carefully and without haste. I should confess that at first I was not too happy with his exceedingly deliberate progress in Soviet-American affairs, which was especially evident in disarmament negotiations. He was at first unfamiliar with the substance, but more important, he clearly had no authority to engage in any quest for agreement. He seemed to be playing for time. I was especially put on guard by his outright unwillingness to participate in the confidential channel, although there were times he would readily talk with me.

But his laconic, official way of speaking made it very difficult to fathom the administration's intentions, which was anything but the best way of communicating between Washington and Moscow, especially during those crucial times when our relations were touch and go. Reporters found this placid and stolid man equally hard to draw out and nicknamed him the Sphinx. Obtaining information that he did not want to impart was like trying to squeeze water from a stone. He was no stranger to supporting foreign policy by force and would bluntly declare that force and diplomacy were no antagonists. In that sense, he was a true representative of the Reagan administration.

However, my opinion of Shultz gradually changed for the better. A businesslike and intelligent man, he spent a great deal of time struggling against those who were trying to control American foreign policy and diplomacy from outside the State Department and was forced to defend his turf against Weinberger and four successive national security advisers: Clark, Robert McFarlane, John Poindexter, and Frank Carlucci. Even Reagan sometimes bypassed the secretary of state under pressure from these advisers, so that Shultz learned about some important matters such as the strategic defense initiative only at the last moment. During Shultz's first years in office, the intrigue and struggles for power within the president's entourage gave him little choice but to act slowly but surely, and to my mind, he personally made a substantial if not decisive contribution to the gradual evolution of Reagan's views.

On issues of U.S.-Soviet diplomacy, George Shultz became the definite leader of the pragmatist group in Reagan's administration. It included McFarlane; Michael Deaver, the president's chief image maker; James Baker, his chief of staff; Vice President Bush; and in her own way Nancy Reagan. Their opponents in the conservative group included among others Weinberger, Clark, Counselor Edwin Meese, CIA Director William Casey, and Jeane Kirkpatrick. Both groups had allies in Congress, the media, and the bureaucracy. The State Department was a base for the pragmatists, but the department's important Arms Control and Disarmament Agency under its outspoken conservative director Kenneth Adelman was on the other side. Publicly conservative groups, using the political climate in the country, were much more vocal. The speechwriting department in the White House was a dedicated conservative enclave. But the main voice of the administration, of course, was President Reagan himself.

On November 4, I was awakened early in the morning by the head of the embassy's coding service, who solemnly handed me a personal cable from Brezhnev. The telegram said I had been awarded the title of Hero of Socialist Labor and the gold medal of the Hammer and Sickle; the Soviet leadership congratulated me, for this was the highest civil decoration in the Soviet Union. I was the first and remain the only ambassador to be honored in this way throughout the long history of Soviet diplomatic service.

Needless to say, I was extremely pleased, but I confess also greatly surprised. Such high government awards were normally timed to national holidays, the signing of important international agreements, some official event or official birthday, or the birthday of the person honored with the award. But there was nothing of the kind happening on that day, at least not that I knew of. I wondered what had prompted the timing.

Within several days, I received quite a number of telegrams from official and public figures, fellow diplomats, and friends and relatives. We staged a friendly dinner with our embassy staff. These events left pleasant memories.

When I asked Gromyko about it some time later, he merely said the government decided to show its appreciation of my ambassadorial work of many years in the difficult conditions of our relations with the United States. But there was one more thing, both curious and tragic, that I learned later when they gave me the medal in the Kremlin. It so happened that the decree awarding me the high title turned out to be the last official document signed by Brezhnev in the capacity of president of the Supreme Soviet. He died unexpectedly a week later, on November 10.

## Brezhnev and Andropov

When Brezhnev's death was announced, the administration reacted promptly and with dignity. On November 11, I received a phone call from William Clark, who conveyed both official condolences and his own. He said the president was considering sending a high-ranking delegation to attend the funeral led by Vice President George Bush and including Shultz, and that the president himself would come to the embassy the following morning to sign the condolence book. Shultz suggested to Reagan that he attend the funeral and meet Brezhnev's successor Yuri Andropov; but the president was not ready for summitry of any sort and did not like to attend funerals anyway.

The next day at 10 A.M.—it was a Saturday—the president arrived, accompanied by Clark and Deaver. He wrote the following entry: "I express my condolences to the family of President Brezhnev and the people of the Soviet Union. May both our peoples live jointly in peace on this planet. Ronald Reagan."

The president, who was visiting the Soviet Embassy for the first time, was noticeably excited by this voyage to the outpost of the "evil empire" and even inadvertently repeated one of the words in his condolence message. I showed him the rooms and halls where President Nixon had negotiated and dined with Brezhnev. Reagan inspected them and examined the photographs with great interest. Although guarded and very inhibited when entering the embassy—he seemed to be wondering what kind of place it was—he felt more in his element by the end of his visit and talked in a more free and indeed friendly manner, although we often had to repeat what was said because he was somewhat hard of hearing. He said he hoped to call on us again, but on a more auspicious occasion.

There are some who say that the historic turn in our relations began with this visit, and others who believe it did not come until Reagan's speech more than a year later when he invoked a metaphorical Ivan and Anya and Jim and Sally comparing their lives and hoping for peace. When we at the embassy heard the speech on January 16, 1984, we could not decide whether it was genuine or mere campaign oratory. But in any case things started to move after Brezhnev's death, first in Moscow, then in Washington.

Yuri Andropov was elected by the Politburo and approved by the Plenum of the party to succeed Brezhnev as general secretary of the Soviet Communist Party on November 12. His first public statement was somewhat aggressive in tone, characteristic of his mood at the moment and fully reflecting the general sentiment of the Soviet leadership. "We know very well," he said, "that peace cannot be obtained from the imperialists by begging for it. It can be upheld only by relying on the invincible might of the Soviet armed forces."

I had not infrequently dealt with Andropov when he was the head of the KGB—the State Security Committee, which also put him in charge of our intelligence service abroad. He knew as much about foreign policy problems as Gromyko and knew more than Gromyko did about Soviet domestic policy, such as the problems of dissidents and emigration from the Soviet Union. He also was familiar with foreign reaction to these sensitive subjects through the KGB's foreign intelligence network. Gromyko virtually ignored them.

Andropov's feelings and views were mixed. He was no anti-Semite. There were quite a few people of Jewish origin among his fellow workers and friends. I never heard him tell any jokes or anecdotes about Jews, quite the contrary to some of our other leaders. He would express some liberal views in private conversations, but he was not liberal. He was a convinced opponent of the dissident movement in the Soviet Union, believing that it caused considerable damage not only at home, but also to our relations with the rest of the world.

It was Andropov, of all people, who suggested exiling Sakharov to the city of Gorky. I happened to be present at a Politburo session discussing the Sakharov case (I was called to report on another subject). Andropov's main reason was that Sakharov and his wife had turned into a constant focus of anti-Soviet campaigning abroad and therefore must be deprived of all access to foreigners through exile to a place closed to foreign reporters. But when some members of the Politburo—Chernenko, Grishin, Solomentzev—suggested various distant cities in Siberia, Andropov named Gorky, the third-largest city in the Soviet Union. He noted that the climate differed little from Moscow, something Sakharov's doctors strongly recommended. Nobody argued with Andropov as nobody spoke against Sakharov's exile in general. He was considered a nuisance to the regime if not a direct enemy.

Andropov's views on foreign policy were close to Gromyko's, and they often successfully presented joint memos to the Politburo. Not infrequently they were joined by Defense Minister Dmitri Ustinov, and together these three constituted the core of the Politburo in determining foreign policy. Andropov had the advantage of familiarity with both foreign policy and military issues from the KGB's broad sources of information, so he defended his point of view with competence. Gromyko and Ustinov were authorities in their respective domains but laid no special claim to each other's fields in the way that Andropov felt comfortable in both.

Last but not least, Andropov had a long record of work in the Central Committee and enjoyed the support of its staff. All that taken together, along with his detailed knowledge of the domestic situation in the Soviet Union, marked him out among the rest of the Soviet leadership, although, thanks to his character and indisputable intellect, he sought to remain on an equal footing with other leaders and did not try to overshadow them. That decided his election as general secretary.

Andropov was always interested in the state of our relations with the United States. Whenever I was in Moscow, he invited me for a long private conversation. His interests ranged over a great variety of things: politics, economics, culture, social life, and especially, the American elite and the Washington official establishment. Like Gromyko, but in contrast to the emotional Ustinov, Andropov did not favor confrontation with the United States, but he believed Reagan to be a dangerous individual whose actions might trigger a military conflict between us. Hence Andropov's guarded attitude toward Reagan and his determination to maintain the Soviet Union's defense capability.

Still I think that, given a favorable international situation, he would have been ready for serious agreements with Washington, especially in limiting nuclear arms. In this he somewhat resembled Mikhail Gorbachev, who was his protégé. Both were intellectuals among the supreme party leadership, each in his own way. Characteristically, during his first days in power, Andropov ordered our delegation at the disarmament talks to stop hinting at our possible withdrawal from the talks—a bluffing tactic sometimes employed by Gromyko—but to persist with the negotiations. However, it was fated that Andropov would never really fulfill himself as leader of the party and the country because his incurable and eventually fatal kidney disease allowed him only about fifteen months in power.

When the American delegation headed by Vice President Bush arrived in Moscow on November 14 for Brezhnev's funeral, Andropov received them for a separate conversation. It was his first meeting with high-ranking American officials. The thrust of his remarks was that the Soviet Union was prepared to improve relations between the two countries, but he did not go into detail. There was not enough time and he was not ready to deal with concrete subjects.

On his return from Moscow Shultz asked me to convey the thanks of the delegation to Andropov for taking time to meet and talk despite the demands of the state funeral and his transition to power. "Of course, you can hardly solve any serious problem during a short meeting," Shultz said, "but we believe it important that we have established a personal relationship with General Secretary Andropov, and we appreciate the fact." Shultz then suggested we meet in private later to conduct an unofficial review of our relations, which I accepted.

On November 23, I had dinner with Shultz at his invitation. He was the seventh secretary of state with whom I had met and dined in the same office. The time was passing by so quickly. The conversation was held in private and was quite open. I reminded Shultz of Andropov's commitment to dialogue and asked how Reagan had reacted to it. Shultz said the president had authorized him to reply that he was also sincerely in favor of more constructive relations. While not disguising the fact that he was still committed to making America militarily strong—"Mr. Andropov, I understand, is committed to the same idea concerning the Soviet Union," Shultz quoted the president—Reagan had instructed him to tell me that he was ready to search for areas that might lead to more constructive relations.

I asked how they would suggest conducting a practical dialogue, because up to now, I reminded him, the administration had made the unacceptable demand that we repay it for normalizing relations by making unilateral concessions. Shultz evaded discussing any definite questions, such as negotiations on nuclear arms. He said that both sides often differed on priorities. "For instance," he said, "the question of human rights. We agree with the Soviet side that interference in your internal affairs is unacceptable. The administration believes the problem is not so much important in itself, but because of the widespread domestic reaction it causes, which the White House cannot possibly ignore." He told me Nixon had recommended that the administration deal with us on this question privately, and Reagan agreed. He continued: "The only thing we are calling upon the Soviet leadership to do—and we don't make our demands public—is to examine the remaining applications to emigrate. They are few, yet they are well known in the United States, and at least some of them should be solved one way or another." Reagan's position on human rights was more quiet and flexible than Carter's.

After that conversation with Shultz I recommended to Moscow that we involve him in a more active dialogue. Andropov agreed. On December 6, I had another meeting with Shultz, this time on Moscow's instructions, and told him that having thought about his suggestions, I wanted to share some of my ideas, which I then proceeded to do in the hope of engaging him in a concrete and positive discussion. Having heard me out, he said in his characteristically cautious manner that while not all of our views coincided, he believed that the very process of exchanging them was rather useful and he would report that to the president.

My conversations with Shultz left me with the impression that he was putting out his personal feelers to see if there was a chance of conducting a meaningful dialogue in the future. He was, so to speak, on his own exploratory mission while for the time being the White House had not yet made a decision in favor of concrete discussions. It was not accidental that every time we came to specific questions such as arms reduction or a summit meeting, the secretary of state kept silent or ducked the point by making general statements or promising to talk about it later.

Later it became clear that within a few weeks of Andropov's ascension to leadership, Shultz asked Reagan for authority to explore cautiously the opportunities across the range of our relationship, and then Shultz without haste began to launch what he called a "work program" with me to review our differences in a systematic manner.

But this would take time, and by the end of the year our relations were still stagnant. On December 30 the American journalist Kingsbury Smith received, in response to his questions, written replies that summarized among other things our position on nuclear disarmament. In general, he proposed freezing the levels of strategic arms and then reducing them by one-quarter to a position of equality. This equality also was to apply in Europe. The Reagan administration showed no interest in these ideas and also announced it had no plans for a Soviet-American summit.

Did this amount to a complete deadlock? Not exactly. Brent Scowcroft told me that at his last meeting with Reagan, the president expressed an intuition that something was wrong with his policy toward the Soviet Union but he did not know where the fault lay. In any case he was prevented from discovering it not only by his own internal arsenal of anti-communist clichés but by the narrowness of his own close advisers, who would be the last to come up with concrete recommendations for improvement. He had to look somewhere else, and as it turned out, he turned to the one person whose self-confidence and determination had guided his political career from the start—himself.

# III. "More Deeds, Less Words"

*A Personal Discussion with Reagan, at Last*

At 5 P.M. on February 15, 1983, I arrived at the State Department for what I assumed would be a routine talk with Shultz. He informed me that President Reagan wanted to talk with me in person at the White House right away. I was certainly mystified but accepted at once.

It was a frosty, foggy evening and Washington was still recovering from a huge weekend snowfall. My visit was utterly shrouded in secrecy. We went in Shultz's car from the basement garage to the White House, entering through the East Gate, where official visitors are rarely received. From there we were conducted not to the president's office in the West Wing but to the second floor of the White House and the president's private apartment, which was nicely decorated and comfortable, and where Reagan preferred to hold informal chats. Only the three of us were there, and Shultz confined himself to occasional remarks.

We exchanged the usual greetings. Coffee was served. The president had been fully briefed on Shultz's conversations with me and especially on Andropov's statements to the U.S. delegation at Brezhnev's funeral, and he wanted to continue with me along those lines. First of all, he said, it would be useful to establish a personal and confidential channel of communication with the general secretary, over the heads of "the bureaucracy," in order to conduct a frank exchange of views. The channel could operate through contacts between Shultz and the Soviet ambassador as it had under past presidencies in a way that he understood had been worthwhile.

The president went on to say that while Andropov had told Bush and Shultz that he favored good relations with the United States, and "you, Mr. Ambassador, have also told Shultz about that on behalf of the Soviet leadership, please tell Andropov that I am also in favor of good relations with the Soviet Union. Needless to say, we fully realize that our lifetime would not be long enough to solve all the problems accumulated over many years. But there are some problems that can and should be tackled now. Probably, people in the Soviet Union regard me as a crazy warmonger. But I don't want a war between us, because I know it would bring countless disasters. We should make a fresh start."

"I noted," continued the president, "that Andropov is clearly committed to the maxim: 'More deeds, less words.' It is easier for a newcomer, who is not burdened with the load of the past, to make the first step even if it is a symbolic one."

Reagan suggested a small gesture that was to figure with unusual symbolism in the turn in our relations. He asked the Soviet Union to grant exit visas for seven Pentecostal Christian fundamentalists who had been living in the basement of the American Embassy since 1978, when they had pushed their way past the guards and taken sanctuary there. If these people were allowed to emigrate, the American public would welcome the Soviet move with greater enthusiasm than any other bilateral agreement, said the president. "It may sound paradoxical, but that's America." (President Reagan was right in his own way, given the very special way American public opinion focuses on individual stories.) Reagan also said the Jackson-Vanik amendment linking Jewish emigration with trade was wrong, but it had been passed by Congress and he could not cancel it. If Congress revoked it, he would not stand in the way.

Reagan paused as if inviting me to express my opinion. I said that since the president and the American government were prepared to improve our relations, they could rely on reciprocity from us. But we believed it important to know exactly how the American side was going to go about it.

The president replied by raising his fundamental point about security and American benevolence, which he had raised in his first handwritten message to Brezhnev. He asked me if the Soviet Union indeed believed the United States posed a threat to the Soviet Union—could the United States attack the Soviet Union and start a nuclear war? He went on to recall the time after World War II when the United States had a monopoly on nuclear weapons, its military industry was prepared for war, and everything was in place for America to dominate the world. Who then could have stopped us? But America did not take the opportunity.

When Brezhnev replied to those questions, he reminded Reagan the Soviet Army had dominated the whole European continent right after the Americans went home at the end of World War II, yet the Soviet Union had honored its commitments to its wartime allies and did not consider expansion into Western Europe. I enlarged on that in my reply by asking Reagan to look at things from our angle: the numerous American military bases around the Soviet Union, their new nuclear missiles, and the arms race now being pursued by the American government. "As to the question of whether we believe that the United States poses a military threat to the Soviet Union," I said, "let me put it bluntly. We regard the huge rearmament program in the United States now under way amidst political tension between the two countries as a real threat to our country's security. Do the American people want a war? The answer seems clear to us: it does not, no more than any other people. As for us, every family in the Soviet Union knows what a war is like and what disasters it can bring to us all. We proceed from the belief that the American president clearly realizes that."

Reagan said he certainly did, but speaking frankly, the American people regarded as its main threat the principal political idea of the Soviet Union, which was based on the fundamental Marxist-Leninist teaching that the world would surely become communist. The Soviet Union therefore justified its encouragement and support for revolutions in any country, especially if they affected American interests. In short, the Soviet Union proceeded from the assumption that the future belonged to it exclusively, while the United States had no future, even though its social system was supported by a majority of its population and its standards of living were the highest in the world.

"We believe in our future, and we will fight for it," the president said.

I told Reagan that he sounded sincere but unrealistic. We were not going to impose our views and convictions by force of arms. Let history be the supreme arbiter of our competition in the conditions of peaceful coexistence. "We are not proclaiming a world crusade against capitalism," I said. "We are ready to accept the verdict of history without making wars or any rash moves that might lead to a disastrous war, particularly between the United States and the Soviet Union. It is in the two countries' interests to avert it. To achieve that we should work jointly with a view to normalize our relations."

Reagan remarked that the subject required more than one discussion and joked that he had received quite a rap across the knuckles for reciting a so-called series of ten commandments of world conquest ascribed to Lenin after reading them in a California newspaper and using them in a speech. It turned out that they did not exist, and had less to do with Lenin than with Reagan's habit of borrowing dubious quotations to support his political assessments, to the intense puzzlement of the public, the press, and his own White House officials, to say nothing of the Kremlin.

I told the president I wanted to seize this surprise opportunity of talking with him to present a practical approach to the future that could be continued with the secretary of state. Reagan was ready to hear me out, and I spoke in detail on nuclear disarmament, both the strategic arms limitation talks and dispute about nuclear arms in Europe. Reagan reiterated the American position on Euromissiles, where clearly his attention was focused.

"Let the delegations keep on working," he said succinctly. "I should like to repeat in conclusion that, like Andropov, I favor good relations between our countries. I want to remove the threat of war in our relations. I want a positive turn. Please communicate this to the general secretary and the whole Soviet leadership."

The meeting lasted almost two hours, unusually long for him; his attention span was notoriously short, but not this time. Shultz and I returned to the State Department to continue our detailed review.

This was not only my first private meeting with Reagan, but it was his first substantive conversation as president with any senior Soviet representative and—as far as I know—at any time in his long career as an aggressive opponent of communism and the Soviet Union. The very decision to hold our meeting was remarkable, as Reagan made it only in the third year of his presidency, which showed his personal desire finally to examine Soviet-American affairs more closely.

Shultz writes in his memoirs that except for his wife Nancy, Deaver, and Shultz himself, the president's entire entourage opposed the meeting, but Reagan decided to go ahead nevertheless. For him this first attempt at face-to-face diplomacy with a representative of the "evil empire" was evidently of major significance. For the first time Reagan was trying to be a negotiator with the Soviet Union. The very fact of the meeting was kept a complete secret by the White House. It was of principal importance to Shultz, as he told me, because once the president himself began a dialogue with the Soviet ambassador, the secretary of state could more confidently tackle Soviet-American affairs, regardless of the opposition from inside the White House and elsewhere. The meeting thus provided the crucial opening that Shultz had been seeking.

I sent Moscow my report about the conversation, recommending that we continue working patiently to bridle Reagan's extremist views. I pointed out that small, inch-by-inch steps toward establishing a personal relationship with Reagan could, at the initial stage, play a more positive role than any major projects for which I believed he was as yet psychologically unprepared. As a first step, I recommended that we clear up the problem of the Pentecostals, which was long overdue anyway.

A month later, Shultz told me that the American Embassy in Moscow reported the Soviet government had made its first step toward letting the Pentecostals emigrate, although it would take some time to complete things.

But more important, Reagan had expressed his satisfaction when Shultz passed on the news. This episode, however small, was interesting from a psychological point of view. For President Reagan, his request was a sort of personal test of the Soviet government's goodwill: Were the communists in Moscow prepared to respond to his appeal even about small matters? For the Soviet leadership, Reagan's request looked distinctly odd, even suspicious. After almost three years in office and at his first meeting with the Soviet ambassador, the president actually raised only one concrete issue—the Pentecostals—as if it were the most important issue between us. This request was rather disappointing to them and was not welcomed enthusiastically in Moscow. But it was a matter of attitude and psychology.

For months afterward, high American officials, including Bush and Shultz, repeatedly cited this case as the first symbolic breakthrough in the president's conviction that it was impossible to deal with the Russians. During my long stay in Washington I came to consider psychological factors a very important part of the relations between the leaders of both countries. Unfortunately, the leaders themselves did not pay enough attention to psychology, preoccupied as they were with geopolitical and ideological conflicts, and often extremely dogmatic ones.

It was evident from Shultz's behavior during our White House conversation and long afterward that Reagan was the real boss, and the secretary of state carried out his instructions. Shultz hardly intervened in the conversation and ostensibly agreed with Reagan throughout. I even had the impression, perhaps an erroneous one, that the secretary of state was somewhat afraid of the president. From Shultz's memoirs, it is clear that at the start of his tenure he did not meet with the president often in private but contacted him through his aides. When I observed Reagan and Shultz during the meeting, I did not sense any personal rapport between them, in contrast to the relationship between Brezhnev and Gromyko.

As for the confidential channel, I think Reagan simply had no idea at the moment about how to use it or even how it functioned. He knew from Nixon that the channel played a considerable role in ensuring a private dialogue between the leadership of the two countries. Shultz echoed the president's words during our White House conversation but he, too, showed little interest in the confidential channel and did little to put it into operation. There seemed to be several reasons for this. Shultz probably feared the channel might be commandeered by one of the president's aides. But he also was reluctant to manage it single-handedly, since it really worked only if the private talks within the channel were used by each side to sound out the other on concrete issues for compromise solutions, and Shultz was not prepared for that kind of exploration. Unlike Kissinger, Shultz, especially at the beginning, was kept on a short leash and had to consult the president in advance about nearly every conversation with me. Besides, Shultz had not yet mastered the detailed nuances of the disarmament talks, which was one of the principal subjects that kept the channel going in the past.

Whenever Shultz wanted to discuss the state of the arms negotiations with me, he always had competent officials and experts by his side even when he had already mastered the material. No confidential dialogue was possible under such circumstances. I had far fewer private conversations with him than with Vance, Kissinger, or Rusk, although I dare say my personal relationship with Shultz was friendly enough. On the whole, he was certainly a true representative of the Reagan administration and defended its positions consistently and stubbornly.

Looking back now and reading Shultz's memoirs, it is clear that he had much stamina and perseverance, patiently pushing against Reagan and his entourage to promote his ideas of compromise. He sought cautiously to develop a long-term policy toward the Soviet Union. It was not an easy task, given Ronald Reagan's essential ambivalence and shifting moods about the Soviet Union and the endless disputes about Soviet policy within his administration. It was difficult for them to create an integrated policy. Fragmentary actions that were approved from time to time by the president prevailed. The policy acquired a more solid basis only when Gorbachev came to power in Moscow two years later and when Reagan with the support of Shultz was prepared to impart a new dynamism to Soviet-American relations.

### Did the Soviet Union Fear an American Nuclear Attack?

One of the elements of Reagan's rhetoric was his air of injured innocence about whether the United States posed a military threat to the Soviet Union. Could anyone even imagine that the United States could launch a nuclear attack on the Soviet Union? He posed this same question at our White House meeting and thus raised an important matter of principle.

I can testify that the possibility of a nuclear war with the United States was considered seriously indeed by Khrushchev, Brezhnev, Andropov, and Konstantin Chernenko, who was the last leader of the old school. All these leaders and their associates proceeded from the assumption that the United States did pose a real military threat to our country's security in the long term. Hence our military planning was keyed to an overwhelming strategy of defense based on the possibility of retaliating by inflicting unacceptable damage. But with the probable exception of Andropov, they did not believe an attack could take place unexpectedly at any moment, like Hitler's attack on the Soviet Union or the Japanese attack on Pearl Harbor in 1941. Such apprehensions were minor on our side, because we knew that the existing political and social structure of the United States was the best guarantee against an unprovoked first strike against us. We knew that the two superpowers had no history of confrontations that led to military clashes, with the possible exception of the Cuban crisis of 1962, and that crisis itself helped define the limits that actually prevented open warfare. In any case I personally never believed that any president was ever planning a nuclear attack on the Soviet Union; this conviction settled in me as I lived for years in the United States.

Moscow's apprehension of military confrontation grew less out of the fear of sneak attack that seems to sit in the American historic consciousness and more from what happened in Cuba—some tense political conflict that might develop and escalate unpredictably at some unforeseen time in the future. Considering the continuous political and military rivalry and tension between the two superpowers, and an adventurous president such as Reagan, there was no lack of concern in Moscow that American bellicosity and simple human miscalculation could combine with fatal results. Andropov once said to me in a very private conversation: "Reagan is unpredictable. You should expect anything from him." All in all, the Kremlin leaders took Reagan seriously—perhaps far more so than he took his own antics—and they therefore watched him with increasing vigilance. Our intelligence services were also more on alert than during other presidencies to pick up any advance signals of U.S. military action.

While still head of the KGB, Andropov did believe that the Reagan administration was actively preparing for war, and he was joined in this belief by Ustinov, the defense minister. They persuaded the Politburo to approve the largest peacetime military intelligence operation in Soviet history, known by its code name of Operation Ryon, an acronym of the Russian words *Raketno-Yadernoye Napadenie*—Nuclear Missile Attack. In 1983 all KGB residents received urgent and detailed instructions to collect any evidence of plans for an American first strike. Only in the following year, when Reagan's policy began to turn, did Moscow give a less paranoid interpretation to the evil empire, Star Wars, and the like. The Foreign Ministry did not inform our ambassadors about this operation, leaving it to the KGB. I learned about it from the KGB resident in Washington. We both remained skeptical but he forwarded what he could get (mostly rumors and guesses) to Moscow.

The Soviet political leadership and military high command felt they had no choice but to reckon with the possibility of a nuclear war because they were certain that a serious military conflict between the Soviet Union and the United States, if it ever were to happen, would inevitably lead to the use of nuclear weapons. For all their patriotic propaganda, they did not really believe that a nuclear war might be winnable, and they profoundly hoped that the supreme military leadership in Washington believed as they did. But they were by no means confident that their potential opponents really felt the same way, and the incessant American attempts to attain strategic superiority made them fear otherwise. Hence our determination to make irreversible the nuclear parity we had achieved.

The American public reacted to the threat of nuclear war somewhat more strongly than the Soviet people; Americans were continuously reminded of it by the mass media and Hollywood reveling in the horrors of nuclear war. But the Soviet people experienced a deeper and persistent feeling of danger, having personally endured terrible suffering during World War II. If you had been able to poll the Soviet populace at that time and asked who they thought was more likely to push the nuclear button first—Brezhnev and Andropov or Reagan, the answer would probably have been practically unanimous—Reagan. If you asked the same question of the American people, most would have said Brezhnev—but more than a few would have been just as apprehensive about their own president. That certainly was my impression, and although I never took any poll I talked to plenty of Americans.

A prime and literally strategic example of this anxiety was provided by Marshal Sergei Akhromeyev, the chief of the General Staff of the Soviet Army during the 1980s. He was one of the most intelligent and knowledgeable military leaders I knew, and impressed his opposite numbers in the Pentagon when he later visited the United States. During one of my visits to Moscow, he suggested to me that we review our relations with the United States together. I welcomed the idea because I was curious about the military aspects. The conversation took place in his impressive office, with all kinds of maps covering the walls.

I asked the marshal to give me a short summary of our military situation vis-à-vis the United States. He ran his pointer along our borders, particularly in the West where the Soviet Union was close to the NATO countries. In this sector, he said as he pointed, we had enough forces, but in another we needed three or four divisions for reinforcements and additional fortifications would have to be built. At some points our forces ought to be reinforced with tanks, aircraft, mechanized infantry, and so forth. "You can't do that overnight," he said, "and we are short of funds. We'll have to ask the Politburo again. The General Staff believes we should be prepared along all our lines."

I asked him straight out, "Do you indeed believe the United States and NATO could attack us some day?"

"It's not my mission to believe, or not to believe," he replied emphatically. "I can't depend on you diplomats and all your conferences or whatever you call them. You seem to agree with Washington on some point today, but a new outbreak of hostility in the world or in Soviet-American relations tomorrow can put the clock back to the time of the Cold War or even cause a military conflict. Suffice it to remember the Arab-Israeli conflict of 1973, when the United States put its armed forces on high combat alert against us. Incidentally, that happened in the period of detente under Nixon. Now, does President Reagan inspire more confidence? That is why my motto as chief of General Staff is 'National military security along all azimuths.' We proceed from the worst conceivable scenario of having to fight the United States, its West European allies, and probably Japan. We must be prepared for any kind of war with any kind of weapon. Soviet military doctrine can be summed up as follows: 1941 shall never be repeated."

It was also interesting to hear his response to my question about why we needed to have large concentrations of our mechanized units stationed in Central Europe, which was the subject of long controversy at the Vienna negotiations on conventional arms reduction. Akhromeyev sketched out the historical background. Our relations with the United States were strained under President Truman right after World War II. Reports coming to Moscow said that Truman considered using nuclear weapons in case of a serious conflict with the Soviet Union, and at that time the United States had clear nuclear superiority. Under the circumstances the Soviet military designed a doctrine of retaliation, which was approved by Stalin. In the center of Europe (where our armies were still present), we created a powerful force of armored divisions capable of delivering a lightning blow crushing America's European allies and occupying their territory all the way to the English Channel and the Atlantic coast of Western Europe. Stalin believed that armored threat would counter the American nuclear threat, and that is what it was doing there—although in Western eyes it was seen as a potentially aggressive spearhead always ready to be launched for conquest. Soviet troops continued to be positioned in this way even after the Soviet Union had reached nuclear parity with the United States, partly because of pure inertia, but also to maintain stability in Eastern Europe, where democratic movements had begun to develop.

Akhromeyev remarked in strict confidence that he believed it feasible to reduce our troops and arms in Central Europe. A year later, he submitted his proposals to Gorbachev, stressing that we should insist on adequate concessions from the American side in return. When Gorbachev and his foreign minister Eduard Shevardnadze were actively seeking rapprochement with the West, the marshal often engaged in interdepartmental debates arguing against being too hasty in making concessions to the United States at disarmament talks. He stressed measured steps in that direction, which turned him against Gorbachev; he supported the coup of 1991, and when it failed he committed suicide. His tragic death was the result of his sincere conviction that the policy of the then Soviet rulers drained the strength and dignity of our army.

I have no doubt that our marshal's American counterparts in the Pentagon also proceeded from "the worst conceivable scenario." One can hardly imagine what would have happened to humanity if these scenarios had actually been played out, although Thomas Watson, who served as U.S. ambassador to Moscow, confided to me that he once looked into the American military mind and found it similarly bleak.

When Watson headed IBM, President Carter asked him to serve on a panel of American industrialists studying American preparedness for nuclear war. They studied all aspects of the U.S. nuclear triad and the command structure of the Pentagon. At the final meeting with the Pentagon generals, he asked them to tell his group how they would wage a nuclear war against the Soviet Union. With huge maps and lighted charts lining the walls, they showed him more than a thousand targets on Soviet territory marked for destruction during the first hours of war. Soviet casualties would be more than one hundred million.

"And what about our casualties?" Watson asked.

They replied that about eighty million Americans and many major industries would be destroyed, just as in the Soviet Union.

"And what would you do after almost everything was destroyed?" Watson persisted.

The generals looked at each other and did not have much to say.

Several days later Watson presented his report to the president with the principal conclusion that questions of nuclear war should not be left to generals. They could wage such a war, he explained, but they do not consider it their business to be concerned about what humanity—or what would be left of it—would do afterward.

## The Evil Empire and Star Wars, the Elections, and the Summit

What seemed most difficult for us to fathom were Reagan's vehement public attacks on the Soviet Union while he was secretly sending—orally or through his private letters—quite different signals seeking more normal relations. On March 8, less than a month after our first White House conversation when he seemed to be trying to open a working relationship with the Soviet leadership, he publicly described the Soviet Union, in a phrase both memorable and notorious, as the evil empire. It came straight from Hollywood—the *Star Wars* series by the master filmmaker George Lucas, whose film title would shortly enter international politics but with a sarcastic edge. The venue was an address to the National Association of Evangelical Christians at Orlando, Florida, which included many die-hard conservative supporters. The speech was not designed to be a history-making event in foreign policy, and according to Shultz no one outside the White House, including him, had a chance to review the text in advance, but the phrase quickly spread throughout the world.

The entire episode demonstrated a certain paradox about Ronald Reagan: contradiction between words and deeds that greatly angered Moscow, the more so because Reagan himself never seemed to see it. In his mind such incompatibilities could coexist in perfect harmony, but Moscow regarded such behavior at that time as a sign of deliberate duplicity and hostility. The Soviet leadership was at times extremely thin-skinned, forgetting that they also engaged in the same kind of propaganda against the United States from time to time. He was giving them a dose of their own medicine.

Next came Star Wars itself, formally known as the Strategic Defense Initiative when proposed by the president. It so happened that I called on Shultz on March 23 to give him a message from Andropov urging Reagan to speed up the Vienna talks on the reduction of conventional arms in Central Europe. As the conversation was about to close, Shultz unexpectedly handed me the text of a speech Reagan was shortly to deliver on television. I was still reading it when he said he was in a hurry to get to the president, who in his speech intended to give the world "hope against the threat of nuclear weapons" in the form of a long-range research program that would eventually be able to develop laser-guided and other sophisticated defensive weaponry to neutralize missiles by shooting them out of the sky.

I asked Shultz at once if that meant that the American government was ready to break the agreement between us limiting our antiballistic missile installations. He reassured me "officially" that the American government would observe its obligations under the agreement and the American research and development program would be conducted within the framework of the ABM agreement. I replied that although I still had to read through the text, it looked to me that the United States was launching another round of the arms race in a new field, namely, in space. Reagan announced the research program in a characteristically dramatic speech on national television.

The Star Wars program—it got its name from critics who thought it was all science fiction—had been outlined by American military scientists led by the prominent physicist Edward Teller and the Pentagon's top officers, who gradually sold the president the idea. Characteristically, the State Department and Shultz himself were informed about the speech and its subject only a couple of days before. They had not been consulted in advance and barely managed to include a mention of the ABM agreement in the prepared text, since the White House and Pentagon speechwriters simply forgot about its existence.

Some American historians wrote that this new initiative was the product of Reagan's imagination, but the more important point was that he simply could not accept the fact that the United States—with all that money they had spent for all that military equipment—had no defense against Soviet missiles. He was easily convinced that American ingenuity could overcome great technological obstacles. Hence Reagan's mistaken assumption that the United States could protect itself from nuclear attack. Missile defense become one of the few issues that actively engaged Reagan once he was in the White House.

Reagan's speech aroused a controversy in the country and the world. Most Americans welcomed it, although scientists and some in Congress were skeptical. Europeans feared that if the United States could eventually hide behind an SDI shield it would sacrifice European interests for its own protection—exactly the fear of "decoupling" that the planting of new American Pershing missiles was supposed to avoid. In terms of military competition and stability, the SDI represented the most radical challenge to existing orthodoxies in arms control since negotiations had begun almost three decades before. It became a principal bone of contention between the United States and the Soviet Union, and our relations were deeply affected by it.

Moscow regarded Reagan's decision primarily as a move designed to destabilize the strategic situation and create a large-scale antimissile defense system for American territory, in order to deprive the Soviet Union of the chance to retaliate in case of a nuclear war. Andropov immediately declared that the new concept would extend the arms race to outer space and warned that the United States was embarking on a very dangerous road. Moscow of course could not immediately evaluate all the military and political consequences of the SDI but feared that the United States had achieved a technological breakthrough. It goes without saying that our own military designers quickly pressed their own claims for permission to catch up, with the vigorous support of Defense Minister Ustinov. Our physicists, headed by Academician Yevgeny Velikhov, were as skeptical as many of their American counterparts, but their views hardly carried much weight at that emotional moment. Our leadership was convinced that the great technical potential of the United States had scored again and treated Reagan's statement as a real threat.

I began to see some American domestic political considerations in this new Reagan initiative when I was approached at a diplomatic dinner on March 26 by Michael Deaver, the president's confidant. He was known to me as one of the few people close to the president who took a pragmatic stand on relations with the Soviet Union. Deaver began by putting to me a surprising question for a Soviet ambassador. With my long experience in the United States, how did I view Reagan's chances for reelection next year?

I replied that I thought it would depend primarily on three factors: first, the condition of the American economy; second, the Democratic nominee; third, the state of Soviet-American relations. I added that the confrontational course being pursued by the president would hardly help him. And now the new SDI program created a new controversy.

Deaver said it was difficult to discuss all this in detail at a general reception, but I was curious about his approach because it evidently came in the wake of my conversation with Reagan. I was interested in Deaver's view of SDI. He saw it as a campaign issue because it held out hope to American voters that the nuclear threat would be neutralized, blunting Democratic attacks on Reagan as a warmonger.

Several days later I had a more poignant electoral conversation with Vice President Bush. He confided to me that Reagan was determined to run for a second term, and his announcement could be expected in June or July. With a measure of bitterness in his voice, he admitted that he would have to adjust his personal plans, but if Reagan changed his mind for any reason, he would be the likeliest Republican nominee. The trouble was, Bush was opposed by right-wing conservatives who saw him as too liberal, but he still thought that if Reagan decided not to run again, he would be best placed as vice president to win it.

Then Reagan was likely to support him, I remarked. Bush replied that was not necessarily so. "I don't expect Reagan to support me vigorously. The best I can expect is his benevolent neutrality. He is likely to speak in my favor to his conservative friends, but that will be it. That may be just as well, depending on the general domestic atmosphere at the election day."

Bush continued that while the president was fully aware of the importance of the economy to his reelection, he apparently did not see the significance of improving relations with the Soviet Union, since the voters were scared by the president's rhetoric and he went right on with his principal objective of rearming America. Paradoxical as it might seem, Reagan had told Bush on several occasions that he would like to come to terms with Andropov and conclude at least one of the agreements on nuclear arms being negotiated in Geneva, and that could be the subject of a summit.

But Reagan had another fixed idea—that the Soviet leadership would not concede him a single point, however trifling it might be, Bush said. "It may sound bizarre to the Soviet government, but Reagan attaches great significance to the Pentecostals' case. It has advanced somewhat, but not completely. To Reagan, it has become a kind of a litmus test of the Soviet leadership's attitude to his personal request. I recommend that you solve this question once and for all. It is not all that important, but it probably could help shift Reagan from his fixed position in relation to the Soviet Union."

The vice president felt that the most important thing was to make Reagan revise his notions, the almost unimaginable ideas and prejudices he brought to the White House from his past. When Bush got closer to him in the initial months of his presidency, he was simply amazed to see to what extent Reagan was dominated by Hollywood clichés and the ideas of his wealthy but conservative and poorly educated friends from California. Unfortunately, many deep-seated stereotypes remained in the president's head, and they were reinforced by the conservatives in Reagan's White House entourage.

"Well, he's hard, very hard indeed," Bush repeated of Reagan, "But I think he wouldn't be altogether hopeless if Soviet-American relations came to be the focus of the election campaign."

In April Indira Gandhi made a public proposal for a meeting of heads of government at the United Nations to discuss the arms race. In a private message, Andropov declined because, although he favored a Soviet-American summit, the Reagan administration was obviously unprepared for real discussions and he feared Reagan might turn it into "small talk" for his own political purposes, which would only open up the Soviet Union to criticism by the Democrats for favoring the president. Prime Minister Gandhi received this message with understanding.

But Reagan tried to maneuver Andropov to the UN by saying in public that he was ready to meet with him, without privately asking us. Moscow remained silent. After a long break Reagan unexpectedly decided to send a private letter to Andropov. I find it hard to say whether the gesture was prompted by electoral considerations or a genuine desire to improve relations, but it was written in his own hand, put in a sealed envelope, and forwarded on July 21 in strict confidence via the American ambassador in Moscow.

Reagan's letter sought to convince Andropov that various American proposals already advanced on a number of issues made sense. It was a typical message, outwardly benevolent, without his customary public attacks, but again without any new proposals or possible compromises, save for a generally expressed readiness to conduct confidential exchanges from time to time.

Reagan's original draft, I learned later, had proposed talks leading to the elimination of all nuclear weapons, a goal that his horrified advisers made him delete. Here was a characteristic Reagan paradox: starting a huge new military program while considering huge cuts in nuclear arms. The final version concluded with this peroration:

> We both share an enormous responsibility for the preservation of stability in the world. I believe we can fulfill that mandate, but in order to do so, it will require a more active level of exchange than we have heretofore been able to establish. There's much to talk about with regard to the situation in Eastern Europe and South Asia and particularly this hemisphere as well as in such areas as arms control, trade between our two countries and other ways in which we can expand East-West contacts.

> Historically our predecessors have made progress when they communicated privately and candidly. If you wish to engage in such communication you will find me ready. I await your reply.

The letter met with a mixed reception in Moscow, where there was a controversy over its motives, but Andropov decided to respond in the same tone. His response on August 1 also was sent in a sealed envelope, and was handed to Clark, the president's assistant for national security affairs. It stressed the specifics of limiting nuclear arms in Europe "on an equal basis" and thus averting a regional nuclear arms race. It concluded:

> I did not seek to raise many questions in this letter, but only selected what I believe to be the ones on which we could focus. I shall welcome a concrete and frank exchange of views with you on these and other questions. I agree to conduct it confidentially if our dealings require it. For my part I propose to do this through the Soviet ambassador in Washington and any person you choose to appoint for the purpose.

There was a handwritten phrase below: "I sincerely hope, Mr. President, that you will give my ideas your most serious attention and respond in a constructive spirit."

Andropov's attempt to revive the confidential channel arose from a conversation we had in Moscow during my regular trip home for my summer vacation. He asked what I thought about the prospects for reopening these secret contacts, and I replied that the Reagan administration did not seem to care because it had no intention of working out any agreements with us. And in any case who exactly could work their end of the channel? Nearly all the White House assistants knew little of what we might achieve, Clark had nothing to suggest, and while I said Shultz was "not hopeless," he "won't stick his neck out," although he was not opposed to better relations. I suggested cooperating with him more closely if possible, although he was very different from his predecessors, Kissinger and Vance. The key was Reagan himself.

Andropov found Reagan a puzzle. "Is he just playing his game and being a hypocrite, or does he really realize that for all our ideological disagreements, you just cannot bring about a confrontation in the nuclear age?" Because of the president's contradictory behavior, I could not venture a definite answer. Andropov summarized the discussion by saying: "We should keep on persistently working with Reagan. We should be vigilant, because he is unpredictable. At the same time we ought not to ignore any signs of his readiness to improve our relations. We should make the confidential channel operate, but we should not press the matter too hard."

## Diplomatic Oxymoron

For me, the real litmus test of the administration was to be found in the debate about Euromissiles and arms control. These questions represented the only familiar and available ground from which to plumb the genuine intentions of the president, even after all the private expressions of goodwill that began in his upstairs living room back in February.

The genesis of the Euromissile debate lay not only in Washington or Moscow but in Europe itself. The American Pershings and cruises really were not primarily military but political weapons and were offered to America's allies, first by Carter then by Reagan, as an earnest expression of America's will to defend them. Under the Reagan administration's policy of confrontation, Europe's willingness to accept the missiles on its soil became a political touchstone of whether it had the backbone, like Reagan's America, to stand fast against the Soviet Union. But Reagan's own behavior provoked a broad pacifist wave across Europe, which made his task of winning popular support that much more difficult and our efforts to counter him correspondingly easier.

The Reagan administration's negotiating position of the zero option was an attractive phrase, but after it was rejected by us, Reagan proposed something called the intermediate option in a speech in Los Angeles at the end of March 1983. Assuming a more flexible stand to deflect criticism, the president offered a new scheme providing for equal numbers of nuclear warheads carried by medium-range missiles on both sides in Europe, but no exact figure. In explaining it to the European NATO ambassadors in Washington, Reagan said that Moscow was unlikely to agree to anything before NATO's December deadline for deployment, so it would probably go ahead, at which point the Russians, being stubborn but realistic, would accept his halfway deal in 1984 in order to prevent full deployment of the

American missiles—and that agreement might lead to a summit. (In this, he proved correct.)

But to us, the proposal boiled down to the same thing: we would dismantle some of our missiles while the United States was entitled to deploy its own—and neither the U.S. air bases nor the British and French nuclear weapons would be counted. I told Shultz it really meant that the United States was supposed to arm and the Soviet Union to disarm.

The episode illustrated a characteristic feature about the proposals on nuclear arms reductions made by both sides during that period. They would be made public with great pomp, fanfare, and explanation to allies, media, and the like by the leaders themselves rather than being discussed through the confidential channel or during working meetings of the two delegations where they could be subjected to a discreet examination. The Soviet-American arms control debate turned into a personal and public battle between the two supreme leaders—the exact opposite of the main idea of a summit, which calls for a mutual and confidential quest for agreement publicized only after it has been reached.

I must admit that the Kremlin found itself dealing with something new and deeply disturbing, a transparently one-sided set of objectives that were put straightforwardly enough by President Reagan: arms control must result in nothing less than a top-to-bottom overhaul of the Soviet arsenal to accomplish changes in the nuclear balance that the United States had not been able to bring about through its own defense programs. In Soviet eyes, arms control was a means of regulating military competition and codifying parity, a process combining continuity with quiet diplomacy. We therefore believed Reagan was not serious about arms control, and many in the West and even in the United States shared that impression. The administration was of course eager to dispel it, and Shultz became especially active in his contacts with us.

On April 17, I went to the State Department for a very unusual meeting. Apart from Shultz himself, all his senior assistants were present: Lawrence Eagleburger, Kenneth Dam, Richard Burt and—the real surprise—Weinberger, who had come over from the Pentagon. I was accompanied by Oleg Sokolov, my embassy counselor. We were definitely outnumbered.

Weinberger first took the floor and made a number of concrete and practical proposals: modernizing the hot line, linking both war departments so they could keep abreast of each other's maneuvers and missile launches, exchanging information on terrorist activity, particularly the seizure of nuclear material, and establishing more effective communication between American and Soviet embassies with their capitals. Weinberger was concise, but having presented his proposals, he took practically no part in our conversation, as if he was not very much interested in it.

Shultz then proposed that while their Geneva arms negotiators were in Washington during recess I should meet with them. Gromyko having already rejected the latest American proposals, I immediately asked, "What exactly are they supposed to discuss with me? Go over it again? Or are they prepared to discuss fresh ideas?" Shultz gave no concrete reply and raised the possibility of improving the provisions in the 1976 and 1979 agreements—which had been signed long ago. He suggested consultations on South Africa, Afghanistan, the Middle East, but also did not elaborate.

Then he turned to Reagan's favorite subject, the Pentacostals. Moscow had already given permission for one to leave for the United States. Shultz hinted that as more were given exit visas the American government would extend the 1976 fishing agreement by another year and conclude a long-term grain agreement (thus lifting the embargo imposed by Reagan himself in 1981 after martial law was declared in Poland).

In Moscow there was a mixed reaction to this unusual meeting. On the one hand, they were impressed by the presence of two leading ministers, but on the other they could not avoid noting that the discussion itself centered on minor questions and carefully avoided anything of substance on the key issues of arms limitation. The Politburo decided to go along with the procedure, hoping for a change for the better. It also agreed to begin consultations on two of Weinberger's suggestions, upgrading the hot line and counterterrorist exchanges. The other two were blocked by the conservatism of our secret services, whose members were acutely conscious of the higher quality of American equipment.

But when on April 14 Shultz invited me for a long discussion on reducing strategic weapons, it got nowhere because there were no signs of compromise on his side. Similarly fruitless meetings followed on Euromissiles, and meanwhile the American public relations machine—the administration described it with a virtual oxymoron, "public diplomacy"—went into operation. Reports about private meetings between the secretary of state and the Soviet ambassador were leaked to the Washington press and diplomatic corps, creating the impression of a genuine effort by both sides to overcome the impasse. But the confidential channel actually had stalled, and I said as much to Shultz's disappointed deputy Kenneth Dam at one point, explaining that his boss had used the channel essentially for raising the same questions that had been discussed repeatedly in Geneva, rather than searching out new solutions as we had during previous administrations.

Shultz must have gotten the message, in form if not in substance, because a fortnight later he invited me to a private meeting. It took place on

May 19 and was our first unwitnessed talk. He said he needed to talk in private to reassure the Soviet side that President Reagan fully realized the great importance of Soviet-American relations, but he wondered whether Moscow really believed that. I said the public in the United States, in the Soviet Union, and the world over was deeply convinced that Reagan was the most anti-Soviet American president for twenty years and his views bordered on fanaticism. Shultz argued that Soviet-American relations were not as dangerous as they might appear. Yes, I agreed sarcastically, things could be worse, and more dangerous, too, but I wondered what changes for the better he could cite in the administration's first two years. Upon reflection he could cite only two: our decision on the Pentecostals and an agreement to resume negotiations on grain sales to the Soviet Union. He could not remember anything else. These were hardly world-shaking events. For all his efforts, it was evident that there had been no essential change.

On June 18 we went through another ritual meeting designed and conducted with President Reagan's consent in three stages: a private conversation on Euromissiles; a second stage at which we were joined by his principal assistants (Dam, Eagleburger, and Burt) and my counselors (Victor Isakov and Sokolov) on human rights, arms control, and bilateral agreements; and finally a return to face-to-face on the Middle East and Central America, while his three assistants gave my two counselors additional information concerning our bilateral relations. The two principal arms negotiators in Geneva also joined the second stage, so we were quite a crowd.

This epidemic of diplomacy evidently was meant to demonstrate a more flexible, carrot-and-stick policy and was an innovation of sorts for an administration which up to then had aimed at confrontation. But the latest meeting looked like a three-act diplomatic play and left me perplexed. The secretary of state did not outline a basic strategy or select any basic directions. He merely presented, and without much discussion, a set of proposals and issues of varied importance and mixed chances of agreement. I was nevertheless encouraged by all the activity, and perhaps that was one of its purposes. Unfortunately, U.S.-Soviet relations soon reached a new low that had nothing to do with this elaborate diplomatic minuet.

## The KAL007 Incident: Bitter Memories

Around midnight of August 31, Soviet chargé d'affaires Oleg Sokolov received an urgent telephone call from Assistant Secretary of State Richard Burt, who told him that a South Korean airliner, Flight 007, from New York en route to Seoul with 269 passengers on board including an American member of Congress, was lost somewhere in the region of Sakhalin Island.

Burt said the plane had probably violated Soviet airspace accidentally and made an emergency landing. No other information was available to American surveillance services at the moment.

The events were developing as fast as in a movie. It so happened that Shultz was the only high-ranking official in Washington at that time, while Reagan, with his aides, was in California, where he was on vacation at his ranch. At 6:30 in the morning of September 1, Shultz was called up at home and informed that the South Korean airliner was missing, probably shot down by the Soviets. Shultz immediately got busy. He talked with American intelligence and with Japanese officials. (A secret installation in the north of Japan intercepted Soviet radio messages and was run jointly by the Americans and the Japanese.)

At 10:45 A.M. Shultz called a press conference and made an emotional announcement describing the reaction to the Soviet attack as one of revulsion. There was a heavy toll of human lives, he said, and nothing could justify the horrible massacre. Shultz knew nothing yet about the Soviet official reaction and had no conclusive evidence. Although he was normally cautious and phlegmatic, this time he was in a hurry. His emotional press conference set the tone for the American official reaction and uproar in the mass media.

On September 2, Sokolov visited Eagleburger to hand over a Soviet government note accusing the South Korean plane of a "gross violation of the state border of the Soviet Union" and complaining of "the slanderous campaign against the Soviet Union launched in the United States" with the participation of American officials.

In this counteraccusation the Soviet government made, in my opinion, a very serious blunder. It did not have enough courage to recognize publicly and immediately with deep regret that the plane had been shot down over Soviet territory by a tragic mistake. Moscow tried to produce an impression that the Soviet Union knew nothing about the missing plane—and this was simply not true. The government waited until September 6, when a Tass statement finally acknowledged that the passenger plane had been mistakenly shot down by a Soviet fighter. But by that time a great deal of damage had already been done to the long-term interests of the Soviet Union. The seeds of an anti-Soviet campaign, always present in the West, immediately sprouted and rapidly took on new life.

President Reagan was quick to join in. Speaking on television, he claimed the Soviet pilot had known it was a passenger plane but shot it down anyway. This was not true, because our pilot really thought it was an American reconnaissance aircraft. The Soviet government issued a statement that went: "In spite of the false claims made by American president. . . ."

First Reagan and later Andropov found themselves unnecessarily and personally involved in a heated campaign of public recrimination.

In short, it grew into a major crisis in American-Soviet relations. At first glance the matter might seem out of proportion, since the plane was not an American one and it was indisputably over Soviet territory and off course. But it proved a catalyst for the angry trends that were already inherent in relations between Washington and Moscow during the Reagan presidency. It also illuminated the difficult relations and lack of communication between our civilian leaders and our military establishment, the generals being even more isolated from the rest of the world than politicians.

I was on vacation in the Crimea, and Andropov urgently called me to Moscow. When I entered his office, he looked haggard and worried. He said my vacation had to be cut short and ordered: "Return immediately to Washington and try to do your utmost to dampen this needless conflict bit by bit. Our military made a gross blunder by shooting down the airliner and it probably will take us a long time to get out of this mess." He phoned Defense Minister Ustinov in my presence and ordered him to arrange a briefing for me.

In the course of the conversation with me Andropov cursed "those blockheads of generals who care not a bit for grand questions of politics" and put our relations with the United States on the verge of a complete break. "Just think of all the effort we have put in to improve them, and there they are making a mess of the whole thing," Andropov said. At that point he sincerely believed the incident had begun with an attempt by the American secret services to assess our radar installations in the area—and he was angry with President Reagan for publicly defending what Andropov saw as a provocation. But even that, he said, was no excuse for our air force command shooting it down instead of forcing the plane to land at one of our airfields. Andropov was actually ready to admit the mistake publicly, but my colleague Georgi Kornienko, who was Gromyko's deputy, later told me that Ustinov talked the general secretary out of it. It is possible that Andropov's indecision was at least in part the result of his poor health, but it was also unusual at that time for the Soviet government to accept it had made any kind of error. This would have meant admitting the government and high command had acted irresponsibly.

When I arrived at Ustinov's office in the Ministry of Defense, I found him strongly scolding the top generals who had been summoned from the Far East. His anger was caused, among other things, by a hole in our own radar defenses. A complex radar system for tracking foreign aircraft was under construction on the Kamchatka Peninsula and Sakhalin Island, to the

West across the Sea of Okhotsk. Despite Ustinov's urgent orders, construction had been delayed, and it so happened that the South Korean jet passed undetected over the unconnected radars and flew for almost an hour in the dead zone not covered by them. Hence the Far Eastern air command was edgy as the plane headed past Kamchatka for neutral waters toward Sakhalin and ordered it held because it had overflown a specially forbidden zone. Our fighter pilot in his report claimed that in poor visibility at night he mistook the airliner for an American reconnaissance plane because their silhouettes were identical. My visit to our own Pentagon did not leave me with a favorable opinion of our high command. Ustinov himself was confused and very angry.

The next day I returned to Washington. I thought both sides had gone slightly crazy in the way they were handling the incident and what they were saying. Shultz had gone out on an emotional limb; he made his charges without any detailed investigation.

On September 8 Eagleburger officially informed me of American sanctions as "punishment" for shooting down the Korean airliner: the Aeroflot offices in Washington and New York would be closed by government order. In the private conversation that followed Eagleburger wondered who exactly had taken the decision to destroy the plane. Had the situation been reported to Andropov as general secretary? I replied that the regulations stipulated that decisions on preventing violations of Soviet borders were to be made by the Air Defense Commands of the local military districts without prior consultation with Moscow, especially if time was short. So this violation had not been referred to the Kremlin in advance.

Eagleburger was curious, asking "strictly personally"—we had known each other well for years and had frank conversations in better times—about the general mood of the Soviet leadership in Moscow and its view of the prospects of our relationship with the Reagan administration. I told him frankly that Moscow was growing increasingly convinced that, as the Russian saying goes, "one can't cook porridge together." That certainly would be true for the next several months because of the KAL007, he said, but he was still hoping for a better future.

As a witness to those events I can testify that the Soviet leadership was convinced that the invasion of Soviet airspace by the South Korean airliner was a thoroughly planned American reconnaissance operation; the only thing that was unclear to us was whether Reagan or Shultz knew about it beforehand. The Korean airliner's black box was later fished from the ocean by Soviet divers but their discovery was kept top secret. It was not until 1993 that the government of Russia gave the flight recorder to the International Civil Aviation Organization for an expert investigation sponsored by the governments of Russia, the United States, Japan, and South Korea. Ten years after the tragic disaster, the ICAO findings were published and failed to establish conclusively why the South Korean passenger airliner, with up-to-date navigation equipment and well-trained pilots, mysteriously deviated from its course between Anchorage and Seoul and strayed into Soviet airspace for several hours. No evidence was found that the Soviet fighter pilot actually knew he was attacking a passenger plane when he fired on KAL007 at night over the Soviet territory.

Yet, it was exactly the idea of a premeditated Soviet attack against a civilian passenger plane that was at the basis of the public accusations made by high American officials. On what grounds did they make these hasty and dangerous accusations?

The whole grievous event left a lasting and bitter memory in our relations with the United States and with President Reagan personally. Our leaders were convinced that he deliberately and disproportionately used the incident against them, and that American secret services were involved one way or another. Andropov considered Reagan's reaction "hysterical." In September, the first meeting between Gromyko and Shultz took place at the final stage of the Madrid Conference on Security and Cooperation in Europe. The atmosphere was explosive and left a deep impression on me. Shultz in his prepared speech made hostile attacks on the Soviet Union. Gromyko publicly rebuffed him. Following the two speeches, tension at the Madrid conference reached its peak.

On the next day Shultz and Gromyko held a personal meeting that had been arranged before the KAL007 incident. It began in a narrow circle, and Shultz started talking on the subject of human rights in the Soviet Union. Gromyko refused to discuss it, insisting as always that it was an internal matter. Nevertheless, Shultz repeated his piece almost word for word. To make it sound more convincing, he added that the president had entrusted him with making that statement at the beginning of the meeting. Gromyko declined to take up the subject again. So they had to go to another room where the conversation proceeded in the presence of the two delegations.

No sooner had Shultz got to the table then he began to speak loudly about the plane crash, conscious of the broader audience. Ignoring Gromyko's proposal to arrange for the order of business, he spoke at length about the incident, again referring to the president's instructions. There was a sharp exchange of accusations. At one point Gromyko even lost his invariable cool and flung his glasses on the table, almost breaking them. There was neither time nor inclination left for other problems.

The exchange, Gromyko wrote in his memoirs, was the most intense of all he had conducted with fourteen secretaries of state during his years of diplomatic service. To us, his closest associates, Gromyko said after the meeting that he believed Shultz had probably tried to provoke him to please Reagan. I cannot confirm that guess, but I can testify that the emotional behavior of the secretary of state went beyond the normal limits at a ministerial meeting and far beyond the limits of self-control he usually set for himself, though the truth may simply be that he was really angry.

The complications persisted. On September 18, Moscow announced that the American authorities offered no guarantee of Gromyko's safety when he came to New York for the UN General Assembly session. The governors of New York and New Jersey refused to accept his special plane at their airports on the pretext that he could just as well travel on a regular passenger plane. The Politburo canceled Gromyko's trip, and although he looked angry, I presume that deep down he welcomed the cancellation because the auguries for a trip to the United States at that point certainly were not good.

### Andropov: Illusions Dispelled

On September 29, *Pravda* published a statement by Andropov sharply criticizing Reagan's policies on nuclear arms in Europe and attacking the administration's anti-Soviet campaign following the shooting down of the Korean airliner. The key phrase was that "if anybody ever had any illusions about the possibility of an evolution to the better in the policy of the present American administration, these illusions are completely dispelled now." The word "completely" was emphasized. The Soviet leadership had collectively arrived at the conclusion that any agreement with Reagan was impossible. Andropov himself initiated a Politburo review, probably because his own illusions had vanished. But for the whole of the Politburo, the statement incorporated an attitude that had been gathering momentum for some time.

Of course, Andropov's statement drew the immediate attention of the Reagan administration and others. On October 1, Kissinger told me that he had been invited to the White House for consultations. They had taken special note of Andropov's remark about his vanished illusions, so they obviously got his point. Kissinger recommended to Reagan that unless he wanted to aggravate relations even more, he would have to show the utmost restraint and moderate the anti-Soviet attacks in his speeches. At the White House, he likened the Soviet Union to "a heavy fly-wheel, hard to turn at first; but even harder to stop after gaining momentum."

Eagleburger later told me privately that the White House and the president himself had drawn the conclusion that the Soviet leadership, for some reason or other, was unwilling to deal with Reagan by making practical agreements on major issues, particularly on nuclear arms. Prospects for our relations therefore were bleak. I replied that this seemed to have been prompted by the desire to shift blame on us; Andropov's statement made it clear we wanted to relax tensions and curb the arms race—"But what about President Reagan?" Eagleburger said that some time ago Kissinger had told Reagan he was deeply convinced that quiet diplomacy and the confidential channel were very useful with the Soviet leadership, and Reagan seemed willing to try. But the idea "got lost somewhere midway between Shultz and Clark."

Reagan's unique view of the world continued to blanket policy. The Saudi Arabian ambassador, Prince Bandar bin Sultan, met with Reagan on behalf of the Saudi Arabian king, who mediated a cease-fire between the armed factions in Lebanon. The ambassador was amazed to find that Reagan saw all events in the region only through the prism of Sovet-American rivalry. Reagan believed that everything done by Syrian President Hafiz al Assad in Lebanon was prompted or even dictated by Moscow—"all but by Andropov himself," Prince Bandar said. Even disputes between the Arabs were seen by Reagan as Moscow's intrigues or as a chance for the Soviet Union to profit at America's expense. Other ambassadors assessed White House policy likewise.

On October 28, I was invited to lunch with Shultz. He observed that this was the first time that he had lunched alone with a foreign ambassador. (It would have been undiplomatic and bad mannered for me to have mentioned that I had had dozens of lunches like this with his predecessors for twenty years.) He wanted to talk about our relations "from a philosophical angle." Both sides were pursuing an ideological struggle and would continue to do so, he said, but the president nevertheless believed we should look for common ground wherever possible.

I asked the secretary of state to tell me frankly who was doing his best, publicly and officially, to poison our relations. The truth of it was not even denied in the United States. I cited the speech made by the president only the previous day on national television accusing the Soviet Union of causing trouble in Lebanon and Grenada. What made him try to fool the American people into believing in the myth of a sinister role played by the Soviet Union in both countries? We were not even present there.

Finally he launched into a "philosophical discourse" about the confidential channel and its significance, but saying nothing definite about how he would use it. He asked my opinion. I replied that the question for us remained quite simple: everything depended upon the contents of the channel—that is, what was communicated through it and whether both sides really used it for compromise. Shultz said he would talk with Reagan about the confidential channel during their trip to the Far East from November 9 to 15.

I wondered why he should postpone the conversation until the trip rather than clear up the matter with Reagan right away. The secretary of state said rather unexpectedly that he normally had more unobstructed opportunity to discuss policy with the president during foreign trips when they were not distracted by pressing domestic problems and the White House staff. I was quite surprised to hear Shultz confess that his opportunities to talk with the president in Washington about vital political issues were somewhat limited—and that he had to wait for the most convenient time to obtain the president's approval of his ideas, especially in the crucial field of Soviet-American relations.

I wrote in my report to Moscow that although Shultz had been secretary of state for over a year, he was still not fully prepared to discuss important questions authoritatively. It was not so much his ignorance of detail as the fact that Reagan apparently had not decided yet to permit practical discussion. I added that the election year was approaching in the United States, and although campaign considerations had not yet been felt, they undoubtedly would in due course, and we should watch the behavior of the administration for opportunities. Maybe it would start playing a more flexible game.

The deployment of American nuclear missiles in Europe and the impasse reached at the negotiations confronted Moscow with a dilemma. If we continued the talks on limiting the European-based weapons, it would hold out to the public the illusory hope of an agreement. But if we walked out, there would be nothing left to prevent Washington from stationing the full complement of missiles. It was clear that the Soviet strategy of blocking the deployment by negotiation and political and public pressure had not worked. Needless to say, the Kremlin's resentment of Reagan reached a crescendo, and in any case the Soviet leadership had already come to the basic conclusion that there was no way it could reach agreement with him.

After a heated debate, the Politburo decided to withdraw from the European missile talks and simultaneously to launch a huge propaganda campaign to persuade Europeans that the new American missiles only raised the level of nuclear threat. The day after the first American missiles arrived in Europe on November 23, the Soviet media published a statement by Andropov accusing Washington of declaring a crusade against socialism. In order to preserve the military equilibrium, he said, Soviet intermediate-range missiles would be deployed in European Russia, and tactical missiles of intermediate range in the German Democratic Republic and Czechoslovakia. He added that if NATO pulled back the missiles, the Soviet Union would follow suit. Nobody in Moscow expected NATO to reverse its course, but that was put in for public consumption.

I am convinced that our most serious mistake was not seizing the opportunity to reach a mutual compromise before the NATO decision was taken to deploy the American missiles. In the two years before the decision, a window of opportunity had existed, and as late as the summer of 1979, West German Chancellor Helmut Schmidt, who was en route to Tokyo, made a little known special stop in Moscow for an airport meeting with Kosygin to signal a possible compromise: the European members of NATO would not agree to deployment of the new American missiles on their soil if the Soviet Union would assure the West that the number of warheads on new SS-20 missiles would not exceed the number of warheads on the old SS-4 and SS-5 missiles, which the Soviet Union intended to withdraw.

Kosygin reported to the Politburo that Schmidt's idea was worth considering, but Ustinov actively opposed it. The defense minister did not want to reveal to the West the number of SS-20 missiles he planned to deploy, to say nothing about possibly reducing that number. As a rule Brezhnev sided against Kosygin's proposals, but this time he was not quite sure. He looked at Gromyko. But the foreign minister was silent. He had no desire to quarrel with Ustinov and he was not sure whether Schmidt's compromise would work. That was the missed opportunity. In the absence of a Soviet reply to Schmidt's probe, NATO went ahead with its decision in December of 1979.

On December 8, 1983, the Soviet side announced another decision in Geneva. The Soviet Union declined to fix a date for the next round of arms negotiations; Moscow was still cautious not to speak of actually breaking off the negotiations. The Soviet representatives claimed that the American proposals were aimed at more than doubling American superiority in the number of strategic nuclear charges (counting submarine ballistic missiles and cruise missiles) and at destroying the very backbone of Soviet strategic forces by reducing the number Soviet heavy missiles, which was frozen under SALT II. This situation fostered rearmament rather than disarmament, which suited Reagan perfectly because Congress was voting him huge increases in military spending.

The Soviet government's decision to suspend for the first time the nuclear arms limitation talks was, if anything, the lowest point in our relations with the Reagan administration. And in general, the year of 1983—the year of Andropov—turned out to be as difficult a year for him personally as for Soviet foreign policy.

# IV. The Thaw

*How Reagan's Belligerence Backfired*

The impact of the American hard line on the internal debates of the Politburo and the attitudes of the Soviet leadership almost always turned out to be just the opposite of the one intended by Washington. Rather than retreating from the awesome military buildup that underwrote Reagan's belligerent rhetoric, the Soviet leaders began to absorb Reagan's own distinctive thesis that Soviet-American relations could remain permanently bad as a deliberate choice of policy. Only gradually did both sides begin to realize they were doomed to annihilation unless they found a way out. But it took a great deal of time and effort to turn from confrontation and mutual escalation, probably much more than if this course had never been taken in the first place.

It now is clear that the turn began during the presidential election year of 1984. How much the election campaign had to do with it, no one will ever really know. The White House was aware of rising public concern over the threats of war inherent in Ronald Reagan's policies, and a certain peace-loving phraseology began pushing the warlike rhetoric into the background. Even so, occasional slips of Reagan's tongue suddenly seemed to reveal the real man: his rearmament program continued, American missiles were deployed in Europe, and the president showed no inclination of abandoning his latest favorite, the Strategic Defense Initiative.

Moscow therefore felt it had to dig in. Shultz and Gromyko were to meet in Stockholm on January 18 for another session of the Conference on Security and Cooperation in Europe. The Politburo drafted detailed and essentially uncompromising instructions for its foreign minister; these give a clear idea of the deep suspicions that Reagan's long campaign had planted at the very center of the Soviet leadership. In his discussions with Shultz, Gromyko was instructed to characterize Reagan's policies as "permeated by the spirit of militarism and aggression," to inform Shultz that Moscow would not permit a change in the military balance between the superpowers, and to make it clear that the deployment of the Pershing II and cruise missiles had doomed the Geneva talks about them and made strategic arms talks more difficult. He was further instructed to "resolutely condemn" the Reagan administration for stirring up regional conflicts in the Middle East and elsewhere, including the "gangster attack on Grenada," and thus undermining "the established structure of relations between states and the whole world order."

Before leaving for Stockholm, Shultz and I met to discuss terms for resumption of the confidential channel. Moscow was skeptical but was willing to give it a try, and the two foreign ministers planned to talk about details in Stockholm, along with many other questions. I thought to myself that they would have a difficult discussion; God grant it would not turn into an angry quarrel as it did in Madrid. Shultz glumly joked that our relations were in such disrepair that there was plenty of opportunity to improve them with very little effort.

Shultz also showed me an advance draft of a speech Reagan was making on Soviet-American relations on January 16. Shultz had advised Reagan to make it to stress the administration's determination to continue the dialogue with the Soviet Union after it withdrew from the Euromissile talks. Reagan's message had a new twist and a new tone: now that the economic and military might of the United States had revived and its alliance with Europe had been consolidated, the administration was prepared to start settling its differences with the Soviet Union, and the year 1984 was proclaimed one of opportunities for peace. Realism, force, and dialogue were his guiding principles, the president declared, with force and dialogue going hand in hand. He spoke in favor of regular summit contacts and concluded that there would be peace if the Soviet government really wanted it. It was—for Reagan—a remarkably conciliatory television address.

At any other time, such a speech by an American president would have been regarded as a tangible step toward improving relations with the Soviet Union. But with all the other negative factors, to say nothing of the imminent presidential election, it was hard to believe in Reagan's sincerity. The speech did not receive much publicity in the United States and his startling shift in tone was perceived domestically as mere campaigning. In retrospect, it is evident that the speech reflected the beginning of certain evolution in his views on relations with the Soviet Union. In other times, such statements might have been supported by explanations through the confidential channel. But Reagan himself probably was not yet ready to translate his new mood into concrete proposals.

The Shultz-Gromyko meeting in Stockholm did not go all that badly, although it had its tense moments when Gromyko followed his instructions to condemn Washington sharply. Shultz told me later he felt that in spite of

Gromyko's tough line, their personal meeting was much better than the angry one in Madrid. He described it as "ice-breaking," although occasionally they talked at cross-purposes while stating familiar positions. Shultz said, "Gromyko ended by saying that our conversation was indispensable and I fully agree with that."

I found it interesting to watch both ministers in action. Both were strong personalities, with high intelligence and rich experience in life. Both profoundly believed in the superiority of their respective political systems and refused to give up their political principles for the sake of normalizing relations between the two countries. Neither believed our relations could radically improve in the foreseeable future. They were too cautious for that, although both were trying to find their way out of the dangerous impasse which they recognized we had reached. That introduced a certain element of optimism into the otherwise gloomy picture.

All this puts me in mind of some Washington gatherings at the time. One was a grand dinner to mark the seventy-fifth birthday of Dean Rusk attended by all of Rusk's successors, more than two hundred senior officials and American diplomats, and me as the only foreign ambassador. I was pleased to meet again the man with whom I had once enjoyed such close cooperation despite our disagreements in difficult times. At another dinner, the Kennan Institute in Washington commemorated the fiftieth anniversary of Soviet-American relations. There was no lack of criticism of Soviet policy, to which I listened patiently. When I got the floor I began by saying, "I did not come here to say we are all right, and you are all wrong."

I really meant that. I had spent many years in the United States and could see fairly clearly the pluses and minuses of both nations and their social systems. I tried to explain to my government the foreign and domestic policies of the United States as I saw them under different administrations, and to do so without much ideology. Of course some of my analyses were wrong, or too emotional. After all, I, too, was strongly influenced by the philosophy of my country and the policies of my government, which I represented abroad to the best of my ability. But I always tried to be objective and was guided by the desire to improve the relations between our two great nations.

## Reagan as Peacemonger?

Through the first half of the year, the most intriguing challenge for Washington in general and our embassy in particular was to determine just how serious the president was in reaching out to the Soviet Union—if that was in fact what he was doing—and how long he intended to continue. Would this last beyond the November elections? Observations, interpretations, and advice about the phenomenon were many and varied, and often as not they were colored by the interest of those who made them.

But the fact remained that a thaw of some kind was unmistakable when the monthly meeting of the socialist countries' ambassadors took place at our embassy. The "friends" met regularly, and I always made it a point not to act like the chief of the group or coordinate policy—that was done in Moscow—so that we could freely trade diplomatic information and Washington gossip. At our January 31 meeting, all the ambassadors, except for the Cuban, unanimously noted that the American government had adopted a more conciliatory attitude toward their countries following the start of deployment of American nuclear missiles in Europe. They all felt Reagan sounded less hostile as the election season began.

Jimmy Carter paid me an unexpected visit on January 30 to voice concern at the extent of Reagan's arms buildup. He described Reagan's peace rhetoric as a pure campaign maneuver. The former president was "utterly convinced" that there would not be a single agreement on arms control, especially on nuclear arms, as long as Reagan remained in power. (He proved to be a poor prophet.)

I had a similar conversation with Eagleburger, an old colleague of mine. When asked if we should expect any initiatives from the Reagan administration to improve our relations, Eagleburger voiced frank doubt, saying that Reagan believed his conciliatory tone was enough to placate the voters. Senator Charles Percy, a liberal Illinois Republican, told me that on January 6 Reagan and his aides had met to discuss the "Soviet theme" of the election campaign. They decided that the voters were well aware of the essence of Reagan's anti-Soviet position, so he would do nothing to make voters feel he was a warmonger but also would not raise their hopes of major agreements with the Soviet Union.

Even the Vatican was interested. Father Felix Morlion, who kept in touch with me privately with the Vatican's knowledge, confided that Cardinal Casaroli, the Vatican secretary of state, had met with Reagan and got the impression he would restrain his anti-Soviet ardor during the election campaign. This would gratify American priests who were reporting that their congregations had been alarmed by the threat of war during Reagan's three years. But Casaroli also found Reagan holding fast to his hard line, partly in the belief that deployment of American missiles in Europe would induce the Soviet Union to be more flexible.

George Kennan, the distinguished historian and diplomat who designed the Cold War policy of containing the Soviet Union, also believed Reagan had started speaking for electoral purposes because he had to take into account the country's fear of nuclear war. He remarked that Andropov's warning of the dangers of Reagan's policy had combined in a peculiar way with the wave of films about the horrors of nuclear war, especially *The Day After* watched by about eighty million people, plus books, articles, and statements by American political and religious figures. All this was producing an uncanny effect, striking fear into the hearts of Americans. With Reagan trying to present himself to the voters as a peace candidate, Kennan advised us to take the president at his word, put him on the defensive and publicly demonstrate our readiness for a mutually advantageous agreement "even under Reagan." Since he was testing the Soviet leadership, we likewise had to put him to test by selecting a few issues where rapid progress was possible and press for action.

Henry Kissinger of course had his opinion, too. He said Reagan and his entourage did not want to exacerbate Soviet-American relations during the election campaign. He reported that the White House and the State Department were discussing various actions to send signals to the Soviet Union, but the whole business was haphazard because there was no one to organize it properly. He stressed that the Reagan administration had no coherent program to deal with the Soviet Union because Reagan had never thought about it seriously, and the State Department was characteristically lacking in initiative and courage to suggest new ideas.

At an official dinner I ran into Thomas P. (Tip) O'Neill, the speaker of the House and an old acquaintance. As always, he was critical of Reagan but he asked me whether what we heard from the White House should lead him to believe that relations with the Kremlin were really improving. I replied that he shouldn't: Soviet-American relations remained as bad as before. O'Neill said he also thought so, although administration officials tried at the Capitol to create the contrary impression by referring to private contacts with the Soviets. O'Neill said no effort should be spared to prevent "that demagogue Reagan" from being reelected. "If that happens," he continued in a somewhat agitated manner, "Reagan will give vent to his primitive instincts and give us a lot of trouble, probably, put us on the verge of a major armed conflict. He is a dangerous man."

Then in May I got from Eagleburger what I think was the first of several definitive answers to my lingering doubts about the real nature of the White House strategy. He had just left the State Department to work for Kissinger's consulting firm at a salary considerably better than the $65,000 a year he earned in the government, which was insufficient to pay for his children's college educations.

In a sort of debriefing on what he had learned before leaving, he said the White House had already decided that during the election campaign

Reagan should exploit to the fullest the Soviet refusal to continue the Geneva arms negotiations. They reasoned this would give credibility to his defense against Democratic attacks that he had failed to reach any major arms agreements with the Soviet Union, unlike his Republican predecessors. All that was supposed to be accompanied by the thesis about Soviet expansionist policy and the Soviet military threat. Almost identical information came to the embassy from other sources and we passed it to Moscow, which failed to develop effective propaganda countermeasures.

Eagleburger also shared with me his impressions of Reagan as a person and as an administrator. The president was still guided by his "inborn instinct" of which he was very proud, although it had not generated a great variety of ideas, and those few it did produce were strongly colored with ideological clichés or plain propaganda. His command of foreign policy was still mediocre after more than three years in office, especially complex nuclear policy problems, and he was just unwilling to go into details. So his aides spared him the trouble of examining lengthy papers, which he simply would not read. Reagan insisted that the only recommendations he would consider approving were those already agreed upon by his advisers. He hated to take decisions that meant choosing between two opposing camps in his administration.

This practice consolidated the role of the Pentagon and Weinberger in foreign policy, particularly in relations with the Soviet Union and China. Taking advantage of Reagan's friendly disposition toward the military, Weinberger could in fact veto any proposals made by the State Department or at least had splendid opportunities to push through his ideas. Schultz had become more active in defending the State Department's point of view before Reagan. But military considerations always weighed heavily in any interagency coordination that the State Department needed "to pass through" before reporting to the president—such questions as disarmament and arms control agreements.

The State Department's diplomacy was severely obstructed by highly formalized procedures imposed by the White House for dealing with the Soviet Union. Instructions were written in such a way as to put tight constraints on what diplomats could say in negotiations or even in the traditionally less structured exchanges of views with Soviet official representatives. Since such instructions arrived only occasionally, American representatives had no backup positions appropriate for sounding out their opposite numbers and continuing an informal dialogue. They had no flexibility and were confined to giving Soviet representatives a strictly approved message, period. This went a long way toward explaining Schultz's noncommittal and guarded behavior. It also explained why there was virtually no chance of conducting a confidential exchange of views, which in the past had assisted diplomats in both capitals to find their way around stalemates.

Eagleburger said Reagan and his entourage would not even hear about using the experience of other administrations with the Soviet Union. So, once the president sensed that his confrontation with Moscow had gone too far, he resorted to improvisations prompted by the narrow circle of his closest aides, who were experts in television image-making but knew little or nothing at all about the workings of the Kremlin and how to conduct a dialogue with it.

Senator Percy told me the White House was busily spreading the word that the president had done his best to improve relations with Moscow but had been blocked by the Kremlin's walkout from the nuclear arms talks. I cited a number of our disarmament proposals and these proved a revelation to Percy, who asked why we did not publicize them. I replied that high-level correspondence was supposed to be confidential. Percy shook his head, saying: "You are just playing into Reagan's hands."

But perhaps the most decisive if not the most rational demonstration of Reagan's character emerged, as it so often does in life, by accident. While testing for the recording of his regular weekly radio address to the nation on August 11, President Reagan joked: "My fellow Americans, I am pleased to tell you today that I've signed legislation that will outlaw Russia forever. We begin bombing in five minutes." He did not know that his microphone was on.

The Soviet government was not amused by this kind of joke, and issued a strong official statement through Tass. The remark did not exactly go down well in America either. The State Department, hurrying to sweep the whole thing under the rug, accused the Soviet Union of blowing the incident out of proportion to use it for propaganda. Perhaps. But of all the remarks that I have recalled here from my notes of the time in attempting to determine the president's genuine feelings and motives, it is unquestionably the one that everyone, including me, remembers most vividly.

## Transition: Andropov Dies; Chernenko Succeeds Him

I met Andropov for the last time in his office at the Central Committee during my vacation in Moscow late in the summer of 1983. He looked unwell but was still energetic in discussing the state of affairs with the United States. He criticized Reagan for his policy and especially his public attacks against the Soviet Union, which Andropov realized made it impossible for him to reach even a small measure of reconciliation with Washington. "I am unlucky to get exactly this American president to deal with. Just my bad luck," he said to me lightly, but there was a measure of bitterness in his words.

During the winter Shultz inquired tactfully about Andropov's health by remarking that "all sorts of speculations" about his disease were reaching the White House. I replied that to the best of my knowledge, the general secretary continued to occupy himself with affairs of state although he had to be careful about his health. His hospitalizations became increasingly frequent, but all information was kept secret from the public, although there were occasional rumors. The first alarming sign was his absence from the December Plenum of the Communist Party when the traditional report from the general secretary was read out for him. Soviet ambassadors, including myself, had no idea how grave his illness was.

Andropov died on February 9. I had linked my hopes for a gradual improvement in Soviet-American relations to him. His intellectual abilities were certainly a cut above those of Brezhnev and Chernenko. Under the right circumstances, he would have been able to make considerable adjustments to improve our relations and he certainly wanted to. Some of his initial views on this were borrowed by his protégé Mikhail Gorbachev, who developed them in his own way, but Andropov himself never got the opportunity nor had the physical energy to change Soviet foreign policy. Besides, the international situation did not allow it. The inertia was too great to overcome within a short period. On February 12 Reagan visited our embassy and signed the condolence book.

Konstantin Chernenko's succession as general secretary was confirmed by an emergency meeting of the Central Committee on February 13, 1984. In the Kremlin the next day, he received George Bush, who led the American delegation to Andropov's funeral. There was a short exchange, and Chernenko told Bush that the two sides "were not born enemies." Bush answered that Reagan was prepared for a real dialogue.

The election of Chernenko at the age of seventy-two, when he was already weakened by emphysema, did not bring about any serious changes in Soviet foreign policy. However, Gromyko regained his dominant position in foreign policy making after losing relative power under Andropov, who knew the subject. But there were in fact no great differences between them and they had already come to recognize the need for a way out of the blind alley with Washington, especially in nuclear arms limitation talks. Chernenko felt it as much, but, lacking in initiative, did not want to introduce drastic changes. Chosen by the Politburo as a deliberately transitional figure, he usually joined the majority of the Politburo's members and guided himself by their mood. He was the most feeble and unimaginative Soviet leader of the last two decades.

The first series of exchanges between Chernenko and Reagan reminded me of an elaborate ritual dance in which both sides wrote letters making obeisance to the need for peace and disarmament but did little to advance either. Reagan made an official visit to China in the spring, made there public statements against the Soviet Union, and clearly was looking to China as a counterweight. He declared he would never sign any agreement with the Soviet Union to reduce or eliminate nuclear weapons in Europe unless the United States could ensure they would not be shifted to Asia. The trip in general consolidated the Soviet leadership's suspicions about the general hostility of the administration.

New complications appeared in the old issue of dissidents in the Soviet Union, which our government continued to handle clumsily through a steadfast and mindless policy of reprisals against individual dissidents. First we would allow a case to reach a point where it turned into a public scandal abroad that damaged our relations, and then we would give in. The Kremlin leaders really believed that almost the entire dissident movement had been inspired and developed with the help of Western intelligence services.

Consider the case of Andrei Sakharov and his wife Yelena Bonner. Reagan and Shultz let me know that Sakharov was planning a hunger strike unless she was allowed to go abroad for medical treatment. They wanted us to deal with her request before it became yet another anti-Soviet cause célèbre. On May 19, a Saturday morning while I was at home, I got a call from the president himself from Camp David. He said he wanted to make a personal and confidential request to Chernenko to permit Bonner to leave for medical treatment. Some reports said she was in very poor health, and God forbid that she should die now. If so, Reagan thought, angry American public opinion would drive our very difficult relations to the lowest conceivable level. Reagan remarked that he did not question the high level of Soviet medical science, but, "What if she dies in the Soviet Union? There will be no end of trouble. If she is to die, let her die here. At the very least nobody, hopefully will blame me for that."

Reagan added in a conciliatory tone that, of course, he was not in a position to judge just how critical Bonner's condition was but he was acting only on unofficial information he had. I promised to relay his request to Moscow promptly. I considered Reagan's intervention as something of a goodwill gesture.

Within a week I phoned back President Reagan with Moscow's answer in a message signed by Gromyko. It said that "the lady and her accomplices" were deliberately trying to dramatize the situation to discredit the Soviet Union, and her real state of health was "good enough for her to outlive many of her contemporaries." This was, he insisted, "evident from the authoritative conclusion drawn by highly qualified medical experts."

The president calmly noted that he was not interested in worsening our relations just to help Bonner, but he could not stop the hue and cry about her health. He said he feared it would "arise again with the help of Jewish organizations" in the United States who supported her.

Bonner was not allowed to visit the United States until the following year under the regime of Gorbachev. The Politburo discussed her request on August 29, 1985. Victor Chebrikov, chairman of the KGB, spoke in favor of granting the application but categorically opposed permitting Sakharov to accompany her because of his knowledge of the development of Soviet nuclear weapons in minute detail. If Sakharov got a laboratory abroad, he would be able to go on with military research, Chebrikov said. Then he remarked, "Sakharov's behavior is shaped by his wife's influence." Gorbachev exclaimed: "There, that's what Zionism is like!" Bonner in fact was only half-Jewish. But because most of the dissidents were Jewish—Sakharov was not—and many Jewish organizations abroad made common cause with them through the Helsinki Watch Committees and other human rights groups, Bonner's case seemed an extension of Zionist influence in the mind of Gorbachev and much of the Politburo. Yelena Bonner was allowed to leave, but not her husband. Thereafter she made several trips abroad.

Relations continued to drift. In May Moscow refused to attend the Olympics in Los Angeles; they were looking for some way to express their dislike of Reagan and remembered the Carter boycott of the 1980 Moscow Olympics. Republicans in the Senate passed a resolution calling for the earliest possible Soviet-American summit, something the average anxious voter could understand, as opposed to the complexities of arms control.

On June 20 Shultz invited me for another conversation. This time it lasted more than three hours and was attended by Assistant Secretary Richard Burt and our embassy counselor Victor Isakov. Shultz said that the president could well understand the disappointment and bitterness on both sides; he wanted to improve relations, but how? A summit meeting with Chernenko could be useful and he did not rule it out, and meanwhile he suggested making an inventory of all our problems.

So Shultz and I went down a long list: nuclear arms control, ratification of past arms agreements, talks on a complete nuclear test ban, banning weapons from outer space, major ABM systems, the Stockholm conference proposals on abjuring force to settle international disputes, limiting naval weapons, banning chemical warfare, improving the hot line. We touched briefly on regional problems such as South Africa, the Middle East, and the Iran-Iraq war; humanitarian questions; and specific bilateral problems. We took stock of all controversial and unsettled questions, but made no attempt even to outline solutions. The discussion undoubtedly proved useful for putting all our affairs in systematic order. But what next?

It turned out to be a surprising invitation from the White House for Gromyko to resume his annual autumn visits to the White House for a conversation with the president. Thomas Simons, chief of the State Department's Soviet Affairs division, delivered the invitation late in August "on the understanding that the conversation should be serious and would not be used for propaganda purposes." He explained to our chargé d'affaires in strict confidence that this curious and unusual passage apparently reflected "present paranoia" among Reagan's entourage, which seriously feared that Moscow might plant some kind of propaganda time-bomb at the meeting that could affect the elections, although the White House was certainly interested in the meeting for its own sake. He added that the government had ordered necessary security measures for the Soviet foreign minister, including an armored car (they knew that Gromyko always paid close attention to his personal safety).

Meanwhile, a new theme began to appear in Reagan's election campaign: that his policy had worked and he now could be more accommodating toward the Soviet Union. By contrast, Soviet leaders continued their public attacks on the American administration, claiming that the danger of war was growing. They would have liked to offer rhetorical assistance to the campaign of the Democratic candidate, Walter Mondale—not because they knew him but because they preferred anybody to Reagan. But Mondale failed to play the question of war and peace to his advantage, and I think that was because he was not sure whether the Soviet factor would turn in his or Reagan's favor by election day. With patriotism and anti-communism deeply rooted in the country, did the American people want their president to stand up to the Soviets in a political, military, and ideological rivalry? Or did they want him to have a summit meeting with the Russians and make some adjustments and concessions for the sake of better relations? Mondale never found a clear answer.

Inside the Politburo, a controversy raged over the best way for us to behave during the final stages of the campaign. Moscow asked my opinion, and I recommended that we keep criticizing Reagan in response to any attacks as a matter of principle, but not to overdo it in practice. Our criticism had to be measured and careful, because American history clearly demonstrated that any foreign interference in elections would most likely backfire. It was also no less important that we reckon on Reagan as the likely winner, and it was simply bad politics to be too brutal toward someone we would probably have to deal with for another four years. The Politburo came to essentially the same conclusion.

But it regarded Gromyko's meeting with Reagan of such importance that it drafted special instructions for him. They stressed the Kremlin's desire for Moscow and Washington above all to discuss mutual security problems and to show their readiness to freeze or reduce nuclear weapons stocks, renounce the production and deployment of destabilizing new weapons, and agree to demilitarize outer space.

The Soviet Union thus had changed its approach from confronting Reagan to starting to try to reach agreements with him. They wanted to take advantage of his more conciliatory attitude during the election campaign in hopes of exploiting it afterward. They were right to move fast because, in retrospect, there was no certainty that this electoral window of opportunity would stay open. Shultz reports in his memoirs that until the very end of 1984 a fierce debate raged around the president on U.S.-Soviet relations. When Reagan decided to receive Gromyko he asked Shultz not to tell anyone beforehand because the people around him would give him no peace and insist on his changing his mind.

## Gromyko Returns to the White House

The reception accorded Gromyko by the president at the White House on September 26 was, in terms of protocol, more appropriate to a head of government than a foreign minister. The president posed for photographs with him in the Oval Office. There were so many press representatives that they had to be divided into three separate pools, all of them shouting questions at the top of their lungs.

Nancy Reagan appeared during the cocktail party before lunch. Gromyko, after the introductions, proposed a toast to her. He had cranberry juice, her glass was filled with soda water. "We both are certainly fond of drinking," he remarked with his characteristic dry humor.

Gromyko had a short chat with the president's wife. "Is your husband for peace or for war?" he asked. She said that he of course was all for peace. "Are you sure?" Gromyko wondered. She was one hundred percent sure. "Why, then, does not he agree to our proposals?" Gromyko insisted. What proposals? she asked. Someone interrupted the conversation, but right before lunch Gromyko reminded Mrs. Reagan, "So, don't forget to whisper the word 'peace' in the president's ear every night." She said, "Of course I will, and I'll also whisper it in yours, too." I must report that Gromyko got a kick out of this exchange and recounted it to the Politburo with great animation.

The negotiations between Reagan and Gromyko started in the Oval Office. Their conversation lasted for two hours and continued at lunch. The American side was represented by top officials—Bush; Shultz; Weinberger; Treasury Secretary Donald Regan; presidential aides Baker, Meese, and Deaver; and Robert McFarlane, the new national security adviser. Gromyko was accompanied by Deputy Foreign Minister Georgi Kornienko and myself.

Reagan began the meeting with a lengthy speech about America's hopes for peace and his explanation of why the American people saw the Soviet Union as a threat to those hopes. Reagan explained that he saw the political philosophy of Marxism-Leninism animating a Soviet policy of world revolution, and this provided for the destruction of the capitalist system in the United States and other Western countries. He reasoned that the United States must arm itself or be forced to choose between surrender or death.

Gromyko was at pains to disabuse him. Yes, he said, the objective course of history meant that one form of society would inevitably be replaced by another, and the capitalist system would surely be succeeded by the socialist system, but this was in no way a cause of the arms race. The Soviet leaders do not believe in political or military intimidation, and nobody should accuse us of trying to change America's social structure by force, he said. "We have no such plans and never have had."

Reagan suggested talking with Gromyko in private before lunch. Reporting later to us about the brief conversation, Gromyko observed that he did not quite understand what the excitement was all about. The president emphatically told him, as if this was a big secret, that his personal dream was a "world without nuclear arms." Gromyko answered that nuclear disarmament was "the question of all questions." Both agreed that the ultimate goal should be the complete elimination of nuclear weapons. And that was about all there was to the private meeting.

I do not rule out that Reagan was personally eager to make the Soviet foreign minister believe that a world without nuclear arms was really his dream. Reagan did refer to it in public time and again, but he realized that there were few people, even in his own entourage, who believed it.

Several presidential aides confirmed to us that Reagan had told them in advance that he wanted a face-to-face conversation alone with Gromyko during the break, but he did not tell them what it would be about and apparently did not fill them in afterward. When Reagan and Gromyko went into the office by themselves, the door was left slightly ajar so the duty officer could peep in case the president summoned him. Having duly exchanged those few words about a nuclear-free world with the Soviet foreign minister, Reagan retired to his personal bathroom, emerged, and then asked Gromyko if he wanted to use it. Gromyko did. The officer did not hear what was said, so the presidential aides were not sure whether the president just forgot his intention of talking with Gromyko in private, changed his mind, or had only intended from the beginning to have a short talk.

On the whole, the exchange proceeded reasonably well and even in a friendly atmosphere, without unnecessary outbreaks of temper both in the presence of other officials and at lunch. But both sides stuck to their guns.

Speaking later on the radio, the president described his conversation with Gromyko as useful, and so it was, but primarily in terms of his campaign for reelection.

Gromyko told the press that his discussion with President Reagan "does not enable us, unfortunately, to conclude that practical positive changes have taken place in the direction of the foreign policy of the American administration."

The statement served to confirm that the Soviet assessment of the administration remained unchanged. But Gromyko was satisfied with his reception. Before leaving Washington by plane he told me that while he found Reagan incorrigibly dogmatic—this was Gromyko talking, of all people!—he might be more disposed toward agreements following the election, and maybe even before Gromyko's next meeting with the president the following autumn. Little did Gromyko know that it was his last visit to the White House and that a hitherto obscure member of the Soviet Politburo, Mikhail Gorbachev would after becoming general secretary kick him upstairs to the mostly ceremonial Soviet presidency and replace him with a younger and more flexible politician.

Gromyko's trip to the United States confronted the Soviet leadership with the cardinal question of how further to develop our relations with Reagan. We had hoped that the popular movement against American missiles in Europe would make the United States and NATO drop the plan. But events had clearly proven us wrong; the missiles were firmly stationed in Europe. It was necessary to search for a compromise by resuming negotiations, and this applied to nuclear weapons in space. Otherwise we would miss the train. Moscow started a painful reassessment of its policy which lasted until mid-November. Then we proposed to Reagan to start a new round of negotiations after the U.S. elections.

As for Ronald Reagan, he felt he had surmounted a hurdle in meeting the formidable Andrei Gromyko. Arthur Hartman, the career diplomat who was the American ambassador to the Soviet Union, told me that immediately after meeting with Gromyko, Reagan had a conversation with his associates, Hartman among them. Reagan looked noticeably relieved; the meeting with Gromyko was over. The president said jokingly that debating Gromyko, a firm opponent of the United States and a convinced defender of the Soviet position, was much harder than debating Mondale. Hartman got the impression that Reagan was satisfied at having passed the "Gromyko test," which even enhanced his self-esteem.

Summing it all up, Reagan expressed the view that it would be an illusion to believe that Soviet-American relations could return to the conditions of Franklin Roosevelt's day; both country's views on each other's social system were irreconcilable and formed a part of their continued rivalry. But Reagan formed the impression that the Soviet Union was really keen on agreements to slow the arms race, and the opportunity for that would appear after November.

Hartman said it appeared that, once reelected, Reagan would become more involved in disarmament problems. Until now his formula for the security of the United States had been to introduce new military programs. But now he was increasingly thinking that American security interests would best be met by combining new arms programs with possible arms control agreements with the Soviet Union. Reagan had so far ignored the second half of this policy because he was up to his ears implementing the first half. But there was a chance he would move to the second part, although it would be wrong to cherish any great illusions.

More along these lines came from Vice President Bush just before the election at a quiet dinner at his house. He was confident of victory and brushed aside one of the latest Washington stories, that a couple of years after a victory Reagan might retire voluntarily in favor of Bush. Bush laughed heartily, saying that he would expect an earthquake in Washington before a voluntary retirement by Ronald Reagan, who very much liked being president with all the attributes of power that went with the office. I wanted to know what was behind Reagan's campaign speeches favoring better relations with the Soviet Union and his references to the possibility of arms agreements. Bush replied that Reagan usually believed sincerely in what he said, but when it came to the specifics of what he had in mind and how he would accomplish them, that was quite another matter. The White House had not yet developed any concrete approach.

## A New Atmosphere in Outer (and Inner) Space

The test of the administration's concrete intentions was played out with Reagan's favorite project, the Strategic Defense Initiative. This was to be the subject on which the administration would at last start to talk, but only after the election and on terms that proved to be narrowly drawn. In the summer before the elections, Moscow and Washington had already started a long discussion under the heading of the militarization of space. About ten private letters were exchanged on SDI by Reagan and Chernenko, and their tone became quite lively indeed. Jack Matlock, the National Security Council's Soviet specialist who later became U.S. ambassador to the Soviet Union, told me that Reagan was carefully examining the pros and cons of negotiations with the Soviet Union. The main obstacle was that he did not want to become a scapegoat if they foundered on the issue of verification.

In due course Star Wars became an issue worldwide and Washington could not resist. The diplomatic struggle was waged on the issue of a precise name for the negotiations, which we proposed calling "negotiations on prevention of the militarization of space." Washington would not accept the word "prevention." This was far more than a diplomatic quibble or a semantic debate, since the very word implied that the negotiations could result in banning SDI. Moscow would not agree to withdraw the term, because what would be left might effectively legitimize the arms race in space by the very process of controlling it.

Early in September the American side declared its readiness to start negotiations in Geneva about "arms control in space." Simultaneously, it proposed discussing the reduction of nuclear arms along with the possibilities for verification. The first part of the American proposal still implied a possibility of putting weapons in space because the question was practically reduced to the means of control. The second part was designed to overcome the Soviet refusal to negotiate on strategic weapons following the deployment of American Pershings in Europe. Reagan elaborated on it in his speech to the UN General Assembly September 24, which in effect put him publicly in favor of resuming SALT talks that had been broken off by the Soviet Union.

In retrospect, American diplomacy deserves credit for its persistence in trying to reduce the number of strategic nuclear weapons to much lower levels. This was finally accomplished in 1993, but in 1984 the White House needed that proposal to blazon its policy on disarmament and its readiness to resume talks, and they put the ball firmly in the Kremlin's court. Moscow decided to wait until after the presidential elections, and in mid-November, the Politburo agreed to new negotiations "on nuclear and space weapons," the phrase it preferred. The decision was prompted in no small measure by Reagan's landslide reelection, which awarded a complete mandate to his foreign and domestic policies. The Politburo instructed Gromyko to try to win a better deal from Shultz on the title.

Inside the administration, there was also a debate over SDI that mirrored the public struggle. The main criticism was that our relations and the strategic balance might be wrecked even before SDI could be developed to shoot incoming missiles out of the sky—the feasibility of which many noted scientists doubted anyway. The internal debate was joined most obviously and fiercely between Shultz and Weinberger. These former close colleagues in government and in private business disagreed on many things, to the point where, right after Reagan's reelection, Shultz privately demanded that the president choose between him and Weinberger.

Reagan, however, could not make up his mind, saying he needed both of them. Ideologically and personally, he was closer to Weinberger and more often followed his recommendations. But after the election, he wanted to speed up contacts and negotiations with Moscow, especially on nuclear arms control, so Shultz's role became more important to him. Robert McFarlane, the new and more pragmatic national security adviser who had replaced the ideological William Clark, told me privately that Shultz began to study disarmament questions thoroughly after the election; he had understood them only superficially until then. So Shultz started methodically to prepare for negotiations with Gromyko; until then the administration made every attempt to avoid them.

On November 23 the Soviet Union and the United States announced a new set of arms control negotiations linking discussions on START, intermediate-range missiles in Europe, and weapons in space, with a meeting of Gromyko and Shultz in Geneva on January 7–8, 1985. They would set the concrete agenda for future talks.

When we met again, Shultz seemed quite upbeat about the possibilities for negotiation. Change was in the air. He was going to Camp David, where Reagan was to meet Margaret Thatcher. They were looking forward to a report about her recent meeting in London with Gorbachev, a new political figure whom she had anointed on the steps of No. 10 Downing Street as someone with whom she could "do business," an unprecedented public accolade from her for any Soviet official. The curiosity of these die-hard American anti-communists had definitely been aroused. "What on earth did he do to fascinate the Iron Lady?" Shultz wondered out loud, and with a smile.

Perhaps I should have told him. I had first met Gorbachev the previous summer during my visit to Moscow. I did my usual rounds among the Politburo and virtually no one asked me anything beyond the usual: How are things going? But Gorbachev plied me with questions—twenty or thirty of them. He had been reading everything he could find about the United States and there was plenty that he wanted to know.

As I walked from Shultz's office, I ran into Simons, the State Department's Soviet specialist. He warned me that the American position being prepared for the Geneva meeting fell short of the Soviet side's expectations. It emphasized strategic offensive weapons, pushing space to the background. Besides, the State Department was still poorly informed about all of the Pentagon's space programs. In his methodical way, Shultz had asked for a detailed Pentagon briefing on SDI but failed to get it. Simons told me the briefing was conducted by Lieutenant General Leslie Abrahamson, the Star Wars program director. As the briefing proceeded, Shultz realized that the general was speaking in the kind of generalities he might have used if he were giving an interview to a newspaper.

"I want to know the particulars," Shultz said, asking the general some specific questions. Abrahamson, not in the least embarrassed by the presence of Shultz, asked his assistant if the secretary of state had a security clearance for this top-secret material. Shultz was indignant. This story, true or not, revealed the mood in the State Department that showed that the military in the United States was no more forthcoming than our own generals in giving their secrets even to the ranking diplomats on their own side.

In Moscow, the Politburo devoted a special session to the guidelines for Gromyko in Geneva. He received firm instructions to obtain the clearest possible commitment that the talks would aim at banning space weapons and be linked with the negotiations on nuclear weapons. All this was directed at making it impossible for the Americans to avoid discussing space weapons, since they evidently wanted to talk mainly about reducing strategic nuclear weapons. Gorbachev chaired the Politburo session, which he was increasingly doing because of Chernenko's declining health. While Reagan doggedly stuck to his Strategic Defense Initiative, Gorbachev convinced himself and the rest of the Soviet leadership that it had to be thwarted at all costs. The clash of these two opposing but fixed positions dominated our security negotiations for years to come, and the question was magnified by emotional involvement of the two leaders.

Shultz went to Geneva with different and not very clear-cut instructions. He had received them from Reagan after a dispute with Weinberger, who strongly opposed any talk at all with Gromyko on space weapons. (At that point SDI was the Pentagon's fastest growing program.) Shultz reasoned that without any talk of Star Wars the whole Geneva meeting would be senseless and so informed the president. Reagan resolved the dispute like Solomon. He said it was all right to start discussing the subject with the Soviet Union but Shultz should proceed "without surrendering anything."

At the meeting in Geneva, Shultz would not commit himself to a clear-cut formula defining the talks in terms of space and Reagan's SDI program, and he also opposed linking the talks on space with nuclear weapons. Thus the discussion with Gromyko proceeded with great difficulty, especially when it came to the wording of a final communiqué. I witnessed the whole process, and I can report that Gromyko displayed enviable perseverance in carrying out his instructions. At last they reached a compromise. The joint statement said the negotiators would be split into three groups covering "a complex of questions concerning space and nuclear weapons, both strategic and intermediate-range" so as to solve them "in their interrelationship . . . to work out effective agreements aimed at preventing an arms race in space and terminating it on earth, at limiting and reducing nuclear arms, and at strengthening strategic stability."

For all its labyrinthine verbiage, this declaration gave a start to new and important negotiations between the Soviet Union and the United States on three key groups of nuclear and space weapons—strategic weapons, intermediate-range missiles in Europe, and the weapons of Star Wars. True, the American side tried to amend the wording later to its own advantage. But the negotiations did proceed.

The public atmosphere around our relations also began to clear after the elections. Early in December I hosted Edgar Bronfman, the president of the World Jewish Congress and a prominent businessman, who pointed out that Jews and blacks were the only two ethnic groups to have voted against Reagan. He said he represented moderate sections of the American Jewish community, who tried to take a realistic approach to Soviet-American relations and did not want the Jews to become hostages of a new Cold War. Most American Jews realized that in a nuclear age their survival meant first of all prevention of a nuclear war between the Soviet Union and the United States, he said, and that gave them an interest in supporting detente. The leadership of the World Jewish Congress was prepared to oppose the arms race and support detente, better relations with the Soviet Union, and closer ties with its Jewish community. Bronfman also expressed a wish to visit the Soviet Union as a businessman dealing with food, chemical, and oil-extracting industries. We established a good personal relationship, and I helped arrange his trip.

Economic links also began to revive. Dwyane Andreas, cochairman at the Soviet-American Trade and Economic Council, visited me the following week. He told me about his trip to Moscow and a meeting with Gorbachev. He was convinced that the Soviet Union was prepared to develop economic relations with the United States, and he would bring it to the attention of the administration. I would like to do justice to Andreas, a consistent champion of better relations between our countries who commands high respect from political and business leaders. He does his work without much publicity but with great conviction and efficiency. We have long been friends, and our families remain in contact with each other.

Armand Hammer called on me several days later. With characteristic enthusiasm he told me about his reception in the Kremlin and a long conversation with Chernenko. The Reagan administration, he claimed, was interested in his trip, and the president invited Hammer to visit him and tell him about the meeting. Hammer asked me to tell Chernenko that he was trying to obtain a U.S. government license to sell offshore oil drilling equipment that could operate in Arctic conditions but was banned for export to the Soviet Union. He had managed to obtain a special exemption to export coal-carrying equipment, but permission for oil-drilling was harder to get. As was evident from his invitation to see Reagan he was, as always, starting at the top.

What accounted for this new and less confrontational atmosphere? Just before Christmas, I had dinner with McFarlane to discuss the outlook for the coming year, and while I welcomed the change, Moscow still could not be sure it was not just for the elections.

McFarlane gave his assessment: Reagan believed that he had fulfilled the basic task of his presidency, which was to restore the potential of the American armed forces. He was going to continue to support the military, but now he believed it was high time to improve relations with the Soviet Union gradually and reach agreements on reducing nuclear arms. His opinion about communism had not changed, and he firmly believed that free enterprise was the best way to develop a nation's potential, but he would no longer engage in a public debate about it. His priority, McFarlane said, was to lessen the threat of nuclear war and therefore to seek out the possibilities for nuclear agreements with the Soviet Union in 1985.

I looked somewhat skeptical, and McFarlane commented that the president was really undergoing an evolution of his views on the Soviet Union, although the process was not evident to those who did not associate with him daily.

# V. The Beginning of the End of the Cold War

## *What the Geneva Summit Meant*

The Geneva summit of November 1985 was the first in almost six years between the leaders of the Soviet Union and the United States. History may regard it as the beginning of the end of the Cold War. While the administration gave no hint that it was abandoning its basic principles, changes appeared in the thinking of Reagan about the Soviet Union. He began to depart from unconditional confrontation and display some sense of realism toward negotiation. This change resulted from a number of factors.

Washington regarded the Geneva meeting as, first and foremost, the fruit of its military buildup, which in turn underwrote its tough diplomacy. But the Reagan policy of a naked military buildup and diplomatic confrontation did not bring the desired results. Its principal utility lay in rebuilding confidence within the United States and in the very mind of the president himself. It never was a realistic possibility that the new weapons could force the Soviet Union to surrender its national interests or would be used to fight the Soviet Union to the death, which is the way the president's own rhetoric sometimes made it sound. In reality, both external and domestic pressure combined to undermine the Reagan strategy. Abroad, the United States came under pressure from its allies to resume a dialogue with the Soviet Union. At home, it became increasingly difficult to ignore the concern of the American people about the dangerous state of Soviet-American relations, and this was closely reflected in the public opinion polls. Furthermore, whatever may have been the effect of the administration's military programs, they had already reached their maximum because they were well under way or nearing successful completion. It would have taken another huge turn of the screw by the Pentagon's arms planners to reach another and more threatening plateau.

The Strategic Defense Initiative was welcomed by the military-industrial complex and the right wing in the United States as a tool to shift the strategic balance in favor of the United States, and at the same time as a tactic to force the Soviet Union to spend itself into bankruptcy, whatever might be the eventual military effectiveness of this technological fantasy. At first Mikhail Gorbachev nibbled at this bait. He made SDI the number one target of his diplomatic and public attacks and proceeded with a cheaper Soviet version, though his main target always remained the same: to kill or neutralize Star Wars through diplomatic negotiations.

The process of change in the Soviet Union was no less complex. Before Konstantin Chernenko died on March 10, 1985, Gorbachev and the other members of the Politburo were pursuing the same old foreign policy, although he began to think cautiously about the necessity of change from confrontation to businesslike relations with the West, primarily the United States. But he had to watch his step in the beginning and needed time to consolidate his power, especially in the Politburo and among the top military proponents of continued confrontation. His situation was further complicated by the fact that he was never sure what Reagan would do next, and the president's unpredictability remained a dominant factor in the Politburo's thinking right through its final session before the November summit.

When Gorbachev got control of Soviet foreign policy, it became increasingly dynamic and played a significant role in paving the way for the turn that took place at the Geneva summit. Gorbachev knew how to take propaganda advantage of the openings provided by Reagan and follow them up with major new initiatives to curb the arms race. No less important was the intensive exchange with the administration at all levels. This included personal letters between Gorbachev and Reagan; meetings and correspondence between Gorbachev's new and pragmatic Soviet foreign minister, Eduard Shevardnadze, and both the secretary of state and the president; and active working contacts through diplomatic channels that had previously been almost completely blocked.

### Washington Decides to Do Business with Gorbachev

From Mikhail Gorbachev's first appearance on the international stage as a rising star in the Soviet leadership, the American administration displayed growing interest in him. At their meeting in Geneva in January 1985 to negotiate the resumption of disarmament talks, Shultz told Gromyko in private (with Reagan's approval) that even though Gorbachev was not yet general secretary, if he wanted to pay a working visit to the United States he would be received by Reagan and Shultz. Gromyko, jealous, did not bother to disguise his displeasure at the American initiative. The old guard in the Politburo regarded Gorbachev with suspicion. Shultz left it at that. Gromyko had been entrusted entirely with the conduct of foreign policy by

Chernenko, who had no interest in it. As Chernenko's health declined early in 1985, there were rumors in the Kremlin that Chernenko would be relieved of his post as chairman of the Supreme Soviet so Gromyko could fulfill its mainly ceremonial duties as president of the nation while also remaining foreign minister, which would have meant additional authority for him. Chernenko would still have retained his top post in the party. But his death changed all these plans.

Gorbachev was elected general secretary of the Communist Party on March 11, the day after Chernenko's death. The old guard was unhappy with the nomination of such a young and energetic leader—he was fifty-four—but had no plausible candidate of its own. Gromyko played a major role by suddenly suggesting Gorbachev at the crucial Politburo session, thus strongly weakening the opposition by betting on the winning horse, as he had done throughout his career. But within six months Gorbachev had fired Gromyko as foreign minister because of his inflexibility and kicked him upstairs. He finally got the presidency, but without the foreign ministry.

At the time of his election, Gorbachev had no clear-cut foreign policy, although he was dissatisfied with the lack of dynamism and the absence of room for broad strategic maneuver. Reagan's public displays of uncompromising anti-communism made it difficult for Gorbachev to develop new initiatives toward the United States with any speed.

On the very day Gorbachev was elected general secretary, we received our first hint of the changes that he might expect from the Reagan administration. Shultz visited the embassy on March 11 to sign the condolence book for Chernenko, arriving twenty minutes before President Reagan to talk with me in private. Shultz told me he and the president had met in the White House earlier that day with McFarlane and Donald Regan, the new White House Chief of Staff. The president summed up by saying that a new situation with new opportunities was emerging in Soviet-American relations and it would be unforgivable not to take advantage of it, although the outcome was hardly predictable. Just as he was starting his second term as president, a new Soviet leader had taken the helm who by all appearances would manage foreign and domestic affairs energetically. Relations with Moscow would therefore be high on the president's list of priorities. With the Geneva arms control negotiations starting, Reagan added, results were crucial.

Reagan therefore wanted to establish a dialogue at the highest level from the very beginning, and with this end in view, the president had decided to send a personal letter to Gorbachev. It would be delivered by Vice President Bush, who would head the American delegation to Chernenko's funeral in Moscow. The letter would contain an invitation to the new general secretary to visit the United States. Needless to say, Gorbachev would be received by the American government and the president himself as a guest of the highest rank, and the White House would arrange for him to tour the country at his convenience and on an itinerary of his choice. Shultz remarked that it was the Soviet leader's "turn" to visit the United States, but if Gorbachev did not find it feasible for his own reasons to leave the Soviet Union and would prefer to invite the American president to visit the Soviet Union first, Reagan would understand.

When the president arrived he did not raise these questions with me, but I took note of his remark that it was his third visit to the embassy in the course of three years on occasions of grief. "But," he added, "I hope to come to the embassy next time on a happier occasion." He also asked me to convey his personal regards to Gorbachev.

I was certainly impressed by the news I got from Shultz, and so was Gorbachev. For the first time during his presidency, Reagan had chosen to express openly, albeit through his characteristically guarded secretary of state, his desire for a summit meeting. Gorbachev instantly noted the extraordinary signal from Washington, the more so because it fitted his own plans.

The next day, McFarlane came to the embassy to sign the condolence book and repeated much of Shultz's message. He stressed that the president hoped Gorbachev would not delay the meeting so their first summit could be "mutually introductory." The prospects of a summit and the degree to which they affected American public opinion could be seen from McFarlane's remarkable confession that if the meeting were to be held at that moment Congress would be most unlikely to approve the billions being requested for the MX missile because it would see the summit as a clear turn toward better relations. He also remarked that as the president became more personally involved in U.S.-Soviet dealings, things might come to the point where the confidential channel between the White House and the Kremlin could again be put into operation. That was news, indeed.

Gorbachev received Bush on March 13 at about 10 P.M. in a majestic Kremlin hall, attended by Gromyko and Shultz. Their discussion lasted for an hour and a half. Gorbachev emphatically confirmed the Soviet Union was ready to promote good relations with Washington if it felt likewise. Bush relayed Reagan's invitation to visit the United States, for which Gorbachev thanked him but gave no definite reply because the matter had to be discussed by the Politburo. Instead he focused his attention on the talks on nuclear and space weapons which had just begun between the Soviet Union and the United States in Vienna and showed little promise.

"Is the United States really interested in achieving results at the talks or does it need them to implement its rearmament programs?" Gorbachev asked bluntly. He stressed that the Soviet Union had never had any plans to fight the United States and had no such intention now. "There has never been any such madman in the Soviet leadership," he said. At the same time, he declared that the Soviet people would not admit to anyone lecturing them about how they should live, nor would they lecture anyone for that matter. Let history pass its judgment, he said.

Both sides left satisfied by the frank and lively conversation and convinced that the dialogue was certainly worth continuing even if it had not thrown up any new ideas and occasionally threw up contradictory thoughts. "Gorbachev is radically different from any Soviet leader I have ever met," Shultz told the press afterward.

Early in the morning of March 15, Shultz phoned me. He had arrived from Moscow a few hours before and was on his way to report to Reagan. He confirmed that Gorbachev had made a good impression with his straightforwardness, expertise, and obvious readiness to improve Soviet-American relations, and he would report all that to the president. The next day, at the annual reception in the State Department for the diplomatic corps, Shultz drew me aside to inform me that Reagan had asked him to characterize Gorbachev on the basis of their talk and compare him with other world figures. Shultz told me he had given Gorbachev high marks as a competent and dynamic leader, undoubtedly aware of his foreign policy goals and determined to spare no effort to achieve them.

The president asked Shultz to enumerate a few concrete issues that could justify a summit before American and Soviet public opinion. ("The president would hate to miss the chance," Shultz said.) Shultz suggested a resumption of Aeroflot flights, opening consulates in New York and Kiev, and agreements on cultural exchange, transport, energy, and the environment. Reagan said all that could provide an adequate basis for a first meeting, considering the tension of the last four years. I asked Shultz why the major questions of controlling the arms race on earth and in outer space were missing from his agenda, and he replied that they certainly could be discussed but there was hardly any hope of solving them at the first summit. All this sounded like a serious commitment.

Then I heard more praise from Vice President Bush, who approached me on March 19 on the White House lawn before an official welcoming ceremony which I was attending as dean of the diplomatic corps. Bush said Reagan was looking forward to Gorbachev's reply to his summit invitation, but in the meantime, his irrepressible anti-Soviet sentiments had reasserted themselves in a speech on a trip to Canada the previous day. I told Bush that, frankly speaking, the president's eagerness for a summit sounded far from convincing when listening to his official speeches; he seemed to favor the meeting in words but not deeds.

Bush shrugged and advised against exaggerating the importance of the president's rhetoric, which was sometimes careless. Said Bush: "Reagan is still Reagan." And indeed, as the ceremony began, the president in his welcoming speech made yet another attack on "Marxist-Leninists" and their intrigues in Central America, the Sandinista government in Nicaragua, and support from the Soviet Union and Cuba.

But despite Cold War detours—Weinberger made much of the tragic killing of an American liaison officer in East Germany by a Soviet sentry, which aroused American public opinion—the administration still seemed to be following the route to the summit. On April 3, I had a talk with Senator Bob Dole, an influential Republican leader whose impression was that the White House increasingly believed that a summit would take place sooner or later, which Dole saw as a big plus because it would mean a collapse of the policy advocated by the extreme right-wingers around Reagan. Meeting Gorbachev at the summit would amount to an admission by Reagan that the policy of confrontation he had followed during his first term had not quite worked and had to be adjusted. Dole therefore saw a summit as potentially very important for the next presidential election because it would weaken the wave of bellicose ultraconservatism in the country. I particularly appreciated such statements from the lips of that intelligent yet fairly conservative-minded man.

Inside the Kremlin, a summit became a matter of active debate. Gorbachev did not share the view of the former Soviet leadership that such a meeting had to deliver a serious agreement to be counted a success.

"If you make it a rule," Gorbachev told his fellow members of the Politburo, "the summit will not be held earlier than in two or three years. Probably, it will not take place at all. Now, time is short. We need a summit to get to know Reagan and his plans and, most important, to launch a personal dialogue with the American president."

His point of view did not appeal to Gromyko, but the foreign minister was in no position to impose his views upon the new and energetic general secretary. Gorbachev began his side of the correspondence with Reagan by endorsing a summit, and his letter was free of polemics. Gorbachev urged a businesslike approach and said a summit would not necessarily have to adopt any major documents; the main thing was to create mutual understanding on the basis of equality and each other's legitimate interests. This represented a turning point from the old Kremlin position on summits, and it was perceived as such by Reagan and Shultz, and Gorbachev came out publicly for a summit on April 8 in *Pravda*. The Soviet people welcomed it.

Before I left for Moscow to attend the Central Committee Plenum Shultz invited me to discuss the reply they were preparing for Reagan, which he promised would be as constructive as Gorbachev's letter. While Reagan would not insist on signed agreements, he would suggest a businesslike approach to our disputes, cooperation in regional problems, and other opportunities in the Geneva negotiations, the Stockholm conference, nonproliferation of nuclear weapons, the Vienna talks on troop reductions in Central Europe, and controls on chemical warfare. The letter itself was drafted skillfully to examine our positions critically and exert pressure on us. Although Gorbachev was looking for new ways, he was not yet prepared for concrete moves because he had to follow Gromyko's well-beaten diplomatic path until he could map out his own and obtain the approval of the Politburo.

## Gorbachev Addresses Soviet Foreign Policy

During the Plenum on April 23, Gorbachev made a routine attack on Reagan's foreign policy for increasing world tension and expressed the hope that it would shift enough to open the way for his personal meeting with the president. When he invited me for a private chat, he showed himself to have a mixture of traditional attitudes and great personal curiosity with a distrust of our dogmatic ways and the potential for flexibility. It was my first private and informal conversation with him as general secretary. His manner was artless and natural. He easily shared his views on Soviet-American relations and asked many questions. He was interested in every minor detail about America.

Two of Gorbachev's ideas stand out, and they were not all that unconventional for a Soviet leader. First, he strongly believed we could not gain victory "over imperialism" by force of arms, nor could we solve our domestic problems without ending the arms race. Second, we had to try to oust the maximum possible number Americans troops from Western Europe. The most effective way to achieve that was to ease international tension and carry out a stage-by-stage withdrawal of Soviet and American troops from Europe. For the Americans, that would mean returning home across the ocean; but for us, a withdrawal only several hundred kilometers behind our borders, where the presence of our troops would be felt almost palpably by European states. These were the first shoots of Gorbachev's new thinking in foreign policy.

As for the United States, he told me we should spare no effort to reverse the hostility in our relations, avoid arguments about ideology, and focus on normalizing and broadening our relations with Washington. I was to be guided by this in my capacity as ambassador, and my first task was to arrange a summit with Reagan. He emphasized that these were his personal instructions; for me they were like a gust of fresh air in the dense fog of recent years.

Gorbachev was keenly interested in knowing what kind of man Reagan was. He did not doubt Reagan's anti-Soviet predisposition, but was the president open to persuasion or was he just hopeless? Was he an anti-communist fanatic or a pragmatist? Could one come to terms with him or would it be worthless to try?

I told him that for all the hostility we had seen in Reagan's first term, during the past year or so, the first signs of pragmatism had begun to appear, and even a vague and unstable measure of interest in establishing contacts with the Soviet Union at the highest level. Could it be that, in his own peculiar way, he had undergone the same sort of evolution in relation to the Soviet Union as Nixon? Maybe, but it was hard to say. My personal experience showed me that it was possible to talk reasonably enough with Reagan. "But then," I noted to Gorbachev, "Reagan had not held a single meeting with Soviet leaders, except for Gromyko—who is a peculiar man himself. One has to have a way with him."

I recommended strongly to Gorbachev that he meet with Reagan. "It goes without saying you cannot guarantee good results," I added, "but I think we can win much more than we lose as far as our bilateral relations are concerned."

Gorbachev agreed. As we talked, he did not hide his displeasure at Gromyko's conservative, dogmatic approach to the vital problems of Soviet foreign policy, particularly in relation to the United States. He evidently had already decided to replace him and had not forgotten Gromyko's criticisms of his trip to Britain, where Gorbachev, who had not yet been elected general secretary, was the first Soviet party leader in the postwar era to evoke a genuinely benevolent reaction. Gromyko had been unusually careless in telling some of his old Politburo colleagues that he believed Gorbachev had behaved as a publicity-seeker. Gromyko simultaneously reprimanded several Soviet ambassadors in Western countries, including me, for too positive reporting back to Moscow with the favorable Western response to Gorbachev's visit. Gorbachev soon found out about these reproaches and long remembered them.

I should note that members of the Politburo were keenly and even competitively interested in their foreign press notices. Embassies relayed foreign press reports and comments about their trips abroad and the visits of foreign dignitaries to Moscow, and so would our news agency Tass. Its reports would be edited in Moscow and when necessary sanitized before being distributed, but the full versions would be passed to the Politburo, where they would be read as a measure of success or failure by the member who had made the trip or received the visitor.

Soon after becoming general secretary, Gorbachev symbolically departed from the habits of his predecessors and began to entrust foreign policy issues not only to Gromyko, but to Boris Ponomarev, the Central Committee secretary for international party relations. He did not do this because he especially appreciated Ponomarev's work (he did not), but mostly to make it clear to Gromyko that the party had its own foreign policy department and it could provide different views for the general secretary, who could accept them. That deliberate snub showed Gromyko's monopoly on foreign policy was near its end.

Shultz and Gromyko met in Vienna on May 14 amidst festive celebrations of a quarter-century of Austria's postwar independence. They discussed a broad range of problems but focused on the Geneva negotiations on nuclear and space weapons. The conversation lasted for six hours and was detailed yet fruitless. It was not until the end of the conversation that the question emerged that was on everybody's mind, that of the summit. Neither wanted to be first to raise it lest he display an undiplomatic zeal, so the two ministers played essentially an unnecessary diplomatic game. Shultz outlasted him.

Since Gromyko had clear instructions from Gorbachev to discuss the matter, he finally was forced to raise the question of the place and time. Gorbachev was proposing a summit in November in Moscow. Shultz said it was the Soviet leader's turn to come to Washington. Gromyko declined, proposing Europe instead because Gorbachev, only a few months in office, was unwilling to go to Washington lest it appear that he was paying court to Reagan.

Shultz reported back to Reagan, which touched off a debate within the administration. While mid-November was acceptable for the meeting, Reagan urged Gorbachev to hold it in one of the two capitals. He also promised to restrain himself from verbal attacks and join in the preparation of agreements.

Thus the summit was taking shape, and as it did, Weinberger and conservatives in the administration and Congress attacked the Soviet Union for failing to comply with the SALT II agreements (whose ratification they themselves had opposed). They called on Reagan to ignore the agreements and withdraw from the ABM Treaty as long as they stood in the way of the U.S. military buildup. Reagan issued an ambiguous statement, saying he would not ignore the agreements as long as the Soviet Union stood by them but left himself the option of commissioning a new nuclear submarine whose missiles would exceed the SALT II limits. Tass then issued a statement warning that if Reagan abrogated the treaty it could have serious consequences, and matters degenerated again into a kind of diplomatic trench warfare.

Finally on June 17 I had a meeting with Shultz that showed we were heading into the final stages of a summit arrangement. With McFarlane and Paul Nitze present, Shultz said the president reluctantly accepted Gorbachev's proposal to meet in a third country, and suggested Geneva. Then he read from a text which boiled down to the idea that the United States was ready to slow its Star Wars program in exchange for a Soviet agreement to make sizable cuts in its strategic missiles. The rationale for this was that if the Soviet force of offensive missiles were reduced, the United States could then justify slowing down SDI, which it regarded as a defensive project. This was really a sort of compromise within the administration between Shultz and Weinberger rather than a compromise with us, because Weinberger had started out by refusing to accept any limits at all on SDI. We of course had always assumed that the size of missile forces would be on the table in negotiations.

But there was another attraction for us. Shultz said he was authorized by the president to propose that he and I conduct through the confidential channel a discussion "in a broad, philosophical sense" of the key arms control questions already under negotiation in Geneva. The exchange could be continued by him and Gromyko late in July, when the two foreign ministers were due to meet in Helsinki for the next Conference on Security and Cooperation in Europe.

I recommended to Moscow that we accept this framework for discussion because it meant that Shultz proposed to reactivate the confidential channel. I thought it meant that the administration was serious about dialogue following Reagan's reelection, although that remained to be proven. Two weeks later Moscow accepted November 19–20 in Geneva as the date and place for the summit, but declined the confidential discussions in favor of continuing to work through the regular Geneva arms negotiators.

Shultz described our reply as disappointing. What he did not know was that it had been drafted by Gromyko, who refused to countenance any repetition of secret personal negotiations in the style developed by Kissinger and me, and which he personally disliked because it devalued his own role. He had convinced Gorbachev that philosophical discussions would only result in drawing us into protracted negotiations—and eventually into tacitly acquiescing in Star Wars simply by agreeing to talk about Reagan's pet project.

## The Turn Begins

When the announcement of the summit was published in the two capitals early in July, Moscow added a piece of news that attracted every bit as much attention worldwide. Gromyko was to be relieved of his job as foreign minister. Because of Gromyko's help in electing Gorbachev, he was not forced to retire—that happened three years later—but was elected chairman of the Supreme Soviet of the Soviet Union, formally the highest position in the state but with no great political influence and largely ceremonial duties. Gorbachev, on the eve of his first serious dialogue with the United States, thus rid himself of a minister who was a burden to him, whom he disliked, and whose presence and authority stood in the way of the incipient new thinking prompted by Gorbachev in Soviet foreign policy.

Gromyko's departure after almost thirty years marked the end of an epoch. Speaking from long and close personal experience, I can testify that behind his stern and forbidding appearance was a rather kind-hearted man, loyal to his fellow workers, devoted to his work, and displaying high professional competence. For all his shortcomings, he earned the respect of his associates and foreign counterparts. In his own way, Gromyko was convinced of the correctness of the policy of his time and showed rare perseverance, talent, and skill in implementing it. His chief priority was the defense of our national interests as he saw them and, first of all, upholding our gains of the hard war that defeated Nazi Germany. A disciple of Stalin's, he did not attach much importance to moral aspects of foreign policy such as human rights, although he was an honest and decent man. He did not believe that such abstract notions could be a serious factor in policy, or in the possibility of early and radical agreements with the West.

His persevering and stubborn conduct in negotiations was legendary. If he had a fallback position approved by the Politburo, he would only show his hand when his partner was about to get up and end the conversation. This occasionally was carried too far and turned into an extreme lack of flexibility, which in the last analysis often left him without results to show for all his determination. He missed several opportunities to speed up the conclusion of the SALT Treaty in negotiations with Kissinger and Vance. Yet within the Politburo Gromyko was a principal initiator of disarmament talks, whether they covered conventional or nuclear arms.

Gromyko did not support unnecessary and dangerous confrontation, especially with the United States, and he struggled persistently against the threat of a new war, particularly a nuclear war. That did not prevent him from being a prominent Soviet Cold War crusader, especially when he believed that our interests were threatened. He was a committed member of the party, loyally upheld communist ideas and believed in their final victory. All that was deeply rooted in his thinking and his code of conduct. But when new developments and a rapid transformation of the world called for a new approach, he gradually became an obstacle to the Soviet diplomacy he had directed for so many years. He finally realized this and suffered for it in his heart of hearts, but he knew there was no way he could reform himself.

The old-line thinking was of course not just a failing of Gromyko. Boris Ponomarev, head of the international department of the party's Central Committee, for instance, drafted the foreign policy section of the Politburo reports to the Twenty-Seventh Congress early in 1986. But the editing committee criticized it for failing to reflect the new approach and our "new thinking" in foreign policy and falling back on old clichés. Indignant, Ponomarev replied, "What new thinking? Our thinking is right. Let the Americans change their thinking. What Gorbachev says abroad is meant exclusively for them, for the West!"

In choosing Gromyko's successor, Gorbachev reverted to an old tradition in the Soviet Union and many Western countries of picking a politician instead of a diplomat. I was later told by members of the Politburo that my name and that of Georgi Kornienko, Gromyko's deputy were mentioned by Gorbachev as good possibilities. But then he told the Politburo that it was time for foreign affairs to be managed directly by the party and that is why the job had to be filled by a member of the party leadership.

But by party leader he did not mean a Kremlin insider. Quite the contrary. Much to everyone's surprise, he named Eduard Shevardnadze, the first secretary of the Communist Party of the Soviet Republic of Georgia, and evaluated him very highly to the amazement of Politburo members. Shevardnadze had never held any positions in Moscow and had spent his career in Georgia. Besides, he had no diplomatic experience whatever. Gorbachev did not attach much importance to that and said, "He'll live to learn." He believed it important to have an intelligent man by his side who was not burdened by the old policy stereotypes and was ready to put his new designs into practice. Gorbachev also needed a like-minded man in the Politburo, where his new thinking in foreign policy was by no means universally shared.

Gorbachev knew that he could completely rely on Shevardnadze. They were old acquaintances dating back a quarter of a century to their days in the Young Communist League and had become friends while working as party secretaries in large neighboring regions in the south of the Soviet Union, Gorbachev in Stavropol and Shevardnadze in Georgia. That Shevardnadze did not have his own connections inside the Kremlin leadership network suited Gorbachev, because the new foreign minister's position as an outsider helped ensure his personal loyalty to the general secretary.

They worked hand in glove. It was not long before the Gorbachev-Shevardnadze tandem came to determine the country's foreign policy in its entirety, gradually pushing the rest of the Politburo into the background, where its collective opinion was no longer of crucial importance. This was especially evident during the last years of Gorbachev's rule, until Shevardnadze resigned his post in 1990. But the actions of this dynamic tandem were not always well thought out, not by a long shot, and in no small measure that was due to Shevardnadze's readiness to follow Gorbachev's rush to compromise for agreements with the West without much expertise provided by professional diplomats from the Foreign Ministry.

The same Plenum that replaced Gromyko as foreign minister—he remained a Politburo member until his retirement in 1988—elected two new secretaries of the Central Committee: Boris Yeltsin, the former first secretary of the Sverdlovsk region, who was charged with construction, and Lev Zaikov, who was given control of the defense industry. Zaikov later became the head of the Politburo troika overseeing negotiations on nuclear and conventional weapons. The other two members were Shevardnadze and Defense Minister Sergei Sokolov, representing the two ministries who were locked in competition over arms policy (just as in Washington). Zaikov, and later his successor Dmitri Yazov, were instructed by Gorbachev to reconcile the positions of the two departments and compromise.

I first met Shevardnadze, who was already serving as minister, during my summer leave in Moscow, and he made a favorable impression on me. He inquired about the United States in minute detail and was interested in our relations. I noted that he was not so much interested in the problems as such, but in the ways that they might be solved through mutual compromise. I somehow found a common language with him much faster than with Gromyko, whose long-established views were hard to change. I also liked the way Shevardnadze did not try to hide his lack of diplomatic experience and felt free to ask all kinds of questions without heed to his ministerial prestige.

Shevardnadze suggested that I accompany him to the foreign ministers' conference at the end of July marking the tenth anniversary of the Helsinki Final Act, to help him in his diplomatic baptism of fire abroad. I of course agreed. He was surprised at the tone of a speech Shultz had made there on human rights in the Soviet Union which he felt had exceeded all the habitual limits of hostility. Shevardnadze was more conciliatory, and when he finally met Shultz at Helsinki, he asked his American counterpart, "Did you really have to make such a speech?"

Shultz seemed very complacent and quite satisfied by the mass of publicity the speech had received in the United States. But Shevardnadze clearly realized that such public statements by the secretary of state made it more difficult for him and Gorbachev to search within the Politburo for a flexible new approach toward the Reagan administration. Shultz also seemed interested in scoring points on Gorbachev's decision to ban all Soviet nuclear explosions starting August 6, which had been announced in Moscow. The secretary of state responded publicly that unless the nuclear tests were put under control, there was no way of knowing whether the Soviet Union was observing its own moratorium. Moscow angrily retorted that it was better to discontinue nuclear explosions than monitor the way they were being carried out.

The private meeting dealt mostly with preparations for the Gorbachev-Reagan summit. Shultz and Shevardnadze came no closer to resolving the problems that divided us, but the atmosphere was noticeably more friendly than during similar meetings with Gromyko, and Shevardnadze came away with an appreciation of Shultz's professionalism and the personal contact with him. At the end of the meeting, Shevardnadze thanked me, confiding that many senior diplomats in the Foreign Ministry were treating him coolly and not offering help as I had.

## A Frustrating Climb Toward the Summit

When I returned to Washington I called on Shultz on September 10 to discuss preparations for the summit. The essence of our problem was that the administration in general and Ronald Reagan in particular still did not yet have a clear vision of the summit, its agenda, and its possible results. The State Department and the Pentagon held different views; if the former wanted some agreement or at least a generally positive outcome, the latter had no interest at all. Weinberger's followers fought to the last to prevent their president from yielding on what they believed were his most deeply held principles, and first of all on SDI.

It was evident that Reagan and his wife were more concerned with the atmospherics of the summit than its essential issues, and this was to bedevil our preparations until the very moment we arrived in Geneva. Shultz told me that the president preferred not to host his dinner in the "sterility" of the U.S. mission in Geneva but at the Aga Khan's villa for an easy chat. In Washington Shultz handed me a personal letter from Nancy Reagan to Raisa Gorbachev expressing her hope for an early meeting and confidence that "we, the wives" were eager to do their utmost to improve relations between the Soviet and American people.

But on substantive questions, I got no reply. Shultz said the administration was not yet prepared even to discuss a joint declaration on the nonproliferation of nuclear weapons—which had been proposed by the Americans themselves. It was evident that the State Department was still awaiting summit instructions from the White House. Senator Robert Byrd informed me of a struggle over the main question of concessions on SDI in exchange for a radical reduction of strategic missiles. The hard-liners opposed any agreement and had reduced the matter to a propaganda battle; they believed Gorbachev had scored more points and now Reagan should do his utmost to catch up.

On September 16, I had another conversation with Shultz, who insisted that the president was serious about a successful meeting. But he confessed that the American leadership was still in the dark about what results it expected. Frankly speaking, his own inactivity seemed inexplicable to me. Foreign ministers were supposed to play a leading role in preparing summit meetings, or at least they always did in the past, but I did not fully realize that his hands were tied by the struggle around the president.

Ambassador Hartman, who was back from Moscow for consultations, told me that Reagan would pay due attention to disarmament problems but he also intended to stress the need for mutual restraint by one side in regions where the other had important interests, a strategy persistently advocated by Richard Nixon. But Hartman also told me something about Reagan's preparations that helped explain why we had made so little progress with the summit only about two months away. In order to keep abreast of the times, Reagan was examining history to obtain a better idea of "the Russian soul," the Soviet Union, and the motives behind its policy. Almost daily he leafed through illustrated booklets about the Soviet Union—he disdained thick books—and read official summaries prepared for him. But he preferred oral reports and stories from people who had lived in the Soviet Union, especially those who had met Soviet leaders. Hartman remarked in passing that Reagan's choice of storytellers might appear dubious but that was up to the president; among them were dissidents who had settled in the United States.

While Shultz seemed to be unhurried, Weinberger lost no time pressing ahead with Star Wars. He convinced Reagan to take another step, and on September 23 the White House announced the organization of the American Armed Forces' United Space Command. All that caused irritation in Moscow. Shevardnadze declared before the United Nations that all responsibility for the crisis in international relations lay with the United States.

But Gorbachev had no intention of engaging in a fruitless public wrangle with Reagan and preferred to maintain his diplomatic initiative. On September 27 he had Shevardnadze hand the White House new Soviet proposals for the summit and for the Geneva negotiations on nuclear and space weapons that were already under way. First he formally proposed a tradeoff:

cut in half the number of long-range nuclear missiles capable of reaching each other's territory in exchange for a complete ban on weapons that could strike from outer space; that would mean a reduction of up to six thousand nuclear warheads. Then he suggested separate negotiations on medium-range missiles in Europe drawing in Britain and France; meanwhile the Soviet Union was putting a ceiling on the number of its SS-20 missiles on combat alert in Europe, and scrapping or removing its obsolete SS-4 and SS-5 missiles. Europe, said Gorbachev, was entitled to expect the United States to respond in kind.

The Soviet proposals had been designed to reach a compromise, and they put the American administration in a difficult position. On October 4 a White House spokesman angrily said the United States did not intend to respond in public, and the next day Weinberger reaffirmed doggedly that the American administration could not negotiate with the Soviet Union about SDI. Shultz made no public statement at all.

Gorbachev's proposals divided the administration anew. Shultz saw the propaganda advantages to the Soviet Union if the Soviet proposal were to be rejected by Washington. He suggested the United States respond to some degree positively because drastic cuts in Soviet strategic forces would be beneficial for the United States. Weinberger and the Pentagon insisted on their crash program for SDI. Reagan could not make up his mind. The intensifying debate within the administration focused on the 1972 ABM agreement, which through more than a decade had been interpreted narrowly by all administrations as not legitimizing a star wars system. Pentagon lawyers argued otherwise, giving a broader interpretation. The controversy spread through the administration, Congress, and the media.

In October a Solomonic solution was worked out by Shultz and McFarlane and approved by Reagan. It said that from a legal point of view the broad interpretation was well justified, but the SDI program would be developed within the traditional narrow interpretation. Still the struggle went on, to the alarm of the European allies over the future of the ABM agreement. It goes without saying the Soviet Union vigorously supported the narrow interpretation, and meanwhile the Gorbachev proposals consolidated our propaganda positions.

McFarlane admitted to me late in September that the president believed Gorbachev was waging a propaganda war in the hope of forcing him into concessions on vital questions of nuclear arms. The president had to give Gorbachev his due: unlike his predecessors, the new Soviet leader could skillfully use public opinion against his foreign opponents, even in their own countries. But McFarlane warned us not to overestimate the influence of public opinion on the president. Reagan was a man of stubborn views and would hardly make concessions under public pressure. To me it was evident that the White House was for the first time feeling a thrashing by the very weapons of propaganda it knew how to wield so well.

That may have made Reagan consider more serious negotiations. During their last meeting in September, Reagan and Shevardnadze raised the subject of establishing a confidential channel to prepare for the summit, but Reagan had failed then to name the person he wanted to operate the American end. Now McFarlane was authorized by the president to say it would be him and me. He remarked fleetingly that the president felt Shultz, who was very busy with other matters, had not used it in full measure. But McFarlane intended to make the utmost use of the channel.

I knew that McFarlane was a kind of White House buffer between the rival views of Weinberger and Shultz, although he leaned toward the views of the secretary of state. After Reagan's reelection McFarlane began to convince the president that his summit with Gorbachev would benefit the United States—a mood that was evident during my conversations with him. The president's wife was also eager for the summit to succeed and ensure her husband's place in history. Had it not been for their personal pressure on Reagan, Shultz alone would have found it difficult to bring the president successfully to the summit.

George Bush played a role in the summit because he saw it as part of a determined campaign to succeed Reagan as president at the next election in 1988. We talked frankly on October 9, and it was evident that he was looking for help from the Soviet Union to create a better atmosphere. Bush said he would like to establish a closer relationship with Gorbachev and added in a light but unmistakable tone that it ought to matter to the general secretary what kind of president he would have to deal with in the future for four or perhaps eight years. Bush proposed visiting the Soviet Union in 1986 as vice president to meet Gorbachev, thus promoting his chances of nomination and election and simultaneously promoting an important agreement on nuclear disarmament between the Soviet Union and the United States the following year. In all frankness he did not see any chance for an agreement at the Geneva meeting because Reagan was not yet prepared for an important agreement that might limit his favorite creation, SDI.

The main thing, Bush said, was to draw a dividing line between the permissible and the impermissible. I immediately replied that the ABM agreement made it possible to draw that line.

"That may be so," Bush remarked, "but Reagan is convinced, or he has let someone convince him, that the line should begin by deploying, rather than developing and testing, the weapons systems."

After some hesitation, Bush mentioned another of Reagan's congenital peculiarities: the president found it hard simultaneously to think and to express his own ideas. This meant that whenever Reagan was ardently advocating an idea be it right or wrong, he hardly grasped what his opponent was saying. He needed some time to digest the ideas and arguments coming at him from the other side. For that reason, Bush believed the first summit should above all put into Reagan's head some different ideas from the ones that he held so tenaciously. In short, another summit would be needed to reach more tangible agreements unless world events were to spring some surprises in the interim. I had to admit he had a good point.

Bush also discussed his political problems. He knew that serving as Reagan's vice president had cost him much of his identity in the eyes of the public and thus damaged his acceptability by the center and even those to the left of center. He said he meant to regain that identity in a year or two to create a broader political base with the help of better and deeper connections with the Republican Party on the local level than Jack Kemp, Bob Dole, and Howard Baker, who lacked international experience and financial support. Bush asked me to inform Gorbachev about our conversation and hoped to visit him for a detailed talk. I believed Bush had good presidential prospects, and I so informed Gorbachev.

One reason was that he was a politician who could swing with the wind. Several months later, in February of 1986, we met at a reception and chatted again about politics. I joked that I was not sure whether to congratulate or commiserate with him about his sudden conversion to a strong conservatism that had earned praise from even from those who had never before been his political allies. Bush said I knew enough about America's political morals to understand his behavior. "I don't conceal the fact," he went on, "that I want to be president. But, like it or not, America has swung strongly to conservatism. A man who is reputed to be a liberal now has no chance to become president, let alone the Republican nomination, which he won't gain under any circumstances. I have no choice but to reckon with that."

Bush told me that he had not changed his views on the need to improve relations with the Soviet Union although for obvious reasons he did not publicize them. "I follow the activity of your new general secretary with great interest," he said. "He has political imagination and boldness. Our roads may meet some day, for all I know." Bush's words came true, although both of them had to wait several years.

Despite all this internal pressure on Reagan, there was little evidence of give-and-take in Washington as the summit date neared. On October 10, before I left for a brief visit to Moscow to discuss preparations, I met with Shultz, who suggested that it might be useful for him to visit Moscow to discuss the summit. He informed me of some housekeeping details such as the meeting at which Reagan and Gorbachev would exchange gifts, and the composition of the American delegation. Three days later Reagan went on the radio to discuss arms limitation. He came out with the same old claim that the United States was lagging behind the Soviet Union in the strategic nuclear arms race and that the strategic balance had to be restored first of all.

When I returned from Moscow I told Shultz his prospective visit was being considered and things looked positive. Shultz told me that "these White House guys," lacking any interest in a productive Geneva summit, had prepared a draft speech for Reagan at the jubilee session of the United Nations with a reference to "bombs against the Soviet Union." But Reagan, much to Shultz's satisfaction, rejected the draft because it was likely to spoil his relationship with Gorbachev, provoke a public quarrel, and probably make a mess of the summit.

Still no definite statements on space and disarmament appeared, and instead Shultz talked up the president's common sense, his desire to continue the dialogue with Gorbachev after the summit, and his eagerness—along with Nancy Reagan's—to visit Moscow before the end of his presidential term. Shultz made a personal request if permission for his Moscow trip came through: he wanted to buy a couple of icons. Historic value was secondary; what mattered was they must look handsome. One was for him, the other for Nancy Reagan, who longed to have one of these famous Russian religious objects. I told him that could be arranged.

On October 22, McFarlane told me at dinner that Reagan had finally started to prepare for the summit in earnest. He had already examined eleven reference materials about Gorbachev and his political views and had gone through several rehearsals for their talks. A number of NSC meetings had been devoted to preparations for the summit. Reagan also consulted his old California adviser Richard Nixon.

Gorbachev then decided to take charge of our summit preparations and invited Shultz to Moscow. He arrived November 4, accompanied by McFarlane. Gorbachev invited me to take part in the meeting the next day in his fairly modest office in the Central Committee rather than in the grandeur of the Kremlin, thus accentuating the businesslike character of the meeting.

Gorbachev was somewhat agitated. One hour before the meeting he called in Shevardnadze and me. He was obviously irritated that while only two weeks remained before his meeting with Reagan, its agenda and possible outcome were still unclear despite preparatory meetings with Shultz and even Reagan himself. "We hear nothing from the Americans but generalities," said Gorbachev, stressing that a mere introductory meeting with the president to satisfy protocol would not suit him. He wanted something more substantial, more tangible to convince the skeptical members of the Politburo that the meeting was worthwhile. At the same time, Reagan's public statements sometimes sounded as if nothing was happening at all.

Gorbachev also wondered why the confidential channel was virtually out of operation, and I explained that quiet diplomacy was basically alien to the Reagan administration, although it seemed to be changing. "We'll see," I said. "What Reagan says in that channel is what counts in the final analysis." I urged Gorbachev to press Shultz strongly to find out what was on the president's mind. Gorbachev agreed and said, "Well, let's see what Secretary of State Shultz has got to tell us."

We had a long and difficult discussion. Gorbachev and Shultz spent some time on an almost philosophical discussion of the erroneous illusions cherished by both their governments about each other's weaknesses, which each tried to use to its own advantage. Gorbachev was especially critical of this tactic. He also spoke emphatically in favor of better relations and stressed the need to reach agreement on nuclear and space weapons. He put special emphasis on SDI and criticized it severely—overdoing it, I thought, because that would merely reinforce Reagan's belief in its importance.

However, all Gorbachev's attempts were of no avail to search out areas of agreement for the summit with Shultz, who talked in his characteristic generalities, making noncommittal declarations about the importance of the summit in itself. He also did not fail to raise the subject of human rights, which Gorbachev simply declined to discuss again. It certainly gave Gorbachev a more realistic view of what to expect. Later Gorbachev told me he liked Shultz's general ideas about economic problems, upon which they touched during the conversation and which were increasingly attracting his interest. On that subject he willingly would talk with Shultz in the future.

Shultz for his part was impressed by Gorbachev's dynamism. Our embassy learned that after his meeting in Moscow Shultz sounded worried that the summit might be marked by new, still stronger pressure from Gorbachev on disarmament; that would put Reagan in a difficult position and give the propaganda advantage to Gorbachev. Once he learned that, Gorbachev told me he did not want Reagan to regard the summit as a great propaganda battle. On the contrary, he felt the summit should be an introductory, get-acquainted meeting to sound out Reagan's intentions and avoid confrontational talk, although Gorbachev was certainly going to state his views clearly. After all, the Geneva summit was meant to be more of a springboard to develop new relations with Reagan. "You can't expect much yet," Gorbachev stressed.

When he reported to the Politburo on his meeting with Shultz, the disappointed Gorbachev admitted that he had failed to engage the secretary of state in a concrete conversation about the key questions; it appeared that Shultz "did not have serious baggage" for the summit. These impressions enabled him to reduce the unduly high expectations in the Politburo, which gave him a free hand to have a more informal talk with the president.

Shultz was satisfied, even relieved, when I briefed him back in Washington on November 7 about Gorbachev's approach to the summit. I told Shultz that the president could expect a solid conversation without each side trying to corner the other or arguing for the sake of arguing, although the essential questions were to be discussed frankly and in detail, with all the seriousness they deserved.

He told me that he had reported to the president on his Moscow meeting with Gorbachev, and Reagan had asked many questions. He was curious about the substance of the discussion and about Gorbachev's manner, his tolerance to objections, the quickness of his mind and reaction, his sense of humor, his expertise in various subjects. Reagan told Shultz it would be good to arrange for Gorbachev's visit to Washington in July of the following year, on the understanding that the president's turn to visit Moscow would come next. This I reported to Moscow with the recommendation that a public declaration agreeing to regular summit meetings would in itself be a worthy result of the summit. The Politburo approved.

Then Shultz and I conducted a detailed review of all the questions on the agenda, concentrating on possible agreements and joint documents. The basic document would be a joint statement to be drafted by officials of his department and my embassy. And so it was done.

But on November 13 Shultz told me about a new and unexpected obstacle. Summit opponents within the administration had fed Reagan arguments against preliminary joint drafting of the communiqué even though much work had already been done. But the president bought the argument that it was wrong to work on the text of a communiqué before a meeting because that meant the diplomats would be imposing on the two leaders something they had not yet discussed themselves. Embarrassed, Shultz said that the president believed this work should be stopped pending the summit. Then it would be decided what to do next. When I asked why foreign ministers could not do the necessary preparatory work with the knowledge of the heads of state, Shultz confined himself to referring to the president's instructions.

It goes without saying that Moscow was very unpleasantly surprised. Meetings with other American presidents had always involved useful preliminary work by both sides on the communiqué. I was urgently instructed to meet with Shultz on the next day. I told him that to Moscow it looked like the American side was beginning to backpedal at the last moment, freezing many of the most important ideas on which we had been working jointly. But I got nowhere, and once again the administration turned from substance to mere form. More than that, Shultz said the president opposed a joint press conference because he found it humiliating for the heads of the two super-powers to be exposed to attacks "of impudent reporters" trying to shout each other down, which Reagan had witnessed "with disgust" at the press conference given by Gorbachev and Mitterrand. Reagan clearly feared losing the propaganda battle before the television cameras.

I knew that Richard Nixon had shared his own summit experience with Reagan, and just before we left for Geneva Donald Kendall filled me in on the former president's reactions. (McFarlane had sounded out Kendall as a possible U.S. ambassador to Moscow; he would have been a good choice but it would have been a thankless task under Reagan and he pleaded the press of business obligations anyway.) Nixon was critical of the way Reagan prepared for the summit: Reagan had a poor knowledge of details, especially concerning disarmament, and had to depend on his aides and experts. McFarlane strongly recommended that the president conduct a general, essentially philosophical conversation, believing that would be on safe ground from which he could defend himself against Gorbachev and avoid discussing concrete points. Nixon reported that many presidential aides were inclined to regard the summit mostly as a photographic session of the two superpower leaders of the contemporary world. They were trying to persuade Reagan to look at the meeting that way.

Nixon described Shultz as a more positive, serious, and knowledgeable figure, but blamed him for not exerting enough pressure on the president. Shultz was too careful, although he was one of the principal American participants preparing Reagan for the summit. Nixon talked Reagan out of taking Weinberger along, as the Secretary of Defense had come to be a symbol of uncompromising hostility toward the Soviet Union even in the United States.

Finally Nixon said with nostalgia that he wished he were in Reagan's place because he had a historic chance to accomplish a turn in Soviet-American relations with the new general secretary, but he feared Reagan might not use it to the full.

The Soviet leadership and indeed Gorbachev himself approached the Geneva summit with high anxiety, uncertain what it would produce because it was the first one in the five years of a presidency characterized by virulent anti-Sovietism. Shultz's visit to Moscow failed to dispel these fears. The Foreign Ministry, the Ministry of Defense, and the KGB prepared the usual joint memorandum that would form the basis of Gorbachev's instructions for the summit after discussion and approval by the Politburo. The memo, dated November 11, 1985, represented the full assessment by the Soviet leadership of our relations with the United States and President Reagan. It reflected the main ideas and thoughts developed by Gorbachev since coming to power, his cautious compromising mood toward the summit and, in contrast to previous documents of this sort, in language closer to ordinary speech.

It declared that the principal aim of the summit "is to try, however slim the chance may be, to find a common language with the American president on the key question of his preparedness to build relations with the Soviet Union on an equal footing, without aiming to reform each other or import ideological differences into relations between nations." It conceded from the start that no agreements could be expected to resolve the principal Soviet-American differences, and "the best we can expect is a joint statement that both sides will proceed from the assumption that nuclear war is unacceptable and unwinnable." This in fact, was the one thing that Gorbachev hoped to take home. He was instructed to press the fact that security and nuclear and space weapons were the dominant problems facing both countries.

The memo also warned that "Reagan will repeat his old claims against us" in regional conflicts, so consultations by both countries would at least confirm a Soviet role in these areas. And even if no concrete agreements were reached, "the summit still should end on a mutual note of readiness to keep the dialogue alive. . . . It certainly would not be bad to have a joint document summarizing the results of the summit. But obtaining it should not be an idée fixe. We might do just as well without a final statement."

As is clear from these guidelines given to Gorbachev, Moscow did not pin great hopes on the summit. The minimum program approved by the Politburo authorized him to act at his discretion if circumstances allowed. The ambitious Gorbachev, as we who accompanied him to Geneva knew, had an additional goal: to try to convince Reagan to ban space weapons with a simultaneous reduction of strategic nuclear weapons by half.

On November 17, on the eve of the summit, the *New York Times* published a secret memorandum by Weinberger for President Reagan. The secretary of defense strongly recommended that the president reject any steps toward disarmament such as a promise to observe the SALT II Treaty or concessions on Star Wars. Weinberger was trying to torpedo the summit at the last moment.

## The Geneva Summit

Gorbachev's plane arrived in Geneva at 11:45 A.M. on November 18, and his talks with Reagan began the next day. The talks were the fourteenth summit between Soviet and American leaders since the Teheran meeting of Stalin, Roosevelt, and Churchill in 1943. Gorbachev, at fifty-four, was just beginning his dynamic career as the Soviet leader; Reagan, at seventy-four, was an anti-communist veteran at the height of his presidential glory. Both recognized the deep differences between the Soviet Union and the United States, but both hoped deep down to give a fresh start to relations between their nations. They also shared a total belief in who they were and what they stood for, and in their personal ability to convince others.

But for all their inherent self-confidence, both were somewhat nervous and uneasy, conscious of the responsibilities they carried to that summit. And each had his reasons to try at all costs to make the summit a success, or at least look like a success—Reagan to justify the policies of a lifetime which boiled down to peace through strength, Gorbachev to gain international stature for the reforms upon which he was just embarking.

All this was imprinted on their behavior. They pinned their hopes on their four private talks, including one in a summer cottage on the bank of Lake Geneva. They talked by the fireside in a cozy informal atmosphere. They also took part at the meetings of the two delegations. But more than half the time only the two leaders and their interpreters were involved. This made life miserable for the enormous press corps, which had to live with a news blackout until the end of the summit.

From the very beginning, Reagan demonstrated his singular knack for publicity through the use of the symbols of protocol. The first meeting was to take place on Tuesday, November 19, at Fleur d'Eau, a nineteenth-century lakeside chateau where Reagan was staying. The president was the official host for the first day. It was a cold November morning with a cutting wind blowing off the lake. Gorbachev wore an overcoat and a winter hat. When he arrived, Reagan came out to greet him in a suit without a topcoat or hat, posing together with Gorbachev for photographers. Numerous photos published in the press showed Reagan looking youthful, energetic, and physically strong against Gorbachev, who was bundled up against the cold. They looked the same age. We learned later from Reagan's aides that the president had been waiting for Gorbachev in the hall, also dressed in an overcoat. But as soon as he saw Gorbachev through the window, he pulled off his coat and walked outside to meet the Soviet leader. Reagan's instinct worked, and Gorbachev quickly made a mental note of it. When it was our turn and Reagan came to our residence, Gorbachev also came out coatless to meet him.

So the summit opened at 10:00 A.M. With a half dozen advisers on each side (including foreign ministers) waiting in a separate conference room, Reagan took Gorbachev and their two interpreters into a pale-blue sitting room for a private conversation. Gorbachev had asked my opinion how best to handle this first important meeting, because I had already had several meetings with Reagan. I told him that first impressions were important to Reagan and could be crucial for their further talks. It was important that Reagan see him first of all in human terms even when they disagreed profoundly. I advised him to use his own sense of humor and at the beginning not to rely too heavily on detailed knowledge of concrete subjects in order not to corner Reagan or embarrass him. Gorbachev himself was a very good actor, and he understood all this quite well.

As a result the initial private meeting of the two leaders lasted more than an hour instead of the planned fifteen minutes. They reviewed their differences freely and agreed, "without formalities" in a frank but friendly manner with a touch of lightheartedness. In general, their first meeting could be considered a success in creating good human chemistry.

Then Gorbachev and Reagan joined their foreign minsters and other experts in the first plenary session in the chateau's ornate salon. Both leaders expressed with their own eloquence their basic ideological convictions about the Cold War, based on their long-standing contradictory views of each country's political and social systems. In many aspects it was a repetition of the private correspondence between Reagan and the Soviet leaders during the past five years of his administration. The two leaders, of course, did not convince each other, but the discussion of familiar views was carried on in a businesslike atmosphere without mutual irritation. It was useful for each to listen to the other.

After lunch with their respective staffs, the two leaders got down to work on arms control at the Tuesday afternoon session. It was no surprise that the discussions about SDI and nuclear arms reductions proved complex and difficult. The atmosphere became heated and emotional. Reagan suggested they get a breath of fresh air. Gorbachev quickly agreed and they bundled up against the cold, walked together toward the lake and the waiting summerhouse with its big fireplace, which gave the Geneva meeting the name of "the fireside summit."

There Reagan handed Gorbachev his proposals in the form of "guidelines" or joint instructions to be issued to our negotiators at the Geneva arms talks. The first point was a fifty percent reduction in strategic forces, to which Gorbachev agreed. The second point was an interim agreement to reduce medium-range nuclear missiles in Europe and eventually eliminate them entirely. Gorbachev raised questions about the role of British and French missiles and airborne nuclear weapons, which Reagan had omitted in his proposals.

But the most controversial point lay in the third proposal for "a greater reliance on defensive systems"—which in Reagan's language meant SDI and ducked the question of whether they would be covered by the long-standing agreement to limit ABM systems. Worse, the statement seemed to imply that the Soviet Union agreed with SDI in principle and that there might even be some possibility that we would cooperate in this "defense program." Gorbachev immediately reminded Reagan that it had been agreed at the Shultz-Gromyko meeting in January that there must be an "interrelationship" between cuts in offensive arms and halting weapons in space. Where was this relationship in Reagan's proposals? The president said he didn't see that the subjects were linked.

The heated debate between the two lasted an hour by the fireplace. Sensing a deadlock, both decided to drop the question for the moment and return to the residence. On the way back, Reagan asked if they could hold another summit meeting in the United States. Gorbachev immediately accepted, proposing in turn to host the third summit in the Soviet Union. Reagan was pleased to accept. It was an important result. After Gorbachev and his party had departed the president gleefully informed the U.S. team that the next summit meetings were already agreed upon. What is not known to historians who have written about this meeting is that both Reagan and Gorbachev had been prepared for this exchange in advance through the confidential channel. It was one of the rare cases in this administration where it had worked smoothly: well before Geneva, Reagan had let Gorbachev know through me about his proposal for later summits.

Most of those present did not know about the confidential exchange, so they were greatly surprised and much relieved that Gorbachev and Reagan had arranged to hold two additional meetings in both capitals regardless of the results of this one. That important agreement showed the determination of the two leaders to continue and develop their mutual dialogue and search for normal relations. The press broadly welcomed this agreement.

The next day, on Wednesday, November 20, at 11:30 A.M. at the Soviet Mission, Gorbachev and Reagan continued their dispute over space weapons in the presence of their advisers. It was a dramatic encounter between the two leaders. Reagan vehemently defended the SDI program: "It's not an offensive system. I am talking about a shield, not a spear." Gorbachev countered that "the reality is that SDI would open a new arms race."

Gorbachev continued to press Reagan: "Why don't you believe me when I say the Soviet Union will never attack? . . . Why then should I accept your sincerity in your willingness to share SDI research when you don't even share your advanced technology with your allies? Let's be more realistic. We're prepared to compromise. We've said we'll agree to a separate agreement on intermediate-range missiles. We'll talk about deep cuts in START. But SDI has got to come to an end."

There was a long and distressing silence. We participants could see that both leaders were very angry. Gorbachev was the first to realize the need to put down all passion.

"Mr. President," he said calmly, "I disagree with you, but I can see you really believe it. Maybe this has grown a bit heated. I was just trying to convey to you the depth of our concern on SDI."

After that session Gorbachev told his advisers that he had decided to cut off the discussion when he realized that there would be no way at this summit to persuade Reagan to drop his SDI research program. He set that task for future summits lest he bring the present one to ruin.

The two leaders discussed other questions, including the controversial problems of regional conflicts and human rights. But these and other questions were of subordinate importance here, mostly because there was not enough time to cover them all—but there were some nuances in the discussion. Reagan as usual strongly denounced the Afghan war. But professional diplomats from the American side were surprised by Gorbachev's low-key, emotionless defense of Soviet policy in Afghanistan, as if saying that he had no personal responsibility for it. The Soviet side, for its part, noticed that Reagan was far more timid on human rights than the usual American official representatives.

The preparation of the final statement caused serious disagreement. There was a sharp clash between Shultz and Kornienko, who had continued from Gromyko's regime as Shevardnadze's first deputy. (Shevardnadze himself was not very active at the Geneva meeting.) A supplementary session of senior diplomats, lasting well into the early hours of the next morning, was needed to devise a compromise. It was reached just several hours before the final meeting of the heads of state, thanks to the intervention of Gorbachev himself. Reagan took no part in the quibble over the wording, which involved genuine disagreements over meaning.

The major point of disagreement centered on the fact that the American side did not want any links between nuclear and space arms, while the Soviet side insisted on it, refusing otherwise to agree to a joint statement. There was also a dispute on whether to mention SDI and the ABM Treaty; ultimately references to both were omitted.

Final compromises on the document were reached at 4:30 A.M., only a few hours before the closing ceremony at 10:00 A.M. On arms issues the U.S. team agreed to fall back on the language of Gromyko and Shultz on January 8, which at first the Americans did not even want to repeat. The final statement on these issues said:

The president and the General Secretary discussed the negotiations on nuclear and space arms. They agreed to accelerate the work at these negotiations, with a view to accomplishing the task set down in the Joint U.S.-Soviet Agreement on January 8, 1985, namely to prevent an arms race in space and terminate it on earth, to limit and reduce nuclear arms and enhance strategic stability.

The diplomatic draftsmen produced a reasonably good document, the first of its kind between Washington and Moscow while Reagan was in the White House. The joint statement was a major political document declaring that a nuclear war should never be unleashed and was unwinnable. Both sides stressed the importance of preventing any war between them, whether nuclear or conventional, and declared that they would not seek military superiority. From our point of view, the minimal program outlined in the Politburo memorandum to Gorbachev was fulfilled. Besides, Shultz and Shevardnadze signed an agreement on scientific, educational, and cultural exchanges, the result of two hundred hours of previous negotiations in sixty-five meetings over fifteen months.

Gorbachev made a surprise move by agreeing to include in the final statement a phrase committing us to "resolving humanitarian cases in the spirit of cooperation." Thus, for the first time in a joint document, we gave some sign of a shift on this vexed question of human rights.

Because of our radical differences about SDI, the final statement essentially ignored it. Gorbachev believed that Reagan's dogged commitment to the project blocked progress toward strategic arms reductions. Although Shultz said that after the heated discussion about SDI he felt Gorbachev finally accepted the inevitability of research on it, the truth is that Gorbachev did not accept it at all and recognized that the best they could do at Geneva was to agree to disagree. The summit had made no progress toward Gorbachev's principal goal of halting Star Wars, and its promises of nuclear arms reduction therefore were vague. Gorbachev hoped that in time he would manage to overcome or somehow weaken Reagan's stubborn position. So he played for time in arranging the next summit in Washington, but he did not want to come home empty-handed. He therefore arranged an interim meeting in Reykjavik the following year, which only confirmed once again that it was anything but easy to shake Reagan's determination to realize his Star Wars dream.

I came away from the Geneva summit with a somewhat different and more uncomfortable impression, which was that Gorbachev had gotten himself unreasonably fixated on American military research on space weapons and converted it into a precondition for summit success. Reagan thus drove us into a deadlock, and later we ourselves had to search for an exit.

Looking back on the many summits in which I participated, I must admit that the first meeting between Gorbachev and Reagan was quite extraordinary. No joint documents were prepared beforehand, and their differences on the principal questions of arms control were so large that it was virtually impossible to agree on how to structure the conversation in advance in order to facilitate a discussion of this complex issue in an orderly manner. As a result, they eventually had no choice but to agree to regard the summit as a get-acquainted meeting. It turned out to be a first step in the process of cooperation, which was completely new to them.

Reagan and Gorbachev virtually refused to follow the agenda that had been prepared by their aides and instead engaged in a free-form discussion. Given the historical background, they were probably right. It served them well in avoiding an impasse on things they could not possibly resolve and thus avoided personal confrontation, which was especially important for their first meeting.

Coupled with the agreement to meet again and the final statement on nuclear war, this represented no small advance. Through the establishment of the first personal relationship with a Soviet leader during the five years of Reagan's presidency, a certain psychological barrier was overcome, first of all by Reagan himself with the realization that it was possible to do business directly with the Soviet leadership and the evil empire, after all. This laid foundations for further advances, although the relations themselves remained complex. The first Reagan-Gorbachev summit could therefore be considered a success. It was not a strategic breakthrough, but it did unquestionably yield a certain moral and political benefit and paved the way for the summits that followed. I got the impression, as I observed both leaders, that they had found ways of communicating with each other.

On the plane home Gorbachev said that Reagan had impressed him as a complex and contradictory person, sometimes frankly speaking his mind, as when he defended SDI, and sometimes, as usual, harping on propaganda dogmas in which he also believed. He was stubborn and very conservative. But still Gorbachev found it possible to establish contact with him and discovered a man who was not as hopeless as some believed. And to Gorbachev that meant he was ready to work with him.

Reagan's entourage left no doubt that he came away with a positive impression of Gorbachev as a leader who differed from all predecessors and was even ready by their second mutual dinner in Geneva to address him by first name, a typical American accolade of friendship. (Cautious aides told him he had better wait a bit.) The White House triumphantly presented the "fireside summit" to the public through the mass media, and Reagan gave a dramatic and favorable report to Congress. The president's approval rating in the polls promptly hit its high mark of 84 percent, a point not lost among the political ideologues in the White House.

In Moscow, the Politburo devoted a special session to the results. Gorbachev was palpably pleased to report on his talks and share his vivid personal impressions; after all, it was the first meeting for any of our leaders with the notoriously anti-Soviet American president.

Gromyko was the first to congratulate Gorbachev on the skillful and successful accomplishment of his difficult mission in Geneva. Other members of the Politburo followed Gromyko's example, more by tradition of praising a general secretary than by conviction. Only the minister of defense and chairman of the KGB, despite their praise, added that Reagan was still Reagan and we should be vigilant in dealing with him. Gorbachev readily agreed, saying that his meeting in Geneva was not yet a breakthrough but, hopefully, the beginning of better relations with Reagan, which we should explore and develop. His main hope in making the Cold War die gradually was in agreeing with the United States to reduce and finally end the arms race. After a lively discussion, the Politburo formally noted the positive significance of the meeting and subscribed to the policy of persisting in efforts to develop our relations with the Reagan administration. A special mention was made about the value of new summits, and in his report to the Supreme Soviet session on November 27, Gorbachev publicly described the Geneva meeting as "necessary and useful."

In the course of the summit Gorbachev successfully shaped and demonstrated his personal style of conducting diplomatic talks, even though at the time, he had no coherent political program and had not yet thought through his concepts of security in relation to the United States. The most important thing was his adoption of a course of cooperation with Reagan which was also endorsed by his political colleagues. This led to profound changes in Soviet-American relations later. Last but not least, Gorbachev and Reagan also reached a mutual if tacit understanding that the spirit of Geneva should not be allowed to vanish into thin air.

# VI. Good-bye to Washington

## *Goodwill and Diplomacy*

**O**f the six American presidents I dealt with during my career in Washington, none presented more contradictions than Ronald Reagan. To us he was an enigma when he tried to restart the Cold War, remained one when he refought it, and was even more so when he and his opponent Mikhail Gorbachev conspired in their own way to end it. He had no head for details and never seemed to realize that goodwill alone was not enough to settle disputes. He grasped matters in an instinctive way but not necessarily in a simple one, and Americans often failed to realize the complexity of his character. He stubbornly believed what he wanted to believe about himself, about other people, and about the realities of the world. When by some mysterious process he had convinced himself that the world and our relations could and should be changed, he would act on his new conviction, and this eventually enabled him to convert from the commitment to the Cold War and the battle against communism that had dominated the latter part of his adult life.

I can think of no better example of the president's unique way of thinking than one episode involving me personally. When Shultz informed him in March of 1986 that I was being promoted to the rank of secretary of the Communist Party and would be returning to Moscow to head the Central Committee's International Relations Department, Reagan, amazed, asked: "Is he really a communist?" He and I had gradually developed a friendly personal relationship, and the president did not seem to know, or perhaps did not want to know, that all Soviet diplomats without exception had to be party members. Intentionally or not, the sentiments underlying his question surely were complimentary, but the question itself revealed that we were not dealing with an ordinary politician.

When I returned to Washington from Geneva we saw more of this behavior in his personal letter to Gorbachev, dated November 28. He had written it by hand to accentuate its confidential and indeed personal character. The letter contained an official invitation to visit the United States in the second half of 1986. Its comments are rather extensive, so I will only quote some passages from it. They are translated back into English from our record of it in Russian.

> Now that we are both home and facing the task of leading our countries into a more constructive relationship with each other, I wanted to waste no time in giving you some of my initial thoughts on our meetings. . . . There are some things I would like to convey very personally and very privately:

> First, I want you to know that I found our meetings of great value. We had agreed to speak frankly and we did. As a result, I came away from the meeting with a better understanding of your attitude. . . . Obviously there are many things on which we disagree . . . very fundamentally. But, if I understand you correctly, you, too, are determined to take steps to see that our nations manage their relationship in a peaceful fashion. If this is the case, then this is one point on which we are in total agreement—and it is after all the most fundamental one of all.

As if continuing the discussion in Geneva, Reagan again argued in favor of the Strategic Defense Initiative and its connection with the reduction of offensive nuclear weapons. He also described regional conflicts as another key issue. He continued:

> The United States does not believe that the Soviet Union is the cause of all the world's ills. We do believe, however, that your country has exploited and worsened local tensions and conflicts by militarizing them. . . . While we both will undoubtedly continue to support our friends, we must find a way to do so without use of armed force. . . .

> Both of us have advisers and assistants, but, you know, in the final analysis, the responsibility to preserve peace and increase cooperation is ours. Our people look to us for leadership and nobody can provide it if we don't.

On December 5, I discussed with Shultz the results of the Geneva summit. In good humor and unusually uninhibited, the secretary of state said Reagan had gone through a process of education of sorts. During his preceding years in power, Reagan had viewed all Soviet statements as blatant propaganda designed simply to mislead the West, Shultz said, but Reagan had changed his mind following his personal talks with Gorbachev, admitting that the Soviet leader had deep convictions of his own. For Reagan, this admission represented a major advance. It had been especially useful for the president to have to listen to an eloquent explanation of Soviet motives and intentions for five hours from someone who was by definition the most unimpeachable source. While they still disagreed on many things, Reagan had begun to recognize the right of other points of view to exist, rather than just waving them aside as he so often did. In that sense, Shultz said, Gorbachev did a good job. As if summarizing Reagan's impressions, the secretary of state quoted the president as saying to his closest associates right after the Geneva meeting was over: "This man is a convinced communist, but you can do business with him."

Gorbachev responded to Reagan's letter with a message looking toward a second summit. He concentrated on untangling the knot of nuclear weapons and weapons in space but ended on a positive note by expressing the hope that the president would regard his letter as another fireside chat. He added: "We would like to preserve the atmosphere of our Geneva meetings and indeed develop our dialogue. I see our correspondence as the most important channel in preparing our new meeting."

The day after Christmas I received a call from President Reagan in California. He had not yet received Gorbachev's letter but had received a personal one from me expressing my hope for better relations. After some flattering words and compliments, Reagan said I could rely on his personal support in my work preparing for a new summit. He also asked me to convey his and his wife's best wishes to Mikhail and Raisa Gorbachev and assure them they would be warmly welcomed in the United States. When I told him that a letter from Gorbachev was on his way to him, he jocularly asked if it was a good one. I replied in the same vein: "It is a good Christmas letter."

The goodwill exchanges continued into the New Year. Gorbachev and Reagan exchanged television addresses to the American and Soviet people on January 1. It was Reagan's idea, but Gorbachev accepted without a moment's hesitation as a symbolic gesture of the evolving new thinking: the chief imperialist was being permitted a direct address to the people of the evil empire.

The president found himself less well prepared when confronted by serious proposals for disarmament that could not be answered with a mere smile and a good chat at the fireside but demanded a careful calculation of the national interest and a considered diplomatic response.

Some time before the Geneva summit, without consulting their bosses, the first deputy foreign minister, Georgi Kornienko, and the chief of the Army's General Staff, Marshal Sergei Akhromeyev, privately started to develop the broadest possible program of nuclear disarmament on their own initiative. Neither Gromyko nor his successor Shevardnadze, nor the successive ministers of defense, nor Gorbachev himself knew anything about it until after the meeting with Reagan. It was only then that their plan worked its way up through the ministries to Gorbachev, who was away from Moscow on a short vacation. Shevardnadze was attracted to it but hesitated to commit himself until he had heard Gorbachev's reaction.

The essence of the idea was that both the United States and the Soviet Union would be just as secure against each other—and far safer—with much smaller stockpiles of nuclear weapons, which even then would be more than sufficient to cause the gravest damage to an enemy. This very simple idea was seen as extraordinary because, like so many simple ideas, it had never been tried. Gorbachev accepted it with enthusiasm, although it demanded his great skills of persuasion to win the approval of the Politburo. He had the complete support of the Foreign Ministry under Shevardnadze and Kornienko, and although there was less backing from the Defense Ministry he also had Akhromeyev, whose plan helped neutralize the conservative military. Nevertheless, under pressure from Gorbachev the process moved relatively swiftly and took not much more than a month, by which time it was ready to be presented to the Americans and the world.

On January 15 I met with Shultz to hand him an urgent message from Gorbachev to Reagan containing his disarmament plan. I realized that when compared to earlier correspondence on the subject, this was of outstanding significance, and I tried to get that across. Gorbachev was proposing "a stage-by-stage program leading to a comprehensive and universal nuclear disarmament by the beginning of the next century"—or a program for the year 2000, which was soon publicized throughout the world.

The program set out a three-stage schedule for reducing nuclear arms, both delivery systems and warheads, until they were completely eliminated. It covered in much detail both strategic and tactical nuclear weapons and banned offensive weapons in space or "space strike weapons." The program also proposed staged reductions in conventional arms. The program was the first adequate and realistic Soviet disarmament program covering a broad range of weapons and laying out a concrete schedule applying to both sides in a balanced way. It took into account the latest American proposals and provided a visible and practical basis for compromise, although negotiations would certainly be needed.

Shultz was unmistakably impressed. He asked questions but would not comment on the substance. He clearly could not wait to take it to the experts and report their opinion to Reagan.

Some hours later Gorbachev disclosed the plan in public, stressing the goal of ridding the planet of nuclear weapons within the next fifteen years, a simple point that caught the public's fancy. Although it would not be honest to deny that Gorbachev's proclamation carried elements of propaganda, the fact remained that the American government could not just shrug it off. For the first time, the Soviet Union was ready to agree to far-reaching cuts in strategic nuclear weapons, on which Reagan had long insisted, and the leaders of American foreign policy had no choice but to recognize that. Answering questions the next day about the Gorbachev plan, Reagan expressed satisfaction that the complete elimination of nuclear arms was being proposed by the Soviet Union for the first time.

A couple of days later, Donald Kendall told me about a conversation with Donald Regan, the White House chief of staff, who admitted to him that the Gorbachev program had caught the entire administration unawares. The president had already been assured by the U.S. Embassy in Moscow that Gorbachev was fully occupied with domestic affairs in his preparations for the party congress. Now the White House had to rack its brains for an answer to Gorbachev when his proposals were concrete and in a number of cases seemed close to the ideas already put forward publicly by the president himself. They could not be brushed aside as mere propaganda, and the Reagan administration unexpectedly found itself facing more vigorous and resourceful Soviet diplomacy than ever before on the most important questions of nuclear disarmament.

It took President Reagan several days to react, and when he did, the best he could do was to say that the United States and its allies would "carefully examine" the Gorbachev proposals, some of which seemed to him to be constructive. He tried to shift the focus of attention to the negotiations on medium-range nuclear weapons in Europe, which were taking place in Geneva but had degenerated into a typical round of name-calling. Meanwhile Weinberger, in his usual highly negative way, publicly rejected Gorbachev's proposal for a moratorium on nuclear tests.

The Gorbachev initiative also caused a small earthquake in American domestic politics. After I handed copies of his statement to leaders on Capitol Hill, Senator Strom Thurmond of South Carolina, notorious like most of his Southern conservative colleagues for his invariable hostility toward the Soviet Union, said rather unexpectedly to me that our countries could and should agree on peace and disarmament, and "it is high time we got down to business." He went as far as to invite some home state reporters to mark his first meeting with the Soviet ambassador and later sent me favorable articles and photos clipped from the South Carolina newspapers, a rare event indeed in those days.

The Democratic Party also began to worry that it was being left high and dry by the joint peace offensive Gorbachev and Reagan had begun at their summit. Senator Edward Kennedy wanted to ascertain Gorbachev's feelings and decided to visit Moscow. Calling on me on January 23 before his departure, he voiced some mild criticism of our policy toward Reagan: it had helped promote a sharp growth in Reagan's popularity in the United States, allayed Americans' concerns over the threat of nuclear confrontation, weakened the vigorous antiwar movement, and neutralized Reagan's opposition in Congress and in the nation as a whole. Kennedy pointed out that Reagan had not been forced to give up a single arms program; on the contrary, he continued to press for their development as bargaining counters in negotiations with the Soviet Union. He was unwilling to accept even a moratorium on nuclear explosions, as a minimum gesture of goodwill.

Then Shultz asked to speak to me on February 11 for one of our rare private conversations. He said he was using the confidential channel "with the president's knowledge" to convey some ideas to Gorbachev. The president wanted Gorbachev to know that the absence of a response to his disarmament proposals did not mean that he was ignoring them, but he wanted to develop his responses in a reply seeking common ground. Shultz gave a somewhat more detailed reply stressing medium-range missiles.

The approach he outlined followed a sharp debate within the administration, and it boiled down to this: without rejecting the Gorbachev program directly, the administration would select those parts of it that looked attractive and try to negotiate in those areas without linking them to the other, less attractive, parts of the program. When Reagan's formal reply was delivered February 22 in Moscow it followed this pick-and-choose strategy. The president welcomed the stage-by-stage program of nuclear disarmament but buried it in countersuggestions following American positions. For example, he praised Gorbachev's proposal to eliminate medium-range nuclear missiles in Europe, but also insisted on their elimination in Asia. The reduction of strategic arsenals would have to depend on Soviet acceptance of the Star Wars program and unilateral cuts in Soviet conventional weapons. Nuclear tests were described as necessary as long as nuclear arms were part of the deterrent arsenal.

There seemed to be no strict discipline or clear guidance within the administration in dealing with the Soviet Union, and its members seemed to delight in staging petty conflicts, to Moscow's irritation. On March 7 the administration ordered a sizable reduction in the staff of the Soviet Mission to the United Nations in New York after highly publicized spy cases on both sides. On March 13, American warships staged a demonstration of naval might off the Crimean Peninsula. There were occasional outbreaks of anti-Soviet rhetoric from top administration officials. On May 27 Reagan declared that he would no longer abide by the strategic arms levels established by the SALT II Treaty.

Not only the Soviet Union, but also the American Congress and European allies sharply criticized that last decision. Shultz argued in private against the move, but this paragon of discipline and obedience supported it after Reagan's statement. Our relations seemed to be sliding back to the road of mounting confrontation.

## My Life Changes

Early in March I left Washington to attend the Twenty-Seventh Congress of the Soviet Communist Party, which radically changed the direction of Soviet foreign policy, shifting from the idea of class warfare as the basis for the relationship between capitalist and communist states to a concept of security shared by East and West at much lower and less dangerous levels of arms. It firmly supported the disarmament plan that had been unveiled January 15. I was highly satisfied with these new ideas in our foreign policy. I was given an advance draft of Gorbachev's report to the congress for my comments. I welcomed the radical change in our policies, which were long overdue, and some of which I had quietly long advocated.

In addition to marking a radical change in our policies, the congress brought a radical change in my life.

I had been a delegate to party congresses more than once. As usual I participated in two or three sessions daily, and in between I visited the Foreign Ministry and other ministries to try to resolve the huge number of bureaucratic problems and policy disputes that always piled up at our embassy in Washington. I had quite a few private meetings with friends and top party and government officials who wanted to hear the latest news from America. This way I also expanded my wide circle of friends during the many years I served as the Soviet ambassador to the United States. These meetings also served a very useful purpose for me because they kept me in touch with the current mood and the plans for the future within the leading circles of the Soviet Union, which was of no small importance to an ambassador in faraway Washington.

With all this to do, two weeks simply flew by, and I began to prepare for my return to Washington. On the last day of the congress, there was a long break before the concluding session, at which the Politburo and the party secretaries were to be elected. To pass the time I took a walk around the Kremlin and Red Square. I returned ten minutes before the start of the session, but no sooner had I entered the Palace of Congresses than one of Gorbachev's security guards ran up to me, panting. He told me they had been looking for me for half an hour; the general secretary urgently wanted to speak with me. I followed him behind the main meeting hall to Gorbachev's private office, where he was preparing for the final session.

There were only five minutes to go, and the first bell had already rung to summon the delegates back to the hall.

We shook hands. Straightaway Gorbachev told me that "there was an opinion"—there was that same anonymous but implacable party phrase that had announced the commencement of my diplomatic career four decades before—that I was to be nominated for election as secretary of the Central Committee for international affairs and would return to Moscow to head its International Department. It came as a complete surprise.

Frankly speaking, the flattering offer did not appeal to me at all, I would rather have remained abroad because I simply liked working as an ambassador. I liked the United States and still do. I liked the comparative independence and autonomy of my job and the distance from the Moscow bureaucracy. I had a rare opportunity to express my opinion and views directly to the general secretary (five of them in succession) and to the Politburo, and thus to some extent influence events and decisions in our relations with the United States from the Soviet Union's most important diplomatic post. Worst of all, the International Department of the Central Committee, to the best of my knowledge, had in reality little to do with foreign policy and diplomacy but mostly occupied itself with promoting cooperation and ties with communist parties and left-wing organizations in other countries. I had neither the experience nor the taste for that, and I told that to Gorbachev in just those words.

Gorbachev dismissed my argument. By electing an experienced ambassador to run the International Department of the Central Committee, he said, the party leadership specifically meant to boost its prestige. Right now it was doing practically nothing in foreign policy, although that was what it was supposed to do. As for dealing with foreign communist parties, Gorbachev said, "You'll have several experienced assistants who have been doing that for a long time, so just let them go on doing it. Your main responsibility will be foreign policy."

The second bell rang. Gorbachev congratulated me on my new appointment and walked to the podium.

The rest passed like a dream. I sat there trying to come to my senses as Gorbachev announced the composition of the top bodies of the Central Committee. There was my name among the candidates. I was elected to the new position. That was the end of my work as the Soviet ambassador to the United States.

Actually, Gorbachev had made his first attempt to bring me back to a job in Moscow the year before. During a short break at the Geneva summit he asked what I would say to Shevardnadze's request to work with him as his deputy. I was on good personal terms with Shevardnadze and had done my best to help him at his first meetings with American officials. I replied that it would be a privilege and I very much appreciated the offer, but I would rather keep my ambassadorial position because the prospect of working on the staff of the ministry did not really appeal to me. Gorbachev laughed and said he would think about it, but did not raise the subject again.

So, my life was entering a new stage. I told Gorbachev, and he agreed, that I had to return to Washington to pay farewell visits to the president, the secretary of state, and other American officials. Early in April, I flew to Washington, and for the first time I realized the importance of my new position. Under regulations existing at the time, members of the Politburo and secretaries of the Central Committee were obliged to make their official trips abroad on special planes. My wife and I were the only passengers on the big airplane, and I confess that I was rather ill at ease.

## A Round of Farewells

For my final round of conversations in Washington I brought with me a letter from Gorbachev to Reagan expressing our disquiet at the lack of any concrete improvement in our relations since the summit five months before. On April 7, the evening before my farewell meeting with Reagan at the White House, Shultz had me to dinner with the new national security adviser, John Poindexter.

They asked me for a frank description of Moscow's attitude toward Soviet-American relations after the party congress. I told them that the Soviet leadership could not but notice that once again our negotiations on disarmament and other questions were stuck, and to us that unfortunately showed the administration's deeds were falling far short of its declared intentions to work for the next summit.

This was to be our last private conversation before I left Washington, and Shultz voiced his personal regret that the Reagan administration had again failed to use the confidential channel between him and me actively, in spite of what had been arranged in Geneva at the summit. "I can see now," Shultz said, "it was due to our own failure to appreciate its advantages. The experience of the preceding administrations, especially in using the channel during preparations for summit meetings, is clear proof." As it turned out, they continued with precisely the opposite procedure. The president himself put forward the agenda, and virtually no exploratory work had been done at a more private and flexible level.

The next day I held a farewell meeting with Reagan at the White House. The weather was excellent: sunny and warm instead of the cold winter evening when I visited Reagan in 1983. It was a full-dress affair attended by Shultz; Poindexter; Donald Regan; Jack Matlock, the president's aide for Soviet affairs; and Rozanne Ridgway, the assistant secretary of state for European affairs. On our side, my embassy counselors Bessmertnykh and Sokolov were present at the meeting. We talked with the president for an hour and a half without interpreters.

The president, consulting extensive notes in his hand as was his habit during serious talks, said he wanted to make some suggestions. He turned out to be far more specific and detailed than his aides. It became clear to me why the secretary of state had not been specific on the night before I meet the president; they evidently decided that all explanations of their position through me to Gorbachev should be given by the president himself. Reagan said he was determined to improve our relationship, which had already been improved since the Geneva summit by increasing exchanges and contacts. But like us, he was not generally satisfied. He was particularly concerned about regional conflicts, especially Libyan-based terrorism and the war in Afghanistan.

Reagan said further that each side should suggest the best practical options for arms control and together we should seek agreements. He agreed that a nuclear test ban was a priority but did not take up Gorbachev's proposal for a special summit. He suggested a discussion by experts on improving the monitoring of nuclear explosions more effectively as a basis for agreement at the next summit.

Reagan went on to summarize quite a number of what he described as "optimal yet real goals." He proposed agreements cutting the number of strategic weapons by half, leading toward the elimination of intermediate-range nuclear weapons, removing the threat of a nuclear first strike and of the deployment of offensive weapons of mass destruction in outer space; banning chemical warfare; devising a process to reach the peaceful settlement of regional conflicts; and improving the political atmosphere to broaden trade and economic cooperation.

Reagan's proposed timetable for us was to reach concrete agreements on the key elements during the current year, thus making it possible to negotiate the formal agreements by the next summit meeting scheduled for 1987. That in turn would allow time for ratification before the 1988 presidential election campaign, after which Reagan would have to leave office. Besides, these agreements would constitute a kind of scheme to implement the first stage of Gorbachev's proposals of January 15, 1986. He also said he was ready to work in a constructive manner on a reduction in the armed forces in Central Europe and more effective confidence-building measures.

Reagan conducted the conversation peacefully and benevolently; if anyone doubted that his time in office had radically changed the attitude and method of this fierce anti-communist crusader in dealing with the Soviet Union, those doubts should be removed by this record of his conversation. He wound up by asking me to tell Gorbachev that he was looking forward to his first visit to the United States this year and hoped he would stay at least a week. He promised: "I'll accompany him personally during his tour of the country."

But however extensive his agenda and reasonable his manner, Reagan's summit agenda gave no explanation of how to approach the important problems he raised. It also ignored what Reagan called defensive space weapons, the SDI and the ABM, which came to be the focus of the Reykjavik summit. His proposals did not represent a comprehensive program, only separate elements that left out important issues. All this I told Reagan, assuring him that everything he said would be reported to Gorbachev personally and that he would reply. I repeated to him the essence of Gorbachev's message asking for an end to sharp anti-Soviet rhetoric and urging careful summit preparation instead of "improvisation" at the highest level.

Nevertheless President Reagan—probably for the first time in our dialogue with him—demonstrated that he recognized that summits should have a broad agenda and that he should be personally involved in the deliberations. It was a good omen. But at the same time his thoughts were not concentrated on a minimal practical agenda and a sense of priority. Once again all the preparatory work for the summit was left to improvisation at the last moment. Gorbachev for his part grew impatient for a meeting, gambling on making a major gain. When they arrived at Reykjavik there was only one item: nuclear and space weapons. But it had not been thoroughly prepared, and no compromises were in the minds of either side. Everything was left for two leaders to discuss and solve by themselves. And they failed.

After the formal conversation the president asked me to stay and talk privately with him. Reagan said it appeared that both leaders had to give an additional push to preparing the summit. One way was to intensify the negotiations in various forums and in particular to involve Shultz and Shevardnadze more personally. Another would be finally to operate a strictly confidential channel, which had proven useful in preparing for Geneva. But Reagan did not give any idea of how the new channel would work; I was going back to Moscow, and he promised to think about how to revive it, but that never happened after I left Washington. One reason was that our ambassadors were changed too often—four in the next five years of the remaining Reagan and succeeding Bush presidency.

The president walked with me to my car. He clearly wanted to give me as much attention as possible by the highest standards of protocol. We had developed good personal chemistry between us during the previous six years. He asked me again to give his regards to Gorbachev, whom he hoped to see in the United States even before the end of the year. "We've got something to talk about," he said, once again wishing me success in my new position. I still keep a White House photograph of the scene sent to me by Reagan. The president and I are walking down the path from the Oval Office through the White House garden. We are talking pleasantly and behind us are my two diplomatic comrades-in-arms, Aleksandr Bessmertnykh and Oleg Sokolov.

Gorbachev had sent a personal message to Reagan expressing his appreciation of "the activity of A. F. Dobrynin as Soviet Ambassador in Washington for many years and his vigorous efforts in establishing good mutual relations between our peoples." Reagan gave me a photograph of us together with our wives in the White House with his own inscription. Richard Nixon sent me a warm letter saying that "not a single ambassador of all those I have known for forty years served his country with more devotion than you. . . . But for your activity, it would have been impossible to develop new mutual relations between our countries that culminated in the 1972 summit." Jimmy Carter sent me his new book inscribed "To my friend Anatoly Dobrynin." Robert Byrd, the Senate majority leader, gave a rather extraordinary lunch in my honor attended by leading senators, both Democratic and Republican: Sam Nunn, Claiborne Pell, Edward Kennedy, Strom Thurmond, John Warner, Joseph Biden, and others. Then he sent me a kind personal letter.

There were many other farewell meetings, conversations, lunches, and receptions. Our embassy staged a farewell reception attended by administration officials, members of Congress, the diplomatic corps, public and political figures, businessmen, newspaper columnists, and reporters—all my broad circle of friends, acquaintances, and business contacts I had made over so many years. Shultz made a warm speech, and I gave my farewell speech.

It left me a bit sad, having to say good-bye to everybody, to my embassy, and to end the many years in Washington, full of work, moving personal experiences, and unforgettable impressions. It was hard to part with all of that. I spent my last night at the embassy almost without sleep. After all, it was not easy to say good-bye to twenty-four years of being ambassador to such a difficult but wonderful country.

## Ronald Reagan and Soviet-American Relations

Through the succession of American administrations during the latter two-thirds of this century runs an irregular but wavelike line characterizing their attitudes toward the Soviet Union. Franklin D. Roosevelt cemented the Soviet-American alliance during World War II. Truman symbolized the start of the Cold War which escalated during his presidency. Eisenhower sought to ease confrontation by the end of his term. Kennedy had to undergo the Cuban missile crisis to start searching for detente. Under Johnson, our relations were marked by instability but not confrontation. Under Nixon, detente developed and reached its culmination. Ford's presidency was characterized by uncertainty, although a certain measure of the status quo was preserved. Under Carter the foundations of detente were shaken, and this brought about its collapse. Reagan's first term, from 1981 to 1984, can be characterized as a period linked to a deep crisis in the policy of detente. In simple terms, the dissatisfaction with detente in the United States in the late 1970s gradually led to the confrontation of the early 1980s, but thereafter signs appeared of a possible turn toward a crisis-free period in our relations. Ultimately, Reagan's achievements in dealing with the Soviet Union could certainly compare favorably with, and perhaps even surpass, those of Richard Nixon and Henry Kissinger.

The contradictions inherent in Ronald Reagan's character and policies are a permanent subject of controversy. He was the most unusual American president in the postwar history of our relations. My compatriots perceived him as a peculiar yet vague political leader. Ordinary Soviet citizens found it hard to digest the transformation of the warmonger and enemy into a pleasant man strolling hand in hand in Red Square with the general secretary of the Communist Party and concluding a number of important agreements with the Soviet Union on limiting strategic arms. Few in the West were prepared to understand it, either.

It is worth examining the paradox of Ronald Reagan. It is a fascinating story of how Reagan's vision of nuclear apocalypse and his deeply rooted but almost hidden conviction that nuclear weapons should ultimately be abolished, would ultimately prove more powerful than his visceral anticommunism.

When Reagan took office, there was no question in Moscow whether detente or confrontation was the preferable policy no matter what his record was. The Soviet leadership clearly preferred the detente of the 1970s. Nor was there any debate on that subject in Soviet public opinion. The question facing the Politburo in the first half of the 1980s was not whether to choose between detente or confrontation, but what course the Reagan administration itself would adopt and how we could meet the challenge. Despite successive changes in the Soviet leadership during Reagan's first term as president, Moscow continued its attempts to renew the process of detente and limit armaments, all the while criticizing the United States for its refusal to follow the course of detente, arms control, and negotiations. The Reagan administration openly and enthusiastically chose confrontation over detente and military superiority over arms limitations. The actions of the Soviet Union during that period were dictated by the need to react to Reagan's aggressive posture to a much greater degree than the West was prepared to admit.

I must confess that from the very beginning I was intrigued by President Reagan's psychology in general and his attitude toward the Soviet Union and its leaders in particular. It was a problem of almost mathematical complexity, the more so because our minds were unquestionably dominated by his anti-Soviet image. What attracted my attention and puzzled me somewhat was the apparent incompatibility of the hostile policies he proclaimed toward the Soviet Union with some things he did or said in his private contacts with Soviet leaders and me that were completely unknown to the American public and even the political establishment.

For instance, Reagan saw nothing contradictory in publicly—and I think sincerely—attacking the Soviet Union as the evil empire and describing its leadership in rather uncomplimentary terms, while in the next moment writing personal letters in his own hand to the general secretary of the Soviet Communist Party very privately expressing his desire for a nonnuclear world, better Soviet-American relations, and a summit meeting with the world's chief communist and atheist. There is no reason to believe he was not just as sincere in these wishes. But at the same time I am not sure he fully realized or even cared that his loose anti-Soviet rhetoric, which was occasionally unreasonable and even wanton, caused serious damage to our relations. All those things combined incomprehensibly yet harmoniously in his mind. He gave the impression that he did not give much thought to those contradictions, nor that he much cared how they would look to the Soviet leadership.

At the initial stage of his presidency Moscow regarded Reagan's ways as the behavior of a convinced enemy. Information or assurances about his intentions to improve relations were not considered as serious but as deceptive and exclusively designed for propaganda purposes. Even Reagan's attempts to sound out the views of the Soviet leadership concerning a probable summit, which were made privately at the end of his first term, were received with skepticism in the Kremlin, where they were dismissed as an electoral maneuver.

The Reagan administration moved bit by bit from its opening stance of uncompromising confrontation toward hesitant attempts to open a diplomatic dialogue from 1984 to 1986. During his 1984 campaign for reelection Reagan made several speeches stressing the need to combine force with dialogue or negotiations with the Soviet Union. He privately discussed the subject of a possible summit. Reagan began to understand the danger of basing foreign policy solely on ideology; he combined militancy with a growing degree of pragmatism toward the Soviet Union, and his main diplomatic principle became negotiation from strength. In September of 1984 Reagan told the UN General Assembly session: "America has restored its might. . . . We are prepared for constructive negotiations with the Soviet Union." After Reagan's reelection and Gorbachev's accession to power, the dialogue about their possible meeting intensified. Yet despite all these contradictions, their face-to-face meeting in Geneva in 1985 was successful enough to give important impetus to a new process of detente, the old process having been destroyed by Carter and then by Reagan himself.

One of the keys to the puzzle of this unique personality was that opponents and experts alike clearly underestimated him. The president proved to be a much deeper person than he first appeared. There is no denying that Reagan had a poor conception of our relations and did not like examining their intricacies, especially those concerning arms negotiations, or that his ideological prejudices sometimes prevented him from realistic assessments and pushed him toward damaging confrontational rhetoric. Yet he struck it lucky, and more often than any other president. His supposedly guileless personality also helped him to get away with many things; he fully deserved the nickname of the "Teflon president" conferred on him by admiring Americans.

Reagan was endowed with natural instinct, flair, and optimism. His imagination supported big ideas like SDI. He presented his own image skillfully, and it appealed to millions. In no small measure it was rooted in his confident and promising nature, which was not necessarily prompted by wisdom and knowledge but by personal conviction and character. He skillfully manipulated public opinion by means of strong illustrative catchwords that oversimplified complex questions and therefore flew straight over the heads of the professionals into the hearts and minds of the millions, for good or ill. Not infrequently he was accused of trying to apply a primitive approach that made him reluctant to examine questions properly and conscientiously. These accusations were largely justified.

But his overriding strength lay in his ability, whether deliberate or instinctive I was never quite sure, to combine the incompatible in the outward simplicity of his approach and in his conviction that his views were correct, even if they were sometimes erroneous or untenable. The point is, he knew they were nevertheless supported by the population and by his own evident stubborn and even dogged determination to put his ideas into effect.

Consider, for example, his successful defense of the zero option for medium-range missiles in Europe. When he first made his proposal to wipe all of them out, no one believed the idea would last, not even the Americans. It appeared too biased in America's favor to be acceptable to anyone. But Reagan stuck to his guns against all Soviet attempts to block the deployment of the American missiles by diplomatic negotiation, propaganda pressure on the West European public, and a long and fierce public debate. There is no escaping the fact that under this pressure Moscow gradually revised its views on general strategic parity and its approach to the negotiations on limiting nuclear missiles. More than that, the treaty was the first in history to actually *reduce* nuclear arms and not just limit them. In short, the Soviet leadership had to accept the zero option as it applied to its own SS-20s as the most suitable under the circumstances, although at the end of the day it meant that billions of rubles had been wasted because of our own hasty decision to deploy the missiles in the first place.

This example can hardly be described as embodying the general failure of arms control and a triumphant victory for Reagan's rearmament policy. In fact these problems would not have appeared at all, had it not been for Carter's and Reagan's own arms buildup, which pushed the Soviet Union into striving to preserve nuclear parity. This cost both countries enormously in military spending and seriously hampered our search to normalize our relations and the world situation and to reverse the arms race. Yet one of the moments at which strategists in the Soviet Union started to reconsider their positions was when Reagan announced his SDI program in 1983. We realized we were approaching a very dangerous situation in the strategic balance. Perhaps we overestimated the military significance of Star Wars, but its unveiling made us think about the situation once again and thus brought us closer to arms control.

Reagan's perseverance in demanding verification in the process of reducing nuclear arms—*doveryai no proveryai,* trust but verify, an incantation he never tired of repeating in Russian—also contributed to the development of joint control systems, which had been a stumbling block for Soviet leaders from Khrushchev to Chernenko.

Consider also the problem of the elimination of strategic missiles. Reagan sometimes shared with the public his dream of a world without them, but no one, not even the closest members of his entourage, took him seriously. His appeals were dismissed as rhetoric, and indeed they were not without propaganda content. But as it later transpired, Reagan really meant it. The whole world had a chance to see this when Reagan, much to his European allies' surprise and dismay, told Gorbachev in Reykjavik that under certain conditions he was ready for both nations to get rid of all their long-range nuclear missiles. It was both his fanatical conviction that SDI was not a bargaining chip and Gorbachev's intransigence that prevented them from reaching an agreement on major nuclear missile reductions. Gorbachev at that moment was far more alarmed by Reagan's commitment to SDI than he was encouraged by his unexpected readiness to make sharp reductions in nuclear arsenals. But it was at Reykjavik nevertheless that Gorbachev put away passion and decided that he could and would work with Reagan. He saw in him a person capable of taking great decisions, and Gorbachev himself told me so when we returned to Moscow.

A careful examination of Reagan's political career shows that he was essentially pragmatic and more flexible than his rhetoric would lead anyone to believe. That helps explain the turn in his policy toward the Soviet Union, which both his fondest supporters and most committed opponents believed unthinkable.

I do not think he made serious changes in his general ideological outlook. He evolved by gradually accepting the truth that in the real world of both the Soviet Union and the United States, important changes were taking place, and that one-sided confrontation was against the spirit of the time. Moreover, he realized his unbending opposition would hamper his own plans which, in the final analysis, were aimed at finding a proper place in American history by creating a safer world. And finally, whatever its huge cost, his rearmament program gave him the self-confidence to face the Soviet Union at the negotiating table.

Some Americans, especially those seeking to justify Reagan's enormous arms buildup and tough foreign policy, still maintain that it was the principal cause of the disintegration of the Soviet Union. I cannot agree with that. Reagan's second term coincided with the appearance of a new Soviet leader, Mikhail Gorbachev. Without Gorbachev, there is no way that the Cold War would have ended. But if Reagan had also been far-sighted enough to divine the Soviet Union's true motives and agreed to the disarmament treaties that were already on the table, that would have ended the Cold War without the crushing military expenditures he laid on the backs of the American people.

Instead, the four summit meetings between Reagan and Gorbachev became the important milestones as both leaders and their nations gradually changed direction. Both played their part in the turn. Reagan was followed by George Bush, who participated even more vigorously in improving our relations, and it was during that period that the Cold War ended. Our relations were even better at that point than during the first years of detente. The suspicious Soviet leadership became convinced that the road to international security lay through agreements with the United States on drastic reductions of nuclear and conventional weapons. The windows of opportunity for international cooperation were wide open. And then, suddenly, the Soviet Union disintegrated within days in 1991. Was it the result of foreign intervention or influence? Had the evil empire been brought down at last by the policies of the Reagan administration, as its supporters still believe?

Even under the worst possible scenario, which would have been the continuation of the Cold War and the arms race up to the very end of Reagan's presidency, the answer would still be no. Had the implacable pressure of an arms race continued, the Politburo under Gorbachev or anybody else who advocated a tough, militaristic policy would have had no lack of support from the military-industrial complex and, more important, from the whole country. If it had been necessary, the Soviet people would have fallen in with a massive rearmament program against a restored enemy number one in the United States. If the leaders of the Soviet Union had pictured the American military buildup as a threat to the existence of the nation, the Soviet people would have responded, I have no doubt about it, with patriotic understanding because all Russians bear the memory of the horrors of World War II—or what we call the Great Patriotic War. The Soviet Union was a totalitarian state, and it is unrealistic to believe that any political opposition would have been able to stage, let alone win, a debate over the relative merits of military versus civilian spending, especially against anything seen as a threat to the Motherland. Soviet citizens would have tightened their belts and seen it as part of a war for national survival.

Sadly for the ardent followers of Reagan, the increased Soviet defense spending provoked by Reagan's policies was not the straw that broke the back of the evil empire. We did not bankrupt ourselves in the arms race, as the Caspar Weinbergers of this world would like to believe. The Soviet response to Star Wars caused only an acceptable rise in defense spending. Throughout the Reagan presidency, the rising Soviet defense effort contributed to our economic decline, but only marginally, as it had in previous years. The troubles in our economy were the result of our own internal contradictions of autarky, low investment, and lack of innovation, as even Western economic specialists at the World Bank and elsewhere now believe.

It may sound like a historical paradox, in particular for Reagan's admirers, but if the president had not abandoned his hostile stance toward the Soviet Union for a more constructive one during his second term, Gorbachev would not have been able to launch his reforms and his "new thinking." Quite the contrary, Gorbachev would have been forced to continue the conservative foreign and domestic policies of his predecessors in defense of the nation against America. And who knows how the world then would have developed?

All this does not of course mean that the Cold War and the Reagan presidency had no impact on the Soviet Union, its economy, and its problems. They did. But it is senseless to consider the huge changes in the Soviet Union and then in Russia as the fulfillment of a scenario written in the interests of the United States. Ascribing any role, let alone a crucial one in the life of a nation, to the policy pursued by a particular American president would be a great exaggeration and indeed a historical error. The fate of the Soviet Union was decided inside our country, in which no small part was played by Mikhail Gorbachev himself, its first and last president.

All great powers from the Roman to the British Empire have disintegrated because of internal strife and not because of pressure from abroad. Nobody won the Cold War, and both sides paid a great price, but the end of the Cold War is our common victory.

# AFTER
# WASHINGTON

# I. Gorbachev: The First and Last President of the Soviet Union

The Soviet Union that Gorbachev inherited in 1985 was a global power, perhaps somewhat tarnished in that image, but still strong and united and one of the world's two superpowers. But in just three years, from 1989 to 1991, the political frontiers of the European continent were effectively rolled eastward from the center of Europe to the Russian borders of 1653, which were those before Russia's union with the Ukraine. How did all this happen?

The roots of the demise of the Soviet Union must be found mainly at home, in our political struggles, in our incompetent but highly ambitious leaders, and in the unbelievably quick chain of domestic events in which the great majority of the population did not participate and still does not really understand. These dramatic and tragic days in the history of my country await a thorough and impartial study, but I will briefly tell my part of the story as I lived it.

## Life as a Secretary

On the first day after I returned to Moscow from the United States in March of 1986 to become a secretary of the party, I felt as if I were in a very special world. I was visited by a representative of the Ninth KGB Department, which provided members of the Politburo and Party Secretariat not only with security but with all kinds of services. As a secretary of the party, I learned that I was allocated four personal bodyguards, a large ZIL limousine with a radio telephone, and a state-owned country house in Sosnovy Bor; it was appropriately called "Sosnovka," that is, "The Pines." The house had its own staff: three cooks, four waitresses, two gardeners, and a guard.

I was greatly surprised to learn that this particular house used to belong to the famed Marshal Georgi Zhukov, to whom it was given by Stalin during World War II. After Khrushchev dismissed him from his post of defense minister, the marshal lived there till his death. It was a spacious two-story building with a large dining room, living room, library, and several bedrooms, and even its own room for screening movies. On the premises there were a tennis court, a sauna, and a greenhouse, as well as a fruit garden. All this was more than sumptuous by Moscow standards or, indeed, by the standards of my life as an ambassador.

For their trips around the country and abroad, all of the approximately twenty-five members of the Politburo and the Party Secretariat were free to use a special squadron of airplanes. Each of us had two local and one international "hot line," through which we could get in touch with any Soviet official wherever he might be. There was also a special, well-protected telephone network among ourselves.

The weekly Politburo meetings were held regularly on Thursdays, and sometimes Gorbachev called urgent meetings. With rare exceptions, these meetings were attended by all party secretaries, who had a right to take part in a discussion, but not to vote. Not that the Politburo often resorted to voting; when the general secretary sensed impending discord, he would suggest that we "finalize" the issue in question at a later meeting, using this time to pressure dissenting members into accepting his position.

Gorbachev reveled in rhetoric and would speak extensively on nearly every issue. As a result a meeting that had started at 11 A.M. might end at 6 or even 8 P.M. Everyone who had something to say was given the floor. Gorbachev was a dynamic individual and usually dominated the Politburo meetings, the more so as there were few who would seriously want to contradict a general secretary. When he presided, as he did at all Politburo meetings, his mental outlook and his logic were impressive, and he usually succeeded in making the Politburo accept his decisions eventually, although he was not an authoritarian ruler and had to take into account the general mood. Yet, he met with no direct or organized opposition in the Politburo. One person stood out for his independent conduct, Boris Yeltsin, the then secretary of the Moscow party committee. He could stubbornly defend his viewpoint although he usually preferred to keep silent, especially when the issue under discussion was not directly connected with his area of authority. Still, one felt some apprehension by Gorbachev toward Yeltsin, whom the general secretary had previously promoted.

During the regular recess of thirty minutes to an hour, all those present would dine together at a long table in one of the Kremlin halls. One could choose between just two simple menus without any elaborate dishes and without liquors (only tea and coffee were served). The conversation would center on the news and the topics of the day.

No official records of the Politburo meetings were kept, although Gorbachev's aide would confidentially make some notes. Politburo decisions were issued in the form of official documents and circulated to a restricted

list of officials for implementation and oversight. They were kept in the secretary general's department filed in a "special folder."

The agenda was always made up by the general secretary himself.
Politburo members had a right to propose additional items and changes but
seldom did so. The discussion papers were distributed a day or two before
the meeting by the General Department of the Central Committee, the
principal executive body under the general secretary.

This General Department had a special place in the Central
Committee's apparatus. It was headed by those closest to the general secretary. For Gorbachev, it was Anatoly Lukjanov and later Valery Boldin.
Lukjanov was an intelligent and friendly man, but Boldin was known as a
haughty, narrow-minded mandarin, who, to many people's surprise, exer-
cised some influence on Gorbachev. (Boldin showed his real face when he
not only took part in the August putsch of 1991 but came to Foros, the vacation retreat where Gorbachev was confined, at the head of the delegation
that brought an ultimatum to his former benefactor.) Boldin had daily access
to Gorbachev, commenting on his mail and providing his chief with the latest news and rumors about the *nomenklatura,* which was our word for the list
of those who really ran the country. It was he who recommended the agenda
for Politburo meetings, which was then reviewed and approved by
Gorbachev.

Formally, Gorbachev had no deputy in the Politburo, yet his de facto
number two was Yegor Ligachev, who stayed by Gorbachev until he abandoned him at the end of his rule. Ligachev managed the party's everyday
business and thus assumed substantial nationwide influence. He presided at
all Secretariat meetings.

Ligachév was also in charge of ideology, assisted by Aleksandr Yakovlev,
another secretary of the party. Ligachev was orthodox, never wavering in his
adherence to principles of Marx and Lenin. At the beginning of my work in
the Secretariat Gorbachev told me frankly that he valued Ligachev's talent as
a party organizer, which relieved him of routine business. But as for ideology
and cultural development, Gorbachev said, Ligachev was "not exactly an innovator" because his overall theoretical learning was far from substantial. Yet
he was perfectly capable of preserving the ideological purity of the party.

These shortcomings of Ligachev were subsequently used by Aleksandr
Yakovlev who won Gorbachev's confidence and, being an intelligent and
well-educated person, established a high intellectual level in his private conversations with the general secretary. This enabled Yakovlev to become
Gorbachev's trusted conversation partner and to infiltrate Ligachev's ideological domain.

As a result of his maneuvering, Yakovlev managed to gain control over the ideology, which was ultimately entrusted to him after Gorbachev made him a full-fledged Politburo member and his closest associate. Yakovlev became Gorbachev's mastermind of the political reforms in the party and the country, which, in a historic paradox, sapped Gorbachev's power and ultimately bankrupted him politically.

Gorbachev himself never remained too close or too long with any of his associates. He could easily abandon a former colleague, leaving him bitter and disappointed. It was not by accident that after his fall, not a single one of the Politburo members defended the former general secretary and president.

There was no personal friendship among the Soviet leaders, neither did their families maintain close contact. To some extent, this can be explained by the psychological factor of being constantly accompanied and monitored by the KGB. We all met only at official parties devoted to national holidays, or at dinners in honor of high-ranking foreign guests, or at annual dinners given by the Gorbachevs at their summer place near Yalta in the Crimea. All Politburo members and party secretaries who happened to be vacationing at the resort were always invited.

The wooden house where these dinners took place had been built for Stalin on the territory of the summer residence of Czar Alexander III. The atmosphere at dinner was quite amicable. The only thing that somewhat spoiled it was the tradition for everyone in turn to pronounce a toast to the general secretary and his spouse. Gorbachev seemed to like it. Gromyko, the eldest among us, would be the first to start the ceremony with a solemn but dull toast.

Gorbachev's major lever of power was his right to nominate top government, party, and military officials at Politburo meetings. This nomination was tantamount to the final appointment, for nobody wanted to contradict him. He tried to place his people everywhere.

Apart from approving the nominations, the Politburo discussed all kinds of questions of foreign and domestic policy, industrial development, and party affairs. Only military issues were not discussed in detail; for these there was a special restricted body, the Supreme Military Council, again headed by Gorbachev. Because of this, not all Politburo members were aware of what was going on in the military field. This perfectly suited the military-industrial complex, which covertly exerted its influence on the general secretary. As time went by, however, Gorbachev started to take the top brass in hand in a way that Brezhnev rarely if ever did.

## The International Department

When I was appointed as the head of the Central Committee's International Department I did not have a clear idea about its functions. It had a staff of about two hundred virtually covering the globe. I had thought the department played an active and important role in Soviet foreign policy, but I soon realized it dealt mostly with communist and other left-wing parties as well as radical international organizations and mass movements, both in the West and in the Third World. All contacts with the socialist countries of Eastern Europe were handled by a separate department of the Secretariat. I was surprised to discover the International Department was really not involved with Soviet foreign policy outside the Third World and would therefore come to prominence only occasionally, in such countries as Angola, Somalia, Ethiopia, Afghanistan, and so on. The department did not concern itself with our relations and negotiations with the United States and Western Europe and was not active in dealing with them. It was also outside the arms control process. I looked up the old charter of the department, which had been approved many years ago, and found it dealt only with similar parties in other countries. Nothing about foreign policy.

There were historical reasons for this. At the start of the Soviet regime Lenin declared there would be two policies—those of the Narkomindel (the Foreign Ministry) and the Comintern (the Communist International)—and when they did not contradict each other, they were to be pursued with equal fervor. But when they were in conflict, the ideological interests of the Comintern were to be subordinated to the normal foreign policy goals of the Soviet state as pursued by the Narkomindel. However, the two lines of policy were always present and often got mixed up in the minds of the Soviet leaders—suffice it to recall the tangle of our relations with Hanoi during the Vietnam War. Some policies were the direct result of ideology, and the propaganda associated with them did not always produce the best image of the intentions of the Soviet Union. Foreigners could easily ascribe to the Masters of Moscow some global conspiracy or sinister expansionist plot.

By inertia the International Department followed the line of the Comintern while the Foreign Ministry handled the foreign policy of the country.

I spoke with Gorbachev about the absurdity of this, and he asked me to draft a new charter reflecting his new policies. In May of 1986 I gave him a detailed memo with a draft charter, which he approved quickly. In addition to its traditional relations with foreign parties of the left, it was charged with maintaining and implementing the party line—that is, Gorbachev's new line—in "cardinal questions of foreign policy and questions of all international relations in general." To strengthen the department's new structure, I obtained Gorbachev's permission to transfer several diplomatic heavyweights and specialists from the Foreign Ministry, including Georgi Kornienko, who had been Gromyko's deputy and continued as first deputy to his successor as foreign minister, Eduard Shevardnadze. Kornienko became my first deputy. I was also joined by Vitaly Churkin, an able diplomat who later became deputy foreign minister. We also brought in some experts on arms control negotiations.

This was a good start to move us into foreign policy, and the department began to participate in negotiations with the United States and preparations for the Soviet-American summit meetings. I was personally entrusted with delicate missions that sent me to confidential talks with President George Bush in Washington, Chancellor Helmut Kohl in Bonn, Prime Minister Rajiv Gandhi in New Delhi, Fidel Castro in Havana, the Afghan leader Najibullah in Kabul, and others. Later I worked in the chancellery of the Soviet president. I visited the president of South Korea in Seoul and arranged for his meeting with Gorbachev in San Francisco. I also headed several Soviet delegations to international conferences, all of which kept me quite busy in my new career in Moscow.

Most important, this was the period when Gorbachev was beginning to formulate what he called his "new thinking" in foreign policy. On the eve of the Geneva summit of 1985, as I watched him, his mind was still fastened on some of the class mythology and ideology that obscured the world and led him into inconsistencies. But at Geneva he quickly realized the prime importance of constructive relations with the United States, and after Geneva he staked much on a direct dialogue with the Americans at the highest level, aiming first of all at agreements on mutual security and arms control.

## The Summit at Reykjavik

In 1986 Gorbachev emphasized the importance of maintaining "the spirit of Geneva" and announced his disarmament program for a "non-nuclear world by the year 2000." He wanted a second meeting with Reagan and was restless and impatient; during the previous year an active personal correspondence of more than twenty-five messages had developed between them. Gorbachev had enjoyed the great publicity he received from the summit. But this time he wanted a meeting with significant results. He mentioned it several times to the Politburo in the first half of 1986, but without going into details of what the agenda might be, although Star Wars was constantly on his mind as a potential obstacle to success.

By the end of February 1986 he confided to some of his assistants: "Maybe it is time to stop being afraid of SDI? The United States is counting on our readiness to build the same kind of costly system, hoping meanwhile that they will win this race using their technological superiority. But our scientists tell me that if we want to neutralize the American SDI system, we only would have to spend 10 percent of what the Americans plan to spend." He said this could be accomplished by building more intercontinental missiles instead of our own SDI system, which would cost more than 500 billion rubles, a huge sum.

But under the influence of our military-industrial complex, Gorbachev gradually began to revert to his insistence on Reagan's withdrawal from SDI as the condition for the success of a new summit on disarmament. He was persuaded that an SDI system would give the United States a first-strike advantage in nuclear conflicts.

No final decision on the summit had been taken by the Politburo by the time Gorbachev left for his summer vacation in the Crimea. While there he telephoned me—I was on vacation, too—to say that he decided to propose to Reagan that they meet during the autumn at some point between Moscow and Washington, perhaps London or Reykjavik. Their principal subject would be nuclear disarmament. Shevardnadze had already approved the idea, and Gorbachev was asking my opinion before submitting it to the Politburo.

I supported the idea but asked Gorbachev exactly what it was about nuclear disarmament that he wanted to discuss with Reagan. He answered that he intended to propose really deep cuts in strategic arms if the president would abandon SDI. I told him I was not so sure that Reagan would abandon his favorite project, but Gorbachev said he would insist on it. Who knows—he wondered—maybe Reagan would ultimately yield on SDI in exchange for the huge reductions in nuclear weapons he professed to want. If not, Gorbachev still hoped to gain worldwide publicity for his radical ideas on nuclear disarmament.

Gorbachev met Reagan in Reykjavik on October 11–12, 1986, and both came away bitterly disappointed.

The meeting itself was highly dramatic. For the first time in the history of our relations, there appeared the possibility of an agreement on the substantial reduction of strategic nuclear arms. Surprisingly, Reagan agreed to the idea of substantial cuts and even complete elimination of strategic missiles after a decade. But he refused to undertake obligations under the antiballistic missile treaty that could have prevented the United States from pursuing the Star Wars project. Gorbachev tried hard to persuade Reagan to moderate his position but without success.

One episode remains pinned in my memory. Gorbachev and Reagan had ended their long and heated negotiations at midnight without agreement and left the conference building together, walking in silence. They stopped to bid each other good-bye as they reached the president's car. I happened to be nearby and served as impromptu interpreter. A short conversation followed in the cold Icelandic night.

Gorbachev, his voice ringing with bitterness he could hardly hide, said: "Mr. President, you have missed the unique chance of going down in history as a great president who paved the way for nuclear disarmament."

Reagan replied gloomily, "That applies to both of us."

On the drive to the airport Reagan was silent for a long time. His chief of staff, Donald Regan, rode with him and later told me that the president finally broke the silence by saying: "Don, together with Gorbachev we were very close to agreement. It's a shame." Then he raised his thumb and index finger half an inch apart: "We were that close." The president was shattered.

At that very moment I was riding with Gorbachev to meet the press in a separate building. He was very angry with Reagan's stubbornness on SDI, which he considered the major reason for the failure of the meeting. Gorbachev was eager to denounce Reagan at his press conference; we who were with him were trying to calm him down. After a ride of ten or fifteen minutes he regained his self-control. He told us that he was going to criticize Reagan strongly, but he would not close the door to future meetings lest the press characterize the meeting as a total failure instead of the first step toward an agreement. It was a fair summary of the Reykjavik summit.

As an eyewitness at Reykjavik, I feel Gorbachev was no less responsible than Reagan for its failure because he held SDI hostage for the success of the meeting. He held good cards with impressive disarmament proposals, and he could have played them far better if he had not been as stubborn on SDI as Reagan. It could have been postponed for further consideration if they had reached agreement on a deep reduction of nuclear weapons, and as a matter of fact Gorbachev followed that bargaining strategy in later negotiations toward the end of the Reagan administration.

At the Politburo meeting to review Reykjavik, Gorbachev was still angry at Reagan but said the meeting with him was worthwhile after all. First, it showed to the world that the Soviet leadership was really prepared for serious discussion of disarmament; second, Reagan unexpectedly demonstrated his readiness to negotiate nuclear arms reduction; third, America's NATO partners in Europe would be critical of Reagan's insistence on continuing SDI at all costs while remaining ready to discuss nuclear arms reduction with Moscow but not consult them.

Gorbachev was in fact already looking toward his next meeting with

Reagan. The old guard in the Politburo and the military-industrial complex covertly opposed his "new thinking" and his plans for accommodation with the United States, but he overcame them by proclaiming his firm intention to carry out his new foreign policy, fully aware that he could count on the party and on the public support he then enjoyed.

## Gorbachev in a Hurry

Gorbachev's manner of handling the work of the Politburo was gradually changing. His style became more authoritarian and commanding. The discussion of foreign policy questions by the Politburo had undergone transformations under Gorbachev. Initially the agendas for all the meetings Gorbachev had scheduled with foreign leaders, especially the Americans, and whether in Moscow or abroad, were minutely discussed by the Politburo. Gromyko had usually presented the foreign ministry's discussion papers, drafts of documents to be signed, and other paraphernalia of such international meetings. But when Shevardnadze became foreign minister, fewer papers were presented or discussed. Gorbachev clearly strove to avoid Politburo guidelines and directives and sought a free hand in dealing with foreign heads of state. Ultimately, with Shevardnadze's help, Gorbachev reached his goal. In fact if not in form, he single-handedly devised the foreign policy of the country and implemented it as well.

This could clearly be seen from his personal handling of the strategic arms limitation talks with American Presidents Reagan and then Bush. Gorbachev increasingly improvised and without consulting our experts would agree to sudden compromises which were often regarded by our military as one-sided concessions to the Americans. One example of Gorbachev's style stands out in my memory.

In April of 1987 Secretary Shultz came to Moscow to negotiate with Gorbachev on Euromissiles. The Soviet leadership was prepared to trade off its SS-20 missiles and other weapons of its range for the comparable U.S. missiles that had been deployed in Europe since 1983. The Euromissiles we were discussing had ranges from 500 to 1,500 kilometers. Under the proposed deal both sides would destroy these intermediate-range missiles, but the military insisted on keeping our modern arsenal of more than one hundred SS-23s, with a range of only 400 kilometers. Before Shultz's arrival, Gorbachev had asked Marshal Akhromeyev and me to prepare a negotiating memo with a summary of both sides' positions. Akhromeyev specifically recommended that if Shultz tried to include the SS-23, Gorbachev should refuse because its range was below that covered in the treaty draft.

In our earlier negotiations, the American side attempted but did not press for including the SS-23s. But when Shultz arrived, he was more insistent on scrapping the new missiles. At first Gorbachev ignored this, but toward the end of the meeting, Shultz raised the SS-23 again. He stressed that if Gorbachev would agree to include these missiles, he could say with confidence that we would be very close to a treaty that could soon be signed in Washington at the coming summit meeting between Gorbachev and Reagan in Washington.

After a moment of hesitation, Gorbachev, to the great surprise of Akhromeyev and myself, said to Shultz, "It's a deal." He shook hands with Shultz, and the principals departed.

Akhromeyev was stunned and asked if I knew why Gorbachev had shifted his position at the last moment. I was as mystified as he was. The marshal turned and rushed to the general secretary's office. Half an hour later he returned and told me a bizarre story. When he asked Gorbachev why he had so suddenly ceded a whole class of missiles and gained nothing in exchange, Gorbachev first said that he had probably made a mistake because he "forgot the warning" in our memo. Akhromeyev then suggested that someone be dispatched quickly to Shultz, who had not yet left Moscow, to correct our position. Gorbachev became very angry and shouted at him: "Do you suggest that we tell the American secretary of state that I, the general secretary, am incompetent in military questions and that after correction from my generals I now am changing my position and going back on my word?"

That was the end of the story; normally Gorbachev had an excellent memory, and things like this did not slip his mind unless there was a reason. Akhromeyev strongly suspected that everything had been staged by Gorbachev because he knew the general staff did not want him to yield on the SS-23s, and the Politburo would support the military. For that reason, he preferred to present his concession to the leadership later as the removal of the final obstacle to the treaty.

Gorbachev was in Washington from December 8 to 10 for the third summit with Reagan, where he signed the treaty on intermediate missiles and again yielded a major point without any serious bargaining or consultation. Gorbachev agreed not only to destroy all our SS-20s deployed in Europe, but those in the Asian part of the Soviet Union as well. In Asia the SS-20s were part of our strategic defenses against China as well as the American bases in Japan and the Indian Ocean, so this certainly represented a major concession. Politically the treaty sent an important signal to the world that both superpowers tacitly and at long last recognized that the arms race did not strengthen their national security and that controlling their armaments did.

Gorbachev believed that his concessions would keep up the momentum of his foreign policy and the negotiations with the West. But our military command as well as some members of the political leadership were decidedly unhappy about Gorbachev's zeal in making deep concessions in order to achieve agreements with Washington. They also saw that Gorbachev was greatly encouraged by Shevardnadze, who was in permanent conflict with the Defense Ministry, a point not lost on Secretary of State Baker, as he discloses in his memoirs.

This struggle came to a head in the Politburo between Shevardnadze and the defense minister, Sergei Sokolov. The work of these ministries' joint committee on Soviet-American disarmament talks was at a dead end: the representatives of the departments followed their ministers' orders, which could not be harmonized. Shevardnadze constantly complained about the military to Gorbachev, who repeatedly had to reconcile the two parties.

Then Gorbachev put Lev Zaikov at the head of the joint ministerial committee preparing our positions for the disarmament negotiations, on which I served as a member. Zaikov, a Politburo member, had long dealt with the arms industry and had good relations with the military but as a party veteran was loyal to the general secretary. Nevertheless, Gorbachev had to talk to him privately and at length to win him over, and Zaikov maintained a reasonable balance between Shevardnadze and Sokolov. The commission began to move forward, but still not as fast as Gorbachev and Shevardnadze desired.

Gorbachev, though impatient, at first was cautious and wanted to avoid a direct clash with the military. Suddenly an extraordinary incident played right into his hands. On May 29, 1987, a small one-engine West German aircraft violated Soviet airspace undetected by the Soviet air defense system, reached Moscow, and made a sensational landing right in Red Square. The plane was flown by a young amateur pilot, Mathias Rust. This event shook the Soviet leadership, which had been convinced it was impossible to penetrate Soviet airspace without being caught. It left the Defense Ministry in complete disarray.

Gorbachev made perfect use of the military's state of confusion and its badly damaged prestige. On the day after Rust's landing, which was a Sunday, he called an urgent meeting of the Politburo. Opening the session, Gorbachev strongly condemned "the complete helplessness of the Defense Ministry, which still has to explain this extraordinary incident to the party and the people." He demanded immediate explanations from the ministry officials.

General Ivan Lushev, the deputy defense minister, reported to the Politburo and admitted that the event was, indeed, unheard of. He tried to justify the malfunctions in the air defense system by saying that it had been designed to intercept only modern military aircraft and was unable to detect a small plane flying at 150–170 kilometers an hour and at an altitude of not more then 300 or 400 meters. This did not sound very convincing, and Lushev had to admit that the sole responsibility for what happened lay with the Defense Ministry. Sokolov, the minister, acknowledged that the ministry had not developed any means of intercepting single low-altitude targets. He also admitted that the air defense units themselves were not operating in close cooperation.

After a heated debate Gorbachev took the floor. He spoke about the grave situation in the army whose top leaders were "apprehensive of the party's turn toward *perestroika* and the new thinking" and urged them to remedy the situation without delay. He urgently demanded stronger leadership at the defense ministry "to increase the military establishment's sense of political responsibility." Then turning to the defense minister, he said, "I don't question your personal integrity, Sergei Leonidovich. But under the present circumstances, if I were you, I would resign at once."

Sokolov, profoundly shaken, stood at attention and resigned on the spot. Gorbachev did not hesitate to accept the resignation "on behalf of the Politburo" adding that it would be announced as a retirement to ease the sting.

After a fifteen-minute break Gorbachev proposed appointing General Dmitri Yazov, Sokolov's deputy, as defense minister. He had already been summoned by arrangement with Gorbachev. At the time Yazov was in charge of the ministry's Personnel Department, so he was closely connected with the party's Central Committee. Yazov was far more obedient to Gorbachev than Sokolov, and thus Gorbachev accomplished a quiet coup. The new defense minister knew little about disarmament talks, and had nothing to do with them. With Yazov as defense minister, Shevardnadze felt much more at ease during the talks. Opposition by the military became more moderate. Sokolov was followed into retirement by about one hundred generals and colonels, conservative military leaders who also opposed Gorbachev's reforms and his concessions to the Americans. But the military establishment by and large remained discontented with Gorbachev, and this would show time and again.

Having gained control of the military establishment, Gorbachev became more active and confident in dealing with disarmament. He wanted to reach his objectives as soon as possible. He was fascinated by the huge challenge of the task and carried away by the cheering international audience. He began to believe in his own exceptional role in history, so he moved forward without seriously contemplating the consequences. Here lay his weakness. He was either unable or in too much of a hurry to think about the prospective turn of events. Very often, he did not have a detailed plan for implementing his designs, only a fascinating outline. At Politburo meetings, when someone expressed cautious concern about his rapid innovations, Gorbachev would cut him off for "contradicting the spirit of the new thinking and *perestroika*." What made him rush? Variety? A desire for a perpetually active foreign policy? Or was it a subconscious awareness that history gave him too little time for his reforms? Only he can answer these questions.

Before going to the UN General Assembly in New York in 1988 Gorbachev urgently pushed through the Politburo a bold unilateral reduction of our armed forces by half a million men. The domestic and foreign political effect of this demobilization was good, and Gorbachev himself was highly praised. But the Soviet government had no practical plans for reintegrating such a huge number of men into the civilian economy. Then in 1990 Gorbachev signed a treaty between the NATO and Warsaw Pact countries on conventional forces in Europe that demanded further deep reductions in our armed forces. Fine as it was in principle, this policy created a serious domestic crisis with the mass withdrawal of Soviet forces from Germany and Eastern Europe. The country was faced with the difficult problem of where to put the troops, and this tragic task was passed on later to the Russian Federation. Where would they live? What would they do? There was no winter housing for them, nowhere for their families to live but in the most elemental conditions. Gorbachev proved to be a poor organizer; thus the proper and indeed necessary idea of reducing the size of our army and bringing it home has proven a severe and lasting burden for the country because of clumsy planning.

As a result, the Soviet population—faced with drastic changes in Europe but no coherent explanation of them from its own government—was at first puzzled and then angry. Morale declined in the armed forces, and military and civilians alike wondered how the Soviet army, still seen as the European victors of World War II, could be rushed home as if it had simply been thrown out. This is an inglorious heritage of the Gorbachev era.

## Gorbachev, Bush, and Germany

From 1990, Gorbachev's popularity fell rapidly in the party, in the army, and among ordinary people; it was propelled further downward by the country's economic problems. Abroad, however, his popularity soared. Hadn't he played the leading role in the turn of Soviet foreign policy toward constructive new thinking? Without question. He also deserved credit for a rapid accommodation with the United States and an impressive process of negotiation that radically reduced nuclear and conventional arms.

But looking back, it now is clear that in its execution Gorbachev's diplomacy often failed to win a better deal from the United States and its allies. Outmaneuvered on the treaty to limit Euromissiles, Gorbachev also had to agree to a heavier burden of reductions and relocations of Soviet forces in the Treaty on Conventional Forces in Europe signed on June 14, 1991, in Vienna. The cost was paid in upheavals along Russia's troubled southern borders and in the Caucasus, where the number of Russian troops is limited and all attempts by Moscow to renegotiate this provision of the treaty have had little success.

The Strategic Arms Reduction Treaty (START I) signed at the Moscow summit on July 31, 1991, was basically a good treaty, but once again the military advantage went to Washington. More important, because of U.S. objections there were no commitments to observe the agreements limiting anti-ballistic missiles, long a goal of Soviet diplomacy. At first Gorbachev wanted to declare unilaterally that were the ABM Treaty to be violated, Moscow would feel free to drop its obligations under the START I Treaty, but then he decided not to complicate the signing ceremony. As a result, years after Ronald Reagan left office, voices were still heard in the United States proposing the revival of his favorite Strategic Defense Initiative.

In exchange for the generous Soviet concessions Gorbachev and his devoted lieutenant Shevardnadze offered the West, they could and should have obtained a more important role for the Soviet Union in European security and a stronger Soviet voice in European affairs. But they did not. Able but inexperienced, impatient to reach agreement, but excessively self-assured and flattered by the Western media, Gorbachev and Shevardnadze were not infrequently outwitted and outplayed by their Western partners. On occasion they went further than necessary in concessions in agreements on arms control, Eastern Europe, and German unification, without receiving something substantial in return. Gorbachev in addition distorted the mechanisms of Soviet diplomacy by running a kind of personal back channel with high American officials to avoid criticism by his colleagues in the Politburo and our corps of professional diplomats. They were increasingly kept in the dark. (The confidential channel I ran and all the deals struck on behalf of Moscow with Washington had to pass through the entire Politburo for discussion and approval.) From 1989 on, Soviet diplomacy became progressively less effective because of the urgent pressure of Gorbachev's domestic political agenda and his efforts to sustain his weakening reputation at home by what appeared to be successes abroad. The result was a dramatic reduction in our capacity to adapt to the fast-changing international environment, provoked in no small degree by Gorbachev himself.

The role of the International Department of the party also diminished after its brief revival in 1986. It gradually returned to its old role. In 1988

Gorbachev ordered the department to explain the meaning of his reforms to communist parties and other foreign organizations and movements "because they do not understand them and are confused." But we were confused, too.

No small part in the downgrading of this department was played by Shevardnadze, who wanted to monopolize foreign policy and avoid competition from our department. Thus the department, and I as its head, were no longer actively involved in foreign policy on an everyday basis. From time to time Gorbachev used me as his personal adviser on Soviet-American relations, especially for his remaining meetings with Reagan and then George Bush. He occasionally sent me as his personal representative to discuss matters confidentially with high American officials up to the president, but I was no longer systematically involved in Soviet-American affairs. These and other major issues of foreign policy were handled by virtually only two men: Gorbachev and Shevardnadze.

Gorbachev began to emerge as a virtual monarch bypassing the traditional policy-making institutions and increasingly making important decisions by himself and directing the nation's course abroad with the eager assistance of Shevardnadze. Ironically, by that time Bush and his Secretary of State James Baker also were operating U.S. foreign policy in an intensely personal and informal fashion, interacting freely with foreign leaders face to face or by telephone. Neither the American president nor the Soviet general secretary seemed to feel the need to consult their governments or explain to their people the full direction and import of their policies, which were shaping the future of the world after the Cold War.

At the core of Gorbachev's foreign policy stood the sound priority of values common to all countries—preventing nuclear catastrophe and ending the Cold War. This did not deny the existence of national interests in our diplomacy, and its general restructuring along these lines provided the necessary flexibility and imagination to overcome old dogmas. The majority of the Soviet diplomatic corps welcomed this with enthusiasm, as I did.

But soon they became confused and frustrated. Gorbachev frequently frittered away the negotiating potential of the Soviet state. His practical interpretations of what he publicly characterized as "the interests of all mankind" were increasingly transformed into personal decisions that ignored important Soviet interests for the sake of hasty agreements with the West. Few Russians were prepared to forgive him for this, especially as the West certainly did not forget its own interests. On March 13, 1989, shortly after George Bush's assumption of the presidency, the National Security Council adopted a confidential document stating that U.S. policy toward the Soviet Union should not be aimed at "assisting" Gorbachev but at dealing with the Soviet Union so "as to push it into the direction desirable for us."*

And the Bush administration pushed it quite successfully. Arms control aside, Washington together with Bonn managed to extract important concessions from Gorbachev in the vital areas of German reunification and European security, as the two blocs that had divided Europe for forty years in a system that had provided the foundation for Soviet security policy, began collapsing along with the Berlin Wall at the end of 1989.

Much earlier in that year our Ministry of Foreign Affairs actively began exploring new ideas to discuss with the West on global and regional security systems. We thought they should exist worldwide within the framework of the United Nations, and in Europe as a regional system within the framework of the Conference on Security and Cooperation. This was a general goal of Soviet policy, especially in Europe, and Gorbachev was fully behind it. He enthusiastically developed his own image for the idea of regional security—a "common European home" where all the nations of Europe would live together peacefully in condominium apartments, so to speak, with the United States and Canada on the same street if not the same building. Washington did not share his enthusiasm but did not object publicly. It occupied itself exploring quietly with its allies the possibility of reunifying Germany.

Gorbachev met President Bush at their first summit meeting at Malta on December 2 and 3, 1989. German reunification was officially not on the agenda. Just before his arrival at Malta Gorbachev declared at his press conference in Italy that German reunification could be considered in the "distant future but as of now it does not have any urgency. Nobody should push or impose this question. History will decide it." But the idea was on everyone's mind because the Berlin Wall had come down less than a month before and East and West Germans were mingling freely for the first time in half a century. Bush cautiously sounded out Gorbachev on reunification in casual conversation. (This was Bush's favored method of starting a negotiation; he would gently trail an idea past his partner without pressure, sometimes try it again, and wait to see if he got a bite.)

Gorbachev responded in a general way that our policy was founded on our adherence to an all-European process and the evolutionary construction of a "common European home" in which the security interests of all countries

---

* Michael Beschloss and Strobe Talbott, *At the Highest Levels: The Inside Story of the End of the Cold War* (Boston: Little, Brown, 1993), p. 92.

should be respected. But he did not specify how it could or should be done, although he had with him a confidential memorandum by our Foreign Ministry outlining a concrete policy: German reunification should be the final product of a gradual transformation of the climate in Europe during which both NATO and the Warsaw Pact would shift their orientation from military to political and be dissolved by mutual agreement. There were no more discussions about German unification in Malta, but it was important for Bush and for the West in general that Gorbachev had not rejected unification as a subject for discussion—as both Washington and Bonn feared we might.

No less important for the future of Eastern Europe was a casual confirmation by Gorbachev to Bush that "the Brezhnev doctrine is dead." This remark was interpreted by the American leadership as a very important assurance by Gorbachev that the Soviet Union would not defend the socialist system in Eastern Europe by force. But it was said when no concrete steps had been taken to create a new, balanced security system throughout the whole of Europe. Who knows? Perhaps that was the moment when, in the secrecy of the chanceries of the West, the contentious idea of moving NATO eastward was conceived.

Did Gorbachev understand the potential danger of such unilateral assurances before there was any chance to trade German unification for a concept of all-European security? This undermined the balance of power and stability in Europe. Did Bush charm him with promises not to take advantage of the Soviet Union's own weakened position in Eastern Europe? Or was he charmed by what he saw as the success of his own policy of "new thinking" toward the West? But the fact remains that at that decisive moment he stood aside from the upheavals in Eastern Europe. "What is happening there," he declared to the Politburo on January 2, 1990, "should not push us aside from our course, neither in thought nor in action."

Within a week after Malta Bush sent Gorbachev a personal message again raising the question of the reunification of Germany. The president wrote that it should proceed under a process of self-determination without prejudging how the Germans themselves would decide, and be part of a growing integration of the European community that would be "peaceful, gradual and carried on in the framework of an evolutionary process."

So both sides actually agreed that German unification was part of a general process that would lead to a new form of European security and stability, which for forty years had been guaranteed by the firm structure of two opposing blocs in balance. This position in favor of evolutionary change to a new all-European system was supported by the Politburo and our European and German experts. Disagreement with the West remained concerning what politico-military structure would replace NATO and the Warsaw Pact, and what would be the status of a united Germany. But then there was a metamorphosis in Gorbachev's behavior. Amid turbulent events at home, he began to waver and handle all the negotiations on Germany virtually by himself or in tandem with Shevardnadze, sweeping aside our professional diplomats and scarcely informing the Politburo, who still favored an evolutionary process. Under Western pressure through confidential channels, he began to uncouple German unification from the general problem of European security.

True, during his summit meeting with Bush in Washington on May 31 to June 2, 1990, he tried to improvise by coming up with ideas of neutralizing a united Germany or offering it simultaneous membership in both NATO and the Warsaw Pact, while the two blocs would gradually merge their structures. But his hesitations soon ended. As Western countries intensified the pressure for unification and his domestic reforms began stalling, Gorbachev began yielding his position, banking on cooperation with the West as his best chance to survive and consolidate his authority at home. By the end of his meeting with Bush in Washington, Gorbachev suddenly agreed to permit Germany itself to decide whether to remain in NATO as a united nation, which was tantamount to Moscow's acceptance of what would soon be an established fact. Even Baker, as he writes in his memoirs, saw that this concession "shocked the rest of the Soviet delegation," and he attributes it to Gorbachev's personal relationship with Bush.

To the surprise of the West, during a blitz meeting with Chancellor Helmut Kohl in July of 1990 at a remote vacation area of the Caucasus far from public attention, Gorbachev removed all his conditions and agreed to Germany's membership in NATO as a unified nation, even though there was still fairly strong opposition within the Politburo. I was later told by one of President Bush's assistants that Kohl was, in his own words, stunned by Gorbachev's sudden agreement. The German chancellor, like the West as a whole, had been prepared for prolonged and difficult discussions with Gorbachev and had come prepared with several fallback positions on different parts of any deal. On the flight home he and his entourage celebrated this historic event, which had been totally unexpected so early in the bargaining. Washington did not conceal its pleasure either. The issue of German unification was of paramount importance to the Americans, and they also had been expecting hard bargaining with Moscow. So I was later told by Bush, Baker, Kissinger, and other prominent Americans.

Thus what was to have been a gradual process of evolution took Gorbachev only half a year. Why did he rush it? He of course correctly understood that the reunification of Germany was historically inevitable. But the process had to be completed in such a way as to ensure the security and stability of the Soviet Union and the whole of Europe. After all, Germany started two world wars. Under pressure at home and abroad, his main aspiration remained a new Europe built on the cooperation between the Soviet Union and the West. After the rapid reunification of Germany, the consequence was a dramatic narrowing of Soviet options and a significant reduction in Moscow's ability to shape its mode of adjustment to new and quickly changing circumstances.

At the start Gorbachev had the right idea: the unification of Germany should be synchronized with the formation of a new security structure for Europe. But he did not fight for this grand design, especially as the regimes in Eastern Europe began to crack and the region grew increasingly unstable. In fact he did not try to translate this grand strategy into concrete action, and although it may be difficult to believe, did not even discuss this troublesome situation as a whole in the Politburo as change shook the Warsaw Pact countries. He was completely frustrated by events. Lacking any strategy of their own, his confused colleagues—some angry, some merely passive—watched as one by one these countries broke loose from the iron frame of a political and military alliance that, however hated it may have been, had held their ethnic and other self-destructive conflicts in check for two generations. The discussions in the Kremlin were chaotic and dominated by Gorbachev's empty rhetoric. He accused the communist leaders of Eastern Europe of failing to reform and adapt themselves to "new thinking." Sometimes on the spur of the moment he hurried to visit those leaders and lectured them, but this only expedited the disintegration of the local regimes, especially in the German Democratic Republic.

I believe that Gorbachev never foresaw that the whole of Eastern Europe would fly out of the Soviet orbit within months or that the Warsaw Pact would crumble so soon. He became the helpless witness to the consequences of his own policy. Our worried general staff sounded the alarm over this disintegration to the Politburo and to Gorbachev and asked how to deal with the security problems. The Kremlin as a whole was confused; there were no contingency plans for such disintegration. Military intervention was ruled out. Gorbachev desperately repeated his main theme of a joint search with the West for a new security system in a "new Europe." But Gorbachev had thrown away his best card in rushing to agree to German reunification and the West was not in a hurry to help him.

By 1989 Shevardnadze privately held much more pessimistic views than Gorbachev. At one point while the foreign minister was vacationing on the Black Sea in Georgia, his personal assistant reported to him about an urgent cable from Nicolae Ceausescu, the Romanian president, who demanded a Warsaw Pact military intervention in Poland because the anti-communist party Solidarity had won the national elections. Moscow promptly refused, but there on the beach a melancholy Shevardnadze said to his surprised assistant that inevitably Moscow would lose control of the Warsaw Pact and more than that, the logic of events would force the breakup of the Soviet Union, especially the secession of the Baltic republics. One of his collaborators from Georgia later remarked that he was never very fond of the Soviet Union anyway and that deep in his heart what he had always wanted was independence for his native Georgia and to be the head of that country.

In Washington, neither the Reagan nor the Bush administrations were especially optimistic about Gorbachev's chances of succeeding with his reforms. During her visit to Moscow in the spring of 1987 Margaret Thatcher remarked casually to Gorbachev that some high officials she had recently visited in Washington considered *perestroika* a misstep that could disrupt the entire economic structure of such a big country, especially if Gorbachev moved too quickly. She counseled caution—even she had run into trouble privatizing British state industries—but she wished him luck. Reporting this to the Politburo, Gorbachev joked about those unnamed "ultraconservative" Americans but added that they might have a point, and in any case he thought it would take at least fifteen to twenty years to reorganize the Soviet economy. But this was only an afterthought, because he did not act on it.

Early in 1989, as part of the preparations for his first full summit at Malta, Gorbachev had sent me to Washington with a personal letter to Bush and instructions to discuss summit topics with the new president, whom I had known for twenty years. (Gorbachev had first met Bush in December of 1988 at a lunch organized by Reagan, who was ending two terms in office. Gorbachev hoped to talk with the president-elect, but they only managed to have a short private conversation—I was the interpreter—because Reagan stole the show. They agreed to start an active private communication.) Bush confessed to me that the recent "turbulent events" in the Soviet Union had prompted him to review Soviet history for a greater understanding of the Communist Party's role in the power structure of the nation. The president asked me a "not a very diplomatic, but a very direct question"—would Gorbachev be able to survive these tumultuous times? He wanted Gorbachev as his negotiating partner but was unsure about Gorbachev's political future. Bush inquired about the legal and judicial means, and the political rules and traditions, that could ensure Gorbachev's continued leadership "irrespective of some sudden party decision" of the kind that deposed Khrushchev. He apologized for the intrusive nature of his question and assured me he would not divulge the contents of the conversation to anyone.

I told Bush that he was right about the complexity of the situation; *perestroika* was creating instability and that made it hard to take a long view. Gorbachev, I said, had just been elected president, and not even the supreme organs of the party now could dismiss him from that post and deprive him of his powers. But the situation was unique and many things were unclear because the party was always the ultimate power in the country. So what would happen now? It looked like Gorbachev would remain Bush's partner in foreign policy at least in the near future, and as such was willing to conclude far-reaching agreements with the United States, especially in disarmament.

Two days later Bush gave me a handwritten letter for Gorbachev stressing the importance of their personal contacts and "the significance of *perestroika* not only for the Soviet people but for his own children and grandchildren." Bush had evidently decided to count on Gorbachev.

But in fact Gorbachev's dominance of events was nearing its end. During his first four years in power, he was the unquestionable leader of his country, and until the end of 1989 he retained a degree of control over the forces of change he had so boldly set in motion. But by 1990 the situation in the Soviet Union had deteriorated, and Gorbachev began to feel he was losing ground. He sought desperately to strengthen his position and, although it is not well known, he spared no effort to secure financial and moral support for his reforms from the United States and from the new president, Bush, personally as one way of supporting his regime and his popularity at home.

On the eve of the Malta meeting in December of 1989 the Kremlin leadership was still not sure whether Bush backed Gorbachev's reforms. Reflecting these suspicions, Shevardnadze on November 8 sent Gorbachev a strictly confidential personal memo saying that "Bush looked like an indecisive leader" torn by different forces and had not yet decided on his attitude toward the most important issue for the Soviet leadership: its reforms in the Soviet Union. Shevardnadze said Bush evidently would not mind using Moscow's difficulties with *perestroika* for his own benefit, so it was of prime importance at Malta for Gorbachev to obtain Bush's public commitment to the reform program in the interests of both countries. The Politburo considered this a main task for the summit, and I can personally testify that at Malta Gorbachev actively worked in that direction. Both leaders seemed to like each other.

Gorbachev left Malta with the impression that he had won Bush's support for his program and regarded it as the most important result of their meeting. On January 21, 1990, in his report to the Politburo, he welcomed Bush's "readiness to give us certain practical aid in the sphere of the economy"—this never materialized—as well as "a mutual understanding of the necessity for Soviet-American cooperation as a stabilizing factor in the current and crucial moment of developments in the world."

In mid-May of 1990, just before Gorbachev's visit to the United States, Secretary of State Baker visited Moscow. Gorbachev had a long private conversation with him about our domestic problems. Baker sounded very sympathetic. Gorbachev was especially encouraged when Baker told him that the Bush administration was in favor of *perestroika* because it "fully corresponded with U.S. interests" and that "Washington had changed course in Soviet-American relations from rivalry to dialogue and cooperation." Gorbachev was easily carried away by such reassurances.

But in fact several days previously, Jack Matlock, the U.S. ambassador in Moscow, had briefed the visiting governor of Maryland, William Schaefer, that the Soviet Union was suffering from a declining economy, ethnic tensions, rising crime, and even the threat of a military coup. Although there was hope of a gradual democratization, Matlock reckoned it would take from half to three-quarters of a century to implant itself. So while the United States wanted to support Gorbachev, Matlock frankly said it also was interested in using his visit to Washington to promote American interests by moving a weakened Soviet Union toward accepting political and economic concessions, including the reunification of Germany.

Back home after his trip to Washington, from May 31 to June 2, Gorbachev again spoke with satisfaction to his colleagues. He said Bush understood "our domestic difficulties" and gave his private reassurances "that the United States would never pose any danger to the Soviet Union." Gorbachev stressed that he "did not feel any more danger from Washington" and declared that he had succeeded in using Bush's and indeed America's support for *perestroika* to convince Washington that the changes in the Soviet Union would benefit the United States. On Germany he spoke more vaguely—that despite serious differences over the military and political status of a unified Germany, both sides sought a solution that would be part of an all-European process. But he concealed his desire for a quick agreement with the West to help him out of his domestic difficulties, which made him all too ready to acquiesce to the West's demands. He accepted them the following month at his meeting with Kohl.

Bush played a particularly soothing and reassuring role, keeping in close touch with Gorbachev and on occasion flattering him quite openly. In the crucial days of July 1990, when the question of Germany's unity hung in the balance, Bush first spoke by telephone and then sent Gorbachev a personal letter about the Group of Seven summit of the largest Western industrialized nations in London. All the leaders of the seven, he wrote, agreed that the "positive and quick changes" in Europe were mostly the result "of your sagacious foreign policy" and—adding what he knew Gorbachev wanted to hear—that "NATO was ready to cooperate in building with you a new Europe." Bush said that he as president was also thinking about "the gradual transformation of NATO itself." All this sounded very encouraging to Gorbachev.

In his lengthy reply on August 6, 1990, Gorbachev expressed "confidence in a close cooperation [with Bush] in solving these historic tasks." One month later, during their meeting at the Helsinki conference in September 1990, Bush again praised Gorbachev's foreign policies, to the great pleasure of Gorbachev and Shevardnadze. Their glowing conclusion, in a confidential memo to the Politburo, was that Bush and Baker "very definitely staked their firm support on our efforts for cardinal reform of Soviet society in this difficult time." They soon began to entertain doubts about the support, but they kept their skepticism private.

None of Gorbachev's optimistic hopes for broad American support ever materialized. The failure of his political agenda, the increasing crisis in the country, the disarray of foreign and defense policy, were all destroying Soviet potential. At that critical, final moment of the Cold War, Gorbachev and Shevardnadze had no coherent, balanced, and firm foreign policy to end it in a fitting and dignified way on the basis of equality. As the Cold War had begun to wind down in the second part of the 1980s, this balance of power with the West was widely recognized and could have created a base from which international relations could evolve into a new and nonconfrontational era. With an inexplicable rush, they actually gave away vital geopolitical and military positions that we had, instead of using them to achieve a new era of stability and equal cooperation, which could have ended the Cold War decisively sooner.

By weakening the might and international influence of his country, Gorbachev missed his great opportunity and missed it badly. The magic wand didn't work. His western partners played their own realpolitik. His dream of a new Europe with a new security system encompassing all states, including Russia, did not come true. The problem of European security has remained very much a conundrum after the end of the Cold War. The joint efforts of Europe, Russia, and the United States are needed more than ever.

Gorbachev also played a prominent role in launching the important process of liberalization and democratization in our country, and in the turn toward transforming our centrally planned system into a market economy. But his "new thinking," especially in domestic economic policy, turned out to be significantly less successful than in the international arena. In some ways, it was catastrophic. His thoughts were contradictory. Until his last days in power, his motto was "more socialism, more democracy." He believed strongly in socialism and resisted drastic changes in our economic structure while he had nevertheless become convinced of the need to introduce elements of a market system to raise our standard of living.

His policy was one of the convergence of socialism with capitalism, although he rejected that definition in public, most notably at a meeting in Washington in 1987 with a group of American intellectuals. He never mentioned the word "capitalism" while describing his economic plans, and his successors in the Russian Federation continued avoiding the word. But Gorbachev's fundamental failing was that he did not really understand economic problems and the policies to deal with them. He was always looking for advice, especially from foreigners and academicians, none of whom had ever been practically involved in economic management on a large scale. From 1986 to 1989, when I worked in the Politburo and participated in its deliberations, I never once heard Gorbachev present any broad and detailed plan for reforming the economy—whether one-year, or five-year, or some other kind of plan that had really been thought through. There were always improvisations, sometimes after his trips abroad or his talks with famous economists and prominent Western industrialists. Li Peng, the Chinese prime minister, confessed to our ambassador in Beijing, Oleg Troyanovsky, that Gorbachev changed his views so rapidly that the Chinese could not properly study them.

At the start of the reforms in 1986, Gorbachev explained his economic credo to the Politburo in this way: the Soviet economy certainly needed reforms, and although we did not know precisely how to achieve them, we must begin. He told the Politburo that they must all be guided by the words of Lenin: "The most important thing in any endeavor was to get involved in the fight and in that way learn what to do next." We got into a fight, all right, but for the years afterward even the new leaders of Russia did not know exactly what to do next.

As a domestic reformer, especially of the state and its economic system, Gorbachev showed himself increasingly helpless in the face of practical problems and tried to solve them by taking spontaneous, feverish, rash steps. I cannot help remembering Winston Churchill's words to Nikita Khrushchev when he visited Britain in 1956 and the two met at a Soviet Embassy reception. The great British statesman said: "Mr. Khrushchev, you are launching reforms in your country. That is good, indeed. But I should like to urge you not to be too rash. It is not easy to cross a chasm in two leaps. You can fall in."

A decisive blow to Gorbachev's political power was the disintegration of the Communist Party in the Soviet Union and most important, his own failure to create in its stead a new structure of power and authority as a successor. However undemocratic it may have been, the party, with its local branches throughout the country, was the governing backbone from the high leadership in Moscow to the villages and factories. As general secretary of the party, Gorbachev was the country's undisputed ruler, and he therefore continued until 1989 to emphasize the leading role of the party in all things, including his own reforms.

But then his attitude toward the party began to change because, once he had opened the Pandora's box of *glasnost* and democracy, criticism naturally arose also from within the party's own ranks. His own Politburo was not unanimous in support of his reforms, and Gorbachev could not forget that Khrushchev had been summarily dismissed in a party coup. Fearful of losing control in the party and thus of losing supreme power in the country, at the end of 1988 he switched to creation of a parliamentary rule via the presidency, a post from which the party could not dismiss him. But these were essentially backroom political maneuvers, and they served only to weaken Gorbachev's position in the party and in the country. And in August 1991, after an attempted coup by his former associates, parliament banned the Communist Party and threw its support to Yeltsin, leaving Gorbachev with no followers.*

In the end Mikhail Gorbachev did not have a clear vision or the concrete national priorities to go with it at home or abroad. I suspect that he will not be entirely comfortable with the suggestion that his endeavor to introduce new thinking unleashed forces that he was unable to control. The political and economic chaos created by Gorbachev's own confusion over how to go about the difficult task of necessary reform, combined with the upheavals of the latter part of 1991, led to his personal political downfall and the collapse of the Soviet Union. Having begun a great reformation, he failed to carry it through successfully.

With the reforms directed skillfully and appropriately, with all positive achievements reasonably preserved and major shortcomings and mistakes of the past eliminated in a carefully planned and evolutionary way, our coun-

---

* On August 19, 1991, I was working alone in my office in the Foreign Ministry, anxious as an attempted coup d'état was unraveling just a few turbulent blocks away. The phone rang, and I heard a voice that was familiar but at that moment highly incongruous with its Texas accent: "Hello, Anatoly, It's me, Bob Strauss. I just arrived in Moscow [as the new American ambassador] and I can't find any Soviet officials. They've all disappeared. I tried to call the foreign minister [Bessmertnykh] but he's also not in. What shall I do?" I told him to lay low for a few days, during which I promised to organize a meeting, which in fact I arranged the very next day by overcoming the hesitation of my old colleague Bessmertnykh who was staying at home. Strauss was thus officially able to get started in his new job. He soon met President Gorbachev. But the days of the president were already numbered. By the end of the year he was forced to resign.

try renewed, reformed, and oriented toward a new course of development, would not only have mastered its challenges but, I am convinced, also would have ranked high among the democratic countries of the world. I do deeply believe it will achieve that in the future, despite the terrible trials as we find our new way.

Gorbachev and Bush last had a meeting together on October 29, 1991, during the Middle East peace conference in Madrid. Gorbachev, remembers Baker, was as "unfocused as I had ever seen him; he seemed like a drowning man, looking for a life preserver. It was hard not to feel sorry for him." But nobody, for one reason or another, threw Gorbachev that life preserver. In any case, it was too late.

On December 13, 1991, President Bush phoned Gorbachev. In answer to Bush's question, Gorbachev tried to minimize the importance of the last fateful events in his country. He insisted that the agreement the heads of Russia, the Ukraine, and Belarus reached on December 8 in Bison Forest on the Belarus–Polish border about the transformation of the Soviet Union was only a "sketch" and that the transformation should have a legal basis.

In order to get information firsthand, Bush sent Baker to Moscow. After he arrived on December 15, he was able to make a sort of farewell gesture in Gorbachev's favor. He had heard confidentially that Gorbachev's immediate assistants feared that if he were to lose the title of president, he would be arrested and tried for the crisis he had created.

During the meeting held the next day with Yeltsin, Baker mentioned the rumors he had heard of possible criminal proceedings against Gorbachev. Such a move would be a mistake that would not be understood by the international community, he said. The Americans hoped the transfer of power could be done in a dignified way—as in the West. Humiliating Gorbachev would serve no purpose, he added. As Baker would write later, Yeltsin took the point and indicated his agreement, despite his clear personal antipathy for Gorbachev.

The meeting between Yeltsin and Baker took place in St. Catherine's Hall in the Kremlin, a room in which previously only Gorbachev had received foreign visitors. Yeltsin, noted Baker in his book, was obviously ready to show who was boss. Yeltsin gave a vivid description of the most recent events in his country, of its transformation from the Soviet Union into the Commonwealth of Independent States, and of the transfer of power from Gorbachev to himself. When they were alone, Yeltsin gave a detailed explanation of how the machinery that controlled the "nuclear button" worked under the new leadership at the Kremlin.

Half an hour later, Baker met with Gorbachev in the same hall. In his report to the president that night, Secretary Baker said that his day had been "filled with contrast" between Yeltsin's energy and confidence and Gorbachev's anxiety and concern. The latter's worries over the unclear future of his country were frequently interrupted by flashes of anger against Yeltsin. This was the last meeting President Gorbachev had with a high-ranking member of the U.S. government.

After Moscow, Baker made a blitz trip to Kyrgyzstan, Alma-Ata, Minsk, and Kiev, observing the disintegration of the Soviet Union.

On December 25, 1991, Gorbachev announced on national television his resignation from the post of the Soviet president. After his statement, the red state flag of the Soviet Union was lowered in the Kremlin: The U.S.S.R. ceased to exist. Gorbachev, the first and the last president of the Soviet Union, forever left the Kremlin.

A couple of hours before his resignation, Gorbachev had had a brief farewell talk by telephone with President Bush. That was also the end of an uneasy but historically important era of Soviet–American relations.

## Instead of an Epilogue

It is difficult to judge the past by today's events. But the lessons of the past should always be remembered.

Now that we have dropped our grand expectations and illusions about rapid economic recovery through the free-market system and a close association with the West, especially the United States, to help our economic reforms, Russia has begun to accommodate itself to the complicated experience of dealing with the outside world. We are passing through an agonizing period of shaping a new image of Russia with new domestic and foreign policies.

This process will depend to a certain degree on Russian-American relations and on whether and how the United States recognizes the proper role of a new Russia in the international community. In the West voices are still heard saying that a strong Russia would be an unpredictable and dangerous adversary and that the balance of power would be better served by moving NATO to the East, closer to Russia. But it would be unrealistic and, moreover, dangerous to stake the future on driving Russia down or creating frontiers for old or, indeed, new antagonisms to fester in Europe. With its human and intellectual resources, its natural riches, its unique geographic position on two continents, and finally its abiding determination as a nation, Russia will always remain a great country. It would be a grave error to believe that even the huge difficulties of a transition period had deprived us of our standing in the world. For the United States and indeed the whole world it is better to have a strong and confident friend and partner than an unfriendly country with a huge nuclear arsenal.

It is also important to remember that our people do not feel they have been defeated by America. The Soviet totalitarian regime was defeated inside our own country by our own efforts and not by foreign liberators as was Nazi Germany or militarist Japan. So there are no victors and no vanquished now. We are equal partners in international affairs.

The Russian and American people can learn from each other. Just as Americans are constantly trying to reform capitalism—Franklin Roosevelt's name is still revered in Russia, and it was he who believed that a market system needed correction by the state from time to time—we Russians are on a difficult and painful road toward modernizing our society and our economy. Russia favors democracy. But just like the market, there are many different understandings of what it really is. Even in America this has always been the case, as Abraham Lincoln said in Baltimore in 1864: "We all speak in favor of democracy, but when we use the word we do not always mean the same thing."

Now Russia is ready for a constructive alliance with the United States, and this is in no way an alliance against anyone else. Our countries share common values and both strive for peace. But the peoples of Russia, like the American people, want to defend their historical and cultural identities and will defend their national interests. Not by force at the expense of other countries, but by the reasonable convergence of interests through traditional political and diplomatic means. This path will not ever be smooth; the United States often experiences difficulty and competition even with its own allies.

But historically, the interests of our two countries have rarely if ever collided. The Cold War was a temporary perversion, based as it was on ideology and not essential national interest, and we must now get rid of the Cold War mentality. Now, for the first time in history, a democratic America meets a democratic Russia. Both countries have much more in common than ever before and new relations are being developed, but they will take time. We should be candid and not easily discouraged when our views do not coincide. From time to time our interests may even clash. But a return to the Cold War must be completely excluded. We should always be able to find a way to disagree without damaging a profoundly important strategic cooperation. This is a fundamental lesson I have learned from my own long life of close association and diplomatic experience with the United States. And it is the lesson I have tried to capture in the pages of this book.

# Appendix

*Excerpts from Andrei Gromyko's Foreign Policy Memorandum of*
*January 13, 1967, Approved by the Politburo*

The experience of recent years shows the great complexity of the task of coexisting with the United States. On the whole, international tension does not suit the state interests of the Soviet Union and its friends. The construction of socialism and the development of economy call for the maintenance of peace. In the conditions of detente it is easier to consolidate and broaden the positions of the Soviet Union in the world.

The main foreign policy principle of Kennedy and Johnson is to preserve the status quo in the world. The American concept of "spheres of vital interest" for the United States and the Soviet Union, and of a "third sphere" generally reflects the fact that American ruling circles have to acknowledge the present correlation of forces and the achievements of socialism. However, the American government has set out to prevent communism from further spreading all over the world, which is, of course, impossible.

Accordingly, in the present situation the leaders of the socialist countries and international working movement have to take into consideration, one way or another, the real state of affairs. This concerns, in particular, their approach to the questions of European security, West Berlin, etc.

The forces of the left in the United States are still relatively weak. That is why the policy of coexistence has to be oriented more at the moderate and liberal circles in the American ruling class and also at those elements in the government who essentially favor the status quo. It is true, these circles' eagerness to preserve the status quo may sometimes lead to sharp differences and indeed crises in individual regions, as further major progressive changes in the world are historically inevitable. Besides, the very forces in the United States that champion the status quo, combine their policy with the continuation of the arms race and with readiness for local armed conflicts.

In this respect, we should stress the immense importance of the October 1964 Plenum of the CPSU Central Committee which put an end to the voluntarism and verbiage in the foreign policy of the Soviet Union.

If we consider relations between the Soviet Union and the United States in a broad perspective, rather than against a background of the current unfavorable state of our relations caused by the U.S. aggression against Vietnam, it can be said that in the present epoch of transition the question is, in the final analysis, just how the transition of countries and nations from capitalism to socialism will proceed: under the conditions of world peace or amidst a world war. However, the answer to the question of whether a global nuclear missile war should break out, without any doubt depends just on the state of Soviet-American relations.

This, in its turn, proves the correctness of the conclusion made in the CPSU Program that at the present historical stage a world war is not fatally inevitable. We must resolutely continue to dissociate ourselves politically and ideologically from adventurous schemes of the Chinese leaders, who have pinned their hopes on the inevitability of an armed confrontation between the socialist countries headed by the Soviet Union and the United States within 8 to 10 years. The opinion that the Americans are out for war anyway and, consequently, a war with the United States is inevitable, would reflect precisely the position of the Chinese. The concentration of our main efforts on domestic purposes is fully in line with Lenin's statement that the final victory of socialism over capitalism will be ensured by the creation of a new, much higher level of labor productivity.

While not ruling out in principle the possibility of coordinated Soviet-American actions aimed at maintaining peace and ensuring the solution of some major international issues, we must, of course, avoid creating the impression that in recognizing the special weight of the two powers we have neglected the interests of other states.

Under certain conditions the Soviet-American dialogue, suspended in 1963, can be resumed on even a far larger scale. This possibility and appropriate arrangements must be thought out as systematically and profoundly as was the case from 1942 throughout World War II in relation to the postwar organization of the world.

We should not cut off the possibility of diplomatic maneuver for ourselves in relations with individual Western countries, including the United States, by adhering to a one-sided view on imperialism. In certain cases it is necessary to draw a more distinct line between the activity of the Comintern and that of the foreign ministry, the difference stressed by Lenin. In order to make our policy more flexible and effective in relation to the United States, the official foreign political statements and actions of the Soviet government should be predominantly and more clearly based on the interests of relations with other countries. Inasmuch as it does not affect relations with other countries, the sociological and ideological aspects of the struggle between the two systems, and the criticism toward the policy of the United States and other Western imperialist states from the ideological point of view, should be conducted predominantly through the party, public organizations, and the press.

As regards the American aggression against Vietnam and its effect on bilateral relations, we should go on rendering comprehensive assistance to the DRV in consolidating its defense capacity to repulse the aggression, without getting directly involved in the war. We must give the Americans to understand that further escalation in the military actions against the DRV will compel the Soviet Union to render its assistance to this country on an ever-growing scale, and that the only way out of the present situation is reaching a political solution on the basis of respecting the legitimate rights of the Vietnamese people. Nevertheless, putting an end to the Vietnam conflict would undoubtedly have a positive effect on Soviet-American relations and open up new possibilities for solving certain international problems.

We should not avoid agreements with the United States on questions of our interest if such agreements do not contradict our position of principle in regard to Vietnam. Needless to say, we should avoid a situation where we have to fight on two fronts, that is against China and the United States. Maintaining Soviet-American relations on a certain level is one of the factors that will help us achieve this objective.

The struggle for the unity of socialist countries is the main means of countering American efforts to split the socialist community.

As to our objective of weakening U.S. positions in Western Europe, we should consistently hold to the principle that European problems can only have "European solutions." We must tirelessly promote the idea that Europe itself can and must ensure its security and consolidate confidence in the relations between Eastern and Western Europe.

Cuba: Our main and long-term task remains rendering economic and political assistance to

Cuba, as well as strengthening its defense capability. We should avoid any actions or statements putting in question the assurances of the U.S. leaders that they will not attack Cuba.

The issues of the national liberation movement: The line of the Twenty-Third Congress of the CPSU for all-round support of this movement meets our foreign policy interests in every way. Considering the shortage of our reserves, we should focus on economic cooperation with the most progressive countries that have embarked on the road of noncapitalist development, such as Egypt, Syria, Algeria, Mali, Guinea, Burma, Congo, Tanzania, and the countries of strategic importance to us (Afghanistan, Turkey, Pakistan, and Iran). We must pursue our activities in other countries of Asia and Africa in such a manner so as to build our economic and trade cooperation with them increasingly on the principle of mutual benefit and commerce.

Considering the experience of Vietnam and the Middle East, we should take timely measures to relax tension in the ganglions in the three continents where sharp conflicts are possible which, in turn, can combine to lead to an "acute situation." In this connection we should, while supporting the Arab countries in their struggle against Israel's expansionist policy, flexibly dampen the extremist trends in the policy of certain Arab states, e.g., Syria, orienting them toward the domestic consolidation.

Disarmament: We should keep our active stand on disarmament. Along with a further struggle for universal and comprehensive disarmament which is expected to take a long period of time, we must pay special attention to some limited measures, first of all, to reaching an agreement on the nonproliferation of nuclear weapons. It is necessary to complete our dialogue with the United States and seek the conclusion of such an agreement in order to prevent any access of the FRG and other nonnuclear states to nuclear arms.

Simultaneously, it is essential to continue to exert pressure on the United States in favor of the measures that the American administration has declared unacceptable, but which are met with understanding by world public opinion and help expose the imperialist course of the United States. These measures include liquidation of foreign military bases, withdrawal of armed troops from foreign territories, and cutting of military budgets.

On possibilities to influence the alignment of political forces in the United States: All our ways and means should be brought into play to broaden the gap between the moderate politicians and the maniacs in the United States, to isolate the "war party" in order to prevent the aggressive forces of imperialism from unleashing a nuclear world war in the future. In this regard a replacement of President Johnson by a Republican (through elections) could hardly meet our interests, as all known Republican candidates are even more rightist than Johnson. Accordingly, when conducting our foreign policy actions involving the United States we should avoid situations when these actions may consolidate the positions of his opponents among the ultras. Simultaneously, it is useful to keep in touch with the "loyal opposition" to Johnson (Senators Fulbright, R[obert] Kennedy, [Dick] Clark, etc.). It is also expedient to broaden, through our public organizations, our contracts with liberal and democratic forces, as well as cultural exchanges and exchanges in the sphere of art and education.

*Excerpts from an Assessment of the Course of Foreign Policy
and the State of Soviet-American Relations, Submitted by
Foreign Minister Gromyko on September 16, 1968,
and Approved by the Politburo*

A. The main foreign policy objective of the Soviet Union is to consolidate the socialist community and develop multiform, ever deepening cooperation between the Soviet Union and fraternal socialist countries. The present situation calls for the integration of socialist countries to be as broad and solid as that created in the West through a network of multilateral organizations connected with NATO or related to it (EEC, European Parliament, etc.). We should proceed to the actual confederation by stages and by various ways. This is the objective to be kept constantly in view by socialist countries in the present international situation. We should not expect the United States to launch any actions in this connection, which would seriously aggravate world tension.

B. We should persist in our efforts at ensuring the most favorable conditions for the construction of communism. This should particularly include measures aimed at curbing the arms race etc.

C. Our aid to national liberation movements should be commensurate with our resources. We should wage a struggle against neocolonialism. As to our economic relations with developing countries, they should be built in such a way as to be beneficial to the Soviet Union. The need for the strict observance of this principle for such bilateral relations is determined by the fact that the Soviet Union can remain powerful in the international arena primarily through its domestic stability, just as the United States is powerful thanks to its domestic stability and pursues its global policy on this basis.

D. Our relations with the United States. There is an evident growth of military and reactionary forces against a background of the Vietnam war and a certain aggravation of the situation in Europe over the events in Czechoslovakia, which involves a danger of greater aggressive trends in the foreign policy of the United States. Simultaneously, there is a growing awareness of the fact that the development of today's international life sets certain limits to the United States' potential, especially in the spheres where broad Soviet and American interests clash directly or indirectly.

The development of our relations with the United States calls therefore for combining the necessary firmness with flexibility in pursuing a policy of strength and for actively using means of diplomatic maneuver. While there is a threat of war, a nuclear war is not fatally inevitable.

The events in Czechoslovakia are regarded by American ruling circles as sufficient ground for them to launch politically and ideologically subversive activities against the Soviet Union in order to damage the international prestige of our country and its foreign policy and to undermine the positions of communist parties in capitalist countries. On the other hand, the determination with which the Soviet Union acted in relation to the Czechoslovak events made the leaders of the United States consider more soberly their potential in the region and see once again the determination of our country's leadership in defending the vital interests of the Soviet Union.

. . . The Soviet-American dialogue of 1961–1963 was not, however, accidental; the reasons that gave rise to it are still in force today. That is why under certain conditions the dialogue can be resumed even on a broader range of issues. The preparations for this dialogue should be conducted systematically and purposefully even now.

# INDEX

Kennedy, Robert, 6, 61*n*, 110–11, 651
  and assassination of Kennedy, 113–14
  confidential channel and, 54–56, 63,
    97–98, 104
  Cuban missile crisis and, 78–79, 84–93,
    95, 100
  nuclear test ban and, 102, 105
  planned Soviet visit of, 62–63
  presidential campaign of, 173
  and Soviet military aid to Cuba, 71–73,
    84–85
  and stalemate over Germany and Berlin,
    66–67, 102
  temper of, 63, 115
Khan, Ayub, 242
Khrushchev, Nikita, 4, 15, 22, 31–33,
    62–64, 100–107, 116–18, 120–21,
    123–24, 137, 224, 473, 475, 615, 621
  arms control process doubted by, 152
  and assassination of J. Kennedy, 113–15
  comparisons between Brezhnev and,
    134–35
  confidential channel and, 54–56, 62–63,
    96–98, 104, 114–15
  Cuban missile crisis and, 74, 79, 81–96,
    98, 100–102
  dismantling detente and, 478, 480
  dismissal of, 96, 132–34, 138, 640, 645
  and Dobrynin's appointment as U.S.
    ambassador, 48, 53–54, 61–62
  and Dobrynin's last meeting with J.
    Kennedy, 109–10
  espionage and, 362
  on foreign policy procedures, 47–48
  Geneva summit and, 38–39
  and Hammarskjold's Soviet visit, 35
  hot line and, 100–101
  and Jewish emigration from Soviet
    Union, 272
  J. Kennedy respected by, 54
  Laotian crisis and, 125–26
  Nixon's kitchen debate with, 202
  nuclear test ban and, 104–10
  Paris summit and, 41–43, 256
  and purposes of U.S.-Soviet summits, 37
  reforms of, 644–45
  relations between Molotov and, 31–32
  R. Kennedy's planned Soviet visit and,
    62–63
  and Soviet fears of nuclear attack, 528
  and Soviet military aid to Cuba, 70–77,
    81–84
  and stalemate over Germany and Berlin,
    66–70, 102–3, 116, 124–25, 238

Thompson's corn plot and, 64
U-2 affair and, 40–43
Vienna summit and, 44–47, 54, 69–70,
    116–17, 127, 384, 430
Vietnam War and, 120, 125, 133
Khvostov, Vladimir, 17–19
Kirkpatrick, Jeane, 513, 516
Kissinger, Henry, 5–8, 183, 199–200,
    201*n*, 204–13, 225–35, 239, 262–64,
    323–30, 332–33, 381–88, 407, 461,
    469–71, 489, 612, 638
  ABMs and, 218–19, 225
  and agreement on preventing nuclear
    war, 278, 282
  Angola and, 366–69, 373–74
  anti-Sovietism of, 470
  attempts on life of, 363–64
  Berlin issue and, 222, 225–28, 234–35
  Brzezinski criticized by, 402
  Carter's election and, 383–86
  China visited by, 229, 231, 239, 246,
    248, 262, 290
  in comparing Ford and Nixon, 344–46
  comparisons between Brzezinski and,
    388, 469
  comparisons between Shultz and,
    527–28, 538
  comparisons between Vance and, 387
  confidential channel and, 55, 204–6,
    208–9, 213, 215–16, 218–20, 228,
    237, 240–42, 245, 265, 273, 275,
    277, 283, 292, 294–96, 302, 313,
    491, 547, 579
  dismantling detente and, 475–77
  and Dobrynin's dinner with Rockefeller,
    328–30
  Dobrynin's relationship with, 7–8
  and doctrine of limited nuclear war, 312
  espionage and, 361–63
  and first use of nuclear weapons, 283
  Ford's presidential campaign and, 353,
    355–56, 372–74
  Ford's relationship with, 324–25, 332
  friction between Rogers and, 209
  on Gromyko's policy decisions, 135
  Helsinki Conference and, 352
  Hollywood visit of, 264–65
  hot line between Dobrynin and, 255
  human rights and, 385–86
  and impossibility of agreement with
    Reagan, 546
  India-Pakistan war and, 240–43
  and Jewish emigration from Soviet
    Union, 273–74, 317, 340–41, 343

and troop reductions in Europe, 431–32
Vienna summit and, 426, 429, 431–32
U-2 incident, 40–43, 256

Valenti, Jack, 122–23
Vance, Cyrus, 5–6, 380, 385–89, 528, 538
Carter's Naval Academy speech and, 416
Carter's presidential campaign and, 451–52, 454–55, 458–59
and Chinese invasion of Vietnam, 424
comparisons between Brzezinski and, 387, 391–92
comparisons between Kissinger and, 387
confidential channel and, 491
and confusion about detente, 414–17
Cuban mini-crisis and, 433–34
espionage and, 362
first-strike doctrine and, 475
human rights and, 385–86, 391, 395–96, 415, 418, 503
Iranian crisis and, 387, 442, 458–59
in meeting with Kissinger and Dobrynin, 385
Middle East peace negotiations and, 400, 403
and NATO's attempts to achieve military superiority over Warsaw Pact, 436
resignation of, 387, 458–60, 463
SALT and, 385–86, 393–404, 414–15, 418–19, 422, 425, 429, 432, 459, 580
and Soviet invasion of Afghanistan, 451–59, 462
on Third World confrontations, 421
U.S.-China relations and, 414–15, 454
Vienna summit and, 402–3, 418, 422, 424–27
Vietnam War and, 179
and war between Ethiopia and Somalia, 408, 410–12, 414
Vanik, Charles, 274, 371
Vasev, Vladlen, 5, 62, 443
Vienna:
Austrian State Treaty anniversary celebrated in, 459, 462
European troop reduction talks in, 281, 350, 436, 477, 531, 533, 576
SALT talks in, 208, 216, 218
space weapons talks in, 573–74, 578
Vienna summit (1961), 43–47, 54, 61–62, 67, 69–70, 79, 116–17, 127, 384, 430
Vienna summit (1979), 398, 407, 418–19, 422–34, 440n, 450–51, 459
agenda of, 426
Carter's push for, 422–24

delay in holding of, 430
domestic implications of, 426
SALT and, 402–3, 419, 422–25, 427–30
and Soviet invasion of Afghanistan, 496
U.S.-China relations and, 430–31
Vietnam, 468
Cambodia invaded by, 420, 423
Chinese invasion of, 423–24
Vietnam War, 60, 118–22, 124–26, 133, 136, 138–50, 154, 172–81, 185, 189–95, 199–200, 203–5, 232–33, 238, 244–56, 276, 326, 347–50, 377, 380–81, 447, 473, 625
arms control and, 157–58
bombing of north in, 139–40, 142–47, 149–50, 160–61, 169, 174, 176–77, 179–80, 190, 224, 244, 249–54, 256, 262, 268
bombing pauses in, 143–44, 160, 190–91, 262, 268
dismantling detente and, 475–76
enemy escalations in, 139–40, 248–51
and fall of Saigon, 348–50
Glassboro summit and, 167–69, 172
and Gromyko's assessments of foreign policy, 162–63, 649–52
and Johnson's campaign for additional summit, 190–92
Laotian crisis and, 126, 141
mining and blockading ports in, 251–52
Moscow summit and, 215, 223–24, 244, 248–55, 259–60
negotiating settlement of, 140, 142–50, 160–61, 167, 169–70, 174–76, 178–80, 190, 194, 205, 211, 235, 244, 246, 248–51, 253, 255, 262, 265–68, 349–50, 363, 373, 475–76, 650
and 1968 presidential campaign, 173, 177–78
Nixon's reelection campaign and, 262–63, 266
peace treaty in, 268–69
public opinion on, 146, 151, 177–78, 246, 350
and reducing U.S. military presence in Europe, 151, 174
and safety of Soviet vessels and sailors, 252
and Soviet invasion of Czechoslovakia, 189
U.S.-China relations and, 229
U.S. escalations in, 146–47, 160–61, 169–70, 173–74, 251–52